Frommer's

Y 2002

Denmark

Here's what the critics say about Frommer's:

"Amazingly easy to use. Very portable, very complete."
                                        —*Booklist*

♦

"The only mainstream guide to list specific prices. The Walter Cronkite of guidebooks—with all that implies."
                                        —*Travel & Leisure*

♦

"Complete, concise, and filled with useful information."
                                        —*New York Daily News*

♦

"Hotel information is close to encyclopedic."
                                        —*Des Moines Sunday Register*

♦

"I use a lot of travel guides when preparing my trips, but I have learned to especially trust Frommer's when it comes to picking lodgings."
                                        —*The Orange County Register*

Frommer's®

1st Edition

Denmark

by Darwin Porter and Danforth Prince

MACMILLAN • USA

914.89

ABOUT THE AUTHORS

Coauthors **Darwin Porter,** a native of North Carolina, and **Danforth Prince,** of Ohio, are veteran travel writers, having produced many editions of *Frommer's Scandinavia.* They have also written numerous best-selling Frommer's guides, notably to England, France, the Caribbean, Italy, and Germany. Here they focus their attention on the recent touristic explosion occurring in tiny Denmark, reviewing hundreds of hotels, inns, restaurants, museums, and natural sights, dozens of which are making their appearance for the first time in any guidebook.

MACMILLAN TRAVEL USA

A Pearson Education Macmillan Company
1633 Broadway
New York, NY 10019

Find us online at **www.frommers.com**

ISBN 0-02-862721-0
ISSN 1098-1551

Editors: Philippe Wamba, Jeff Soloway, Vanessa Rosen
Production Editor: Michael Thomas
Photo Editor: Richard Fox
Design by Michele Laseau
Page Creation: John Bitter, Angel Perez, David E. Pruett
Staff Cartographers: John Decamillis, Roberta Stockwell
Additional Cartography: Hans G. Andersson

SPECIAL SALES

Bulk purchases (10+ copies) of Frommer's and selected Macmillan travel guides are available to corporations, organizations, mail-order catalogs, institutions, and charities at special discounts, and can be customized to suit individual needs. For more information write to Special Sales, Macmillan General Reference, 1633 Broadway, New York, NY 10019.

Manufactured in the United States of America.

Contents

List of Maps

AN INVITATION TO THE READER

In researching this book, we discovered many wonderful places—hotels, restaurants, shops, and more. We're sure you'll find others. Please tell us about them, so we can share the information with your fellow travelers in upcoming editions. If you were disappointed with a recommendation, we'd love to know that, too. Please write to:

Frommer's Denmark, 1st Edition
Macmillan Travel
1633 Broadway
New York, NY 10019

AN ADDITIONAL NOTE

Please be advised that travel information is subject to change at any time—and this is especially true of prices. We therefore suggest that you write or call ahead for confirmation when making your travel plans. The authors, editors, and publisher cannot be held responsible for the experiences of readers while traveling. Your safety is important to us, however, so we encourage you to stay alert and be aware of your surroundings. Keep a close eye on cameras, purses, and wallets, all favorite targets of thieves and pickpockets.

WHAT THE SYMBOLS MEAN

✪ Frommer's Favorites

Our favorite places and experiences—outstanding for quality, value, or both.

The following abbreviations are used for credit cards:

AE	American Express	EC	Eurocard
CB	Carte Blanche	JCB	Japan Credit Bank
DC	Diners Club	MC	MasterCard
DISC	Discover	V	Visa
ER	enRoute		

FIND FROMMER'S ONLINE

Arthur Frommer's Budget Travel Online (**www.frommers.com**) offers more than 6,000 pages of up-to-the-minute travel information—including the latest bargains and candid, personal articles updated daily by Arthur Frommer himself. No other Web site offers such comprehensive and timely coverage of the world of travel.

Denmark

0 — 40 km
— 24 mi
N

North Sea

Skagerrak

Skagen
Hirtshals
Hjørring
Frederikshavn
SWEDEN
Laesø
Hanstholm
Aalborg
Thyborøn
Nykøbing
Kattegat
Skive
Holstebro
Viborg
Randers
Grenå
JUTLAND
Ringkøbing
Silkeborg
Århus
Ebeltoft
Herning
Helsingør
Jelling
Hillerød
Vejle
Samsø
Varde
Kalundborg
Copenhagen ★
Esbjerg
Fredericia
Roskilde
Fanø
Kolding
Odense
ZEALAND
Køge
Ribe
Nyborg
Korsør
Slagelse
Ringsted
Malmö
Rømø
FUNEN
Fåborg
Tønder
Abenrå
Svendborg
Ærøskøbing
MØN
Maribo
FALSTER
LOLLAND
Nykøbing

GERMANY

Baltic Sea

100 m →
Bornholm

Ferry Routes - - - - -

The Best of Denmark

Denmark presents visitors with an embarrassment of riches, everything from exciting Copenhagen to historic castles, unusual offshore islands, quaint villages, and more. To help you decide how best to spend your time in Denmark, we've compiled a list of our favorite experiences and discoveries. In the following pages you'll find the kind of candid advice we'd give our close friends.

1 The Best Travel Experiences

- **A Day (and Night) at Tivoli:** These 150-year-old pleasure gardens are worth the airfare to Copenhagen all by themselves. They offer a little bit of everything: open-air dancing, restaurants, theaters, concert halls, an amusement park . . . and, oh yes, gardens as well. From the first bloom of spring until the autumn leaves start to fall, they're devoted to lighthearted fun. The gardens are worth a visit any time but are especially pleasant at twilight when the lights begin to glint among the trees. See chapter 5.
- **Down on the Farm in Denmark:** The best way to see the heart of Denmark and meet the Danes is to spend a week on one of their farms. Some 370 farms all over the country take in paying guests. Take a pin and stick it anywhere on a map of Denmark away from the cities and seacoast, and you'll find a thatched and timbered farm or perhaps a more modernized homestead. Almost anyplace makes a good base from which you can explore the rest of the country on day trips. You join the host family and other guests for meals. You can learn about what's going on at the farm—or even pitch in and help with the chores if you like. Activities range from bonfires and folk dancing to riding lessons, and even horse-and-buggy rides. To arrange a farm holiday, contact **Danish Farmhouse Holidays** (Urlaub auf dem Bauernhof), Søndergade 26, DK-8700 Horsens (☎ **75-60-21-20**; fax 75-60-21-90). The experience is a great bargain too, since the cost may be as low as 200 DKK ($29.00) per person per night.
- **On the Trail of the Vikings:** Renowned for three centuries of fantastic exploits, the Vikings explored Greenland to the north, North America to the west, and the Caspian Sea to the south and east from roughly A.D. 750 to 1050. Their legacy lives on in Denmark. Relive the age at the Nationalmuseet in Copenhagen,

which displays burial grounds of the Viking period, along with the largest and richest hoards of treasure, including relics from the "Silver Age." Even Viking costumes are exhibited. At Roskilde, explore the Viking Ship Museum, containing five vessels found in a fjord nearby, the largest of which was built in Ireland around 1060 and manned by 60 to 100 warriors. At Jelling, see two enormous mounds (the largest in Denmark), one of which was originally the burial ground of King Gorm. And if you're in Ribe, check out the Museum of the Viking Age, where a multimedia room, "Odin's Eye," introduces the visitor to the world of the Vikings through a vivid sound and vision experience. See chapters 5, 6, and 10.

- **Biking in Denmark:** Since Denmark is relatively flat, it's one of the best countries in Europe for touring on two wheels. Green hills, half-timbered villages, castles, manor houses, beech forests, and lakes provide the backdrop as you roll along on your own power. Cyclists are given high priority in traffic. Of course, you can set out on your own, but a company that's loosely affiliated with the Danish Tourist office is **Bike Denmark,** Åboulevard 1, DK-1635 Copenhagen (☎ **35-36-41-00**), whose offerings are depicted on their Web page **www.bikedenmark.com**. The company offers eight different bike tours of Denmark, some of which depart from Copenhagen, others of which cover parts of Jutland and in some cases, southern Sweden. Tours last between 5 and 10 days, and cover between 12½ and 37 miles per day. Detailed maps and directions are provided to each cyclist, who proceeds at his or her own pace along itineraries specially routed to cover sites of historic interest or natural beauty. Luggage is transported ahead of time along the route, so that it's waiting for participants in their hotel rooms at the end of a long day of cycling.

- **In the Footsteps of H. C. Andersen:** To some visitors, this storyteller is the very symbol of Denmark itself. The fairy tale lives on in Odense, on the island of Funen, where Andersen was born the son of a shoemaker in 1805. His childhood home, a small half-timbered house on Munkemøllestræde, where he lived from 1807 to 1817, has been turned into a museum. You can also visit the H. C. Andersens Hus, where much of his memorabilia is stored (including his walking stick and top hat), and take a few moments to listen to his tales on tape. But mostly you can wander the cobblestone streets that he knew so well, marveling at the life of this man—and his works—that, in the words of his obituary, struck "chords that reverberated in every human heart," as they still do today. See chapter 9.

2 The Best Scenic Towns & Villages

- **Dragør:** At the very doorstep of Copenhagen, this old seafaring town once flourished as a bustling herring port on the Baltic. Time, however, passed it by, and for that we can be grateful, because it looks much as it used to, with half-timbered ocher and pink 18th-century cottages topped with thatch or red-tile roofs. The entire village is under the protection of the National Trust of Denmark. A 35-minute ride from the Danish capital will take you back two centuries.

- **Ærøskøbing:** This is storybook Denmark, a little village on the country's most charming island (Ærø), lying 18-miles across the water south of Svendborg. A 13th-century market town, it is a Lilliputian souvenir of the past, complete with little gingerbread houses. You expect Hansel and Gretel to arrive at any moment. See chapter 9.

- **Odense:** The birthplace of Hans Christian Andersen is visited by thousands of the storyteller's fans every year. Denmark's third-largest city still has a medieval core, and you can walk its cobblestone streets and admire its half-timbered houses, including H. C. Andersens Hus. Other than its associations with the writer, Odense is a worthwhile destination in its own right, filled with attractions (including St. Canute's Cathedral), both within the city limits and nearby. On the outskirts you can explore everything from the 1554 Renaissance castle, Egeskov, to a 72-foot-long 10th-century Viking ship at Ladby, 12 miles to the northeast of Odense. See chapter 9.
- **Ribe:** Located on the island of Jutland, this is the best-preserved medieval town in Denmark—known for its narrow cobblestone lanes and crooked, half-timbered houses. An important trading center during the Viking era, it's known today as the town where the endangered stork—often the subject of European myth and legend—nests every April. The medieval center of Ribe is protected by the National Trust. From April until mid-September a night watchman circles Ribe, spinning tales of the town's legendary days and singing traditional songs. See chapter 10.
- **Ebeltoft:** On Jutland, this well-preserved town of half-timbered buildings is the capital of the Mols hill country. It's a town of sloping rowhouses, crooked streets, and local handcraft shops. The Town Hall looks as if it had been erected for kindergarten children to play in; here in Ebeltoft you can also visit the 1860 frigate *Jylland,* the oldest man-of-war in Denmark. See chapter 11.

3 The Best Active Vacations

- **Golfing:** In recent years golf has become quite popular in Denmark. There are as many as 114 clubs throughout the country, most of which welcome visitors (all you need is a membership card from your club at home). Several clubs have a pro trainer, a golf shop, a clubroom, and a cafe restaurant. Golfing vacations are available from $110 per day, which includes half board, hotel, and greens fees. Contact **Borton Overseas** (☎ 800/843-0602) for more information. One of Denmark's best courses is at the **Rungsted Golf Klub** in Copenhagen. See chapter 5.
- **Fishing:** For centuries, much of Denmark's diet relied on the sea and whatever the country's fishers could pull out of it. Since then, no *smørrebrød* buffet would be complete without a selection of shrimp, herring, and salmon, and Danish techniques for preparing plaice, cod, eel, perch, and trout are culinary art forms in their own right. The seas off the 680-mile coastline of Funen, especially within the Great Belt, have yielded endless tons of seafood, a tradition that has encouraged anglers and sport enthusiasts to test their luck in the rich waters of the Baltic. You'll find many different outfitters in Denmark who, for a fee, can expose you to the mysteries of fresh and saltwater fishing. One of the most consistently reliable maintains a permanent headquarters facing the Great Sound on the island of Funen, **Ole Dehn,** Søndergard 22, Lohals, DK-5953 Tranekær (☎ 62-55-17-00). This outfitter's most popular fishing experience involves half-day deep sea fishing tours on the Great Sound, priced at 195 DKK ($28.30) per person for a 6-hour fishing experience that's conducted whenever business warrants it, from 8am to 2pm.

  The lakes around the town of Ry in Central Jutland are particularly good fishing spots. See chapter 11.
- **Biking:** A nation of bikers, Denmark has organized its roads to suit this national sport. Bikers can pedal along a network of routes and paths protected from heavy

traffic, and much of the terrain is flat. Packaged bicycle vacations are available as inclusive tours, covering bike rental, ferry tickets, and accommodations en route. Some deluxe bike tours transport your luggage from one hotel to the next. For more information, contact the **Danish Cycling Federation,** Rømersgade 7, DK-1362 Copenhagen (☎ **33-32-31-21**). We particularly recommend cycling in the Lake District in Central Jutland (see chapter 11) and on the island of Bornholm (see chapter 8).

- **Camping:** There are a number of pleasant, well-equipped campgrounds near Copenhagen and elsewhere—a total of 528 throughout the country. For information about campsites and facilities, contact the tourist information office in your home country or in your chosen destination in Denmark, or write to a nation-wide organization devoted to the marketing of Danish campgrounds to the rest of the world at large, the **Campingraadet,** Hesseløgade 16, DK-2100 Copenhagen (☎ **39-27-88-44**).
- **Horseback Riding:** Riding schools throughout Denmark rent out horses. Local tourist offices can offer advice on this. Our favorite place for riding is on the Isle of Læsø (off of Jutland), which you can explore on the back of an Icelandic pony. After you gallop along past salt marshes and bird life, you can stop from time to time to relax on the beach. For more information, contact **Krogbækgaard,** Byrum, DK-9940 Læsø (☎ **98-49-15-05**). Boats sail to Læsø from the port of Frederikshavn in North Jutland. See chapter 12.

4 The Best Festivals & Special Events

For more information on these festivals, see the "Calendar of Events" in chapter 3.

- **Aalborg Carnival:** Celebrated on May 21, this is one of the great spring events in Denmark. The streets are filled with happy folk in colorful costumes. Almost 10,000 take part in the celebration, honoring the victory of spring over winter. The whole city bursts with joy.
- **July 4 Festival** (Rebild, near Aalborg): This is one of the few places outside the United States to honor U.S. independence. Each year Danes and Danish-Americans gather in these hills to celebrate the day with picnic lunches, outdoor entertainment, and speeches.
- **Copenhagen Jazz Festival:** One of the finest jazz festivals in Europe takes place in July. Some of the best jazz musicians in the world show up to jam in the Danish capital. Indoor and outdoor concerts—many of which are free—are presented.
- **Viking Festival** (Frederikssund): During this annual 4-week festival (June 19 to July 15), Nordic sagas are revived by bearded Vikings in an open-air theater. After each performance, a traditional Viking banquet is served.
- **Fire Festival Regatta** (Silkeborg): This is the country's oldest and biggest festival, with nightly cruises on the lakes and illumination provided by thousands of candles on shore. On the final night, the fireworks display is without equal in Europe, and Danish artists provide the entertainment at a large fun fair. Usually held the first week in August.

5 The Best Castles & Palaces

- **Christiansborg Palace** (Copenhagen): The queen receives official guests here in the Royal Reception Chamber, where you must don slippers to protect the floors.

The complex also holds the Parliament House and the Supreme Court. From 1441 until the fire of 1795, this was the official residence of Denmark's monarchy. You can tour the richly decorated rooms, including the Throne Room and banqueting hall. Below you can see the well-preserved ruins of the 1167 castle of Bishop Absalon, founder of Copenhagen. See chapter 5.

- **Rosenborg Castle** (Copenhagen): Founded by Christian IV in the 17th century, this red-brick Renaissance castle remained a royal residence until the early 19th century when it was converted into a museum. It still houses the crown jewels, and its collection of costumes and royal memorabilia is unequaled in Denmark. See chapter 5.

- **Kronborg Slot** (Helsingør): Shakespeare never saw this castle, and Hamlet (if he existed at all) lived centuries before it was ever built. But Shakespeare set his immortal play here—the Bard has spoken, and that's that. Its cannon-studded bastions are full of intriguing secret passages and casemates, and it often serves as the backdrop for modern productions of *Hamlet*. The brooding statue of Holger Danske sleeps in the dungeon, but, according to legend, this Viking chief will rise again to defend Denmark if it is endangered. See chapter 6.

- **Frederiksborg Castle** (Hillerød): Known as the Danish Versailles, this moated *slot* (castle) is the most elaborate in Scandinavia. It was built in the Dutch Renaissance style of red brick with a copper roof, and its oldest parts date from 1560. Much of the castle was constructed under the direction of the "master builder," Christian IV, from 1600 to 1620. The castle was ravaged by fire in 1859 and had to be completely restored. It is now a major national history museum. See chapter 6.

- **Egeskov Castle** (Kværndrup): On the island of Funen, this 1554 Renaissance "water castle" is set amid splendid gardens. It's the most romantic example of Denmark's fortified manors. Built in the middle of a moat, it's surrounded by a 30-acre park. The best-preserved Renaissance castle of its type in Europe, it has many attractions on its grounds, including an airplane museum and a vintage automobile museum. See chapter 9.

6 The Best Offbeat Experiences

- **People-to-People Contacts:** If you'd like to meet Scandinavians with similar interests and backgrounds to yours, the best "bridge" is **Friends Overseas,** 68-04 Dartmouth St., Forest Hills, NY 11375 (☎ **718/544-5660**). A fee of $25 is charged for your "hook-up" in Scandinavia, but for many it's worth the money to have this close encounter with the bright, articulate, and often sensitive and caring people of Scandinavia, among the most educated in the world. For more information, refer to chapter 3.

- **Journeying Back to the 1960s:** If you're nostalgic for the counterculture of the 1960s, it lives on in Christiania, a Copenhagen community located at the corner of Prinsessegade and Badsmandsstræde on Christianshavn. Founded in 1972, this is an anarchists' commune that occupies former army barracks; its current residents preach the gospel of drugs and peace. Christiania's residents have even organized their own government and passed laws, for example, to legalize drugs. They're not complete anarchists, however, since they venture into the city at least once a month to pick up their social welfare checks. Today you can wander about their community, which is complete with a theater, cafes, grocery stores, and even a local radio station. See chapter 5.

- **Looking Behind the Scenes in Denmark:** Denmark has often led the world in advanced social thinking. The Danes have accepted same-sex marriages and take seriously the need to provide excellent child care centers. Now a tour group, **Benns Rejser,** Nørregade 51, DK-7500 Holstebro (☎ **97-42-68-00**), will take interested visitors behind the scenes to see what's being done in such areas as environmental protection, care of the elderly, agriculture, education, social welfare programs, and developments in alternative (non-nuclear) energy programs. Established in 1963, the company has developed a reputation for showcasing Denmark's sometimes advanced, sometimes controversial positions on social progress during academic and intra-industry study tours that usually average around 5 days each.
- **Exploring Erotica:** Denmark was the first country to "liberate" pornography, in 1968, and today there's a museum in Copenhagen devoted to the subject. In the Erotica Museum (at Købmagergade 24), you can learn about the sex lives of such famous figures as Nietzsche, Freud, and even Duke Ellington. Founded by a photographer of nudes, the exhibits range from the tame to the tempestuous—everything from Etruscan drawings to pictures of venereal skin disease and sadomasochism videos. See chapter 5.
- **Calling on Artists and Craftspeople:** In West Jutland there are many open workshops where you can see craftspeople in action; you can meet the potter, the glassblower, the painter, the textile designer, and even the candlestick maker. Local tourist offices can let you know which studios are open to receive guests in such centers as Tønder, Ribe, Esbjerg, Varde, Billund, Herning, Struer, and Skive. One of our favorites is the studio of Havlit Stentøj, Inga V. Sørenson, and Asger Kristensen, at Vesterballevej 1 on Jutland, 22-miles north of Ho, DK-6857 Blåvand or Esbjerg (☎ **75-27-95-93**). At this pottery workshop you can see unique pieces being made. The potters take their inspiration from the rugged landscape of West Jutland, expressing it in urns, pots, and reliefs in which lines, colors, and patterns create a harmonious finished product. See chapter 10.

7 The Best Buys

- **Danish Design:** It's worth making a shopping trip to Denmark. The simple but elegant line that became fashionable in the 1950s has made a comeback. Danish modern chairs, glassware, and even buildings have returned. "Old masters" such as Arne Jacobsen, Hans Wegner, and Poul Kjærhom are celebrated; their designs from the 1940s and 1950s are sold today in antiques stores. Wegner, noted for his sculptured teak chairs, for example, is now viewed as the grand old man of Danish design. Younger designers have followed in the "old masters'" footsteps, producing carefully crafted items for the home—everything from chairs, desks, and furnishings, to table settings and silverware. For the best display of Danish design today, walk along the pedestrians-only Strøget, the major shopping street of Copenhagen. The best single showcase for modern Danish design may be **Illums Bolighus,** Amagertorv 10 (☎ **33-14-19-41**). See chapter 5.
- **Crystal & Porcelain:** Holmegaard crystal and Royal Copenhagen porcelain are household names, known for their beauty and craftsmanship. These items cost less in Denmark than in the United States, although signed art glass is always extremely costly. To avoid high prices, you can shop for seconds, which are discounted by 20% to 50% (sometimes the imperfection can be detected only by an expert). The best centers for these collectors' items in Copenhagen

are: **Royal Copenhagen** and **Bing & Grøndahl Porcelain,** Amagertorv 6
(☎ **33-13-71-81**), and **Holmegaards Glasværker,** Amagertorv 6 (☎ **33-12-
44-77**). See chapter 5.
• **Silver:** Danish designers have made a name for themselves in this field. Even with
taxes and shipping charges, you can still save about 50% when purchasing silver
in Denmark as compared with in the U.S. If you're willing to consider "used"
silver, you can get some remarkable discounts. The big name in international
silver—and you can buy it at the source—is **Georg Jensen,** Amagertorv 6,
Copenhagen (☎ **33-11-40-80**). See chapter 5.

8 The Best Hotels

• **Kong Frederik** (Copenhagen; ☎ **800/44-UTELL** in the U.S., or 33-12-59-02):
An intimate hotel of charm and style, this is a sibling of the highly ranked
d'Angleterre (see below). Ultra-chic, it has a devoted following—almost like a private club. Comprised of two separate hotels in 1850, the King Frederick is now a
harmonious whole—graced with traditional and often antiques-filled rooms and
known for the excellent cuisine of its Queen's Garden Restaurant. See chapter 4.
• **Hotel d'Angleterre** (Copenhagen; ☎ **800/44-UTELL** in the U.S., or 33-12-
00-95): Some critics rate this as the finest hotel in Denmark. As it drifted toward
mediocrity a few years back, a massive investment was made to save it. Now the
hotel is better than ever—housing a swimming pool and a nightclub. Behind its
Georgian façade, much of the ambience is in the traditional English mode. Service is among the finest in Copenhagen. See chapter 4.
• **Falsled Kro** (Falsled; ☎ **62-68-11-11**): Not only is this Funen Island's finest
accommodation, but it's the quintessential Danish inn, with origins going back
to the 1400s. A Relais & Châteaux property, it has been elegantly furnished and
converted into a stellar inn as well as a top-quality restaurant, rivaling the very
best in Copenhagen. See chapter 9.
• **Hotel Hesselet** (Nyborg; ☎ **65-31-30-29**): This stylish modern hotel on Funen
Island occupies a woodland setting in a beech forest. The spacious bedrooms are
artfully decorated, often with traditional furnishings. A library, Oriental carpets,
and an open fireplace add graceful touches to the public areas. Many Copenhagen residents book in here for a retreat, patronizing the hotel's gourmet restaurant at night. See chapter 9.
• **Hotel Dagmar** (Ribe; ☎ **800/528-1234** in the U.S., or 75-42-00-33): Jutland's
most glamorous hotel was converted from a private home in 1850, although the
building itself dates back to 1581. This half-timbered hotel encapsulates the
charm of the 16th century, with such adornments as carved chairs, sloping
wooden floors, and stained-glass windows. Many of the bedrooms are furnished
with antique canopy beds. A fine restaurant, serving both Danish and international dishes, completes the picture. See chapter 10.

9 The Best Restaurants

• **St. Gertruds Kloster** (Copenhagen; ☎ **33-14-66-30**): This is the capital's most
romantic restaurant—and it also serves the most refined cuisine. In 14th-century
underground vaults which have no electricity, you dine by the light of some
1,500 flickering candles. Once a medieval monastery, the restaurant now offers a
delectable international cuisine, including a velvety *foie gras* with black truffles or
venison with green asparagus. See chapter 4.

- **Kommandanten** (Copenhagen; ☎ **33-12-09-90**): A house built by a Danish commander for his family in 1698 now accommodates this restaurant. The menu, drawn freely from some of the finest continental and Mediterranean influences, includes such dishes as *foie gras* with a lobster and truffle sauce or pigeon sautéed with bacon, cabbage, and cherries. Fresh seafood is served in every conceivable way. The wooden floors and beams date back to the 17th century, but the Warhol modern art gives the restaurant a trendy edge. See chapter 4.
- **Divan II** (Copenhagen; ☎ **33-12-51-51**): This early 19th-century slate house was constructed when the lush Tivoli Garden grounds were being laid out. In this romantic setting, you can enjoy both a meal and a view over the lake across from the fairytale Hans Christian Andersen Castle. The chefs prepare the gardens' most refined cuisine—a world of gastronomic delights—ranging from rack of Danish lamb roasted with garlic and sage to *mousseline* of lobster baked with turbot and served with asparagus spears. See chapter 4.
- **Marie Louise** (Odense; ☎ **66-17-92-95**): Glittering with crystal and silver, this dining room on a pedestrian street is one of the finest on the island of Funen. In an antique house, this Danish/Franco alliance offers a cuisine that's the epitome of taste, preparation, and service. Seafood and fish are the favored dishes. See chapter 9.
- **Falsled Kro** (Falsled; ☎ **62-68-11-11**): Even if you don't stay here, consider enjoying a meal here. A favorite among well-heeled Europeans, this restaurant produces a stellar French-inspired cuisine, often using seasonal produce from its own gardens. The succulent salmon is smoked on the premises in one of the outbuildings, and the owners breed quail locally. Such care and attention to detail make this one of Denmark's top restaurants. See chapter 9.

Getting to Know Denmark 2

The Danes may live in a small country, but they usually extend an enthusiastic welcome to visitors. The late British novelist Evelyn Waugh called the Danes "the most exhilarating people of Europe." Few Danes would dispute this—and neither would we.

Made up mostly of islands, Denmark is a heavily industrialized nation, known for its manufactured products as well as its arts and crafts. However, it also boasts a quarter of a million farmers.

1 Denmark Today

Denmark has been called a bridge since it links northern Europe with the Scandinavian peninsula. The smallest of the Scandinavian countries, its total land mass equals about 16,000 square miles (about half the size of Maine), most of which is located on the peninsula of Jutland, which borders Germany. The major islands are Zealand, Funen, and Bornholm. Denmark has adequate space for its population of 5.5 million people, but its population density is much greater than that of the other Scandinavian countries. About 1.4 million Danes live in the capital city, Copenhagen, on the island of Zealand.

About 98% of all native-born Danes belong to the Danish Lutheran Church, the state church, although church attendance is actually low. The second-largest group is Catholics (30,000), and there are about 6,500 Jews.

As Denmark faces the millennium, surveys have shown that at least 4.5% of the population is made up of immigrants, including refugees identified as Palestinians, Somalis, Bangladeshis, Kurds, and Iraqis, among others. Vietnamese immigrants seem rather popular, but Muslim and Arab immigrants tend to experience hostility.

Historically, Denmark has been ranked among the most tolerant nations on earth. The king, for example, chose to wear a yellow star during the entire Nazi occupation of Denmark in World War II. Nevertheless, it is currently experiencing a wave of anti-immigrant and anti-refugee feeling. In recent months, the well-scrubbed and apple-cheeked Danes have been making unattractive world headlines, including one on the front page of the *International Herald Tribune:* "A Xenophobic Weed is Growing in Denmark's Tidy Little Garden." This feeling has been growing so alarmingly that many expect that some time before the millennium the far-right ultra-nationalist Danish

People's Party will emerge from parliamentary elections as Denmark's third largest political force. However, Danes apparently still reject the tenets of this right-wing Danish People's Party and its leaders, shown at an anti-racist rally in the late autumn of 1997, which was the largest such mass outpouring in the decade.

Much of the growing xenophobic anger focuses on the fact that in this welfare state, a refugee family from Iraq, for example, with 11 children, can receive the same cash allotment as a native-born Dane who has worked for 50 years, paying taxes into the system. Danes also complain that immigrants, who are mainly relegated to certain areas, are creating ghetto-like conditions in some Danish cities. In response, many Danes have moved to other areas, and moved their children into private or public schools where Danes are still in the majority.

Erling Olsen, a speaker of Parliament and a senior figure in the Social Democratic Party, which leads the minority government, saw it this way: "Our challenge is to remain humanist while seeking to limit abuses in the area of immigration. It's a small country but a little megalomaniac. We have to find a solution, a tolerant one."

Technically, Denmark is a parliamentary democracy and constitutional monarchy. Its territories include the Faroe Islands (an autonomous area under the Danish Crown) and Greenland (which was granted regional autonomy in 1985). The sovereign is Queen Margrethe II, who ascended the throne in 1972; her husband is a Frenchman, Prince Henrik. Margrethe is the first woman sovereign in Denmark in six centuries. Real power is vested in the unicameral parliament (the Folketing), which is elected every 4 years by citizens over the age of 23. The royal family functions primarily in a ceremonial capacity.

Although a NATO member since 1949, Denmark does not permit nuclear weapons to be deployed on its soil. It's also an active member of the European Union and enjoys harmonious relations with its Scandinavian neighbors as well as other European countries.

Denmark enjoys one of the world's highest standards of living plus a comprehensive social welfare system, which is funded through extremely high taxes. Danes enjoy 7½-hour work days, cradle-to-grave security, state-funded hospitals and schools, and even a month-long vacation every year. During their vacations Danes tend to travel extensively. By and large the Danes are extremely well educated; they have pioneered

❓ Did You Know?

- Denmark is a nation of nearly 500 islands.
- The reigning queen, Margrethe II, also designs postage stamps and opera and ballet sets.
- Second only to the Bible, the writing of Hans Christian (H. C.) Andersen are the most widely translated literary works in the world.
- Some historians argue that the fairy tale writer Andersen wasn't the son of a poor cobbler, but the child of the 19th century Danish king Christian VIII.
- Denmark has the largest proportion of female clerics per population.
- The country has a celebration honoring America's Fourth of July.
- Chilly Denmark used to grow grapes for wine-making in the Middle Ages.
- Danes pay the highest taxes on earth and have the highest suicide rate (although these two facts are not necessarily linked!).

the establishment of adult education centers (for those ages 18 to 35), and this movement has spread to other countries of Europe as well.

No country in the European Union has less poverty or a fairer distribution of wealth than Denmark. Both the poor and the rich get richer, and in most cases young people have little trouble finding employment. And in fact, unemployment rates are falling.

Although a progressive, modern, and liberal state (it was the first country to recognize same-sex marriages, and the first NATO country to grant women the right to serve in front-line military units), Denmark has its share of problems. Drug use among young people is a growing concern, and the institution of marriage is increasingly being rejected by the young, so common-law relationships are becoming the norm. Also, the divorce rate is rising.

In spite of those headlines about "Xenophobic Weed," Denmark in the late 1990s is building bridges to the world. On June 14, 1998, Queen Margrethe II cut a ribbon before driving across the Great Belt Bridge, linking the island of Zealand (on which Copenhagen sits) with the island of Funen. Because Funen is linked by bridge to Jutland (mainland Europe), Copenhageners can now drive into Germany without having to rely on ferryboats, cutting travel time across the "Belt" by more than an hour.

That's not all. The "Øresund Fixed Link" between Denmark and Sweden is set to be completed in the year 2000. A new artificial island 2½-miles long will be constructed halfway across Øresund to connect a 2-mile rail and motorway tunnel and a 4.8-mile two-level bridge. Bridging the divide between Copenhagen and Malmø (Sweden), this link should promote cultural, educational, and research exchanges, as well as making business and travel between the two nations easier than ever before. With three million people living within a 31-mile radius of the link, this combined region of Denmark and Sweden has the largest population density in the Nordic world.

2 The Natural Environment

Denmark has more than 4,500 miles of irregular coastline. Linked geologically with northern Europe, especially Germany, Denmark is nevertheless part of Scandinavia, although not anchored there quite as solidly as Sweden and Norway.

Denmark is a low-lying country—its highest elevation is only 565 feet above sea level. But that doesn't mean that the country is totally flat. Most of its terrain consists of folds, undulations, small and often steep hills, and long, low rises. There are also forests, small rivers, lakes, and even beaches, many of which are excellent for swimming, although the water may be too cold for some people.

The west coast of Jutland is washed by the North Sea, but it's not suitable for exploration by ship since it's obstructed by sand dunes and small sandbanks. "Island hills" that rise from sandy plains represent the oldest glacial terrain in Denmark. Much of this landscape was formed during the last Ice Age when ancient icebergs carved the country into its present shape. On the east coast of Jutland there are fjords (such as Lim and Mariager), although they lack the drama of those on the west coast of Norway. The longest river in Denmark is the Gudenå—80-miles long—which rises in north-central Jutland and feeds into Lake Lanso on the eastern side of the peninsula.

Winters in Denmark tend to be mild along the North Sea coast, although harsh in the interior of Jutland. In general, eastern Denmark receives more precipitation than the west, although in winter that situation is reversed.

To Denmark's east lies the Baltic Sea, which surrounds the small offshore island of Bornholm. The flora of Bornholm differs from that found elsewhere in the country.

If I were a dictator, I would not occupy Denmark for fear of being laughed to death.
                                                              — John Steinbeck

Denmark's vegetation resembles that of the continent. The woods in southern Denmark are largely deciduous, with oak and birch forests. Major reforestation is under way, especially with the planting of coniferous forests, mostly pine and spruce. The most beautiful beech forests are on the island of Møn.

Humans and agriculture have reduced the living space for Denmark's native fauna. However, roe, red deer, badgers, and foxes are still found. Fallow deer are also widely scattered throughout the country. Birders will be able to spot woodpeckers, robins, tits, chaffinches, and some thrushes in the Danish wetlands, which survive more or less in their natural state. The greatest place for bird-watching is near the Limfjord in North Jutland.

Denmark, which is a leader among environmentally conscious nations, has set aside 3.5% of its land mass as a protected nature reserve, including Rebild National Park in North Jutland, the chalk cliffs of Møn, and the tidal sands off the west coast of Jutland—one of the world's most valued wetlands.

3 The Regions in Brief

Zealand   Home to Denmark's capital, **Copenhagen,** Zealand draws more visitors than any other region of the country. The largest island, Zealand is also the wealthiest and most densely populated. Other cities include **Roskilde,** 20-miles west of Copenhagen, which is home to the Roskilde Cathedral (burial place of many Danish kings) and a collection of Viking vessels that were discovered in a fjord. The medieval town of **Køge** was a place where witches were burned in the Middle Ages. One of the most popular attractions on the island is **Helsingør** (Elsinor in English), about 25-miles north of Copenhagen, where visitors flock to see "Hamlet's Castle." Off Zealand's southeast corner lies the island of **Møn**, home to Møns Klint, an expanse of white cliffs that rise sharply out of the Baltic.

Jutland   The peninsula of Jutland links the island nation of Denmark with its neighbor, Germany. Jutland's miles of coastline feature some of northern Europe's finest sandy but chilly beaches. Giant dunes and moors abound on the west coast, whereas the interior has rolling pastureland and beech forests. Jutland's more interesting towns and villages include **Jelling,** heralded as the birthplace of Denmark and the ancient seat of the Danish kings; here you can see an extensive collection of Viking artifacts excavated from ancient burial mounds. The Viking port of **Ribe** is the oldest town in Denmark. It's known throughout the world as the preferred nesting grounds for numerous endangered storks. The resort of **Fanø**, with its giant dunes, heather-covered moors, and forests, is an excellent place to bird-watch or view Denmark's varied wildlife. The university city of **Århus** is Jutland's capital and second only to Copenhagen in size. **Aalsborg,** founded by Vikings more than 1,000 years ago, is a thriving commercial center in northern Jutland and lies close to Rebild National Park and the Rold Forest.

Funen   The island of Funen, with an area of 1,150 square miles, is Denmark's second-largest island. Called the garden of Denmark, Funen is known to the world as the birthplace of Hans Christian Andersen. Its rolling countryside is dotted with orchards, stately manors, and castles. **Odense,** Andersen's birthplace, is a mecca for fairytale writers and fans from around the world. Nearby stands Egeskov Castle, resting on oak columns in the middle of a small lake. It's Europe's best-preserved Renaissance castle. Funen has a number of bustling ports, including **Nyborg** in the east and **Svendborg** at the southern end of the island. **Ærøskøbing** is a medieval market town that's a showplace of Scandinavian heritage.

Bornholm   In the Baltic Sea, southeast of Zealand, close to Sweden, lies the island of Bornholm. Here the countryside is peppered with prehistoric monuments and runic stones, and numerous fishing villages dot the shoreline. On the northern coast, near **Hammerhus,** the Bornholm Animal and Nature Park is home to many native species as well as some that have been introduced from other parts of Scandinavia. Some of Europe's largest castle ruins dot this region of the island. The town of **Rønne** is the site of Denmark's oldest regional theater; many concerts and shows are performed here year round. The island of **Christiansø,** off the coast of Bornholm, had been the site of Denmark's penal colony, built in 1825 and in use for most of the 19th century. Danish criminals sentenced to life imprisonment were deported to the island where they spent their lives in slavery.

Møn, Falster & Lolland   Called "the South Seas of Denmark" (a bit of an exaggeration), this trio of islands lie off the coast of South Zealand, to which all three are connected by bridges. Møn, the only "South Sea island" we cover in this guide, is the most popular of the three destinations, visited chiefly for its unique chalk cliffs. Falster is known for its fine white sandy beaches, and Lolland for its rolling agricultural landscape and yachting harbors. The best base for Møn is the main town and commercial center of **Stege,** one of Denmark's wealthiest towns during the Middle Ages. Falster's single large town is **Nykøbing F** (the "F" stands for Falster and is used to differentiate this Nykøbing from other towns in Denmark of the same name). **Gedser,** at the tip of Falster, is Denmark's southernmost point. The town of **Maribo** is the geographical and commercial center of Lolland.

4 History 101

Composed of a flat and sandy peninsula and a cluster of islands, Denmark is tiny, with less than 7% of the land mass of Texas. But despite its small size, its strategic position at the mouth of the Baltic has made Denmark one of the most coveted terrains in the world. Consequently, Denmark's struggles to secure its sovereignty and independence from the larger, stronger, military forces that surround it on every side have repeatedly shaped Danish history. And although modern Danes are somewhat embarrassed when confronted with their country's militaristic past, Denmark used to be known as a fiercely aggressive nation, jockeying for territory, prestige, and strategic advantage with other such empire-building nations as England, Austria, and the precursors of modern-day Germany.

Dateline

- **810** The reign of the first recorded Danish king, Godfred, ends.
- **811** The southern boundary of the Danish kingdom is established at the banks of the Eider River, where it remains for almost a thousand years.
- **800–950** Vikings emerge to plunder the monasteries and settlements of England, France, and Russia.
- **940–985** Harald Bluetooth brings Christianity to Denmark.

continues

- **1013–43** The crowns of Denmark and England are united.
- **1104** The foundation is laid for a Danish national church that's distinctly different from that within German lands to the south.
- **1397** The Union of Kalmar, under the leadership of Queen Margaret, unites Denmark, Norway, and Sweden. Meanwhile, high percentages of Danes are allowed to work their own farmland, forming the basis of Denmark's eventual strength as an agrarian nation.
- **1471** Sweden abandons the union; Denmark and Norway remain united under Christian I (1426–81).
- **1530** Lutheran preachers bring the Reformation to Denmark.
- **1536** After a siege of Copenhagen, most of the lands and assets owned by the Catholic church are seized by the Danish crown.
- **1577–1648** The long reign of Christian IV brings prosperity, but ends in a losing war with Sweden.
- **1675–1679** The Skane War, wherein Denmark loses large territories to Sweden, including the "château country" of southern Sweden.
- **1801–7** England, in a black chapter of its foreign policy, bombards Copenhagen and confiscates the ships of Denmark's navy as a means of ensuring that the Danes don't cooperate with Napoléon.
- **1813** The national treasury of Denmark, faced with punitive clauses in the treaty at the end of the Napoleonic Wars, goes bankrupt.

continues

PREHISTORIC DENMARK AND THE ROMANS   The mystery that surrounds early Denmark stems from the fact that the Romans and their legions never managed to transform it into a colony. Consequently, while former Roman provinces like France and Germany were described by numerous historians, including Julius Caesar himself, very little was ever recorded about ancient Denmark. There is evidence of early trade, though. Amber found only in the Baltic has been identified within Egyptian jewelry, and some historians cite Danish trade with the Eastern Mediterranean, in which the Danes exchanged fur and slaves for bronze utensils and gold jewelry.

Concentrations of bones from various grave sites, and stone implements that archeologists estimate as 80,000 years old, have been unearthed in various regions of Jutland, but despite those discoveries, Denmark has never produced the wealth of archeological finds that are commonplace, say, in Greece, Italy, or Egypt. Part of the reason might stem from the great ice sheets that made much of Denmark uninhabitable for thousands of years.

Later, as the ice sheets receded northward, hunter-gatherers eked out a modest living, although their communal grave sites and the stone dolmen that mark their entrances show proficiency at erecting large stone lintels and markers.

Ironically, the high acid and iron content within Denmark's peat bogs has had the macabre effect of preserving the bodies of at least 160 unfortunates, all of whom died violently, in some cases many thousands of years ago, and all of whom appear to have been unceremoniously dumped into bogs. Among the most famous of these is the well-preserved, 2,000-year-old body of the Grauballe Man, who was probably strangled to death, and whose body was discovered in the 1950s in a Jutland peat bog. His body revealed some clues about what life was like in prehistoric Denmark: A wool cap covered his head, stubble on his chin and cheeks indicated the fashion at the time involved shaving, and the remains within his stomach showed that his last meal consisted mostly of barley.

And as for literary references, other than a few cryptic comments that appear within such early English sagas as *Beowulf,* and the cryptic descriptions by the medieval Scandinavian historian Saxo Grammaticus of a long line of (otherwise undocumented) early medieval Danish warlords, there isn't a lot of documentation about post-Roman Denmark. Historians conclude that Denmark was a land of frequent migrations, frequent annihilations of one tribal unit by another, and frequent changeovers of the racial texture of the peninsula as one group of tribespeople were either annihilated or ousted by others.

VIKINGS TERRORIZE EUROPE Denmark developed a reputation for violence as the Vikings ravaged regions of central and southern Europe.

So ironically, the country with one of the least controversial images in Europe today was originally a hell-raising land that, along with such other Viking areas as Norway and Sweden, was associated with terror for the rest of Europe. Lustfully pagan and undeterred by the belief that Christian churches and monasteries were sanctified, they exacted rich plunder from whatever monastery or convent they happened to judge as weak enough to be attractive.

Their longboats were especially feared: Measuring about 60 feet from the dragon-shaped prow to its stern, longboats were powered by 30 oars and a sail, but were still light enough that its crews could drag them across land, thereby "hopping" from rivers to lakes, across sandbars, and across ithsmuses that would otherwise have been unnavigable. It's small wonder that the Danes would eventually become proficient as both mariners and traders.

Through rape and intermarriage, the Vikings mingled bloodlines with future English, French, Germans, and Russians. Despite the mayhem they unleashed on conquered lands, Vikings brought with them regimented rituals; for example, unlike most European peoples at the time, they bathed every Sunday, regardless of temperature or weather.

The most distinct threat to Danish territoriality came from Charlemagne, whose Frankish empire covered what is today France and Germany. If Charlemagne hadn't focused most of his territorial ambitions on richer, more fertile lands within central Europe and Spain, it's likely that what's known today as Denmark would have become a vassal state of the Franks. As it was, the Franks only took a slight imperial interest in Jutland. In fact, Godfred, the first recorded Danish king, died in 810 after spending most of his reign battling the Franks.

Godfred's successor, Hemming, signed a treaty with the Franks marking the Eider River, an east-west stream that flanks southern Jutland, as the southern boundary of his sovereignty. That boundary functioned more or less as the Danish border until 1864.

- **1810–1830** The golden age of Danish literature, as defined by the creation of works by Sören Kierkegaard and Hans Christian Andersen.
- **1849** Simultaneous with revolutions that break out across Europe, liberal reforms are activated in the form of a new Danish constitution.
- **1866** Denmark loses Schleswig-Holstein to Prussia.
- **1890s** Many liberal reforms in education and health insurance act as precursors of the liberal social policies of Denmark in the 20th century.
- **1914** Denmark struggles to maintain neutrality in World War I.
- **1915** A new constitution gives Denmark universal suffrage.
- **1916** Denmark sells what later becomes known as the U.S. Virgin Islands for $25,000,000.
- **1926–1940** Worldwide depression causes great suffering in Denmark.
- **1940–45** Denmark is invaded and occupied by Nazi Germany.
- **1949** Over some protests, Denmark joins NATO.
- **1953** A new constitution provides for a single-chamber parliament.
- **1972** Denmark joins the European Economic Community; Margrethe, daughter of Frederik IX, becomes queen of Denmark.
- **1982** Poul Schluter becomes the first Conservative prime minister since 1894.
- **1989** Denmark leads the world in certain social policies: The first NATO country to allow women in front-line military units, and the first country to recognize same-sex marriages.

continues

■ **1992** Denmark votes against the Maastricht Treaty, which established the framework for the European Economic Union.

■ **1993** Denmark votes to support the Maastricht Treaty and then presides over the European Union for the first half of the year.

■ **1996** Copenhagen is designated the "Cultural Capital of Europe"; the "Copenhagen 96" festival attracts artists and performers from all over the world, with more than 25,000 performances staged.

■ **1998** By a narrow margin, Denmark votes to enlarge its ties with the European Union.

Two famous kings emerged from Denmark during the 10th century, Gorm the Old (883–940), and his son, Harald Bluetooth (940–985). Their reigns resulted in the unification of Denmark with power centralized at Jelling in Jutland. Harald, through the hard work of a core of Christian missionaries trained in Frankish territories to the south (especially in Hamburg), also introduced Christianity, which eventually became the country's predominant religion. As part of his attempt to obliterate Denmark's pagan past, he transformed his father's tomb, which honored a roster of pagan gods and spirits, into a site of Christian worship.

Harald eventually extended Danish influence as far as neighboring Norway. The links he established between Denmark and Norway weren't severed, at least politically, until the 1800s. Harald's son, Sweyn I, succeeded in conquering England in 1013, more than 50 years before the Norman invasion in 1066. The Normans, ironically, were also of Danish origin, through invasions several centuries before.

Under Sweyn's son, Canute II (994–1035), England, Denmark, and part of Sweden came under the rule of one crown. After Canute's death, however, the Danish kingdom was reduced to only Denmark. Canute's nephew, Sweyn II, ruled the Danish kingdom, and upon his death his five sons governed Denmark successfully. In 1104, the foundation was laid for a Danish national church that was distinct from the ecclesiastical administration in Hamburg.

THE BALTIC: A DANISH "LAKE"   The few remaining links between Denmark and the Frankish Holy Roman Empire were severed under Archbishop Eskil (1100–82) and King Waldemar I (1131–82). During a celebration at Ringsted in 1190, the Danish church and state were united, partly because of the influence of Archbishop Absalon (1128–1201), a soldier and statesman who is honored today as the patron saint of Copenhagen. Inspired by monarchical ideas, Absalon became a fierce and militaristic guardian of Danish independence. The hostilities became a religious confrontation, pitting the Christian Danes against the pagans to the south, as well as a territorial conflict. Absalon's most dramatic disfigurement of a pagan god occurred on the now-German island of Rügen around 1147, when he chopped the four-headed wooden figure (Svantevit) into little pieces and distributed them as firewood among his Danish (nominally Christian) soldiers.

In 1169, Denmark began what would evolve into a long series of conquests and influence-peddling within city-states along the Baltic, including the ports of Estonia (which was conquered by the Danes in 1219), Latvia, eastern Germany, Poland, Sweden, and Russia. Part of Denmark's military and mercantile success derived from the general weakness of the German states to the south; part of it was because of a population explosion within Denmark, which increased the pressure for colonization.

Valdemar II (1170–1241) strengthened Denmark's control over the Baltic and came close to transforming it into a Danish lake. Grateful for their help, he ennobled many of his illegitimate sons and empowered many of his military cohorts with aristocratic titles and rewarded them with land.

"Denmark"

It was during the early Middle Ages that the name "Denmark" was introduced to the consciousness of northern Europe. The name was inspired by the word for a primitive stone and earth barricade, known as the *Dannevirk* or *Danewerk*, which was erected in an ultimately futile attempt to shut out invaders from the south.

The result was a weakening of the monarchy in favor of an increasingly voracious group of nobles, whose private agendas conflicted with those of the king. Valdemar's son, Eric IV (also known as Eric Ploughpenny; 1216–50), argued with church bishops and with his brothers over royal prerogatives, and was assassinated by his younger brother, Duke Abel of Schleswig, who proclaimed himself king of Denmark in 1250.

Civil wars ensued, and three of the four successive kings were killed in battle. Eric VI (1274–1319) also waged wars with Norway and Sweden, which led to Denmark's debilitation and the mortgaging of large parcels of the kingdom to pay for unsuccessful military campaigns.

Between 1332 and 1340, Denmark had no king and was ruled by an uneasy coalition of nobles. Valdemar IV Atterdag (1320–75) retained his grip on the Danish throne only by signing the peace treaty of Stralsund with the towns of the Hanseatic League (a federation of free towns in northern Germany and adjoining countries formed around 1241 for economic advancement and mutual protection) in 1370. Its enactment did a lot to improve the fortunes of the city-states of the Hanseatic League, as it granted them enviable commercial privileges. The resulting prosperity of the Hanseatic League led to architectural enhancements, whose effects were visible all around the Baltic.

A UNITED SCANDINAVIA   Valdemar IV died in 1375, leaving Denmark without a male heir. Finally, Olaf (1375–87), the infant son of Valdemar's daughter Margaret through her marriage with King Haakon VI Magnusson (1339–80) of Norway, came to the throne. (Through a complicated chain of bloodlines, the infant Olaf was the nominal heir to all of Norway, Denmark, and Sweden.)

During his infancy, Margaret ruled the country as regent. When both her husband, Haakon, and 12-year-old Olaf died, she was acknowledged as queen of Norway and Denmark. A patroness of the arts and a savvy administrator of the national treasury, she was eventually granted wide political leeway in Sweden as well.

Although the three nations had already been combined under the stewardship of Margaret, they were merged into a united Scandinavia in 1397 under the guise of The Union of Kalmar. One of the largest political unions since the collapse of the Roman Empire, it extended from Iceland and the fledgling communities in Greenland as far east as the western coast of Finland. It included the entire Danish archipelago as well as the Faroe, Shetland, and Orkney islands.

Acknowledging her advanced age and the need for a male figurehead at the reigns of power, Margaret arranged for her nephew, Eric of Pomerania (1382–1459), to be crowned king of all three countries as Eric VII. Margaret, however, firmly committed to the superiority of Denmark within the trio, continued to rule behind the scenes until her death in 1412. (A contemporary historian said of Margaret's comportment at public events, "All the nobility of Denmark were seized by fear of the wisdom and strength of this lady.") Despite later attempts to expand the Scandinavian union within northeastern Germany, the concept of a united Scandinavia was never again as far-reaching or powerful as it was under Margaret, much to the chagrin of 19th- and 20th-century visionaries who hoped for the eventual unification of "the three separate nations of the Scandinavian north."

Margaret's designated heir, Eric VII, was childless. He was dethroned in 1439, and replaced by his nephew Christopher of Bavaria. His reign lasted only about 9 years, after which Sweden pressed for autonomy. It elected Karl Knutson (Charles VIII) as its Stockholm-based king in 1471. Denmark and the relatively weak Norway shared King Christian I (1426–81). Although Christian I lost control of Sweden, he did gain sovereignty over Schleswig and Holstein, ancient territories to the south of modern-day Denmark. But it was a troubled and culturally ambiguous acquisition that would vex the patience of both Denmark and the German states for centuries to come, as its citizens waffled in their allegiances.

Throughout the rest of the 15th century, the Danish church accumulated great wealth, and the merchant class profited from increases in agricultural production. By around 1500, about 12,000 Danes were estimated to own their own farms; about 18,000 Danes operated farms on land leased by the Danish king, and some 30,000 Danes maintained lease lands belonging to either Danish nobles or to the increasingly wealthy (tax-exempt) Catholic church. Denmark became an exporter of foodstuffs, especially beef and grain, and livestock, especially horses.

The early 15th century marked a fundamental change in the definition of nobility. Prior to that, any Dane could become a noble by contributing a fully equipped private army, invariably composed of feudal-style serfs and vassals, to the king's war efforts. In exchange for this, he would be granted an exemption from all taxes generated by his estates. After around 1400, however, only nobles who could prove at least three generations of aristocratic lineage could define themselves as noble, with all the attendant privileges that such a title implied. With no new blood coming into the pool of Danish aristocrats, the number of noble families decreased from 264 to 140 between 1450 and 1650. The names of two of those families, the Rosenkrans and the Gyldenstjernes, were borrowed by Shakespeare for his drama about the mythical Danish prince, Hamlet.

The 16th century also saw changes in Danish religious practice as critiques of Catholicism began to gain currency across Europe. One of Denmark's most devoted Reformation-era theologians was Paul Helgesen, a staunch opponent of the corruption of Denmark's church. He was appointed to a position of academic prominence within the University of Copenhagen in 1519, and was a particularly vocal critic of the idea of buying salvation through the sale of indulgences. Ironically, Martin Luther's break with the Catholic church in 1521, from a base in nearby Germany, transformed the reputation of Paul Helgesen into something of an arch-conservative defender of Danish Catholicism.

THE 16TH CENTURY   Christian II (1481–1559) ascended the throne in 1513. Sympathetic to the common man during his regency over the throne of Norway, he was mistrusted by conservative nobles. Their distrust was exacerbated by his commitment to seeking financial and military advice from commoners. He went so far as to turn over control of the kingdom's finances to his mistress's mother, Sigbrit Villoms, the frugal and canny widow of a Dutch burgher. A former alchemist who claimed to have a telepathic hold over the king, she contributed to a reign alternating between bouts of genius and bouts of blood-soaked madness. Despite the massacre of more than 600 Danish and Swedish nobles in the "bloodbath of Stockholm" in 1520 and other violent atrocities, many Renaissance-style reforms were activated under Christian II's reign, without which Denmark might have erupted into full-fledged revolution.

Christian II recaptured Sweden in 1520 but was defeated by the Swedish warrior-king Gustavus Vasa a year later. Christian was deposed in 1522, whereupon he fled to the Netherlands. In the spring of 1532, he returned to Denmark, where he was incarcerated until his death, first restricted to Sönderborg Castle and then to Kalundborg castle.

His successor, Frederik I (1471–1533), signed a charter granting the nobility many privileges. Under his regime, the Franciscans, an order of Roman Catholic monks associated with St. Francis, were expelled from their conspicuously wealthy houses of worship, and Lutheran ministers were granted the freedom to roam throughout Denmark preaching. Upon Frederik's death, the Reformation took earnest hold within Denmark. Conflicts between Lutherans and Catholics erupted in a civil war, with Catholic power centered in Copenhagen and with Lutherans mainly based on the islands of Funen and Jutland. The war ended in 1536 with the surrender of Copenhagen. In the process vast Catholic-owned estates were forfeited to the Danish crown.

The Danish Lutheran Church was founded in 1536 during the reign of Christian III (1534–59). Before the end of the 1570s, Protestantism was firmly entrenched within Denmark, and virtually every vestige of Catholicism had been ousted by a Danish church that was organized according to German Lutheran models. Disciples of Martin Luther were brought in to organize the new Reformed Church of Denmark, which soon took on patriotic and nationalistic overtones, as hymn books, liturgies, and sermons were eventually conducted exclusively in vernacular Danish. As for the monarchy, its finances were vastly improved at the end of the Reformation thanks to its confiscation of the vast wealth formerly controlled by the Catholic church.

WARS WITH SWEDEN   Much of the 17th century in Denmark was consumed with an ongoing series of wars with its arch-enemy, Sweden. Despite that, the reign of the Danish king Christian IV (1577–1648) was one of relative prosperity. The Danes worked hard, investing time and money in the development of their "overseas territory," Norway. That territory's capital, Christiania (now known as Oslo), was named after their king.

Sweden was understandably concerned about Denmark's control of the entrance to the Baltic, the sea on which Sweden and many members of the Hanseatic League depended. Denmark, thanks to its control of the narrow straits near Copenhagen, its ownership of such Baltic islands as Ösel and Gotland, and, within the Atlantic, its control of Iceland and the Faroe Islands, could be accused of being far more imperial than its small size, and present-day pacifism, would imply.

Denmark continued to meddle in German and English politics throughout the 1600's, notably in the Thirty Years War that ripped apart the principalities of Germany.

Tensions between Denmark and Sweden also intensified during this period and were exacerbated by Sweden's emperor Charles V, who argued that Sweden held the right of succession to the Danish throne.

Sweden invaded Jutland, quickly defeating the Danes. Military scholars attribute the victory to Sweden's reliance on well-trained Swedish peasants who filled the ranks of the Swedish army. The Danes, in contrast, relied on paid, and less committed, mercenaries. By the Treaty of Christianople, Denmark was forced to cede to Sweden many of its former possessions, including scattered communities in Norway and the Baltic island of Gotland.

Simultaneous with the loss of its territories in southern Sweden, was the completion of two of Denmark's most-photographed castles: Frederiksborg in Hillerod, and Rosenborg in Copenhagen, both under the regime of Christian IV.

Danish king Frederik III (1609–70) tried to regain the lost territories when Sweden went to war with Poland, but he was defeated by Charles X. Frederik ended up giving Sweden additional territory, including the island of Bornholm. Charles X attacked Denmark in an attempt to take control of the whole country, but this time Denmark won, regaining its lost territories. Sweden ended the war after the death of Charles X in 1660.

The Skane War (1675–79) was an ill-advised military campaign started by the Danish king Christian V (1646–99). Its outcome included Denmark's loss of Skane, a valuable territory within southern Sweden which, because of its architectural appeal, is known today as Sweden's "château country." After the signing of the peace treaty that ended the war, Denmark managed to retain its claim on the island of Bornholm, and cities within northern Norway, such as Trondheim.

Frederik IV (1671–1730), Christian V's successor, resumed the war with Sweden in 1699. Named the "Great Northern War," it raged, more or less inconclusively, from 1699 to 1730. Southern Sweden was not recovered, but part of Schleswig-Holstein (northern Germany) was ceded to Denmark by the German states.

During the 18th century, Denmark achieved many democratic reforms. Thanks to its navy and its seasoned core of merchant vessels, it also gained control of a group of islands in the West Indies (now the U.S. Virgin Islands) as well as the barren, snowy expanse of Greenland. Agriculture and trade prospered, and Copenhagen developed into a quietly prosperous but formidable guardian of the western entrance of the Baltic Sea.

THE 19TH CENTURY AND THE NAPOLEONIC WARS   At the start of the Napoleonic wars, with France squarely opposed to most of the other nations of Europe, Denmark was engaged in a booming business of selling grain to both England and France. Despite the sweeping changes in the map of Europe engendered by Napoléon's military campaigns, Denmark strongly defended its right to remain neutral, and, as such, worked hard to ensure free passage of ships from other neutral nations within the Baltic.

This refusal to take sides, and also the rich contracts that Danish merchants were able to acquire transporting supplies between hostile parties, infuriated England—the sworn enemy of Napoléon's France. In 1801, fearing that Denmark's formidable navy might be persuaded to cooperate with the French, England destroyed part of the Danish fleet in a battle at sea.

In 1807, as the threat of Napoléon's conquest of Europe became more and more of a reality, in one of the most arrogant acts of coercion in 19th-century history, England ordered the Danes to transfer their navy to British rule within 8 days, or be bombarded. When the Danes refused, English warships opened fire on Copenhagen, destroying the city's cathedral, its university, and hundreds of private homes. Denmark's treatment by England forced the youthful king Frederik VI (1808–39) to ally Denmark with France and the militaristic policies of Napoléon. Later, after all of Napoléon's European allies abandoned him, Denmark remained loyal.

This led to a series of humiliating disasters for Denmark, especially when Napoléon was roundly defeated by an alliance of European countries in 1814. Because of England's embargoes on Denmark, and the destruction of many Danish ships, Denmark lost control over its overseas colony of Norway, and its trade came to an almost complete standstill after the loss of its navy.

At a treaty that was signed at Kiel the same year, Denmark was forced to yield Norway to Sweden and Heligoland to England. The only remaining gems within Demark's once-mighty overseas empire included Greenland, Iceland, and the Faroe Islands.

Without a navy and partially crippled by huge debts and a loss of much of its prestige, Denmark sank into poverty. In 1813, the national treasury went bankrupt. Several years later, especially between 1818 and 1824, the price of grain virtually collapsed, culminating in many farm failures and a massive exodus from Denmark, through Copenhagen, to the New World. The country's precarious financial and military position also put a virtual end to any hope of liberal reforms.

Following the Napoleonic wars, the rulers Frederik VI and his successor Christian VIII formed very conservative governments. In 1848, as revolts and revolutions broke out across Europe, the Danes demanded a more liberal constitution. Absolute rule on the part of the Danish monarchs was tempered by representatives elected under a new constitution that was signed on June 5, 1849.

The liberal reforms inaugurated in 1849 eventually applied to a smaller, more compact nation. In 1850, after a 2-year revolution, Schleswig-Holstein successfully seceded from Denmark and allied itself with its German-speaking neighbor to the south, Prussia. After several years of indecisive referendums and military interventions and the intense politicking of such other European nations as Austria, Schleswig-Holstein was officially ceded to Prussia in 1866 under the Treaty of Prague.

On July 28, 1866, a new constitution was adopted, but it was more conservative than the earlier one (1849), and granted more power to those who paid the highest taxes, in other words, the landowners.

Throughout the rest of the 19th century, Denmark's conservatives struggled against reform-minded liberals. Conservatives pledged to build up trade incentives and military fortifications around Copenhagen. In the event of war, liberals argued most of the Danish countryside would be sacrificed to the invaders, and only Copenhagen would be defended.

Members of the left favored social reforms, a downsizing of the Danish army, and an official allegiance to political neutrality. Despite opposition, a process of liberalization continued apace with the changes wrought by the Industrial Revolution. In 1891, a system of old-age pensions was introduced; in 1892 came an early form of health insurance; and in 1899, funds were allocated for the acquisition of farmland by individuals who qualified for assistance from the Danish government. Universal suffrage for men and women, regardless of their social rank, began only in 1915, during the most confused and indecisive days of World War I.

WORLD WAR I & ECONOMIC CHAOS   When World War I broke out, Denmark found itself on a razor's edge and struggled to remain neutral, but its position astride the shipping lanes favored by both England and Germany made this especially perilous. On August 14, 1914, Germany lay mines in the sea channels of southern Denmark, and then strongly implied that Denmark would be well-advised to lay other mines in the channels leading toward Copenhagen. Fearing that if they didn't comply, Germany would lay the mines anyway and then commandeer parcels of Danish soil for installation of German naval bases, Denmark began laying mines.

Danish king Christian X had the unfortunate task of phoning his cousin, the king of England, about the situation. England agreed not to interpret Denmark's action as a direct act of hostility. Consequently, all the waters around Denmark were peppered with high-powered explosives, a situation that had a disastrous effect on Danish trade and the Danish treasury. Later, German U-boats sank at least 30% of Denmark's merchant fleet.

Eventually, through cooperation and joint commitments with Sweden and Norway, Denmark managed to retain its fragile hold on wartime neutrality, but at a high price in terms of unemployment, higher taxes, and endless neuroses and self-doubts.

Partly in reaction to the traumas of their untenable situation, the Danes signed a new constitution on June 5, 1915, establishing a two-chamber parliament and granting equal voting rights to men and women. In 1916, a law was passed that compelled industries to insure their workers against accidents. In 1916, a financially strapped Denmark concluded a treaty with the United States, selling the Danish colonies in the Caribbean (later known as the U.S. Virgin Islands) for $25,000,000.

In 1919, a land reform act resulted in the breakup of many large estates, with lands passing into the hands of greater numbers of farmers.

Because Germany was defeated in World War I, many people felt that all of Schleswig should be returned to Denmark, and that the details should be hammered out during the Versailles Conference. But in an act that was later interpreted as remarkably callous, Denmark, because of its official neutrality during World War I, was not invited to the conference, despite the extreme losses its navy and merchant marine had suffered. Under extreme pressure, the conventioneers eventually agreed to return North Schleswig, but not South Schleswig or Holstein, to Denmark.

A new treaty was drawn up between Iceland and Denmark in 1918. Although they functioned as separate, sovereign states, the two countries were united under one king, with Iceland under Denmark's protection. Danish ships were appointed as the official inspectors of Icelandic fisheries, and plans were laid for Iceland's eventual independence.

Denmark participated in the creation of the League of Nations and officially joined it in 1920. A crisis arose when Norway claimed jurisdiction over the territory of Greenland. However, in April 1933, the Permanent Court of International Justice granted Denmark sovereignty over Greenland, nullifying Norway's claim.

Although the Great Depression didn't begin in the U.S. until October 1929, Denmark was plunged into high levels of unemployment (30%) as early as 1926. Poor harvests and a 1926 tariff imposed on Danish grain by Germany, one of Denmark's largest trading partners, contributed to Denmark's fiscal woes. By 1932, a fiscal collapse of the Danish government seemed imminent. Fueled by the uncertainty, Danish branches of both the Fascist and the Nazi Parties had been established by the mid-1930s, although they remained relatively small. Part of their lack of success derived from the Danish government's policy of forbidding the civilian use of any kind of uniform in public, with the exception of the Boy Scouts. As a result, no mass demonstrations in the style of what the Germans later developed into the Third Reich ever took place on Danish soil.

THE COMING OF HITLER & NAZI OCCUPATION   In May of 1939, Hitler asked Denmark to sign a non-aggression pact. Denmark accepted it; Norway and Sweden did not, and as such, any semblance of a united Scandinavian front collapsed. The pact specified that Denmark and Germany would not go to war with each other for 10 years, and that Denmark would not give aid or assistance to any nation with which Germany was at war. When war broke out in 1939, Denmark declared its neutrality. Denmark's ties with Iceland were severed, and Greenland and the Faroe Islands were occupied by the United States and Great Britain, respectively.

Despite the non-aggression pact, Nazi forces invaded and occupied Denmark in 1940. In 1943, Hitler sent General Hermann von Hanneken to impose martial law on Denmark, and commandeered two Danish destroyers. Heroic Danish resistance continued against the German occupying forces, often in the form of sabotage of German-controlled industries and military installations. In many cases, Danish sailors scuttled their own ships to prevent them from falling under Nazi control. Danish Jews and homosexuals were arrested and sent to concentration camps beginning in 1942, but most, aided by the brave Danish people, were able to escape to Sweden. Danish civil servants tended to remain at their posts, as a means of ensuring an orderly administration of the country during terrible times.

In September 1944, many members of the Danish police, suspected (often correctly) of helping the Danish resistance, were imprisoned. The same year, a general strike among the Danes generally crippled Copenhagen, until the Germans accepted an uneasy compromise, and the Nazi troops became less visible within the capital.

On March 21, 1945, the Gestapo's headquarters (in what had been the Danish headquarters for Shell Oil) were demolished during an Allied air raid, sending most of the Gestapo's archives up in flames, much to the regret of later historians. Later, the Gestapo's Danish strongholds in Odense and Århus were also bombarded.

Beginning in February 1945, as the defeat of Germany appeared imminent, thousands of refugees from Germany poured across the border, seeking safety in Denmark. When Germany surrendered in 1945, British troops occupied most of Denmark. The island of Bornholm, however, was occupied by Soviet troops, who bombed parts of the island in a successful effort to dislodge the occupying Nazi forces. After the war, Denmark subsequently joined the United Nations.

POST-WAR DENMARK   After 1945, the Liberal Party under Knud Kristensen assumed control of Denmark. In 1947, Kristensen resigned. The country was then governed by the Social Democratic Party, who governed under Frederik IX. The economy remained sluggish until 1948.

In 1949, Denmark joined NATO. In 1953, the Scandinavian Council was formed, comprised of Denmark, Norway, Sweden, and Iceland; the council lasted until 1961. Also in 1953, Denmark adopted a new constitution, providing for a single-chamber parliament.

In 1972, Denmark became the sole Nordic member of the EEC. That same year, Queen Margrethe, born in 1940 (the year of the Nazi invasion), became queen of Denmark upon the death of her father, Frederik IX.

In 1982, Denmark seemed to abandon its long-cherished liberalism when it elected Poul Schluter, its first Conservative prime minister since 1894. However, by 1989 Denmark was leading the world in the development of a liberal social agenda. It became the first NATO country to allow women to join front-line military units. Later, it became the first country to recognize marriages between partners of the same sex.

The early 1990s were dominated by Denmark's continuing debate over its role (or lack thereof) in the European Union. In 1992, Denmark rejected the Maastricht Treaty, which had established a framework for the European Economic Union. However, in a 1993 referendum Denmark reversed its position (by a very close vote), voting to support the Maastricht Treaty and its own limited involvement in it. Denmark presided over the European Union for the first part of that year.

In 1993 Denmark also observed the 50th anniversary of the virtual overnight rescue of 8,000 of its Jewish citizens, who were smuggled out of the country in 1943 into neutral Sweden. That same year the Tivoli Gardens celebrated its 150th year, and *The Little Mermaid* statue, inspired by the famous character from H. C. Andersen's fairy tales, turned 80.

In 1996, Copenhagen was named the "Cultural Capital of Europe." Following in the footsteps of other European cities (including Athens, Florence, Paris, and Madrid), Copenhagen celebrated with a year of festivities. A massive campaign of restorations and new construction revitalized the city.

In May 1998, Denmark held a referendum on extending its ties and connections with the European Union. In a tight race that was too close to call, Danes, Greenlanders, and Farose voted for enlargement of its position within EU. But the margin was extremely narrow, indicating how divided Danes remain on this important issue.

5 Danish Cuisine: From Smørrebrød to Rødgrød med Fløde

Danish food is the best in Scandinavia—in fact, it's among the best in Europe.

Breakfast is usually big and hearty, just right for a day of sightseeing. It usually consists of homemade breads, Danish cheeses, and often a boiled egg or salami. In most establishments you can order bacon and eggs, two items that are well stocked here. However, you may prefer a simple continental breakfast of Danish *wienerbrød* (pastry) and coffee. The "danish" is moist, airy, and rich.

The favorite dish at midday is the ubiquitous *smørrebrød* (open-faced sandwiches)—a national institution. Literally, this means "bread and butter," but the Danes stack this sandwich as if it were the Leaning Tower of Pisa—and then throw in a slice of curled cucumber and bits of parsley or perhaps sliced peaches or a mushroom for added color.

Two of these sandwiches can make a more-than-filling lunch. They're everywhere—from the grandest dining rooms to the lowliest pushcart. Many restaurants offer a wide selection; guests look over a checklist and then mark the ones they want. Some are made with sliced pork (perhaps a prune on top), roast beef with béarnaise sauce and crispy fried bits of onion, or liver paste adorned with an olive or cucumber slice and gelatin made with strong beef stock.

Smørrebrød is often served as an hors d'oeuvre. The most popular, most tempting, and usually most expensive of these delicacies is prepared with tiny Danish shrimp, on which a lemon slice and caviar often perch, perhaps even with fresh dill. The "ugly duckling" of the *smørrebrød* family is anything with a cold sunny-side-up egg on top of it.

For dinner, the Danes tend to keep farmers' hours: 6:30pm is common, although restaurants remain open much later. Many main-course dishes are familiar to North Americans, but they're prepared with a distinct flourish in Denmark—for example, *lever med løg* (liver and fried onion), *bøf* (beef, in a thousand different ways), *lammesteg* (roast lamb), or that old reliable staple, *flæskesteg med rødkål* (roast pork with red cabbage).

Danish chefs are really noted for their fresh fish dishes. The tiny Danish shrimp, *rejer,* are splendid; herring and kippers are also greeted with much enthusiasm. Really top-notch fish dishes include *rodspætte* (plaice), *laks* (salmon), *makrel* (mackerel), and *kogt torsk* (boiled cod).

Danish cheese may be consumed at any meal, then eaten again on a late-night *smørrebrød* at Tivoli. Danish bleu is already familiar to most people. For something softer and milder, try Havarti.

Danish specialties that are worth sampling include: *frikadeller,* the Danish meatballs or rissoles (prepared in various ways); a Danish omelet with a rasher of bacon covered with chopped chives and served in a skillet; and Danish hamburger patties topped with fried onions and coated with a rich brown gravy.

Two great desserts are Danish apple Charlotte, best when decorated with whipped cream, dried breadcrumbs, and chopped almonds; and *rødgrød med fløde*—basically a jellied fruit-studded juice, served with thick cream.

As for drinks, Carlsberg or Tuborg beer are Denmark's national beverages. A bottle of pilsner costs about half the price of the stronger export beer with the fancy label. Value-conscious Danes rely on the low-priced *fadøl* (draft beer); visitors on a modest budget might want to do the same.

You may gravitate more toward *aquavit* (schnapps, to the British), which comes from the city of Aalborg in northern Jutland. The Danes, who usually drink it at mealtime, follow it with a beer chaser. Made from a distilling process using potatoes, *aquavit* should only be served icy cold.

For those with a daintier taste, the world-famous Danish liqueur, Cherry Herring, is a delightful drink; made from cherries, as the name implies, it can be consumed anytime except with meals.

6 Recommended Books

HISTORY AND PHILOSOPHY

A Kierkegaard Anthology, Roger Bretall (editor), Princeton University Press (1974). This book explores the work of the Copenhagen-born philosopher who developed an almost pathological sense of involvement in theology. It includes a representative selection of some of his most famous or more significant works.

Copenhagen, A Historical Guide, Torben Ejlersen. Published in 1989, by Høst & Søn in Denmark (and available at most bookstores there), this 88-page guide takes you on a brief tour of the city that began as a ferry landing and became one of the most important capitals of Europe.

Of Danish Ways, written by two Danish-Americans, Ingeborg S. MacHiffic and Margaret A. Nielsen, Harper & Row, 1984. This delightful account of a land and its people has a little bit of everything: history, social consciousness, customs, food, handcrafts, art, music, and theater.

LITERATURE

Andersen's Fairy Tales, by Hans Christian Andersen, Price, Stern, Sloan Publishing (1997). Also, *The Complete Hans Christian Andersen Fairy Tales,* Gramercy Publishing (1993). The most translated writer in the world, this author published his first children's stories in 1835—and the rest is history. He became the most famous children's storywriter of all time, and these anthologies include all his classics.

Out of Africa (Modern Library, 1992); *Letters from Africa* (University of Chicago Press, 1984), and *Seven Gothic Tales* (Modern Library, 1994)—all by Karen Blixen (Isak Dinesen). Blixen gained renewed fame with the release of the 1985 film, Out of Africa, which starred Meryl Streep and Robert Redford. One of the major authors of the 20th century, twice nominated for the Nobel Prize, Blixen's world lives on in these almost flawless stories. *Seven Gothic Tales* is her masterpiece. Other titles by Blixen include *Winter's Tales* (Vintage Books, 1993).

The Liar, Martin A. Hansen, Sun and Moon Press, 1995. Hansen, of course, was one of the best-selling authors—and in some ways the most perceptive—of the post-war generation, who wrote in the difficult years after Denmark was liberated at the end of World War II. This novel takes place in the 1950s, and has wisely been re-released after all these years. *The Liar* explores the inner thoughts of a lonely schoolteacher living on a tiny Danish island, and does so exceedingly well.

Smilla's Sense of Snow, Peter Høeg, Delta, 1995. This book deservedly became an international bestseller, establishing Høeg as one of Denmark's major writers of the 1990s. Published in America as *Miss Smilla's Sense of Snow,* it's a thriller dealing with the Danish colonialism of Greenland and deeply exploring the confusing issue of cultural identity.

Winter's Child, published by the University of Nebraska Press, 1987, explores modern Danish society as viewed through the eyes of a number of women working in the maternity ward of a hospital on the outskirts of Copenhagen.

3 Planning a Trip to Denmark

In the following pages, we've compiled all of the practical information you' need to plan your trip in advance—airline information, what things cost, a calendar of events, and more.

1 Visitor Information & Entry Requirements

VISITOR INFORMATION

In the United States, contact the **Scandinavian Tourist Board,** 655 Third Avenue, 18th Floor, New York, NY 10017 (☎ **212/ 949-2333**), for maps, sightseeing information, ferry schedules, or whatever.

In the United Kingdom, contact the Danish Tourist Board at 55 Sloane Street, London SW1X 9SY (☎ **0171/259-5959**).

You might also try the following World Wide Web address: **www.city.net/countries/Denmark.**

If you get in touch with a **travel agent,** make sure that the agent is a member of the American Society of Travel Agents (ASTA), so that— in case a problem arises—you can complain to the ASTA Consumer Affairs Department at 1101 King Street, Alexandria, VA 22314 (☎ **703/706-0387**).

ENTRY REQUIREMENTS

PASSPORTS & VISAS Every U.S. traveler entering Denmark must hold a valid passport. It is not necessary to obtain a visa unless you're staying longer than 3 continuous months.

In the **United States,** you can apply for passports in person at 1 of 13 regional offices or by mail. To apply, you'll need a passport application form, available at U.S. post offices and federal court offices, and proof of citizenship, such as a birth certificate or naturalization papers; an expired passport is also accepted. Two identical passport-size photographs are required. First-time applicants for passports pay $60 ($40 if under 15 years of age). Persons 18 or older who have an expired passport that's not more than 12 years old can reapply by mail. The old passport must be submitted along with new photographs and a pink renewal form (DSP-82). The fee is $40. For an additional $35 a passport can be renewed within 3 business days. Call ☎ **202/647-0518** at any time for information. Information can also be obtained on the

Internet at **http://travel.state.gov** or by calling the **National Passport Information Center (NPIC)** at ☎ **900/225-5674.** The cost is 35¢ per minute for 24-hour automated service, or $1.05 per minute from 9am to 3pm for live operator service.

You can also write to Passport Service, Office of Correspondence, Department of State, 1111 19th Street NW, Suite 510, Washington, D.C. 20522-1075.

In **Canada**, citizens can go to one of 28 regional offices, or mail an application to the Passport Office, External Affairs and International Trade Canada, Ottawa ON K1A 0GE (☎ **613/996-8885**). Applicants residing in a city where a passport office is located are requested to submit their application in person. Passport applications are available at passport offices, post offices, and most travel agencies. All requirements for obtaining a passport are outlined on the application form. The fee is $60 Canadian. Passports are valid for 5 years. For travel information, call ☎ **800/267-6788,** or ☎ 800/267-8376 for general information.

In **Great Britain,** British subjects may travel to Denmark and any other European Union country with only an identity card. A passport is not necessary. British visitors who wish to own a passport can do so at a cost of £21 for a 10-year passport. Basic documentation is available at any post office in Great Britain. For more information regarding fees, documentation requirements, and to ask for an emergency passport, telephone the London Passport office at ☎ **0990/210410.**

In **Australia,** citizens can apply for a passport at the nearest post office. Provincial capitals and other major cities have passport offices. Application fees are subject to review every 3 months. Call ☎ **02/13-12-32** for the latest information. An adult's passport is valid for 10 years; for people under 18, a passport is valid for 5 years.

In **New Zealand,** citizens should contact the nearest consulate or passport office to obtain an application. One can file in person or by mail. Proof of citizenship is required, and the passport is good for 10 years. Passports are processed at the New Zealand Passport Office, Documents of National Identity Division, Department of Internal Affairs, P.O. Box 10-526, Wellington (☎ **0800/22-50-50**). The fee is NZ$80.

In **Ireland,** write in advance to the Passport Office, Molesworth Street, Dublin 2, Ireland (☎ **01/671-16-33**). The cost is IR£45. Applications are sent by mail. Irish citizens living in North America can contact the Irish Embassy, 2234 Massachusetts Avenue NW, Washington, D.C. 20008 (☎ **202/462-3939**). The embassy can issue a new passport or direct you to one of the three North American consulates that have jurisdiction over a particular region; the charge is $75 to $81 depending upon the consulate.

In **South Africa,** citizens can apply for a passport at any Home Affairs office. Passports issued are valid for 10 years, costing SAR80. For children under 16, passports are valid for only 5 years, costing SAR60. For further information, contact your nearest Department of Home Affairs Office.

2 Money

Traveler's checks, while still the safest way to carry money when traveling abroad, are going the way of the dinosaur. The aggressive evolution of international computerized banking and consolidated ATM networks has led to the triumph of plastic throughout Europe, including Denmark—even if cold cash is still the most trusted currency.

Never rely on credit cards and ATMs alone, however. Though you should be safe in most hotels and many restaurants, smaller towns and cheaper places are still wary of "virtual money," and occasionally the phone lines and computer networks used to verify your plastic can go down and render your cards useless. Always carry some local currency and some traveler's checks for insurance.

The Danish Krone

For American Readers   At this writing, $1 = approximately 6.78 kroner (or 1 krone = 14 ½ ¢); this was the exchange rate used to calculate the dollar values given in this edition, rounded to the nearest nickel.

For British Readers   At this writing, £1 = approximately 11 ½ kroner (or 1 krone = 8.7 pence); this was the exchange rate used to calculate the pound values in the chart below.

Note: Throughout this guidebook, Danish kroner are abbreviated as DKK. Since international exchange rates fluctuate over time because of various political and economic factors, they may not be the same when you travel to Denmark. Therefore, this table should be used only as a guide.

DK	US$	UK£	DK	US$	UK£
1	0.15¢	0.09	75	10.88	6.53
2	0.29¢	0.17	100	14.50	8.70
3	0.44¢	0.26	125	18.13	10.88
4	0.58¢	0.35	150	21.75	13.05
5	0.73¢	0.44	175	25.38	15.23
6	0.87¢	0.52	200	29.00	17.40
7	1.02	0.61	225	32.63	19.58
8	1.16	0.70	250	36.25	21.75
9	1.31	0.78	275	39.88	23.93
10	1.45	0.87	300	43.50	26.10
15	2.18	1.31	350	50.75	30.45
20	2.90	1.74	400	58.00	34.80
25	3.63	2.18	500	72.50	43.50
50	7.25	4.35	1000	145.00	87.00

CURRENCY   For currency, the Danes use the **krone** (crown), kroner in the plural, which breaks down into 100 **øre.** The international monetary designation for the Danish kroner is expressed as DKK. (Note: the currency in Sweden is also the kronor but is spelled with an "o" instead of an "e"). At press time, 1 krone equals about 14½ ¢ U.S., or 6.78 DKK to the U.S. dollar. Of course, these rates are subject to change, and you should check the current rates shortly before you go.

Banknotes in circulation include 50, 100, 200, 500, and 1,000 kroner. Coins are minted in denominations of 25 øre, 50 øre, 1 krone, and 2, 5, 10, and 20 kroner. Still in circulation (but being phased out) are 5- and 10-øre coins.

CURRENCY EXCHANGE   When converting your currency into Danish kroner, be aware of varying exchange rates. In general, banks offer better rates than currency-exchange bureaus, but they do charge a commission for the service. Danish banks charge a substantial 20KR ($3.10) per traveler's check, with a minimum 40KR ($6) fee. If you are cashing American Express checks, go to the American Express office, where you won't have to pay a commission. Try not to exchange money at your hotel; you'll get the worst rates there.

Most large cities have 24-hour ATMs that allow travelers to withdraw small amounts of local cash as needed. Many banks, however, impose a fee every time a card is used at an ATM in a different city or bank. Check the fees and restrictions of your ATM card before you use it extensively abroad.

TRAVELER'S CHECKS   Traveler's checks are the safest way to carry cash while traveling. Most banks will give you a better exchange rate for traveler's checks than for cash. Checks denominated in U.S. dollars or British pounds are accepted virtually anywhere.

American Express (☎ **800/221-7282** in the U.S. and Canada) is one of the largest and most immediately recognized issuers of traveler's checks. It will refund checks if lost or stolen, provided that you produce documentation. When purchasing checks, ask about refund hotlines. No commission is charged to members of the American Automobile Association and to holders of certain types of American Express cards. For questions or problems arising outside the United States or Canada, contact any of the company's many regional representatives. We'll list locations throughout this guide. The following agencies also issue traveler's checks:

Citicorp (☎ **800/645-6556** in the U.S. and Canada, or ☎ 813/623-1709, collect, from anywhere else in the world) issues checks in several different currencies.

Thomas Cook (☎ **800/223-7373** in the U.S. and Canada, or ☎ 609/987-7300, collect, from anywhere else in the world) issues MasterCard traveler's checks denominated in several currencies; not all currencies are available at every outlet.

Interpayment Services (☎ **800/221-2426** in the U.S. and Canada, or ☎ 212/858-8500, collect, from most other parts of the world) sells Visa checks denominated in several major currencies.

CREDIT & CHARGE CARDS   These are useful throughout Scandinavia. American Express, Diners Club, and Visa are widely recognized. If you see a Eurocard or Access sign, it means that the establishment accepts MasterCard. With an American

What Things Cost in Copenhagen	U.S. $
Taxi from the airport to the city center	18.85
Subway from Central Station to outlying suburbs	1.60
Local telephone call	.35
Double room at the Hotel d'Angleterre (very expensive)	300.90
Double room, with bath, at the Copenhagen Admiral Hotel (moderate)	137.75
Double room, without bath, at the Hotel Boulevard (inexpensive)	72.50
Lunch for one at the Els (moderate)	34.35
Lunch for one at the Ida Davidsen (inexpensive)	15.00
Dinner for one, without wine, at Kommandaten (expensive)	84.10
Dinner for one, without wine, at L'Alsace (moderate)	44.20
Dinner for one, without wine, at Nyhavns Færgekro (inexpensive)	21.05
Pint of beer (draft pilsner)	6.45
Coca-Cola	3.40
Cup of coffee	3.40
Admission to Tivoli	5.05
Movie ticket	8.50
Roll of ASA 100 color film, 36 exposures	10.50
Theater ticket (at the Royal Theater)	8.70-87.00

Express, MasterCard, or Visa card, you can also withdraw currency from cash machines (ATMs) at various locations. Always check with your credit- or charge-card company about using your card to access cash before leaving home.

ATM NETWORKS   Plus, Cirrus, and other networks connected with automated teller machines operate throughout Denmark. You can usually use your home bank card to get Danish currency. The exchange rate is excellent, but your home bank will probably charge a fee every time you use an ATM machine abroad.

If your credit card has been programmed with a PIN (Personal Identification Number), you can probably use your card at Scandinavian ATMs to withdraw money as a cash advance on your card. Always determine the frequency limits for withdrawals and check to see if your PIN code must be reprogrammed for usage on your trip abroad. Discover cards are accepted in the United States only. For **Cirrus** locations abroad, call ☎ **800/424-7787.** For **Plus** usage abroad, check the Plus site on the World Wide Web (**http://www.visa.com**) or call **800/843-7587.**

MONEYGRAM   If you find yourself without money, an American Express wire service can help you secure emergency funds from willing family members or friends. Through **MoneyGram,** 7501 W. Mansfield, Lakewood, CO 80235 (☎ **800/926-9400**), money can be sent abroad in less than 10 minutes. Senders should call Amex to learn the address of the closest MoneyGram outlet. Cash, credit/charge card, or sometimes a personal check (with ID) are acceptable forms of payment. Amex's fee is $10 for the first $300, with a sliding scale for larger amounts; the fee enables the sender to include a short telex message and make a 3-minute phone call to the recipient. At the outlet where money is received, the recipient must present a photo ID.

3 When to Go

CLIMATE

Denmark's climate is mild for a Scandinavian country—New England farmers experience harsher winters. Summer temperatures average between 61° and 77°F. Winter temperatures seldom go below 30°F, thanks to the warming waters of the Gulf Stream. From the weather perspective, mid-April through November is a good time to visit.

Denmark's Average Daytime Temperatures

	Jan	Feb	Mar	Apr	May	June	July	Aug	Sept	Oct	Nov	Dec
°F	32	32	35	44	53	60	64	63	57	49	42	37
°C	0	0	2	7	12	15	18	17	14	9	6	3

HOLIDAYS

Danish public holidays are: January 1 (New Year's Day), Maundy Thursday, Good Friday, Easter Sunday, Easter Monday, May 1 (Labor Day), Common Prayers Day (fourth Friday after Easter), Ascension Day (mid-May), Whitsunday (late May), Whitmonday, June 5 (Constitution Day), December 25 (Christmas Day), and December 26 (Boxing Day).

DENMARK CALENDAR OF EVENTS

May
- **Ballet and Opera Festival.** Classical and modern dance and two operatic masterpieces are presented at the Old Stage of the Royal Theater in Copenhagen. For tickets, contact the Royal Theater, Box 2185, DK-1017 København (☎ **33-69-69-69**). Mid-May through June.

- **Aalborg Carnival.** This is one of the great spring events of Denmark. The streets are filled with locals in colorful costumes. Almost 10,000 take part in the celebration, honoring the victory of spring over winter. For information, call ☎ **98-12-60-22.** May 21.
- **Carnival in Copenhagen.** A great citywide event. There's also a children's carnival. For information, call ☎ **33-11-13-25.** May 30–31.

June

- **Viking Festival,** Frederikssund (8-miles southwest of Hillerød). For 2 weeks every summer "bearded Vikings" present old Nordic sagas in an open-air setting. After each performance, a traditional Viking banquet is held. Call ☎ **42-31-06-85** for more information. June 19–July 15.
- **Midsummer's Night.** This age-old event is celebrated throughout Denmark. It is the longest day of the year. Festivities throughout the tiny nation begin around 10pm with bonfires and celebrations along the myriad coasts of Denmark. June 21.
- **Roskilde Festival.** Europe's biggest rock festival celebrated its 29th anniversary in 1998, and this central Zealand town is prepared for another 90,000 visitors scheduled to arrive for its 1999 blast. Beside major rock concerts, which often draw "big names," scheduled activities include theater and film presentations. For more information, call the Roskilde Festival at ☎ **46-36-66-13.** June 25–28.

July

- **Funen Festival.** Marking its 24th year in 1999, this annual musical extravaganza is often headlined by some big international groups. The festival's music is often hard-core rock, but there are gentler, classical melodies presented as well. It all takes place in the city of Odense on the island of Funen, the hometown of Denmark's most famous writer, Hans Christian Andersen. For more information, call the Odense Tourist Bureau at ☎ **66-12-75-20.** July 1–5.
- **Fourth of July.** The Danish town of Rebild, near Aalborg, is one of the few places outside the United States that honors America's Independence Day. For more information, contact the Aalborg Tourist Office, Østerågade 8, DK-9000 Aalborg (☎ **98-12-60-22**). July 4.
- **Copenhagen Jazz Festival.** Features international jazz musicians in the streets, squares, and theaters. Pick up a copy of *Copenhagen This Week* to find the venues of various performances. For information, call ☎ **33-93-20-13.** July 3–12.
- **Sønderborg Tilting Festival.** Dating back to the Middle Ages, the "tilting at the ring" tradition has survived only in the old town of Sønderborg, on the island of Als in southern Jutland. While riding at a gallop, the horseman must use his lance to see how many times (out of 24 attempts) he can take the ring. The festival also features parades, music, and entertainment. For more information, contact the Turistbureau, Rådhustorvet 7, DK-6400 Sønderborg (☎ **74-42-35-55**). July 10–13.

August

- **Fire Festival Regatta,** Silkeborg. Denmark's oldest and biggest festival features nightly cruises on lakes illuminated by thousands of candles along the shores. On the last night there's a fireworks display, the largest and most spectacular in northern Europe. Entertainment is provided by popular Danish artists at a large fun fair. For more information, contact the Turistbureau, Godthåbsuej 4, DK-8600 Silkeborg (☎ **86-82-19-11**). August 2–4.
- **Fall Ballet Festival.** The internationally acclaimed Royal Danish Ballet returns home to perform at the Old Stage of the Royal Theater, just before the tourist season ends. For tickets, contact the Royal Theater, Box 2185, DK-1017 København (☎ **33-69-69-69**). Mid-August through September 1.

- **Århus Festival Week.** This festival presents a wide range of cultural activities, including opera, jazz, classical music, folk music, ballet, and theater. This is the biggest recurring annual festival of culture in Scandinavia. Sporting activities and street parties abound as well. For more information contact Århus Tourist Office, Rådhuset, Århus C, DK-8000 Århus (☎ **86-12-16-00**). August 28– September 26.

4 The Active Vacation Planner

BEACHES   With some 5,000 miles of coastline, Denmark has many long strips of sandy beaches. In many cases, dunes protect the beaches from sea winds. Most of these beaches are relatively unspoiled, and the Danes like to keep them that way (any polluted beaches are clearly marked). Many Danes like to go nude at the beach. Nudist beaches aren't clearly identified; often you'll see bathers with and without clothing using the same beach. The best beach resorts are those on the north coast of Zealand and the southern tip of the island of Bornholm. Beaches on the east coast of Jutland are also good, often attracting Germans from the south. Funen also has a number of good beaches, especially in the south.

BIKING   A nation of bikers, the Danes have organized their roads to suit this national sport. Bikers can pedal along a network of biking routes and paths protected from heavy traffic. The Danish landscape is made for this type of vacation. Most tourist offices publish biking tour suggestions for their own district, a great way to see the sights and get in shape at the same time. The **Dansk Cyklist Forbund** (Danish Cycling Federation), Rømersgade 7 in Copenhagen (☎ **33-32-31-21**), also publishes excellent guides covering the whole country. They can also provide information about a number of pre-packaged biking vacations that are available.

FISHING   Since no place in Denmark is more than 35 miles from the sea, fishing is a major pastime. And Denmark also has well-stocked rivers and lakes, including fjord waters around the Limfjord. Anglers between the ages of 18 and 67 must obtain a fishing permit from the Danish Ministry of Fisheries for 100 DKK ($14.50); these are available at any post office. Jutland is known for its good trout fishing; salmon is also available, but it is found more readily in Norway. Anglers who fish from the beach can catch eel, mackerel, turbot, sea trout, plaice, and flounder. For more information about fishing in Denmark, contact **Sportfiskerforbund,** Worsåesgade 1, DK-7100 Vejle (☎ **75-82-06-99**).

GOLF   In recent years this has become a very popular sport in Denmark. Denmark's undulating landscape is ideal for the construction of golf courses. Prospective golfers should bring with them a valid golf club membership card from home. For information on the best courses near where you're staying, contact local tourist offices.

HANGGLIDING & PARAGLIDING   Although Denmark is a relatively flat country, good possibilities for practicing wind-gliding do exist. The Danish Union of Windgliders provides information about suitable locations. As a rule, the union has arranged with local landowners that a slope or some other suitable place may be used. Since equipment cannot be rented in Denmark, clients must bring their own. More information is available from **Dansk Drageflyver Union,** ☎ **74-82-20-15.**

SAILING   Denmark has about 600 harbors, both large and small, including the island of Bornholm. Those who like to sail have many opportunities to do so, especially in the open waters of the Baltic or in the more sheltered waters of the South Funen Sea between Lolland/Falster and Zealand. The Limfjord in North Jutland is also ideal for sailing. Many sailing boats are available for rent, as are cruisers. For information, contact the tourist office or **Odense Sejiklub,** Heltzengade 4, DK-5000 Odense (☎ **66-14-88-07**).

WALKING   About 100 pamphlets have been published describing walks of short or long duration in Danish forests. Twenty of these are printed in English, and are available from local tourist offices.

5 Adventure/Alternative Travel

ADVENTURE TRAVEL OPERATORS IN THE U.K.

The oldest travel agency in Britain, **Cox & Kings,** Gordon House 10, Greencoat Place, London SW1P 1PH (☎ **0171/873-5006**), was established in 1758; at that time, the company served as the paymasters and transport directors for the British armed forces in India. Today the company sends large numbers of travelers from Britain throughout the rest of the world, specializing in unusual, if pricey, holidays. Its offerings in Scandinavia include cruises through the region's spectacular fjords and waterways, bus and rail tours through sites of historic and aesthetic interest, and visits to the region's best-known handcraft centers, Viking burial sites, and historic churches. The company's staff is noted for their focus on tours of ecological and environmental interest.

Those who would like to cycle their way through the splendors of Scandinavia should join Britain's oldest and largest association of bicycle riders, the **Cyclists' Touring Club,** 69 Meadrow, Godalming, Surrey GU7 3HS (☎ **01483/417-217**). Founded in 1878, it charges £25 ($40) a year for membership, which includes information, maps, a subscription to a newsletter packed with practical information and morale boosters, plus recommended cycling routes through virtually every country in Europe. The organization's information bank on scenic routes through Scandinavia is especially comprehensive. Membership can be arranged over the phone with an appropriate credit card (such as MasterCard, Visa, Access, or Barclaycard).

LEARNING VACATIONS

The **Det Danske Kultur Institutu** (Danish Cultural Institute), Kultorvet 2, DK-1175 København (☎ **33-13-54-48**; fax 33-15-10-91), offers summer seminars (in English), including a course in Danish culture. Credit programs are available, but many courses are geared toward professional groups from abroad. An especially interesting course for those with some knowledge of Danish is "Danmark, Danskerne, Dansk," which includes language instruction.

An international series of programs for persons over age 50 who are interested in combining travel and learning is offered by **Interhostel,** developed by the University of New Hampshire. Each program lasts two weeks, is led by a university faculty or staff member, and is arranged in conjunction with a host college, university, or cultural institution. Participants may stay longer if they wish. Interhostel offers programs consisting of cultural and intellectual activities, with field trips to museums and other centers of interest. For information, contact the University of New Hampshire, Division of Continuing Education, 6 Garrison Ave., Durham, NH 03824 (☎ **800/733-9753** or ☎ 603/862-1147).

Another good source of information about courses in Denmark is the **American Institute for Foreign Study (AIFS),** 102 Greenwich Ave., Greenwich, CT 06830 (☎ **800/727-2437** or ☎ 203/869-9090). This organization can set up transportation and arrange for summer courses, with bed and board included.

The largest organization for higher education in Europe is the **Institute of International Education (IIE)**, 809 United Nations Plaza, New York, NY 10017 (☎ **212/883-8200**). A few of its booklets are free; but for $36.95, plus $4 for postage, you can purchase the more definitive *Vacation Study Abroad*. Visitors to New York may use the resources of its Information Center, which is open to the public Tuesday through Thursday from 11am to 4pm. The institute is closed on major holidays.

One well-recommended clearinghouse for academic programs throughout the world is the **National Registration Center for Study Abroad (NRCSA)**, 823 N. 2nd St., P.O. Box 1393, Milwaukee, WI 53201 (☎ **414/278-0631**). The organization maintains language study programs throughout Europe.

HOME STAYS

Friendship Force, 57 Forsyth St. NW, Suite 900, Atlanta, GA 30303 (☎ **404/522-9490**), is a nonprofit organization that encourages friendship among people worldwide. Dozens of branch offices throughout North America arrange visits, usually once a year. Because of group bookings, the airfare to the host country is usually less than the cost of individual APEX tickets. Each participant spends two weeks in the host country, one as a guest in the home of a family and the second traveling in the host country.

Servas, 11 St. John Street, Suite 411, New York, NY 10038 (☎ **212/267-0252**), is an international nonprofit, nongovernmental, interfaith network of travelers and hosts whose goal is to help promote world peace, goodwill, and understanding. (Its name means "to serve" in Esperanto.) Servas hosts offer travelers hospitality for two days. Travelers pay a $55 annual fee and a $25 list deposit after filling out an application and being approved by an interviewer (interviewers are located across the United States). They then receive Servas directories listing the names and addresses of Servas hosts.

HOME EXCHANGES

One of the most exciting breakthroughs in modern tourism is the home exchange. Sometimes the family automobile is included. Of course, you must be comfortable with the idea of having strangers in your home, and you must be content to spend your vacation in one place.

Home exchanges cut costs. You don't pay hotel bills, and you can also save money by shopping in markets and eating in. One potential problem, though, is that you may not get a home in the area you request.

Intervac, U.S., 30 Corte San Fernando, Tiburon, CA 94159 (☎ **800/756-HOME** or ☎ 415/435-3497), is part of the largest worldwide exchange network. It publishes four catalogs a year, containing more than 10,000 homes in more than 36 countries. Members contact each other directly. The cost is $65 plus postage, which includes the purchase of three of the company's catalogs (which will be mailed to you), plus the inclusion of your own listing in whichever one of the three catalogs you select. If you want to publish a photograph of your home, there is an additional charge of $11.

The Invented City, 41 Sutter St., Suite 1090, San Francisco, CA 94104 (☎ **800/788-CITY** or ☎ 415/252-1141), is another international home-exchange agency. Home-exchange listings are published three times a year—in February, May, and November. The $75 membership fee allows you to list your home, with your own description; you can also give your preferred time to travel, your occupation, and your hobbies.

Vacation Exchange Club, P.O. Box 650, Key West, FL 33041 (☎ **800/638-3841** or ☎ 305/294-7766), will send you five directories a year for $88. You'll be listed in one of the directories.

PEOPLE TO PEOPLE

Established in 1971, **Friends Overseas** places American visitors to Scandinavia in touch with Scandinavians who would like to meet people with similar interests and backgrounds. Names and addresses are given to each applicant, and letters must be written before the visitors depart; Scandinavians may not be able to meet visitors unless they have ample time to plan. For more information, write to Friends Overseas, 68-04 Dartmouth St., Forest Hills, NY 11375 (☎ **718/544-5660,** after 5pm). Send a self-addressed, stamped, business-size envelope, including your age, occupation or occupational goals, approximate dates of your visit, and names of your traveling companions. The service costs $25.

6 Health & Insurance

HEALTH

You will encounter few local health problems while traveling in Denmark. The water is safe to drink, the milk is pasteurized, and the health services of each country are excellent. Occasionally a change in diet may cause minor diarrhea, so you may want to take some anti-diarrhea medicine along. In summer, arrive at buffets early so that your smørrebrød (open-faced sandwiches) or salads made with mayonnaise are fresh.

Put all your essential medicines in your carry-on luggage, and bring enough of any prescription medication to last during your stay. Bring along copies of your prescriptions written in the generic form.

If you need a doctor, your hotel will find one for you. You can also obtain a list of English-speaking doctors from the **International Association for Medical Assistance to Travelers (IAMAT),** 417 Center St., Lewiston, NY 14092 (☎ **716/754-4883**), or in Canada, Regal Rd., Guelph, ON N1K 1B5 (☎ **519/836-0102**).

If you suffer from a chronic illness, talk to your doctor before taking the trip. For conditions such as heart trouble, epilepsy, or diabetes, wear a Medic Alert Identification Tag, which will immediately alert any doctor to your condition. The tag also provides Medic Alert's 24-hour hotline number so that a foreign doctor can obtain your medical records. The initial membership costs $35, plus a $15 yearly fee. Contact the **Medic Alert Foundation,** 2323 Colorado Ave., Turlock, CA 95381-1009 (☎ **800/ 825-3785**).

In case of a sudden illness or the aggravation of a chronic disease, Denmark will provide free treatment to foreign visitors provided the visitors were not deliberately seeking free treatment and that they cannot immediately return home. Transportation home is the visitors' responsibility.

INSURANCE

Before purchasing any additional insurance, check your homeowner's, automobile, and medical insurance policies, as well as the insurance provided by credit- and charge-card companies and auto and travel clubs.

Remember, Medicare covers U.S. citizens traveling in Mexico and Canada only.

Also note that to submit any claim you must always have complete documentation, including all receipts, police reports, medical records, or other data.

If you're prepaying your vacation or are taking a charter or any other flight that imposes high cancellation penalties, consider getting cancellation insurance.

One final note: The restrictions tied to most of these policies are sweeping. Check the restrictions very carefully. Chances are you won't be covered if you're injured in an activity that could be even remotely deemed "athletic." Also, check with your local insurance agent to see if you already have a policy that would cover what these additional policies claim to cover.

The following companies can provide helpful information:

Travel Guard International, 1145 Clark St., Stevens Point, WI 54481 (☎ **800/ 826-1300** or ☎ 715/345-0505), offers comprehensive insurance programs starting as low as $44. The program covers basically everything, including emergency assistance, accidental death, trip cancellation and interruption, medical coverage abroad, and lost luggage. There are restrictions, however, that you should understand before you purchase the coverage.

Travelers Insured Company Inc., P.O. Box 280568, Hartford, CT 06128-0568 (☎ **800/243-3174** in the U.S., or ☎ 860/528-7663 outside the U.S. between 7:45am and 7pm EST), provides trip cancellation and emergency evacuation policies costing $5.50 for each $100 of coverage. Travel accident and illness insurance start from $10 for 6 to 10 days; $500 worth of coverage for lost, damaged, or delayed baggage costs $20 for 6 to 10 days; and trip cancellation goes for $5.50 for each $100 worth of coverage (written approval is necessary for cancellation coverage above $10,000).

Travelex, 11717 Burt St., Suite 202, Omaha, NE 68175 (☎ **800/228-9792** in the U.S.), offers insurance packages priced from $59 per person for a tour valued at $1,000. Packages include financial protection against trip cancellation, trip interruption, and flight and baggage delays, as well as coverage for accident-related medical costs, accidental death and dismemberment, and medical evacuation.

Healthcare Abroad (MEDEX), c/o Wallach & Co., 107 W. Federal St. (P.O. Box 480), Middleburg, VA 20118 (☎ **800/237-6615** in the U.S., or ☎ 703/687-3166), offers coverage for 10 to 120 days at $3 a day. This policy includes accident and sickness coverage up to $100,000, medical evacuation, and a $25,000 accidental death and dismemberment compensation. Provisions for trip cancellation can also be written into this policy at a nominal cost.

Access America, 6600 W. Broad St., Richmond, VA 23230 (☎ **800/284-8300** in the U.S.), offers comprehensive travel insurance and assistance packages, including medical expenses, on-the-spot hospital payments, medical transportation, baggage insurance, trip-cancellation/interruption insurance, and collision-damage insurance for rented cars. Its 24-hour hotline connects you to multilingual coordinators who can offer advice and help on medical, legal, and travel problems. Varying coverage levels are available.

Travel Assistance International by Worldwide Assistance Services, Inc., 1133 15th St. NW, Suite 400, Washington, D.C. 20005 (☎ **800/821-2828** in the U.S., or ☎ 202/331-1596), is another option. It offers on-the-spot medical-payment coverage up to $15,000, $30,000, or $60,000 for emergency care practically anywhere in the world, as well as unlimited medical evacuation/repatriation coverage back to the United States if necessary. For an additional fee you can be covered for trip cancellation/disruption, lost/delayed luggage, and accidental death and dismemberment. Fees are based on the length of your trip and the coverage you select. Prices begin at $65 per person ($85 per family) for a 1- to 8-day trip.

INSURANCE FOR BRITISH TRAVELERS   Most big travel agencies offer their own insurance and will probably try to sell you their package when you book a holiday trip. Think before you sign up. Britain's Consumers Association recommends that you insist on seeing the policy and reading the fine print before you buy travel insurance.

You should also shop around for better deals. You might contact **Columbus Travel Insurance Ltd.** (☎ **0171/375-0011** in London), or, for students, **Campus Travel** (☎ **0171/730-3402** in London).

7 Tips for Travelers with Special Needs

FOR TRAVELERS WITH DISABILITIES

IN THE UNITED STATES   Before you go, you might want to contact an agency that can provide advance-planning information. One is the **Travel Information Service** at the Moss Rehab Hospital in Philadelphia (☎ **215/456-9603,** or ☎ 215/456-9602 for TTY), which provides information to telephone callers only.

For a $25 annual fee, you can join **Mobility International USA,** P.O. Box 10767, Eugene, OR 97440 (☎ **541/343-1284**). Besides answering questions on various destinations, it offers discounts on videos, publications, and programs it sponsors. One of the best organizations serving the needs of persons with disabilities is **Flying Wheels Travel,** 143 W. Bridge St. (P.O. Box 382), Owatoona, MN 55060 (☎ **800/535-6790** or ☎ 507/451-5005); it offers various international escorted tours and cruises.

You might also want to take an organized tour that's geared to travelers with disabilities. You can obtain the names and addresses of such tour operators and miscellaneous travel information by writing to the **Society for the Advancement of Travel for the Handicapped,** 347 Fifth Ave., New York, NY 10016 (☎ **212/447-7248**). Annual membership dues are $45, or $30 for senior citizens and students. Send a stamped, self-addressed envelope.

For the blind or visually impaired, the best source of information is the **American Foundation for the Blind,** 11 Penn Plaza, New York, NY 10001 (☎ **800/232-5463** or ☎ 212/502-7600). It offers information on travel and various requirements for the transport and border formalities for seeing-eye dogs. It also issues identification cards to those who are legally blind.

IN BRITAIN   British travelers with disabilities can contact **RADAR (Royal Association for Disability and Rehabilitation),** Unit 12, City Forum, 250 City Rd., London EC1V 8AF (☎ **0171/250-3222**), for useful annual holiday guides. *Holidays and Travel Abroad* costs £5, *Holidays in the British Isles* goes for £7, and *Long Haul Holidays and Travel* is £5. RADAR also provides holiday information packets on such subjects as sports and outdoor holidays, insurance, and financial arrangements for people with disabilities. Each of these fact sheets is available for £2. All publications can be mailed outside the United Kingdom for a nominal fee.

Another good British service is the **Holiday Care Service,** 2nd Floor Imperial Buildings, Victoria Road, Horley, Surrey RH6 7PZ (☎ **01293/774-535**; fax 01293/784-647), which advises on accessible accommodations. Annual membership costs £15 (U.K. residents) and £30 (abroad), and includes a newsletter and access to a free reservations network for hotels throughout Britain and—to a lesser degree—Europe and the rest of the world.

If you're flying around Europe, the airline and ground staff can help you on and off planes and reserve seats for you with sufficient leg room, but you *must* arrange for this assistance *in advance* by contacting the airline.

IN DENMARK   Denmark is one of the Scandinavian countries that provides services for people with disabilities. In general, trains, airlines, ferries, and department stores and malls are accessible. For information about wheelchair access, ferry and air travel, parking, and other matters, your best bet is to contact the **Scandinavian Tourist Board** (see "Visitor Information & Entry Requirements," earlier in this chapter).

In Denmark, useful information for people with disabilities is provided by **Disabled People's User Service** (run by the Danish Council of Organizations of Disabled People), Kloeverprisvej 10B, DK-2650 Hvidovre, København (☎ **36-75-17-93**).

FOR GAY MEN & LESBIANS

IN THE UNITED STATES   To learn about gay and lesbian travel throughout Scandinavia in advance, you can obtain publications or join data-dispensing organizations. Men can order *Spartacus,* the international gay guide ($32.95), or *Odysseus 1999, The International Gay Travel Planner,* a guide to international gay accommodations ($27). Both lesbians and gay men might want to pick up a copy of *Gay Travel A to Z* ($16), which focuses on general information, listing bars, hotels, restaurants, and places of interest for gay travelers throughout the world. These and other books are available from **Giovanni's Room,** 1145 Pine St., Philadelphia, PA 19107 (☎ **215/ 923-2960**).

Our World, 1104 N. Nova Rd., Suite 251, Daytona Beach, FL 32117 (☎ **904/ 441-5367**), is a magazine devoted to options and bargains for gay and lesbian travel worldwide. It costs $35 for 10 issues. *Out and About,* 8 W. 19th St., Suite 401, New York, NY 10011 (☎ **800/929-2268**), has been hailed for its "straight" reporting about gay travel. It profiles the best gay or gay-friendly hotels, gyms, clubs, and other places at worldwide destinations. It costs $49 a year for 10 information-packed issues. It writes specifically for the upscale gay male traveler, and it has received praise from *Travel & Leisure* and the *New York Times,* among others. Both these publications are generally available at most gay and lesbian bookstores.

The **International Gay Travel Association (IGTA),** 4331 N. Federal, Suite 304, Fort Lauderdale, FL 33308 (☎ **800/448-8550** for voice mail, or ☎ 954/776-2626), encourages gay and lesbian travel worldwide. With around 1,200 member agencies, it specializes in putting travelers in touch with appropriate gay-friendly service organizations or tour specialists. It offers a quarterly newsletter, marketing mailings, and a membership directory (updated four times a year). Travel agents who are IGTA members are included in this organization's vast information resources.

IN DENMARK   The Danish organization for gay men and lesbians is **Landsforeningen for Bøsser og Lesbiske,** Teglgaardstræde 13, 1007 København (☎ **33-13-19-48**); there are branches in Århus, Aalborg, and other cities.

FOR SENIORS

IN THE UNITED STATES   Many senior discounts are available, but some may require you to be a member of a particular association (such as the AARP). For information before you go, try to obtain a copy of the free booklet *101 Tips for the Mature Traveler,* available from **Grand Circle Travel,** 347 Congress St., Suite 3A, Boston, MA 02210 (☎ **800/221-2610** or ☎ 617/350-7500).

SAGA International Holidays, 222 Berkeley St., Boston, MA 02116 (☎ **800/ 343-0273**), organizes all-inclusive tours for seniors, mostly for those 50 years of age or older. Insurance is included in the price.

The **American Association of Retired Persons (AARP),** 601 E St. NW, Washington, D.C. 20049 (☎ **202/434-AARP**), is the best U.S. organization for seniors. It offers discounts on car rentals and hotels.

Information is also available from the **National Council of Senior Citizens,** 8403 Colesville Rd., Suite 1200, Silver Spring, MD 20910 (☎ **301/578-8800**), which charges $13 per person or per couple, for which you receive a bimonthly magazine, part of which is devoted to travel tips. Reduced discounts on hotel and auto rentals are available.

Mature Outlook, P.O. Box 9390, Des Moines, IA 50306 (☎ **800/336-6330**; fax 847/286-5024), is a travel organization for people over 50. Members are offered discounts at ITC-member hotels and a bimonthly magazine. The $14.95-to-$19.95 annual membership fee entitles members to coupons for discounts at Sears, Roebuck & Co.

Elderhostel, 75 Federal St., Boston, MA 02110-1941 (☎ **617/426-8056**), offers an array of university-based educational programs for senior citizens throughout the world, including Scandinavia. Most courses abroad last about 3 weeks and offer remarkable value since the modest cost includes airfare, accommodations in student dormitories or modest inns, all meals, and tuition. The courses, which require no homework, tend to be in the liberal arts. Participants must be at least 55 years old; spouses of any age may attend, but companions must be at least 50. Meals consist of the basic, no-frills fare found in educational institutions worldwide. Elderhostel programs provide a safe and congenial environment for older single women, who comprise about 67% of the enrollment.

Interhostel offers international educational and cultural programs for those over 50 who want to combine travel and education. Developed by the University of New Hampshire, Division of Continuing Education, 6 Garrison Ave., Durham, NH 03824 (☎ **800/733-9753** in the U.S., or ☎ 603/862-1147), each program lasts 2 weeks, is led by a university faculty or staff member, and is arranged in conjunction with a host college, university, or cultural institution. Participants may stay longer if they wish.

Uniworld, 16000 Ventura Blvd., Encino, CA 91436 (☎ **800/733-7820** or ☎ 818/382-7820), specializes in single tours for the mature person. It arranges for you to share an accommodation with another single person or gets you a low-priced single supplement. Uniworld specializes in travel to certain districts of England, France, Spain, Italy, and Scandinavia, including Denmark.

IN BRITAIN   Wasteels, Victoria Station (opposite Platform 2), London SWIV 1JZ (☎ **0171/834-6744**), will sell a Rail Europe Senior Pass to bona-fide residents of the U.K. for £5. With it, a British resident over 60 years of age can buy discounted rail tickets on many of the European rail lines. To qualify, British residents must present a valid British Senior Citizen rail card, which can be obtained at any BritRail office by showing proof of age and British residency and paying £16.

IN DENMARK   Seniors receive discounts on rail travel and the ferries to Sweden plus certain attractions and performances, including those at the Royal Theater. However, you may have to belong to a seniors organization to qualify for certain discounts.

FOR FAMILIES

"Family Travel Time" is a newsletter about traveling with children. The cost is $40 for four issues. Subscribers can also call in with travel questions, but only on Wednesday from 10am to 1pm Eastern Standard Time. Contact **TWYCH** (which stands for "Travel With Your Children"), 40 Fifth Ave., New York, NY 10011 (☎ **212/447-5524**).

The best deals for British families are often package tours put together by some of the giants of the British travel industry. Foremost among these is **Thomsons Tour Operators.** Through its subsidiary, **Skytours** (☎ **0171/387-9321**), it offers dozens of air/land packages that have a pre-designated number of airline seats reserved for free use by children under 18 who accompany their parents. To qualify, parents must book airfare and hotel accommodations for trips lasting two weeks or more, and book as far in advance as possible. Savings for families with children can be substantial.

FOR SINGLES

Unfortunately for the 85 million or so single Americans, the travel industry is far more geared toward couples, and so singles often wind up paying the penalty. It pays to travel with someone. One company that resolves this problem is **Travel Companion,** which matches single travelers with like-minded companions. It's headed by Jens

Jurgen, who charges $99 for a 6-month listing in his well-publicized files. People seeking travel companions fill out forms stating their preferences and needs, and receive a listing of potential travel partners. Companions of the same or opposite sex can be requested. A bimonthly newsletter averaging 46 large pages also gives numerous money-saving travel tips of special interest to solo travelers. A sample copy is available for $5. For an application and more information, contact Jens Jurgen at **Travel Companion,** P.O. Box P-833, Amityville, NY 11701 (☎ **516/454-0880**; fax 516/454-0170).

Since single supplements on tours carry a hefty price tag, some tour companies will arrange for you to share a room with another single traveler of the same gender. One such company that offers a "guaranteed-share plan" is **Cosmos.** Book through your travel agent or call ☎ **800/221-0090.**

In the United Kingdom, a tour operator whose groups are usually comprised of at least 50% unattached persons is **Explore Worldwide, Ltd.,** 1 Frederick St., Aldershot, Hampshire GU11 1LQ (☎ **01252/344-161**), with a well-justified reputation of assembling offbeat tours. Groups rarely include more than 20 participants, and children under 14 are not allowed.

FOR STUDENTS

IN THE UNITED STATES   A subsidiary of the Council on International Educational Exchange, **Council Travel** is America's largest student, youth, and budget travel group, with more than 60 offices worldwide. The main office is at 205 E. 42nd St., New York, NY 10017 (☎ **212/822-2600;** fax 212/822-2699). International Student Identity Cards, issued to all bona-fide students for $19, entitle the holder to generous travel and other discounts. Discounted international and domestic air tickets are available.

Through Council Travel you can also book Eurotrain rail passes, YHA (Youth Hostel Association) passes, weekend packages, overland safaris, and hostel/hotel accommodations. Council Travel sells a number of publications for young people, including: *Work, Study, Travel Abroad: The Whole World Handbook; Volunteer: The Comprehensive Guide to Voluntary Service in the U.S. and Abroad;* and *Going Places: The High School Student's Guide to Study, Travel, and Adventure Abroad.*

For real budget travelers it's worth joining **Hostelling International/IYHF** (International Youth Hostel Federation). For information, contact Hostelling Information/American Youth Hostels (HI-AYH), 733 15th St. NW, Suite 840, Washington, D.C. 20005 (☎ **202/783-6161**). Membership costs $25 annually; those under age 18 pay $10, and those over 54 pay $15.

IN BRITAIN   Campus Travel, 52 Grosvenor Gardens, London SW1W 0AG (☎ **0171/730-3402**), open 7 days a week, is Britain's leading specialist in student and youth travel worldwide. Founded to meet the needs of students and young people, it provides a comprehensive travel service specializing in low-cost rail, sea, and air transportation; holiday breaks; travel insurance; and student discount cards. No matter what kind of trip you have in mind, the experienced staff at Campus Travel can assist you.

8 Getting There

BY PLANE

Scandinavia's off-season is winter (from about November 1 through March 21). Summer (generally June through September) is the peak season and the most expensive; shoulder season (spring and fall) lies in-between. In any season, midweek fares (Monday to Thursday) are the lowest, though you'll often pay a premium if you don't stay at least one Saturday night.

REGULAR AIRFARES & APEX FARES

Regular airfares include, in order of increasing price: economy, business class, and first class. These tickets carry no restrictions. In economy you pay for alcoholic beverages (although juices and soft drinks are free), and the seats are not spacious; in business all drinks are free, and the seats are wider; in first-class, amenities and services are the best.

Currently the most popular discount fare is the **APEX** (advance-purchase excursion), which usually carries restrictions—advance-purchase requirements, minimum and/or maximum stays abroad, and cancellation or change-of-date penalties.

In addition, airlines often introduce special **promotional discount fares.** Always check the travel sections of your local newspapers for such advertisements.

THE MAJOR AIRLINES

FROM NORTH AMERICA   Only three airlines offer nonstop flights from the United States to Copenhagen. **SAS** (Scandinavian Airlines Systems; ☎ **800/ 221-2350** in the U.S.; **www.flysas.com**) has more nonstop flights to Scandinavia from more North American cities than any other airline, and more flights to and from Denmark and within Scandinavia than any other airline in the world. From Seattle and Chicago SAS offers nonstop flights to Copenhagen daily in midsummer and almost every day in winter; from Newark, New Jersey, there are daily flights year round to Copenhagen. SAS's recent agreement with United Airlines, dubbed the "Star Alliance," has allowed SAS to connect their flights with other U.S. cities such as Boston, Dallas/Fort Worth, Denver, Houston, Los Angeles, Minneapolis/St. Paul, New York City, San Francisco, and Washington, D.C. These flights, aboard United, connect with SAS at its three U.S. gateway cities.

SAS offers some of the lowest fares to Copenhagen from New York. Flying during specific off-peak seasons, round-trip tickets can cost as little as $406 for those who pay for their tickets within 2 days after booking and stay abroad between 7 and 30 days—but no refunds or changes in flight dates are permitted. Similar round-trip tickets between Chicago and Copenhagen cost $528. Both tickets cost $60 more for travel on Friday, Saturday, or Sunday. These prices can—and almost certainly will—change during the lifetime of this edition, so you should confirm these prices before booking your ticket.

TWA (Trans World Airlines; ☎ **800/221-2000** in the U.S.; **www.twa.com**) also flies to Copenhagen daily from New York's JFK Airport.

Likewise, **Delta** (☎ **800/241-4141** in the U.S.; **www.delta-air.com**) features daily nonstop flights to Copenhagen from JFK in New York, and usually has competitive prices.

Nonstop flights to Copenhagen from New York take about 7½ hours; from Chicago, around 8 ½ hours; from Seattle, 9 ½ hours.

FROM THE U.K.   There are more options for traveling to Copenhagen by air for those coming from Britain or elsewhere in Europe. **British Airways** (☎ **800/ AIRWAYS; www.british-airways.com**) offers convenient connections through two of London's airports (Heathrow and Gatwick) to Copenhagen, with a price structure (and discounted prices on hotel packages) that sometimes makes a stopover in Britain less expensive than you might have thought. **SAS** offers five daily nonstop flights to Copenhagen from London's Heathrow Airport (1 ¾ hours), two daily nonstops from Glasgow (2 hours), and three daily nonstops from Manchester (2 ⅓ hours). Other European airlines with connections through their home countries to Copenhagen include **Icelandair** (☎ **800/223-5500** in the U.S.; **www.icelandair.is**), **KLM** (☎ **800/374-7747** in the U.S.; **www.klm.nl**), and **Lufthansa** (☎ **800/645-3880** in the U.S.; **www.lufthansa-usa.com**).

BUCKET SHOPS, CHARTERS & OTHER OPTIONS

BUCKET SHOPS   More politely referred to as "consolidators," these agencies purchase large blocks of unsold seats from the airlines and sell them to the public often at dramatic discounts (from 20% to 35% off regular fares). The terms of payment may vary from the last minute to 45 days in advance. Here are some recommendations to get you started.

In New York, try **TFI Tours International,** 34 W. 32nd St., 12th Floor, New York, NY 10001 (☎ **212/736-1140** in New York state, or ☎ 800/745-8000 elsewhere in the U.S.). This tour company offers service to 177 cities worldwide.

Travel Avenue, 10 S. Riverside Plaza, Suite 1404, Chicago, IL 60606 (☎ **800/ 333-3335**), is a national agency headquartered in the Midwest. Its tickets are often cheaper than those sold by most shops.

Another possibility is **TMI (Travel Management International),** 1129 E. Wayzata Blvd., Wayzata, MN 55391 (☎ **612/476-0005**; fax 612/476-1480). It offers a wide variety of discounts, including youth fares, student fares, and access to other kinds of air-related discounts.

One of the biggest U.S. consolidators is **Travac,** 989 Sixth Ave., New York, NY 10018 (☎ **800/TRAV-800** or ☎ 212/563-3303). It offers discounted seats from points throughout the United States to most cities in Europe on TWA, United, Delta, and other major airlines.

UniTravel, 1177 N. Warson Rd., St. Louis, MO 63132 (☎ **800/325-2222**), offers tickets to Europe at prices that may be lower than what airlines charge if you order tickets directly from them. UniTravel is best suited for providing discounts to passengers who want (or need) to get to Europe on short notice.

Another option suitable for clients with flexible travel plans is available through **Airhitch,** 2641 Broadway, 3rd Floor, Suite 100, New York, NY 10025 (☎ **212/ 864-2000**). You let Airhitch know which five consecutive days you're available to fly to Europe, and Airhitch agrees to fly you there within those days. It arranges for departures from the East or West Coast, the Midwest, and the Southeast, and tries, but cannot guarantee, to fly you to and from the cities of your choice.

You can also try **800-FLY-4-LESS,** a discount domestic and international airline ticketing service. Travelers unable to buy their tickets three weeks in advance can utilize this service to obtain low discounted fares with no advance purchase requirements. 800-FLY-4-LESS is a nationwide airline reservation and ticketing service that specializes in finding only the lowest rates.

CHARTER FLIGHTS   Strictly speaking, a charter is a one-time-only flight between two predetermined points, for which the aircraft is reserved months in advance. Before you pay for a charter, check the restrictions on your ticket or contract. You may be asked to purchase a tour package and pay for it far in advance, and there will be a stiff penalty (or ticket forfeit) if you cancel. Some charter ticket sellers offer an insurance policy for a legitimate cancellation (such as hospitalization or a death in the family). Be aware that a charter might be canceled if the plane cannot be filled.

Some charter companies have proved to be unreliable in the past. Recommended charter flight operators include **Council Charter,** a subsidiary of the Council on International Educational Exchange, 205 E. 42nd St., New York, NY 10017 (☎ **212/ 2-COUNCIL** or ☎ 212/882-2900). It can arrange charter seats to most major European cities on regularly scheduled aircraft.

REBATORS   Rebators are firms that pass along to a passenger part of their commission, although many assess a fee for their services. They are not the same as travel agents but can sometimes offer similar services. Most rebators offer discounts averaging from

10% to 25%, plus a $25 handling charge. **Travel Avenue,** 10 S. Riverside Plaza, Suite 1404, Chicago, IL 60606 (☎ **800/333-3335** or ☎ 312/876-6866), is one of the oldest agencies of its kind. It offers up-front cash rebates on every ticket over $300 it sells. In a style similar to a discount brokerage firm, the agency does not offer travel counseling. Instead, it sells airline tickets to independent travelers who have already worked out their travel plans. Also available are tour and cruise fares, plus hotel reservations, usually at prices less expensive than if you had reserved them on your own. Another major rebator is **The Smart Traveller,** 3111 SW 27th Ave., (P.O. Box 330010), Miami, FL 33133 (☎ **800/448-3338** or ☎ 305/448-3338), which also offers discounts on package tours, including hotels, car rentals, and Rhine/Danube cruises.

TRAVEL CLUBS   Travel clubs are another possibility for low-cost air travel, offering discounts usually in the range of 20% to 60%.

After you pay an annual fee, you're given a hotline number to call to find out what discounts are available. Of course, you're limited to what's available, so you have to be fairly flexible. Two travel clubs are **Moment's Notice,** 7301 New Utrecht Ave., Brooklyn, NY 11204 (☎ **718/234-6295; www.moments-notice.com**), which charges $25 per year for membership and is geared toward impulse purchases and last-minute getaways; and **Travelers Advantage,** 3033 S. Parker Rd., Suite 1000, Aurora, CO 80014 (☎ **800/548-1116** in the U.S.), which, for a $49 annual membership fee, offers members a quarterly catalog, maps, discounts at select hotels, and a limited guarantee to match equivalent packages by other travel organizations.

Encore Travel Club, 4501 Forbes Blvd., Lanham, MD 20706 (☎ **800/ 638-8976**), charges $59.95 a year for membership and offers up to a 50% discount at more than 4,000 hotels, sometimes during off-peak periods; it also offers substantial discounts on airfare, cruises, and car rentals through its volume-purchase plans. Membership includes a travel package outlining the company's many services and use of a toll-free telephone number for advice and information.

GOING AS A COURIER   Couriers are hired by overnight air-freight firms hoping to skirt the often-tedious Customs delays that regular cargo faces at the other end. For the service, the courier pays the firm a fee much lower than the cost of the ticket, and sometimes can fly free. Don't worry, the service is legal—you won't be asked to handle illegal drugs. Also, you don't actually carry the merchandise you're "transporting"; you just carry a shipping invoice to present to Customs when you arrive.

This cost-saving approach is not for everyone—there are lots of restrictions, and courier opportunities are hard to come by. You're allowed only one piece of carry-on luggage, since your checked-baggage allowance is used by the courier firm to transport its cargo.

For courier services, check with **Halbart Express,** 147-05 176th St., Jamaica, NY 11434 (☎ **718/656-5000** or ☎ 718/656-8189 daily from 10am to 3pm). Also try **Now Voyager,** 74 Varick St., Suite 307, New York, NY 10013 (☎ **212/431-1616**), Monday to Friday from 10am to 5:30pm, Saturday from noon to 4:30pm. An automatic telephone-answering system announces last-minute specials and the firm's fees for the round trip. Courier services are also listed in the yellow pages or in advertisements in newspaper travel sections.

For an annual membership of $45, the **International Association of Air Travel Couriers,** P.O. Box 1349, Lake Worth, FL 33460 (☎ **407/582-8320**), will send you six issues of its newsletter, *Shoestring Traveler,* and about a half dozen issues of *Air Courier Bulletin,* a directory of air-courier bargains around the world. The fee also includes access to their 24-hour "Fax-on-Demand" update of last-minute courier flights available for those who can travel on short notice.

A NOTE FOR BRITISH TRAVELERS

Since regular airfares from the U.K. to Scandinavia tend to be rather high, savvy Brits usually call a travel agent for a "deal"—either a charter flight or some special air-travel promotion. These so-called deals are often available because of Scandinavia's popularity as a tourist destination. If you can't get a deal, the next best choice is an APEX ticket. Although these tickets must be reserved in advance, they offer a discount without the usual booking restrictions. You could also inquire about a "Eurobudget ticket," which carries restrictions or length-of-stay requirements.

British newspapers typically carry lots of classified advertisements touting "slashed" fares from London to other parts of the world. One good source is *Time Out,* a magazine published in London. London's *Evening Standard* has a daily travel section, and the Sunday editions of almost all British newspapers run ads. Although competition is fierce, **Trailfinders** (☎ **0171/937-5400** in London) is one well-recommended company that consolidates bulk ticket purchases and then passes the savings on to its customers. It offers tickets on such carriers as SAS, British Airways, and KLM. You can fly from London's Heathrow or Gatwick airports to Copenhagen, Oslo, Stockholm, and Helsinki.

In London, there are many bucket shops around Victoria Station and Earl's Court that offer low fares. Make sure that the company you deal with is a member of the IATA, ABTA, or ATOL. These umbrella organizations will help you out if anything goes wrong.

CEEFAX, a British television information service (included on many home and hotel TVs), runs details of package holidays and flights to Europe and beyond. Just switch to your CEEFAX channel and you'll find a menu of listings that includes travel information.

Make sure that you understand the bottom line on any special deal you purchase— that is, ask if all surcharges, including airport taxes and other hidden costs, are included, before you commit yourself to purchase it. Upon investigation, people often find that some of these "deals" are not as attractive as advertised. Also, make sure you understand what the penalties are if you're forced to cancel at the last minute.

Cyberdeals for Net Surfers

More savvy travelers are finding excellent deals on everything from flights to whole vacation packages by searching the Internet. Although Web sites tend to change as fast as the Internet itself, a good beginning is to engage your favorite search engine, such as Yahoo or AltaVista, and search for the keyword, "travel." Here are some particularly useful sites.

Microsoft's **www.expedia.com** features a "Fare Tracker" that allows you to search for the cheapest flight to a certain destination, and even to subscribe to an e-mail service that gives you updated information on the cheapest flight every week. **www.travelocity.com** offers a similar service. **www.travelcom.es** allows you to search travel destinations to decide on that perfect vacation, and offers links to travel agency sites all over the world and in all 50 states. **www.moments-notice.com** promotes itself as a travel service, not an agency. New vacation deals are offered every morning—many of them are snapped up by the end of the day. A drawback is that these vacations may require you to drop everything and go almost immediately.

BY CAR

You can easily drive to Denmark from Germany. Many drive to Jutland from such cities as Hamburg, Bremerhaven, and Lübeck. Jutland is linked to the central island of Funen by bridge. And since 1998 it's been possible to take a bridge across the Great Belt from Funen to the island of Zealand, site of the city of Copenhagen. The bridge lies near the Danish city of Nyborg. Once in West Zealand you'll still have to drive east across the island to Copenhagen.

Car-ferry service to Denmark from the United Kingdom generally leaves passengers at Esbjerg, where they must then cross from Jutland to Copenhagen. From Germany, it's possible to take a car-ferry from Travemünde, northeast of Lübeck, which will deposit you at Gedser in Denmark. From here, connect with E55, an express highway north to Copenhagen.

BY TRAIN

If you're in Europe, it's easy to get to Denmark by train. Copenhagen is the main rail hub between Scandinavia and the rest of Europe. For example, the London-Copenhagen train via Ostende (Belgium) or Hoek van Holland (a port town in Holland) leaves four times daily (22 hours). About 10 daily express trains run from Hamburg (Germany) to Copenhagen (5 ½ hours). There are also inter-city trains on the Merkur route from Karlsruhe (Germany) to Cologne, Hamburg, and Copenhagen. The Berlin-Ostbahnhof-Copenhagen train (8 ½ hours) connects with Eastern European trains. Two daily express trains make this run.

If you plan to travel a great deal on Danish railroads, it's worth securing a copy of the *Thomas Cook European Timetable of European Passenger Railroads.* It's available exclusively in North America from **Forsyth Travel Library,** 226 Westchester Ave., White Plains, NY 10604 (☎ **800/FORSYTH**), at a cost of $27.95, plus $4.50 postage (priority airmail) in the United States or $5 U.S. to Canada.

RAIL PASSES FOR NORTH AMERICAN TRAVELERS

SCANRAIL PASS   If your visit to Europe will be primarily in Scandinavia, the Scanrail pass may be better and cheaper for you than the Eurailpass. This pass allows its owner a predetermined number of days of free rail travel within a larger time block. (Presumably, this allows for days devoted to sightseeing scattered among days of rail travel.) For example, you could choose a total of any 5 days of unlimited rail travel during a 15-day period, 10 days of rail travel within a 1-month period, or 1 month of unlimited rail travel. The pass, which is valid on all lines of the state railways of Denmark, Finland, Norway, and Sweden, offers discounts or free travel on some (but not all) of the region's ferryboat lines as well. The pass can be purchased only in North America, at any office of **RailEurope** (☎ **800/361-RAIL**) or at **Scanam World Tours,** 933 Highway 23, Pompton Plains, NJ 07444 (☎ **800/545-2204**).

Depending on whether you choose first- or second-class rail transport, the pass costs from $182 to $228 for the 5 days of travel in 15 days pass, $292 to $364 for the 10 days of travel in 1 month pass, and $426 to $532 for the 1 month of unlimited travel pass. There are 20% discounts off of these prices for senior citizens and students.

EURAILPASS   If you're going to be traveling extensively in Europe, the **Eurailpass** might be a good bet. It's valid for first-class rail travel in 17 European countries. With one ticket, you travel whenever and wherever you please; more than 100,000 rail miles are at your disposal. The pass is sold only in North America. A Eurailpass good for 15 days of travel costs $538, a pass for 21 days costs $698, a 1-month pass costs $864, a 2-month pass costs $1,224, and a 3-month pass goes for $1,512. Children under 4 travel free if they don't occupy a seat (otherwise, they're charged half fare); children under 12 are charged half fare. If you're under age 26, you can purchase a **Eurail Youthpass,** which entitles you to unlimited second-class travel for 15 days for $376, 1 month for $605, or 2 months for $857. Travelers considering purchasing a 15-day or 1-month pass should estimate rail distances before deciding if such a pass is worthwhile. To take full advantage of the tickets for 15 days or a month, you'd have to spend a great deal of time on the train. Eurailpass holders are entitled to substantial reductions on certain buses and ferries as well. Travel agents in all towns, and railway agents in such major cities as New York, Montréal, and Los Angeles, sell all these tickets. A Eurailpass is available at the North American offices of CIT Travel Service, the French National Railroads, the German Federal Railroads, and the Swiss Federal Railways.

The **Eurail Flexipass** allows greater flexibility in European travel. It's valid in first class and offers the same privileges as the Eurailpass. However, it provides a number of individual travel days that can be used over a much longer period of consecutive days. Using this pass makes it possible to stay longer in one city and yet not lose a single day of travel. There are two Flexipasses available: 10 days of travel within 2 months for $634, and 15 days of travel within 2 months for $836.

The **Eurail Saverpass** offers discounted tickets for groups of two or more people traveling together—but you must travel together at all times. The price of a Saverpass, valid all across Europe in first class only, is $458 for 15 days, $594 for 21 days, and $734 for 1 month. Even more freedom is offered by the **Saver Flexipass,** which is similar to the Eurail Saverpass with the exception that you are not confined to consecutive days of travel. For travel on any 10 days within 2 months the fare is $540; for any 15 days within 2 months the fare is $710.

The cheaper **Eurail Youth Flexipass** has many of the same qualifications and restrictions as the previously described Flexipass but is sold only to travelers under age 26. It allows 10 days of travel within 2 months for $444 and 15 days of travel within 2 months for $585.

RAIL PASSES FOR BRITISH TRAVELERS

Thousands of trains run from Britain to the Continent every month, and at least some of them are routed directly across or under the Channel, through France or Belgium and Germany into Denmark. For example, a train leaves London's Victoria Station daily at 9am, arriving the next day in Copenhagen at 8:25am. Another train leaves London's Victoria Station at 8:45pm, arriving the next day in Copenhagen at 8:20pm. Both go via Dover-Ostende, or via a connection at Brussels. Once you're in Copenhagen, you can make good rail connections to Norway, Finland, and Sweden.

If you plan to do a lot of exploring, you might prefer one of three rail passes designed for unlimited train travel within a pre-designated region during a predetermined number of days. These passes are sold only in Britain and several other European countries.

An **InterRail Pass** is available to passengers under age 26 of any nationality who can prove residency in a European or North African country (Morocco, Algeria, and Tunisia) for at least 6 months prior to purchasing the pass. The pass allows unlimited travel through all of Europe except Albania and the republics comprising the former Soviet Union. Prices are complicated and vary depending on the countries you want to include. For pricing purposes, Europe is divided into seven zones and the cost depends on the number of zones you include. The most expensive option, priced at £259, allows 1 month of unlimited travel in all seven zones (BritRail staff refer to this as a "global").

Passengers aged 26 and over can buy an **InterRail 26-Plus Pass,** which unfortunately, is severely limited geographically. Many countries do not honor this pass, including France, Belgium, Switzerland, Spain, Portugal, and Italy. The pass is, however, suitable for travel through Denmark, Finland, Norway, and Sweden. Second-class travel with the pass costs £339 for 15 days or £349 for 1 month. The same residency requirements apply to this pass that apply to the InterRail Pass described above.

For information on the purchase of individual rail tickets or any of the above-mentioned passes, contact **British Rail International,** Victoria Station, London (☎ **0990/ 848-848** or ☎ 0171/839-3341, for information). Tickets and passes are also available at any of the larger railway stations as well as selected travel agencies throughout Britain and the rest of Europe.

BY SHIP/FERRY

Liners carrying both cars and passengers operate between Denmark and ports in several other countries, including England, Germany, Poland, Norway, and Sweden. Check with your travel agent for details.

FROM BRITAIN   Scandinavia Seaways (☎ **800/533-3755** in the U.S., or ☎ 0171/616-1400 in London) runs vessels year-round between Harwich, England, and Esbjerg in West Jutland. The crossing takes between 16 and 20 hours. The same line also sails from Newcastle upon Tyne to Esbjerg, but only in the summer, as part of a passage that takes 22 hours. Overnight cabins and space for cars are available on both routes.

FROM NORWAY/SWEDEN   The **Bergen Line** (☎ **800/323-7436** in the U.S., or ☎ 212/319-1300) operates vessels between Oslo and Hirtshals in North Jutland.

The **Stena Line** runs much-frequented sea links between Oslo and Frederikshavn, North Jutland (11 ½ hours), and between Gothenburg, Sweden, and Frederikshavn (3 hours). For information, schedules, and fares, contact **EuroCruises,** 303 W. 13th St., New York, NY 10014 (☎ **800/688-3876** in the U.S., or ☎ 212/691-2099).

FROM GERMANY   From the Baltic coast of Germany, ferries operate between Kiel and Bagenkop on the Danish island of Langeland. Reserve tickets at **Langeland-Kiel Touristik,** Oslokai 3, in Kiel (☎ **431/97415-0**).

PACKAGE TOURS

For those travelers who feel more comfortable if everything is prearranged—hotels, transportation, sightseeing excursions, luggage handling, tips, taxes, and even meals— a package tour is the obvious choice, and it may even help save money.

One of the best tour operators to Denmark, Sweden, and Norway is **Bennett Tours,** 342 Madison Ave., New York, NY 10073 (☎ **800/221-2420** in the U.S., or ☎ 212/ 697-1092). It offers land packages with experienced guides and a wide range of prices.

Other reliable tour operators include **Olson Travelworld,** 1145 Clark St., Stevens Point, WI 54481 (☎ **800/826-4026**)), and **Scantours, Inc.,** 3439 Wade St., Los Angeles, CA 90006 (☎ **800/223-7226,** or ☎ 310/636-4656).

9 Getting Around

BY PLANE

The fastest way to get around the whole of Scandinavia is to take advantage of air passes.

SAS's VISIT SCANDINAVIA FARE   Scandinavia's vast distances encourage air travel between some of its most far-flung points. SAS's **Visit Scandinavia Pass** is one of the most worthwhile promotions 'available. This pass, available only to travelers who fly SAS across the Atlantic, includes up to six coupons, each of which is valid for any

SAS flight within or between Denmark, Norway, and Sweden. Each coupon costs $85, a price that's especially appealing when you consider than an economy-class ticket between Stockholm and Copenhagen can cost as much as $250 each way. The pass is especially valuable if you plan to travel to the far northern frontiers of Sweden or Norway; in that case, the savings over the price of a regular economy-class ticket can be substantial. For information on purchasing the pass, call **SAS** (☎ **800/221-2350**).

BY PLANE WITHIN DENMARK   For those in a hurry, **SAS** (☎ **32-32-00-00** in Copenhagen) operates daily service between Copenhagen and points on Jutland's mainland. From Copenhagen it takes about 40 minutes to fly to Aalborg, 35 minutes to Århus, and 30 minutes to Odense's Beldringe Airport.

Fares to other Danish cities are sometimes included in a transatlantic ticket at no extra charge, provided that the additional cities are specified when the ticket is written.

BY TRAIN

Flat, low-lying Denmark, with its hundreds of bridges and the absence of mountains, has a large network of railway lines that connect virtually every hamlet with the largest city, Copenhagen. For **information, schedules,** and **fares** anywhere in Denmark, call ☎ **33-14-88-00.** A word you're likely to see a lot is *Lyntog,* which is basically the Danish word for "express trains."

On any train within Denmark, children between 4 and 11 are charged only 50% of the fare; of course, they must be accompanied by an adult.

Adults 65 or older receive a 20% to 33% discount on one-way or round-trip tickets at all times. No identification is needed when you buy your ticket, but the conductor who checks your ticket might ask for proof of age if there's any doubt.

The Danish government offers dozens of different discounts on the country's rail networks—depending on the type of traveler, days or hours traveled, and destination. Because these discounts change quite often, it's always best to ask for a discount based on your age and the number of days (or hours) you intend to be traveling.

BY BUS

By far the best way to visit rural Denmark is by car, but if that's not possible, you can usually travel by bus. In much of Scandinavia, buses take passengers to destinations not served by the train; therefore, the bus route often originates at the railway station. The arrival of trains and departure of buses are usually coordinated.

For seniors age 65 and over, round-trip bus tickets are sometimes offered at one-way prices (excluding Saturday, Sunday, and peak travel periods around Christmas and Easter). Most discounts are granted only to seniors who are traveling beyond the city limits of their point of origin.

BY CAR

RENTALS   Avis, Budget, and Hertz offer well-serviced, well-maintained fleets of cars in Denmark. You may have to reserve and prepay for your rental car within a reasonable time (usually within 2 weeks, but occasionally as little as 48 hours in advance) in order to obtain the lowest rates. Unfortunately, if your trip is canceled or your arrival date changes, you may have to fill out a lot of forms to arrange a refund. All three companies may charge slightly higher rates to clients who reserve less than 48 hours in advance and decide to pay for their rental at the time of pickup. The highest rates are charged to walk-in customers who arrange their rentals after they arrive in Denmark.

Before you rent, you should know that the Danish government imposes a whopping 25% tax on all car rentals. Agencies that encourage prepaid rates will almost

Parking

Parking charges in most European countries have risen so high in recent years that they now have to be factored into the cost of a European trip if you're planning to drive. Increasingly, unless you want to use expensive garages and the very limited sites available at most big city hotels, parking is harder and harder to find on the streets of Europe.

Fortunately, Denmark is different. Except for Copenhagen and a few cities such as Århus or Aalborg, almost no one pays to park at a Danish hotel or inn. Parking is generally free wherever you travel, although during the day you may have to put kroner into parking meters along city streets.

Out in the country and especially on the offshore islands, you just pull up at the door and park. All this cuts down considerably on your road costs, of course.

---

never collect this tax in advance—instead, it will be imposed as part of a separate transaction when you pick up the car. Furthermore, any car retrieved at a Danish airport is subject to a one-time supplemental tax of 100 DKK ($14.50); thus, you might prefer to pick up your car at a downtown location instead, presumably after you've recovered from jet lag and had the opportunity to become oriented to the city. Membership in certain travel clubs or organizations (such as AAA or AARP) might qualify you for modest reductions.

Avis (☎ **800/331-2112** in the U.S.) maintains two offices in Copenhagen, one at the arrivals hall of the Copenhagen airport and another at Kampmannsgade 1 (☎ **33-15-22-99**). The rate for its smallest car—a Ford Festiva—is $262 per week (with unlimited mileage) if you prepay 2 weeks before your departure. Avis warns that "walk-in" clients who don't reserve from North America may be charged double the above-mentioned rates, so reserving in advance is quite important.

Budget (☎ **800/527-0700** in the U.S.) has about 14 rental locations in Denmark, fewer than either Avis or Hertz, although they tend to be in the cities and regions most frequented by foreign visitors. Budget's rate for the cheapest car—a Ford Fiesta—is $315 per week with unlimited mileage if it's prepaid in North America, and considerably higher for walk-in customers who have not reserved and prepaid. Budget maintains a large branch at the Copenhagen airport (☎ **32-52-39-00**).

Hertz (☎ **800/654-3001** in the U.S.) charges a prepaid rate of $351 for a Ford Festiva and about $388 for those who have not prepaid. Hertz's office in central Copenhagen is at Ved Vesterport 3 (☎ **33-17-90-20**); another office is located at the airport (☎ **32-50-93-00**). These rates are subject to change at any time without notice.

When inquiring about a Danish rental car, consider the services of a small company based in Harrison, N.Y.—**Kemwel** (☎ **800/678-0678** in the U.S.). As the North American representative for two Denmark-based car companies—Van Wijk and Hertz—Kemwel may be able to offer attractive rental prices to North Americans who pay in full at least 10 days before their departure. Seniors and members of AAA get a 5% discount. Another excellent rental company is **Auto-Europe** (☎ **800/223-5555**; **www.autoeurope.com**).

INSURANCE   Each of the rental companies builds a certain amount of insurance into the rates, which is adequate for most drivers and most accidents. If you have a mishap, however, and didn't purchase additional insurance to cover the cost of repairs to your rental car, you'll be responsible for an amount that varies from 15,000 DKK to the full value of the car. Of the big three, Budget usually offers the most favorable insurance arrangements.

The cost of additional insurance is about 80 DKK ($11.60) per day at Budget (for its least expensive car) and a bit more for equivalent vehicles at the other two companies. Advance payment with certain types of credit cards may eliminate (or at least reduce) the need for additional insurance, depending upon the card issuer. Be sure to read your card's coverage policy carefully.

10 Organized Tours

If you'd rather leave the driving and the details to someone else, there are lots of package tours available to show you the highlights of Denmark.

BUS TOURS   Scanam World Tours (☎ **800/545-2204**) offers a tour through the "Heart of Fairy Tale Denmark." You can choose a 3- or 6-day trip through Hans Christian Andersen country, including a visit to Odense (his birthplace), and an excursion to Legoland. Tours begin at $410.

SELF-DRIVE TOURS   Several companies offer self-drive tours which usually include accommodations, rental cars, and a customized itinerary. **Scantours Incorporated** (☎ **800/223-7226**) features the 7-day "Royal Tour of Denmark," which is available year-round on request. It begins at $950. This company also sponsors a tour of Danish inns. The 4-day self-drive tour includes accommodations in Danish inns, breakfast, car rental, and an itinerary priced from $299.

DUCK-HUNTING TOURS   Sports enthusiasts may be interested in a duck-hunting excursion. **Transmarine** (☎ **800/206-8936** in the U.S.) offers 3 days of duck hunting at various manors throughout southern Denmark. Tours cost $1,500 and up, depending on the accommodations and location of the hunt, and include all meals and hunting permits.

BICYCLE TOURS   An excellent way to explore the flat, rolling Danish countryside is on a bicycle. Numerous organizations (including **Scantours International** and **Scanam Tours**) sponsor bike tours through various regions of the country. You can choose one that covers the castles, beaches, and fjords of northern Denmark; the southern Funen islands; the beaches and marshland of western Jutland; or the lake country in eastern Jutland. **Blue Marble Travel** (☎ **973/326-9533**) offers 7-day excursions of H. C. Andersen country and several small islands in the Baltic for $1,450. **Dansk Cyklist Forbund,** Rømersgade 7, DK-1362 København K (☎ **33-32-31-21**), can provide the latest information on cycling tours in Denmark.

SUGGESTED ITINERARIES

If You Have 1 Week

Days 1–3   Spend your first 3 days in Copenhagen. After the first day recovering from the flight, have dinner at Tivoli (in summer) or at Nyhavn (in winter). Spend the morning of the second day taking one of our walking tours (see chapter 5); then, if it's summer, spend the afternoon wandering through Tivoli Gardens, listening to the free music. Devote Day 3 to more serious sightseeing, including visits to Christiansborg Palace and the Ny Carlsberg Glyptotek.

Day 4   Leave Copenhagen and head north, stopping over at the modern art museum, Louisiana, before heading to Helsingør, site of the Kronborg Castle of *Hamlet* fame. Either spend the night in Helsingør or return to Copenhagen.

Day 5   Journey to Odense on the island of Funen, birthplace of Hans Christian Andersen. Spend the rest of the day and evening exploring its many attractions.

Day 6   Stop in Roskilde to see its cathedral and Viking Ship Museum. Return to Copenhagen and spend the night.

Day 7   Try another walking tour, and schedule visits to Rosenborg Castle and, if you have time, the National Museum. Return to Tivoli for a farewell drink.

If You Have 2 Weeks

Day 1   Recover from jet lag and have dinner at Tivoli (in summer) or at Scala (a restaurant complex across from Tivoli) if it's off-season.

Day 2   In the morning, take our first walking tour (see chapter 5). Spend the afternoon wandering around Tivoli Gardens (in summer).

Day 3   Take another walking tour and visit Christiansborg Palace and the Ny Carlsberg Glyptotek.

Day 4   Head north from Copenhagen, visit the modern art museum, and have lunch at Helsingør, site of the Kronborg Castle of *Hamlet* fame. Spend the night in Helsingør.

Day 5   Explore North Zealand, with visits to the royal palace at Fredensborg and the 17th-century Frederiksborg Castle at Hillerød. Spend the night in Helsingør.

Day 6   Return to Copenhagen and visit Rosenborg Castle and the National Museum.

Day 7   Still in Copenhagen, explore the other attractions of Zealand, journeying outside the capital to the open-air museum, Frilandsmuseet. Head to Roskilde for lunch, visiting the cathedral, the Viking Ship Museum, and the Iron Age Village at Lejre.

Day 8   Head south from Copenhagen to explore South Zealand. Visit the old market town of Køge, Vallø Castle, and Selso Slot. Spend the night in a typical inn on Zealand.

Day 9   Go west, crossing mid-Zealand. At Korsør, cross the bridge to Nyborg. Visit Nyborg Castle before driving to Odense to explore the city of Hans Christian Andersen. Stop overnight in Odense.

Day 10   Spend time exploring more of Odense. Then visit the Viking ship at Ladby and Egeskov Castle outside Odense.

Day 11   Drive south from Odense to Svendborg. Explore the nearby islands of Thurø and Tåsinge.

Day 12   From Svendborg, board a ferry (make a reservation) and head for the island of Ærø. Spend the night in the capital, Ærøskøbing, or at an island inn.

Day 13   Leave Ærø and return to Svendborg by ferry. Drive north toward Odense along Route 9 until you connect with E20 west, the highway that will take you into Jutland. In Jutland, take Route 32 at the junction with E20 to Ribe. Spend the night in Ribe.

Day 14   Leave Ribe in the morning and drive to Silkeborg to view Sky Mountain. Ride on a paddle-wheel steamer on the Silkeborg Lakes. Visit the Silkeborg Museum. From Silkeborg, drive to Århus, where you can explore the Old Town. Have fun at Århus's Tivoli amusement park. Spend the night.

If You Have 3 Weeks

Days 1–12   Follow the first 12 days of the above itinerary.

Day 13   Leave Ærø in the morning and return by ferry to Svendborg. From Svendborg, take Route 44 west to Fåborg to explore the largely bucolic southwestern corner of the island.

Day 14   From Fåborg, go along Route 43 north to Odense and connect with the express highway, E20, heading west to Jutland. Drive to Jelling, seat of the 10th-century kings of Denmark. Accommodations are limited in Jelling, so stay overnight in Vejle, a short drive southeast of Jelling.

Day 15   From Jelling, take E45 and Route 32 cross country to Ribe, of stork's-nest fame. Explore its attractions, including the cathedral and the smallest house in Denmark. Spend the night.

Day 16   Drive northwest from Ribe to Esbjerg. Take the 20-minute ferry ride to Fanø, an island of heather-covered moors and windswept sand dunes. Stay overnight at one of the *kros* (inns) on the island.

Day 17   From Fanø, board the return ferry to Esbjerg and head north along various routes to Silkeborg. Visit Sky Mountain and enjoy a ride on a paddle-wheel steamer on the Silkeborg Lakes. Also visit the Silkeborg Museum. Stay overnight in Silkeborg.

Day 18   From Silkeborg, drive east to Århus. Explore its many attractions, including Den Gamle By (the Old Town). Spend the night in Århus.

Day 19   Leave Århus and drive to Ebeltoft, 32-miles northeast. Continue on to Randers for the night or, for more atmosphere, spend the night at the Hvidsten Kro, on the outskirts of Hvidsten, between Randers and Mariager.

Day 20   Head north to Aalborg, where you can visit Lindholm Hoje, the largest Scandinavian burial site of the Viking period, the Aalborg Zoo, and yet another Tivoli.

Day 21   After Aalborg, spend the rest of the day exploring North Jutland, going to either Frederikshavn, Hirtshals, or Skagen for an overnight stop. Skagen is at the northern tip of Jutland. At Frederikshavn you can take a car-ferry to Oslo to begin exploring Norway or a car-ferry to Gothenburg if you're ready for Sweden.

FAST FACTS: Denmark

Area Code   The country code for Denmark is **45.** There are no city area codes. Each telephone number dialed in Denmark has eight digits.

Business Hours   Most **banks** in Denmark are open Monday to Friday from 9:30am to 4pm (on Thursday to 6pm), but outside Copenhagen, banking hours vary. **Stores** are generally open Monday to Thursday from 9am to 5:30pm, on Friday from 9am to 7 or 8pm, and on Saturday from noon to 2pm; most are closed Sunday.

Camera & Film   Film is so expensive that we suggest you bring what you'll need from home. Film processing is also expensive, so wait until you're home to develop your pictures. There are no special restrictions on taking photographs, except in certain museums (signs are generally posted). When in doubt, ask.

Customs   Nearly all items that can safely be viewed as "personal" are allowed in duty-free. Tobacco is limited: You can bring in either 250 cigarettes or 250 grams of tobacco. You can also bring in 1 liter (a standard bottle) of spirits or 2 liters of strong wine, depending on whether you're coming into Denmark from an EU or non-EU country. There are no restrictions on the import of currency into Denmark. However, nonresidents cannot take out more Danish kroner than they brought in, unless they can prove they obtained it by converting foreign currency.

Upon leaving Denmark, U.S. citizens who have been outside their home country for 48 hours or more are allowed to take home $400 worth of merchandise duty free—if they have claimed no similar exemption within the past 30 days. If you make purchases in Denmark, keep your receipts.

Doctors   Most areas have doctors on duty 24 hours a day on Saturday, Sunday, and holidays; weekday emergency hours are 4pm to 7:30am. Every doctor speaks English.

Drug Laws   There are severe penalties in Denmark for the possession, use, purchase, sale, or manufacturing of drugs. The quantity of the controlled substance is more important than the actual type of substance someone might possess. Danish police are particularly strict with any cases involving the sale of drugs to children.

Drugstores   They're known as *apoteker* in Danish and are open Monday to Thursday from 9am to 5:30pm, on Friday from 9am to 7pm, and on Saturday from 9am to 1pm.

Electricity   Voltage is generally 220 volts AC, 50 to 60 cycles, but in many camping sites 110-volt power plugs are also available. Adapters and transformers may be purchased in Denmark. It's always best to check at your hotel desk before using any electrical outlet.

Embassies   All embassies are in Copenhagen. The embassy of the **United States** is located at Dag Hammarsjölds Allé 24, DK-2100 København (☎ **35-55-31-44**); the embassy of the **United Kingdom,** at Kastelsvej 40, DK-2100 København (☎ **35-44-52-00**); the embassy of **Canada,** on Kristen Berniskowsgadei, DK-1105 København K (☎ **33-12-22-99**); the embassy of **Australia,** at Strandboulevarden, DK-2100 København (☎ **39-29-20-77**), and the embassy of **Ireland,** at Østbanegade 21 (☎ **31-42-32-33**).

Emergencies   Dial **112** for the fire department, the police, an ambulance, or to report a sea or air accident. Emergency calls from public telephone kiosks are free (no coins needed).

Holidays   See "When to Go," earlier in this chapter.

Language   Danish is the national tongue. English is commonly spoken, especially among young people. You should have few, if any, language barriers. The best phrase book to buy is *Danish for Travellers,* published by Berlitz.

Liquor Laws   To consume alcohol in Danish bars, restaurants, or cafes, a customer must be 18 or older. However, there are no restrictions on children under 18 who drink at home or, for example, from a bottle in a public park. Danish police tend to be lenient unless drinkers become raucous or uncontrollable. There is no leniency, however, in the matter of driving while intoxicated. It's strictly illegal to drive with a blood-alcohol level of 0.8 or more, which could be produced by two drinks. If the level is 1.5, motorists will pay a serious fine. If the blood-alcohol level is more than 1.5, drivers can lose their license. If the level is 2.0 or more (usually produced by six or seven drinks), a prison term of at least 14 days might follow.

Package stores are closed on Sunday, but some bars stay open until 5am on Sunday.

Mail   In general, post offices are open Monday to Friday from 9 or 10am to 5 or 6pm and on Saturday from 9am to noon; they're closed on Sunday. All mail to North America will be sent airmail without extra charge. The cost for 20 grams (.175 ounces) is 3.75 DKK (55¢). All mailboxes are painted red and display an embossed crown and trumpet of the Danish Postal Society.

Maps   The best map for touring Denmark is part of the series published by Hallwag. It can be purchased at all major bookstores in Copenhagen, including the most centrally located one, **Boghallen,** Rådhuspladsen 37 (☎ **33-11-85-11**), in the Town Hall Square.

Newspapers & Magazines   English-language newspapers are sold at all major news kiosks in Copenhagen but are much harder to find in the provinces. London papers are flown in for early-morning deliveries, but you may find the *International Herald Tribune* or *USA Today* more interesting. Pick up a copy of *Copenhagen This Week,* printed in English, which contains useful information.

Police   Dial **112** for police assistance.

Radio & TV   There are no English-language radio or TV stations broadcasting from Denmark. Only radios and TVs with satellite reception can receive signals from countries such as Britain. News programs in English are broadcast Monday to Saturday at 8:30am on Radio Denmark, 93.85 MHz. Radio 1 (at 90.8 MHz VHF) features news and classical music. Channels 2 and 3 (96.5/93.9 MHz) broadcast some entertainment, light news items, and light music. Most TV stations transmit from 7:30am to 11:30pm. Most films (many of which are American) are shown in their original languages, with Danish subtitles.

Rest Rooms   All big plazas, such as Town Hall Square in Copenhagen, have public lavatories. In small towns and villages, head for the marketplace. Hygienic standards are usually adequate. Sometimes both men and women patronize the same toilets. Otherwise, men's rooms are marked *herrer* or *H,* and women's rooms are marked *damer* or *D.*

Safety   Denmark is one of the safest countries of Europe for travelers. Copenhagen, the major population center, naturally experiences the most crime. Muggings have been reported in the vicinity of the railway station, especially late at night, but crimes of extreme violence are exceedingly rare. Exercise the usual precautions you would when traveling anywhere.

Taxes   Denmark imposes a 25% VAT (value-added tax) on goods and services. In Denmark it's known as *MOMS* (pronounced "mumps"). Special tax-free exports are possible, and many stores will mail goods home to you, circumventing the tax. If you want to take your purchases with you, look for shops displaying Danish tax-free shopping notices. Such shops offer tourists tax refunds for personal export. This refund applies to purchases of 300 DKK ($43.50) and up for U.S. and Canadian visitors. To apply, the 300-kroner purchase must be made at a single store participating in the tax-free plan. Your tax-free invoice must be stamped by Danish Customs when you leave the country. You can receive your refund at Copenhagen's Kastrup International Airport when you depart. If you depart by land or by sea, you can receive your refund by mail. Requests for refunds should be sent by mail to **Danish Tax-Free Shopping A/S,** H. J. Holstvej 5A, DK-2605 Brøndby, Denmark. You'll be reimbursed by check, cash, or credit- or charge-card credit in the currency you wish.

For the refund to apply, the 300 DKK must be spent in one store, but not necessarily at the same time. Some major department stores allow purchases to be made over several days or even weeks, at the end of which receipts will be tallied. Service and handling fees are deducted from the total, so actual refunds come to about 18%. Information on this program is available from the Danish Tourist Board (see "Visitor Information & Entry Requirements," earlier in this chapter).

A 25% MOMS is included in your hotel and restaurant bills, service charges, and entrance fees, as well as on repair of foreign-registered cars. No refunds are possible on these items.

Heritage—The Search for Roots

More than 12 million North Americans have Scandinavian roots, many in Denmark. To help you trace your ancestry, Danish consulates can furnish fact sheets. Many original Danish records are available on microfilm from **The Family History Museum,** 35 North West Temple, Salt Lake City, UT 84150 (☎ **801/ 240-2331**).

Established in 1992, the **Danish Immigrant Museum,** Elk Horn, Iowa (☎ **712/764-7225**), is devoted to telling the story of Scandinavian migration to the United States. It also collects and preserves a vital chapter in Danish-American history.

In Denmark itself the major archives concerning immigration are held at **Det danske Udvandrerarkiv** (Danes' Worldwide Archives), Arkivstræde 1, P.O. Box 1731, DK-9100 Aalborg (☎ **98-12-57-93;** fax 98-10-22-48).

Telephone   The country code for Denmark is **45.** This two-digit number should precede any call made to Denmark from another country.

Danish phones are fully automatic. Dial the eight-digit number; there are no city area codes. At public telephone booths, use two 50-øre coins or a 1-krone or 5-krone coin only. Don't insert any coins until your party answers. You can make more than one call on the same payment if your time hasn't run out. Remember that it can be expensive to telephone from your hotel room. Emergency calls are free.

Time   Denmark operates on Central European Time—1 hour ahead of Greenwich Mean Time and 6 hours ahead of Eastern Standard Time (so when it's 1pm in New York, it's 7pm in Copenhagen). Daylight Savings Time is observed from the end of March to the end of September.

Tipping   Tips are seldom expected, but when they are, you should give only 1 or 2 DKK. Porters charge according to fixed prices, and tipping is not customary for hairdressers/barbers. Hotels, restaurants, and even taxis impose a 15% service charge in the rates they quote; thus, service is built into the system. Since there's a built-in service charge, plus the 25% MOMS, you'll probably end up paying an additional 40% for some services!

Consider tipping only for special services—actually, some Danes could feel insulted if you offer them a tip.

Water   Tap water is safe to drink throughout Denmark.

4 Introducing Copenhagen

Copenhagen, the capital of Denmark, got its name from the word *køben-havn,* which means "merchants' harbor." It grew in size and importance because of its position on the Øresund (the Sound), the body of water between Denmark and Sweden, guarding the entrance to the Baltic. From its humble beginnings, Copenhagen has become the largest city in Scandinavia, home to 1 ½ million people. It's the seat of one of the oldest kingdoms in the world.

Over the centuries Copenhagen has suffered more than its share of disasters. In the 17th century the Swedes repeatedly besieged it, and in the 18th century it endured the plague and two devastating fires. The British attacked twice during the Napoleonic wars in the early 1800s. Its last major disaster occurred in 1940 when the Nazis invaded Denmark and held it in their grip until 1945 when the British army moved in again, this time as liberators.

Copenhagen is a city with much charm, as reflected in its canals, narrow streets, and old houses. Its most famous resident was Hans Christian Andersen, whose memory still lives on. Another of Copenhagen's world-renowned inhabitants was Sören Kierkegaard, who used to take long morning strolls in the city, planning his next addition to the collection of essays that eventually earned him the title, "father of existentialism."

Copenhagen still retains some of the characteristics of a village. If you forget the suburbs, you can cover most of the central belt on foot, making it a great place to visit. It's almost as if the city was designed for strolling, as reflected by its Strøget, the longest and oldest pedestrians-only street in Europe.

1 Orientation

ARRIVING

BY PLANE   You arrive at **Kastrup Airport** (☎ **32-54-17-01**), 7¼ miles from the center of Copenhagen. Beginning in 1998, air-rail trains for the first time have linked the airport with the Central Railway Station in the center of Copenhagen. The ride takes only 11 minutes, and costs 16.50 kroner ($2.40). Located right underneath the airport's arrivals and departure halls, the Air Rail Terminal is just a short escalator ride from the gates. It is equipped with more than 30 check-in counters, ticketing offices, information desks, restaurants, and fast-food chains. You can also take an SAS bus to the city terminal; the fare is 35 DKK ($5.05). Even cheaper is a local bus, no. 250S, which leaves from the international arrivals terminal every 15 or 20 minutes for Town Hall Square in central Copenhagen and costs 15 DKK ($2.15). A taxi to the city center costs around 130 DKK ($18.85).

BY TRAIN   Trains arrive at the **Hoved Banegård** (Central Railroad Station) (☎ **33-14-17-01** for rail information), in the very center of Copenhagen, near Tivoli Gardens and the Rådhuspladsen. The station operates a luggage-checking service, but room bookings are available only at the tourist office (see "Visitor Information," below). You can also exchange money at Den Danske Bank (☎ **33-12-04-11**), open daily from 7am to 8pm.

From the Central Railroad Station, you can connect with the **S-tog,** the local subway system; trains depart from platforms in the terminal itself. The information desk is near tracks 5 and 6.

BY BUS   Buses from Zealand and elsewhere in Denmark also pull into the Central Railroad Station. For bus information, call ☎ **36-45-45-45** daily from 7am to 9:30pm.

BY CAR   If you're driving from Germany, a car-ferry will take you from Travemünde to Gedser in southern Denmark. From Gedser, get on E55 north, an express highway that will deliver you to the southern outskirts of Copenhagen. If you're coming from Sweden and crossing at Helsingborg, you'll land on the Danish side of Helsingør. From there, take express highway E55 south to the northern outskirts of Copenhagen.

BY FERRY   Most ferryboats land at Havnegade, at the southern tip of Nyhavn, a short walk from the center of Copenhagen. Taxis also wait here for ferry arrivals. Most arrivals are from Malmö, Sweden; ferries from continental Europe usually land in South Zealand.

VISITOR INFORMATION

The **Copenhagen Tourist Information Center,** Bernstorffsgade 1 (☎ **33-11-13-25**), across from Tivoli's main entrance, dispenses information. It's open in July and August, daily from 8am to 11pm; May, June, and September 1 through 15, daily from 9am to 9pm; and September 16 through April, Monday to Friday from 9am to 4:30pm and Saturday from 9am to 1:30pm.

CITY LAYOUT

MAIN ARTERIES & STREETS   The heart of Old Copenhagen is a warren of pedestrian streets, bounded by Nørreport Station to the north, Rådhuspladsen (Town Hall Square) to the west, and Kongens Nytorv to the east. **Strøget,** the longest continuous pedestrians-only route in Europe, goes east from Town Hall Square to Kongens Nytorv, and is made up of five streets: Frederiksberggade, Nygade, Vimmelskaftet, Amagertorv, and Østergade. **Strøget** is lined with shops, bars, restaurants, and in summer, sidewalk cafes. **Pistolstræde** is a maze of galleries, restaurants, and boutiques, all housed in restored 18th-century buildings.

Fiolstræde (Violet Street), a dignified street with antiques shops and bookshops, cuts through the university (Latin Quarter). If you turn into Rosengaarden at the top of Fiolstræde, you'll come to **Kultorvet** (Coal Square), just before you reach Nørreport Station. Here you join the third main pedestrian street, **Købmagergade** (Butcher Street), which winds around and finally meets Strøget at Amagertorv.

At the end of Strøget you approach **Kongens Nytorv** (King's Square). This is the site of the Royal Theater and Magasin, the largest department store in Copenhagen. This will put you at the beginning of **Nyhavn,** the former seamen's quarter that has been gentrified into an upmarket area of expensive restaurants, apartments, cafes, and boutiques.

The government of Denmark is centered on the small island of **Slotsholmen,** which is connected to the center by eight different bridges. Several museums, notably Christiansborg Castle, are found here.

The center of Copenhagen is **Rådhuspladsen** (Town Hall Square). From here it's a short walk to the Tivoli Gardens, the major attraction of Copenhagen, and the Central Railroad Station, the main railroad, subway, and bus terminus. **Vesterbrogade,** a wide boulevard, passes by Tivoli until it reaches the Central Railroad Station. **H. C. Andersens Boulevard,** another major avenue named after Denmark's most famous writer, runs along Rådhuspladsen and Tivoli Gardens.

FINDING AN ADDRESS   All even numbers are on one side of the street, all odd numbers on the other. Buildings are listed in numerical order. A, B, or C are often inserted after the street number.

NEIGHBORHOODS IN BRIEF

For a map of Copenhagen, see page 66.

Tivoli Gardens   These amusement gardens were built on the site of former fortifications in the heart of Copenhagen, on the south side of Rådhuspladsen. Some 160,000 flowers and 110,000 electric lights set the scene. Built in 1843, Tivoli is made up of a collection of restaurants, dance halls, theaters, beer gardens, and lakes.

Strøget   This pedestrians-only street begins at Rådhuspladsen. The most interesting parts are Gammeltorv and Nytorv, "old" and "new" squares, lying on either side of Strøget. They're the sites of fruit and vegetable markets, as well as stalls selling bric-a-brac and handmade jewelry. The word "Strøget" doesn't appear on any maps. Instead, Strøget encompasses five streets: Frederiksbrerggade, Nygade, Villelskaftet, Amagertorv, and Østergade.

Nyhavn   This is the harbor area, for years the haunt of sailors looking for tattoos and other diversions. Nowadays it's one of the most elegant sections of the city, site of the deluxe hotel d'Angleterre and many prestigious restaurants. The Royal Theater stands on Kongens Nytorv.

Indre By   This is the name given to the Old Town, the heart of Copenhagen. Once filled with monasteries, it's a maze of old streets, alleyways, and squares. If you cross Gammeltorv and Nørregade, you'll be in the university area, nicknamed the Latin Quarter, as in Paris. The Vor Frue Kirke (cathedral of Copenhagen) is found here, as is the Rundetårn (Round Tower).

Slotsholmen   This island, site of Christiansborg Palace, was where Bishop Absalon built the first fortress in the city in 1167. Today it's the seat of the Danish parliament and the site of Thorvaldsen's Museum, among others. Slotsholmen is linked to Indre by bridges. You can also visit the Royal Library, the Theater Museum, and the Royal Stables. The 17th-century Børsen (stock exchange) is also here.

Christinashavn   This was the "new town" ordered by master builder Christian IV in the early 1500s. The town was originally constructed to house workers in the shipbuilding industry. Visitors come here today mainly to see the Danish Film Museum on Store Søndervoldstræde, and Vors Frelsers Kirke, on the corner of Prinsessegade and Skt. Annægade. Sightseers can climb the spire of this old church for a panoramic view.

Christiania   This offbeat district, once a barracks for soldiers, is within walking distance of Vor Frelsers Kirke at Christianshavn. You can enter the area on Prinsessegade.

There are craft shops and restaurants here; merchandise and food are fairly cheap because the residents refuse to pay Denmark's crippling 25% tax. In 1971 many young and homeless people moved in without the city's permission, proclaiming that Christiania was a "free city." It has been a controversial place ever since.

Vesterbro   The main street of this district, Istedgade, runs west from the main rail depot in the center of town. It passes through various neighborhoods. At first, the blocks are lined with rather respectable hotels but they soon give way to Copenhagen's red-light district. In the early 1970s when Denmark legalized pornography, visitors from all over the world flocked to this district. Now that pornography is readily available in many places, Vesterbro has lost its original allure, although the porn shops and seedy nightclubs remain. In the 1990s, many immigrants to Copenhagen, especially those from Turkey and Pakistan, have settled in the neighborhood, filling it with plenty of indigenous craft shops and ethnic restaurants.

Nørrebro   Adjacent to Vesterbro (see above), Nørrebro takes the immigrant overflow, and is also rich in artisan shops and ethnic restaurants, especially Turkish and Pakistani. This area has been a blue collar neighborhood since the middle of the 19th century. However, the original Danish settlers have long since departed, replaced by immigrants who are not always greeted with a friendly reception in Copenhagen. The area also abounds with artists, students, and musicians who can't afford the high rents elsewhere. There are so many second-hand clothing stores—especially around Sankt Hans Torv—that Nørrebro is taking on the flavor of a Middle Eastern bazaar. Antique shops (believe us, many of the furnishings and objets d'art aren't authentic) also fill the area. Most of these "antique" stores lie along Ravnsborgade. On Saturday morning a flea market is in full swing along the wall of Assistens Kirkegård, to the west of Nørrebrogade.

Frederiksberg   If you head west from the inner city along Vesterbrogade, you will reach the residential and business district of Frederiksberg. It grew up around Frederiksberg Palace, constructed in the Italianate style with an ocher façade. A park, Frederiksberg Have, surrounds the palace. To the west of the palace is the Zoologisk Have, one of the largest zoos in Europe.

Dragør   Dragør is a fishing village south of the city that dates from the 16th century. Except for Tivoli, this seems to be everybody's favorite spot. It's especially recommended if you only have time to see the Copenhagen area and not the countryside at large. Walk its cobblestone streets and enjoy its 65 old red-roofed houses, which have been designated as national landmarks.

2 Getting Around

Copenhagen is a walker's paradise, neat and compact. Many of the major sightseeing attractions are close to one another.

BY PUBLIC TRANSPORTATION

A joint zone fare system includes Copenhagen Transport buses and State Railway and S-tog trains in Copenhagen and North Zealand, plus some private railway routes within a 25-mile radius of the capital, enabling you to transfer from train to bus and vice versa with the same ticket.

BASIC FARES   A *grundbillet* (basic ticket) for both buses and trains costs 11 DKK ($1.60). You can buy 10 tickets for 70 DKK ($10.15). Children 11 and under ride for half fare; those 4 and under go free on local trains; and those 6 and under go free on buses. For 70 DKK ($10.15) you can purchase a ticket allowing 24-hour bus and train travel through nearly half of Zealand; it's half price for children 7 to 11, and free for children 6 and under.

What strikes me now most as regards Denmark is the charm, beauty, and independence of the women.

—Arnold Bennett, Journal 1913.

DISCOUNT PASSES   The **Copenhagen Card** entitles you to free and unlimited travel by bus and rail throughout the metropolitan area (including North Zealand), 25% to 50% discounts on crossings to and from Sweden, and free admission to many sights and museums. The card is available for 1, 2, or 3 days and costs 140 DKK ($20.30), 255 DKK ($36.95), and 320 DKK ($46.40), respectively. Children 11 and under are given a 50% discount. For more information, contact the Copenhagen Tourist Information Center (see "Orientation," earlier in this chapter).

Students who have an **International Student Identity Card (ISIC)** are entitled to a number of travel breaks in Copenhagen. A card can be purchased in the United States at any **Council Travel office** (for the office nearest you, call **800/GET-AN-ID**).

For information about low-cost train, ferry, and plane trips, go to **Wasteels,** Skoubogade 6 (☎ **33-14-46-33**), in Copenhagen. It's open Monday to Friday from 9am to 7pm and Saturday 10am to 3pm.

Eurail passes (which must be purchased in the U.S.) and Nordturist Pass tickets (which can be purchased at any train station in Scandinavia) can be used on local trains in Copenhagen.

BY BUS   Copenhagen's well-maintained buses are the least expensive method of getting around. Most buses leave from Rådhuspladsen. A basic ticket allows 1 hour of travel and unlimited transfers within the zone where you started your trip. For information, call ☎ **36-45-45-45.**

BY S-TOG (SUBWAY)   The S-tog connects heartland Copenhagen with its suburbs. Use of the tickets is the same as on buses (see above). You can transfer from a bus line to an S-tog train on the same ticket. Eurail pass holders generally ride free. For more information, call ☎ **33-14-17-01** at any time.

BY CAR

Because of the widespread availability of traffic-free walkways in Copenhagen, and because of its many parks, gardens, and canal-side promenades, the Danish capital is well suited to pedestrian promenades. It's best to park your car in any of the dozens of city parking lots, then retrieve it when you're ready to explore the capital's suburbs. Many parking lots are open 24 hours a day, but a few close between 1am and 7am; some close on Saturday afternoon and on Sunday when traffic is generally lighter. The cost ranges from 11 to 20 DKK ($1.60 to $2.90) per hour or 55 to 85 DKK ($8 to $12.30) for 24 hours. Two centrally located parking lots are **Industriens Hus,** H. C. Andersens Blvd. 18 (☎ **33-91-21-75**), open Monday to Friday from 7am to 12:45am, and Saturday and Sunday from 10am to 12:45am; and **Statoil,** Israels Plads (☎ **33-14-37-76**), open daily around the clock.

BY TAXI

Watch for the FRI (free) sign or green light to hail a taxi. Be sure the taxis are metered. **Københavns Taxa** (☎ **35-35-35-35**) operates the largest fleet of cabs. Tips are included in the meter price: 22 DKK ($3.20) at the drop of the flag and 10 DKK ($1.45) per kilometer thereafter, Monday to Friday from 6am to 6pm. From 6pm to 6am, and all day on Saturday and Sunday, the cost is 11 DKK ($1.60) per kilometer. Many drivers speak English.

BY BICYCLE

To reduce pollution from cars (among other reasons), many Copenhageners ride bicycles. For 40 DKK ($5.80) per day, you can rent a bike at **Københavns Cyklebors,** Gothersgade 157 (☎ **33-14-07-17**). Hours are Monday to Friday 8:30am to 5:30pm and Saturday 10am to 1:30pm.

FAST FACTS: Copenhagen

American Express   American Express's office is more limited in Copenhagen than within equivalent capitals of Europe, as it only offers facilities for foreign exchange and customer service for Amex cardholders who lose their cards or need traveler's checks. The small, temporary office is located at Nørregade 7A, 3rd floor (☎ **33-12-23-01**). It's likely that a new address, with the same phone, will be operational before the millennium. In the meantime, anyone needing the services of a travel agent can contact Amex's affiliate, **Profile Travel,** Gamie Kongevej 2 (☎ **77-33-55-66**). Corporate clients can make arrangements for group travel at yet another travel agency, **Neiman & Schultz,** Norregade 7A (☎ **33-13-11-81**). All agencies are open Monday to Friday from 9am to 5pm, and on Saturday from 9am to noon (to 2pm between May and August).

Area Code   The country code for Denmark is **45.** There are no city area codes. Each telephone number dialed in Denmark has eight digits.

Baby-sitters   Try **Students Baby-sitting Agency** (☎ **70-20-44-16**), open Monday to Friday 1 to 4pm in summer or 10am to 3pm the rest of the year. The cost is 245 DKK ($35.55) for 1 to 5 hours, with a charge of 35 DKK ($5.05) for each additional hour. Transportation is extra.

Bookstores   One of the best and most centrally located is **Boghallen,** Rådhuspladsen 37 (☎ **33-47-27-60**). Hours are Monday to Saturday 10am to 5pm.

Business Hours   Most banks are open Monday to Friday from 10am to 4pm (on Thursday to 6pm). **Stores** are generally open Monday to Thursday from 9am to 6pm, on Friday from 9am to 7 or 8pm, and on Saturday from 9am to 2pm; most are closed Sunday. **Offices** are open Monday to Friday from 9 or l0am to 4 or 5pm.

Car Rentals   See "Getting Around," in chapter 3.

Currency Exchange   Banks are generally your best bet. When banks are closed, you can exchange money at **Forex** (☎ **33-11-29-05**) in the Central Railroad Station, daily from 8am to 9pm, or at the **Change Group,** Østergade 16 (☎ **33-93-04-55**), Monday to Saturday from 9am to 10pm and on Sunday from 9am to 8pm.

Dentists   During regular business hours, ask your hotel to call the nearest English-speaking dentist. For emergency dental treatment, go to **Tandlægevagten,** Oslo Plads 14 (☎ **35-38-02-51**), near Østerport Station and the U.S. Embassy. It's open Monday to Friday from 8am to 9:30pm and on Saturday, Sunday, and holidays from l0am to noon. Be prepared to pay in cash.

Doctors   To reach a doctor, dial ☎ **33-93-63-00** from 9am to 4pm, or ☎ **38-88-60-41** after hours. The doctor's fee is payable in cash. Virtually every doctor speaks English.

Drugstores   See "Pharmacies," below.

Emergencies   Dial **112** to report a fire or to call the police or an ambulance. State your phone number and address. Emergency calls from public telephones are free (no coins needed).

Eyeglass Repair   The largest and oldest optical chain in Denmark is **Synoptik,** Købmagergade 22 (☎ **33-15-05-38**), with 80 other branches throughout Denmark. Most glasses can be replaced in 2 or 3 hours. Bifocals can take 10 to 14 days. They also specialize in soft and hard contact lenses, with hundreds of different types in stock. Hours are Monday to Thursday 9:30am to 6pm, Friday 9:30am to 7pm, and Saturday 9:30am to 4pm.

Hairdresser   **Stuhr Coiffeur,** Scala, Axeltorv 21 (☎ **33-15-11-44**), is located on the second floor of the shopping complex across from Tivoli. Services are available for both men and women. You should call for an appointment. Hours Monday to Wednesday are 10am to 6pm, Thursday 9:30am to 7:30pm, Friday 9:30am to 6pm, and Saturday 8:30am to 2pm.

Hospitals   In case of a sudden illness or accident, even foreigners are entitled to free medical treatment in Denmark. One of the most centrally located hospitals is **Rigshospitalet,** Blegdamsvej 9 (☎ **35-45-35-45**).

Laundry/Dry Cleaning   There are laundromats in all neighborhoods, some independent, others part of the **Vascomat** and **Møntvask** chains that seem to dominate the business. Some of the most convenient ones are found at Borgergade 2, Nansensgade 39, and Istedgade 45. They are open daily from 8am to 10pm. Your clothes can be dry-cleaned at **Dry Cleaning,** Vester Farimagsgade 3 (☎ **33-12-45-45**), a block from the Central Railroad Station. It's open Monday through Friday from 8am to 6pm and on Saturday from 9:30am to 3pm.

Libraries   Try the **Københavns Bibliotek** (Copenhagen Library), located at Krystalgade 15 (☎ **33-73-60-60**). Open Monday to Friday from 10am to 7pm, and on Saturday from 10am to 2pm, it has a large collection of English-language publications.

Lost Property   The Lost and Found Property office at Slotsherrensvej 113, 2720 Vanløse (☎ **38-74-88-22**), is open Monday to Thursday from 9am to 5:30pm and on Friday from 9am to 2pm. For property lost on buses, phone ☎ **36-45-45-45;** on trains, ☎ **33-16-21-10.** These numbers can only be called Monday to Friday from 9am to 4pm (until 6pm on Thursday).

Luggage Storage/Lockers   Luggage can be stored in rental lockers at the Central Railroad Station. Lockers are available daily from 4:30am to midnight. The cost is 10 to 20 DKK ($1.45 to $2.90) for 24 hours. For information, call ☎ **33-14-17-01.**

Newspapers   Foreign newspapers, particularly the *International Herald Tribune* and *USA Today,* are available at the Central Railroad Station in front of the Palladium movie theater on Vesterbrogade, on Strøget, and at the newsstands of big hotels.

Pharmacies   An *apotek* (pharmacy) open 24 hours a day in central Copenhagen is **Steno Apotek,** Vesterbrogade 6C (☎ **33-14-82-66**).

Photographic Needs   The biggest photography shop and camera supply center in Denmark is **Kontant Foto,** Købmagergade 44 (☎ **33-12-00-29**). It's open Monday through Thursday from 9am to 5:30pm, on Friday from 9am to 7pm, and on Saturday from 10am to 2pm.

Police   In an emergency, dial **112**. For other matters, go to the police station at Halmtorvet 20 (☎ **33-25-14-48**).

Post Office   For information about the Copenhagen post office, phone ☎ **33-33-89-00**. The main post office, where your *poste restante* (general delivery) letters can be picked up, is located at Tietgensgade 35–39, DK-1704 København (☎ **33-33-89-00**). It's open Monday to Friday from 11am to 6pm and on Saturday from 10am to 1pm. The post office at the Central Railroad Station is open Monday to Friday from 8am to 10pm, on Saturday from 9am to 4pm, and on Sunday from 10am to 4pm.

Religious Services   You can attend services at St. Ansgar's Roman Catholic Church, Bredgade 64 (☎ **33-13-37-62**); the English Church of St. Alban's (Anglo-Episcopalian) on Langelinie (☎ **39-62-77-36**); the American Church (Protestant and interdenominational) at the U.S. Embassy, Dag Hammarskjølds Allé 24 (☎ **35-55-31-44**); and the synagogue at Krystalgade 12 (☎ **33-12-88-68**). The International Church of Copenhagen (affiliated with the American Lutheran church) holds services at the Vartov Church, Farvergade 27 (☎ **39-62-47-85**), across from the Town Hall.

Rest Rooms   Some public toilets can be found at Rådhuspladsen (Town Hall Square), the Central Railroad Station, and at all terminals. Look for the markings *TOILETTER, WC, DAMER* (women), or *HERRER* (men). There is no charge.

Safety   Compared with other European capital cities, Copenhagen is relatively safe. However, since the early 1990s, with the increase of homelessness and unemployment, crime has risen. Guard your wallet, purse, and other valuables as you would when traveling in any big city.

Shoe Repair   Go to **Magasin,** Kongens Nytorv 13 (☎ **33-11-44-33**), a leading Danish department store, which has a great shoe-repair franchise in its basement, Mister Minit. This service is available Monday to Saturday 10am to 7pm.

Taxes   Throughout Denmark you'll come across MOMS on your bills, a government-imposed value-added tax of 25%. It's included in hotel and restaurant bills, service charges, entrance fees, and in repair of foreign-registered cars. No refunds are given on these items. For more information, see "Shopping," in chapter 5.

Telegrams and Telex   The main telegraph office is located at Købmagergade 37 (☎ **33-41-02-00**). To send a telegram by phone, dial **0022**. There are telex booths at the telegraph office, Købmagergade 37. Hours are Monday to Friday 9:30am to 6pm, Saturday 10am to 2pm.

Transit Information   Day or night, phone ☎ **36-45-45-45** for bus information or **33-14-17-01** for S-tog (subway) information.

3 Accommodations

Peak season in Denmark is summer, from May to September, which pretty much coincides with the schedule at Tivoli. Once Tivoli closes for the winter, lots of rooms become available. Make sure to ask about winter discounts.

Nearly all doubles come with a private bath. Find out, though, whether this means a shower or a bathtub. You can undercut these prices by requesting a room without bath at moderate and inexpensive hotels. Ask if breakfast is included (usually it isn't).

Several inexpensive hotels in Copenhagen are known as **mission hotels;** they were originally founded by a temperance society, but now about half of them are fully licensed to serve alcohol. They tend to cater to middle-class families.

A word of warning: In most moderate and nearly all inexpensive hotels in Copenhagen, the bathrooms are cramped, and there's never enough room to spread out all your stuff. Many of the bathrooms were added as a later architectural device to older buildings that weren't designed for baths. Also, get used to towels that are much thinner than you might like—not the thick, fluffy types the late Sinatra was always giving maids an extra $100 to bring him more of.

RESERVATIONS SERVICE   At Bernstorffsgade 1, across from the Tivoli's main entrance, the Tourist Information Center maintains a useful hotel-booking service **Værelsænvisningen** (☎ **33-12-40-45**). The charge for this service, whether you book into a private home, a hostel, or a luxury hotel, is 35 DKK ($5.05) per person. A deposit, about 8.6% of the accommodation cost, must be paid, but it will later be deducted from your room rent. You'll also be given a city map and bus directions. This particular office doesn't accept advance reservations; it can arrange private accommodations if the hotels in your price range are already full. The office is open April 19 through September 30, daily from 9am to 9pm and October through April 18, Monday to Friday from 9am to 5pm and on Saturday from 9am to 2pm.

In the same building is another service—the **Hotel Booking Service** (☎ **33-25-38-44**)—that will reserve hotel rooms in advance.

NEAR KONGENS NYTORV & NYHAVN

Once the home of sailor joints and tattoo parlors, Nyhavn is now a chic, up-and-coming section of Copenhagen. The central canal, filled with 19th-century boats and the 18th-century façades of the buildings around it, contributes to the area's special ambience.

VERY EXPENSIVE

✪ **Hotel d'Angleterre.** Kongens Nytorv 34, DK-1050 København. ☎ **800-44-UTELL** in the U.S., or ☎ 33-12-00-95. Fax 33-12-11-18. E-mail: anglehot@remmen.dk. 130 units. A/C MINIBAR TV TEL. 2,075–2,900 DKK ($300.90–$420.50) double; 3,450–12,000 DKK ($500.25–$1,740) suite. AE, DC, MC, V. Parking 150 DKK ($21.75). Bus: 1, 6, or 9.

At the top of Nyhavn, this Leading Hotels of the World member is the premier choice in Denmark, even though it's a bit staid and stodgy—impeccably bourgeois and correct. Although it's not particularly imaginative, there's no better address in Copenhagen. The seven-story hotel was built in 1755 and extensively renovated in the 1980s. Guests have included H. C. Andersen and almost every celebrity who has ever visited Denmark. It's a medley of styles: Empire, Louis XVI, and modern. The bedrooms are beautifully furnished with art objects and occasional antiques. Light color schemes, subdued lighting, and modern amenities continue to make this a desirable address. Rooms vary in size and exposure, but each unit has a high ceiling along with marble baths complete with robes, hair dryers, phones, thick towels, and scales. The most deluxe rooms are in front, but those facing the courtyard are more tranquil and also receive a fair amount of sunlight—that is, when the sun is shining.

Dining/Diversions: The evening begins at the Bar, where everyone from rock stars to CEOs meets for a drink. Wiinblad, the hotel's moderately priced restaurant, caters to the young and beautiful, while Restaurant d'Angleterre is acclaimed for its French cuisine and vintage wines. Light lunches and snacks are also available.

Amenities: Room service (24 hours), laundry, valet parking, in-house video, banquet and meeting facilities, health club, swimming pool, sauna, Turkish bath, solarium.

✪ Phoenix Copenhagen. Bredgade 37, DK-1260 København. ☎ **33-95-95-00.** Fax 33-33-98-33. E-mail: phoenix@avip.cybercity.dk. 212 units. MINIBAR TV TEL. 1,490–2,390 DKK ($216.05–$346.55) double; 2,800–6,000 DKK ($406–$870) suite. AE, DC, MC, V. Parking 90 DKK ($13.05). Bus: 1, 5, 9, or 10.

More than any other hotel in Copenhagen, this top-of-the-line hotel poses a serious challenge to the discreet grandeur of the nearby Hotel d'Angleterre. Opened in 1991 after 3 years of intensive rebuilding, the Phoenix rose from the ruined neoclassicism of a royal guesthouse originally built in the 1700s to accommodate the aristocratic courtiers of the Amalienborg Palace. During World War II the building was the home of a battalion of Nazi officers, and between 1945 and 1988, in much reduced circumstances, it was the headquarters of the now-almost-defunct Danish Communist Party. Beginning in 1988, tons of white and colored marble were imported to create the Louis XVI decor that has so impressed guests ever since. The bedrooms are tastefully elegant utilizing discreet interpretations of Louis XVI style. Beds are large with firm mattresses, and wool carpeting and chandeliers add graceful notes. The Italian marble baths are large enough to serve their purpose and contain hair dryers, robes, and plenty of towels. The very best accommodations also have faxes, trouser presses, and even phones in the baths.

Dining/Diversions: A Danish/French restaurant, the Von Plessen, is on the premises, as well as an English-inspired pub, Murdoch's. Menus are often based on dishes served in old Danish manor houses.

Amenities: Concierge, room service (24 hours), massage, laundry. The staff is every bit as professional as that of the Angleterre. Hairdresser/barber/beautician next door.

EXPENSIVE

Hotel Neptun. Skt. Annæ Plads 14–20. DK-1250 København. ☎ **800/528-1234** in the U.S., or ☎ 31-13-89-00. Fax 33-14-12-50. www.hotel-copenhagen.dk/neptun.htm. E-mail: info@Neptunhotel.group.dk. 133 units. MINIBAR TV TEL. 1,415–1,775 DKK ($205.15–$257.40) double, 1,775–2,065 DKK ($257.40–$299.40) suite. Rates include buffet breakfast. AE, DC, MC, V. Free parking. Bus: 1, 6, 9, or 28. Closed Dec 19–Jan 4.

Modernized in 1990, the interior of this hotel, originally built in 1854, resembles an upper-class living room, with English-style furniture, warm colors, paneling, and even a chess table. Some rooms overlook two quiet, covered-interior courtyards. In the summertime you can order drinks on the hotel's outdoor terrace on the 6th floor. The bedrooms are tastefully furnished in a modern style and have radios, trouser presses, and hairdryers. Other extras include safes. Closets are small and the tiled baths are only modest in size—some without tubs. Only some of the units are air conditioned. Ask for an accommodation opening onto the courtyard as they are the brightest during the day and the most tranquil in the evening. Suites, most often booked by business people, have data ports and faxes.

Dining: The Gendarmen Café/Restaurant is in an 1840s building with a cozy, rustic atmosphere. Here you can enjoy a version of regional Danish fare. A leading Danish food critic recently awarded this restaurant five stars out of a possible five.

Amenities: 24-hour room service, babysitting, business center, access to nearby health club, and dry cleaning/laundry.

Sophie Amalie Hotel. Skt. Annæ Plads 21. DK-1250 København. ☎ **33-13-34-00.** Fax 33-11-77-07. www.remmen.dk/hsa.ktm. E-mail: anglehot remmen.dk. 134 units. A/C TV TEL. 1,030–1,080 DKK ($149.35–$156.60) double, 1,230–1,685 DKK ($178.35–$244.35) suite. Winter discounts available. AE, MC, V. Free parking. Bus: 1, 10, or 28.

Copenhagen Accommodations

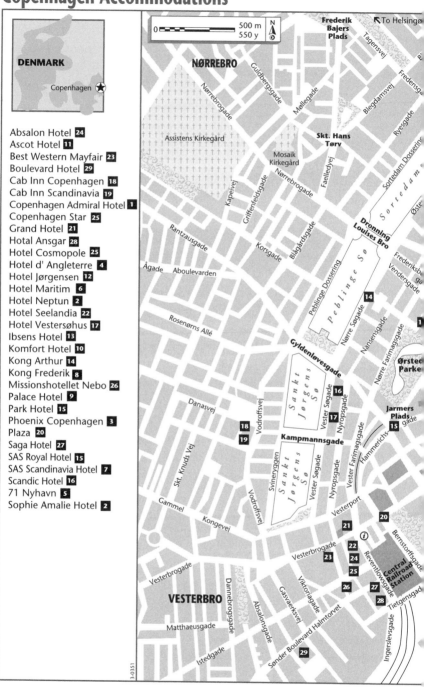

Absalon Hotel **24**
Ascot Hotel **11**
Best Western Mayfair **23**
Boulevard Hotel **29**
Cab Inn Copenhagen **18**
Cab Inn Scandinavia **19**
Copenhagen Admiral Hotel **1**
Copenhagen Star **25**
Grand Hotel **21**
Hotal Ansgar **28**
Hotel Cosmopole **25**
Hotel d' Angleterre **4**
Hotel Jørgensen **12**
Hotel Maritim **6**
Hotel Neptun **2**
Hotel Seelandia **22**
Hotel Vestersøhus **17**
Ibsens Hotel **13**
Komfort Hotel **10**
Kong Arthur **14**
Kong Frederik **8**
Missionshotellet Nebo **26**
Palace Hotel **9**
Park Hotel **15**
Phoenix Copenhagen **3**
Plaza **20**
Saga Hotel **27**
SAS Royal Hotel **15**
SAS Scandinavia Hotel **7**
Scandic Hotel **16**
71 Nyhavn **5**
Sophie Amalie Hotel **2**

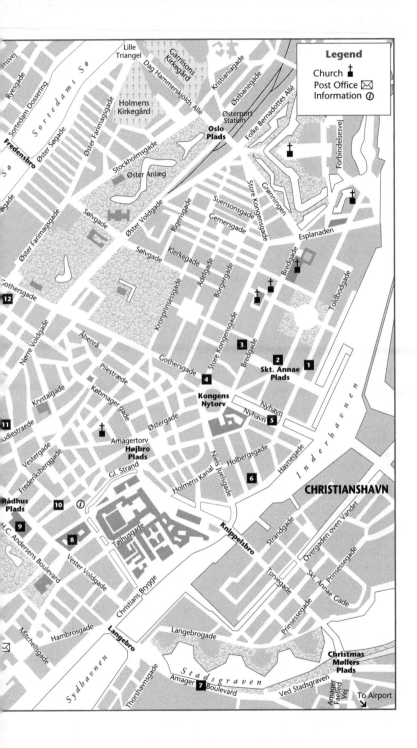

Legend
Church ✝
Post Office ✉
Information ⓘ

Lille Triangel

Carnisons Kirkegård

Dag Hammerskjölds Allé

Kristianiagade

Østbanegade

Holmens Kirkegård

Østerport Station

Oslo Plads

Folke Bernadottes Allé

Forbindelsesvej

Øster Søgade

Stockholmsgade

Øster Anlæg

Grønningen

Store Kongensgade

Suensonsgade

Rigensgade

Gernersgade

Esplanaden

Øster Voldgade

Øster Farimagsgade

Sølvgade

Sølvgade

Klerkegade

Adelgade

Borgergade

Bredgade

Toldbodgade

Gothersgade

Kronprinsessegade

12

Nørre Voldgade

Abenrå

Pilestræde

Gothersgade

Store Kongensgade

3

Bredgade

2

1

Skt. Annae Plads

Købmagergade

4

Kongens Nytorv

Krystalgade

Østergade

Amagertorv

Højbro Plads

Nyhavn

Nyhavn

5

11

Vestergade

Frederiksberggade

Gl. Strand

Niels Juelsgade

Holbergsgade

Holmens Kanal

Havnegade

Inderhavnen

CHRISTIANSHAVN

Rådhus Plads

10

ⓘ

6

9

8

H.C. Andersens Boulevard

Vester Voldgade

Tøjhusgade

Knippelsbro

Strandgade

Overgaden oven Vandet

Skt. Prinsessegade

Christians Brygge

Torvegade

Skt. Annae Gade

Prinsessegade

Mitchellgade

Hambrosgade

Langebro

Langebrogade

Christmas Møllers Plads

Sydhavnen

Thorshavnsgade

Stadsgraven

Amager **7** Boulevard

Ved Stadsgraven

Amager Fælled Vej

To Airport

Fredensbro

Ryesgade

Sortedam Dossering

Sortedams Sø

Gothersgade

67

The Sophie Amalie is a first-class hotel situated along the harbor front and close to Amalienborg Castle. From the rooms facing north you can see Amalienborg, the residence of Queen Margrethe II. The hotel is named for Sophie Amalie (1628–85), a German duke's daughter who married King Frederik III at the age of 15. Within walking distance of Nyhavn, it's conveniently close to the business and shopping districts of the capital. Dating from 1948, the hotel has been vastly improved and upgraded over the years. Its bedrooms are furnished with the best of Scandinavian modern design. Double-glazed windows cut down on street noise. The beds are rather narrow but contain firm, comfortable mattresses. Closets are large but baths are small with mosaic tiles and hair dryers (but not enough room to store your stuff). In the 6th-floor suites, a curved staircase leads from the living room to the bedroom.

Dining/Diversions: The Restaurant Sophie serves Danish cuisine. If you'd like to dine at your hotel one night, the chef here is quite good. We've enjoyed his mussels steamed in sorrel and garlic, his young rooster with basil and tomato, and ravioli filled with truffles. For dessert, when was the last time you had a rhubarb soup with a parfait of licorice and caramel? In addition, Sophie's Bar is a snug little retreat with a charming and relaxing atmosphere if you'd like to meet someone for an off-the-record drink.

Amenities: The hotel is equipped with a sauna and solarium, and provides laundry-service and baby-sitting.

MODERATE

Copenhagen Admiral Hotel. Toldbodgade 24–28, DK-1253 København. ☎ **31-11-82-82.** Fax 33-32-36-07. E-mail: admiral@-hotel.dk. 366 units. TV TEL. 950–1,210 DKK ($137.75–$175.45) double; from 1,750 DKK ($253.75) suite. AE, MC, V. Free parking. Bus: 1, 9, 10, 28, or 41.

Only 2 blocks from the Nyhavn Canal, this hotel was originally built as a granary in 1787 but was turned into a hotel in 1988 and last renovated in 1997. Even though the guestrooms are showing wear, many readers have reported that they prefer this hotel to the highly touted 71 Nyhavn nearby. The building still features thick timbers and stone arches, though modern partitions have created a series of well-furnished first-class bedrooms. Although the guestrooms lack a certain coziness and charm, they're well maintained, and some have harbor views. Some of the units are smoke free, and some open onto French balconies. The split-level 6th-floor suites (actually studios) are the best here, with large sitting areas, upgraded furnishings, and views of the water. Baths are small but have bidets, tile floors, marble walls, and hair dryers.

A popular luncheon buffet is served in the hotel restaurant. At night, guests are greeted with formal service and an international cuisine. Services include laundry, limited room service, and baby-sitting; among the facilities are a sauna and a solarium.

✪ **71 Nyhavn.** Nyhavn 71, DK-1051 København. E-mail: arp@isa.dknet.dk. ☎ **33-11-85-85.** Fax 33-93-15-85. 82 units. MINIBAR TV TEL. Mon–Thurs 1,350–1,550 DKK ($195.75–$224.75) double. Fri–Sun 950–1,150 DKK ($137.75–$166.75) double. Suite 2,695 DKK ($390.80) all week. AE, DC, MC, V. Free parking. Bus: 650.

On the corner between Copenhagen harbor and Nyhavn Canal, this hotel, its redbrick walls rising above the wooden hulls of ships anchored in the adjacent canal, is a restored old warehouse dating from 1804. It was one of the few buildings in the area spared by an 1807 British bombardment. The warehouse was converted into a hotel in 1971, and it was thoroughly renovated in 1997.

All the bedrooms have been redecorated with all modern facilities, although the old Pomeranian pine beams are still in place. Most of the rooms have a view of the harbor and canal. Nice touches in the rooms include trouser presses and double glazing on the windows. The best units are also equipped with ironing boards, faxes, and bathrobes, and electrical cords to plug in laptop computers are available at the reception desk. Non-smoking accommodations are available. Mattresses are firm but the beds are narrow. Baths are rather small but are tiled and contain hair dryers; most have a stall shower.

Dining/Diversions: In the cellar of the 1804 warehouse, the Restaurant Pakhuskælderen offers rustic charm, plenty of atmosphere, and good food. The menus are constantly changed to reflect seasonal supplies, and the wine list is among the finest in the city. Both French and Danish specialties are offered. The hotel also has a small bar area.

Amenities: Room service, money exchange, concierge, and dry cleaning/laundry.

INEXPENSIVE

Hotel Maritim. Peder Skrams Gade 19, DK-1054 København. ☎ **33-13-48-82.** Fax 33-15-03-45. 64 units. TV TEL. 950 DKK ($137.75) double, 1,275 DKK ($184.90) triple. AE, DC, MC, V. Bus: 1, 6, or 9.

Frankly, although the bedrooms within this three-star hotel are comfortable and tastefully conservative in their style, you might be put off by a pretentious and somewhat rigid staff who are not as well-rehearsed in their roles as you might have wanted. Despite that, the place has an enviable location near hotels that cost a lot more money, in a neighborhood midway between high glamour (Kongens Nytorv, site of the very expensive Hotel d'Angleterre) and the Nyhavn Canal, a testimonial to the seafaring Copenhagen of long ago. Built more than a century ago, it was converted into a hotel in 1953, but bedrooms were completely renovated in 1996. Four of its floors are devoted to bedrooms. The uppermost floor contains a conference center, and the street level offers a restaurant.

NEAR RÅDHUSPLADSEN & TIVOLI

Some of the most expensive hotels in Copenhagen are located here. In the heart of the city, centered around Rådhuspladsen (Town Hall Square), Tivoli Gardens, and the Central Railroad Station, you'll be near all public transportation and many attractions.

VERY EXPENSIVE

Palace Hotel. Rådhuspladsen 57, DK-1550 København. ☎ **800/448-8355,** or ☎ 33-14-40-50. Fax 33-12-75-86. www.dkhotellift.dk/palace.html. E-mail: principal@euroconnect.dk. 162 units. MINIBAR TV TEL. 1,725–2,025 DKK ($250.10–$293.65) double; from 2,500 DKK ($362.50) suite. Rates include buffet breakfast. Discounts of 25% may be available on weekends and in midwinter, depending on occupancy. AE, DC, MC, V. Parking 80 DKK ($11.60). Bus: 2, 30, 32, 33, 34, or 35.

Opened in 1910 and declared a historic landmark in 1985, the Palace Hotel has been visited by countless celebrities seeking seclusion. Although the hotel has tried to keep abreast of the times, it's no longer the frontrunner it once was (this distinction now belongs to other Copenhagen hotels, including the Kong Frederik). The modern rooms are attractively furnished in a traditional style, with many amenities, such as trouser presses and hair dryers. Most of the bathrooms contain a shower (not a tub) and are somewhat cramped. Thoughtful extras, however, include a hair dryer. The best rooms are on the top floor, away from street noise. Even if you're assigned a room on floors 2 and 3, you are still in luck as they contain high ceilings and tasteful furnishings and appointments. The reception desk is especially helpful in arranging for theater tickets, tours, and transportation.

Dining/Diversions: The Palace Bar on the ground floor has a Hollywood-style atmosphere, and the restaurant, Brasserie on the Square, serves both Danish and international food. There's also a roof terrace.

Amenities: Valet, laundry, safe-deposit box in rooms, parking garage, executive meeting rooms, and health club (with sauna, solarium, and massage).

SAS Royal Hotel. Hammerichsgade 1, DK-1611 København. ☎ **33-14-14-12.** Fax 33-42-61-00. 265 units. A/C MINIBAR TV TEL. 2,190 DKK ($317.55) double, 2,395 DKK ($347.30) Business Club, 5,995 DKK ($869.30) suite. AE, DC, MC, V. Parking 150 DKK ($21.75). Bus: 14 or 16.

Long favored by business travelers, this international deluxe hotel lies in the city center, near Tivoli and the Town Hall Square, and it's filled with facilities and conveniences. The hotel has an aura of sleek modern Danish styling throughout. The accommodations are beautifully furnished and well maintained with such extra amenities as trouser presses and hair dryers. Baths are tiled and rather spacious, except for those in the single units, which are small and often lack tubs. At the Business Club on the top floors, guests are pampered with electronic safes, a lounge with complimentary refreshments, speedier check-ins, and free admission to the hotel facilities.

Dining/Diversions: The hotel has the prestigious Summit Restaurant on the top floor. There's also the Café Royal, a lobby bar.

Amenities: 24-hour room service, three-hour laundry service, massage, hairstylist. SAS airline check-in, "Office-for-a-day," gym, sauna, solarium.

EXPENSIVE

Grand Hotel. Vesterbrogade 9A, DK-1620 København. ☎ **31-31-36-00.** Fax 31-31-33-50. 151 units. MINIBAR TV TEL. 1,295–1,695 DKK ($187.75–$245.75) double; 2,195–2,795 DKK ($318.25–$405.30) suite. Rates include buffet breakfast. AE, DC, MC, V. Bus: 1, 6, 16, 27, 28, or 29.

Originally built in 1880, this surprisingly elegant landmark hotel near the Central Railroad Station underwent a recent renovation that gave it a new life. The charm of the old building was preserved, while the bedrooms and baths were updated—each tastefully furnished and well maintained. Baths are quite superior, generous in size and clad in marble, and furnished with hair dryers. Singles opening onto the courtyard are more tranquil but don't have views. The corner rooms are the best and most expensive because they have been recently renovated and are larger in size. Amenities such as in-room movies were added.

Dining/Diversions: The Grand Bar overflows in summer onto a sidewalk cafe, and Oliver's Restaurant serves freshly prepared Danish specialties.

Amenities: Concierge, room service, laundry.

✪ **Kong Frederik.** Vester Voldgade 25, DK-1552 København. ☎ **800/44-UTELL** in the U.S., or ☎ 33-12-59-02. Fax 33-93-59-01. 110 units. MINIBAR TV TEL. 1,450–1,650 DKK ($210.25–$239.25) double; 3,000–6,000 DKK ($435–$870) suite. AE, DC, MC, V. Parking 85 DKK ($12.35). Bus: 1, 6, or 28.

The smallest of the ultra-chic hotels in Copenhagen, the Kong Frederik still has the feeling of an unpretentious but elegant private club because of its discreet service, dark paneling, and labyrinth of antiques-filled lounges. Many discriminating guests feel that it's much cozier than the Angleterre. Originally built around 1850 as two separate hotels, and then combined around a central courtyard about 1990, it has always appealed to glamorous representatives of showbiz. Renovated in 1996, the rooms are conservatively decorated in a wide array of styles with striped fabrics, overstuffed chairs, and antique prints. The hotel has some of the best bathrooms in town, with good lighting, top brand toiletries, and hair dryers. The accommodations in the front are brighter.

Dining/Diversions: The Restaurant Queen's Garden is recognized for its fine cuisine and excellent service. A sliding glass roof lets in the sun and breezes, creating a Mediterranean-style atmosphere. Surrounded by the mellow panels of the Queen's Pub, you can order both food and drink (see "Discovering Copenhagen," in chapter 5).

Amenities: Room service (24 hours), valet parking, same-day dry cleaning, laundry.

Plaza. Bernstorffsgade 4, DK-1577 København. ☎ **800/223-5652** or ☎ 33-14-92-62. Fax 33-93-93-62. MINIBAR TV TEL. www.phg.dk. E-mail: plaza-group euroconnect.dk. 93 units. MINIBAR TV TEL. 1,580–1,980 DKK ($229.10–$287.10) double. 2,850–5,850 DKK ($413.25–$848.25) suite. AE, DC, MC, V. Closed Dec 27–Jan 1. Parking 120 DKK ($17.40). Bus: 1 or 6.

Set close to the railroad station, and richly imbued with a sense of turn-of-the-century nostalgia, this successful overhaul of an older hotel has pleased many clients thanks to its mahogany paneling, first-class comfort, and antique furnishings. Opposite the Tivoli Gardens, the hotel was commissioned to be built by King Frederik VIII in 1913, and since that time has entertained its share of celebrities and royalty. Plaza bedrooms resemble what you might find in an English country house—traditional, yet with all the modern amenities. They vary greatly in size, however. Antiques, double glazing on the windows, and views from many units make this a good choice. There are some smoke-free accommodations as well. Rooms on the top floor have dormered windows. Baths are generous in size, completely tiled, and contain such equipment as hair dryers and make-up mirrors.

Dining/Diversions: The Library Bar provides one of the most charming oases in Copenhagen for a drink. Off the lobby, the Flora Danica Restaurant serves not only a sumptuous Scandinavian buffet for breakfast, but also a good lunch featuring such dishes as roast beef sandwiches, cognac-flavored blini, and American rib eye steak with stuffed potato.

Amenities: Access to nearby health club, room service, dry cleaning/laundry, secretarial services.

SAS Scandinavia Hotel. Amager Blvd. 70, DK-2300 København. ☎ **33-11-23-24.** Fax 33-96-55-55. 593 units. MINIBAR TV TEL. 1,545–1,845 DKK ($224–$267.50) double; 2,045 DKK ($296.50) Business Club, from 2,245 DKK ($325.50) suite. Rates include buffet breakfast. One child free per room. AE, DC, MC, V. Free parking. Bus: 5, 11, 30, or 34.

A five-minute walk east of Tivoli, this international deluxe hotel is rated as the finest and largest modern hotel in the Danish capital, catering primarily to businesspeople. First-class bedrooms are attractive and comfortable, with many amenities such as a VCR with international movies, trouser press, tiled baths, and hairdryer. Greater comfort is found on the top floors at the Business Club, where guests receive such extra privileges as free admission to all hotel facilities.

Dining/Diversions: Papa's Restaurant is one of several dining facilities at the hotel. It's known for serving steaks from the grill, including T-bone and tournedos, and for its fish from the North Sea, including Norwegian salmon. A traditional English mixed grill is also served. Other hotel dining options include a Thai restaurant, the Blue Elephant, and an Italian restaurant, Mama's. There's also a Japanese restaurant, Kyoto, which is popular among the growing number of Japanese customers. Gamblers enjoy the Casino Copenhagen, the only gambling room in town.

Amenities: Room service, concierge, massage, secretarial assistance, SAS airline check-in, express laundry, health club with indoor swimming pool, Business Service Center, conference facilities, business-class rooms, Danish designer shops, sauna, solarium, and baby-sitting.

Scandic Hotel. Vester Søgade 6 (Box 337), DK-1601 København. ☎ **33-14-35-35.** Fax 33-32-12-23. www.scandic-hotels.com. E-mail: copenhagen@scandic-hotels.se. 462 units. A/C MINIBAR TV TEL. Sun–Thurs 1,595 DKK ($231.25) double; from 2,600 DKK ($377) suite. Fri–Sat 950–1,200 DKK ($137.75–$174) double; from 1,400 DKK ($203) suite. Rates include continental breakfast. AE, DC, MC, V. Parking 40 DKK ($5.80). Bus: 1 or 14.

One of the tallest buildings in the neighborhood, this 18-story steel-and-glass member of a hotel chain makes a good impression in the Danish capital. We prefer it to the SAS hotels. Built near the Tivoli Gardens in 1972, it's a favorite among business executives, partly because of the concierge staff, who can arrange for typists, translators, and other business services quickly and conveniently. The bedrooms are outfitted in soothing colors with modern conveniences, including at least eight international TV channels. The most expensive accommodations are located on the hotel's top two floors. The 6th floor is reserved exclusively for nonsmokers. Baths for the most part tend to be small, with showers often instead of tubs, but with hair dryers and marble surfaces.

Dining/Diversions: The Blue Garden is the hotel's most prestigious dining room, while simple platters can be ordered in the Red Lion Pub.

Amenities: Concierge, room service (24 hours), manicures and pedicures, massage, laundry, secretarial services, parking, sauna and massage, shopping arcade, and car rental.

MODERATE

Ascot Hotel. Studiestræde 61, DK-1554 København. ☎ **33-12-60-00.** Fax 33-14-60-40. www.dkhotellist.dk. E-Mail: hotel@ascot-hotel.dk. 143 units. TV TEL. 920–1,390 DKK ($133.40–$201.55) double; 1,090–2,090 DKK ($158.05–$303.05) suite. Rates include buffet breakfast. Winter discounts available. AE, DC, MC, V. Free parking. Bus: 14 or 16.

On a side street about a 2-mile walk from Town Hall Square, the Ascot Hotel was originally built in 1902 on 492 wooden pilings rescued from a section of a medieval fortification that had previously stood on the site. In 1994 the hotel annexed an adjacent building that had been designed as a boathouse in the 19th century, and whose black marble columns and interior bas-reliefs are considered historically important. The bedrooms were renovated and modernized, and the resulting structure is one of the best small hotels in Copenhagen. The furniture is rather standard and the finest units open onto the street, and, the rooms in the rear get better air circulation and more light. Bathrooms are generous in size and tiled. The atmosphere is inviting and well maintained. Same-day laundry and dry cleaning are available. There's also a bar, a fitness center, and a solarium, but no restaurant.

Komfort Hotel. Løngangstræde 27, DK-1468 København. ☎ **33-12-65-70.** Fax 33-15-28-99. E-mail: principal@euroconnect.dk. 201 units. TV TEL. 1,250 DKK ($181.25) double. Additional bed 225 DKK ($32.65). Rates include buffet breakfast. AE, DC, MC, V. Parking 90 DKK ($13.05). Bus: 1, 5, or 6.

In the heart of Copenhagen, close to the Town Hall, the Komfort Hotel offers good value and is surprisingly large. In just two minutes you can walk over to the Tivoli Gardens. All its refurbished bedrooms have a modern Danish design, and contain such thoughtful extras as a radio and writing desk. Traditional Danish lunches or dinners are served in the hotel's restaurant, Hattehylden. Also on site is the John Bull Pub, the oldest English pub in the city, which even has a pool room. Just two minutes away is the Komfort's sibling hotel, the Palace, where you can enjoy its roof terrace in summer.

✪ **Kong Arthur.** Nørre Søgade 11, DK-1370 København. ☎ **33-11-12-12.** Fax 33-32-61-30. www.dk.hotellist.dk/kongarthur.htm. E-mail: hotel@kongarthur.dk. 107 units. MINIBAR TV TEL. 750–1,145 DKK ($108.75–$166) double; from 2,700 DKK ($391.50) suite. Rates include buffet breakfast. AE, DC, MC, V. Free parking. Bus: 5, 7, or 16.

Originally an orphanage when it was built in 1882, this hotel sits behind a private courtyard next to the tree-lined Peblinge Lake in a residential part of town. It's a terrific value. It has been completely renovated into a contemporary hostelry; a new wing with more spacious rooms, including 20 non-smoking rooms, was added in 1993. Each of the comfortably furnished and carpeted bedrooms is freshly painted and has an in-house video and safe. Baths are tiled, spacious, and contain hair dryers. The hotel is equipped with a sauna and provides 24-hour room service and baby-sitting. Breakfast is served in a large greenhouse-like room that's filled with sunshine on sunny days. The hotel's Restaurant Brøchner is recommended for its reasonably priced Danish and French cuisine. A Japanese restaurant, Sticks 'n' Sushi, offers sushi and yakitori. There's a pleasant bar that offers 24-hour service and a glass-covered breakfast room that overlooks a back garden.

Park Hotel. Jarmer Plads 3, DK-1551 København. ☎ **33-13-30-00.** Fax 33-14-30-33. 61 units. TV TEL. 1,075 DKK ($155.90) double. Winter discounts available. Rates include breakfast. AE, DC, MC, V. Bus: 14 or 16.

The Park Hotel houses our favorite breakfast room in Copenhagen. One wall is adorned with radiator covers from six vintage automobiles while other walls have an airplane propeller from 1916, a collection of antique auto headlights, and lots of machine-age posters and engravings. The bedrooms have tasteful furniture, marble-covered baths, thick carpeting, and lithographs, and amenities such as clock radios and hairdryers are available.

INEXPENSIVE

Boulevard Hotel. Sønder Blvd. 53, DK-1720 København. ☎ **33-25-25-19.** Fax 33-25-25-83. 20 units, none with bath. TV TEL. 500 DKK ($72.50) double. AE, MC, V. Bus: 10.

Simple but well kept, this five-story hotel is about a 10-minute walk from the Central Railroad Station. Renovated in the late 1980s from an older core, it's unpretentious and unassuming, with bright and acceptably decorated bedrooms. Each has a sink with hot and cold running water; the toilets and showers are in rooms off of the central corridors. Breakfast is the only meal served.

Hotel Vestersøhus. Vester Søgade 59, DK-1601 København. ☎ **33-11-38-70.** Fax 33-11-00-90. 44 units (40 with bath, 12 with kitchenettes). TV TEL. 650 DKK ($94.25) double without bath; 1,050 DKK ($152.25) double with bath; 1,150 DKK ($166.75) double with bath and kitchenette. AE, DC, MC, V. Bus: 29.

One of the best features of this simple, relatively inexpensive hotel is the fact that about half of its bedrooms overlook a canal-shaped body of water that the Danes refer to as "the lakes," actually Skt. Jørgens Lake. (The other rooms look over the quiet, but more prosaic-looking back yard.) Set in the heart of town, behind a redbrick façade, the hotel was originally built around 1900 as an apartment house. Today, all seven floors (which are linked with an elevator) contain simple, pastel-colored bedrooms that are small, clean, and comfortable, if furnished in a way that's not particularly imaginative. If your heart is set on doing your own cooking while you're in town, be advised that the rooms that contain kitchens are usually booked far in advance to business travelers setting up medium-term lodgings in the capital. Other than breakfast, no meals are served.

Missionhotellet Nebo. Istedgade 6, DK-1650 København. ☎ **33-21-12-17.** Fax 33-23-47-74. www.nebo.dk. E-mail: nebo@email.dk. 150 units, 72 with bath. TV TEL. 600 DKK ($87) double without bath, 840 DKK ($121.80) double with bath. Additional bed 200 DKK ($29) extra. AE, DC, MC, V. Parking 25 DKK ($3.60). Bus: 1, 6, 16, 28, or 41.

This hotel near the railroad station is a quiet retreat, with clean, up-to-date, although Spartan, rooms. The lobby is tiny, and a lounge opens onto a side courtyard. The

> ### ⓘ Family-Friendly Accommodations
>
> **Hotel d'Angleterre** (see p. 64)   This elegant hotel contains a swimming pool and in-house video; both help keep children entertained.
>
> **Hotel Seelandia** (see p. 76)   This well-maintained, tidy hotel offers laundry facilities and baby-sitting services at affordable rates. It's a clean, safe environment.
>
> **Kong Arthur** (see p. 72)   Once a home for Danish orphans, this is a safe haven in a residential section near tree-lined Peblinge Lake.

rooms are small, furnished in a functional, Nordic style. There are bathrooms on all floors.

ON HELGOLANDSGADE & COLBJØRNSENSGADE

Copenhagen's main accommodations street, Helgolandsgade, is near the Central Railroad Station. The many moderately priced hostelries in this area can be booked through a **central reservations office** at Helgolandsgade 4 (☎ **31-31-43-44**), adjacent to the Triton Hotel. The service is operated jointly by the well-recommended Absalon Hotel, which lies close to the Central Railroad Station. Admittedly, most people who phone this service are referred to this hotel, but if it's full, lodgings are found at other acceptable hotels in the neighborhood. Colbjørnsensgade, which runs parallel to Helgolandsgade, is the second major street for accommodations. From either street, you're within easy walking distance of Rådhuspladsen and the Tivoli Gardens.

In the 1970s this area behind the railroad station became one of the major pornography districts of Europe, but subsequent hotel renovations, much-publicized civic efforts, and the gradual decline of the porno shops have led to a continuing gentrification. Today, with the original 19th-century façades generally still intact and often gracefully restored, the district is safer than you might think and offers some of the best hotel values in Copenhagen.

MODERATE

Best Western Hotel Mayfair. Helgolandsgade 3, DK-1653 København V. ☎ **800/ 528-1234** in the U.S., or ☎ 31-31-48-01. Fax 31-23-96-86. 106 units. MINIBAR TV TEL. 1,125 DKK ($163.15) double; 1,700 DKK ($246.50) suite. Rates include breakfast. AE, DC, MC, V. Bus: 6, 16, 28, 29, or 41.

This is an older, much-respected three-star hotel that retains some of its original architectural detailing despite a radical overhaul that brought it up to modern-day standards about a decade ago. Set 2 blocks west of Copenhagen's main railway station, it boasts a conservative, well-planned decor that might remind you of furnishings within a well-heeled private home in England. The decorative theme in the lobby, with its carpeting, exposed wood, and conservative sense of tradition, reflects the style of the bedrooms upstairs. Each of the rooms is comfortable and clean, representing better-than-expected value in a hotel that's rated three stars by the Danish government, and four stars by the Best Western chain to which it belongs. Guest accommodations are classically appointed with good carpeting and quilted fabrics, along with safes, trouser presses, and coffeemakers. The marble baths with tubs are adequate in size and contain hair dryers. Some recently upgraded accommodations have the added advantage of containing sitting areas. Unfortunately, there aren't any amenities (bar, health club, etc), and other than breakfast, no meals are served.

Copenhagen Star. Colbjørnsengade 13, DK-1652 København. ☎ **33-22-11-00.** Fax 33-21-21-86. 134 units. MINIBAR TV TEL. 1,190 DKK ($172.55) double, 1,500 DKK ($217.50) suite. Rates include breakfast. AE, DC, MC, V. Bus: 6, 16, 28, 29, or 41.

Located a short walk from the railroad station, this hotel was created in 1990 when a simple older hotel was connected to a neighboring building and upgraded into a comfortable and stylish whole. Its neoclassical façade was originally built around 1880. The outside is lit with neon, and the hotel design is definitely postmodern, as reflected by an interior decor that features leather chairs, teakwood tables, and an abundance of granite columns. Bedrooms are traditionally furnished and well maintained with such extras as a hair dryer and a trouser press. The suites come with Jacuzzis. There is a bar on the premises, but the only meal served is breakfast.

Hotel Cosmopole. Colbjørnsensgade 5–11, DK-1652 Kobenhavn. ☎ **33-21-33-33.** Fax 33-31-33-99. 208 units. TV TEL. 950 DKK ($137.75) double. Winter discounts available. Rates include breakfast. AE, DC, MC, V. Bus: 6, 10, 16, 28, or 41.

Operated by a chain that manages several other Danish tourist hotels, the large but unpretentious Hotel Cosmopole is composed of two connected 19th-century buildings identified as Cosmopole I and Cosmopole II. (Cosmopole is known to many local residents as the Hotel Union.) The rooms are simple, efficient, and modern, and include such amenities as clock radios and hairdryers. There's a bar on the premises, plus the Restaurant City, which serves Danish specialties daily from 5 to 11pm. Laundry service and baby-sitting can be arranged.

INEXPENSIVE

Absalon Hotel. Helgolandsgade 15, DK-1653 København. ☎ **33-24-22-11.** Fax 33-24-34-11. E-mail: absalon-hotel@city.dk .179 units. 700–1,100 DKK ($101.50–$159.50) double; 1,100–1,500 DKK ($159.50–$217.50) suite. Rates include an all-you-can-eat buffet breakfast. AE, DC, MC, V. Closed Dec 18–Jan 2. Bus: 6, 10, 16, 27, or 28.

The four thick-walled townhouses that the Nedergaard family joined into one building became a hotel in 1938. Its origins are based on a love story that unfolded at the nearby railroad station. Shortly after the father of the present owners began his first job as a door porter at a neighboring hotel, he was asked to go to the station to pick up a new baby-sitter who had just arrived from Jutland. They fell in love, married, and bought the first of what would eventually become four connected buildings and one of the best-managed hotels in the neighborhood. Two of their children were born in Room 108 of the present hotel, including one of the brothers you'll probably meet behind the reception desk today.

   You'll find a spacious blue-and-white breakfast room and an attentive staff directed by Eric and Mogens Nedergaard. The bedrooms are simple and modern but cramped. Those with private bathrooms also have TVs, trouser presses, and hair dryers. There are also laundry facilities. Adjoining the hotel, under the same management, is the Hotel Triton. Its accommodations are more basic and don't include baths. Double rooms cost 400 DKK ($58).

Hotel Ansgar. Colbjørnsensgade 29, DK-1652 København. ☎ **33-21-21-96.** Fax 33-21-61-91. 87 units (68 with bath). TEL. 500 DKK ($72.50) double without bath, 800 DKK ($116) double with bath. Additional bed 200 DKK ($29) extra. Rates include buffet breakfast. AE, DC, MC, V. Bus: 6, 10, 28, or 41.

Although this five-story hotel was built in 1885, its comfortable and cozy rooms are decorated with modern Danish furniture. There are showers and baths on each floor (no charge for use). A dozen large rooms that can accommodate up to six are perfect for families, and are available at negotiable rates. There is often free parking outside the hotel after 6pm. Guests arriving at Kastrup Airport can take the SAS bus to the Air Terminal at the Central Railroad Station, walk through the station, and be inside the hotel in less than 4 minutes.

Hotel Seelandia. Helgolandsgade 12, DK-1653 København. ☎ **31-31-46-10.** Fax 31-31-46-10. www.hotel-seelandia.dk. E-mail: hotel-seelandia@city.dk. 87 units, 57 with bath. TV TEL. 540 DKK ($78.30) double without bath, 850 DKK ($123.25) double with bath. Rates include breakfast. AE, DC, MC, V. Closed Dec 20–Jan 2. Bus: 1, 6, 10, 14, 16, 27, or 28.

Solidly built in 1928 behind the railroad station, the Hotel Seelandia was given a new, comfortably modern format in 1992. A longtime favorite of budget-conscious families, it's well maintained and clean. The furnishings are simple, in a modern Scandinavian style. Laundry facilities are available, and baby-sitting can be arranged. A good Danish breakfast is served in a ground-floor room.

Saga Hotel. Colbjørnsensgade 18–20, DK-1652 København. ☎ **33-24-99-67.** Fax 33-24-60-33. 78 units (24 with bath). TV TEL. 380–580 DKK ($55.10–$84.10) double without bath, 500–870 DKK ($72.50–$126.15) double with bath. Additional bed 150–200 DKK ($21.75–$29) extra. Modest discounts offered in winter. Rates include breakfast. AE, DC, MC, V. Bus: 6, 10, 16, 28, or 41.

This is a reasonably priced and solidly acceptable choice among the hotels on this sometimes-troublesome street. About half of its accommodations tend to be booked by groups of foreign visitors in the summer, and by organized groups of Danes (such as students and conventioneers) in winter. The hotel was established in 1947 when a pair of late 19th-century apartment buildings were joined together and given a unifying coat of dark red paint. The bedrooms, renovated in 1989, are unusual in that each one has its own unique size and layout. This five-story building has no elevator, so hauling luggage upstairs might present a problem for the elderly. Both the reception and the breakfast areas are situated one floor above street level. Breakfast is the only meal served.

NEAR NØRREPORT STATION
MODERATE

Ibsens Hotel. Vendersgade 23, DK-1363 København. ☎ **33-13-19-13.** Fax 33-13-19-16. E-mail: hotel.ibsenshotel.dk. 103 units. TV TEL. 950–1,050 DKK ($137.75–$152.25) double. Rates include buffet breakfast. AE, MC, V. Bus: 5, 14, or 16.

Preferred by budget-conscious travelers and families, Ibsens Hotel, built in 1906 and completely renovated in 1998, offers clean, comfortable, well maintained, traditionally furnished bedrooms. Most rooms are doubles or triples, and each now has a private bath, although they are cramped and supplied with rather thin towels.

Breakfast is the only meal served, but there are many restaurants and cafes nearby.

INEXPENSIVE

Hotel Jørgensen. Rømersgade 11, DK-1362 København. ☎ **33-13-81-86.** Fax 33-15-51-05. 24 units; 13 dormitory rooms (72 beds). TV TEL. 580 DKK ($84.10) double; 115 DKK ($16.65) per person in dormitory. Rates include breakfast. MC, V. Parking free overnight. Bus: 14, or 16.

Back in 1906 this building was a publishing house for school textbooks, but in 1984 it was transformed into Denmark's first gay hotel. This white stucco establishment, located on a busy boulevard in central Copenhagen, obviously appeals to gay men and lesbians, but it also welcomes straight guests. The staff is most helpful. Prices are reasonable, and the bedrooms are conventional and well organized. The 13 barracks-style dormitories, which accommodate 6 to 14 people each, are segregated according to gender.

Wittrup Motel on Copenhagen — Roskilde Highway. Family run. Very clean + comfortable.

IN FREDERIKSBERG
INEXPENSIVE

Cab Inn Copenhagen. Danasvej 32–34, DK 1910 Frederiksberg (Copenhagen). ☎ **33-21-04-00.** Fax 33-21-74-09. 82 units. TV TEL. 600 DKK ($87) double. Rate includes breakfast. AE, DC, MC, V. Parking 30 DKK ($4.35). S-tog: Vesterport (plus a 5-minute walk). Bus: 29.

This is one of three members of a small Danish chain of low-cost hotels that many readers have found cozy, comfortable, and affordable. Set within the township of Frederiksberg, a half-mile south of Copenhagen's Town Hall, it was built in a tasteful but low-budget format in the early 1990s. Rising three stories above the cityscape around it, it has almost no facilities or amenities other than a coffee shop set near the lobby. Bedrooms are simple, streamlined, illuminated with small windows overlooking the street life outside, and outfitted in shades of either soft red or blue. Baths are small with not much room to spread out your stuff.

If this hotel is overbooked on the night of your arrival, fear not, as its larger (201 room) sibling hotel lies within about a block. Here, at **Hotel Cab Inn Scandinavia,** Vodroffsvej 57, DK-1900 Frederiksberg (☎ **35-36-11-11;** fax 35-36-11-14), you'll find a four-story format within a building that's about two years newer. It offers the same prices, the same amenities, the same décor, the same kind of coffee shop in the lobby, and the same streamlined, contemporary look. Despite the fact that it can appear understaffed when it's busy, it has managed to capture the imagination of budget-conscious travelers from around Europe.

4 Dining

It's estimated that Copenhagen has more than 2,000 cafes, snack bars, and restaurants. Most of the restaurants are either in Tivoli or situated around Rådhuspladsen (Town Hall Square), the Central Railroad Station, or in Nyhavn. Others are located in the shopping district, on streets that branch off from Strøget.

You pay for the privilege of dining in Tivoli; prices are always higher. Reservations are not usually important, but it's best to call in advance. Nearly everyone who answers the phone at restaurants speaks English.

NEAR KONGENS NYTORV & NYHAVN
VERY EXPENSIVE

✪ **Kommandanten.** Ny Adelgade 7. ☎ **33-12-09-90.** Reservations required. Main courses 240–270 DKK ($34.80–$39.15); fixed-price menu 580 DKK ($84.10). AE, DC, MC, V. Mon–Fri noon–2pm, and Mon–Sat 6–10pm. Bus: 1 or 6. INTERNATIONAL.

Built in 1698—the former residence of the military commander of Copenhagen—Kommandanten is the epitome of Danish chic and charm. Enjoy an apéritif in the bar before you go upstairs to one of the elegant rooms, painted cobalt blue and gray.

The menu offers a mouth-watering array of classical dishes as well as innovative selections. Each dish is given a pleasing personal touch. No rough edges mar the kitchen's virtuoso handling of flawless seasonal foods. The finest ingredients are used, and the menu changes every 2 weeks. You might be offered the grilled catch of the day, breast of duck with port-wine sauce, braised turbot with an olive sauce, or a gratinée of shellfish. The service is the best in Copenhagen. Before leaving, look at the three valuable Andy Warhol originals of Margrethe II in the downstairs dining room.

✪ **Kong Hans Kælder.** Vingårdsstræde 6. ☎ **33-11-68-68.** Reservations required. Main courses 265–335 DKK ($38.40–$48.55); fixed-price menu 465–725 DKK ($67.45–$105.10). AE, DC, MC, V. Mon–Sat 6pm–midnight. Closed July 15–Aug 15 and Dec 24–26. Bus: 1, 6, or 9. INTERNATIONAL.

Copenhagen Dining

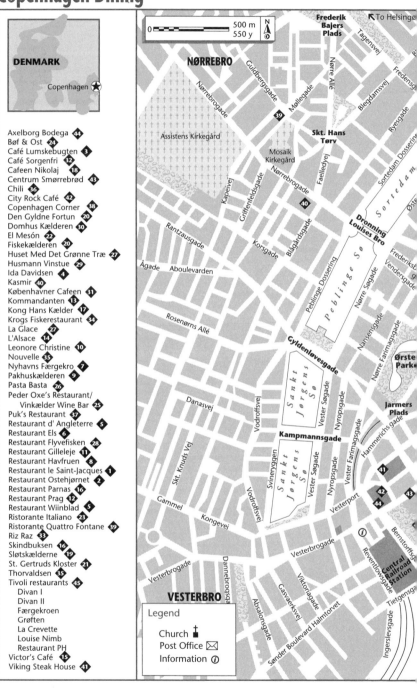

DENMARK

Copenhagen ★

Axelborg Bodega **44**
Bøf & Ost **24**
Café Lumskebugten **3**
Café Sorgenfri **32**
Cafeen Nikolaj **18**
Centrum Smørrebrød **43**
Chili **36**
City Rock Café **42**
Copenhagen Corner **38**
Den Gyldne Fortun **20**
Domhus Kælderen **30**
El Mesón **22**
Fiskekælderen **20**
Huset Med Det Grønne Træ **27**
Husmann Vinstue **29**
Ida Davidsen **4**
Kasmir **40**
Københavner Cafeen **31**
Kommandanten **13**
Kong Hans Kælder **17**
Krogs Fiskerestaurant **34**
La Glace **27**
L'Alsace **14**
Leonore Christine **10**
Nouvelle **35**
Nyhavns Færgekro **7**
Pakhuskælderen **9**
Pasta Basta **26**
Peder Oxe's Restaurant/
    Vinkælder Wine Bar **25**
Puk's Restaurant **37**
Restaurant d' Angleterre **5**
Restaurant Els **6**
Restaurant Flyvefisken **28**
Restaurant Gilleleje **11**
Restaurant Havfruen **8**
Restaurant le Saint-Jacques **1**
Restaurant Ostehjørnet **2**
Restaurant Parnas **16**
Restaurant Prag **12**
Restaurant Wiinblad **5**
Ristorante Italiano **23**
Ristorante Quattro Fontane **39**
Riz Raz **33**
Skindbuksen **16**
Sløtskælderne **19**
St. Gertruds Kloster **21**
Thorvaldsen **35**
Tivoli restaurants **45**
    Divan I
    Divan II
    Færgekroen
    Grøften
    La Crevette
    Louise Nimb
    Restaurant PH
Victor's Café **15**
Viking Steak House **41**

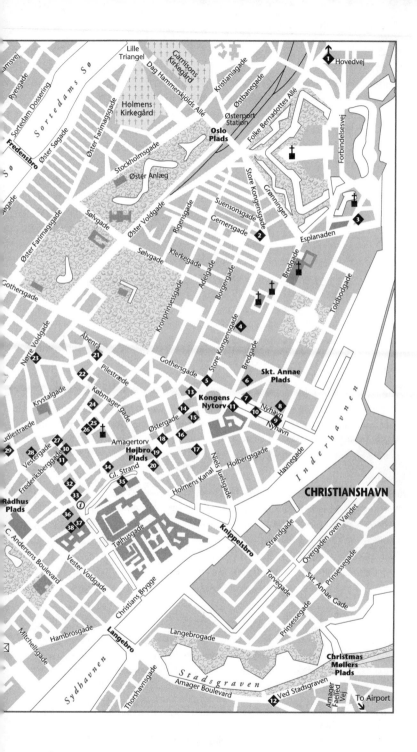

This vaulted Gothic cellar, once owned by King Hans (1455–1513), may be the best restaurant in Denmark. Its most serious competition is the Kommandanten, which many discriminating critics claim is the best. Five centuries ago the site of this restaurant was a vineyard. Located on "the oldest corner of Copenhagen," the building has been carefully restored and is now a Relais Gourmands (a member of an exclusive society of gourmet restaurants). Hans Christian Andersen once lived upstairs and even wrote some of his finest stories here.

The chef creates dishes that one critic claimed "to have been prepared by Matisse or Picasso." You might prefer to order the fixed-price menu; one is offered at lunch and another at five in the evening. A typical three-course dinner would include smoked salmon from the restaurant's own smokery, breast of duck with bigarade sauce, followed by plum ice cream with Armagnac for dessert. The a la carte menu is divided into "country cooking," which includes such items as *coq au vin* (chicken with wine) from Alsace and daube of beef; and *les spéialités,* which feature tournedos with *foie-gras* sauce or fresh fish from the daily market, perhaps beginning with an essence and ballotine of quails with truffles.

✪ **Restaurant d'Angleterre.** In the Hotel d'Angleterre, Kongens Nytorv 14. ☎ **33-12-00-95.** Reservations recommended. Lunch main courses 58–288 DKK ($8.40–$41.75); dinner main courses 235–288 DKK ($34.05–$41.75). Set menus 395–495 DKK ($57.30–$71.75). AE, DC, MC, V. Daily 11:30am–10pm (last order). Bus: 1, 6, or 9. FRENCH/INTERNATIONAL.

Equipped for no more than 25 diners at a time, this is the most upscale of the two restaurants in the most upscale hotel in Denmark. As such, it has entertained virtually everyone of high-ranking social or fiscal status in Denmark, and carries a cachet that's hard for other, less formidable, restaurants to even approach. Within a plushly upholstered setting that includes carefully oiled mahogany, 18th and early 19th-century French furniture, and dark colors, you can sample from a menu that changes virtually every day. The set menus seem devoted to showcasing the culinary skill of the chef, who scours the local market for ingredients early every morning. A la carte items include a filet mignon of reindeer served with a terrine of *foie gras,* a breast of young roasting chicken sautéed and baked with sun-dried tomatoes and fresh basil, and a dessert fantasy composed of a *confit* of blackberries with vanilla ice cream. The quality of the ingredients is first rate, as is the preparation. Reservations two to three days in advance are a good idea at this place, where the upscale glamour-of-the-moment is exceeded only by the Restaurant Kommandanten (see above).

EXPENSIVE

Leonore Christine. Nyhavn 9. ☎ **33-33-50-40.** Reservations required. Main courses 195–245 DKK ($28.30–$35.55), four-course fixed-price menu 395 DKK ($57.30). AE, DC, MC, V. Mon–Fri noon–3pm and 6–10pm, Sat–Sun noon–4pm and 6–10pm. Bus: 1, 6, or 9. DANISH.

This restaurant, on the sunny (south) side of the canal, is the best in Nyhavn. The building itself dates from 1681. The restaurant is open year-round, but seems at its best in summer when the terrace is open and you can dine overlooking the canal and the milling throngs of passersby. It's named Leonore Christine after the sister-in-law and bitter enemy of Sophie Amalie, the 17th-century queen of Denmark and wife of Frederik III. As sister of the king, Leonore was virtually "the lady of the land"—until Sophie Amalie arrived to replace her. Although the menu changes frequently, you might try such stellar dishes as oven-baked halibut with mussels and saffron, North Sea turbot with fjord shrimp and asparagus, tournedos with spinach and a red-burgundy sauce, or warm smoked trout with lump fish roe and Danish caviar. For dessert, you might be served white-chocolate cake with mango sorbet. There is mastery of cookery here, pure harmony, and lots of flavor.

Pakhuskælderen. In the Nyhavn 71 Hotel, Nyhavn 71. ☎ **33-11-85-85.** Reservations recommended. Main courses 188–198 DKK ($27.25–$28.70); set-menus 298–328 DKK ($43.20–$47.55). AE, DC, MC, V. Mon–Sat 6–10:30pm. Closed July. Bus: 650. INTERNATIONAL.

Much of the allure of this restaurant derives from a decor that combines the massive timbers of its original construction in 1804 with well-prepared food and an undeniable stylishness. And despite the glamour that is sometimes displayed here, something about the raw bulk of the exposed beams and trusses evokes maritime 19th-century Denmark at its most vivid. The menu is deliberately limited to fewer than a half-dozen main courses and starters, each of which changes every 2 weeks. On a recent visit, the menu offered such starters as a ballotine of salmon, whitefish baked with pesto and fried tomatoes, and grilled zander with a tapenade of black olives. Main courses might include guinea fowl cooked with sea scallops and dill, tournedos layered with *foie gras,* and sea devil braised with lemons. Over the years we have found the cuisine consistently reliable here. The menu is concise and to the point. The kitchen always uses the finest ingredients and never extends itself beyond its capability, preparing time-tested dishes that have won approval on previous menus. Donald Trump, author of the famous quote, "only losers take lunch," would definitely approve of their dinner only policy.

MODERATE

Café Lumskebugten. Esplanaden 21. ☎ **33-15-60-29.** Reservations recommended. Main courses 168–250 DKK ($24.35–$36.25); three-course fixed-price lunch 275 DKK ($39.90); four-course fixed-price dinner 465 DKK ($67.45). AE, DC, MC, V. Mon–Fri 11am–10:30pm, Sat 5–10:30pm. Bus: 1, 6, or 9. DANISH.

This restaurant is a spic-and-span, well-managed bastion of Danish charm, with an unpretentious elegance that's admired throughout the capital. It was established in 1854 as a rowdy tavern for sailors by a now-legendary matriarch named Karen Marguerita Krog. As the tavern's reputation grew, aristocrats, artists, and members of the Danish royal family came to dine. Today a tastefully gentrified version of the original beef hash is still served.

Two glistening-white dining rooms are decorated with antique ships' models, oil paintings, and pinewood floors. (Two additional smaller rooms are usually reserved for private functions.) The food and service are excellent. Menu specialties include a tartare of salmon with herbs, Danish fish cakes with mustard sauce and minced beet root, fried platters of herring, sugar-marinated salmon with mustard-cream sauce, and a symphony of fish with saffron sauce and new potatoes. At lunchtime, a Danish platter of assorted house specialties is offered for 185 DKK ($26.85); most patrons consider it a meal in itself.

L'Alsace. Ny Østerg 9. ☎ **33-14-57-43.** Reservations recommended. Main courses 150–200 DKK ($21.75–$29). Set lunch 236 DKK ($34.20); set dinner 305–386 DKK ($44.20–$55.95). AE, DC, MC, V. Mon–Sat 11:30am–10:45pm. Bus: 5. CONTINENTAL.

Established in the 1970s by an entrepreneur from Austria, within a venerable 18th-century building on a cobble-covered courtyard, this restaurant offers dishes that provide a welcome change from too constant a diet of Danish food. Amid a striking collection of modern paintings, you can order dishes from across the culinary divides of Europe. Many derive from eastern France (Alsace), including sauerkraut studded with pork knuckles and pork sausages, and a terrine of *foie gras.* There are also oysters from the Atlantic coast of France, Weiner schnitzels, *tafelspitz* (Habsburg-style boiled beef with horseradish), Austrian-style roulades of beef, pepper steaks, roasted duck with orange sauce, and other items that change according to the whim of the chef and the seasonality of the ingredients. Pastries inspired by France and Austria are featured at dessert. What's our beef about the place? We only hope that former diners Elton John, Queen Margrethe, and even Pope Paul II got better service than we did on our last visit.

Restaurant Els. Store Strandstræde 3 (just off Kongens Nytorv). ☎ **33-14-13-41.** Reservations recommended. Fixed-price menu 178 DKK ($25.80) for one course, 237 DKK ($34.35) for two courses, 296 DKK ($42.90) for three courses ("anniversary" menu), 382 DKK ($55.40) four courses. AE, DC, MC, V. Daily noon–3pm and 5:30–10pm. Closed July. Bus: 1, 6, or 10. DANISH/FRENCH.

Restaurant Els preserves its original 1854 decor. Several 19th-century murals believed to be the work of Christian Hitsch, the 19th-century muralist who adorned parts of the interior of the Danish Royal Theater, are displayed. Hans Christian Andersen was a regular here.

Each day there's a different fixed-price menu, but a selection of Danish open-faced sandwiches is offered at lunch for those who want a lighter meal. The cuisine at night is French, accompanied by excellent wines. The menu is based on what's fresh at the market.

A fish menu is featured nightly, including, for example, such perfectly prepared dishes as honey-smoked salmon, lobster ragoût in puff pastry, fillet of Dover sole with saffron sauce, followed by black-currant sorbet with cassis. A la carte dishes are likely to include a truffle-baked chicken-liver parfait with red currants, fresh mussels steamed in white wine with herbs, honey-fried guinea hen with ginger and peppers, beef rib eye steak with escargots, tournedos of veal baked with black poppyseeds and served with quail sauce, breast of squab in puff pastry with tarragon sauce, and several variations of Danish bay shrimp on toast with lemon and butter.

Restaurant Gilleleje. Nyhavn 10. ☎ **33-12-58-58.** Reservations required. Main courses 155–235 DKK ($22.45–$34.05). AE, DC, MC, V. Bus: 8, 9, or 10. DANISH/INTERNATIONAL.

The nautical decor is appealing but diners come mainly for the endless procession of meats, fish, spices, garnishes, and sauces made so deftly by a skilled kitchen staff. The chefs here aren't afraid of adding flavor to the food. You get tasty vittles and plenty of it. You might start with the specialty, a velvety, smooth lobster soup that will make you want to order a second helping, although that would fill you up too quickly. Other special dishes include the Danish herring platter, which many habitués like to order to launch their meal. The fish soup is always savory, as is the whisky steak flambé with grilled tomatoes. For dessert (and only if you have room), the Danish crêpes with vanilla ice cream will make you fall in love with Copenhagen.

Restaurant Havfruen. Nyhavn 39. ☎ **33-11-11-38.** Reservations recommended. Lunch main courses 135–140 DKK ($19.60–$20.30); dinner main courses 140–240 DKK ($20.30–$34.80). DC, MC, V. Daily 11:30am–5pm and 5–11pm. Bus: 1, 6, or 9. SEAFOOD.

Small and usually full because of its reputation for good fish, this restaurant is a cozy, nautically outfitted hideaway whose atmosphere is enhanced by the carved wooden mermaid hanging from the heavy ceiling beams. Lunches are less complicated, and less expensive, than dinners, and offer a more limited choice of food, with an emphasis on salmon, different preparations of herring, and shellfish such as clams and oysters. Dinner is fancier, with platters of whatever fish arrived fresh that day in the market. Especially flavorful is the Greenland turbot in a *beurre blanc* (white butter) sauce, which tastes wonderful when served with a fruity white wine from the Loire valley. The staff can get rather hysterical when the place fills up.

Restaurant Wiinblad. In the Hotel d'Angleterre, Kongens Nytorv 14. ☎ **33-12-00-95.**
Reservations recommended. Lunch main courses 60–130 DKK ($8.70–$18.85); dinner main
courses 155–225 DKK ($22.45–$32.65). Set menus 295–350 DKK ($42.80–$50.75). AE, DC,
MC, V. Daily 11:30am–5pm and 5–10pm (till 11pm Fri–Sat). Bus: 1, 6, or 9. DANISH/
INTERNATIONAL.

This is the less formal of the two restaurants within the ultra-upscale Hotel
d'Angleterre, and as such, many clients actually prefer it to its more restrictive (and
more expensive) sibling, Restaurant d'Angleterre. It was named after Bjorn Wiinblad,
an artist who is beloved throughout Denmark for his whimsical illustrations of children's fables, and who fulfills better than any living Dane the outward impression of
a tactful and sensitive guardian of the childhood fantasies of Danes of all ages. The
mostly-blue decor here—walls, furniture, lighting, and place settings—was for the
most part designed and executed within Wiinblad's studios, usually featuring representations of fanciful characters that show the Danish sense of myth, legend, and fairy
tale at its best. Since he completed the setting, the octogenarian artist himself returns
for a meal at least twice a month. Menu items are considerably more formal in the
evening than at lunchtime. Lunches might consist of *smørrebrød* (open-faced sandwiches), salads, and Danish platters that combine three oft-changing ingredients into
a single very satisfying lunch. Dinners are more elaborate, and might include grilled
salmon with a lobster-flavored saffron sauce, shrimp served with Thai-style lemon
grass, and a tenderloin of Charolais beef with lobster tail and drawn butter. This hotel
has long been known for selecting some of Copenhagen's finest chefs, and chances are
you won't be disappointed.

Victor's Café. Ny Østergade 8. ☎ **33-13-36-13.** Reservations recommended. Restaurant,
main courses 215–235 DKK ($31.15–$34.05). Café, *smørrebrød* (served only at lunch) 50–
80 DKK ($7.25–$11.60). AE, DC, MC, V. Mon–Thurs 9am–midnight, Fri 9am–2am, Sat
9am–5am. Bus: 1, 6, or 9. DANISH/FRENCH.

Hip, artsy, and boasting Parisian decor and service, this is a Danish version of a
bustling French bistro. There's a cafe at one end and a restaurant at the other. The arts-
oriented crowd can sit at the curved, illuminated bar or at a table. The popular Victor
Plate, which costs 155 DKK ($22.45), offers three food items. You can also choose
from a variety of open-faced sandwiches. Look for the daily specials posted on the
chalkboard. Try the breast of wild duckling with plums and celery, ragoût of fish with
red peppers, or baked salmon with chervil sauce and artichoke heart. The cooking may
not be the finest in Copenhagen, but the atmosphere and ambience compensate.

ⓘ Family-Friendly Restaurants

City Rock Café (see p. 87)   At this busy cafe, rock 'n roll music from the 1960s
to the 1990s is played against a backdrop of banquettes made from a 1959
Cadillac and a Harley-Davidson motorcycle.

Copenhagen Corner (see p. 85)   A special children's menu features such dishes
as shrimp cocktail and grilled rump steak.

Ida Davidsen (see p. 83)   When at lunch has your kid ever faced a choice of
177 sandwiches? At the "*smørrebrød* queen's" cozy eatery, that's what you get—
almost every conceivable sandwich, ranging from salmon to ham, from shrimp
to smoked duck. Even the queen of Denmark has praised these sandwiches and
ordered them for royal buffets at Amalienborg.

INEXPENSIVE

✪ **Ida Davidsen.** Store Kongensgade 70. ☎ **33-91-36-55.** Sandwiches 45–150 DKK ($6.50–$21.75). DC, MC, V. Mon–Fri 9am–4pm (last order). Bus: 1 or 9. SANDWICHES.

This restaurant has flourished within the Danish psyche since 1888 when the forebears of its present owner, Ida Davidsen, established a sandwich shop. Today, five generations later, the family matriarch and namesake is known as the "*smørrebrød* queen of Copenhagen," selling a greater variety of open-faced sandwiches (177 kinds) than anyone else in Denmark. If you opt for a sandwich here, you'll be in good company: Her fare has even been featured at royal buffets at Amalienborg Castle. You'll select your choice by pointing to it in a glass-fronted display case, after which a staff member will carry it to your table. Naturally, there's a vast selection to choose from, including types made with salmon, lobster, shrimp, smoked duck with braised cabbage and horseradish, liver pâté, ham, herring, and boiled egg. Two of them, accompanied perhaps with a slice of cheese, comprise a worthy lunch. If in doubt, a member of the service team, or perhaps Ida's articulate and charming husband, Adam Siesbye, will offer suggestions. The enlarged photographs that decorate the walls of this place, incidentally, usually come from the Davidsen family's personal scrapbook, and feature *smørrebrød* authorities, in their natural element, from generations past.

✪ **Nyhavns Færgekro.** Nyhavn 5. ☎ **33-15-15-88.** Reservations required. Fixed-price dinner 145 DKK ($21.05); herring buffet 78 DKK ($11.30); *smørrebrød* 39–60 DKK ($5.65–$8.70). DC, MC, V. Daily 11:30am–4pm and 5–11pm. Closed Jan 1 and Dec 24–25. Bus: 1, 6, or 9. DANISH/FRENCH.

The "Nyhavn Ferry Inn" has a long tradition and many loyal fans. The house is old, dating from the final years of the 18th century. In the harbor area, it offers a popular summer terrace where diners can enjoy not only their food but also a view of the 18th-century houses and boats in the canal. Inside, the decor is unusual, with a spiral stairway from an antique tram and a black-and-white "checkerboard" marble floor. Lights serve as call buttons to summon the staff when you want service.

The kitchen prepares a daily homemade buffet of 10 types of herring in different styles and sauces, including fried, *rollmops* (rolled or curled herring), and smoked. Some people make a full meal of the herring. You can also order *smørrebrød*—everything from smoked eel with scrambled eggs to chicken salad with bacon. A true Dane, in the tradition of Nyhavn, orders a schnapps or aquavit at lunch. Denmark has a tradition of making spicy aquavit from the herbs and plants of the land—St. Johns wort from Tisvilde Hegn, sloe-leaf from the wild moors, green walnuts from the south of Funen, and many other varieties. For dinner you can enjoy one of Copenhagen's most tender and succulent entrecôtes.

Restaurant Ostehjørnet. Store Kongensgade 56. ☎ **33-15-85-77.** Reservations recommended. Main courses 92–106 DKK ($13.35–$15.35). DC, MC, V. June and Aug–Sept Mon–Fri 11:30am–6pm, Oct–May Mon–Fri 11:30am–6pm, Sat 11:30am–3pm. Closed July. Bus: 1 or 10. DANISH.

Since this restaurant is so popular at lunchtime that dozens of diners must be turned away, the secret is to arrive early or late. There are a variety of Danish specialties, but we prefer the seafood salads made fresh daily. We recommend the herring salad, the mussel salad, quiche Lorraine, veal Cordon Bleu, smoked turkey, sweetbreads, and the ham-and-cheese omelets. An excellent dessert is a delectable fruit tart with a hint of chocolate. The restaurant is located one floor above street level in an 18th-century building.

Restaurant Parnas. Lille Kongensgade 16. ☎ **33-11-49-10.** Reservations required. Main courses 62–145 DKK ($9–$21.05). AE, DC, MC, V. Mon–Thurs 5pm–3am, Fri–Sat 5pm–5am. Bus: 1, 6, 9, 10, or 29. DANISH.

Opposite the city's largest department store, Magasin, this is a late-night refuge decorated like a warm, rustic, old-fashioned Danish *kro* (inn). Begin with three different kinds of herring or marinated salmon, followed by fried sliced pork with parsley sauce, several different preparations of sole and salmon, or the house specialty—*Parnas Gryde*, which combines grilled sirloin with bacon, marrow, and mushrooms, with béarnaise sauce on the side. This platter has been on the menu since the restaurant opened in the 1930s. After midnight a limited menu is available. Live music begins at 8:30pm.

Skindbuksen. Lille Kongensgade 4, off Kongens Nytorv. ☎ **33-12-90-37.** Reservations not accepted. Main courses 60–100 DKK ($8.70–$14.50). DC, MC, V. Daily 11am–midnight (kitchen closes at 9:15pm). Bus: 1, 6, 10, 27, 28, or 29. DANISH.

This place is more Danish than the queen. Although located in an expensive neighborhood of tiny establishments, it is not only reasonable in price but is a down-home type of place (that is, down-home Danish style). This atmospheric landmark has long drawn beer drinkers in the neighborhood. Many locals, often old men of the sea, swear by its *lobscouse,* the Danish version of a meat and potato stew that has kept many a mariner from starvation over the years. This dish is so popular it's often sold out at noon. A good variety of *smørrebrød* is always a luncheon favorite. You can order other dishes here too, including homemade soups, pâtés, fresh shrimp, and a local favorite, tender beef served with a béarnaise sauce. On Sunday afternoons there is live jazz from 4 to 6:30pm.

NORTH OF CHURCHILLPARKEN
MODERATE

Restaurant Le Saint-Jacques. Sankt Jacobs Pladsen 1. ☎ **35-42-77-07.** Reservations recommended. Lunch main courses 85–100 DKK ($12.35–$14.50); dinner main courses 170–190 DKK ($24.65–$27.55). Set menu 240 DKK ($34.80). DC, MC, V. Daily noon–4pm and 6–10pm. Bus: 1, 6, or 9. FRENCH.

Set in a single dignified dining room, in a building that's at least a century old, this is a well-respected French restaurant with a talent for defining itself as an unofficial embassy of Gallic goodwill. During mild weather, you can escape from the somewhat cramped interior in favor of a table on the street outside, adding a flavor that might remind you of something in the south of France. Menu items change frequently, based on the inspiration of the chef and the availability of the ingredients. Examples include North Atlantic scallops with salmon roe and leeks in a *beurre blanc* (white butter) sauce, fillet of sole with a balsamic glaze, a purée of eggplant served with paper-thin slices of smoked salmon, and fillets of free-range chicken with a cream-flavored morel sauce. There is a steady hand here in the kitchen, and dishes are admirably presented to diners who usually have traditional tastes. Excellent ingredients also go into this skillful cuisine. There is a wide-ranging wine list, which includes vintages from around the world.

NEAR RÅDHUSPLADSEN & TIVOLI
MODERATE

Copenhagen Corner. H. C. Andersens Blvd. 1A. ☎ **33-91-45-45.** Reservations recommended. Main courses 75–225 DKK ($10.90–$32.65); three-course fixed-price menu 285 DKK ($41.30). AE, DC, MC, V. Daily 11:30am–11pm. Bus: 1, 6, or 8. SCANDINAVIAN.

Set amid some of the heaviest pedestrian traffic in Copenhagen, this restaurant opens onto Rådhuspladsen, around the corner from the Tivoli Gardens. Decorated in tones of green and yellow, and outfitted with some of the accessories of a greenhouse-style conservatory for plants, it offers well-prepared and unpretentious meals to dozens of city residents throughout the day and evening.

A perusal of the menu, which offers many Danish favorites, will place you deep in the heart of Denmark, beginning with three kinds of herring or freshly peeled shrimp with dill and lemon. There's even a *carpaccio* of fillet of deer for the most adventurous palates. The soups are excellent here, as exemplified by the consommé of white asparagus flavored with chicken and fresh herbs. The fish is fresh and beautifully prepared, especially the steamed Norwegian salmon with a "lasagna" of potatoes, or the baked halibut with artichokes. Meat and poultry courses, although not always equal to the fish, are tasty and tender, especially the veal liver Provençale.

Restaurant Flyvefisken. Lars Bjørnstr. 18. ☎ **33-14-95-15.** Reservations recommended at dinner. Lunch platters 60–100 DKK ($8.70–$14.50); dinner main courses 95–150 DKK ($13.75–$21.75). Set-price dinners 148–210 DKK ($21.45–$30.45). DC, MC, V. Mon–Sat noon–3pm and 5:30–10:30pm. Bus: 5. DANISH/THAI.

The decor of this restaurant is authentically Danish, complete with colors of the national flag, thick wooden tables, and paneling. And indeed, the lunch you order is likely to focus on *smørrebrød* (open-faced sandwiches), different preparations of herring, grilled steaks with fried onions, and freshly made salads. But beginning at 5:30pm, the culinary repertoire changes radically, and the fiery cuisine of Thailand becomes the norm. Then, expect strong curries and lemon-grass flavors, the hot fish soups of Bangkok, grilled lamb, shark meat in basil sauce, chicken with cashews and fiery peppers, steaming cupfuls of green and black tea, and bottles of Singha beer brewed in Thailand. Although the cuisine has lost some authentic flavor and taste in the long jump from Thailand, it is still a marvelous change of pace from typically Danish fare.

Restaurant Prag. Amagerbrogade 37. ☎ **32-54-44-44.** Reservations recommended. Main courses 158–225 DKK ($22.90–$32.65); fixed-price menu 198–218 DKK ($28.70–$31.60) at lunch, 265–325 DKK ($38.40–$47.15) at dinner; smørrebrød (at lunch) 48–78 DKK ($6.95–$11.30). AE, DC, MC, V. Mon–Fri noon–3pm and 5–10pm, Sat 5–10pm. Closed lunch and all day Mon in July. Bus: 2 or 9. DANISH.

Near the SAS Scandinavia Hotel, east of Tivoli, this famous Copenhagen restaurant has never been better. Established in 1910 as the Café Sonderborg, it was revitalized under the direction of the Michelsen family. It fills the entire block, incorporating an English-style library, and is like a warmly accommodating Danish *kro* (inn), with dark-wood trim, white stucco walls, and impeccable service.

As much attention is paid to the way a dish looks as to the way it tastes. Try the warm leek terrine with a mushroom salad, sautéed fish of the day, lobster bisque with cognac, or fillet of veal with a red-wine sauce and stuffed onions. The wild duck with spinach is also excellent. The cuisine is increasingly assertive, seasonal, and regional. At lunch you can enjoy a tempting selection of *smørrebrød*.

Viking Steak House. Scala, Axeltorv 2. ☎ **33-15-37-99.** Main courses 88–198 DKK ($12.75–$28.70), all-you-can-eat buffet 148 DKK ($21.45). AE, DC, MC, V. Daily 11:30am–midnight. Bus: 1, 6, or 8. STEAK.

Although the name easily evokes a tourist trap, the food here is quite decent and a great value. It's part of a general dining complex close to Tivoli, City Hall, and the Central railway station—all part of the most extensive range of bars, restaurants, cinemas, and nightlife possibilities in the Danish capital. The most expensive dish, naturally, is the lobster from a live tank at the front, but most people come here to sample the Danish beef steak, priced according to weight. Meats are well flavored and grilled to perfection and almost always very tender. You check off the kind of steak you want on a card and return it to a waitress. It's not refined dining, but if you want a fair price, a good piece of meat, and tasty side dishes, this is the place to go.

INEXPENSIVE

Axelborg Bodega. Axeltorv 1. ☎ **33-11-06-38.** Reservations recommended. Main courses 78–115 DKK ($11.30–$16.65). AE, DC, MC, V. Daily 11:30am–9:30am. (Bar, daily 10am–2am.) Bus: 1 or 6. DANISH.

Across from the Benneweis Circus and near Scala and Tivoli, this well-established 1912 Danish cafe has outdoor tables where you can enjoy a brisk Scandinavian evening. Order the *dagens ret* (daily special). Typical Danish dishes are featured, including *frikadeller* (meatballs) and pork chops. A wide selection of club sandwiches is also available, costing 82 DKK ($11.90) each. Although the atmosphere is somewhat impersonal, this is a local favorite; diners enjoy the recipes from grandma's attic.

Café Sorgenfri. Brolæggerstræde 8. ☎ **33-11-58-80.** Reservations recommended for groups of four or more diners. *Smørrebrød* 35–60 DKK ($5.05–$8.70). DC, MC, V. Daily 11am–8pm. Bus: 5 or 6. SANDWICHES.

Don't come here expecting grand cuisine, or even a menu with any particular variety. This place has thrived for 150 years selling beer, schnapps, and a medley of *smørrebrød* (open-faced sandwiches) that appeal to virtually everyone's sense of workaday thrift and frugality. Partly because it contains only about 50 seats, the place is likely to be very crowded around the lunch hour, with somewhat more space during the mid-afternoon. Consider this place even for an early dinner, if it suits you. Everything inside reeks of old-time Denmark, from the potted shrubs that adorn the façade to the well-oiled paneling that has witnessed many generations of Copenhageners selecting and enjoying sandwiches. Between two and four of them might comprise a reasonable lunch, depending on your appetite. You'll find it in the all-pedestrian shopping zone, in the commercial heart of town.

Chili. Vandkunsten 1. ☎ **33-91-19-18.** Main courses 59–103 DKK ($8.55–$14.95); burgers and sandwiches 51–89 DKK ($7.40–$12.90). No credit cards. Mon–Sat 11am–midnight, Sun 11am–11pm. Bus: 5, 14, 16, 28, or 41. AMERICAN.

Boisterous, informal, and with an American theme, this is the most recent incarnation of a once-famous 19th-century establishment known to many generations of Danes as Tokanten. Chili serves at least 17 versions of burgers, available in quarter- and half-pound sizes, whose descriptions read like a map of the world. Choices include Hawaii burgers (with pineapple and curry), English burgers (with bacon and fried eggs), French burgers (with mushrooms in cream sauce), Danish burgers (with fried onions), and all the Texas burgers and chili burgers you would ever want. Also available are sandwiches and grilled steak platters. The dining room is decorated in desert-related colors of earth tones, warm reds, greens, and blues. Service is fast, and the ambience is unpretentious.

City Rock Café. In Scala, Axeltorv 2. ☎ **33-15-45-40.** Burgers, sandwiches, and platters 62–120 DKK ($9–$17.40). DC, MC, V. Daily 11am–11pm. Bar, daily 11am–1 or 2am. Bus: 1, 6, or 8. AMERICAN.

Inspired by the success of the Hard Rock Café chain, this is one of the busiest cafe bars in the Scala shopping and restaurant complex. Rock music from the 1960s to the 1990s is played against a backdrop of banquettes made from the rear end of a 1959 Cadillac, an old-fashioned Wurlitzer jukebox, and an antique Harley-Davidson motorcycle spotlighted and displayed as pop art. Menu choices, which are copious and inexpensive, consist of several kinds of burgers, T-bone steaks (referred to as "Mr. T-bone"), and an array of salads bearing such distinctly non-Danish names as Malibu, Tijuana, and Pacific.

Domhus Kælderen. Nytorv 5. ☎ **33-14-84-55.** Reservations recommended. Lunch main courses 45–108 DKK ($6.50–$15.65); dinner main courses 98–148 DKK ($14.20–$21.45). Set menus 98–148 DKK ($14.20–$21.45). AE, DC, MC, V. Daily 11am–4pm and 5–10pm. Bus: 5. DANISH/INTERNATIONAL.

Its good food, and a location across the square from City Hall, guarantees a strong percentage of lawyers and their clients who are arguing cases within the building's courtrooms. That, coupled with lots of foreign visitors, makes this a bustling and old-fashioned emporium of Danish cuisine. The setting is a half-cellar room illuminated with high-laced windows that shine light down on wooden tables and 50 years of memorabilia. (Prior to its role as a restaurant, the site functioned as a butcher shop.) Menu items at lunch are more conservative and more Danish than at night. Lunch might include *frikadeller* (meatballs), and heaping platters of herring, Danish cheeses, smoked meats and fish, and salads. Dinners might include pickled salmon, prime rib of beef with horseradish, and fine cuts of beef, served with a béarnaise or pepper sauce. Also look for the catch of the day, prepared in virtually any way you like. The food is typically Danish and well prepared. You get no culinary surprises here, but then you are rarely disappointed.

Huset Med Det Grønne Træ. Gammel Torv 20. ☎ **33-12-87-86.** Reservations recommended. Sandwiches and platters 33–101 DKK ($4.80–$14.65). MC, V. Mon–Sat noon–2:45pm (last order). Closed: Sat from May–Aug. Bus: 5. DANISH.

Set within the half-cellar of a brick-fronted building originally erected in 1776, this restaurant's decor has changed very little since the turn of the century. Its only drawback involves the fact that its hours are shorter than those of virtually any other restaurant in the neighborhood, but despite that, it fills up very quickly with shoppers and long-time patrons during the limited hours its kitchen is open. Specialties include artfully crafted sandwiches in the open-faced Danish style. Among the least pretentious of the roster is herring, slices of which are arranged on rough-textured bread with butter. Other versions include hot *smørrebrød* (more like full-fledged platters, really) garnished with chopped beef, horseradish, chopped onions, and pickles. The *pièce de la résistance* is a "sampler platter" composed of the most-loved culinary specialties of Denmark, including herring, chopped beef, liver pâté, potato salad, horseradish, cheese, and—for color and aesthetics—a scattering of radishes, scallions, lettuces, and pickles. Beer tastes wonderful with sandwiches like this, but if you really want to pretend you're Danish, why not opt for a small glass of any of 12 kinds of *aquavit* (schnapps)? Each sells for 24 DKK ($3.50) a glass. The staff will advise you on one that you might find appealing.

Husmann Vinstue. Larsbjørnsstræde 2. ☎ **33-11-58-86.** Reservations recommended. Main courses 35–115 DKK ($5.05–$16.65). AE, DC, MC, V. Daily 11:30am–4pm (last order). Bus: 5. SANDWICHES.

This is the kind of old-fashioned, two-fisted, and bustling lunch stopover that reminds city residents of the way much of Copenhagen was during the 19th century. It was founded in 1888 as a tavern and today boasts a decor that hasn't changed very much since then. In 1912 an injunction issued by a female owner refused admittance to women, a ban that continued as an iron-clad rule here until 1981. Today, it's more liberal in its admittance policies, but still very old-fashioned and appealing. The menu focuses almost exclusively on *smørrebrød,* the Danish open-faced sandwiches that at their best are miniature examples of culinary art. Combination platters, with herring, meatballs, Danish cheeses, and a small piece of steak make especially satisfying meals. The fresh raw materials and the homemade specialties are of the highest quality. Waiters wear black vests, white shirts, and black neckties.

Københavner Cafeen. Badstuestæde 10. ☎ **33-32-80-81.** Reservations recommended. *Smørrebrød* 38–45 DKK ($5.50–$6.50); main courses 89–129 DKK ($12.90–$18.70). AE, DC, MC, V. Daily noon–10:30pm. Bus: 5 or 6. DANISH.

One of the smallest (about 45 seats) restaurants in this pedestrian-only zone, the Københavner works hard to convey a sense of old-time Denmark. There's been an inn on this site since the 12th century, but the current structure dates from the 19th century. The setting is cozy, ensconced in deep red walls, pictures of the Royal Family, and engravings of the Copenhagen of several hundred years ago, and you can enjoy authentically old-fashioned food items whose preparation adheres to methods practiced by many Danish grandmothers. Expect a roster of open-faced sandwiches at both lunch and dinner; *frikadeller* (Danish meatballs); grilled fillets of plaice with butter sauce and fresh asparagus; roasted pork with braised red cabbage; and *biksemal,* a type of seafood hash that was served several times a week in many Danish homes throughout World War II. One of the most appealing items, and a specialty of the house, is a *Københavner platte,* consisting of several preparations of herring, marinated salmon, shrimp, meatballs, fresh vegetables, and fresh-baked, roughly textured bread with butter. The price of this culinary tour through Denmark is 108 DKK ($15.65). Be warned that Santa impersonators might be entertaining the children in the crowd during your visit, even if your visit happens to fall during the month of August.

La Glace. Skoubougade 3–5. ☎ **33-14-46-46.** Reservations not accepted. Pastries 12–24 DKK ($1.75–$3.50), coffee, tea, hot chocolate 30 DKK ($4.35). No credit cards. Mon–Thurs 8am–5:30pm, Fri 8am–6pm, Sat 9am–5pm. Bus: 1, 6, or 8. PASTRIES.

Should you need a place to invite the queen for tea, make it La Glace. This pastry shop has been a Copenhagen tradition since 1870. You can always find an array of Copenhagen matrons here devouring the latest offerings of the pastry chefs. La Glace is known for its hot chocolate—this is not a powdery concoction, it's a drink made with real fresh chocolate, just the thing to fortify you on one of those gray, overcast days in the city, of which there are so many. You can also sample a wide variety of cakes, Danish pastries, and chocolates. One of our favorites is a slice of Sportkage (sportman's cake) made with whipped cream, crumbled nougat, macaroons, and profiteroles that have been glazed in caramel. One of the best chocolate offerings is called Othellokage, a mixture of macaroons, custard cream, and "outrageous" amounts of chocolate, enough to satisfy the taste of the most devoted addict.

Puk's Restaurant. Vandkunsten 8. ☎ **33-11-14-17.** Reservations required in summer and Dec only. Main courses 58–132 DKK ($8.40–$19.15). AE, DC, MC, V. Daily noon–10:30pm. Bus: 5, 28, 29, or 41. DANISH.

Solid and reliable, this restaurant is housed inside the thick stone walls of what was originally a brewery in the 1750s. You can enjoy a drink or two in the establishment's atmospheric pub next door; a pint of Danish beer costs 34 DKK ($4.95). Most serious diners head down a flight of stairs from the street into the cellar-level restaurant. Menu selections include platters of *smørrebrød* (open-faced sandwiches), platters of several kinds of smoked fish, Danish meatballs, herring offered either cold and marinated or fried and served with dill and new potatoes, and tournedos of beef with a sauce made from fresh tomatoes and herbs. This is real Danish cooking—without any particular flair, but hearty and filling.

✪ **Riz Raz.** Kompagnistræde 20 (at Knabrostræde). ☎ **33-15-05-75.** Vegetarian buffet 59 DKK ($8.55) per person; main courses 79–150 DKK ($11.45–$21.75). DC, MC, V. Daily 11:30am–midnight. Bus: 5 or 6. MEDITERRANEAN.

Bustling and unpretentious, this decidedly un-Danish hideaway offers the best all-vegetarian buffet in Copenhagen. You'll help yourself from a sprawling network of buffet tables laden with each of the vegetarian specialties of the Mediterranean world, including Morocco, Egypt, Lebanon, Greece, and Italy, all for a price that by Scandinavian standards is highly reasonable. Carry your selections to a warren of small dining rooms, each of which leads—railroad style—into the next. There's additional seating outdoors during mild weather, or upstairs. Expect a medley of virtually every vegetable known to humankind, prepared either *au naturel,* or as part of a marinated fantasy that might include the antipasti of Italy, the hummus of Lebanon, or an array of long-simmered casseroles inspired by the cuisine of the Moroccan highlands. There's also a selection of pastas, some of them redolent with garlic, oil, and Mediterranean spices, as well as a limited array of meat and fish dishes. These are described on a multi-lingual menu and, when they're ready, they are carried by staff, a la carte style, to your table. Service staff is composed mostly of students from countries around the world. The place is fully licensed to serve alcohol.

Slotskælderne. Fortunstræde 4. ☎ **33-11-15-37.** Reservations recommended. *Smørrebrød* 35–85 DKK ($5.05–$12.35). DC, MC, V. Tues–Sat 11am–3pm. Bus: 1, 6, or 10. DANISH.

A star on the *smørrebrød* circuit, this landmark opened in 1797, but since 1910 has been owned by the same family. Habitués call the place "Gitte Kik," the name of the owner and granddaughter of the founder. Everything—the Danish wood trim, the framed old photographs, and the gold walls—add up to *hygge,* a coziness that has attracted such notables as the prince of Denmark, the king and queen of Sweden, and Victor Borge, the world famous Danish musician and entertainer. Try the marinated salmon, fresh tiny shrimp, or hot *frikadeller* (Danish meatballs). The smoked eel and scrambled egg sandwich is the best of its kind.

NEAR ROSENBORG SLOT
VERY EXPENSIVE

✪ **St. Gertruds Kloster.** Hauser Plads 32. ☎ **33-14-66-30.** Reservations required. Main courses 215–268 DKK ($31.15–$38.85); fixed-price menu 340–750 DKK ($49.30–$108.75); children's menu 90 DKK ($13.05). AE, DC, MC, V. Daily 4–11pm. Closed Dec 25–Jan 1. Bus: 4E, 7E, 14, or 16. INTERNATIONAL.

Near Nørreport Station and south of Rosenborg Castle, this is the most romantic restaurant in Copenhagen. There's no electricity in the labyrinth of the 14th-century underground vaults, and the 1,500 flickering candles, open grill, iron sconces, and rough-hewn furniture create an elegant medieval ambience. Enjoy an apéritif in the darkly paneled library. The chefs display talent and integrity, their cuisine reflecting precision and sensitivity. Every flavor is fully focused, each dish balanced to perfection. Try the fresh homemade *foie gras* with black truffles, lobster served in a turbot bouillon, scallops sautéed with herbs in sauterne, venison (year-round) with green asparagus and truffle sauce, or a fish-and-shellfish terrine studded with chunks of lobster and salmon.

AT GRÅBRØDRETORV
MODERATE

Bøf & Ost. Gråbrødretorv 13. ☎ **33-11-99-11.** Reservations required. Main courses 125–179 DKK ($18.15–$25.95); fixed-price menu 95 DKK ($13.75) at lunch, 235 DKK ($34.05) at dinner. DC, MC, V. Mon–Sat 11:30am–10:30pm. Closed Jan 1 and Dec 24–25. Bus: 5. DANISH/FRENCH.

"Beef & Cheese" is housed in a 1728 building, and its cellars come from a medieval monastery. In summer there's a pleasant outdoor terrace overlooking "Gray Friars

Square." Specialties include lobster soup, fresh Danish bay strips, a cheese plate with six different selections, and some of the best grilled tenderloin in town. One local diner confided in us: "The food is not worthy of God's own table but it's so good for me I come here once a week."

El Mesón. Hausers Pladsen 12. ☎ **33-11-91-31.** Reservations recommended. Main courses 120–155 DKK ($17.40–$22.45). Set-price menu 185 DKK ($26.85). DC, MC, V. Mon–Sat 5–10:30pm. Bus: 5. SPANISH.

This is the best Spanish restaurant in Copenhagen, with an emphasis on fresh food prepared in the Iberian style, and a staff from Murcia, Córdoba, Zaragoza, Madrid, and Valencia. With all that Spanish authenticity, you're likely to fall in love with the country all over again, surrounded as you'll be with a roster of Spanish-made ceramics and art objects. The restaurant is especially appealing later at night, when lots of local Danes indulge themselves in the fond memories of their holidays on Spanish beaches. Menu items include tender cuts of tournedos and *chateaubriand*, a succulent version of lamb chops served with potatoes and fresh vegetables, and Pinco de España, a delightful tenderloin of pork served with paprika and rosemary. The chef's version of paella is one of the most appealing this side of Valencia. All of the wines available at this restaurant, of course, are from Spain, and include impressive lists of Riojas and Ribera del Duero.

Peder Oxe's Restaurant/Vinkælder Wine Bar. Gråbrødretorv 11. ☎ **33-11-00-77.** Reservations recommended. Main courses 69–159 DKK ($10–$23.05); fixed-price lunch 69–89 DKK ($10–$12.90). DC, MC, V. Daily 11:30am–midnight. Bus: 5. DANISH.

In the Middle Ages this was the site of a monastery, but the present building dates from the 1700s. Today it's a restaurant and wine bar that attracts a young crowd. Selections from the salad bar cost 20 DKK ($2.90) when accompanied by a main course, but the offerings are so tempting that many prefer to enjoy salad alone for 56 DKK ($8.10) per person. Dishes include lobster soup, Danish bay shrimp, fresh asparagus, open-faced sandwiches, hamburgers, and fresh fish. The bill of fare, although standard, is well prepared.

INEXPENSIVE

Pasta Basta. Valkendorfsgade 22. ☎ **33-11-21-31.** Reservations recommended. Main courses 67–145 DKK ($9.70–$21.05). No credit cards. Sun–Wed 11:30am–3am, Thurs–Sat 11:30am–5:30am. Bus: 5. ITALIAN.

This restaurant's main attraction is a table loaded with cold antipasti and salads, one of the best deals in town. With more than nine selections on the enormous buffet, it's sometimes called the "Pasta Basta Table." For 69 DKK ($10) you can partake of it, all that you can eat, plus unlimited bread. The restaurant itself is divided into half a dozen cozy dining rooms, each decorated in the style of ancient Pompeii, with tones of russet and deliberately faded frescoes patterned after originals from Italy. The restaurant is located on a historic cobblestone street off the main shopping boulevard, Strøget.

Menu choices include at least 15 kinds of pasta (all made fresh on the premises), raw marinated filet of beef *(carpaccio)* served with olive oil and basil, a platter with three different kinds of Danish caviar (whitefish, speckled trout, and vendace, all served with chopped onions, lemon, toast, and butter), mozzarella with a sauce of pine nuts and fresh basil, fresh mussels cooked in a dry white wine with pasta and a creamy saffron sauce, thin-sliced salmon with a cream-based sauce of salmon roe, and sliced Danish suckling lamb with fried spring onions and tarragon. Dessert offerings include an assortment of Danish, French, and Italian cheeses, *crème brûlée*, and tartufo, an ice cream inspired by a restaurant on the Piazza Navona in Rome.

NEAR KULTORVET
INEXPENSIVE

Ristorante Italiano. Fiolstræde 2. ☎ **33-11-12-95.** Reservations recommended. Pizzas and pastas, 42–69 DKK ($6.10–$10), main courses 52–75 DKK ($7.55–$10.90), three-course fixed price menu 105 DKK ($15.25). AE, DC, MC, V. Daily 11am–2am (kitchen closes at 1am). Bus: 5. ITALIAN.

Patronized mainly by a foreign clientele under age 30 and by students from the nearby University of Copenhagen, this restaurant is boisterous, unassuming, and often very busy. Its specialties include various pizzas and pastas, as well as platters of Italian-style veal and grilled steaks. Both the service and the turnover is rapid. You've probably had better versions of this cuisine elsewhere, but Italiano is a good value and many of the dishes are quite tasty, although never rising to a level where you'd request the recipe.

NEAR CHRISTIANSBORG
EXPENSIVE

Krogs Fiskerestaurant. Gammel Strand 38. ☎ **33-15-89-15.** Reservations required. Main courses 228–395 DKK ($33.05–$57.30); fixed-price menu 385 DKK ($55.80) for three courses, 435 DKK ($63.05) for five courses. AE, DC, MC, V. Mon–Sat 11:30am–4pm and 5:30–10:30pm. Bus: 1, 2, 10, 16, or 29. SEAFOOD.

Krogs Fiskerestaurant, which is a short walk from Christiansborg Castle, is the most famous restaurant in the district, originally built in 1789 as a fish shop. (The canal-side plaza where fishers moored their boats is now the site of the restaurant's outdoor dining terrace.) Converted into a restaurant in 1910, it still serves very fresh seafood in a single large room decorated in an antique style with old oil paintings and rustic colors of faded greens and browns. The well-chosen menu includes lobster soup, bouillabaisse, natural oysters, mussels steamed in white wine, and poached salmon-trout with saffron sauce. Each dish is impeccably prepared and filled with flavor. A limited selection of meat dishes is also available, but the fish is better.

Nouvelle. Gammel Strand 34. ☎ **33-13-50-18.** Reservations required. Main courses 225–295 DKK ($32.65–$42.80); three-course fixed-price lunch menu 275 DKK ($39.90); four-course fixed-price dinner 485 DKK ($70.30). AE, DC, MC, V. Mon–Fri 11:30am–3pm and 6–10pm, Sat 7:30–9pm. Closed Dec 22–Jan 6. Bus: 28, 29, or 41. DANISH.

In an elegant dining-room setting, Nouvelle has been one of the capital's special restaurants since 1950. It's on the first floor of a gray 1870 house beside a canal. The color scheme is dark and light tones of yellow, with gray and purple accents. If you've won the lottery, the restaurant has a special caviar menu, with Sevruga and Beluga. Otherwise you can explore the a la carte menu, which changes frequently but is likely to include goose-liver terrine with three kinds of glazed onions or warm oysters and mussels *gratinée*. The fish dishes are superb, including North Sea turbot grilled or poached and served on a tomato, rosemary, and artichoke parfait. Lobster is served as a *fricassée* with green apples and a curry hollandaise. Meat selections are likely to include grilled goose liver with glazed spring cabbage and curry or lamb medallions with white truffles and new onions.

MODERATE

Den Gyldne Fortun. Ved Stranden 18. ☎ **33-12-20-11.** Reservations recommended. Main courses 155–255 DKK ($22.45–$36.95), three-course fixed-price menu 295 DKK ($42.80) Sun, 325 DKK ($47.15) Mon–Sat. AE, DC, MC, V. Mon–Fri noon–3pm, daily 6–10pm. Bus: 1, 6, or 10. DANISH/SEAFOOD.

Popular at lunchtime, this restaurant opposite Christiansborg Castle is a real "golden fortune," as the name translates. Dating from 1796, it has been visited by Hans

Christian Andersen, Jenny Lind, and Henry Wadsworth Longfellow. You climb green marble stairs to enter the formal restaurant, which resembles an English club. Amid crystal chandeliers, modern lithographs, and bubbling aquariums, you can order the kind of dishes that members of Denmark's royal family have requested during their meals here after shopping expeditions on the nearby Strøget. Menu choices include a Scandinavian version of *bouillabaisse* (served only in winter); fried fillet of plaice in butter sauce; fried Danish lamb with red wine and tarragon sauce; oven-baked salmon with Noilly Prat sauce; halibut with red-wine sauce and herbs; and fillet of turbot with scallops, fresh tarragon, and *beurre blanc* (white butter) sauce. Dessert offerings include the restaurant's well-known sweet plate, with the day's freshest mousses and pastries, or any of a range of exotic sorbets that change almost every week.

✪ **Fiskekælderen.** Ved Stranden 18. ☎ **33-12-20-11.** Reservations recommended. Main courses 145–265 DKK ($21.05–$38.40); three-course fixed-price menu 325 DKK ($47.15). AE, DC, MC, V. Mon–Fri noon–3pm and 5–10pm, Sat–Sun 6–10pm. Bus: 1, 6, 8, or 10. SEAFOOD.

Although the building dates from 1750, Fiskekælderen was established in 1975 and is today the best seafood restaurant in Copenhagen. The restaurant prides itself on very fresh fish, either imported from the Mediterranean or caught in the waters of the North Atlantic. Warmly nautical in decor, it has a bubbling lobster tank and an ice table displaying the fish of the day. Try the lobster bisque with fish and lobster roe, Danish fish soup, stuffed sole poached in white wine and glazed with hollandaise sauce, or a truly delectable *fricassée* of three types of fish in a saffron-flavored bouillon with noodles. Some beef dishes, such as Charolais sirloin, are also served.

INEXPENSIVE

Cafeen Nikolaj. Nikolaj Plads 12. ☎ **33-11-63-13.** Reservations not accepted. Main courses 60–105 DKK ($8.70–$15.25). AE, DC. Mon–Sat 11:30am–5pm. Bus: 2, 6, 10, 27, 28, or 29. DANISH.

This cafe, which to some evokes Greenwich Village in the 1950s, is located at the site which, circa 1530, was the scene of the thundering sermons of Hans Tausen, a father of the Danish Reformation. Today no one is orating any more but instead ordering an array of typically Danish lunches including a tasty variety of open-faced sandwiches along with homemade soups. You can always count on the cook preparing various types of herring. Danish sliced ham on some good homemade bread is a perennial favorite, and there is also a selection of Danish cheese. The place makes no pretensions of being more than it is: a simple cafe for good-tasting food prepared with fresh ingredients and sold at a fair price.

Thorvaldsen. Gammel Strand 34. ☎ **33-32-04-00.** Reservations not accepted. Main courses 60–135 DKK ($8.70–$19.60). AE, DC, MC, V. Mon–Sat 11:30am–4pm. Bus: 28, 29, or 41. DANISH.

This lunch-only restaurant, in the same building as the elegant and far more expensive Nouvelle, is hardly a citadel of grand cuisine, but it offers some of the best tasting and least expensive *smørrebrød* (open-faced sandwiches) in town along with a changing daily array of old-fashioned Danish cookery. Against a backdrop of walls covered with old tapestries, you can partake of this hearty and very filling cuisine. Locals begin with various versions of herring or smoked salmon. You can go on to the typical dishes of the day, which almost invariably include fried plaice. An occasional special appears with flair and flavor, including, for example, free-range Danish roasted chicken with a saffron sauce and accompanied by a helping of risotto. For dessert, opt for the fresh fruit with vanilla ice cream. Tables are placed outside in a courtyard if the weather allows.

IN NØRREBRO
INEXPENSIVE

Kasmir. Nørrebrogade 35. ☎ **35-37-54-71.** Reservations recommended. Main courses 40–98 DKK ($5.80–$14.20). Set menus (served only to two diners or more) 110–160 DKK ($15.95–$23.20). AE, DC, MC, V. Bus: 16. INDIAN.

This North Indian hideaway offers a welcome respite from too constant a diet of herring, *smørrebrød,* and beef with fried onions, and as such, it does a thriving business with local residents. Within an environment where floors and walls are lavishly decorated with hand-made Indian carpets, amid representations of such Indian deities as Shiva, you can order from a long list of dishes from South Asia's most populous country. Most can be ordered to the degree of spiciness you specify, from cool and mild to fiery. Examples include buttered lamb, slow-baked lamb *aloo* that's cooked in a clay pot with spices; a savory tandoori chicken with cumin; several varieties of Indian *nan* (bread); and a wide choice of highly flavorful vegetarian dishes served either in tomato or yogurt sauce.

Ristorante Quattro Fontane. Guldbergsgade 3. ☎ **35-39-39-31.** Reservations recommended. Main courses 78–139 DKK ($11.30–$20.15). No credit cards. Daily 4–11:30pm. Bus: 5. ITALIAN.

This is one of the busiest and most popular Italian restaurants in Copenhagen, with a success that derives in part from its ownership by an Italian-Irish husband-and-wife team who have successfully adapted traditional Italian recipes to Danish tastes. Dining rooms contain marble-topped tables, artwork that celebrates Italian landscapes, and a motif of grape vines that meander across the ceilings. If you're an absolute purist about Italian authenticity, be sure to specify the degree of *al dente* you prefer in your pasta: The Abruzzi-born owner notes that Danish tastes prefer the spaghetti a bit softer than an Italian might have wanted, so communication with a staff member might be a good idea. Menu items include thick-crusted pizzas; sautéed frog's legs in the French style; succulent shrimp with garlic sauce; excellent fish, lamb, and scallopine dishes; tenderloin steaks; and even some platters of grilled vegetables, much appreciated by vegetarians, that celebrate the fruits of the Danish harvest prepared in the Italian style.

IN TIVOLI

Food prices in the Tivoli restaurants are about 30% higher than elsewhere. To compensate for this, skip dessert at your restaurant and buy something less expensive (perhaps ice cream or pastry) later at one of the many stands in the park. Take bus nos. 1, 6, 8, 16, 29, 30, 32, or 33 to reach the park and any of the following restaurants.

Note: These restaurants are open only from May through mid-September.

VERY EXPENSIVE

✪ **Divan II.** Vesterbrogade 3, Tivoli. ☎ **33-12-51-51.** Reservations recommended. Main courses 265–345 DKK ($38.40–$50.05); fixed-price menu 295 DKK ($42.80) at lunch, 385–585 DKK ($55.80–$84.80) at dinner. AE, DC, MC, V. Daily 11am–midnight. DANISH/FRENCH.

This restaurant in a garden setting is the finest in Tivoli, and certainly the most expensive. It was established in 1843, the same year as Tivoli itself, and despite its name—Divan II—it's actually older than its nearby competitor, the less formal Divan I. The service is uniformly impeccable. The cuisine is among the most sophisticated in Copenhagen. The credo of the chefs is to create excellent meals using the best ingredients, but without audacious inventions. The *carpaccio* of Norwegian wild salmon marinated with lemon grass and virgin olive oil is a success, as is the terrine of goose *foie gras* baked with fresh truffles. Everything else is elegant and well prepared, whether it be the redfish braised with saffron and garlic (served with sautéed fennel) or the medallions of free-range poultry from Bresse (France) stuffed with squash and served with a *foie gras* of goose. Many dishes are homegrown, and these are the most likely to achieve taste perfection, as exemplified by the rack and leg of Danish spring lamb (in a truffle cream sauce) or the lightly salted breast of Danish free-range duck with an unusual horseradish *beurre blanc* (white butter). You may think you'll never be hungry again until the waiter starts tempting you with such delights as strawberry Romanoff (strawberries marinated in Smirnoff vodka, Grand Marnier, and orange juice), chocolate mousse, walnut nougat, and a crêpe filled with custard cream and fresh berries, or a spicy cake with raspberry sorbet, all on the same platter. No wonder it's called the chef's "grand dessert."

EXPENSIVE

Divan I. Vesterbrogade 3, Tivoli. ☎ **33-11-42-42.** Reservations required. Main courses 115–325 DKK ($16.65–$47.15), fixed-price menu 175 DKK ($25.40) at lunch, 295 DKK ($42.80) at dinner. AE, DC, MC, V. Mon–Sat noon–11pm. Sun noon–10pm. FRENCH.

This popular garden-like restaurant has been pleasing discriminating diners since 1913. Be assured of a refined French cuisine and excellent service, as well as a good view of the Tivoli Gardens. The chef prepares one of the largest selections of appetizers—both hot and cold—at Tivoli. Try the freshly shelled fjord shrimp, the smoked salmon, or even a crêpe stuffed with sweetbreads and sun-dried tomatoes. A platter of three fish selections served with three different sauces is a delectable seafood symphony. Poultry and meat dishes are likely to include a saddle of Danish lamb with roasted mushrooms and sauce Périgeux, or breast of cock from Bornholm roasted with mustard seeds and served with savory cabbage. Both the cookery and the service are refined at this long-time culinary citadel, and the produce selected is deluxe.

La Crevette. Vesterbrogade 3, Tivoli. ☎ **33-14-68-47.** Reservations recommended. Main courses 195–295 DKK ($28.30–$42.80); three-course fixed-price lunch 285 DKK ($41.30); all-you-can-eat lunch buffet 115 DKK ($16.65); four-course fixed-price dinner 425 DKK ($61.60). AE, DC, MC, V. Daily noon–11pm. SEAFOOD.

This restaurant offers more varied seafood dishes than any of its Tivoli competitors. Housed in a pavilion that was built in 1909, it has an outdoor terrace, a tastefully modern dining room, and a well-trained staff. The seafood is fresh, flavorful, and prepared in innovative ways—for example, pickled slices of salmon come with oyster flan and egg cream with chives, and a bisque of turbot is served with veal bacon and quail's eggs. In their main dishes the chefs reveal a mastery of cookery, pure imagination, and harmony. This becomes apparent as you sample such platters as grilled sea bass and scampi on crispy spinach and sautéed eggplant, or the fried fillet of red mullet with a chive sauce and a perfectly delightful "pyramid" of shellfish. Meat and poultry courses are extremely skimpy on the menu but you don't come here for that. Finish your repast with a selection of cheese from France, Denmark, and Italy (served with marinated prunes, a nice touch), or the fresh pastries of the day. The restaurant has its own confectionery.

Louise Nimb. Bernstorffsgade 5, Tivoli. ☎ **33-14-60-03.** Reservations required. Main courses 198–295 DKK ($28.70–$42.80); fixed-price menu 295 DKK ($42.80) at lunch, 425 DKK ($61.60) at dinner. AE, DC, MC, V. Daily noon–4pm and 5–11pm. DANISH/FRENCH.

Next door to its companion restaurant, La Crevette, this is the most formal restaurant in Tivoli, styled like a Moorish pavilion. It's decorated with antique accessories and looks out over the fountains and flowers of Tivoli. Why the name Louise Nimb?

She's the establishment's long-departed female chef who ladled up soup from the formerly smaller kitchen. Those modest days are long forgotten and the present menu is
one of the most elaborate in the city; the chef uses only the freshest produce from
Denmark and elsewhere throughout Europe. The first course is likely to include
smoked Baltic salmon or freshly peeled fjord shrimp, or even 6 oysters gratiné in a
lemon sabayon. The chef is rightfully proud of his shellfish medley, which includes
Norwegian lobster, mussels, oysters, crab claws, and North Sea shrimp. Other fish
choices include grilled red mullet with chive sauce, or for meat eaters, tournedos of
beef with marrow and a red wine sauce. Live piano music is featured at dinner.

Restaurant P.H. Vesterbrogade 3, Tivoli. ☎ **33-75-07-75.** Reservations recommended.
Main courses 155–245 DKK ($22.45–$35.55). Set-price lunch 145 DKK ($21.05); set-price
dinners 185–398 DKK ($26.85–$57.70). AE, DC, MC, V. Daily noon–10:30pm (last order).
DANISH/FRENCH.

This eatery, one of the most upscale and elegant restaurants in Tivoli, bears the initials
of Paul Hemmingsen (1894–1967), an architect, interior designer, and writer, whose
works are known and understood by virtually every Dane. A relative newcomer to the
Tivoli restaurant scene, where owners and venues change only very, very rarely, this
restaurant has gained a flash of fame since it was established in the late 1990s, thanks
to intelligent cuisine and a freshness of image that older, more jaded restaurants in the
area might have lost. You'll dine within a modern-looking building that Hemmingsen
designed, surrounded by a sun-flooded, cheerfully modern decor illuminated with
lamps that any Danish connoisseur might instantly recognize. Menu items are based
on French and Danish traditions, with touches of Asian pepper and spice to heat
things up just a bit.

   The menu intelligently draws on fine Danish culinary traditions without the heavi-
ness. For starters, try three varieties of homemade pickled herring with onions and
capers, or the more charming smoked Baltic salmon with asparagus. The chefs seem
capable of preparing everything well, even scrambled eggs with Italian summer truffles
on the side. Good choices include the North Sea turbot, with white asparagus and
spring cabbage, or the tomato fondant. If you want something deeply rooted in the old
kitchens of Denmark, try the Danish veal cutlet with a panade of ham and shallots
served with potato baked in a calf's tail confit, and top it off with a creamy morel sauce.

MODERATE

Færgekroen. Vesterbrogade 3, Tivoli. ☎ **33-12-94-012.** Main courses 70–160 DKK
($10.15–$23.20), fixed-price lunch 95 DKK ($13.75). AE, DC, MC, V. Daily 11am–midnight
(hot food 11am–9:45pm). DANISH.

Nestled in a cluster of trees at the edge of the lake, this restaurant resembles a pink
half-timbered Danish cottage. In warm weather, try to sit on the outside dining terrace. The menu offers drinks, snacks, and full meals. The latter might include an array
of omelets, beef with horseradish, fried plaice with melted butter, pork chops with red
cabbage, curried chicken, and fried meatballs. The food, prepared according to old
recipes, is something like what you might get down on a Danish farm. If you like
honest and straightforward fare, without a lot of fancy trimmings, and don't like to
spend a lot of money, this might be the place for you. A pianist provides sing-along
music every evening starting at 8pm.

Grøften. Vesterbrogade 3, Tivoli. ☎ **33-12-11-25.** Main courses 85–168 DKK
($12.35–$24.35). AE, DC, MC, V. Daily noon–10pm. DANISH.

Partly because of its low prices, and partly because it recalls the rustic restaurants
fondly remembered by many Danes from their childhood vacations, this is the most

popular spot in Tivoli. There's room for about 750 diners, equally divided between an outdoor terrace and an indoor dining room decorated in faded green and red, with sometimes-startling old photographs of Tivoli. In 1996 Grøften radically revised and improved its menus yet kept the old-fashioned favorites; it added several dishes that evoke the rich flavors and textures of the Mediterranean. We always get started here with the freshly peeled shrimp, though the smoked salmon with cream of morels is equally tempting. The cold potato soup with bacon and chives is the Danish version of *vichyssoise*. The wisest bet is to ask the waiter for the day's fish offering, based on the latest visit of the fishmonger. The chef's specialty is grilled beef tenderloin with bitter greens, tomatoes, olive oil, and black truffle essence. Old-time Danes have been coming here for years for the skipper's *lobscouse* (Danish hash). Glasses of Danish beer sell for 30 to 45 DKK ($4.35–$6.50), depending on size.

ON THE OUTSKIRTS

Restaurant Paustian. Kalkbrænderilobskaj 2. ☎ **39-18-55-01.** Reservations recommended. Main courses 120–175 DKK ($17.40–$25.40), fixed-price lunch 195 DKK ($28.30). AE, DC, MC, V. Mon–Sat noon–2pm. DANISH.

Amid an industrial landscape 3-miles north of the city center along the North Harbor, this lunch-only restaurant is part of the showroom for a large furniture outlet. In a futuristically modern building, it's worth the excursion. Combine lunch with a shopping trip to survey some of the finest Scandinavian furniture, including reproductions of the old masters such as Charles Eames and Alvar Aalto. The restaurant has cobalt-blue majolica tile, high-tech lighting, and big windows framing cranes and masts of ships in the harbor. The cuisine uses the best of Danish produce. Begin with fresh oysters or mussel soup with leeks and garlic. Then try smoked salmon with spinach or veal kidney with mustard sauce. You might also try the delectable Greenland halibut with a tomato *beurre blanc* (white butter) sauce. All the main courses are served with a selection of fresh vegetables gathered that day at the market. The cuisine here is first class, and we've never had a dish that disappointed.

✪ **Søllerød Kro.** Søllerødvej 35. Holte-Søllerød. ☎ **45-80-25-05.** Reservations required. Main courses 178–245 DKK ($25.80–$35.55). AE, DC, MC, V. Daily noon–3pm and 6–10pm. Motorists take the E4 toward Holte, exiting at Søllerød, or else the S-train to Holte (a taxi the rest of the way). DANISH/FRENCH.

In a historic village 11-miles north of Copenhagen, this traditional 1677 inn with a thatched roof and whitewashed walls is the top-rated restaurant of Zealand outside the capital. Located inside a flower-filled garden with outdoor courtyard dining, the setting is idyllic. Appetizers are often exotic, perhaps a bouillon of duck with deep-fried vegetables and lightly salted hearts of duck, or a terrine of duckling *foie gras* with breast of capon served with brioche. A main-dish specialty features three kinds of fish from Danish seas with hollandaise sauce. You might also try breast of pigeon baked in puff pastry with mushrooms, or Danish lamb served with parsley noodles and a pumpkin gratin. Another offering, beloved by Danish gourmets, is a whole roasted plaice with a creamed parsley sauce, potatoes, and a cucumber salad. The kitchen pays special attention to its pastry desserts, as reflected by the warm apple cake with macaroons and whipped cinnamon ice cream. But in summer we always gravitate to the vanilla ice cream (which tastes homemade) with fresh berries from the Danish countryside.

5

Discovering Copenhagen

Copenhagen is a city of amusement parks, glittering shops, beer-drinking cellars, gardens, and bustling nightlife. But the city is also proud of its vast storehouse of antiquities, and holds its own with the other capitals of Europe.

The "fun, fun" slogans and the "wonderful, wonderful" Copenhagen melodies tend to detract from this important fact: the Danish capital is an excellent center not only for pleasure seekers, but for the visitor who wants to inspect art galleries, museums, and castles.

In the morning, you can wander back to classical or Renaissance days in such showcases of art as Thorvaldsen's Museum.

In the afternoon, you can head south to the little town of Dragør on the island of Amager, long connected to the mainland and now almost a suburb of Copenhagen. Here, in the museums and architecture, you'll see strong evidence of the Dutch inhabitants who lived and farmed on the island for some 300 years.

On a summer evening, visitors can stroll through the Tivoli pleasure gardens, which seem to have emerged intact from the days when the world was young . . . and so were we. Apparently, the Danes loved childhood too much to abandon it forever, no matter how old they got—so Tivoli keeps alive the magic of fairy-lights and the wonder of yesteryear.

SUGGESTED ITINERARIES

IF YOU HAVE 1 DAY Take our walking tour through the old city (found later in this chapter), which isn't too taxing if you're still recovering from jet lag. Spend the late afternoon at Christiansborg Palace (on Slotsholmen), where the queen of Denmark receives guests. Early in the evening, head to Tivoli.

IF YOU HAVE 2 DAYS For your first day, follow the suggestions given above. On Day 2, visit Amalienborg Palace, the queen's residence. Try to time your visit so that you can see the changing of the guard. Continue beyond the palace to the statue of the Little Mermaid. In the afternoon, see the art treasures of Ny Carlsberg Glyptotek. At night, visit Scala, the restaurant-and-shopping complex.

IF YOU HAVE 3 DAYS For your first 2 days, follow the suggestions given above. On the morning of Day 3, visit the 17th-century Rosenborg Castle, summer palace of Christian IV. Afterward, wander through the park and gardens. Have lunch at one of the restaurants lining the canal at Nyhavn, the old seamen's quarter of Copenhagen. In the afternoon, go to the Rundetårn (Round Tower) for a panoramic view of the city and, if time remains, stop in at the National Museum.

IF YOU HAVE 4 OR 5 DAYS   For the first 3 days, see "If You Have 3 Days," above. On Day 4, head north from Copenhagen to Louisiana, the modern-art museum, and continue on to Helsingør to visit Kronborg Castle, famously associated with Shakespeare's *Hamlet*. Return by train to Copenhagen in time for a stroll along Strøget, the longest pedestrians-only street in Europe. For dinner, eat at a restaurant in Dragør.

On Day 5, visit Frilandsmuseet, at Lyngby, a half-hour train ride from Copenhagen. Have lunch at the park. Return to Copenhagen and take the second of our walking tours (later in this chapter). If time remains, tour the Carlsberg brewery. Pay a final visit to Tivoli to cap your adventure in the Danish capital.

1 In & Around the Tivoli Gardens

✪ **Tivoli Gardens.** Vesterbrogade 3. ☎ **33-15-10-01.** Admission 11am–1pm, 35 DKK ($5.05) adults, 20 DKK ($2.90) children 11 and under; 1–9:30pm, 45 DKK ($6.50) adults, 20 DKK ($2.90) children; 9:30pm–midnight, 20 DKK ($2.90) for everyone. Rides 20 DKK ($2.90) each. Daily 11am–midnight. Closed mid-Sept to Apr. Bus: 1, 16, or 29.

Since it opened in 1843, this 20-acre garden and amusement park in the center of Copenhagen has been a resounding success. It features thousands of flowers, a merry-go-round of tiny Viking ships, games of chance and skill (pinball arcades, slot machines, shooting galleries), and a Ferris wheel of hot-air balloons and cabin seats. There's even a playground for children.

An Arabian-style fantasy palace, with towers and arches, houses more than two dozen restaurants in all price ranges, from a lakeside inn to a beer garden. Take a walk around the edge of the tiny lake with its ducks, swans, and boats.

A parade of the red-uniformed Tivoli Boys Guard takes place on weekends at 6:30 and 8:30pm, and their regimental band gives concerts on Saturday at 3pm on the open-air stage. The oldest building at Tivoli, the Chinese-style Pantomime Theater with its peacock curtain, stages pantomimes in the evening.

For more specifics on all the nighttime happenings in Tivoli—fireworks, brass bands, orchestras, discos, variety acts—see "Copenhagen After Dark," later in this chapter.

✪ **Ny Carlsberg Glyptotek.** Dantes Plads 7. ☎ **33-41-81-41.** Admission 30 DKK ($4.35) adults, free for children; free for everyone Wed and Sun. Tues–Sun 10am–4pm. Bus: 1, 2, 5, 6, 8, or 10.

The Glyptotek, behind Tivoli, is one of the most important art museums in Scandinavia. Founded by the 19th-century art collector Carl Jacobsen, Mr. Carlsberg Beer himself, the museum comprises two distinct departments, modern and antiquities. The modern section has both French and Danish art, mainly from the 19th century. Sculpture, including works by Rodin, is on the ground floor, and works of the impressionists and related artists, including van Gogh's *Landscape from St. Rémy*, are on the upper floors. Egyptian, Greek, and Roman art are on the main floor, and Etruscan, Greek, and Cypriot art are on the lower floor. A conservatory separates the two departments. The Egyptian collection is outstanding; the most notable prize is a prehistoric rendering of a hippopotamus. Fine Greek originals (headless Apollo, Niobe's tragic children) and Roman copies of original Greek bronzes (4th-century Hercules) are also displayed, as are some of the noblest Roman busts—Pompey, Virgil, Augustus, and Trajan. The Etruscan art display (sarcophagi, a winged lion, bronzes, and pottery) is a favorite of ours.

In 1996 the Ny Glyptotek added a French Masters' wing. This wing, constructed of white marble and granite, is situated in the inner courtyard, which can only be reached through the Conservatory. In a climate- and light-controlled environment, you'll find an extensive collection of French masterpieces that includes works by Manet, Monet, Degas, and Renoir, as well as an impressive collection of French sculpture, such as Rodin's *The Burghers of Calais*, and one of only three complete sets of Degas bronzes. The display features Cézanne's famous *Portrait of the Artist*, as well as about 35 paintings by former Copenhagen resident, Paul Gauguin.

Rådhus (Town Hall) and World Clock. Rådhuspladsen. ☎ **33-66-25-82.** Rådhus, 30 DKK ($4.35); clock, 10 DKK ($1.45) adults, 5 DKK (75¢) children. Guided tour, Rådhus, Mon–Fri at 3pm, Sat at 10am; tower, Mon–Sat at noon. Bus: 1, 6, or 8.

Built in 1905, the Town Hall has impressive statues of Hans Christian Andersen and Niels Bohr (the Nobel Prize–winning physicist). Jens Olsen's famous **World Clock** is open for viewing Monday to Friday from 10am to 4pm and on Saturday at 1pm. Frederik IX set the clock on December 15, 1955. The clockwork is so exact that it's accurate to within half a second every 300 years. Climb the tower for an impressive view.

To the east of the Rådhus is one of Copenhagen's most famous landmarks, the **Lurblæserne** (Lur Blower Column), topped by two Vikings blowing an ancient trumpet called a *lur.* There's a bit of artistic license taken here. The *lur* actually dates from the Bronze Age (circa 1500 B.C.), while the Vikings lived some 1,000 years ago. But it's a fascinating sight anyway.

2 Amalienborg Palace & Environs

✪ **Amalienborg Palace.** Christian VIII's Palace. ☎ **33-12-21-86.** Admission 35 DKK ($5.05) adults, 5 DKK (75¢) children 5–15, free for children 4 and under. Jan–Apr Tues–Sun 11am–4pm; May daily 11am–4pm, June–Aug daily 10am–4pm, Sept–Oct daily 11am–4pm, Nov–Dec 13 Tues–Sun 11am–4pm, Dec 26–31 daily 11am–4pm. Closed Dec 14–Dec 25. Bus: 1, 6, 9, or 10.

These four 18th-century French-style rococo mansions—opening onto one of the most attractive squares (Amalienborg) in Europe—have been the home of the Danish royal family since 1794 when Christiansborg burned. Visitors flock to witness the changing of the guard at noon when the royal family is in residence. A swallowtail flag on the mast signifies that the queen is in Copenhagen, and not at her North Zealand summer home, Fredensborg Palace.

The Royal Life Guard in black bearskin busbies (like the hussars) leaves Rosenborg Castle at 11:30am and marches along Gothersgade, Nørre Voldgade, Frederiksborggade, Købmagergade, Østergade, Kongens Nytorv, Bredgade, Sankt Annæ Plads, and Amaliegade, to Amalienborg. After the event, the guard, still accompanied by the band, returns to Rosenborg Castle via Frederiksgade, Store Kongensgade, and Gothersgade.

In 1994 some of the official and private rooms in Amalienborg were opened to the public for the first time. The rooms, reconstructed to reflect the period 1863–1947, all belonged to members of the reigning royal family, the Glücksborgs, who ascended the throne in 1863. The highlight is the period devoted to the long reign (1863–1906) of Christian IX (1818–1906) and Queen Louise (1817–98). The items in his study and her drawing room—gifts from their far-flung children—reflect their unofficial status as "parents-in-law to Europe." Indeed, the story of their lives has been called "the Making of a Dynasty." Both came from distant sides of the then-heirless royal family to create a true "love match." The verses for their 1842 wedding song (a Danish tradition) were written by none other than Hans Christian Andersen.

⊘ Frommer's Favorite Copenhagen Experiences

Sitting at an Outdoor Cafe   Because of Copenhagen's long gray winters, sitting at an outdoor cafe in the summer and drinking beer or eating is always a favorite pastime. The best spot is at Nyhavn (New Harbor), beginning at Kongens Nytorv. Enjoy ice cream while admiring the tall rigged ships with bow sprits moored in the canal.

Going to Tivoli   This is the quintessential summer adventure in Copenhagen, a tradition since 1843. It's an amusement park with a difference—even the merry-go-rounds are special, using a fleet of Viking ships instead of the usual horses.

Strolling Strøget   In Danish, the word *strøget* means "to stroll"—and that's exactly what all born-to-shop addicts do along this nearly three-quarter-mile stretch, from Rådhuspladsen to Kongens Nytorv.

Exploring Alternative Lifestyles   Not for everybody, but worth a look, is a trip to the Free City of Christiania, on the island of Christianshavn (take bus no. 8 from Rådhuspladsen). Since 1971 some 1,000 squatters have illegally taken over 130 former army barracks (spread across 20 acres) and declared the area a free city. You can shop, dine, and talk to the natives about this experimental community with its own doctors, clubs, stores, and even its own flag. Exercise caution here, however.

Christian and Louise gave their six children a simple (by royal standards) but internationally oriented upbringing. One daughter, Alexandra, married Edward VII of England; another, Dagmar, wed Tsar Alexander III of Russia. The crown prince, who became Frederik VIII, married Louise of Sweden-Norway; another son became king of Greece, and yet another declined the throne of Bulgaria. In 1905 a grandson became king of Norway.

In the 1880s members of the Danish royal family, numbering more than 50, got together regularly each summer at the Fredensborg Palace, north of Copenhagan. The children, now monarchs in their own right, brought Christian IX and Louise presents—works of art from the imperial workshops and from jewelers such as Fabergé—as well as souvenirs, embroideries, and handcrafts made by the grandchildren. All became treasures for the aging king and queen, and many are exhibited in the museum rooms today.

Also open to the public are the studies of Frederik VIII and Christian X. Thanks to his marriage to Louise of Sweden-Norway, the liberal-minded Frederik VIII (1843–1912), who reigned from 1906 to 1912, had considerable wealth, and he furnished Amalienborg Palace sumptuously. The king's large study, decorated in lavish neo-Renaissance style, testifies to this.

The final period room in the museum is the study of Christian X (1870–1947), the grandfather of Margrethe II, who was king from 1912 to 1947. He became a symbol of national resistance during the German occupation of Denmark during World War II. Along with the period rooms, a costume gallery and a jewelry room are open to the public. The Amalienborg Museum rooms comprise one of two divisions of the Royal Danish Collections; the other is at Rosenborg Palace in Copenhagen.

Den Lille Havfrue (The Little Mermaid). Langelinie on the harbor. Bus: 1, 6, or 9.

The one statue *everybody* wants to see in Copenhagen is the life-size bronze of *Den Lille Havfrue,* inspired by H. C. Andersen's *The Little Mermaid,* one of the world's

Copenhagen Attractions

Alexander Nevsky Church ⑤
Amaliehavn Gardens ⑧
Amalienborg Palace ⑦
Assistens Kirkegård ㊳
Benneweis Circus ㉟
Børsen ㉕
Botanisk Have ⑬
Botanisk Museum ⑫
Charlottenborg Palace ⑲
Christiansborg Palace ㉗
Davids Samling ⑨
Erotica Museum ⑱
Frihedsmuseet ③
Geologisk Museet ⑭
Hirschsprung Collection ⑯
Kastellet ②
Københavns Bymuseum ㊱
Kongelige Bibliotek ㉘
Kongelige Teater ⑳
Kunstindustrimuseet ④
Legetøjsmuseet ㉑
Little Mermaid ①
Louis Tussaud
   Wax Museum ㉞
Marble (Frederik's) Church ⑥
Nationalmuseet ㉚
Ny Carlsberg Glyptotek ㉜
Observatory ⑪
Rådhus ㉛
Rosenborg Castle ⑩
Rundetårn ⑰
Statens Museum for Kunst ⑮
Telefonhus Kirke ㉔
Thorvaldsen's Museum ㉖
Tivoli Gardens ㉝
Tøjhusmuseet ㉙
Tycho Brahe Planetarium ㊲
University ㉓
Vor Frue Kirke ㉒

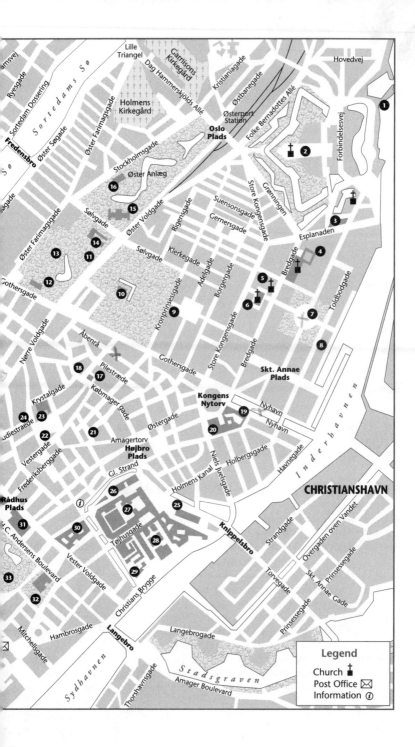

Lille Triangel

Garnisons Kirkegård

Kristianiagade

Hovedvej

Ryesgade

Sortedam Dossering

Dag Hammerskjölds Allé

Østbanegade

Folke Bernadottes Allé

Forbindelsesvej

❶

Sortedams Sø

Holmens Kirkegård

Østerport Station

Oslo Plads

Grønningen

❷

Fredensbro

Øster Søgade

Øster Farimagsgade

Stockholmsgade

Øster Anlæg

❶⑥

❶⑤

Øster Voldgade

Store Kongensgade

Suensonsgade

Gernersgade

Esplanaden

❸

❹

Rigensgade

Øster Farimagsgade

Sølvgade

❶④

❶❸

❶❶

Sølvgade

Klerkegade

Adelgade

Borgergade

Bredgade

❺

Toldbodgade

❶②

❶⓪

Kronprinsessegade

❻

❼

Gothersgade

❾

❽

Nørre Voldgade

Abenrå

Pilestræde

Gothersgade

Store Kongensgade

Bredgade

Skt. Annae Plads

❶⑧

❶⑦

Købmager gade

Krystalgade

Østergade

Kongens Nytorv

Nyhavn

❶⑨

②④

②③

Studiestraede

②②

②①

Amagertorv

Højbro Plads

②⓪

Nyhavn

Vestergade

Frederiksberggade

Gl. Strand

Niels Juelsgade

Holbergsgade

Havnegade

Inderhavnen

CHRISTIANSHAVN

Rådhus Plads

②⑥

Holmens Kanal

②⑤

③①

②⑦

Strandgade

H.C. Andersens Boulevard

③⓪

Tøjhusgade

②⑧

Knippelsbro

Overgaden oven Vandet

③③

Vester Voldgade

②⑨

Torvegade

Skt. Annae Gade

Skt. Prinsessegade

③②

Christians Brygge

Prinsessegade

Mitchellsgade

Hambrosgade

Langebro

Langebrogade

Stadsgraven

Sydhavnen

Thorshavnsgade

Amager Boulevard

Legend

Church ✝
Post Office ⊠
Information ⓘ

103

Danish Design

Despite the massive postwar output of modern furniture in Norway and Sweden, and despite the architectural innovations of such Finnish designers as Alvar Aalto, the streamlined, uncluttered look of modern Scandinavian design tends to be associated with Denmark. This is due in part to innovations made during the 1950s by such local luminaries as Hans Wegner, Poul Kjærholm, and Arne Jacobsen, who were trained as architects. Their mid-century furniture and tableware designs are avidly showcased by connoisseurs who appreciate their radical departures from previous styles.

The original inspiration for Danish design is believed to be the organic curves of art nouveau, where sinuousness and an uncluttered elegance have been defined by critics as "the curved line in love with itself." Danish modern, however, managed to transform art nouveau from a decorative, nonessential adornment into an aesthetically pleasing utilitarian stylistic approach that coincided with the industrial boom in Europe after World War II.

What makes a desirable and sought-after piece of Danish modern design? Some critics have referred to it as "structural vigor," others as "the visual expression of a socially just society" or "aesthetic functionalism," through simple and straightforward materials, including wood (usually oak, maple, ash, and, to a lesser degree, walnut and teak), steel, aluminum, silver, and copper. The best pieces of Danish modern stress flawless craftsmanship, a design that suits the ergonomics of the object's intended use, and subservience of form to its eventual function. Respect for the beauty of the raw components of a piece demands use of the finest materials. And the artful simplicity of each piece is achieved only after laborious hours of mortise-and-tenoning, lathering, polishing, and fitting the components into an artfully simple whole.

As the postwar years progressed, new industrial processes developed experimental materials (which later became mainstream): Bakelite, high-grade plastics,

most famous fairy tales. The statue, unveiled in 1913, was sculpted by Edvard Eriksen. It rests on rocks right off the shore.

In spite of its small size, the statue is just as important a symbol to Copenhageners as the Statue of Liberty is to New Yorkers. Tragedy struck on January 6, 1998. An anonymous tipster called a freelance television cameraman in the middle of the night to check out the four-foot bronze Mermaid. She'd lost her head. Most of the city responded with sadness. "She is part of our heritage, like Tivoli, the Queen, and stuff like that," said local sculptor, Christian Moerk.

The Mermaid was last decapitated on April 25, 1964. The culprits at that time were never discovered, and the head was never recovered. In the early 1900s some unknown party or parties cut off her arm. The original mold exists so it's possible to recast the bronze and weld back missing body parts. The arm was replaced.

Although not taking blame for the last attack in 1998, the Radical Feminist Faction sent flyers to newspapers to protest "the woman-hating, sexually fixated male dreams" allegedly conjured by the statue's bronze nudity. After the last decapitation, the head turned up mysteriously at a TV station, delivered by a masked figure. In the spring, welders put her head back on, making the seam invisible. Today the Little Mermaid—head, fishy tail, and all—is back to being the most photographed nude woman in Copenhagen.

spun aluminum, and spun steel. All these were carefully integrated into the growing canon of tenets associated with Danish modern, especially the integrity of design plus aesthetically pleasing functionalism.

Home design before World War II embodied clunky bourgeois ideals. Following the devastation of the war and its aftermath, the modern design movement emerged from the peculiar corner of the world that was Denmark, a land that during the 1950s found itself uncomfortably positioned between Eastern and Western Europe. Danish *joie de vivre* rose to the challenge. Within the streamlined designs, there's an implicit belief in the intelligence of the consumer as typified in the socialist idealism of the 1930s, and an implied rejection of the romantic ideals, arrogant nationalism, and imperialism that motivated some of the carnage of World War II. There's also an endearing (perhaps even quaint) sense of optimism that science and technology can alleviate many of society's problems and ills.

The style was unusual for what it was, and perhaps even more unusual for what it was not. There wasn't a trace of kitschiness about it—the very fact that the best examples of the style have endured for almost half a century (with few alterations or adaptations) attests to its timelessness. In contrast, the Naugahyde sofas and Eisenhower-era "moderne" accessories that swept across other parts of the world look hopelessly outdated today.

The allure of Danish modern hasn't been lost on art historians: Most visitors to Copenhagen's Museum of Decorative and Applied Art head straight for the Danish modern exhibits, featuring works that were purchased directly from the designers and artists in the 1950s. Hot objects on the auction circuit that fetch high prices today include mid-century cocktail shakers and the ergonomically balanced "egg chairs."

Nearby is the **Gefion Springvandet** (Gefion Fountain), sculpted by Anders Bundgaard. Gefion, a Scandinavian mythological goddess, plowed Zealand away from Sweden by turning her sons into oxen. Also in the area is **Kastellet** at Langelinie (☎ **33-11-22-33**), a citadel constructed by King Frederik III in the 1660s. Some of Copenhagen's original ramparts still surround the structure. The Citadel was the capital's main fortress until the 18th century when it fell into disuse. However, during the Nazi occupation of Copenhagen in World War II, the Germans made it their headquarters. Today the buildings are occupied by the Danish military. You can, however, explore the beautiful grounds of Churchillparken surrounding Kastellet. At the entrance to the park stands St. Albans, the English church of Copenhagen. You can still see the double moats built as part of Copenhagen's defense in the wake of the Swedish siege of the capital on February 10, 1659. The ruined citadel can be explored daily from 6am to sunset. Admission is free.

Frihedsmuseet (Museum of Danish Resistance, 1940–45). Churchillparken. ☎ **33-13-77-14.** Free admission. May–Sept 15, Tues–Sat 10am–4pm, Sun 10am–5pm; Sept 16–Apr, Tues–Sat 11am–3pm, Sun 11am–4pm. Bus: 1, 6, or 9.

This museum reveals the tools of espionage and sabotage that the Danes used to throw off the Nazi yoke in World War II. Beginning softly with peace marches in the early days of the war, the resistance movement grew from a fledgling organization into a highly polished and skilled underground that eventually electrified and excited the Allied world: "Danes Fighting Germans!" blared the headlines.

The museum highlights the workings of the outlaw press, the wireless communications equipment and illegal films, relics of torture and concentration camps, British propaganda leaflets dropped in the country, satirical caricatures of Hitler, information about Danish Jews, and, conversely, about Danish Nazis, and material on the paralyzing nationwide strikes. In all, this moment in history is graphically and dramatically preserved. An armed car, used against Danish Nazi informers and collaborators, is displayed on the grounds.

Kunstindustrimuseet (Museum of Decorative and Applied Art). Bredgade 68. ☎ **33-14-94-52.** Museum, 35 DKK ($5.05) adults, free for children 15 and under; library, free. Museum, Tues–Sun 1–4pm; library, Tues–Sat 10am–4pm. S-tog: Østerport. Bus: 1, 6, or 9.

The Kunstindustrimuseet is in a rococo building consisting of four wings surrounding a garden, a part of the former Royal Frederik Hospital built from 1752 to 1757 under King Frederik V. It was restored in the early 1920s and adapted to house the collections of the museum. These are composed mostly of European decorative and applied art from the Middle Ages to the present, arranged in chronological order. The pride of the place is given to furniture, tapestries, other textiles, pottery, porcelain, glass, and silver. Furthermore, there are collections of Chinese and Japanese art and handcrafts. Several separate exhibitions are shown within the scope of the museum. The library contains around 65,000 books and periodicals dealing with arts and crafts, architecture, costumes, advertising, photography, and industrial design.

Davids Samling. Kronprinsessegade 30. ☎ **33-13-55-64.** Free admission. Tues–Sun 1–4pm. Bus: 10, 17, or 43.

Its status as a privately funded museum, plus the excellence of its collection, make this a most unusual museum. Established by a Danish attorney, C. L. David (1878–1960), shortly after World War II on the premises of his private house across from the park surrounding Rosenborg Castle, the collection features European art, decorative art, and the largest Islamic collection in the Nordic world.

David's other major bequest to Denmark was his summer villa in the northern suburbs of Copenhagen at Marienborg, which is for the use of the Danish prime minister.

3 Rosenborg Castle, Botanical Gardens & Environs

✪ **Rosenborg Castle.** Øster Voldgade 4A. ☎ **33-15-32-86.** Admission 45 DKK ($6.50) adults, 10 DKK ($1.45) children 14 and under. Palace and treasury (royal jewels), June–Aug, daily 10am–4pm; May and Sept to mid-Oct, daily 11am–3pm; mid-Oct to Apr 30, Tues, Fri, and Sun 11am–2pm. S-tog: Nørreport. Bus: 5, 10, 14, 16, 31, 42, 43, 184, or 185.

Founded by Christian IV in the 17th century, this redbrick Renaissance-style castle houses everything from narwhal-tusked and ivory coronation chairs to Frederik VII's baby shoes—all artifacts from the Danish royal family. Officially, its biggest draws are the dazzling crown jewels and regalia in the basement Treasury, which houses a lavishly decorated coronation saddle from 1596 and other treasures. Try to see the Knights Hall (Room 21), with its coronation seat, three silver lions, and relics from the 1700s. Room 3, another important attraction, was used by founding father Christian IV (lucky in love, unlucky in war), who died in this bedroom decorated with Asian lacquer art and a stucco ceiling. The King's Garden *(Have)* surrounds the castle, and the Botanical Gardens are across the street.

Botanisk Have (Botanical Gardens). Gothersgade 128. ☎ **35-32-22-22.** Free admission. Apr–Sept, daily 8:30am–6pm; Oct–Mar, daily 8:30am–4pm. S-tog: Nørreport. Bus: 5, 7, 14, 16, 24, 40, or 43.

Planted from 1871 to 1874, the Botanical Gardens are located at a lake that was once part of the city's defensive moat. Across from Rosenborg Castle, it contains hothouses growing both tropical and subtropical plants. Special features include a cactus house and a palm house, all of which appear even more exotic in the far northern country of Denmark. An alpine garden contains mountain plants from all over the world.

✪ **Statens Museum for Kunst (Royal Museum of Fine Arts).** Sølvgade 48–50. ☎ **33-74-84-94.** Admission 30–50 DKK ($4.35–$7.25) adults, free for children 15 and under. Tues and Thurs–Sun 10am–5pm, Wed 10am–8pm. Bus: 10, 14, 40, 42, 43, or MZE.

This well-stocked art museum—the largest art museum in Denmark— houses foreign painting and sculpture from the 13th century to the present. There are Dutch golden age landscapes and marine paintings by Rubens and his school, plus portraits by Frans Hals and Rembrandt. The Danish golden age is represented by Eckersberg, Købke, and Hansen. French 20th-century art includes 20 works by Matisse. In the Royal Print Room are 300,000 drawings, prints, lithographs, and other works by such artists as Dürer, Rembrandt, Matisse, and Picasso. When it reopened in 1998, following a major renovation, the museum was completely transformed, almost doubling in size. A new modern museum was erected at the rear of the century-old main building. Also brand new is a wing dedicated as a Children's Art Museum.

Den Hirschsprungske Samling (Hirschsprung Collection). Stockholmsgade 20. ☎ **35-42-03-36.** Admission 25 DKK ($3.60) adults, free for children 15 and under; 40 DKK ($5.80) during special exhibitions. Wed 11am–9pm, Thurs–Mon 11am–4pm. Bus: 10, 14, 42, or 43.

This collection of Danish art from the 19th and early 20th centuries lies in Ostre Anlaeg, a park in the city center. Heinrich Hirschsprung (1836–1908), a tobacco merchant, created the collection, and it has been growing ever since. The emphasis is on the Danish golden age, with such artists as Eckersberg, Købke, and Lundbye, and on the Skagen painters, P. S. Krøyer and Anna and Michael Ancher. Some furnishings from the artists' homes are also exhibited.

4 Christiansborg Palace & Environs

✪ **Christiansborg Palace.** Christiansborg Slotsplads. ☎ **33-92-64-92.** Royal Reception Rooms, 37 DKK ($5.35) adults, 10 DKK ($1.45) children; parliament, free; castle ruins, 20 DKK ($2.90) adults, 5 DKK (75¢) children. Reception Rooms, guided tours, June–Aug, daily at 11am, 1pm, and 3pm; May and Sept, Tues–Sun at 11am and 3pm; Oct–Apr, Tues, Thurs, and Sun at 11am and 3pm. Parliament, English–language tours given only mid-June to late-Sept, Sun–Fri 10am–4pm. Ruins, May–Sept, Tues–Fri and Sun 9:30am–3:30pm; closed Oct–Apr. Bus: 1, 2, 5, 8, or 9.

This granite-and-copper palace, located on Slotsholmen—a small island that has been the center of political power in Denmark for more than 800 years—houses the Danish parliament, the Supreme Court, the prime minister's offices, and the Royal Reception Rooms. A guide will lead you through richly decorated rooms, including the Throne Room, Banqueting Hall, and the Queen's Library. Before entering, you'll be asked to put on soft overshoes to protect the floors.

Under the palace, visit the well-preserved ruins of the 1167 castle of Bishop Absalon, founder of Copenhagen.

You can also visit **Kongelige Stalde & Kareter,** Christianborg Ridebane 12 (☎ **33-40-10-10**), the royal stables and coaches. Elegantly clad in riding breeches and jackets, riders exercise the royal horses. Vehicles include regal coaches and "fairytale" carriages, along with a display of harnesses in use by the royal family since 1778. Admission is 10 DKK ($1.45) for adults, 5 DKK (75¢) for children. The site can be visited May to September Friday to Sunday 2 to 4pm. During other months, visits are possible on Saturday and Sunday 2 to 4pm.

✪ **Nationalmuseet (National Museum).** Ny Vestergade 10. ☎ **33-13-44-11.** Admission 30 DKK ($4.35) adults, free for children. Tues–Sun 10am–5pm. Closed Dec 24–25 and 31. Bus: 1, 2, 5, 6, 8, 10, 28, 29, 30, 32, 33, 34, or 35.

A gigantic repository of anthropological artifacts, this museum is divided primarily into five departments. The first section focuses on prehistory, the Middle Ages, and the Renaissance in Denmark. These collections date from the Stone Age and include Viking stones, helmets, and fragments of battle gear. Especially interesting are the *lur* horn, a Bronze Age musical instrument, among the oldest instruments in Europe, and the world-famous "Sun Chariot," an elegant Bronze Age piece of pagan art. The second area is a study of the palace and the history of the museum itself. Exhibits focus on the history of the 18th-century royal palace. The third collection, the Royal Collection of Coins and Medals, displays various coins from antiquity. The fourth collection, the Collection of Egyptian and Classical Antiquities, offers outstanding examples of art and artifacts from ancient civilizations. Here you'll find the Roman holy cups depicting Homeric legends. Finally, the Ethnographic section is devoted to relics of the Eskimo culture and the people of Greenland and Denmark.

Erotica Museum. Købmagergade 24. ☎ **33-12-03-11.** Admission 59 DKK ($8.55). May–Sept, daily 10am–11pm; Oct–Apr, Mon–Fri 11am–8pm, Sat 10am–9pm, Sun 10am–8pm. Bus: 1, 16, or 29.

This is perhaps the only museum in the world where you can go to learn about the sex lives of such famous people as Freud, Nietzsche, and Duke Ellington. Founded by Ole Ege, a well-known Danish photographer of nudes, it's within walking distance of Tivoli and the Central Railroad Station. In addition to providing a glimpse into the sex lives of the famous, it presents a survey of erotica around the world as well as through the ages.

The exhibits range from the tame to the tempestuous—everything from Etruscan drawings and Chinese paintings to Greek vases depicting a lot of sexual activity. On display are remarkable lifelike tableaux created by craftspeople from Tussaud's Wax Museum, as well as a collection of those dirty little postcards Americans tried to sneak home through Customs back in the 1920s and 1930s.

As you ascend the floors of the museum, the more explicit the exhibits become. By the time you reach the fourth (top) floor, a dozen video monitors are showing erotic films, featuring everything from black-and-white films from the 1920s—all made underground—to today's triple X–rated releases in full-bodied color, with the emphasis on "bodied."

Tøjhusmuseet (Royal Arsenal Museum). Tøjhusgade 3. ☎ **33-11-60-37.** Admission 20 DKK ($2.90) adults, 5 DKK (75¢) children 6–12, free for children 5 and under. Tues–Sun noon–4pm. Closed Jan 1 and Dec 24–25 and 31.

The museum features a fantastic display of weapons used for hunting and warfare. On the ground floor—the longest vaulted Renaissance hall in Europe—is the Canon Hall, stocked with artillery equipment from 1500 up to the present day. Above the Canon Hall is the impressive Armory Hall with one of the world's finest collections of small arms, colors, and armor. The museum building was erected during the years 1598–1604.

Thorvaldsens Museum. Porthusgade 2. ☎ **33-32-15-32.** Admission 20 DKK ($2.90) adults, free 14 and under. Free Wed. Tues–Sun 10am–5pm. Bus: 1, 2, 5, 6, 8, 10, 28, 29, or 550S.

This restrained yet decorated museum on Slotsholmen next door to Christiansborg houses the greatest collection of the works of Bertel Thorvaldsen (1770–1844), the most significant name in neoclassical sculpture. Thorvaldsen's life represented the romanticism of the 18th and 19th centuries: he rose from semi-poverty to the pinnacle of success in his day. He's famous for his most typical, classical restrained works, taken from mythology: Cupid and Psyche, Adonis, Jason, Hercules, Ganymede, Mercury—all of which are displayed at the museum. In addition to the works of this latter-day exponent of Roman classicism, the museum also contains Thorvaldsen's personal, and quite extensive, collection, everything from the Egyptian relics of Ptolemy to the contemporary paintings he acquired during his lifetime (for example, *Apollo Among the Thessalian Shepherds*). After many years of self-imposed exile in Italy, Thorvaldsen returned in triumph to his native Copenhagen, where he died a national figure and was buried in the courtyard of his own personal museum.

5 In the Old Town (Indre By)

Rundetårn (Round Tower). Købmagergade 52A. ☎ **33-73-03-73.** Admission 15 DKK ($2.15) adults, 5 DKK (75¢) children. Tower, June–Aug, Mon–Sat 10am–8pm, Sun noon–8pm; Sept–May, Mon–Sat 10am–5pm, Sun noon–5pm. Observatory, Sept 26–Mar 20 only, Tues–Wed 7–10pm. Bus: 5, 7E, 14, 16, or 42.

This 17th-century public observatory, attached to a church, is visited by thousands who climb the spiral ramp (no steps) for a panoramic view of Copenhagen. The tower is one of the crowning architectural achievements of the Christian IV era. Peter the Great, in Denmark for a state visit, galloped up the ramp on horseback, preceded by his carriage-drawn tsarina. On the premises is a Bibliotekssalen (Library Hall), offering changing exhibits on art, culture, history, and science.

Vor Frue Kirke (Copenhagen Cathedral). Nørregade. ☎ **33-14-41-28.** Free admission. Mon–Fri 9am–5pm. Bus: 5.

This Greek Renaissance–style church, built in the early 19th century near Copenhagen University, features Bertel Thorvaldsen's white marble neoclassical works including *Christ and the Apostles.* The funeral of Hans Christian Andersen took place here in 1875, and that of Sören Kierkegaard in 1855.

6 More Museums

Arbejdermuseet (The Workers Museum). Rømersgade 22. ☎ **33-93-25-75.** Admission 30 DKK ($4.35) adults, 15 DKK ($2.15) children. July 1–Nov 1 daily 10am–6pm. Off-season Tues–Sun 10am–6pm. Bus: 5, 7, 14, 16, 17, 24, 43, or 84.

This is one of those "Workers of the World, Unite!" type museums, lying in Nørrebro District. It traces the working class of Denmark from their struggles beginning around 1850 up to the present day. It's not just about the labor movement, however; it re-creates various times and eras. For example, there is a reconstruction of a Danish street in the 1800s, complete with a tram. There's also the re-creation of an apartment that was once inhabited by a worker in a brewery, along with his wife and eight children. The furnishings and artifacts are authentic. In all, it's a homage to the working class, depicting the struggle of laborers to make a living and provide for their families.

Insider Tip: Even if you aren't too turned on by the exhibits, go here for its 19th-century style restaurant where old-fashioned Danish specialties are still served, the kind enjoyed by grandpa and grandma. If that doesn't interest you, head for the 1950s style coffee shop where you'll expect to see the arrival of the Danish versions of Marilyn Monroe and James Dean at any minute.

Den Kongelige Afstøbningssamling. Vestindisk Pakhus, Toldbodgade 40. ☎ **33-91-21-26.** Admission 20 DKK ($2.90) adults, 13 DKK ($1.90) children. Free Wed. Wed–Tues 10am–4pm, Sat–Sun 1–4pm. Closed on other days. Bus: 1, 6, or 9.

Founded in 1895 as part of the Statens Museum for Kunst, the Royal Cast Collection remained on the ground floor of its parent museum until the 1960s. In 1984 the collection was placed permanently in the Vestindisk Pakhus, a rebuilt warehouse overlooking the harbor of Copenhagen, close to Amalienborg Palace.

It is one of the largest and oldest cast collections in the world, comprising some 2,000 plaster-casts modeled after famous sculptures from the past 4,000 years of western culture. The best known original works from antiquity and the Renaissance are now scattered all over the museums of the world, but here they are brought together as a world of plaster—monumental Egyptian sphinxes, gold from Atreus' treasury, *Venus de Milo*, the Pergamon altar, and marble sculpture from the temples of the Acropolis in Athens. Most of the collection was made from 1870 to 1915 by leading European plaster workshops.

Kongelige Bibliotek (Royal Library). Christians Brygge 8. ☎ **33-93-01-11.** Admission free. Mon–Fri 9am–7pm, Sat 10am–7pm. Bus: 1, 2, 5, 6, 8, or 9.

The Royal Library, which reopened in late 1998 after a closure, dates from the 1600s and is the largest library in Scandinavia. Housed in a classic building with high-ceilinged reading rooms and columned hallways, it is a grand and impressive place. It holds some 2 million volumes, everything from sagas of Viking journeys to America (yes, before Columbus allegedly "discovered" the already inhabited continent), and enough prints, maps, and manuscripts to keep the most intense scholar busy for several lifetimes. The library owns original manuscripts by such fabled Danish writers as Hans Christian Andersen and Karen Blixen (more widely known as Isak Dinesen). The library was closed while a gargantuan granite annex was added to accommodate the vast output of Danish works since World War II, and today the library stretches all the way to the waterfront. As a national library, Kongelige Bibliotek owns the world's most complete collection of works printed in Danish, some going as far back as 1482. After viewing the interior of the library, you can wander through its formal gardens, which contain a fish pond and a statue of philosopher Sören Kierkegaard (1813–55).

Musikhistorisk Museum. Åbenrå 30. ☎ **33-11-27-26.** Admission 20 DKK ($2.90) adults, 5 DKK (75¢) children. Fri–Wed 1–3pm. Bus: 5, 7, 14, 16, 17, 24, 31, 42, 43, 50, 84, or 184.

This museum offers a journey through the history of musical instruments in Europe from 1000 to 1900. Exhibits are grouped around a theme, and as you view them you're treated to special recordings. The overall emphasis of the museum is on the effect music has had on Danish culture. Sometimes the museum is the venue of special concerts.

Orlogsmuseet (Royal Naval Museum). Overgaden Oven Vandet 58. ☎ **32-54-63-63.** Admission 30 DKK ($4.35) adults, 20 DKK ($2.90) children. Tues–Sun noon–4pm. Bus: 2, 8, 9, 28, 31, or 350S.

This museum in Søkvasthuset, the former naval hospital, opens onto Christianshavn Kanal. Since it traces the history of the navy, and since Denmark is a maritime nation, this museum practically tells the saga of the country itself. More than 300 model ships, many based on designs that date from as early as the 1500s, are on display. Some of these vessels were actually designed and constructed by naval engineers. They served as prototypes for the construction of actual ships that were later launched into the North Sea. The models are wide ranging—some are fully "dressed," even with working sails, whereas others are merely cross-sectional with their frames outlined. You get a vast array of other naval artifacts here too, including an intriguing collection of figureheads, some of which are actual art works unto themselves. That's not all. Look for the display of navigational instruments and the propeller from the German U-Boat that sank the *Lusitania,* making headlines around the world as war clouds loomed. Finally, there is also a display of naval uniforms worn by Danish officers and sailors over the decades.

Teatermuseet. Christiansborg Ridebane 18. ☎ **33-11-51-76.** Admission 20 DKK ($2.90) adults, 5 DKK (75¢) children. Wed 2–4, Sat–Sun noon–4pm. Bus: 1, 2, 5, 6, 8, 9, 10, 31, 37, or 43.

Theater buffs flock to this museum in the Old Court Theater, which dates from 1767. King Christian VII had it constructed as the first court theater in Copenhagen. At one time Hans Christian Andersen was a fledgling ballet student here, although we can't imagine how this awkward "ugly duckling" looked on stage. In 1842 the theater was overhauled and given its present look, but the curtain went down on it for the last time in 1881.

However, it made a "comeback" as a museum in 1992. The museum traces the history of the Danish theater from the 18th century until modern times. The public has access to the theater boxes, the stage, and the old dressing rooms. Some of the great theatrical performances of Europe, from Italian opera to pantomime, reportedly took place on the stage here. Photographs, prints, theatrical costumes, and even old stage programs tell the story, beginning with Ludvig Holberg and going up to the present day.

Tivoli Museum. Vesterbrogade 3. ☎ **33-15-10-01.** Admission 20 DKK ($2.90) adults, 10 DKK ($1.45) children. Apr 24–Sept 13 daily 11am–6pm. Off-season Tues–Sun 10am–4pm. S-train to Central Station.

Some 150 years of Europe's most famous amusement park are revealed in this offbeat museum spread across three floors. Models, films, 3D displays, pictures, posters, and original artifacts reveal how the Danes and their foreign visitors had harmless fun over the decades. Opening in 1993, the museum became an instant hit with Tivoli devotees. It's a great idea to come here if you have only one chance to visit Copenhagen in a lifetime, and Tivoli has shut down for the year at the time of your visit. Tivoli has hosted many legendary performers over the years—everyone from Marlene Dietrich to a flea circus that ran for 65 years—and their appearances are documented in the museum. Children will delight in the rides of yesterday (some of them good enough to recycle today).

W.Ø. Larsens Tobakmuseet (W.Ø. Larsens Tobacco Museum). Amagertorv 9. ☎ **33-12-20-50.** Admission free. Mon–Thurs 10am–6pm, Fri 10am–7pm, Sat 10am–5pm. Bus: 8, 28, 29, or 41.

For the pipe or cigar smoker, this place is Valhalla. It contains pipes from around the world—in all, 400 years of tobacco and the cigar industry. The museum is crammed with antiquities and rarities pertaining to tobacco. You can see old-fashioned tobacco jars, pipe racks, snuff tins, and old tobacco packaging down through the ages. One tiny pipe is no bigger than an embroidery needle.

7 The Churches of Copenhagen

For a visit to the cathedral of Copenhagen, refer to "In the Old Town," (above).

Holmens Kirke. Holmens Kanal. ☎ **33-13-61-78.** Admission free. May 15–Sept 15 Mon–Fri 9am–2pm, Sat 9am–noon. Bus: 1, 2, 6, 8, 9, 10, 31, 37, or 43.

Built in 1619, this royal chapel and naval church lies across the canal from Slotsholmen, next to the National Bank of Denmark. Although the structure was converted into a church for the royal navy in 1619, its nave was originally built in 1562 when it was first used as an anchor forge. By 1641 the ever-changing church became predominantly Dutch Renaissance in style, an architectural style that is maintained to this day. The so-called "royal doorway" was brought here from Roskilde Cathedral in the 19th century. Inside, look for the baroque altar of unpainted oak and a carved pulpit by Abel Schrøder the Younger. Both of these artifacts date from the mid-17th century. In the burial chamber are the tombs of some of Denmark's most important naval figures, including Admiral Niels Juel, who successfully fought off a naval attack by Swedes in 1677 in the epic Battle of Køge Bay. Peder Tordenskjold, who defeated Charles XII of Sweden during the Great Northern War in the early 1700s, is also entombed here. On a lighter note, this is the church in which Queen Margrethe II chose to take her wedding vows in 1967.

Frederikskirke (called the Marble Church). Frederiksgade 4. ☎ **33-15-01-44.** Admission free to church, dome 20 DKK ($2.90) adults, 10 DKK ($1.45) children. Church: Mon–Tues and Thurs–Fri 11am–2pm, Wed 11am–6pm, Sat 11am–4pm, Sun noon–4pm. Dome: June 15–Sept 1 daily 11am–12:45pm; Oct–May, Sat–Sun 11am–12:45pm. Bus: 1, 6, or 9.

This two hundred year–old church, with its green copper dome—one of the largest in the world—is a short walk from Amalienborg Palace. After an unsuccessful start during Denmark's neo-classical revival in the 1750s, the church was finally completed in Roman baroque style in 1894. In many ways it's even more impressive than Copenhagen's cathedral.

Von Frelsers Kirken (Our Savior's Church). Skt. Annægade 29. ☎ **31-57-27-98.** Admission to tower 20 DKK ($2.90) adults, 10 DKK ($1.45) children; church free. Mar–Aug daily 9am–4pm; Sept–Nov daily 9am–3pm; Dec–Feb daily 10am–2pm.

This baroque church with an external tower staircase dates from 1696. Local legend maintains that when the encircling staircase was constructed curving the wrong way, the architect climbed to the top, realized what he'd done, and then committed suicide by jumping. The green and gold tower of this Gothic structure is a Copenhagen landmark, dominating the Christianshavn area. Inside, view the splendid baroque altar, richly adorned with a romp of cherubs and other figures. There is also a lovely font and richly carved organ case. Four hundred steps will take you to the top, where you'll see a gilded figure of Christ standing on a globe, and a panoramic view of the city.

8 A Glimpse into the Past Right Outside Copenhagen

Frilandsmuseet (Open-Air Museum). Kongevejen 100. ☎ **42-85-02-92.** Admission 30 DKK ($4.35) adults, free for children. Easter–Sept, Tues–Sun 10am–5pm; Oct 1–18, Tues–Sun 10am–4pm. Closed Oct 19–Easter. S-tog: From Copenhagen Central Station to Sorgenfri (leaving every 20 minutes). Bus: 184 or 194.

This reconstructed village in Lyngby, on the fringe of Copenhagen, recaptures Denmark's one-time rural character. The "museum" is nearly 90 acres, a 2-mile walk around the compound, and includes a dozen authentically re-created buildings—farmsteads, windmills, and fishers' cottages. Exhibits include a half-timbered 18th-century farmstead from one of the tiny windswept Danish islands, a primitive longhouse from the remote Faroe Islands, thatched fishermen's huts from Jutland, tower windmills, and a potter's workshop from the mid-19th century.

Organized activities are staged on summer afternoons. On one recent visit, folk dancers in native costume performed, and there were demonstrations of lace making and loom weaving.

The park is about 9 miles from the Central Railroad Station. There's an old-style restaurant at the entryway to the museum.

9 Literary Landmarks

Admirers of **Hans Christian Andersen** may want to seek out the various addresses where he lived in Copenhagen, including Nyhavn 18, Nyhavn 20, and Nyhavn 67. He also lived for a time at Vingårdsstræde 6.

Assistens Kirkegård (Assistens Cemetery). Nørrebrogade/Kapelvej. Free admission. May–Aug, daily 8am–8pm; Mar–Apr and Sept–Oct, daily 8am–6pm; Nov–Feb, daily 8am–4pm. Bus: 5, 7E, or 16.

The largest cemetery in Copenhagen, dating from 1711, it contains the tombs of Sören Kierkegaard, H. C. Andersen, and Martin Andersen Nexø, a famous novelist of the working class. The cemetery is now a public park.

Kobenhavns Bymuseet (Copenhagen City Museum). Vesterbrogade 59. ☎ **31-21-07-72.** Admission 30 DKK ($4.35) adults, 10 DKK ($1.45) children. May–Sept, Tues–Sun 10am–4pm; Oct–Apr, Tues–Sun 1–4pm. Bus: 6, 16, 27, or 28.

The permanent exhibition here presents the history of Copenhagen in artifacts and pictures. A smaller separate department is devoted to Sören Kierkegaard (1813–55), the father of existentialism; here you'll find exhibits of his drawings, letters, books, photographs, and personal belongings.

Special & Free Events

Much of Copenhagen is a summer festival, especially at the **Tivoli Gardens.** Although there's an entrance fee, once you're inside, many of the concerts and other presentations are free. A total of 150 performances each summer are presented at the Concert Hall. Of these, more than 100 are free. Pantomime performances at the Pantomime Theater are also free. Performances on the open-air stage are free every night (closed Monday). Likewise, the other amusement park, **Bakken,** has many free events. And you don't have to pay an admission to enter—only if you patronize the various attractions.

The **birthday of Queen Margrethe** on April 16 is a celebration with the queen and the royal family driving through the pedestrian street, Strøget, in a stagecoach escorted by hussars in gala.

A **Ballet and Opera Festival** (mid-May to June) takes place at the Royal Theater, offering classical and modern dance, as well as operatic masterpieces.

Carnival in Copenhagen (May 29–31) is a great event where dressed-up Copenhageners move about the city in samba rhythm. The event culminates in a children's carnival.

The **Copenhagen Jazz Festival** (July 3–12) features the best of international jazz musicians.

The highly acclaimed Royal Dutch Ballet performs at the Royal Theater for the Fall Ballet Festival (mid-August to September 1).

10 Especially for Kids

Copenhagen is a wonderful place for children, and many so-called adult attractions also appeal to children. If you're traveling with children, **Tivoli** is the obvious choice, as is the statue of **the Little Mermaid** at Langelinie. Try also to see the changing of the Queen's Royal Life Guard at **Amalienborg Palace,** including the entire parade to and from that royal residence. Kids also enjoy **Frilandsmuseet,** the open-air museum. (Details on these sights have been given earlier in this chapter.) Other attractions great for kids include the following:

Bakken Amusement Park. Dyrehavevej 62, Klampenborg. ☎ **39-63-73-00.** Free admission. Daily 1pm–midnight. Closed late Aug to late Mar. S-tog: Klampenborg train from the Central Railroad Station to the Klampenborg station (about a 20-minute ride); then walk through the Deer Park or take a horse-drawn cab.

On the northern edge of Copenhagen, about 7 ½ miles from the city center, this amusement park was created 35 years before the Pilgrims landed at Plymouth Rock. It's a local favorite, featuring roller coasters, dancing, the tunnel of love, and a merry-go-round. Open-air restaurants are plentiful, as are snack bars and ice-cream booths. Proceeds from the amusements support this unspoiled natural preserve. There are no cars—only bicycles and horse-drawn carriages.

Denmark's Aquarium. Strandvejen, in Charlottenlund Fort Park, Charlottenlund. ☎ **39-62-32-83.** Admission 55 DKK ($8) adults, 30 DKK ($4.35) children. Mar–Oct, daily 10am–6pm; Nov–Feb, Mon–Fri 10am–4pm, Sat–Sun 10am–5pm. S-tog: Line C to Charlottenlund. Bus: 6.

Opened in 1939 north of Copenhagen along the Øresund coast, this is one of the most extensive aquariums in Europe. Its large tanks are famous for their decoration. Hundreds of salt- and freshwater-species are exhibited. One tank houses bloodthirsty piranha from South America.

Eskperimentarium (Hands-On Science Center). Tuborg Havnevej 7, Hellerup. ☎ **39-27-33-33.** Admission 69 DKK ($10) adults, 49 DKK ($7.10) children 4–14, free for children 3 and under. Daily 10am–5pm. S-tog: Hellerup or Svanemøllen. Bus: 6, 21, or 23.

Located in the old mineral water–bottling hall of Tuborg breweries, this museum has a hands-on approach to science. Its director claims that it's one of the most extensive and technologically advanced museums of its type in northern Europe. Visitors use not only their hands but all of their senses as they participate in some 300 exhibitions and demonstrations divided into three themes: "Man," "Nature," and "The Interaction Between Man and Nature." Visitors hear what all the world's languages sound like, make a wind machine blow up to hurricane force, check their skin to test how much sun it can take, dance in an "inverted" disco, or visit a slimming machine. Families can work as a team to examine enzymes, make a camera from paper, or test perfume. Exhibitions change frequently.

Louis Tussaud Wax Museum. H. C. Andersens Blvd. 22. ☎ **33-11-89-00.** Admission 58 DKK ($8.40) adults, 25 DKK ($3.60) children. Apr 29–Sept 13, daily 10am–11pm; Sept 14–Apr 28, daily 10am–6pm. Bus: 1, 2, 16, 28, 29, or 41.

Now a part of Tivoli, the Louis Tussaud Wax Museum is a major commercial attraction in Copenhagen. It features more than 200 wax figures—everybody from Danish kings and queens to Leonardo da Vinci. Children can visit the Snow Queen's Castle, or watch Frankenstein and Dracula guard the monsters and vampires.

Tycho Brahe Planetarium. Gammel Kongevej 10. ☎ **33-12-12-24.** Admission 15 DKK ($2.15) adults, 10 DKK ($1.45) children; 45–68 DKK ($6.50–$9.85), depending on the show, for Omnimax films. Daily 10:30am–9:30pm. Bus: 1 or 14.

The marvel of the night sky, with its planets, galaxies, star clusters, and comets, is created by a star projector using the planetarium dome as a screen and space theater. Named after the famed Danish astronomer Tycho Brahe (1546–1601), the planetarium also stages Omnimax film productions. There's an information center and a restaurant.

Zoologisk Have (Copenhagen Zoo). Roskildevej 32, Frederiksberg. ☎ **36-30-25-55.** Admission 60 DKK ($8.70) adults, 30 DKK ($4.35) children. Daily 9am–6pm. S-tog: Valby. Bus: 6, 18, 28, 39, or 550S.

With more than 2,000 animals from Greenland to Africa, this zoo boasts spacious new habitats for reindeer and musk oxen as well as an open roaming area for lions. Take a ride up the small wooden Eiffel Tower, or walk across the street and let your kids enjoy the petting zoo. The zoo is mobbed on Sundays.

WALKING TOUR 1
The Old City

Start: Rådhuspladsen.
Finish: Tivoli Gardens.
Time: 1 ½ hours.
Best times: Any sunny day.
Worst Times: Rush hours (Monday to Friday from 7:30 to 9am and 5 to 6:30pm).

Start at:

1. **Rådhuspladsen** (Town Hall Square), in the center of Copenhagen. You can stop in at the Town Hall, but even more appealing is a bronze statue of Hans Christian Andersen, the spinner of fairy tales, which stands near a boulevard bearing his name. Also on this square is a statue of two *lur* horn players that have stood here since 1914.

   Bypassing the *lur* horn players, walk east along Vester Voldgade onto a narrow street on your left:

2. **Lavendelstræde.** Many houses along here date from the late 18th century. At Lavendelstræde 1, Mozart's widow (Constanze) lived with her second husband, Georg Nikolaus Nissen, a Danish diplomat, from 1812 to 1820.

   The little street quickly becomes Slutterigade.

3. **Courthouses** rise on both sides of this short street, joined by elevated walkways. Built between 1805 and 1815, this was Copenhagen's fourth town hall, now the city's major law courts. The main courthouse entrance is on Nytorv.

   Slutterigade will lead to:

4. **Nytorv,** a famous square where you can admire fine 19th-century houses. Sören Kierkegaard, the noted philosopher (1813–55), lived in a house adjacent to the courthouse.

   Cross Nytorv, and veer slightly west (to your left) until you reach Nygade, part of the famed:

5. **Strøget,** a traffic-free shopping street. At this point it goes under a different name. (Actually it began at Rådhuspladsen and was called Frederiksberggade.) The major shopping street of Scandinavia, Strøget is a stroller's and a shopper's delight, following a three-quarter-mile–long trail through the heart of Copenhagen.

   Nygade is one of the five streets that comprise Strøget. Head northeast along this street, which quickly becomes winding and narrow Vimmelskaftet, which turns into Amagertorv. Along Amagertorv, you'll come across the:

6. Helligåndskirken (Church of the Holy Ghost), on your left, with its 15th-century abbey, Helligåndshuset. This is the oldest church in Copenhagen, founded at the beginning of the 15th century. Partially destroyed in 1728, it was reconstructed in 1880 in a neoclassical style. Some of the buildings on this street date from 1616. The sales rooms of the Royal Porcelain Factory are at Amagertorv 6.

Next you'll come to Østergade, the last portion of Strøget. You'll see Illum's department store on your left.

Østergade leads to:

7. Kongens Nytorv, Copenhagen's largest square, with many interesting buildings surrounding it and the equestrian statue of Christian IV in the center. The statue is a bronze replica of a 1688 sculpture. (For more about this square, see "Walking Tour 2," below.)

At Kongens Nytorv, head right until you come to Laksegade. Then go south along this street until you reach the intersection with Nikolajgade. Turn right. This street will lead to the:

8. Nikolaj Church, dating from 1530, and the scene of the thundering sermons of Hans Tausen, a father of the Danish Reformation.

☕ **TAKE A BREAK**   A mellow spot for a pick-me-up, either a refreshing cool drink or an open-faced sandwich, the **Cafeen Nikolaj,** Nikolaj Plads 12 (☎ **33-11-63-13**), attracts both older shoppers and young people. You can sit and linger over a cup of coffee, and no one is likely to hurry you. You can visit any time in the afternoon, perhaps making it your luncheon stopover.

Not open on a Sunday.

After viewing the church, head left down Fortunstræde to:

9. Højbro Plads, off Gammel Strand. You'll have a good view of Christiansborg Palace and Thorvaldsen's Museum on Slotsholmen. On Højbro Plads is an equestrian statue honoring Bishop Absalon, who founded Copenhagen in 1167. Several handsome buildings line the square.

Continue west along:

10. Gammel Strand, which means "old shore." From this waterfront promenade, the former edge of Copenhagen, you'll have a good view across to Christiansborg Palace. A number of interesting old buildings line this street, and at the end you'll come upon the Ministry of Cultural Affairs, occupying a former government pawnbroking establishment, dating from 1730.

To the right of this building, walk up:

11. Snaregade, an old-fashioned provincial street, typical of the old city. Walk until you reach Knabrostræde. Both these streets boast structures built just after the great fire of 1795. Where the streets intersect, you'll see the Church of Our Lady.

Make your way back to Snaregade, and turn right to:

12. Magstræde, one of Copenhagen's best-preserved streets. Proceed along to Rådhusstræde. Just before you reach Rådhusstræde, notice the two buildings facing that street. These are the oldest structures in the city, dating from the 16th century.

Walk across Vandkunsten, a square at the end of Magstræde, then turn right down Gasegade, which doesn't go very far before you turn left along Farvergade. At this street's intersection with Vester Voldgade you'll see the Vartov Church. Continue west until you reach Rådhuspladsen. Across the square, you'll see the:

13. Tivoli Gardens, whose entrance is at Vesterbrogade 3. Attracting some 4 ½ million visitors every summer, this amusement park has 25 different entertainment choices and attractions and just as many restaurants and beer gardens.

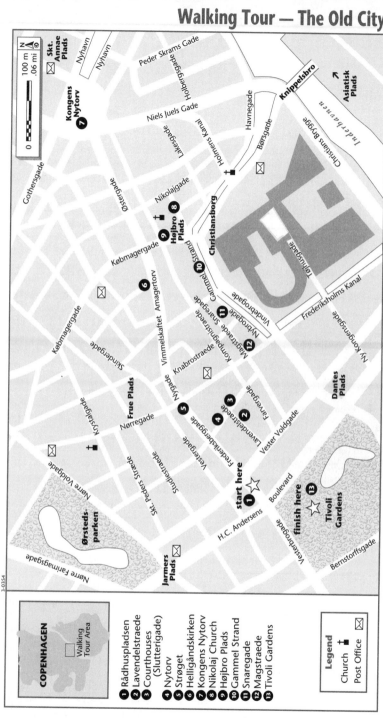

COPENHAGEN

Walking Tour Area

1. Rådhuspladsen
2. Lavendelstraede
3. Courthouses (Slutterigade)
4. Nytorv
5. Strøget
6. Helligåndskirken
7. Kongens Nytorv
8. Nikolaj Church
9. Højbro Plads
10. Gammel Strand
11. Snaregade
12. Magstraede
13. Tivoli Gardens

Legend
Church
Post Office

WALKING TOUR 2
Kongens Nytorv to Langelinie

Start: Kongens Nytorv.
Finish: The Little Mermaid.
Time: 1 ½ hours.
Best Times: Any sunny day.
Worst Times: Rush hours (Monday to Friday from 7:30 to 9am and 5 to 6:30pm).
Although the Nyhavn quarter, once a boisterous sailors' town, has quieted down, it's still a charming part of old Copenhagen with its 1673 canal and 18th-century houses.

To explore the area, begin at:

1. **Kongens Nytorv,** containing Magasin, the biggest department store in the capital, plus an equestrian statue of Christian IV. Kongens Nytorv, which means "King's New Market," dates from 1680. On the northeast side of the square is:

2. **Thott's Mansion,** completed in 1685 for a Danish naval hero and restored in 1760. It now houses the French Embassy. Between Bredgade and Store Strandstræde, a little street angling to the right near Nyhavn, is Kanneworff House, a beautifully preserved, privately owned house dating from 1782. On the west side of the square, at no. 34, is the Hotel d'Angleterre, the best in Copenhagen. There is also an old anchor memorializing the Danish seamen who died in World War II.
   On the southeast side of the square stands the:

3. **Royal Theater,** founded in 1748, where ballet, opera, and plays are presented. Statues of famous Danish dramatists are out front. The present theater, constructed in 1874, is in a neo-Renaissance style.
   With your back to the Hotel d'Angleterre, walk toward the water along:

4. **Nyhavn,** once filled with seamen's bars and lodgings and shipping establishments. Nowadays it has become a restaurant row. First, walk along the north (left) side of Nyhavn. In summer, cafe tables border the canal, and the whole strip takes on a festive atmosphere. At the port end of the canal you can see the Naval Dockyards, and Christianshavn across the harbor. High-speed craft come and go all day here, connecting Copenhagen with Malmö, Sweden.
   On the quieter side of the canal (the south), you can see:

5. **Charlottenborg Palace,** now the Danish Academy of Fine Arts. A pure baroque building, it takes its name from Queen Charlotte Amalie, who lived here in the eighteenth century. Beautiful old homes, antiques shops, and more restaurants line the southern flank. Nyhavn was also the home of Hans Christian Andersen at various times: no. 20 where he wrote his first fairy tales in 1835, no. 67 from 1845 to 1864, and no. 18 where he spent the last 2 years of his life, dying there in 1875.
   Walk to the end of Nyhavn toward the harbor and turn left onto Kvæsthusgade, which will take you to:

6. **Skt. Annæ Plads,** where ferries depart for Oslo. Many consulates, two hotels, and fine old buildings open onto this square. Walking inland along the plads, turn right onto Amaliegade, which leads under a colonnade into the cobblestone Amalienborg Plads, site of:

7. **Amalienborg Palace,** with a statue of Frederik V standing in its core. When the queen is in residence, there's a daily changing of the guard here at noon. The palace is the official residence of the queen and her French prince, but sections of it are open to the public. Four identical mansion-like palaces flank this square. The queen lives in the right wing next to the colonnade.
   Between the square and the harbor are the gardens of:

Walking Tour — Kongens Nytorv to Langelinie

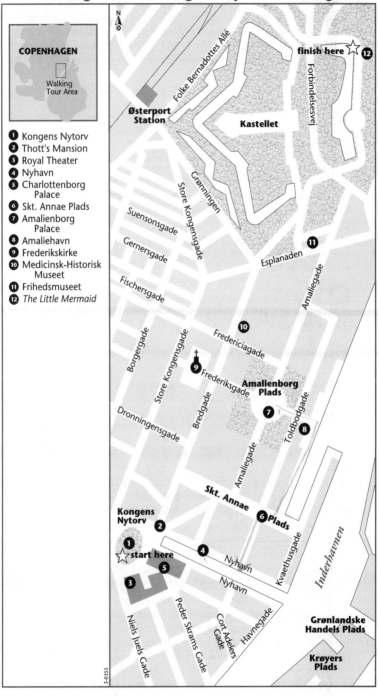

COPENHAGEN

Walking Tour Area

1. Kongens Nytorv
2. Thott's Mansion
3. Royal Theater
4. Nyhavn
5. Charlottenborg Palace
6. Skt. Annae Plads
7. Amalienborg Palace
8. Amaliehavn
9. Frederikskirke
10. Medicinsk-Historisk Museet
11. Frihedsmuseet
12. *The Little Mermaid*

finish here

Forbindelsesvej

Folke Bernadottes Allé

Kastellet

Østerport Station

Grønningen

Store Kongensgade

Suensonsgade

Gernersgade

Fischersgade

Esplanaden

Amaliegade

Fredericiagade

Borgergade

Store Kongensgade

Frederiksgade

Amalienborg Plads

Bredgade

Dronningensgade

Amaliegade

Toldbodgade

Skt. Annae Plads

Kongens Nytorv

start here

Nyhavn

Nyhavn

Kvaethusgade

Inderhavnen

Niels Juels Gade

Peder Skrams Gade

Cort Adelers Gade

Havnegade

Grønlandske Handels Plads

Krøyers Plads

3-0355

8. Amaliehavn. Among the most beautiful in Copenhagen, these gardens were laid out by Jean Delogne, who made lavish use of Danish granite along with limestone imported from France. The bronze pillars around the fountain were the work of Arnaldo Pomodoro, an Italian sculptor.

After viewing the waterfront gardens, walk away from the water, crossing Amalienborg Plads and emerging onto Frederiksgade. Continue along this short street until you reach:

9. Frederikskirke, at no. 1. Often called the Marmorkirken or "marble church," construction of this building, begun in 1740, had to stop in 1770 because of the staggering costs. The church wasn't completed until 1894 (finally, Danish marble was used instead of the more expensive, imported Norwegian marble). The church was modeled on and intended to rival St. Peter's in Rome; indeed, it ended up with one of the largest domes of any church in Europe. Supported on a dozen towering piers, the dome has a diameter of 108 feet.

Facing the church, turn right and head north along Bredgade; stop at no. 22, the:

10. Medicinsk-Historisk Museet (Medical History Museum), which traces the history of medicine. The collection is gruesome, with aborted fetuses, dissected heads, and the like.

☕ **TAKE A BREAK**   Before you approach the Little Mermaid, consider tea and a snack at **Café Lumskebugten,** Esplanaden 21 (☎ **33-15-60-29**) (see chapter 4). Dating from 1854, this cafe offers a cold plate served throughout the afternoon. There are five specialties: beef tartare, fish cakes with mustard sauce, marinated salmon, baked cod, and shrimp.

Bredgade comes to an end at the Esplanaden, which opens onto Churchillparken, a green belt bordering the water. Turn right and walk along Esplanaden until you come to the:

11. Frihedsmuseet, Churchillparken, the Danish resistance museum depicting the struggle of the Danish people against the Nazis from 1940 to 1945.

After leaving the museum, walk toward the water along Langelinie where signs point the way to:

12. The Little Mermaid. Perched on rocks just off the harbor bank, *Den Lille Havfrue* dates from 1913. The bronze figure, by Edvard Eriksen, was modeled after the figure of Ellen Price, a prima ballerina. In time, this much-attacked and abused statue became the symbol of Copenhagen. It's the most photographed statue in all of Scandinavia.

11 Organized Tours

BUS & BOAT TOURS   There are a number of boat and bus sightseeing tours in Copenhagen, ranging from get-acquainted jaunts to in-depth tours. Inexpensive bus tours depart from the *lur* horn-blowers statue at Town Hall Square, and boat trips leave from either Gammel Strand (the fish market) or Nyhavn.

For orientation, try the **1 ½-hour City Tour** (2 ½ hours with a visit to a brewery), which covers major scenic highlights like the Little Mermaid, Rosenborg Castle, and Amalienborg Palace. On weekdays tours also visit the Carlsberg brewery. Tours depart May 30 to September 13 daily at 1pm, and cost 125 DKK ($18.15) for adults, 20 DKK ($2.90) for children.

We heartily recommend the **City and Harbor Tour,** a 2 ½-hour trip by launch and bus, departing from Town Hall Square. The boat tours the city's main canals, passing the Little Mermaid and the Old Fish Market. It operates May 30 to September 13, daily at 1pm. These tours cost 165 DKK ($23.90) for adults, 30 DKK ($4.35) for children.

Shakespeare buffs will be interested in an afternoon excursion to the castles of North Zealand. The 7-hour tour explores the area north of Copenhagen, including visits to Kronborg (Hamlet's Castle); a brief visit to Fredensborg, the queen's residence; and a stopover at Frederiksborg Castle and the National Historical Museum. Tours depart from Town Hall Square, May 2 to October 16, Wednesday, Saturday, and Sunday at 10:15am. The cost is 335 DKK ($48.55) for adults, 40 DKK ($5.80) for children.

For more information about these tours and the most convenient place for you to purchase tickets in advance, call **Vikingbus** (☎ 31-57-26-00) or **Copenhagen Excursions** (☎ 32-54-06-06).

GUIDED WALKS   English-language guided walking tours of Copenhagen are offered during the summer. The price is 40 DKK ($5.80) for adults, 20 DKK ($2.90) for children. For information, contact the **Copenhagen Tourist Information Center,** Bernstorffsgade 1 (☎ 33-11-13-25).

BREWERY TOUR   Free 90-minute tours are offered by the **Carlsberg Brewery,** Ny Carlsberg Vej 140 (☎ 33-27-13-14, ext. 1312), Monday to Friday at 11am and 2pm (take bus no. 6 from Rådhuspladsen). Visitors are escorted through the brew houses and along the production line, and each tour ends with a beer party where guests can sample the products. The swastika on the Carlsberg elephant doesn't mean the company was a Nazi sympathizer—Carlsberg used the symbol long before Hitler. The factory turns out 3 million bottles of beer a day.

12 Active Sports

BICYCLING   The absence of hills plus the abundance of parks and wide avenues with bicycle lanes makes cycling the best way to explore Copenhagen. Bike-rental shops and stands are scattered throughout the city. Two suggestions are **Københavns Cyclebørs,** Track 12, in the Central Railroad Station (☎ 33-14-07-17), and **Urania Cykler,** Gammel Kongevej 1 (☎ 33-21-80-88).

FITNESS   **Form & Fitness,** located at Øster Allé 42E (☎ 35-55-00-78), offers a day pass for 75 DKK ($10.90). Aerobics, various weights, and fitness machines are available Monday to Thursday from 6:30am to 9:30pm, Friday from 6:30am to 8pm, and Saturday and Sunday from 8am to 5pm.

GOLF   Denmark's best-known golf course, and one of its most challenging, is at the **Rungsted Golf Klub,** Vestre Stationsvej 16 (☎ 45-86-34-14). Established in 1937 in the heart of Denmark's "Whisky Trail" (a string of upper-crust homes and mansions known for their allure for retirees), the club's 18 holes are popular among golfers visiting from around the world. Some degree of golf-related competence is required for anyone wanting to play here, so if you're a beginner or intermediate, it might be wise to rehearse your drive swing elsewhere before coming here. If you're an advanced golfer, call for information and to arrange a tee time. Greens fees cost between 325 and 375 DKK ($47.15–$54.35) for a full day's use of the club's 18 holes. To play, you must present evidence of a handicap index of 20 for games on Saturday and Sunday, and 25 for games Monday to Friday. If you give advance notification, they'll rent you a set of clubs for 250 DKK ($36.25). The course is closed between November and March. No motorized buggies (i.e. golf carts) are allowed on the ecologically fragile terrain of this course.

Another course—one that welcomes novice golfers—is **Copenhagen Pay & Play,** Smørum Golfcenter (☎ **44-97-01-11**). This course is open year-round, daily from 8am to 10pm. Greens fees range from 15 to 200 DKK ($2.15–$29).

JOGGING   The many parks and green lungs of Copenhagen provide endless routes for joggers. Our favorite, just west of the city center, circles Lakes Sortedams, St. Jorgens, and Peblinge. The paths that wind through the Frederiksborg gardens are also well suited for joggers.

SWIMMING   Swimming is a favorite pastime among the Danes. The **Frederiksborg Svømmehal,** Helgesvej 29 (☎ **38-14-04-04**), a public swimming pool, is open Monday to Friday from 8am to 8pm, Saturday from 8am to 2pm, and Sunday from 9:30am to 2:15pm. Tickets cost 30 DKK ($4.35). You can also try **Sundby Swimming-pool,** Sundbyvestervej 50 (☎ **32-58-55-68**); **Kildeskovshallen,** Adolphsvej 25 (☎ **39-68-28-22**); or **Vesterbro Swimming Baths,** Angelgade 4 (☎ **31-22-05-00**).

SQUASH   The **Copenhagen Squash Club,** Vestersøhus, Vester Søgade (☎ **33-11-86-38**), rents courts as well as racquets and balls. Courts cost 130 DKK ($18.85) per hour. Call between 3 and 9:30pm to reserve.

TENNIS   Nonmembers and nonguests usually pay a large supplement to play tennis at any of the various hotels and clubs in Copenhagen. There's a high hourly rate, and courts must be reserved in advance. Try the **Hotel Mercur,** Vester Farimagsgade 17 (☎ **33-12-57-11**); visitors pay 130 DKK ($18.85) for the first hour, and 100 DKK ($14.50) for each additional hour. Another club you might try is **København Boldklub,** Peter Nagsvej 147 (☎ **38-71-41-80**).

13 Shopping

Copenhagen is in the vanguard of shopping in Europe, and much of the action takes place on **Strøget,** the pedestrian street in the heart of the capital. Strøget begins as Frederiksberggade, north of Rådhuspladsen, and winds to Østergade, which opens onto Kongens Nytorv. This jam-packed street is lined with stores selling everything from porcelain statues of *Youthful Boldness* to Greenland shrimp to Kay Bojesen's teak monkeys.

Between stops, relax with a drink at an outdoor cafe or just sit on a bench and watch the crowds.

Two other walking areas are nearby—**Gråbødretorv** and **Fiolstræde**—where you can browse through antiques shops and bookstores.

Bredgade, beginning at Kongens Nytorv, is the antiques district of Copenhagen. Prices tend to be very high. **Læderstræde** is another shopping street that competes with Bredgade for antiques.

BEST BUYS   In a country famed for its designers and craftspeople, you'll find your best buys in stainless steel, porcelain, china, glassware, toys (especially Kay Bojesen's wooden animals), functionally designed furniture, textiles (napkins to rugs), and jewelry (decorative, silver, and semiprecious stones).

STORE HOURS   In general, shopping hours are Monday to Thursday from 9:30 or 10am to 5:30pm, until 7 or 8pm on Friday, and until 2pm on Saturday. Most shops are closed Sunday except the kiosks and supermarket at the Central Railroad Station, where you can purchase food until 10pm or midnight. The Central Railroad Station's bakery is open until 9pm, and one of the kiosks at Rådhuspladsen, selling newspapers, film, and souvenirs, is open 24 hours.

SHIPPING IT HOME & RECOVERING VAT   Denmark imposes a 25% tax on goods and services, a "value-added tax" known in Denmark as MOMS (pronounced "mumps"). However, special tax-free exports are possible. Many stores will mail goods to your home so you can avoid paying the tax. If you want to take your purchases with you, look for shops displaying Danish tax-free shopping notices. Such shops offer tourists tax refunds for personal exports. This refund applies to purchases of over 300 DKK ($43.50) for visitors from the United States and Canada. Your tax-free invoice must be stamped by Danish Customs when you leave the country. You can receive your refund at Copenhagen's Kastrup International Airport when you depart. If you depart by land or by sea, you can receive your refund by mail.

The 300 DKK must be spent in one store for the refund to apply, but some major department stores allow purchases to be made over several days or even weeks, at the end of which the receipts will be tallied. Service and handling fees are deducted from the total, so actual refunds come to about 18%. Information on this program is available from the Danish Tourist Board (see "Taxes" in "Fast Facts: Denmark," in chapter 3).

Tax refund questions can be answered by calling **Europe Tax-Free Shopping** at ☎ **33-52-55-66.**

AMBER
The Amber Specialist. Frederiksberggade 28. ☎ **33-11-88-03.** Bus: 28, 29, or 41.

Customers refer to the two owners as "The Amber Twins," two blonde-haired ladies who deal in amber, "the gold of the north." This amber, or petrified resin, originated from the large coniferous forests that covered Denmark some 35 million years ago. The forest disappeared but the amber remained, and is now used to create handsome jewelry. There is a large collection of amber set in 14-karat gold.

ART GALLERIES & AUCTION HOUSES
Bruun Rasmussen. Bredgade 33. ☎ **33-13-69-11.** Bus: 1, 6, 9, or 10.

Established shortly after World War II, this is the leading auction house in Denmark. The new season begins in August with an auction of paintings and fine artworks. July is usually quiet, although the premises remain open for appraisals and purchases. Viewing time is allowed before auctions, which take place about once a month. There are also auctions of wine, coins, books, manuscripts, and antique weapons.

Galerie Asbaek. Bredgade 20. ☎ **33-15-40-04.** Bus: 1, 6, 9, 10, 28, 29, or 41.

This modern-art gallery has a permanent exhibition of the best local artists along with changing exhibitions of Scandinavian and foreign artists. There's a book-shop and a cafe serving French-inspired Danish food. Graphics and posters are available for purchase.

Kunsthallens Kunstauktioner. Gothersgade 9. ☎ **33-32-52-00.** Bus: 1, 6, 9, or 10.

Established in 1926, this is Europe's leading dealer in the pan-European school of painting known as COBRA (the acronym for **Co**penhagen, **Br**ussels, and **A**msterdam, the artists' home cities). These works, produced from 1948 to 1951, were an important precursor of abstract expressionism. The gallery holds 12 auctions yearly, 8 with modern art; the others concentrate on the 19th century.

BOOKS
Boghallen. Rådhuspladsen 37. ☎ **33-11-85-11.** Bus: 2, 8, or 30.

This big store on Town Hall Square carries many books in English, as well as a wide selection of travel-related literature, including maps. You can also purchase books (in English) on Danish themes, such as the collected works of H. C. Andersen.

DEPARTMENT STORES

Illum's. Østergade 52. ☎ **33-14-40-02.** Bus: 1, 6, 9, or 10.

One of Denmark's top department stores, Illum's is located on Strøget. Take time to browse through its vast world of Danish and Scandinavian design. There's a restaurant and a special export cash desk at street level.

✪ **Magasin.** Kongens Nytorv 13. ☎ **33-11-44-33.** Bus: 1, 6, 9, or 10.

The elegant Magasin is the biggest department store in Scandinavia. It offers a complete assortment of Danish designer fashion, a large selection of glass and porcelain, and souvenirs. Goods are shipped abroad tax-free.

FASHIONS

Brodrene Andersen. Østergade 9. ☎ **33-15-15-77.** Bus: 1, 6, 9, or 10.

A distinguished purveyor of "personal furnishings for gentlemen" (and increasingly for women), this store has an atmosphere of quiet dignity. The clothes are mostly German and Italian and, to a lesser degree, French.

Sweater Market. Frederiksberggade 15. ☎ **33-15-27-73.** Bus: 2, 8, or 30.

Take your pick from Scandinavian and Icelandic top-grade cardigans, pullovers, hats, scarves, and mittens, hand-knit in Denmark with pure 100% wool. There's also a large selection of Icelandic wool jackets and coats.

FLEA MARKETS

Det Blå Pakhus. Holmbladsgade 113. ☎ **32-95-17-07.** Bus: 5, or 37.

Copenhagen's largest indoor market place has 325 booths, selling a little bit of everything. The motto of "The Blue Warehouse" is that you can find "everything between heaven and earth here," and they're probably right. It's a flea market paradise, complete with second-hand furniture, antiques, carpets, assorted bric-a-brac, and all sorts of knickknacks. It is only open Saturday and Sunday between 10am to 5pm, and charges an entrance of 5 DKK (75¢).

FURS

✪ **Birger Christensen.** Østergade 38. ☎ **33-11-55-55.** Bus: 28, 29, or 41.

This is one of Scandinavia's leading fur shops. It has its own designer line and also features furs and fashions by some of the world's leading designers, including Sonia Rykiel, Chanel, Hermes, and Donna Karan. You can also purchase—cheaper than the furs—a selection of cashmere or wool blended coats with fur lining and fur trim. This is swank shopping and very, very, expensive.

GLASSWARE, PORCELAIN & CRYSTAL

Danborg. Holbergsgade 17. ☎ **33-32-93-94.** Bus: 1, 6, or 9.

This shop behind the Royal Theatre offers a large selection of Flora Danica porcelain at reduced prices. It also specializes in antique quality Georg Jensen pieces, and you can sometimes save up to 50% on Georg Jensen estate silver. There is also exquisite jewelry sold here.

Holmegaards Glasværker. In the Royal Copenhagen retail center, Amagertorv 6 (Strøget). ☎ **33-12-44-77.** Bus: 1, 6, 8, 9, or 10.

This is the only major producer of glasswork in Denmark. Its Wellington pattern, for example, was created in 1859 and is still available here. The Holmegaard glasses and the Regiment Bar set reflect solid craftsmanship.

Rosenthal Studio-Haus. Frederiksberggade 21. ☎ **33-14-21-01.** Bus: 28, 29, or 41.

There's an array of ceramic works here, especially by well-known Danish artist Bjørn Wiinblad, whose figures we find whimsical and delightful. You can also get some good buys on Orrefors Crystal, including some stunning bowls. The sculptural bas-reliefs, handmade in lead crystal, range from miniatures to giant animal reliefs in limited 199-piece world editions. Often the animals of the far north are depicted.

✪ **Royal Copenhagen and Bing & Grøndahl Porcelain.** In the Royal Copenhagen retail center, Amagertorv 6 (Strøget). ☎ **33-13-71-81.** Bus: 1, 2, 6, 8, 28, 29, or 41 for the retail outlet; 1 or 14 for the factory.

Royal Copenhagen's trademark, three wavy blue lines, has come to symbolize quality in porcelain throughout the world. Founded in 1775, the factory was a royal possession for a century before passing into private hands in 1868. Royal Copenhagen's Christmas plates are collectors' items. The factory has turned out a new plate each year since 1908, most of the designs depicting the Danish countryside in winter. There's a huge selection of seconds on the top floor, and unless you're an expert, you probably can't tell the difference. Visitors are welcome at the **factory** at Smallegade 45 (☎ **31-86-48-48**), where 25 DKK ($3.60) tours are given Monday to Friday at 9am, 10am, 11am, 1pm, and 2pm. (These tours can be arranged by contacting the Royal Copenhagen store at the phone number listed above.) Purchases cannot be made at the factory.

There are also various porcelain and silver retailers in this same location, as well as the Royal Copenhagen Antiques shop, which specializes in buying and selling antique Georg Jensen, Royal Copenhagen, Bing & Grøndahl Porcelain, and Michelson Christmas Spoons.

Skandinavisk Glas/A. B. Schou. Ny Østergade 4. ☎ **33-13-80-95.** Bus: 1, 6, 9, or 10.

This store carries porcelain pieces from Royal Copenhagen, Baccarat crystal, porcelain from Ginovi in Italy, Hummels from Germany, Orrefors from Sweden, Lladro` from Spain, and Wedgwood from England. If you like to comparison-shop among famous competitors, this is the place. The exhibition of collectors' plates is the largest in Scandinavia.

GOOSE DOWN COMFORTERS
Ofelia. Amagertorv 3. ☎ **33-12-41-98.** Bus: 28, 29, or 41.

If you'd like to snuggle under a goose down comforter on a winter's night, head for this cozy shop noted for its traditional craftsmanship and superb quality. You'll find it along the Strøget.

INTERIOR DESIGN
Hanne Gundelach. Bredgade 56. ☎ **33-11-33-96.** Bus: 28, 29, or 41.

At this house of art and design, you can purchase works by David Marshall, the well-known sculptor and designer. Handmade interior design objects are hand-cast in a method dating back to the Romans, producing a rustic appearance. The outlet also represents the well-known artist Guillermo Silva, known for beautiful sculptures, tableware, candlesticks, and bowls.

HOME FURNISHINGS
✪ **Illums Bolighus.** Amagertorv 10 (Strøget). ☎ **33-14-19-41.** Bus: 28, 29, or 41.

This center for modern Scandinavian and Danish design is one of Europe's finest showcases for household furnishings and accessories. Browse through furniture, lamps, rugs, textiles, bedding, glassware, kitchenware, flatware, china, jewelry, and ceramics. The store also sells fashions and accessories for women and men. There's even a gift shop.

Lysberg, Hansen & Therp. Bredgade 3. ☎ **33-14-47-87.** Bus: 1, 6, 9, or 10.

This shop, founded before World War I, is a major interior-decorating center offering fabrics, carpets, and furniture. Admire the decorated apartments furnished with impeccable taste. The company manufactures its own furniture in traditional design and imports fabrics, usually from Germany or France. Try to visit their gift shop, which has many hard-to-find items.

✪ **Paustian.** Kalkbrænderiløbskaj 2. ☎ **39-16-65-65.** S-tog: Nordhavn.

The leading furniture showroom in Copenhagen, located in the somewhat distant industrial Nordhavn section, will ship purchases anywhere in the world. The finest of Scandinavian design is on display, along with reproductions of the classics. There's a well-recommended adjoining restaurant.

MUSIC
Axel Musik. In Scala Center (first floor), Axeltorv 2. ☎ **33-14-05-50.** Bus: 1, 6, or 8.

Known as one of the best-stocked music stores in the Danish capital, Axel also has a newer branch in the city's main railway station.

NEEDLEWORK
Eva Rosenstand A/S—Clara Wæver. Østergade 42. ☎ **33-13-29-40.** Bus: 1, 6, 9, or 10.

Danish-designed cross-stitch embroideries are sold here. The material is usually medium or coarser grades of linen, but cotton is also available. There's also an admission-free needlework museum on the premises, the only one of its kind in Europe.

PEWTER & SILVER
✪ **Georg Jensen.** In the Royal Copenhagen retail center, Amagertorv 6 (Strøget). ☎ **33-11-40-80.** Bus: 1, 6, 8, 9, or 10.

Legendary Georg Jensen is known for its fine silver. For the connoisseur, there's no better address, for it displays the largest and best collection of Jensen hollowware in Europe. The store also features gold and silver jewelry in traditional and modern Danish designs.

Peter Krog. Bredgade 4. ☎ **33-12-45-55.** Bus: 1, 6, 8, 9, or 10.

Peter Krog features fine silver, jewelry, and objets d'art of outstanding quality and value, bought up in the sales of large estates and reconditioned if necessary. Occasionally, in addition to Russian works of art, there are works by Carl Fabergé, and the establishment carries an extensive selection of Georg Jensen used silver. Visits are by appointment only.

SHOPPING CENTERS
In addition to the centers described below, for excellent buys in Scandinavian merchandise, as well as tax-free goods, we recommend the **shopping center at the airport.** A VAT-refund office is located nearby.

Bolten's. Store Kongensgade 5/Gothersgade 8. ☎ **33-32-44-44.** Bus: 1, 6, or 9.

One of the city's more imaginative renovations was named after Baron Bolten, the original occupant of one of the dozen or so 18th-century buildings whose façades were kept intact while the interiors were renovated in 1991. Near Kongens Nytorv and the Hotel d'Angleterre, this small-scale development incorporates private offices and apartments, a series of traffic-free interior courtyards filled with flowers, and a handful of shops, restaurants, and cafes. The half-dozen shops usually sell original merchandise fabricated in-house, including children's clothing, lacy undergarments, hats, and shoes. There are also two discos (the Kitsch and X-Ray Underground) on the premises, as well as a theater for occasional comedy acts or satire, and scattered gallery space (some of it underground) for modern art, which is displayed and sold from time to time. There's also a ticket kiosk that can arrange bookings for cultural events throughout Copenhagen.

VIKING JEWELRY
Museums Kopi Smykker. Frederiksberggade 2. ☎ **33-32-63-60.** Bus: 28, 29, or 41.

This is a shop selling museum jewelry reproductions, all authentic copies of jewelry found in Scandinavia, the Baltic region, and even Germany, Britain, and the Netherlands. The jewelry covers a wide range of periods, including the Bronze and the Iron Ages, although the hottest selling items are from the Viking era. The jewelry is created at Vissenbjerg on the island of Funen where it is cast and handcrafted. This ancient jewelry—often copies of pieces you can see on display in the National and other major museums—is made in bronze, sterling silver, and gold-plated sterling silver, and it also comes in 8- and 14-karat gold.

14 Copenhagen After Dark

Danes really know how to party. A good night means a late night, and on warm weekends, hundreds of rowdy revelers crowd Strøget until sunrise. Merrymaking in Copenhagen is not just for the younger crowd; jazz clubs, traditional beer houses, and wine cellars are routinely packed with people of all ages. Of course, the city has a more highbrow cultural side as well, exemplified by excellent theaters, operas, ballets, and one of the best circuses in Europe.

To find out what's happening at the time of your visit, pick up a free copy of *Copenhagen This Week* at the tourist information center. The section marked "Events Calendar" has a week-by-week roundup of the most interesting entertainment and sightseeing events in the Danish capital.

TIVOLI
In the center of the gardens, the large **open-air stage** books vaudeville acts (tumbling clowns, acrobats, aerialists) who give performances Sunday to Friday at 7 and 10:30pm, and on Saturday at 5, 7, and 10:30pm. Spectators must enter through the turnstiles for seats, but there's an unobstructed view from outside if you prefer to stand. Special arrangements with jazz and folklore groups are made during the season. Admission is free.

The 150-year-old outdoor **Pantomime Theater,** with its Chinese stage and peacock curtain, is located near the Tivoli's Vesterbrogade 3 entrance and presents shows Tuesday to Sunday at 6:15 and 8:30pm. The repertoire consists of 16 different *commedia dell'arte* productions featuring the entertaining trio, Pierrot, Columbine, and Harlequin—these are authentic pantomimes that have been performed continuously in Copenhagen since 1844. Admission is free.

The modern **Tivolis Koncertsal** (concert hall) is a great place to hear famous and talented artists, led by equally famous conductors. Inaugurated in 1956, the concert hall can seat 2,000, and its season—which begins in late April and lasts for more than 4 months—has been called "the most extensive music festival in the world." Performances of everything from symphony to opera are presented Monday to Saturday at

7pm, and sometimes at 9pm, depending on the event. Good seats are available at prices ranging from 200 to 400 DKK ($29–$58) when major artists are performing—but most performances are free. Tickets are sold at the main booking office on Vesterbrogade 3 (☎ **33-15-10-12**).

Tivoli Glassalen (☎ **33-15-10-12**) is housed in a century-old octagonal gazebo-like building with a glass, gilt-capped canopy. Shows here are often comedic/satirical performances by Danish comedians in Danish, and these usually don't interest non-Danish audiences. But there are also musical revues. Tickets range from 205 to 240 DKK ($29.70–$34.80).

THE PERFORMING ARTS

For **discount seats** (sometimes as much as 50% off the regular ticket price), go in person to a ticket kiosk at the corner of Fiolstraede and Nørre Voldgade, across from the Nørreport train station. Discount tickets are sold only on the day of the performance and may be purchased Monday to Friday from noon to 5pm and on Saturday from noon to 3pm.

✪ **Det Kongelige Teater (Royal Theater).** Kongens Nytorv. ☎ **33-69-69-69.** Tickets 60–600 DKK ($8.70–$87), half price for seniors 67 and over and young people 25 and under. Bus: 1, 6, 9, or 10.

Performances by the world-renowned **Royal Danish Ballet** and **Royal Danish Opera,** dating from 1748, are major winter cultural events in Copenhagen. Because the arts are state-subsidized in Denmark, ticket prices are comparatively low, and some seats may be available at the box office the day before a performance. The season runs from August to May.

THE CLUB & MUSIC SCENE
NIGHTCLUBS/CABARET

Fellini. Hammeritchsgade 1. ☎ **33-93-32-39.** Cover charge 50 DKK ($7.25). Bus: 2, 6, 9, or 43.

This is the most luxurious and upscale nightclub in Copenhagen, drawing an international crowd. The club is set inside, but independent from, the SAS Royal Hotel, and its decor is entirely sheathed in shades of mauve and scarlet. You'll find two bars, a dance floor, and a different entertainment theme each week. Previous themes have included African music night, Latin salsa night, and American night (which usually coincides with the arrival of whatever American sports team is in residence that week). Most amusing of all is the "Miss Bikini Denmark" night, in which a roster of Danish women in bikinis promenade during an interlude in the music and are judged by a panel of "experts." It's open Thursday to Saturday from 10pm to 5am. Despite its upscale venue, men aren't expected to wear jackets and ties.

JAZZ, ROCK & BLUES

Copenhagen JazzHouse. Niels Hemmingsensgade 10. ☎ **33-15-26-00.** Cover charge 40–70 DKK ($5.80–$10.15) when live music is performed, depending on the artist. Bus: 10.

The decor is modern and uncomplicated and serves as a consciously simple foil for the music and noise. This club hosts more performances by non-Danish jazz artists than virtually any other jazz bar in town. Shows begin relatively early here, at around 8:30pm, and usually finish early, too. Around midnight on Thursday, Friday, and Saturday, the club is transformed from a live concert hall into a disco. It's closed Mondays; otherwise, it keeps a confusing schedule that changes according to the demands of the current band.

Nighttime Experiences for Free (Well, Almost)

You don't have to go to clubs or attend cultural presentations to experience Copenhagen nightlife. If you want to save money and have a good time, too, consider doing as the Danes do: walk about and enjoy the city and its glittering night lights for free, perhaps stopping at a lovely square to have a drink and watch the world pass by.

Copenhagen's elegant spires and tangle of cobbled one-way streets are best viewed at night, when they take on the aura of the Hans Christian Andersen era. The old buildings have been well preserved, and at night they're floodlit. The city's network of drawbridges and small bridges is also particularly charming at night.

One of the best places for a walk is **Nyhavn** or New Harbour, which until about 25 years ago was the haunt of sailors and some of the roughest dives in Copenhagen. Today it's gone upmarket and is the site of numerous restaurants and bars. In summer you can sit out at one of the café tables watching life along the canal and throngs of people from around the world passing by—all for the price of your Carlsberg. Along the quay you can also see a fleet of old-time sailing ships. Hans Christian Andersen lived at three different addresses along Nyhavn: 18, 20, and 67.

Another neighborhood that takes on special magic at night is **Christianshavn**, whose principal landmark is Christiansborg Slot or Castle, a massive granite pile surrounded by canals on three sides. The ramparts of Christianshavn are edged with walking paths, which are lit at light. This neighborhood, which glows under the soft, forgiving light of antique street lamps, is the closest Copenhagen comes to the charm of the Left Bank in Paris. You can wander for hours through its warren of cobbled streets and 18th century buildings. The area also abounds in cafés, bars, and harbor restaurants, so there are plenty of "refueling stops." Originally the section was conceived by King Christian IV to provide housing for workers in the shipbuilding industry. But in the past decades real-estate prices have soared here, and it's definitely gone upmarket.

For a much more offbeat adventure—although it's not the safest place at night—you can head for the commune of **Christiania**, which lies a few blocks to the east of Vor Frelsers Kirke. This area once housed Danish soldiers in barracks. When the soldiers moved out, the free spirits of Copenhagen moved in, occupying the little village, even though—technically speaking—they are squatters and in violation of the law. They declared the area a "free city" on September 24, 1971. However, Copenhagen authorities have not moved in to oust them in all this time, fearing a full-scale riot. The area is a refuge for petty criminals and other drug dealers. But there has been success in the community as well, evoking the communes of the 1960s. For example, the villagers have helped hundreds of addicts kick heroin habits.

At night adventurous tourists enter Christiana to eat at one of the neighborhood's little restaurants, many of which are surprisingly good. Prices here are the cheapest in Copenhagen, because the restaurant managers refuse to pay taxes. You can also wander through some of the shops selling handmade crafts. Because most establishments are small and personalized, you can also invite yourself in, perhaps to listen to innovative music or see some cultural presentation. Currently your best bet for dining is **Spiseloppen** (no phone). Later you can visit the jazz club, **Loppen**, where you'll hear some of the best jazz in the city. If you're a vegetarian, as are many members of the commune, head for the vegetarian restaurant, **Morgensted**.

La Fontaine. Kompagnistræde 11. ☎ **33-11-60-98.** Cover 40 DKK ($5.80) Fri–Sat only. Bus: 5 or 10.

This is a dive that hasn't changed much since the 1950s, but it's the kind of dive that— if you meet the right partner, or if you really groove with the music—can be a lot of fun. Small, and cozy to the point of being cramped, it functions mostly as a bar, every Tuesday to Saturday from 8pm till 6am or even 8am the next morning. Sunday hours are from 9pm till 1:30am. Live music is performed here, but only on Friday and Saturday, when free-form jazz artists hold court beginning around 11:30pm.

Mojo Blues Bar. Løngangsstræde 21C. ☎ **33-11-64-53.** No cover. Sun–Thurs, 40 DKK ($5.80) Fri–Sat. Bus: 2, 8, or 30.

Mojo is a candlelit drinking spot that offers blues music, 90% of which is performed by Scandinavian groups. It's open daily from 8pm to 5am.

DANCE CLUBS

Baron & Baroness. Vesterbrøgade 2E. ☎ **33-16-01-01.** Cover charge 50 DKK ($7.25) for disco only. Bus: 250E or 350E.

A short walk from Tivoli, this is a relatively upscale nightclub whose decor incorporates *faux-medieval* crenellations, wrought-iron replicas of the bars on boudoir windows, suits of armor, and lots and lots of hunting trophies. It attracts a crowd that's a bit older and more prosperous than nearby competitors catering only to teenagers. Full meals cost from 150 to 250 DKK ($21.75 to $36.25). On nights when there's no disco, you'll find a solo musician playing a fiddle, piano, or harmonica. The bars here are open nightly from 6pm until at least 3am; the restaurant from 6pm to 11pm. There's a disco one floor above the street restaurant Thursday through Saturday, from 10pm until dawn.

Crazy Dayzi. Nørregade 41. ☎ **33-13-67-88.** 50 DKK ($7.25) Fri–Sat. Tram: Nørreport Station.

In the early 1990s a popular provincial nightclub in Jutland broadened its horizons and expanded into 16 other locations in Denmark. Today the Copenhagen branch is the largest and busiest member of the chain, and a serious draw for many of the capital's night owls. No one under age 21 is admitted, but those who make it past the doorman will find a whimsical collection of five bars, each with a distinctly different decorative theme—the American West, ancient Rome, raunchy old Havana, the volcanic jungles of Hawaii, and the Créole earthiness of New Orleans. Pints of beer cost 40 DKK ($5.80) each. The evening usually begins amiably and quietly, but by around 11pm the energy is cranked up to a disco inferno where everybody seems eager to dance. Open only 2 nights a week: Friday and Saturday from 10pm to 5am.

Den Røde Pimpernel. H. C. Andersens Blvd. 7 (near Rådhuspladsen). ☎ **33-12-20-32.** No cover Tues–Thurs, 40 DKK ($5.80) Fri–Sat. Bus: 2, 8, or 30.

The lively, club-like atmosphere of "The Scarlet Pimpernel" makes it a good place for dancing. You'll be admitted only after being inspected through a peephole. A live band plays a variety of dance music. It's open Tuesday to Saturday from 9pm to 8am. A beer will set you back 30 DKK ($4.35), and mixed drinks cost 45 to 50 DKK ($6.50 to $7.25).

Lekitch/The Fever. Gothersgade 8F, Bolthensgaard. ☎ **33-93-74-15.** Cover 50 DKK ($7.25) after midnight. Bus: 1, 6, or 9.

Discos come and go with alarming frequency in the Danish capital, but this remains one of the hotter, more popular venues for a late-night crowd of 25- to 35-year-olds, most of whom are avid fans of whatever musical innovation has just emerged in London or Los Angeles. The decorative themes derive from the 1960s cult classic *A Clockwork Orange*. Looking for insights into the heady world of the Danish arts? Head for the club's lower level, where luminaries from ballet, high fashion, and other fields are likely to be gossiping. Don't be surprised to see deliberately weird costumes, sometimes competing with one another for the most bizarre ensemble of the evening. Despite that (or maybe because of that), the venue is animated, loud, and high-energy—and can be a lot of fun. Beer costs 20 to 40 DKK ($2.90 to $5.80), and whisky begins at 45 DKK ($6.50). The club is open Thursday to Saturday from 11pm to 5am.

Rosie McGee's. Vesterbrøgade 2A. ☎ **33-32-19-23.** Cover 40 DKK ($5.80) imposed only when the place functions as a disco. Bus: 250E or 350E.

Set across the boulevard from Tivoli, this is a funky, American-style nightclub that caters to youthful (aged 18 to 25), high-energy generation X–ers. A jukebox near the entrance, and lots of gum-chewing teeny-boppers with braces, decked out in jeans and sneakers, come here to mingle, compare notes, and dance, dance, dance. There's a simple restaurant on site, serving mostly Mexican food, and frothy, foamy drinks that might help ease the shyness of striking up a conversation with a stranger. The bars and restaurant open nightly from 5:30pm, with the disco featured every Thursday to Saturday from 11:30pm till dawn.

Rust. Guldbergsgade 8. ☎ **35-24-52-00.** No cover Mon–Tues, otherwise 20–40 DKK ($2.90–$5.80). Bus: 5 or 6.

Rust sprawls over a single floor in the Nørrebro district where the clientele is international and high-energy. There's a restaurant, several bars, a dance floor, and a stage where live musicians perform every Tuesday night beginning around 9pm. Meals are served Monday to Saturday from 5:30 to around midnight, and at least someone will begin to boogie on the dance floor after 9:30pm, as drinks flow. The setting is dark and shadowy. There are places to sit, but none are so comfortable that you'll stay in one place for too long. No one under age 21 is admitted but you'll spot very few over age 45. Open from 5:30pm to at least 2am Monday to Saturday.

THE BAR SCENE
PUBS

Det Lille Apotek. Stor Kannikestraede 15. ☎ **33-12-56-06.** Bus: 2, 5, 8, or 30.

This is a good spot for English-speaking foreign students to meet their Danish counterparts. Although the menu varies from week to week, keep an eye out for the prawn cocktail and tenderloin, both highly recommended. The main courses run about 88 to 128 DKK ($12.75 to $18.55), and a beer costs 16 to 32 DKK ($2.30 to $4.65). It's open daily from 11am to midnight; closed December 24–26.

Drop Inn. Kompagnistræde 34. ☎ **33-11-24-04.** Bus: 28, 29, or 41.

This is not a disco, but it does offer live and iconoclastic bands who perform for young people in their late teens and twenties. There's no dress code. The room combines antique and modern oil paintings and a long bar. It's open daily from 11am to 5am. Beer starts at 19 DKK ($2.75).

✪ Library Bar. In the Hotel Plaza, Bernstorffsgade 4. ☎ **33-14-92-62.** Bus: 6.

Frequently visited by celebrities and royalty, the Library Bar was once rated by the late Malcolm Forbes as one of the top five bars in the world. In a setting of antique books and works of art, you can order everything from a cappuccino to a cocktail. The setting is the lobby level of the landmark Hotel Plaza, commissioned in 1913 by

Frederik VIII. The bar was originally designed and built as the hotel's ballroom, and Oregon pine was used for the paneling. The oversized mural of George Washington and his men dates from 1910. It's open Monday to Saturday from 11:30am to 1am and on Sunday from 11:30am to midnight. Beer costs 35 DKK ($5.05); drinks begin at 55 DKK ($8).

Nyhavn 17. Nyhavn 17. ☎ **33-12-54-19.** Bus: 1, 6, 27, or 29.

This is the last of the honky-tonks that used to make up the former sailors' quarter. This cafe is a short walk from the patrician Kongens Nytorv and the d'Angleterre luxury hotel. In summer you can sit outside. It's open Sunday to Thursday from 10am to 2am and Friday and Saturday until 4am. Beer costs 34 DKK ($4.95), and drinks start at 25 DKK ($3.60).

The Queen's Pub. In the Kong Frederik Hotel, Vester Voldgade 25. ☎ **33-12-59-02.** Bus: 1, 2, 6, 8, or 28.

Cozy, traditional, and imbued with a sense of Baltic history, this is the kind of bar where a businessperson could feel at home after a transatlantic flight. The older members of the staff have served nearly every politician and journalist in Denmark here. It's located on the ground floor of one of Copenhagen's most legendary (and discreet) hotels, and its decor includes English walnut, red brocade, and etched Victorian glass. Open daily from 11:30am to 11:45pm. Beer costs 25 to 38 DKK ($3.60 to $5.50); drinks begin at 55 DKK ($8).

A WINE BAR
Hvids Vinstue. Kongens Nytorv 19. ☎ **33-15-10-64.** Bus: 1, 6, 9, or 10.

Built in 1670, this old wine cellar is a dimly lit safe haven for an eclectic crowd, many patrons—including theater-goers, actors, and dancers—drawn from the Royal Theater across the way. In December only, a combination of red wine and cognac is served. It's open Monday to Saturday from 10am to 1am; closed Sunday in July and August. Beer is 30 DKK ($4.35); wine costs 25 DKK ($3.60).

GAY & LESBIAN CLUBS
Café Babooshka. Turensensgade 6. ☎ **33-15-05-36.** No cover. Bus: 5, 7, or 16.

Copenhagen's premier lesbian bar attracts women from around the world. Owned and managed by women, and situated near the Ørsteds Parken and the Gyldenløvesgade, it welcomes sympathetic men (gay and straight), but is primarily a spot where gay women can be themselves. The cafe-style format that prevails during daylight hours is transformed into a disco around 9pm. Glasses of beer and wine cost 34 DKK ($4.95) each. The place is open Monday to Thursday from 4pm to 1am, and Friday to Sunday from 4pm to 2am.

Erik Den Røde. Amagerbrogade 40. ☎ **31-57-87-88.** Bus: 2, 5, 9, 11, 19, 28, or 250S.

At the corner of Holmbladgade, this pub resembles a cozy Danish *kro* (inn). It's a popular venue for both gay and straight businessmen who drop by to enjoy the *frikadeller* (meatballs), filet of plaice, or grilled or roast beef. Main dishes cost from 55 DKK ($8).

The Men's Bar. Teglårdsstræde 3. ☎ **33-12-73-03.** Bus: 2, 8, or 30.

This is the only leather bar in town, filled with an unusual collection of uniforms, leather, and Levis. There's one bar, and the decor consists of shades of gray, black, and stainless steel. It's open daily from 3pm to 2am. A beer will set you back 20 DKK ($2.90).

XXX Copenhagen

The heady "boogie nights" of the 70s, when pornography aficionados flocked to Copenhagen to purchase X-rated materials, are long gone. Copenhagen is no longer the capital of sex, having long ago lost out to Hamburg and Amsterdam. But it's still possible to take a walk here on the wild side any night of the week. Two of the city's streets are **Istedgade** and **Helgolandsgade**, both of them near the rail terminus in the center of the city. Ironically, the sex shops peddling magazines and X-rated films stand virtually adjacent to decent family hotels. Mothers can often be seen hustling their sons past the window displays.

Pan Society. Knabrostræde 3. ☎ **33-13-19-48.** Cafe, free; dance club cover 55 DKK ($8). Bus: 28, 29, or 41.

This nationwide organization was established in 1948 for the protection and advancement of gay and lesbian rights. Its headquarters is a 19th-century yellow building off of the Strøget. A dance club occupies three of its floors, and a modern cafe is situated on the ground floor. Every night is gay night, although a lot of straight folk come here because the music is good. The cafe is open daily from 8pm to 5am. The dance club, however, is open on Wednesday from 11pm to 3am, on Thursday from 10pm to 4am, and on Friday and Saturday from 10pm to 5am, and on Sunday from 11pm to 3am.

GAMBLING

Casino Copenhagen. In the SAS Scandinavia Hotel, Amager Blvd. 70. ☎ **33-96-59-65.** Cover 80 DKK ($11.60); guests at any of Copenhagen's SAS hotels enter free. Bus: 5, 11, 30, or 34.

Danish authorities allowed the country's first fully licensed casino to open in the first class SAS Scandinavia Hotel just after Christmas in 1990. Today gamblers play such popular games as roulette, baccarat, punto banco, blackjack, and slot machines. The whole operation is overseen by Casinos of Austria, the largest casino operator in Europe. It's open daily from 2pm to 4am.

15 Side Trips from Copenhagen

BEACHES

The beach closest to Copenhagen is **Bellevue** (take the S-tog train to Klampenborg), but the water is not recommended for swimming. If you want to take a dip at a sandy beach, take a trip (by train or car) to the beaches of North Zealand—**Gilleleje, Hornbæk, Liseleje,** and **Tisvildeleje.** Although these are family beaches, minimal bathing attire is worn.

To reach any of these beaches, take the train to Helsingør and then continue by bus. Or you can make connections by train to Hillerød and switch to a local train; check at the railroad station for details. If you drive, you may want to stay for the evening discos at the little beach resort towns dotting the north coast of Zealand.

DRAGØR

5km (3 miles) S of Copenhagen's Kastrup Airport

This old seafaring town on the island of Amager is filled with well-preserved half-timbered ocher and pink 18th-century cottages with steep red-tile or thatched roofs, many of which are under the protection of the National Trust.

Dragør (pronounced *Drah*-wer) was a busy port on the herring-rich Baltic Sea in the early Middle Ages, and when fishing fell off, it became just another sleepy little waterfront village. After 1520, Amager Island and its villages—Dragør and Store Magleby—were inhabited by the Dutch, who brought their own customs, Low-German language, and agricultural expertise to Amager, especially their love of bulb flowers. In Copenhagen you still see wooden-shoed Amager locals selling their hyacinths, tulips, daffodils, and lilies in the streets.

ESSENTIALS

GETTING THERE   Take bus no. 30, 33, or 73E from Rådhuspladsen (Town Hall Square) in Copenhagen (a 35-minute trip).

SEEING THE SIGHTS

Amager Museum. Hovedgaden 4–12, Store Magleby. ☎ **32-53-93-07.** Admission 20 DKK ($2.90) adults, 10 DKK ($1.45) children. Apr–Sept, Wed–Sun noon–4pm; Oct–Mar, Wed and Sun noon–4pm. Bus: 30, 33, or 350S.

A rich trove of historic treasures is found in this museum outside Dragør. The exhibits reveal the affluence achieved by the Amager Dutch, with rich textiles, fine embroidery, and such amenities as carved silver buckles and buttons. The interiors of a Dutch house are especially interesting, showing how these people decorated their homes and lived in comfort.

Dragør Museum. Havnepladsen 2–4. ☎ **32-53-41-06.** Admission 20 DKK ($2.90) adults, 10 DKK ($1.45) children. May–Sept, Tues–Fri 2–5pm, Sat–Sun and holidays noon–6pm. Closed Oct–Apr. Bus: 30, 33, or 350S.

The exhibits at this harbor-front museum show how the Amager Dutch lived from prehistoric times to the 20th century. Farming, goose breeding, seafaring, fishing, ship piloting, and ship salvaging are displayed through pictures and artifacts.

WHERE TO STAY

The Hotel Dragør Kro, although primarily a restaurant, has a few rooms to rent.

Dragør Badhotel. Drogdensvej 43, DK-2791 Dragør. ☎ and fax **32-53-05-00.** 20 units (3 with bath). TV. 495 DKK ($71.75) double without or with bath. Rates include breakfast. AE, DC, MC, V. Bus: 30, 33, or 73E.

Built around 1901, this establishment near the sea is more popular as a restaurant than a hotel, yet it offers comfortably old-fashioned rooms with good mattresses and beds, but a shortage of private baths. Naturally, the rooms with private baths are booked first, since they cost no more than units without. You'll get a real feel for a country Danish inn here, yet you're only 20 minutes from the Copenhagen Town Hall. Non-residents are welcome to come in and enjoy the hotel's excellent cuisine. There are six different preparations of herring to get you going, followed by a Dragør Plate of mixed meats and pâtés, meltingly tender schnitzels, homemade soups, and a selection of *smørrebrød* (open-faced sandwiches) at lunch. Main courses cost from 85 to 142 DKK ($12.35–$20.60), and hours are daily from noon to 9pm.

WHERE TO DINE

The Dragør Badhotel (see above) also offers an excellent cuisine.

Café Beghuset. Strandgade 14. ☎ **32-53-01-36.** Reservations recommended. Main courses 128–172 DKK ($18.55–$24.95); three-course fixed-price dinner 248 DKK ($35.95). AE, DC, MC, V. Tues–Sun noon–3pm and 5:30–10pm. Bus: 30, 33, or 73E. DANISH/FRENCH.

This cafe and restaurant on a cobblestone street in the center of town looks like an idyllic cottage. To reach the restaurant section, you walk through the cafe. Although the

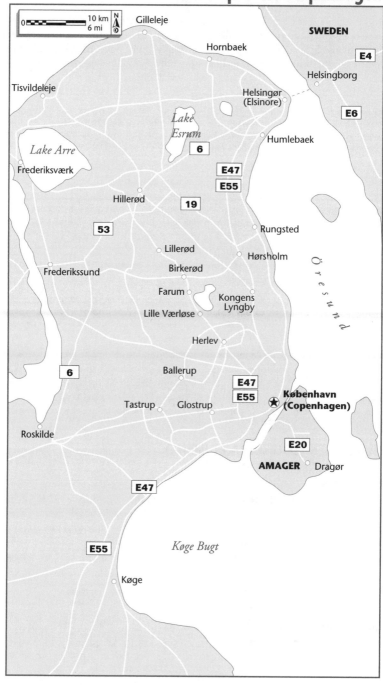

menu changes every 2 to 3 months to accommodate various seasonal items, a weary traveler in search of sustenance will be tempted by selections like fish soup, Swedish caviar, thinly sliced smoked lamb with a balsamic dressing on a bed of seasonal greens, and fresh oysters. Main courses include a perfectly cooked guinea fowl braised in red wine served with bacon of veal (their own invention) and herbs, and Dragør plaice roasted in butter and served with either parsley sauce or a bacon-thyme sauce.

Hotel Dragør Kro. Kongvejen 23, DK-2791 Dragør. ☎ **32-53-01-87.** Fax 32-53-00-53. Reservations recommended. Main courses 100–195 DKK ($14.50–$28.30); fixed-price three-course menu 115–230 DKK ($16.65–$33.35). AE, DC, MC, V. Daily noon–9:30pm (to 10:30pm in summer). Closed Dec 22–Jan 15. Bus: 30, 33, or 73E. DANISH/FRENCH.

This is a particularly beautiful *kro* (inn), and it's one of the oldest continuously operated restaurants in Denmark. The building itself dates from 1650, although the inn was first established in 1721, with a new wing added in 1795. This structure has a series of half-paneled dining rooms. There's a rose-filled courtyard for outdoor dining and drinking. You can select a filet of plaice with white-wine sauce, filet of beef with pepper sauce, or perhaps filet of veal in mustard sauce. "Falling star," boiled or fried fish with caviar and shrimp, is a house specialty.

The hotel rents five attractively furnished and well-maintained double bedrooms, each with a private bath, ranging in price from 800–1,000 DKK ($116–$145) a night.

Strandhotel. Strandlinbyn 9, Havnen. ☎ **32-53-00-75.** Reservations recommended. Main courses 105–188 DKK ($15.25–$27.25); lunch *smørrebrød* 42–88 DKK ($6.10–$12.75); one-course "quick lunch" 75 DKK ($10.90). AE, DC, MC, V. Daily 10am–10pm. Closed Oct–Mar. Bus: 30, 33, 73E, or 350S. DANISH.

One of Dragør's most visible restaurants is the Strandhotel (which, ironically, has no bedrooms). A long-established favorite, it has welcomed such guests as Frederik III (who usually ordered eel soup) and the philosopher Sören Kierkegaard. At lunchtime an ample spread of *smørrebrød* (open-faced sandwiches) is served, although other offerings include filet of pork in paprika sauce, a savory smoked filet of eel, fried or poached plaice, and a delectable trout with almonds.

HUMLEBÆK (LOUISIANA MUSEUM)
32km (20 miles) N of Copenhagen

ESSENTIALS
GETTING THERE **By Train** Humlebæk is on the Copenhagen-Helsingør train line; there are two trains per hour that leave Copenhagen's main railway station heading toward Humlebæk (trip time: 40 minutes). Once you reach Humlebæk, the Louisiana Museum is a 10-minute walk.

By Bus Take the S-tog train, line A or B, to Lyngby station. From there, take bus no. 388 along the coast road. There's a bus stop at the museum.

By Car Follow the Strandvej (coastal road no. 152) from Copenhagen. The scenic drive takes about 45 minutes.

SEEING THE SIGHTS
✪ **Louisiana Museum of Modern Art.** Gl. Strandvej 13. ☎ **49-19-07-19.** Admission 55 DKK ($8) adults, 15 DKK ($2.15) children 4–16, free for children 4 and under. Wed 10am–10pm, Thurs–Tues 10am–5pm. Closed Dec 24–25 and 31.

Established in 1958, this museum is idyllically situated in a 19th-century mansion on the Danish Riviera surrounded by elegant gardens, opening directly onto the Øresund. Exhibits include paintings and sculptures by modern masters (Giacometti and

Henry Moore, to name two) as well as the best and most controversial works of modern art. Look especially for paintings by Carl-Henning Pedersen. The museum name derives from the fact that the first owner of the estate, Alexander Brun, had three wives—each named Louise.

The museum has one of the largest exhibition spaces in Europe, and major exhibitions of contemporary art are staged here. There is also an extensive program of lectures, films, discussions with authors, and public debates. Its concert series is known throughout Denmark. Children find their own haven here, especially at the Børnehuset, or children's house, and the Søhaven, or Sea Garden. The museum's cafe is on the famed terrace with Alexander Calder's playful sculptures.

WHERE TO DINE

Gamla Humlebæk Kro. Ny Strandvej 2A. ☎ **49-19-05-69.** Reservations recommended. Main courses 95–198 DKK ($13.75–$28.70). AE, DC, MC, V. Daily 10am–9:30pm. DANISH.

This is the most obvious luncheon choice for anyone visiting the Louisiana Museum, which is just a short walk away. Built in 1722, the inn is comprised of one large dining room and three hideaway rooms richly adorned with rustically elegant accessories. Food selections include a range of open-faced sandwiches, deep-fried filet of plaice with shrimp and mayonnaise sauce, Wiener schnitzel, medallions of veal with morel sauce, and herring with sherry sauce. The cookery is very satisfying in an old-fashioned sort of way. Market-fresh ingredients are used.

RUNGSTEDLUND: HOME OF KAREN BLIXEN

21km (13 miles) N of Copenhagen

GETTING THERE   From Copenhagen's Central Railroad Station, trains run to Rungsted Kyst every 30 minutes. However, since this rail stop is still half a mile from the museum, it is better to take the train to Klampenborg where you can board bus no. 388, which offers frequent service to a bus stop about a block from the entrance to the museum.

By Car   Head north from Copenhagen along the E4 to Helsingør until you reach the turnoff east marked RUNGSTED.

THE MUSEUM

Since the 1985 release of *Out of Africa,* starring Robert Redford and Meryl Streep, thousands of literary and movie fans have been visiting the former home of baroness Karen Blixen, who wrote under the pen name Isak Dinesen. Her home, Rungstedlund, Rungsted Strandvej III (☎ **42-57-10-57**), is midway between Copenhagen and Helsingør on the coastal road.

Her father, Wilhelm Dinesen, purchased the estate in 1879. Blixen left in 1914 for Kenya when she married Bror van Blixen Finecke, but returned in 1931 and stayed until her death in 1962.

It was at Rungstedlund that Blixen wrote her first major success, *Seven Gothic Tales,* which many literary critics consider more memorable than *Out of Africa.* She also wrote collections of stories, *Winter's Tales* and *Last Tales,* here. Before Dinesen's father acquired the property, it was known as Rungsted Kro (inn), attracting travelers going north from Copenhagen to Helsingør.

Blixen wrote in Ewald's Room, named to honor poet Johannes Ewald, who stayed at the place when it was an inn. Four years before her death, Blixen established the Rungstedlund Foundation, which owns the property and its 40-acre garden and bird sanctuary. The gardens have long been open to the public, but in 1991 the foundation invited Queen Margrethe to open the museum.

In one part of the museum is a small gallery with exhibits in oil, pastel, and char-coal—all works by Blixen. The museum is filled with photographs, manuscripts, and memorabilia that document Blixen's life in both Africa and Denmark.

Visitors pay 30 DKK ($4.35) to enter, although children under 12 go free. It's open May to September, daily from 10am to 5pm; October to April, Wednesday through Friday from 1 to 4pm and on Saturday and Sunday from 11am to 4pm.

Blixen is buried in the grave at the foot of Edwaldshøj.

WHERE TO DINE

✪ **Restaurant Nokken.** Rungsted Havn 44. ☎ **45-57-13-14.** Reservations recommended. Lunch platters 48–125 DKK ($6.95–$18.15); dinner main courses 175–215 DKK ($25.40–$31.15). Set menus 345–445 DKK ($50.05–$64.50). AE, DC, MC, V. Daily noon–4:30pm and 5:30–10:30pm. DANISH/SEAFOOD.

Amid light-grained paneling and nautical accessories, a short walk downhill from Karen Blixen's house, with big-windowed views that extend across the water as far as Sweden, you can enjoy one of the best meals to be found along the Danish Riviera. You'll find it near the sea-battered piers next to the harbors, a fact that gives it a raffish feeling despite its reputation for well-prepared, savory fish and seafood. There's a bar near the entrance that's favored as a hangout by boat owners and local residents, and when you eventually get hungry, head for the dining room. The specialty is a seafood platter piled high with mussels, shrimp, oysters, and lobster. There are also fish dishes, including filets of lemon sole with hollandaise sauce, or you can try the roasted Danish lamb, the scampi with sweet-and-sour sauce or filet of prime beef with thyme. The cuisine is generous, uncomplicated, and always fresh.

North Zealand 6

Close to sea shores, lakes, fishing villages, and woodlands, North Zealand is often called "Royal North Zealand," because of its associations with the royal family of Denmark. In July, the Queen throws open the doors to her summer place at Fredensborg and invites in the public. Of course, many rushed visitors, after seeing Copenhagen, schedule a brief morning's visit to "Hamlet's Castle" at Helsingør—and that's it for North Zealand.

But those with more time and interest will find a wealth of attractions waiting here. Two of the more famous, the Louisiana Museum of Modern Art at Humlebæk and the home of Isak Dinesen (Karen Blixen) at Rungstedlund, are so close to Copenhagen that they're practically viewed as part of the capital itself. For information on them, refer to "Side Trips from Copenhagen" in chapter 5.

It will take days just to see some of the highlights, which range from Frederiksborg Castle at Hillerød (not to be confused with Helsingør); the home of the famous explorer, Knid Rasmussen, near Hundested; and the cathedral and the Viking Ship Museum at Roskilde, the old capital of Denmark.

Don't overlook the possibility of a beach outing, although you may at first think the water is better suited for polar bears. Wherever you stay in North Zealand, you are not far from a beach. A Blue Flag flying over the beach indicates that its waters are clean. Danes don't just use their beaches on summer days. Even on a blustery autumn afternoon, or when the Nordic winds of spring are still cold, you'll find them walking along their beaches, smelling the fresh air and listening to the crashing of waves. They even visit their beaches on crisp, fresh winter days for long walks.

If you can't make it to Norway (see *Frommer's Scandinavia*), you can also sample "Fjord Country" without leaving Denmark. Around the fjords of Roskilde and Isefjord are charming towns such as Hundested with its special light (praised by artists) and its bustling harbor, and Frederiksværk with its lovely canal system. On the gentle banks of Isefjord you'll find such lively commercial centers as Holbæk and Roskilde itself ("the town of kings").

For North Zealand rail information, you can call the main station in Copenhagen (see chapter 4). For bus information in Zealand, call ☎ 36-45-45-45.

1 Hillerød

35km (22 miles) NW of Copenhagen

Hillerød offers some very interesting sights, including one of Scandinavia's most beautiful castles. The ideal time to visit Hillerød is for its summer Viking festival (see below). But there's always something of interest here, as Hillerød lies in the heart of North Zealand, surrounded by some of the most beautiful and extensive woodlands in Denmark.

The city's history goes back four centuries, although its status rose significantly in 1602 when Christian IV began the construction of Frederiksborg Castle (see below).

The wide forests around Hillerød remain as vestiges of the prehistoric North Zealand wilderness. To the south sprawl the woodlands of Store Dyrehave, and to the north stretch the forests of **Gribskov,** the second largest in the country. The forests today are still rich in game, notably the pale tail-less fawn-colored roe deer. Gribskov forest contains some 800 fallow deer distinguished by their white-speckled hide. The great philosopher, Sören Kierkegaard, regularly reveled in the tranquillity of these forests.

Leaflets outlining the best walks and trails to follow in Gribskov and Store Dyrehave are available at the tourist office (see below).

Close at hand is Esrum Sø, a lake popular with bathers, sail-sports enthusiasts, and anglers alike. The western shores of the lake are fringed by Gribskov. The parklands of Fredensborg Palace and Skipperhuset (Skipper's Cabin) lie on the eastern shores, the point of embarkation for a sailing trip on Esrum Sø.

ESSENTIALS

GETTING THERE   The S-train (s-tog) from Copenhagen arrives every 10 minutes throughout the day, taking 40 minutes. Trains also link Hillerød with Helsingør in the east, and there are also rail links with Gilleleje and Tisvildeleje. Hillerød also has good bus connections with the major towns of North Zealand: Bus 305 from Gilleleje, buses 306, 336, and 339 from Hornbæk, and buses 336 and 339 from Fredensborg.

By Car   Take Route 16 north from Copenhagen.

VISITOR INFORMATION   The **tourist office,** located at Slotsgade 52 (☎ **48-24-26-26**), is open June to August, Monday to Saturday from 9am to 6pm; September to May, Monday to Saturday 9am to 4pm.

SPECIAL EVENTS   One of the most important Viking festivals in Scandinavia takes place every year near Hillerød. **Frederikssund** is a little town 8-miles southwest of Hillerød and 30-miles northwest of Copenhagen. It stages a 2-week ✪ **Viking festival** each summer where Nordic sagas are sometimes revived—and the record is set straight about who "discovered" America 5 centuries before Christopher Columbus. *Hamlet* is rarely performed anymore. Instead, the festival features a revolving series of plays, medieval and modern, concerning the Vikings.

The festival begins in mid-June. The traditional play is performed nightly at 8pm, and a Viking banquet follows. Tickets for the festival are 90 DKK ($13.05) for adults, 25 DKK ($3.60) for children 5 to 12 (it's not suitable for children 4 and under). The banquet costs 130 DKK ($18.85) for adults, 75 DKK ($10.90) for children 5 to 12. Trains depart for Frederikssund at 20-minute intervals from Copenhagen's Central Railroad Station. Travel time is 50 minutes, and there are enough trains back to Copenhagen after the spectacle ends to allow commutes from the capital. From the station at Frederikssund, it's a 20-minute walk to the site of the pageant. For details, contact the tourist information office in Copenhagen or phone the Frederikssund Tourist Office (☎ 47-31-06-85).

EXPLORING THE TOWN

✪ **Det Nationalhistoriske Museum på Frederiksborg.** In Frederiksborg Slot. ☎ **48-25-04-39**. Admission 40 DKK ($5.80) adults, 10 DKK ($1.45) children 6–14, free for children 5 and under. May–Sept, daily 10am–5pm; Apr and Oct, daily 10am–4pm; Nov–Mar, daily 11am–3pm. Bus: 701 from Hillerød Station.

This moated *slot* (castle), known as the Danish Versailles, is the major castle in all of Scandinavia, constructed on three islands in the castle lake. Like Kronborg, it was built in Dutch Renaissance style (redbrick, copper roof, sandstone façade). The oldest parts date from 1560 and the reign of Frederik II. However, the main part of the castle was erected from 1600 to 1620 by his son, Christian IV. The castle was used by Danish monarchs for some two centuries. From 1671 to 1840, Danish kings were crowned in Christian IV's chapel, which is used to this day as a parish church. Since 1693 it has been a chapel for the knights of the Order of the Elephant and of the Grand Cross of Danneborg. Standing in the gallery is an old organ built by Esaias Compenius in 1610. Every Thursday between 1:30 to 2pm, the chapel organist plays for museum guests. In 1859 the castle was ravaged by fire, but it has been restored.

Since 1878 the castle has housed the Museum of National History. Founded by the brewer J.C. Jacobsen as a special department of the Carlsberg Foundation, it encompasses the Great Hall and the former Audience Chamber of Danish monarchs. The museum contains the most important collection of portraits and historical paintings in the country. The collection, organized on a chronological basis, illustrates Danish history from the 16th century until today. The modern collection covering the 20th century was added on the third floor in 1993.

The castle is a 15-minute walk or a short taxi ride from the trail station.

✪ **Frederiksborg Castle Garden.** Rendelæggerbakken 3. ☎ **42-26-02-62**. Admission free. May–Aug, daily 10am–9pm; Sept and Apr, daily 10am–7pm; Oct–Mar, daily 10am–5pm; Nov–Feb, daily 10am–4pm. Bus: 701 from Hillerød Station.

This baroque garden north of the castle, laid out by Frederik IV in the early 18th century, became one of the finest in the country. The royal architect and landscape designer, Johan Cornelius Krieger, was responsible for its final appearance.

The gardens were built around a central axis, creating a sense of continuity between building, garden, and the open land. A cascade with water canals and fountains was built along the main axis. Symmetrically surrounding the cascades were avenues, bosquets, and parterres sporting royal monograms. The parterre was planted with box hedges in the exact manner in which King Frederik had seen similar gardens in France and Italy. The garden existed for 40 years, and enjoyed the patronage of three kings, Frederik IV, Christian VI, and Frederik V.

The last remains of the cascade were removed during the reign of Christian VII (1766–1808), presumably because the garden had grown out of style and become too expensive to maintain. In 1993, only the terraced ground, avenues in decay, and deformed box hedges remained from the original baroque garden.

Finally, the baroque garden was re-created when funds became available, and it was inaugurated on June 5, 1996. As many as 65,000 box plants and 166 pyramid-shaped yews have been planted in the parterre, while 375 limes and 7,000 hornbeam plants create the avenues and bosquets. The cascade floor consists of a quarter of a mile of dressed granite stones.

Events in the Garden

During the summer, the Frederiksborg Castle Garden forms the venue for several recurring concerts, May pole celebrations, and other cultural events.

Sophienborg Nordsjællandsk Folkemuseet (North Zealand Folk Museum). Helsingørsgade 65. ☎ **48-24-34-48.** Admission 15 DKK ($2.15) adults, free for children. Museum and supplementary collections, Tues–Sun, 11am–4pm. Closed Nov–Apr.

Collections depict the rural history of North Zealand, with special emphasis on the pre-industrialization era in Hillerød.

There are supplementary displays at **Sophienborg,** Sophienborg Allé (☎ **48-24-34-48**), an estate on the western outskirts of Hillerød. You can easily reach Sophienborg on bus no. 734 from Hillerød station. From here, it's an 8-minute walk. By car, take either Frederiksværksgade or Herredsvejen, turn right at Tulstrupvej, and follow the signs to the Folkemuseet Sophienborg. It keeps the same hours as the folk museum, and admission is on the same ticket.

The **Aebelholt Klostermuseum,** Abelholt 4 (☎ **48-21-03-51**), the ruins of an Augustinian monastery founded in 1175, is 4-miles west of Hillerød. A museum on this site—housed in the ruins—exhibits human skeletons dating from medieval times and provides clues to diseases that were commonplace at the time. Healing methods used by these early monks are also revealed. You can wander through a medicinal garden adjoining the museum. From March 1 to April and in October, hours are Saturday and Sunday 1 to 4pm. From May to August, Tuesday to Sunday 10am to 4pm, and in September, Tuesday to Sunday 1 to 4pm. Closed otherwise. Admission is 15 DKK ($2.15) adults, free for children 16 and under.

SHOPPING   The town is loaded with shopping possibilities. In the town center rises the sprawling **SlotsArkaderne** shopping center, close to Frederiksborg Castle, with an entrance on Nordstensvej. Opened in 1992, its distinctive interior design has been hailed throughout Denmark. It is definitely shopper friendly. Within the center are some 50 specialty shops and a department store, **Obs!** (☎ **48-22-71-00**). In 1993 the center was voted the most beautiful shopping center in Europe, and today it's better than ever. Shops here are open Monday to Friday 10am to 7pm and on Saturday 10am to 4pm.

There are a number of specialty stores throughout the town, including **Samlerhuset,** Helsingørsgade 34 (☎ **43-26-85-40**), specializing in antiques and second-hand goods. Right in front of the castle, **Sweater House**, Slangerupgade 1 (☎ **48-25-51-25**), offers the town's best selection of Scandinavian sweaters, often in blue and white patterns. The best selection of leather goods is found at **Laederhuset Husted,** Helsingørsgade 11 (☎ **48-26-02-54**). Since Danish toys enjoy world renown, you might want to check out the selection at **Fætter BR,** SlotsArkadern 27 (☎ **48-26-07-55**).

WHERE TO STAY

Although the hotel recommended below is fine, many guests prefer the more glamorous Hotel Store Kro at Fredensborg (see below).

Hotel Hillerød. Milnersvej 41, DK-3400 Hillerød. ☎ **48-24-08-00.** Fax 48-24-08-74. 62 units, each with kitchenette. TV TEL. 800 DKK ($116) double. Rates include breakfast. AE, DC, MC, V.

Although there isn't anything particularly historic associated with this hotel, it offers clean, well-maintained accommodations within a modern design, and it's just a short walk south of the town's commercial and monumental core. Low-slung, and evocative of a motel you might find on the outskirts of a large American city, it offers bedrooms with Danish modern furniture, and color schemes of either russet and white or blue and white. Each has a terrace or balcony of its own, plus a small kitchenette. Breakfast is the only meal served.

WHERE TO DINE

Café Havehuset. Rendelæggerbakken. ☎ **48-24-40-85.** Reservations not accepted. Snacks and platters 40–75 DKK ($5.80–$10.90). V. Daily 10am–9pm. Closed: Nov–Apr. DANISH.

Don't expect full-fledged meals in this simple cafe, as its menus tend to focus on drinks; light platters of smoked salmon, smoked turkey, or ham; salads; and pastries. But for a pick-me-up after a visit to the castle, which rises at the opposite end of its baroque gardens, the cafe might make a welcome and worthy addition to your day. The building that houses it was constructed in the 1600s, at about the same era as the castle itself. Depending on the mood of the youthful staff, service is either slow, impossibly blasé, or perky.

Ellegården. Ellegårdsvej 12. ☎ **48-28-66-93.** Reservations recommended. *Smørrebrød* 30–60 DKK ($4.35–$8.70). Main courses 79–160 DKK ($11.45–$23.20). Set-price dinners 98 DKK ($14.20). DC, MC, V. June to mid-Sept, daily noon–9pm. Mid-Sept to May, Thurs–Sun noon–9pm. DANISH.

Set 2 ½ miles west of the town center, a 5-minute drive from Frederiksborg Castle, this charming and well-managed restaurant thrives thanks to the well-intentioned labors of its owner, Les (pronounced "Lees") Gaal. Within a 250-year-old farmhouse that was rebuilt in the 1950s after it was partially destroyed by fire, and surrounded by a garden, it offers flavorful versions of tried-and-true Danish cuisine that includes most of the country's culinary staples. Delectable examples include platters of marinated salmon with *créme fraîche,* shrimp cocktail, fried fillets of plaice with shrimp, and sautéed beefsteak with fried onions.

John F. Kennedy Pub-Café. Torvet 4. ☎ **48-26-04-05.** Set-price meals 40–170 DKK ($5.80–$24.65). AE, DC, MC, V. May–Sept, Mon–Sat 11am–7pm. Oct–Apr Tues–Sat 11am–7pm. Bar until 2am year-round. DANISH/INTERNATIONAL.

Set directly on the main square of Hillerød, its name was selected in 1996 by the owner, an avid fan of virtually everything associated with the memory of the late JFK. During the day this place mainly functions as a cafe and restaurant, where menu items include New Orleans–style barbecue, grilled shrimp on a skewer, club sandwiches, and pastas. After dark, however, when the food service has wound down, beginning around 7pm, it transforms itself into a bar that seems to have been designed for drinking, talking, and flirting. Action spills over onto an outdoor terrace, and every Friday and Saturday, an annex room is transformed into one of Hillerød's most visible discos, Club Annabell. Entry costs 45 DKK ($6.50), and a bottle of Carlsberg goes for 19 DKK ($2.75). No one under age 25 is allowed inside.

Slotsherrens Kro. Frederiksborg Slot. ☎ **48-26-75-16.** Main courses 76–158 DKK ($11–$22.90); fixed-price two-course menu 162 DKK ($23.50); lunch plate 76 DKK ($11); *smørrebrød* 32–68 DKK ($4.65–$9.85). DC, MC, V. Tues 10am–5pm, Wed–Mon 10am–9pm. Closed Dec–Mar. Bus: 701. DANISH.

Since the 1970s this well-managed tavern has flourished here in what were formerly the stables for nearby Frederiksborg Castle. It's the most sought-after dining spot in town for anyone visiting the castle, partly because of its carefully crafted array of open-faced sandwiches. The place also serves grilled meats, salads, and platters of food, which usually comprise a meal in themselves.

Slotskroen. Slotsgade 67. ☎ **48-26-01-82.** Set-price meals 89–126 DKK ($12.90–$18.25). *Smörgåsbord* buffet 138 DKK ($20). AE, DC, MC, V. Daily noon–4pm. DANISH.

Either before or after a visit to the castle, this is the nearest, most convenient, and most appealing luncheon stopover. It has been serving hungry passers-by since 1794, when it was inaugurated as an inn. The main differences between then and now is that the food tastes better, and is served only at lunchtime (although on rare occasions dinner is served as well). Within a trio of cozy and historic-looking dining rooms, some of whose windows open onto direct views of the nearby castle, you can enjoy access to a *smörgåsbord*-style buffet that's laden with hot and cold dishes, several kinds of open-faced Danish sandwiches, *frikadeller* (meatballs), and salads. Otherwise, set-price menus might include any of several kinds of herring, Wiener schnitzel, and a well-flavored version of beefsteak with mushrooms, bacon, bread, and butter. There's also an outdoor terrace for use during warm weather.

HILLERØD AFTER DARK

The best place to go is the **John F. Kennedy Pub-Cafe** (see "Where to Dine," above), which transforms itself into Club Annabell at night.

A CASTLE, AN ART MUSEUM & RUINS

Hillerød makes a good center for exploring neighboring attractions.

From the center of Hillerød, take Route 6 south, following the signs to København. At Route 53, turn west. Thirty-four miles from Hillerød you'll come to **Selsø Slot,** Selsøvej 30 (☎ **47-52-01-71**), Denmark's first Renaissance castle, built in 1576 and renovated in the baroque style in 1733. Located at Hornsherred, east of Skibby, south of Skuldelev, and 35-miles west of Copenhagen, Selsø is one of the few private manor houses on Zealand that can be thoroughly explored.

The Great Hall and adjoining rooms are maintained as they were in 1733, with 14-foot-high marble panels, ornate plaster ceilings, and fine paintings. A children's room with hundreds of tin soldiers, the cellar, vaults dating from around 1560, an old manor kitchen with open fireplace and a scullery, old tools, and a dungeon below the gatehouse—all these features are worth seeing. Cultural events, such as orchestra concerts, are staged annually.

Admission is 40 DKK ($5.80) for adults, 10 DKK ($1.45) for children. The castle is open mid-June to mid-August, daily from 11am to 4pm; and mid-August to late October, Saturday and Sunday from 1 to 3:30pm (closed otherwise).

Frederikssund (see above) is usually visited at the times of its Viking pageant. But the opening of an art museum here in 1957 made the hamlet a year-round attraction. The **J. F. Willumsen's Museum,** Jenriksvej 4 (☎ **47-31-07-73**), is devoted to the paintings, drawings, engravings, sculpture, ceramics, and photographs of the well-known Danish artist, J. F. Willumsen (1863–1958), one of Denmark's leading symbolists. The artist spent most of his creative years in France. During short sojourns in Denmark, he lived mainly in Copenhagen. The museum also displays the works of other artists, mainly foreign, which were once part of Willumsen's private collection. Hours are daily year-round 10am to 4pm. Admission is 20 DKK ($2.90) for adults, 10 DKK ($1.45) for students and children under age 15 (free for age 14 and under). From Hillerød, take Route 6 south, following the signs to Copenhagen. At Route 53 head west. The total distance is 25 miles.

2 Fredensborg

9 1/2 km (6 miles) W of Helsingør; 40km (25 miles) N of Copenhagen

On the southeast shore of Esrum Sø, the country's second largest lake, Fredensborg is visited mainly for its royal palace. Many visitors rush through just for the day, visiting the palace and then departing immediately. However, you can stay and dine in the area, and enjoy a number of other attractions as well (see below).

Naturally, the first inhabitants of the town were people who helped service the royal court. But over the years many others moved in, and today the town is a lively little place even when the Queen isn't in residence. To Denmark, it occupies a position somewhat similar to Windsor in England. The town is home to some 40 specialty shops, each of which can be enjoyed in a pedestrian street environment.

The palace is a major backdrop for events in the life of the royal family—weddings, birthday parties, and the like. Heads of states from many of the countries of the world are received when they pay state visits here. And foreign ambassadors present their credentials to the monarch here as well.

GETTING THERE   From Copenhagen's Central Railroad Station, frequent trains run to Fredensborg. Bus nos. 336 and 384 from Copenhagen's Central Railroad Station go to Fredensborg.

By Car   From Copenhagen, head north on the E55 toward Helsingør, turning west on Route 6.

VISITOR INFORMATION   The **Fredensborg Turistinformation,** Slotsgade 2 (☎ **48-48-21-00**), is open Monday to Friday 10am to 4pm.

✪ **Fredensborg Slot.** Slottet. ☎ **48-48-48-00.** Admission 25 DKK ($3.60) adults, 10 DKK ($1.45) children. Gardens free (open around the clock). Palace only July 1–5pm.

This is the summer residence of the Danish royal family. Although the palace has been extended many times, it still retains its baroque, rococo, and classic features. The palace was particularly celebrated during the reign of Christian IX, who assembled the greats of European royalty here in the days of Queen Victoria. When the queen is in residence visitors assemble at noon to watch the changing of the guard. On Thursdays, except in July, the queen often appears to acknowledge a regimental band concert in her honor.

The palace was built for King Frederik IV by the Danish architect, J. D. Krieger. Originally there was only the main building with a Cupola Hall. Over the years the palace was extended with such additions as the Chancellery House and the Cavaliers Wing.

Frederik IX and Queen Ingrid began the tradition of spending several months of the year at Fredensborg Palace. They preferred spring and autumn. That tradition is still upheld today by Queen Margrethe and Prince Henrik.

Today the palace is hardly one of the impressive royal palaces of Europe, but it has its own charm, especially in the Domed Hall and the Garden Room.

The palace opens onto a 275-year-old baroque garden. A public part of the palace garden is open all year, but the private, reserved royal garden is open only in July, daily from 9am to 5pm. The orangery in the royal garden is also open in July, daily from 1 to 4:30pm.

These are some of the largest and best preserved gardens in Denmark. Note how strictly symmetrical and geometrical the shapes are. The palace gardens were laid out in the 1720s by Frederik IV and J. C. Krieger, drawing on Italian designs for their inspiration. In the 1760s Frederik V redesigned the garden, adding elements from French baroque horticulture.

WHERE TO STAY

Endruplund Country House. Holmeskovvej 5, DK-3480 Fredensborg. ☎ **48-48-02-38.** Fax 48-48-35-17. 20 units (12 with bath). 340 DKK ($49.30) double without bath; 380 DKK ($55.10) double with bath. MC, V. From Fredensborg's center, follow the signs to Helsingør.

Set a mile northeast of Fredensborg's center, this is a circa-1900 summer house that was purchased by the present owner's parents in 1926. Today, you'll find comfortable, charmingly eccentric bedrooms, each personalized by the hardworking efforts of the inn's owner, Karen Windinge, whose critically acclaimed dried flower arrangements are artfully scattered throughout her comfortable and eclectically decorated guesthouse. No meals are served other than breakfast.

✪ **Hotel Store Kro.** Slottsgade 6, DK-3480 Fredensborg. ☎ **48-48-00-47.** 49 units. MINIBAR TV TEL. 1,150–1,350 DKK ($166.75–$195.75) double. Rates include breakfast. AE, DC, MC, V. Bus: 336 or 733E.

A 10-minute walk from the train station and only 5 minutes from Esrum Lake, this is one of the most venerable old inns in Zealand. It was commissioned in 1723 by Frederik IV. Since it was right next door to Fredensborg Castle, many guests of the royal family have stayed here. No two rooms are alike, but each is equally charming. They are color coordinated and stylishly furnished, often with draped beds. Taste and elegance rule throughout. Over the years such modern amenities as private toilets have been added. If available, ask for a room with a view of the palace. Only five such units are available, and they are the most requested. In 1997 President Clinton dropped into the inn for a look when he was visiting the queen at Fredensborg.

Dining: The hotel restaurant is the finest in the area. See "Where to Dine," below.
Amenities: Concierge, billiards, and a dart room.

✪ **Pension Bondehuset.** Sørupvej 14, DK-3480 Fredensborg. ☎ **48-48-01-12.** Fax 48-48-03-01. 15 units. TEL. 1,125 DKK ($163.15) double. Rates include half-board. DC, MC, V.

This compound of Dutch-roofed buildings at the edge of Lake Esrum was originally constructed in the 1700s by the local shipbuilder about a mile south of the center of Fredensborg. For years, it functioned as a boatyard and repair site for watercraft on the lake, but since the administration of the Larsen family, it has been a cozy and sought-after hotel. Part of its allure derives from its plushly furnished public areas, many of which contain oriental carpets and bright colors. Bedrooms are outfitted in a sedate, eminently tasteful motif similar to what you'd expect in a private manor house.

WHERE TO DINE

✪ **Hotel Store Kro Restaurant.** Slotsgade 6. ☎ **48-48-00-47.** Reservations recommended. Main courses 215–270 DKK ($31.15–$39.15). AE, DC, MC, V. Daily noon–3pm and 6–10pm. DANISH/INTERNATIONAL.

When the weather is warm, the lovely garden here is ideal for lunch and dinner; otherwise you can retreat into the elegant dining room where the service and staff are top-rate. The cuisine is refined and prepared with excellent ingredients. The cooking is not only delicious—it's sometimes inspired. You might start with pigeon stuffed with apricots and served with arugula and Balsamic vinegar. Go on to such delights as grilled veal with kidney and spinach, accompanied by a Madeira sauce, or else grilled angler served with a tomato compote and a mussel cream sauce. The specialty here is *canard à la presse,* using the same recipe as the celebrated dish served at the legendary Tour d'Argent in Paris. Here it comes with a red wine sauce, cayenne, lemon and orange flavors, and, of course, *foie gras.* The fresh salmon and monkfish served with beet root, spinach leaves, and salmon roe—delicately flavored with dill—is worthy enough to invite the Queen over from the palace to join you. For dessert, there's nothing better than the meringue pie stuffed with fresh fruit sorbets.

Prinsessen. Slotsgade 3A. ☎ **48-48-01-25.** Reservations recommended. Main courses 115–195 DKK ($16.65–$28.30). DC, MC, V. Daily noon–9:30pm. DANISH/FRENCH.

This small, family-run restaurant a short walk from Fredensborg Castle has a lot of panache, verve, and sensitivity. Originally built in the 1930s, the premises might remind you of a small-scale villa. Inside, you'll find a trio of cozy dining rooms, a cuisine that focuses on Danish and French dishes, and food items that include chateaubriand, Wiener schnitzels, French-style beef with horseradish sauce, several different preparations of herring and salmon, and freshly made dessert pastries. At any time, if the more substantial offerings don't appeal to you, you can order any of at least a dozen artfully contrived *smørrebrod,* the open-faced sandwiches for which the Danes are famous.

Restaurant Skipperhuset. Skipperallée 6. ☎ **48-48-17-17.** Reservations recommended. Main courses 158 DKK ($22.90) each. Set menu 254 DKK ($36.85). AE, MC, V. Tues–Sun noon–3:30pm and 6–9pm (last order). DANISH/FRENCH.

Part of the experience of dining at this restaurant is the pleasant path you'll use to reach it—a long promenade lined with trees that was originally laid out long ago as one of the decorative avenues associated with Fredensborg Palace. The building that contains it was conceived 150 years ago as the boathouse for the royal family's yacht. Today, in a much-altered form, it functions as a well-respected restaurant where cuisine manages to combine elements of both the Danish and the French traditions. The cooks here have experience and an expert sense of precise, clear flavors. Menu items include breast of chicken stewed with young vegetables and summer cabbage; fried mackerel with spinach, apples, olives, and lemon-thyme sauce; and a dessert specialty of stewed rhubarb with sugared biscuits.

EASY EXCURSIONS

Esrum Sø is the second largest lake in Denmark, and it's also exceptionally deep: 72 feet in some places. Since 1949 the land around the lake has been protected by the government. Increasingly it is a winter feeding ground for large numbers of waterfowl. You can enjoy a trip on the lake if for no other reason than to admire the flocks of noble swans—not an "Ugly Duckling" among them.

If there's enough business to warrant its departure, a local outfitter, **Færgefart Bådudlejning på Esrum Sø,** Skipperhuset, in the village of Sørup (☎ 48-48-01-07), leads tours in an open boat through the lake's shallow waters in good weather. The emphasis is on ecology, and the tour is conducted in Danish with halting English and German explanations added afterward. The duration of the tour is around 45 minutes, and the cost of participating is 38 DKK ($5.50) per person.

Esrum Kloster, Klostergade 11, Esrum (☎ 48-36-04-00), was founded in 1151 and has a long and ancient history. Eleven monks arrived to lay the foundation stone of what later became the abbey, surrounded by forest, meadows, lake, and fields. The Middle Ages come alive here as you view the second floor exhibit of the monastic period. Originally, until the Reformation, the cloisters functioned as a Cistercian monastery, one of the most important in the Nordic countries.

The mounted exhibition gives you an idea of the layout of the monastery and the everyday life of the monks. The exhibition on the main floor deals with Esrum Abbey after the Reformation. The cloisters underwent many changes, becoming a royal hunting lodge, a base for a regiment of dragoons, a stud farm for horses, even a post office and district tax office. As a result of King Frederik II's horse-breeding interests, the fabled Frederiksborg horse was produced, highly prized for its riding skills and stamina.

In addition to the exhibitions, regular concerts and even theatrical performances are staged here, both inside and outside the monastery.

The abbey is open May 1 to October 31, Tuesday to Sunday from 10am to 4pm. From November 1 to April 30, it's open only on Saturday and Sunday from 10am to 4pm. It's closed from December 11 to January 8. Admission costs 15 DKK ($2.15) per person.

From Fredensborg, you can get to Esrum by bus (marked "Esrum") getting off at Hovedgaden. From here, walk for less than a quarter-mile along the Klostergade, which leads you to the entrance of the abbey. Motorists can take Route 205 north from Fredensborg.

From Hillerød to Esrum, you can take bus nos. 305, 306, and 331, a 25-minute ride, for around 15 DKK ($2.15).

3 Helsingør (Elsinore): In Search of Hamlet

40km (25 miles) N of Copenhagen; 24km (15 miles) NE of Hillerød; 72km (45 miles) NE of Roskilde

Once you reach Helsingør, usually by train from Copenhagen, you'll be in the center of town and can cover all the major attractions on foot. Helsingør (Elsinore in English) is visited chiefly for "Hamlet's Castle." Aside from its literary associations, the town has a certain charm: a quiet market square, medieval lanes, and old half-timbered and brick buildings—remains of its once-prosperous shipping industry.

In 1429 King Erik of Pomerania ruled that ships passing Helsingør had to pay a toll for sailing within local waters. The town quickly developed into the focal point for international shipping, bringing in a lot of revenue. King Erik also constructed the Castle of Krogen, later rebuilt by Christian IV as the Castle of Kronborg. For a while Helsingør prospered and grew so much that it was the second-largest town in the country.

ESSENTIALS

GETTING THERE   By Train   There are frequent trains from Copenhagen, taking 50 minutes. Buses have been discontinued.

By Ferry   Ferries ply the waters of the narrow channel separating Helsingør (Denmark) from Helsingborg (Sweden) in less than 25 minutes. They're operated around the clock by **Scandlines** (☎ **33-15-15-15**), which charges 21 DKK ($3.05) each way for a pedestrian without a car, and 245 DKK ($35.55) each way for a car with up to five persons inside. Between 6am and 11pm, departures are every 20 minutes; between 11pm and 6am, departures are timed at intervals of between 40 and 80 minutes. The process is simple and straightforward: You simply drive your car on board, and wait in your car in a line that might remind you of the Staten Island ferryboat. Border formalities during the crossing between Denmark and Sweden are perfunctory, and although you should carry a passport, it might not even be asked for.

By Car   Take E-4 north from Copenhagen.

VISITOR INFORMATION   The **tourist office,** at Havnepladsen 3 (☎ **49-21-13-33**), is open Monday to Friday from 9am to 5pm and on Saturday from 10am to 1pm.

SEEING THE SIGHTS

✪ **Kronborg Slot.** Kronborg. ☎ **49-21-30-78.** Admission 30 DKK ($4.35) adults, 10 DKK ($1.45) children 6–14, free for children 5 and under. May–Sept, daily 10:30am–5pm; Apr and Oct, Tues–Sun 11am–4pm; Nov–Mar, Tues–Sun 11am–3pm. Closed Dec 25.

There is no evidence that Shakespeare ever saw this sandstone-and-copper Dutch Renaissance-style castle, full of intriguing secret passages and casemates, but he made

Helsingør

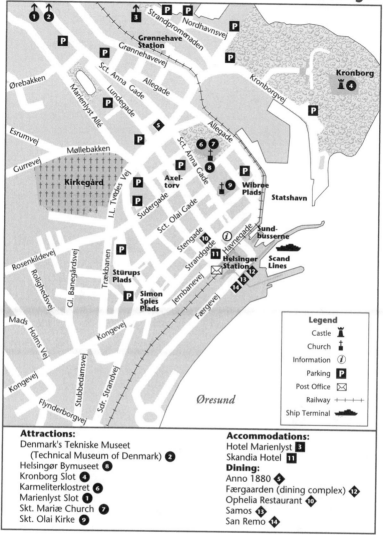

it famous in *Hamlet*. If Hamlet had really lived, it would have been centuries before Kronborg was built (1574–85). Over the years a number of famous productions of the Shakespearean play have been staged here. One great performance was Derek Jacobi's interpretation in 1979. In 1954 the parts of Hamlet and Ophelia were played by Richard Burton and Claire Bloom.

The castle, on a peninsula jutting out into Øresund, was restored in 1629 by Christian IV after it had been gutted by fire. Other events in its history include looting, bombardment, occupation by Swedes, and use as a barracks (1785–1922). The façade is covered with sandstone, and the entire castle is surrounded by a deep moat. You approach the castle via a wooden bridge and by going through Mørkeport, a gate from the 16th century. This will lead you to the main courtyard of Kronborg. Instead of entering the castle at once, you can walk around the moat to the waterfront where you can view a spectacular vista of the Swedish coast. At the platform—backed by massive bronze guns—Hamlet is said to have seen the ghost of his father, all shrouded in pea-soup fog.

The starkly furnished Great Hall is the largest in northern Europe. Originally 40 tapestries portraying 111 Danish kings were hung around this room on special occasions. They were commissioned by Frederik II and produced around 1585. Only seven remain at Kronborg; the rest have disappeared except for seven in the Nationalmuseet in Copenhagen. The church, with its original oak furnishings and the royal chambers, is worth exploring. The bleak and austere atmosphere adds to the drama. Holger Danske, a mythological hero who is believed to assist Denmark whenever the country is threatened, is said to live in the basement. Also on the premises is the **Danish Maritime Museum** (☎ **49-21-06-85**), which explores the history of Danish shipping.

Guided tours are given every half-hour October through April. In summer you can walk around on your own. The castle is half a mile from the rail station.

Karmeliterklostret. Skt. Annagade 38. ☎ **49-21-17-74.** Admission 10 DKK ($1.45) adults, 5 DKK (75¢) children. Guided tours, mid-May to mid-Sept, daily at 2pm.

This well-preserved 15th-century former Carmelite monastery is the best of its kind in Scandinavia. After the Reformation it became a hospital, but by 1630 it was a poor house. It's located at the intersection of Havnegade and Kronborgvej.

Skt. Mariæ Church. Skt. Annagade 38. ☎ **49-21-17-74**. Free admission. May 15–Sept 14, daily 10am–3pm; Sept 15–May 14, daily 10am–2pm.

A monastery complex with late 15th-century frescoes, St. Mary's also contains the organ played by baroque composer Dietrich Buxtehude from 1660 to 1668 (still in use). The church is located near the intersection of Havnegade and Kronborgvej.

Skt. Olai's Kirke. Skt. Annagade 12. ☎ **49-21-04-43**. Free admission. May–Aug, Mon–Sat 10am–4pm; Sept–Apr, daily 10am–2pm.

Built between 1480 and 1559, this christening chapel is worth a visit. The interior of the church, and the baptistry in particular, are one-of-a-kind. The spired church is connected to the Carmelite cloisters. The church lies near the intersection of Havnegade and Kronborgvej.

Helsingør Bymuseet. Skt. Annagade 36. ☎ **49-21-00-98.** Admission 10 DKK ($1.45) adults, free for children. Daily noon–4pm.

Installed in part of the Karmeliterklostret (see above), this museum houses the town's historic archives and various exhibits. Of special interest are 15th-century items related to Helsingør's collection of duties in the sound. The exhibits present materials on the various trades practiced in days gone by, including a printing house. There's also a collection of about 200 antique dolls. The museum also has a fine scale model of the town in 1801. It's a short walk from bus, train, and ferryboat stations.

Marienlyst Slot. Marienlyst Allé 32. ☎ **49-28-37-91.** Admission 20 DKK ($2.90) adults, free for children. Daily noon–5pm.

Marienlyst was built from 1759 to 1763 in a neoclassical style by the French architect N. H. Jardin. The building was intended to be a royal summer home, but was never used as such. Up until 1953 it served as a private residence. Today it's a museum, with well-preserved interiors in the original Louis XVI style and a permanent collection of paintings from Helsingør, along with an exhibit of silver works. Special exhibits are arranged upstairs in summer. The castle is surrounded by a fine park, and there's a panoramic view of the sound from the top of a steep slope behind the castle.

(take in a rock show)

Exploring lost cultures? Carry an **AT&T Direct**® **Service** wallet guide in your pocket.

It's a list of access numbers you need to call home fast and clear from around the world,

using an AT&T Calling Card or credit card. So you can tell everyone back home you saw the stones.

For a list of **AT&T Access Numbers,** take the attached wallet guide.

t's all within your reach.

Denmark's Tekniske Museet (Technical Museum of Denmark). Nordre Strandvej 23. ☎ **49-22-26-11.** Admission 25 DKK ($3.60) adults, 13 DKK ($1.90) children. Daily 10am–5pm.

This museum contains technical, industrial, scientific, and transportation exhibits, including the oldest Danish airplanes and trains, the world's first typewriter, and the world's first electromagnetic sound recorder (tape recorder). There's also an 1888 Danish automobile, Hammelvognen. The museum is next door to the train station.

WHERE TO STAY
❍ **Hotel Marienlyst.** Nordre Strandvej 2, DK-300 Helsingør. ☎ **49-21-40-00.** Fax 49-21-49-00. E-mail: hotel@marienlyst.dk. 233 units. TV TEL. 1,070–1,150 DKK ($155.15–$166.75) double, 1,500–1,700 DKK ($217.50–$246.50) suite. Rates include breakfast. AE, DC, MC, V. Bus: 340.

Located on the western outskirts of town beyond the castle, this hotel is about as close to Las Vegas as you'll get in Denmark. Today comprised of a compound with three buildings, its headquarters and oldest core were built around 1850, while the largest of its annexes went up in the mid-1970s. With a panoramic view over the gray sea toward Sweden, this hotel contains a glossy outbuilding with one of only six gambling casinos in Denmark. Bedrooms are a study in sleek Nordic styling—very comfortable and beautifully maintained. Thoughtful extras include trouser presses and hair dryers. Many of the bedrooms open onto a balcony or a terrace, and 86 of the units have a picturesque view of the sound.

Dining/Diversions: In the Seaside Restaurant you can enjoy regional and international specialties in a dining room with a view of the sound and Kronborg Castle. The kitchen always uses the best raw materials, which it fashions into tasty fare. In the evening you can drink and dance in the Seaside Bar & Night Club, where a live band plays on Friday and Saturday. In the evening you can play casino games of black jack, roulette, oasis, and poker, as well as work numerous slot machines.

Amenities: You can relax under palm trees at the Aqua Park which has a swimming pool with waves, a special pool for children, a water slide, a spa pool, and a sauna. The hotel is also located next to a fine beach. Health club, tennis courts, room service, laundry/dry cleaning, and baby-sitting.

Skandia Hotel. Bramstræde 1, DK-3000 Helsingør. ☎ **49-21-09-02.** Fax 49-26-54-90. 44 units (9 with bath). 540 DKK ($78.30) double without bath, 680 DKK ($98.60) double with bath. Rates include breakfast. AE, DC, MC, V.

Attracting the economy-minded, this hotel provides simple but clean and cost-conscious accommodations in an amply proportioned building erected in 1922. Only half of its rooms have been renovated, so your opinion of this hotel may depend on your room assignment. Naturally, the renovated units go first. Accommodations are neat and functionally furnished. Ask to get a room on the fifth floor if you'd like a good view of the sound. There are no TVs in the rooms but a public TV lounge is available. If you need to make a phone call, you can do so at the reception desk. The hotel lies behind a redbrick façade along a street running parallel to the port near the bus and train station and the departure point for the ferryboat to Sweden.

WHERE TO DINE
Typical Danish hot meals, such as *hakkebof* (hamburger steak), *frikadeller* (Danish rissoles or meatballs), rib roast with red cabbage, cooked or fried flounder or herring, and *æggekage* (egg cake) with bacon, are served in the local restaurants. In Helsingør you'll also find many fast-food places, and you won't want to miss the celebrated ice-cream wafers.

Anno 1880. Kongensgade 6. ☎ **49-21-54-80.** Reservations recommended. Main courses 159–184 DKK ($23.05–$26.70). Set-menu 275 DKK ($39.90). AE, DC, MC, V. Mon–Sat 11:30am–10pm. DANISH.

Set within a long, narrow, half-timbered building that originally functioned as a green-grocer's shop, this is a comfortable and traditional restaurant that's owner-managed and always alert to the freshness of its ingredients. Within old-fashioned dining rooms, you'll enjoy seasonal meals that might include cream of clam soup with saffron; fillets of salmon, haddock, or plaice in butter sauce with herbs; fried steak with fried onions and boiled potatoes; and such desserts as a kirsch-flavored parfait.

Ophelia Restaurant. In the Hotel Hamlet, Bramstræde 5. ☎ **49-21-05-91.** Reservations recommended. Main course 80–170 DKK ($11.60–$24.65). AE, DC, MC, V. Daily noon–9:30pm. Bus: 801 or 802. DANISH/FRENCH.

The Ophelia is one of the most appealing restaurants in town. In the elegantly rustic dining room, photos of various world *Hamlet* productions line the brick walls. Specialties of the house include Hamlet veal steak and richly caloric desserts. Lunches cost only half as much as dinner. Although not overly imaginative, the cookery is very competent, with dish after tasteful dish emerging from the kitchen.

Samos. Stengade 81 (at Færgaarden). ☎ **49-21-39-46.** Reservations recommended. Main courses 108–179 DKK ($15.65–$25.95); all-you-can-eat buffet dinner 108 DKK ($15.65). MC, V. Daily noon–11pm. GREEK.

Situated near Helsingør Castle and the ferryboat terminal for passengers heading back to Copenhagen, this restaurant was inspired by a Greek island *taverna*. It's part of Færgaarden, the former 1770 Customs House that's now a complex of international restaurants and the most popular choice for dining in Helsingør. Amid a color scheme of Ionian blue and white and a decor of fish nets and murals of such monuments as the Acropolis, you can order heaping portions of moussaka, roast lamb, grilled fish, meatballs, tzatziki, and the honey-enriched dessert, baklava. The buffet offers more than 20 items guaranteed to delight your taste buds. Additional seating is available on a breezy outdoor pavilion overlooking the sea.

San Remo. Stengade 53 (at Bjergegade). ☎ **49-21-00-55.** Main courses 30–90 DKK ($4.35–$13.05). MC, V. June–July, daily 9am–9pm; Aug–May, daily 11am–6pm. Bus: 801 or 802. DANISH.

A down-to-earth self-service establishment with crystal chandeliers, the San Remo offers 35 different meals, including *frikadeller* (Ping-Pong sized meatballs) and potatoes. The fare is robust, hearty, filling, and cheap—nothing more. The cafeteria is set in a traffic-free shopping mall half a block from the harbor, in a building dating from 1904 that was inspired by Dutch architecture.

A DINING COMPLEX

Færgaarden is the setting for a trio of international restaurants in what was Helsingør's Customs House back in 1770. (See the previous recommendations of Samos, for one of the most popular choices in town.) This complex enjoys the dining monopoly in Helsingør and is frequented by passengers going to and from Sweden. In addition to Samos, Færgaarden is also the site of **Gringo's Cantina** (☎ 49-26-14-47), a Mexican restaurant where main courses cost 70–150 DKK ($10.15–$21.75), with a fixed-price menu going for 99–149 DKK ($14.35–$21.60). There is also the very competent **Bamboo** (☎ 49-21-22-82), a Chinese restaurant offering main courses for 70–150 DKK ($10.15–$21.75). Both establishments are open daily from noon to 10pm. All of them accept American Express, Diners Club, MasterCard, and Visa.

HELSINGØR AFTER DARK

The major center of nightlife is the previously recommended **Hotel Marienlyst,** which has a casino usually filled with Swedes.

4 Hornbæk

49 1/2 km (31 miles) N of Copenhagen; 12km (7 1/2) miles west of Helsingør

A 500-year-old fishing hamlet turned modern holiday resort, Hornbæk is one of the best places for a vacation on the north coast of Zealand—sometimes called the Kattegat coast. Coastal woodlands, heathlands, and sand dunes make for a uniquely Danish holiday.

Hornbæk has the best beach along the north coast, a wide expanse of soft white sands that runs the full length of the resort, set against a backdrop of beach grass and sand dunes. *Rosa rugosa,* a wild pink rose that seems to flourish in this salty air, blooms here all summer. The beach is pristine and is beautifully maintained; all the kiosks and facilities lie inland from the dunes.

The special light found in Hornbæk attracted and continues to attract artists to this small fishing hamlet. In 1870 the town was discovered by such artists as Kristian Zartmann, P. S. Krøyer, Viggo Johansen, and Carl Locher. Krøyer, for example, depicted among other elements the work of fishermen at sea and down the shore. Locher was so fascinated with his marine subjects that he lived at Hornbæk from 1881 to 1889; his home still stands at Østre Stejlebakke, but is not open to the public.

ESSENTIALS

GETTING THERE   From Helsingør (see above), which has frequent connections to Copenhagen, trains arrive about twice an hour during the day, pulling into the station at Hornbæk after a trip of just 22 minutes. From Helsingør, bus no. 340 journeys here about once an hour, taking 30 minutes.

By Car   Drive NE along the coastal road (Route 237) from Helsingør, following the signs to Hornbæk and/or Gilleleje.

VISITOR INFORMATION   Providing information for the area, **Hornbæk Turistbureau,** Vester Stejebakke 2A (☎ **49-70-47-47**), is found inside the local library. Hours are Monday, Tuesday, and Thursday 2 to 7pm, Wednesday and Friday 10am to 2pm, Saturday 10am to 1pm (until 3pm on summer Saturdays).

GETTING AROUND

You don't really need a car to explore the area. Do as the Danes often do and cycle along on a "voyage of discovery." Bikes can be rented at **Bjærre Cykler,** Nordre Strandvej 338A (☎ **49-70-32-82**). Rental fees are 50 DKK ($7.25) per day.

FUN ON THE BEACH & ELSEWHERE

The beach is the big attraction, and swimming conditions are good. The dunes protect the beach from heavy winds. Danes, often from Copenhagen, flock here in summer, but there's always space for sunbathing. The beach offers lovely views over the sea toward Kullen, the rocky promontory jutting out from the Swedish coast.

The municipality cleans the beach daily, and for several years it has been voted as one of the cleanest beaches in Scandinavia. A host of activities are possible here, including water biking. Windsurfing can be arranged at **Surfudlejning** (☎ **49-70-33-75**), at Drejervej 19. Kiosks sell fast food and drinks; there are toilets, and, for persons with disabilities, catwalks that are wheelchair friendly lead down to the sea.

Insider's Tip

After you've explored the town of Hornbæk and hit the beach, consider taking a trail through a vast track of public forest, **Hornbæk Plantage,** lying 2-miles east of the center of Hornbæk. The tourist office (see above) will give you a free map outlining the best hiking trails. You'll come across Scotch broom, wild roses, and hundreds of pine trees as you follow one of the trails along the coast. We recommend the coastal trail because of its more dramatic scenery, although some of the hiking routes cut inland.

The **Havnen** or **Hornbæk Harbour** is a modern, well-equipped harbor with mooring for 200 boats. It lies next to "shanty town," a collection of huts where fishers check their tackle or hang flatfish out to dry under the eaves. Facilities with showers are beside the harbor master's office. Charters for fishing trips can be arranged here. The harbor here is the starting point of an annual Zealand regatta in June.

If you've arrived by train from Helsingør, the harbor is only a 5-minute walk from the depot. Head down Havnevej. After crossing the dunes, you're on the beach, and we hope the day is a sunny one.

At the harbor, you'll see a monument honoring the poet Holger Drachmann, who died here in 1908.

If you'd like to walk through the village you'll come upon some old fisher's cottages still standing, and a church from the 17th century with many votive ships hanging from the ceiling. Votive ships are scaled-down replicas that have been blessed by a priest or minister and are designed to honor the sacrifices of men who labor at sea. The church was built in 1737 to take the place of two buildings that were blown down in fierce winds. A bit inland, many Danes have erected luxurious summer villas. City officials have planted tree plantations to give shelter from the frequent gales.

SHOPPING   There are at least two antique stores worth a visit, including **Engdalen Antikviteter,** Engdalen 8 (☎ **49-70-48-88**), and its competitor, **Mae Otto Antique,** Ndr. Strandvej 357 (☎ **49-70-11-22**). The best outlet for handcrafts is found at **Sylvest Stentøj,** Klosterrisvej 2, Havreholm (☎ **49-70-11-20**), which specializes in stoneware.

WHERE TO STAY

Ewaldsgaarden. Johs. Ewaldswej 5, DK-3100 Hornbæk. ☎ and fax **49-70-00-82.** 12 units (some with bath). 495 DKK ($71.75) double. Rates include breakfast. Half-board 68 DKK ($9.85) per person extra. V.

Small-scale and deliberately rustic, this hotel prides itself on its role as a simple pension with few if any of the amenities of a full-fledged hotel. Painted an appealing shade of russet and set within a garden, it was originally built in 1814 as a post office, with enough stables to house the horses that would be needed for keeping mail deliveries timely. You'll be thrown into a closer series of contacts with the other guests here than in a more anonymous setting, thanks to the small dimensions and rather cramped bedrooms. Each of these is outfitted with a combination of wallpaper and painted surfaces, sometimes in bright colors, and contain many of the trappings of a thoughtfully decorated private home. Overall, thanks to genuine cheerfulness and thoughtful management, you can have a happy and successful overnight stay here.

Søbakkehus. Hornebyvej 8, DK-3100 Hornbæk. ☎ **49-70-00-33.** 27 units (none with bath). 650 DKK ($94.25) double. Rates include breakfast and dinner. DC, MC, V. Closed: Nov–Mar.

A 12-minute walk from the beach, this is one of Hornbæk's simplest guesthouses, with clean but cramped, ultra-stripped-down bedrooms and the overriding feel—which you might find very appealing—of a summer camp at the seashore. The complex consists of at least four long and narrow buildings, each built between 1920 and 1958, set edge-to-edge in a row that evokes a series of railway cars strung together along a track. Meals are served in a modern dining room ringed with windows. None of the rooms has any particular frills, but a communal TV is positioned in one of the public areas.

Havreholm Slot. Klosterrisvej 4, Havreholm DK-3100 Hornbæk. ☎ **49-75-86-00.** Fax 49-75-80-23. 30 units. MINIBAR TV TEL. Mid-Aug to May, Fri–Sat nights 950 DKK ($137.75) double; Sun–Thurs 1,400 DKK ($203) double. DC, MC, V. Take bus from central Hornbæk marked "Havreholm."

The most elaborate and best-accessorized hotel in Hornbæk occupies what was originally built in the 1870s as the private home of a local lumber baron and paper manufacturer, Valdemar Culmsee. Designed with a mock-fortified tower and vaguely ecclesiastical Victorian-style ornaments, it sits 2 ½-miles south of Hornbæk, within a very large expanse of privately owned field and forest. Overnight accommodations are contained within a series of bungalows, each independent, and set on the hillsides sloping down to a widening of the river on which the property sits. Each is cozy and attractively decorated in a way befitting an upscale private home.

Dining/Diversions: A well-managed restaurant, serving artfully prepared food, is in the mansion's original dining room. (It's recommended separately in "Where to Dine.") There's also a bar.

Amenities: Bicycle rentals, horseback riding, golf, tennis, both indoor and outdoor swimming pools, saunas, Jacuzzis, a squash court, and billiard and pool tables.

WHERE TO DINE
Havreholm Slot. Klosterrisvej 4, Havreholm. ☎ **49-75-86-00.** Reservations recommended. Main courses 170–185 DKK ($24.65–$26.85). Set-course menu 250–335 DKK ($36.25–$48.55). DC, MC, V. Daily noon–2pm and 6–9pm. DANISH/CONTINENTAL.

One of the most appealing restaurants in the region is located within the previously recommended Havreholm Slot hotel, in a grand 19th-century dining room whose original accessories remain for the most part intact. Part of its allure for art historians and Danish nationalists derives from the murals that cover the walls. Commissioned in 1872 by the owner of the house, they were painted by Joakim Skovgaard, a well-known name in the Danish arts. The result was an interpretation of the Creation and the Garden of Eden in 12 panels that are visible from wherever you happen to be seated. In addition to the mural-decked dining room, there are three other dining areas, each with a fireplace of its own. A well-trained chef produces the best food in town, with menu items that change with the seasons. Examples include a salad of fresh mussels; fresh salmon served with a vegetable terrine; breast of chicken cooked with mushrooms and red wine sauce; and, an especially delectable choice, roasted oxtail in red wine sauce.

Hornbæk Bodega. A.R. Friisvej 10. ☎ **49-70-28-88.** Main courses 79–150 DKK ($11.45–$21.75). Set-price daily menu 69 DKK ($10). AE, DC, MC, V. Daily noon–10pm. DANISH/INTERNATIONAL.

Set near the water, in a century-old building in the center of town, this bodega resembles an English pub more closely than virtually anything else in Hornbæk. Surrounded by forest green walls, you'll be seated on the recycled black leather upholstery of what used to serve as the seats for an old-fashioned English train. No one will mind if you drop in here just for a drink—a bottle of Carlsberg costs 19 DKK ($2.75); a half-liter of beer on draft goes for 35 DKK ($5.05). But if you're hungry, menu items include lots of American-derived items such as club sandwiches and burgers, and such Danish standards as *frikadeller* (meatballs), fish fillets with shrimp and asparagus, hot liver pâté with bacon and mushrooms, and plaice fried in butter.

Søstrene Olsen. Øresundsvej 10. ☎ **49-70-05-50.** Reservations recommended. Main courses 150–250 DKK ($21.75–$36.25). Set-price 295 DKK ($42.80). AE, DC, MC, V. Daily noon–10pm. Closed Jan. DANISH/CONTINENTAL.

Set near the sea, close to the center of town, the building that houses this restaurant was originally constructed in the 1880s as the summer home of a wealthy woman who spent most of her winters in Copenhagen. Today, it's one of the most appealing restaurants in town, partly because of its low-key elegance, partly because of the flavorful cuisine that emerges from the hardworking kitchens on steaming platters. The menu changes at least every two weeks, but might include such dishes as a gratin of lobster with green sauce, fillets of monkfish served with shrimp and liquefied spinach, filet of beef with a tomato-cream sauce, fried eel with mashed potatoes, *moules marinière* (mussels marinara), and *crème brulée.*

HORNBÆK AFTER DARK

Two of the busiest and oft-mentioned watering holes in Hornbæk are particularly active during the summer months. The more historic of the two is **Hornbæk Bodega,** A.R. Friisvej 10 (☎ **49-70-28-88**), a previously recommended restaurant (see "Where to Dine," above). Set within what was originally conceived as the town's movie theater, it attracts socializing Danes like a magnet every evening as the dinner service begins to wind down. Come here for a drink of beer or schnapps, or for a taste of disco music if your visit happens to fall on a Friday or Saturday night throughout the year (from 10pm till around 5am). When there's disco, a cover charge of around 25 DKK ($3.60) pays for the first drink. The Bodega's most visible competitor is **Café Paradiso,** Havnevej 3 (☎ **49-70-04-25**). Set in a modern, relatively nondescript building in the town's center, this is a lively and gregarious English-inspired pub that offers live music every Friday and Saturday night from 9pm till at least 2am. No cover.

5 Gilleleje

59km (37 miles) N of Copenhagen; 29 1/2 km (18 1/2) miles NW of Helsingør

The northernmost town in Zealand, Gilleleje offers Blue Flag beaches (meaning non-polluted waters), the leafy glades of the nearby Gribskov forest in the south, and a typical Danish landscape with straw-roofed houses and a large fishing harbor. In all, there are 9 miles of coastline with plenty of sandy beaches for water babies of all ages.

Gilleleje Harbour is the center of local life. As soon as dawn breaks, fishing boats of all sizes make their way into North Zealand's largest industrial port, and can be seen unloading their catch. Look for the fish auction hall to see the night's catch being sold in a unique language understood only by the initiated. There are many smokehouses along the harbor used for smoking the fish.

Later you can go for a walk in the town itself, with its many small and large shops. On Thursdays and Saturdays you can experience a Zealand *mylder,* when the town square becomes a market place with stalls and booths vying to take your kroner. Horse-drawn carriage rides and street music provide an added bonus.

ESSENTIALS

GETTING THERE   During the day, two trains an hour arrive from Hillerød; the trip takes 30 minutes. There is also frequent service from Helsingør; the ride takes about 40 minutes. All the towns of North Zealand are linked by bus. For example, bus no. 340 links Gilleleje with Hornbæk (20 minutes), and with Helsingør (50 minutes). Bus 363 links Gilleleje with Tisvildeleje, but the awkward bus route takes about an hour. The bus and train depot in Gilleleje adjoin each other. It's only a 5-minute walk from the bus and train stations down to the harbor.

By Car   From Helsingør (see above), follow Route 237 west.

VISITOR INFORMATION   The **Gilleleje Turistbureau** is at Gilleleje Hovedgade 6F (☎ 48-30-01-74). From mid-June to August, it's open Monday to Saturday from 10am to 6pm; from September to April, it's open Monday to Saturday from 9am to 4pm; and from May 1 to mid-June, it's open Monday to Saturday from 9am to 5pm.

EXPLORING THE AREA

When you tire of the beaches, take a stroll through the old town center, with its narrow streets and well-preserved old houses, no two alike. In the center of town stands the Sladrebænken or "gossip bench" where you can rest and spread some gossip.

From the harbor you can take the sign-posted Gilbjergstien path, offering panoramic views over the sea. This will take you to the Sören Kierkegaard Stone, a monument to Denmark's most renowned philosopher. As long ago as 1835, he was one of the first tourists to appreciate the beauty and tranquillity of this place.

But most summer visitors come here for the beaches, not to see the sights. Gilleleje has an unbroken coastline on either side, stretching from Gilbjerg to Kullen, running from Kattegat in the north to Øresund in the southeast. The city has lifeguards posted in several places along the coast. Many of the bathing beaches have modern toilets, little kiosks, and, often, proper restaurants. Several beaches also have ramps leading down to the water for the benefit of wheelchair users.

Within a green space adjacent to the sea, an area that forms part of the landscaping around the also-recommended Gilleleje Museum and the town's public library, stands a bronze statue called **Teka Bashofar Gadol,** a Hebrew name meaning "Let the mighty Shofa proclaim." The statue was donated by a wealthy Israeli patron of the arts, Yul Ofer, and was unveiled in the spring of 1997 to commemorate the flight of Danish Jews from the Nazis in 1943. Gilleleje was the point of departure for some 2,000 Jews who fled to Sweden from the town and other places along the North Coast. Risking their own lives, people in the town and country harbored Jews until they could secure passage on a ship to Sweden.

The **Gilleleje Museum**, Vesterbrogade 56 (☎ 48-30-16-31), traces the development of the area from the early Middle Ages, although some exhibits go back before recorded history. Panoramas present both shore birds and migratory birds. The museum, along with Gilleleje's library, are housed in the Pyramiden, the Pyramid cultural center where traditional and modern buildings have been integrated into a harmonious whole.

There is a fascinating exhibit related to the rescue of the Danish Jews in 1943. The museum is open year-round, Wednesday to Monday, from noon to 5pm. Admission costs 10 DKK ($1.45) for adults, 5 DKK (75¢) for children ages 5 to 11 (free for kids age 4 and under).

A mile east of town stands the world's first coal-fired lighthouse, **Nakkehoved Østre Fyr,** Fyrvej 20 (☎ 48-30-16-31). Dating from 1772, it is one of the rarest and best-preserved coal lighthouses in the world. It has been restored and turned into a minor nautical museum. You can always drive there—its location 1 ½-miles east of town is clearly marked from the town center (follow the signs to "Nakkehoved Østre Fyr"). But the more invigorating and preferred method of reaching the lighthouse involves walking along a coastal footpath beginning in Gilleleje at Hovedgade on the east side of the fishing museum. The path goes on for 1 ½ miles before reaching the lighthouse. It's only open from June to September, daily from noon to 5pm, charging an admission of 10 DKK ($1.45) for adults, and 5 DKK (75¢) for children aged 5 to 12 (free for kids age 4 and under).

The Fiskerhuset (Old Fisherman's House) and **The Skibshallen** (Ship Hall) are located at Hovedgade 49 (☎ **48-30-16-31**). This is a fisherman's dwelling from the 1820s, now restored. The hall also presents the history of fishermen in the area from the Middle Ages to the present day, using the fishing hamlets between Hundested and Helsingør as the points of departure. The museum—on the main street—uses a variety of panoramic scenes, models of the boats used in former times, and exhibits on trades associated with fishing, to reveal how the industry has dominated local life. The hours and prices are the same as those previously mentioned for the lighthouse.

One of the most interesting museums in the region is the **Rudolph Tegnersmuseum,** Museumsvej 19, in Villingerød (☎ **49-71-91-77**). Set 4 ½-miles southwest of Gilleleje, you can reach it by driving southwest along the coastal route (no. 237) and then following the signs pointing south to the museum from the hamlet of Dronningmølle. Surrounded by heather-covered hills that might remind you of Scotland (although this region of Zealand is often referred to as "Russia"), this museum is devoted to the artist Tegner. Fourteen of his bronzes are displayed in an adjacent sculpture park, 42,000 acres of protected countryside. The museum houses Tegner's collection of 250 sculptures in plaster, clay, bronze, and marble, some of monumental proportions. Selected pieces of furniture from the artist's home, and a sarcophagus containing Tegner's body, make the museum a monument to this individual and controversial avant garde artist who lived from 1873–1950. To reach the museum, take bus no. 340. It's open Tuesday to Sunday from April 15 to May from noon to 5pm. In June to August it is open Tuesday to Sunday, 9:30am to 5pm. It is also open in September until the third Sunday in October, Tuesday to Sunday noon to 5pm. It's closed the rest of the year. Admission costs 20 DKK ($2.90) for adults, and it's free for children under age 12.

OUTDOOR ACTIVITIES

A wealth of possibilities in North Zealand await you, none finer than the **Gilleleje Golf Klub,** Ferlevej 52 (☎ **49-71-80-56**), one of Denmark's best golf courses, 18 holes situated in gently undulating terrain. The course is of very high quality and often used for both national and international tournaments. On site are a bar, restaurant, and golf shop. Greens fees are 220 DKK ($31.90) from Monday to Friday, rising to 250 DKK ($36.25) on weekends.

The **Gilleleje Tennis Klub,** Øster Allé, lies just a few minutes' walk from the beach. This beautiful tennis complex has 8 hard courts, plus bathing and club facilities.

Many other sporting possibilities are available—the tourist office (see above) has full details. The use of jet skis is prohibited, but the coast of Rågeleje is ideal for windsurfing. The beaches of Gilleleje and Dronningmølle also attract windsurfers, although you must exercise caution to avoid bathers. If you'd like to go horseback riding across heathland and sand dunes, contact the **Enggården Ridecenter,** Hellebjergvej 27, Dronningmølle (☎ **49-70-46-60**), and discuss arrangements.

SHOPPING   For whatever reason, there are more shops in Gilleleje, per capita, than for virtually any other small town in Zealand. At least part of that is attributable to the discretionary income of many of the holiday-makers who flock here from other parts of Denmark, or perhaps it's the tradition of buying and selling antiques that has been a part of the civic consciousness here since the 1960s. In any event, a walk up and down the length of the Vesterbrogade will reveal lots of small boutiques whose inventories, collectively, might enrich the aesthetics of wherever you might opt to display them.

Some of the largest and most unusual of the town's antique dealers include **Gilleleje Antik,** Hillerødvejen 21 (☎ 48-30-09-57), a specialist in antique Royal Copenhagen porcelain and porcelain figurines and a purveyor of 19th-century mahogany furniture from Denmark and, to a lesser extent, England. (There's also a winning collection of 1960s kitsch, including some plywood furniture that was considered experimental, and therefore rare, even when it was made.) Gilleleje Antik competes in a gentlemanly way with a much larger purveyor of antique furniture (much of it mahogany), **J.S. Antiques,** Ferlevej 55–57, Ferle, (☎ 49-71-79-79), one of the biggest and most visible antique stores in town. A smaller, and very choice store, selling antique furniture, decorative accessories, and porcelain, is **Kanalhylden,** Vesterbrogade 31C (☎ 48-35-45-15). And a store that has garnered a devoted clientele from all around the world because of its knowledge of antique Danish porcelain, especially Royal Copenhagen, is **Antik Ulla,** Vesterbrogade 94 (☎ 48-30-07-58). Looking for something more contemporary, but handmade? Check out the modern stoneware and ceramics, especially the depictions of fish and boats, at **Radoor Keramik,** Havnevej 13 (☎ 48-30-20-87).

Know in advance, before you begin your barnstorming of Gilleleje's antique stores, that opening hours of these shops are relaxed to the point of being almost chaotic. In most cases, shops open daily except Monday and Tuesday, from around 11am till around 4 or 5pm, depending on business and the mood of the shopkeeper. Most, however, maintain extensions of the phone numbers listed above that ring within their homes, so a call in advance in many cases will do wonders in opening a shop outside the hours noted above.

WHERE TO STAY

Hotel Strand. Vesterbrogade 4D, DK-3250 Gilleleje. ☎ **48-30-05-12.** Fax 48-30-18-59. E-mail: hotelstr@post.7.tele.dk. home7.inet.tele.dk/hotelstr/index.htm. 25 units (22 with bath). TV. 550–600 DKK ($79.75–$87) double with bath. Rates include breakfast. MC, V.

Because of frequent rebuilding and a radical renovation that was completed in 1984, it's sometimes hard to get a sense of the 1896 origins of this well-established hotel. But despite the fact that most of the old-time architectural embellishments were long ago ripped out, it's still a popular, well managed hotel whose simple, efficiently decorated bedrooms are usually booked fairly heavily throughout the summer. Both the beach and the harbor lie within a 2-minute walk. Breakfast is the only meal served. All of the rooms in the hotel have private bathrooms except for three singles.

WHERE TO DINE

Fyrkroen. Fyrvejen 29. ☎ **48-30-02-39.** Reservations recommended, especially when weather is clear. Main courses 98–145 DKK ($14.20–$21.05); set-price menu 138 DKK ($20). MC, V. May–Aug Tues–Sun noon–10pm; Sept–Dec and Mar–Apr, Thurs–Sun noon–10pm. Closed Jan–Feb. From Gilleleje, drive 2 ½-miles west, following signs to Hornbæk. DANISH.

Much of the allure of this place derives from its historic charm and the fact that it affords diners with panoramic views stretching as far away as the coast of Sweden. It was built in 1772 as a lighthouse marking the position of the dangerous shoals offshore. Today, the low-slung white-painted stone building adjacent to the lighthouse tower contains a well-recommended restaurant where patronage is especially brisk on days with the best visibility. There's an indoor dining room, an outdoor terrace, and a sense of the old-time days of the long-ago sailing ships. Menu items include a medley of soups (especially shrimp, asparagus, tomato, and goulash soups); smoked salmon; several kinds of salads; steaks; and a roster of such fish as halibut, salmon, and perch. The cookery is competent, made with market-fresh ingredients.

✪ **Hos Karen & Marie.** Nordre Havnevej 3. ☎ **48-30-21-30.** Reservations recommended. Main courses 150–189 DKK ($21.75–$27.40). Set-menus 198–238 DKK ($28.70–$34.50). AE, DC, MC, V. Daily noon–4:30pm and 6–9:30pm. DANISH/FRENCH.

This is our favorite restaurant in Gilleleje, thanks to its consistently hardworking staff and a sophisticated international flair that might be the result of the managers' years of experience working on the cruise ships of the Caribbean and the ferryboats plying the waters between Harwich (England) and the Danish port of Esbjerg. The setting is a 110-year-old yellow-brick building—it looks like an antique warehouse—that originally functioned as a general store for the maritime industry. Menu items change with the seasons and the moods of the chef, but focus to a large extent on fish and in virtually every case, at least two meat dishes. Examples include the restaurant's signature dish, a local whole plaice served with parsley sauce and new potatoes. Alternatively, you might appreciate the sea devil prepared with rum, thyme, and basil; or the beef tenderloin served with forest mushrooms and red wine sauce. A worthy beginning to a meal here is virgin lobster bisque garnished with cognac. The restaurant's name, incidentally, derives from two sisters (Karen and Marie) who founded the place in the 1970s, but who are no longer associated with the restaurant in any way.

Kok & Kone. Møllegade 3. ☎ **48-30-16-66.** Reservations recommended. Lunch main courses 75–178 DKK ($10.90–$25.80); dinner main courses 158–178 DKK ($22.90–$25.80). Set dinners 245 DKK ($35.55). AE, DC, MC, V. Tues–Sun noon–midnight. Closed Jan. INTERNATIONAL.

This place is the product of the husband-and-wife efforts of Lars and Jetta Vind, who live up to their restaurant's name ("The Chef and his Wife") through their hardworking efforts in the kitchen and dining room. The building originally functioned as a garage, which was radically transformed into a pair of cozy and well-conceived dining rooms decorated with a changing array of paintings. Exhibitions change every 2 or 3 weeks, and the paintings are for sale, so inquire if you like any of the artwork you see. Menu items also change every 2 weeks, and might include lemon sole *meunière* with a sauce made from a *fumet* of fish, cream, and white wine. There's also a perfectly cooked Charolais steak served with homemade spicy butter, lots of fresh-grilled fish, and such vegetarian dishes as a medley of peppers simmered with olive oil and herbs.

6 Tisvildeleje

59km (37 miles) NW of Copenhagen; 25km (15 1⁄2) miles W of Helsingør; 17 1⁄2 km (11 miles) NW of Hillerød; 70 1⁄2 km (44 miles) N of Roskilde

This is one of the most idyllic seaside villages along the north coast of Zealand. Against a backdrop of low-lying sand dunes, Tisvildeleje—the largest settlement within the region known as Tisvilde—opens onto one of the broadest stretches of white sandy beaches in Zealand, although the waters, even in July, will be too cold for you if you're from Florida. The best beach is less than a mile west of the center of the little resort. It has facilities such as a changing room and toilets and also a spacious parking lot. Those who don't like Danish beaches often come here for walks through **Tisvilde Hegn,** a windswept forest of heather-covered hills and trees twisted by the cold Nordic winds.

ESSENTIALS

GETTING THERE   From Hillerød (see above) trains run to Tisvildeleje at the rate of once an hour during the day. The trip only takes half an hour.

VISITOR INFORMATION   **Tisvilde Turistinformation** is at Banevej 8 (☎ 48-70-74-51), open Monday to Saturday, 10am to 5pm but only from June to August.

GETTING AROUND   Bike rentals are available at **Servicehjørnet,** Hovedgade 54 (☎ **48-70-80-13**). You can rent one for 45 DKK ($6.50) per day.

EXPLORING THE AREA

To the west of the center, running alongside Tisvilde Hegn, Denmark's fifth largest forest, is a ¾-mile stretch of white, family-friendly sandy beaches lapped by clean salty waters and fringed by dunes and woodland. The natural surroundings here are exceptionally clean and unspoiled. Volunteers work to see that this whole area of coastline is the most thoroughly inspected and litter-free in Denmark. A Blue Flag flies over the beach, meaning that the waters are not polluted.

In town you can visit **Tibirke Kirke,** Ved Kirken Vej (☎ **48-70-62-94**), which is open Monday to Saturday from 10:30am to 2:30pm, with Sunday devoted to a church service. Admission is free. This church was probably built around 1120 on a pagan site. In the latter part of the 14th century the church was enlarged and the nave provided with arches. At that time the small Roman windows were replaced with larger Gothic windows. In the middle of the 15th century the original choir was torn down to be replaced by a bigger one. The tower was built during the first half of the 16th century, but has had to be reconstructed many times since. During a period of terrible sand drifts, the church was laid waste. But it was eventually restored, and in 1740 a baroque altarpiece was added, with a picture by J. F. Krügell depicting *The Last Supper.*

At the foot of the church is a spring that may have been the place where pilgrims came in olden days.

Tisvolde Hegn is enchanting and usually wind-blown. The forest is crossed with many trails, our favorite being a dirt path south to Troldeskoven, a distance of about 1 ½ miles. Nordic winds have turned the trees into "sculptures" of rather haunting shapes—one is called "Witch Wood." The tourist office (see above) will provide trail maps.

If you don't want to walk, you can take a horse-drawn carriage through the forest. Starting at the tourist office in Tisvildeleje, the route takes you through the forest to Troldeskoven and along the wooded coastline to the ruins of Asserbo Castle for a look around. Trips last 2 hours and are available every Thursday in July. Carriage rides cost 100 DKK ($14.50) for adults and 50 DKK ($7.25) for children under age 12.

SHOPPING   Some of the most charming objects available within Tisvildeleje are artfully crafted candles, each made of paraffin and/or beeswax. They come in a wide variety of scents and colors at a small but well-stocked shop, **AVL-lys,** Hovegården 65 (☎ **48-70-78-90**).

Every Saturday between June and September, from 10am and 2pm, a large and lively flea market, **Tisvilde Loppemarked** (Tisvilde Flea Market), is held at Birkepladsen, in front of Tisvildeleje's railway station. This is the time locals empty their attics, divesting themselves of things they might have inherited or acquired and don't really want. There's also a collection of crafts and in some cases, used clothing.

WHERE TO STAY

Kildegaard. Hovedgaden 52, DK-3220 Tisvildeleje. ☎ **48-70-71-53.** 23 units (none with bath). 515 DKK ($74.70) double. Rates include breakfast. No credit cards.

This is an engaging and likable small hotel whose owners, the Tetzschner family, work hard to create an intimate and cozy environment for guests who tend to return several years in a row. The centerpiece of the complex is a century-old farmhouse, whose space is supplemented with outbuildings ranging in age from 30 to 70 years. Guests spend their days swimming at the nearby beach, playing volleyball or sleeping in hammocks strung across the garden, and enjoying a menagerie of family pets. Bedrooms are unpretentious and summery, each outfitted with a mishmash of simple contemporary furniture. Dinner platters are served only to residents who request them in advance for a price of around 80 DKK ($11.60). The establishment is located in the heart of town, a short walk from the tourist information office.

Tisvildeleje Strand Hotel. Hovedgaden 75, DK-3220 Tisvildeleje. ☎ **48-70-71-19.** Fax 48-70-71-77. E-mail: tisvildeleje_strandhotel@iname.com. 29 units (8 with bath). 550 DKK ($79.75) double without bath; 700–900 DKK ($101.50–$130.50) double with bath. Rates include breakfast. MC, V.

This is one of the few structures in Tisvildeleje that precedes the building boom of the 1920s, when wealthy Copenhagen families bought up much of the seafront and constructed large summer houses. Originally conceived in 1897 as a grocery store and livery stable, it has been rebuilt and expanded many times since until it reached its present form: Four interconnected buildings encircling a verdant courtyard and a massive chestnut tree. Don't expect a lot of amenities here to amuse and entertain you, as the focus is on beach life (the sea is only 100 yards away) and back-to-the-earth walks in the nearby forest. Bedrooms are simple, summery, and utterly unpretentious. The in-house restaurant is surprisingly good and aggressively international in its tastes and perspectives, and is recommended separately in "Where to Dine" (see below).

WHERE TO DINE

Bio-Bistro. Hovedgården 38. ☎ **48-70-41-91.** Lunch main courses 45–70 DKK ($6.50–$10.15); dinner main courses 155–205 DKK ($22.45–$29.70). DC, MC, V. June–Aug, daily 11:30am–10pm. Sept, Wed–Sun 6–10pm; Oct, Fri–Sun 6–10pm; Nov–May, Fri–Sat 6–10pm. DANISH/INTERNATIONAL.

This well-respected bistro next to a movie theater under the same management offers food that is often praised by the owners of various B&B hotels in town without restaurants of their own. In a setting that's vaguely derived from the kind of brasserie you might have expected in Paris or Lyons, you can order simple lunches (sandwiches, burgers, *croque monsieurs,* etc.), but only during the peak of midsummer. Most of the year, it operates only at night, and only on carefully designated days (see above), thereby guaranteeing that whenever it's open, it's likely to cause a bit of a stir among Tisvildeleje's year-round community. Menus feature a mixture of French and Danish dishes, and usually include chicken with wine sauce, salmon with a mousseline sauce, and several different kinds of steak.

Tisvildeleje Strand Hotel. Hovedgåden 75. ☎ **48-70-71-19.** Reservations recommended. Main courses 65–150 DKK ($9.40–$21.75). MC, V. June to late-Sept, daily 11:30am–10pm. Closed Oct–May. INTERNATIONAL.

Set within a big-windowed area of the previously recommended hotel, this brasserie-like eatery is the most cosmopolitan and most internationally conscious restaurant in town. About the only thing that's Danish here is the clientele; menu options include selections from Thailand, the Philippines, Australia, and France, and all of the well-crafted dishes use very fresh ingredients. Expect an array of stir-fried fish and vegetable dishes; lemon-grass soup and both green and red curry dishes from Thailand; satay skewers of beef and chicken served with peanut sauce; and whenever the chef feels particularly French, an old-fashioned *coq au vin* (chicken in red wine) or pepper steak.

7 Roskilde

32km (20 miles) W of Copenhagen

Roskilde, once a great ecclesiastical seat, was Denmark's leading city until the mid–15th century. Today the twin spires of **Roskilde Cathedral** stand out from the Danish landscape like elegantly tapered beacons. These towers are the first landmark you see when approaching the city that celebrated its 1,000th anniversary in 1998.

Once the capital of Denmark, Roskilde is centuries past its peak. But it is no sleepy museum town either. It's filled with a dynamic student community, boutique-filled walking streets, several landmarks and major sights, and a population of more than 52,000 people who call themselves Roskildenser.

Today Roskilde's cobbled streets and towering cathedral only hint at the power and mystery of its Viking past. Toward the end of the last millennium, the Vikings settled the area, drawn no doubt by its sinuous coastline, where they could launch their ships. In 1957 divers in the Roskilde Fjord came upon shards of wood and reported their findings. Their discovery turned out to be bigger than anyone imagined. Here, sunken and mud-preserved, were five Viking ships that presumably had been put there to block the passage of enemy ships.

Archeologists began the painstaking job of building a water-tight dam and draining that section of the fjord, while keeping the chunks of splinters of wood wet enough so as not to cause them to disintegrate. Splinter by splinter they began the reconstruction and re-assembly of the boats—a process that continues even today. You can see their efforts on display at the **Viking Ship Museum** (see below), a modern museum that contains the five found ships.

Between 990 and 1000 A.D., Roskilde's prominence grew, becoming the home of the royal residence. By the 11th century, a Catholic church and a Bishop's Seat resided at Roskilde, which was to remain Denmark's capital until the Reformation in 1536.

At that time all the parish churches were abolished and the Catholic hierarchy disappeared. The government and the monarchy moved to Copenhagen. Nonetheless, at its peak, Roskilde's importance was expressed in its architecture. By 1150, it was surrounded by an embankment and a moat, inside of which stood 12 churches and a cathedral. In 1170 Bishop Absalon built a new church on the same site where Harald Bluetooth had erected his church 2 centuries before. Though it took 300 years to construct, and was subsequently burned, destroyed, ravaged, and rebuilt, Absalon's cathedral laid the foundation for the existing Roskilde Cathedral or Domkirche, which today is a UNESCO world cultural heritage site.

ESSENTIALS

GETTING THERE   Trains leave three times an hour from Copenhagen's Central Railroad Station on the 35-minute trip to Roskilde.

By Bus   Buses depart from Roskilde several times daily from Copenhagen's Central Railroad Station.

By Car   Take the E-21 express highway west from Copenhagen.

VISITOR INFORMATION   The **Roskilde-Egnens Turistbureau,** Gullandsstræde 15 (☎ **46-35-27-00**), provides pamphlets about the town and the surrounding area. The office is open April to June, Monday to Friday from 9am to 5pm and Saturday from 10am to 1pm; July and August, Monday to Friday from 9am to 6pm, Saturday from 9am to 3pm, and Sunday from 10am to 2pm; and September to March, Monday to Friday from 9am to 5pm, and Saturday from 10am to 1pm. While at the tourist office inquire about a Roskilde card, which costs 100 DKK ($14.50) for adults or 50 DKK ($7.25) for children. The card admits you to the 10 major attractions of the area and is valid for 7 days from the date of issue. Without the card, it would cost 252 DKK ($36.55) to visit these same attractions.

SPECIAL EVENTS   The **Roskilde Festival** (☎ **38-88-70-22**), held outdoors July 1–4 on a large grassy field, attracts fans of rock music. To get information on the festival—dates and performances—call the above number or contact the Roskilde-Egnens Turistbureau (see "Visitor Information," above).

SEEING THE SIGHTS   *Saturday market 9am – 1pm City Centre Squan*

✪ **Roskilde Domkirke.** Domkirkestræde 10. ☎ **46-35-27-00**. Admission 12 DKK ($1.75) adults, 6 DKK (85¢) children. Apr–Sept, Tues–Fri 9am–4:45pm, Sat 9am–noon, Sun 12:30–4:45pm; Oct–Mar, Tues–Fri 10am–3:45pm, Sat 11:30am–3:45pm, Sun 12:30–3:45pm. Bus: 602, 603, or 604.

This cathedral made Roskilde the spiritual capital of Denmark and northern Europe. Today it rises out of a modest townscape, like a mirage—a cathedral several times too big for the town surrounding it. Construction started in 1170 when Absalon was bishop of Roskilde. Work continued into the 13th century, and the building's original Romanesque features gave way to an early Gothic façade. The twin towers weren't built until the 14th century.

Today the cathedral's beauty goes beyond a single architectural style, providing almost a crash course in Danish architecture. Although damaged by a fire in 1968, the cathedral has been restored, including its magnificent altarpiece.

The Domkirke is the final abode of 38 Danish monarchs whose tombs are found here, ranging from the modest to the downright eccentric. Not surprisingly, the tomb of Christian IV, the builder king, who was instrumental in the construction of nearly all of Copenhagen's famous towers and castles, is interred in a grandiose chapel here with a massive painting of himself in combat, a bronze likeness by the Danish sculptor, Bertel Thorvaldsen. In humble contrast is the newest addition, from 1972, of the simple brick chapel of King Frederik IX, which stands outside the church. This chapel is octagonal in shape and decorated with hand-painted tiles designed by the architects Johannes and Inger Exner and Vilhelm Wohlert. Other notable tombs include the white marble sarcophagus of Queen Margrethe I.

In King Christian I's Chapel, which dates from the 15th century, there is a column marked with the heights of several kings. The tallest monarch was Christian I, at 6 feet, 9 inches. This, no doubt, was an exaggeration, as his skeleton measures only 6 feet, 2 inches. The late 18th and early 19th century chapel of King Frederik V is graced by a large, bright cupola. Note also the Gothic choir stalls, each richly and intricately carved with details from both the Old and New Testaments.

The gilded winged altar in the choir was made in Antwerp in the 1500s and was originally intended for Frederiksborg Castle. Pictures on the wings of the altar depict scenes from the life of Jesus, ranging from the Nativity to the Crucifixion. Following the fire, a new altar cloth was created by the renowned artisan, Anna Thommesen.

The most charming aspect of the cathedral is its early 16th-century clock poised on the interior south wall above the entrance. A tiny St. George on horseback marks the hour by charging a dragon. The beast howls, echoing through the cavernous church, causing Peter Doever, "the Deafener," to sound the hour. A terrified Kirsten Kiemer, "the Chimer," shakes in fright but pulls herself together to strike the quarters.

Insider's tip: Free concerts on the cathedral's baroque pipe organ, which dates from the 1500s, are often presented at 8pm on Thursdays in summer. They are presented less frequently throughout the rest of the year. Check with the tourist office.

Roskilde

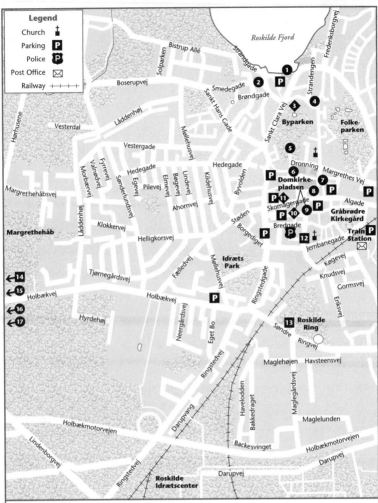

Legend

Church ✝

Parking **P**

Police **P**

Post Office ✉

Railway +++++

Roskilde Fjord

Byparken

Folke-parken

Domkirke-pladsen

Skomagergade

Algade

Gråbrødre Kirkegård

Bredgade

Train Station

Margrethehåb

Idræts Park

Roskilde Ring

Roskilde Idrætscenter

Attractions:
Historisk Arkæologisk Forsøgscenter ⑮
Ledreborg Park og Slot ⑯
Museet for Samtidskunst
  (Museum of Contemporary Art) ⑨
Palæsamlingerne (The Palace Collections) ⑧
Roskilde Domkirke ⑥
Roskilde Museum ⑦
Skt. Hans Kilde ⑤
Skt. Ibs Kirke ④
Skt. Jørgensbjerg Kirke ②
The Tramway Museum ⑰
Vikingeskibshallen
  (Viking Ship Museum) ❶

Accommodations:
Hotel Prinsden ⑫
Scandic Hotel Roskilde ⑬
Svogerslev Kro ⑭

Dining:
Club 42
  (Restaurant Den Hvide Fugl) ⑪
Raadhuskælderen ⑩
Restaurant Toppen ❸

✪ **Viking Ship Museum (Vikingeskibshallen).** Strandengen. ☎ **46-30-02-00.** Admission 40 DKK ($5.80) adults, 25 DKK ($3.60) children 6–16, free for children 5 and under. Family ticket 85 DKK ($12.35). Apr–Oct, daily 9am–5pm; Nov–Mar, daily 10am–4pm. Bus: 605.

Five vessels found in Roskilde Fjord, and painstakingly pieced together from countless fragments of wreckage, are on display here. It's presumed that the craft (dating from 1000–50) were deliberately sunk about 12 ½-miles north of Roskilde at the narrowest section of the fjord to protect the settlement from a sea attack. The discovery was relatively unprotected and unpublicized until 1957 when the Danish National Museum carried out a series of underwater excavations.

A merchant cargo ship used by the Vikings, a small ferry or fishing boat, and a Danish Viking warship similar to the ones portrayed in the Bayeux Tapestry are also displayed, and a "longship," a Viking man-of-war that terrorized European coasts, was also discovered. Copies of Viking jewelry may be purchased in the museum gift shop, and there's also a cafeteria.

To understand the attraction better, you can see a short film, "The Ships of the Vikings," about the excavation and preservation of the ships and the building and navigation of *Roar Ege,* a Viking ship replica.

In 1997 the Viking Ship Museum opened a museum harbor for its collection of Nordic vessels, including *Roar Ege,* plus another Viking ship replica, *Helge Ask.* The museum's restored sloop, *Ruth,* is also moored here. And workshops where you can try your hand at old maritime crafts such as rope- and sail-making, woodwork, and other activities, are located opposite the Boat Yard.

Roskilde Museum. Sankt Ols Gade 15–18. ☎ **42-36-60-44.** Admission 20 DKK ($2.90) adults, free for children. Daily 11am–4pm. Closed Dec 24–25 and Dec 31–Jan 1. Bus: 601, 602, 603, or 605.

Located 100 yards from the Town Square, this museum, set in a former merchant's house, features exhibits of the celebrated Hedebo embroidery, regional costumes, and antique toys. Displays also include an *aurochs* (an ancient European ox) skeleton, a unique Viking tomb, and a large number of medieval finds from the town. The museum also has a grocer's courtyard, with the shop in operation.

Museet for Samtidskunst (Museum of Contemporary Art). Stændertorvet 3A. ☎ **46-36-88-74.** Admission 10 DKK ($1.45) adults, children free. Tues–Fri 11am–5pm, Sat–Sun noon–4pm.

Housed in a beautiful palace from the 18th century, this museum of modern art has frequently changing exhibitions, together with performances, film shows, and modern dance and classical music concerts. It also houses a videotheque presenting programs with Danish and foreign artists. "The Palace Collections" (see below) are also housed on this same site.

Palæsamlingerne (The Palace Collections). Stændertorvet 3E. ☎ **46-35-78-80.** Admission 5 DKK (75¢) adults, 2 DKK (30¢) children. May 15–Aug 9, daily 11am–4pm; off-season, Sat–Sun only 1–3pm.

After a visit to the Museet for Samtidskunst (see above), you can view the collections in Roskilde Palace at the same site. Most of these *objets d'art* and paintings date from the era of great prosperity Roskilde merchants enjoyed in the 1700s and 1800s, when such local families as the Bruuns and the Borchs amassed a great deal of art and antiques, which you can see today.

MORE ATTRACTIONS

The **St. Jørgensbjerg quarter** was originally a small fishing village, and a number of old, half-timbered houses, some with thatched roofs, remain. These houses cluster around **Skt. Jørgensbjerg Kirke,** Kirkegade, which stands on the top of a hill with a panoramic view of Roskilde Fjord. This is one of the oldest and best-preserved stone buildings in Denmark. The nave and choir of the church date from the beginning of the 12th century, but the walled-up north door is even older, possibly dating from 1040. Slender billets, found only in wooden churches, are in the corners of the church and in the center of the nave. A model of a *kogge,* a medieval merchant vessel, has been engraved in a wall. The church is only open Monday to Friday 10am to noon from June 22 to August 31 (closed otherwise). To get there from Roskilde, take bus no. 605 toward Boserup.

The same bus will deliver you to **Skt. Ibs Kirke** ("The Church of St. James"), Skt. Ibs Vej, also in the north of Roskilde. Although no longer in use as a church, this ruin dates from circa 1100. Abolished as a church in 1808, it was later a field hospital and a merchant's warehouse. Regrettably, the merchant destroyed the tower, the chancel, the porch, and the church vaults of this medieval relic, but spared the nave. From sunup to sundown, it is open for visits from April 4 to October 18 (closed otherwise).

NEARBY ATTRACTIONS

Historisk Arkæologisk Forsøgscenter. Slagealléen 2, DK-4320 Lejre. ☎ **46-48-08-78.** Admission 50 DKK ($7.25) adults, 30 DKK ($4.35) children. Daily 10am–5pm. Closed late-Sept to Apr. Take the train from Copenhagen to Lejre, then bus no. 233 to the center. From Roskilde, there are frequent buses to Lejre, then take bus no. 233.

Lejre Forsøgscenter, an archaeological research center 5-miles west of Roskilde, is the site of a reconstructed Iron Age community on 25 acres of woodland. The center features clay-wall and thatch houses built with tools just as they were some 2,000 years ago. Staffers re-create the physical working conditions as they thatch Iron Age huts, plow with "ards," weave, and make pottery by an open fire. They also sail in dugout canoes, grind corn with a stone, and bake in direct fire. Visitors can take part in these activities. Jutland black pottery is produced here, and handcrafts and books are on sale at the gift shop. Tables are available where you can enjoy a picnic lunch.

Ledreborg Park Og Slot. Allé 2, DK-4320 Lejre. ☎ **46-48-00-38.** Admission 45 DKK ($6.50) adults, 25 DKK ($3.60) children 6–16, free for children age 5 and under. Family ticket 100 DKK ($14.50). June–Aug, daily 11am–4:30pm; Sept–May, Sun 11am–4:30pm. From Copenhagen's Central Railroad Station, take the direct train to Lejre, which leaves hourly and takes 35 minutes; from Lejre station, take the 3-minute bus (no. 233) ride to the castle and park. From Roskilde, there are frequent buses to Lejre, followed by the short bus ride to the castle and park.

A baroque manor house and French/English-style park 4½-miles southwest of Roskilde and 27 miles west of Copenhagen, Ledreborg is one of the best-preserved monuments in Denmark. A 33-room house with a landscaped garden and 217 acre park, this manor has been owned by one family, the Holstein-Ledreborgs, for eight generations. It was built by a minister to Christian IV, Johan Ludwig Holstein. Between 1741 and 1757 it was turned from a farmhouse into a baroque manor. Inside is a collection of antiques from the 17th and 18th centuries and a gallery of Danish paintings. It's approached by a 4-mile long *alleé* of lime trees, some 2 centuries old. Near the manor is a grave dating from the late Stone Age, approximately 3000 B.C.

The Tramway Museum. Skjoldenæsholm, Skjoldenæsvej 107. ☎ **53-62-88-33.** Admission 45 DKK ($6.50) adults, 20 DKK ($2.90) children. Late-May to late-June and mid-Aug to late-Oct, Sat 1–5pm, Sun 10am–5pm; late-June to mid-Aug, Tues–Thurs 10am–5pm, Sat 1–5pm, Sun 10am–5pm. Take a train from Copenhagen to Borup, then bus no. 248 or 249 from the station.

Located in the town of Justrup, some 10-miles southwest of Roskilde, in a pleasant woodland area close to Glydenveshj, the Tramway Museum with its collection of antique trams is situated on the highest point on Zealand, 416-feet above sea level. To reach the museum, board an old tram at the entrance and travel the 1,000 feet to the main building.

A BOAT TOUR OF THE ROSKILDE FJORD

You'll get a leisurely waterside view of the southern parts of Roskilde Fjord by partic-ipating in one of the frequent warm-weather tours offered aboard the **Sajafjord,** a many-balconied steamer from the 1950s whose profile evokes a paddlewheel steamer on the Mississippi. You can opt for either a lunch or dinner cruise (2- to 2 ½-hours long, and 3 ½-hours long, respectively), or a shorter mid-afternoon cruise (90 min-utes), depending on your schedule. Regardless of what you select, you'll pay a base rate of 65 DKK ($9.40), after which your (optional) food costs are extra. Platters of food aboard the lunch cruise cost 98 DKK ($14.20) each, and access to a *smörgåsbord*-style luncheon buffet goes for 145 DKK ($21.05). Evening three-course fixed-price menus cost from 215 to 265 DKK ($31.15–$38.40) each. Tours are only conducted between April and October. They operate daily during June, July, August, and September, and between 3 and 5 days a week, depending on the schedule, during April, May, and October. Cruises depart from a prominently sign-posted ("Sagafjord Tours") pier in Roskilde Harbor. For schedules, information, and reservations, contact **Rederiet Sagafjord,** St. Valbyvej 154 (☎ **46-75-64-60**).

SHOPPING

The best streets for shopping are the pedestrian thoroughfares Algade and Skomager-gade. Of these, we find Skomagergade the most interesting. It dates from the 12th century. Its name, "shoemaker street" in English, means that the shoemakers of Roskilde were placed on this street in the Middle Ages.

At either end of the street a triskelion within a circle has been placed in the paving. The symbol is three curved lines radiating from the center. It comes from the coins struck in Roskilde from 1018 to 1047. Today this silver coin has been recreated by one of the goldsmiths of Roskilde and is sold as a piece of jewelry at the tourist office (see above).

The best time for shoppers to be in Roskilde is for the market days every Wednesday and Saturday morning (go after 8am). Bustling activities take place on Stændertorvet, the main square by the cathedral. Fresh fruit and vegetables of the season are sold here along with many stalls hawking fresh fish and Danish cheese. You can purchase many items that are good for a picnic, along with beautiful pieces of jew-elry, and even mugs and pottery. For some reason, vendors also peddle a number of well-made children's clothes.

Roskilde also abounds in specialty shops, notably **Bydr. Lützhøfts,** Købmandsgård, Ringstedgade 6–8 (☎ **46-35-00-61**), a cozy old grocer's shop selling herring and other delicacies across the counter. The interior of the shop is fitted as it looked around the 1920s, and goods for sale are typical of that era. The building at no. 8 Ringstedgade is a butcher's shop, **Slagterbutikken O. Lunds,** selling goods made according to recipes from about 1920. You can also explore the merchant's yard with buildings from the 18th and 19th centuries. Sometimes special exhibitions are staged here—for example, depicting merchants and trade in Roskilde over the past 1,000 years. This shop is open Monday to Friday 11am to 7pm, Saturday 10am to 4pm. But from June to August, it is also open on Sunday from 11am to 5pm. Even if you don't purchase anything, this is one of the town's tourist attractions.

The town also has very excellent buys in handcrafts. Head first for **Glasgallerjet,** Skt. Ibs Vej 12 (☎ **46-35-65-36**), a former gasworks near the harbor which now houses the open workshop of a glassblower. Here the most beautiful glasses, dishes, vases, and other items are shaped by the glassblower, who displays marvelous skill. Spectators are able to watch the transformation of a lump of melted glass into a beautiful Danish handcraft on sale at the gallery.

An unusual selection of crafts is found at **Jeppe,** Skomagergade 33 (☎ **46-36-94-35**), which is run collectively by 20 craftspeople from Roskilde and its environs. They make and sell their own crafts. These are definitely non-factory goods. Exhibitions are always changing.

In the environs you can visit **Kirke Sonnerup Kunsthåndværk,** Englerupvej 62 at Kirke Sonnerup (☎ **46-49-25-77**). From Roskilde it is easily reached by bus no. 219 from Hvalsø St. This is an unusual art center with a gallery and cafe. It is one of the largest galleries in Zealand. Items displayed here are by Danish artists who exhibit their latest works in a brightly-lit showroom. You can shop for glass, ceramics, textiles, jewelry, and even silk scarves and toys, among other items. Light lunches, hot and cold beverages, and homemade cakes are also sold here. Hours are Wednesday noon to 7pm and Thursday to Sunday 10am to 5pm.

SWIMMING *Laundrette open 7am – 9pm just off city centre.

You can swim both in and out of doors in the Roskilde area, although outdoors might be a bit cool if you're not a Dane. There are several small bathing beaches along Roskilde Fjord, notably **Vigen Strandpartk,** directly north of the town. Here you'll find a sandy beach with a jetty, set against the backdrop of green salt meadows. A Blue Flag flies at this beach, a European designation meaning the waters are not polluted.

If you'd like to swim indoors, head for the **Roskilde Badet,** Bymarken 37 (☎ **46-35-63-92**), reached from the center by taking bus no. 601 toward Vindinge. Admission is 16 DKK ($2.30) for adults and 5 DKK (75¢) for children. Hours are Monday and Wednesday 1 to 6pm, Tuesday and Thursday 1 to 8:30pm, Friday 1 to 6:30pm, Saturday 7am to 4pm, and Sunday 8am to 1:30pm. Closed July 1 to 25.

WHERE TO STAY

Hotel Prinsden. Algade 13, DK-4000, Roskilde. ☎ **46-35-80-10.** Fax 46-35-81-10. www.hotelprinsden.dk. 46 units. MINIBAR TV TEL. Mid-June to mid-Aug 785 DKK ($113.80) double, mid-Aug to mid-June 985 DKK ($142.80) double. Rates include breakfast. AE, DC, MC, V. Bus: 602 or 603.

Although its stucco-covered façade looks about a century old, the foundations of this hotel date from 1695 when it functioned as a smaller version of what you'll see today. Most of its interior was renovated in 1994, and today it offers medium-sized, smartly furnished bedrooms—all in all, a cozy nest with neatly tiled bathrooms that are a bit small. Only five accommodations on the top floor have a view of the fjord. There's a rather active bar on site, plus a steakhouse, Le Boeuf, which serves a wide selection of Danish dishes and international specialties from noon to 10pm daily. The beef here is exceptional, but there is also an array of Danish lamb and poultry dishes, although almost no fish. A fixed-price menu, served only in the evening, costs from 220 to 300 DKK ($31.90–$43.50), with main courses going for 120 to 200 DKK ($17.40–$29). In summer if the weather's fair you can dine outside.

Scandic Hotel Roskilde. Søndre Ringvej 33, DK-4000 Roskilde. ☎ **46-32-46-32.** Fax 46-32-02-32. 108 units. MINIBAR TV TEL. Sun–Thurs 1,095 DKK ($158.75), Fri–Sat 750 DKK ($108.75). Suite 1,400 DKK ($203) all week. Rates include breakfast. AE, DC, MC, V.

The best in Roskilde, this chain hotel, built in 1989, still offers a sleek modern decor and good facilities, including a sauna and a solarium. The bedrooms are of average size, and are traditionally furnished and most comfortable, with medium-size baths. The hotel also has a good restaurant serving both Danish and international dishes, plus a bar. Parking is free in front of the three-story hotel, which lies on the ring road about half a mile south of the green belt, Roskilde Ring, on the southern outskirts of the city.

Svogerslev Kro. Hovedgaden 45, Svogerslev, DK-4000 Roskilde. ☎ **46-38-30-05.** Fax 46-38-30-14. 18 units. TV TEL. 575 DKK ($83.40) double. Rates include breakfast. AE, DC, MC, V. Bus: 602 with hourly connections to the town center.

Since 1727 this old-time inn has been welcoming visitors who make the 2 ½-mile journey west of Roskilde's center. The rooms are medium size (some, however, are a bit small) and are decorated in modern Danish styling and well maintained. Baths are a bit cramped. Accommodations are tranquil, many opening onto the inn's garden. The well-respected kitchen serves Danish open-faced sandwiches at lunch and an array of international dishes at night, including regional specialties, with main courses ranging from 135 to 185 DKK ($19.60–$26.85). If you're adventurous, request the fried eel, or else you might happily settle for the breast of guinea fowl with fresh herbs and a red pepper cream sauce. The chef's stew is made with bacon, onions, and mushrooms, in a paprika sauce. You can always count on baked salmon and some good steak dishes.

NEARBY ACCOMMODATIONS

Gershøj Kro. Havnevej 14, Gershøj, DK-4050 Skibby. ☎ and fax **47-52-80-41.** 6 units. TV. 500 DKK ($72.50) double, 1,150 DKK ($166.75) suite for six. Rates include breakfast. AE, DC, MC, V. From Roskilde, drive 9-miles NW, following the signs to Frederikssund. Closed Sept–May. Free parking.

The only problem with this atmospheric hotel involves the fact that it's open to individual travelers only 3 months a year, farming its simple and old-fashioned bedrooms out to members of corporate conventions the rest of the year. If you're lucky enough to arrive during midsummer, however, you'll be welcomed at a circa-1830 inn that's set only a few paces from the docks of the fishing hamlet of Gershøj, 9 scenic miles northwest of Roskilde. Expect old-fashioned charm and a restaurant that's known for the variety of ways in which it prepares a time-tested local favorite, eels hauled in from the harbor. Main courses cost from 100 to 190 DKK ($14.50–$27.55), with most of the eel dishes priced at 172 DKK ($24.95) each. From June to August, the restaurant is open daily for lunch and dinner.

Osted Kro & Hotel. Hovedvejen 151B, Osted, DK-4000 Roskilde. ☎ **46-49-70-41.** Fax 46-49-70-46. 16 units. TV TEL. 600 DKK ($87) double. Rates include breakfast. AE, DC, MC, V. From Roskilde, drive 7 ½-miles south along Route 151, following the signs to Ringsted.

There has been a hotel on this site since 1521, functioning as a refreshment stopover for travelers migrating between Roskilde and Ringsted. The roadside inn you'll see today is much, much newer than that, however, with a much-rebuilt original core and a modern annex (constructed in 1985) that holds the establishment's 16 deliberately old-fashioned bedrooms. Don't expect too many distractions here, since other than a restaurant and bar, there isn't a lot to do. Nonetheless, meals are savory and well-prepared according to old-time Danish recipes, with main courses priced at from 100 to 145 DKK ($14.50–$21.05). Food is served daily from 11:30am to 9:30pm.

Skuldelev Kro. Østergade 2A, Skuldelev, DK-4050 Skibby. ☎ **47-52-03-08.** Fax 47-52-08-93. 31 units. TV TEL. 650 DKK ($94.25) double. Rate includes breakfast. AE, DC, MC, V. From Roskilde, take route 53 for 16 miles, heading north, following the signposts to Skibby.

Solid and reliable, and set behind a pale yellow façade in the hamlet of Skudelev, less than a mile from the sea, this Danish inn was built in 1778, and was radically reconfigured and upgraded from a virtual ruin in the early 1990s. Since its re-opening, several branches of Denmark's governmental bureaucracy have designated it as the site for some of its conferences and conventions. When one of these isn't going on, however, you can rent any of the simple but comfortably furnished bedrooms, each of which has a color scheme of pale red and white and contemporary furniture. There's a restaurant on the premises that's open daily for lunch and dinner, charging 100 to 130 DKK ($14.50–$18.85) per main course. On the premises is an outdoor swimming pool that many residents prefer in lieu of a trek to the beach.

WHERE TO DINE

Club 42 (Restaurant Den Hvide Fugl). Skomagergade 42. ☎ **46-35-17-64.** Reservations recommended. Main courses 100–200 DKK ($14.50–$29); fixed-price three-course menu 168 DKK ($24.35). DC, MC, V. Daily 11am–10pm. DANISH/INTERNATIONAL.

Sandwiched between two similar houses in the heart of town, this brick-fronted building originally housed a blacksmith's shop 300 years ago and was the site where most of the town's horses were fitted with shoes. In a long and narrow interior whose greenhouse-style roof can be opened during mild weather, it offers a selection of open-faced sandwiches, pork ribs prepared in barbecue sauce or in garlic/onion sauce, filet steak with red-wine sauce, a fish platter of the house served with butter sauce, and grilled pepper steak. The place is one of the middle-bracket staples of Roskilde. Although the food is a bit standard, it is well prepared with tasty ingredients.

Raadhuskælderen. Stændertorvet, Fondens Bro 1. ☎ **46-36-01-00.** Reservations recommended. Main courses 138–280 DKK ($20–$40.60). Set-price menu 238 DKK ($34.50). AE, DC, MC, V. Mon–Sat 11am–10pm; Sun 11am–9pm. DANISH.

One of the oldest restaurant venues in Roskilde occupies the street level of a building whose redbrick masonry was erected in 1430, across the street from the town's cathedral. Although it's tempting to remain within the vaulted and arcaded interior (you'll have to descend only about 4 steps to reach it), there's also an outdoor terrace that is pleasant during midsummer, especially because of its view of the cathedral. Menu items are carefully prepared using very fresh ingredients. Examples include lobster soup served with homemade bread, smoked salmon with a small portion of scrambled eggs, tournedos in red wine sauce, and pepper steak that's flambéed at your table. One particularly succulent main course is a *Raadhus teller* that's composed of paprika-dusted pork cutlets with noodles and herbs.

Restaurant Toppen. Bymarken 37. ☎ **46-36-04-12.** Reservations recommended. Main courses 60–95 DKK ($8.70–$13.75). DC, MC, V. Mon–Fri 3:30–10pm, Sat–Sun noon–10pm. Bus: 601. DANISH.

At the top of a 1961 water tower, 274-feet above sea level, Restaurant Toppen offers a panoramic view of the whole town, the surrounding country, and Roskilde Fjord—all from the dining room. Begin with a shrimp cocktail served with dill and lemon, which is accompanied by salad, bread, and butter. Main dishes include sirloin of pork a la Toppen with mushrooms and a béarnaise sauce, accompanied by a baked potato and salad. For dessert, try the chef's nut cake with fruit sauce and sour cream. The cookery has much improved in recent months, and there is a finesse and consistency that wasn't here before. The restaurant lies a mile east of the town center between Vindingevej and Københavnsvej. The water tower doesn't revolve electronically, but some clients, in the words of the management, "Get the feeling that it's turning only if they drink enough." There's a free elevator to the top.

A NEARBY PLACE TO DINE

Langtved Færgekro. Munkholmvej 138, 3-miles SW of Kirke Såby. ☎ **46-40-50-53.** Reservations recommended. Main courses 150–200 DKK ($21.75–$29). No credit cards. Wed–Fri 3–9pm; Sat–Sun noon–9pm. From Roskilde, drive 16-miles NW, following the signs to Holbæk and then to Munkholm Bro. DANISH.

This isolated Danish inn, a short walk from the hamlet of Munkholm Bro, 3-miles southwest of the town of Kirke Såby, was inaugurated 250 years ago when a need arose to feed passengers on a nearby ferryboat route. Today, its black-and-white half-timbered premises are a favored site for clients who appreciate walks in the surrounding forest, or along the nearby shoreline, either before or after a meal within its historic dining room. Menu items have received several awards for their flavors, and are configured as part of a series of culinary choices that change with the seasons. Examples include shrimp cocktails; crêpes stuffed with baby shrimp, feta cheese, and herbs; marinated salmon with homemade bread; steak with fried onions; pepper steak; tournedos with marrow sauce; and either halibut or plaice with hollandaise sauce.

ROSKILDE AFTER DARK

Two of the busiest and most appealing night spots in Roskilde each offer their share of available Danes, both male and female, who might agree to strike up a dialogue with a stranger. **Club Exami,** Algade 25A (☎ **46-36-10-06**), offers an all-purpose singles bar, dance floor, and restaurant that reflects the low-key permissiveness of the Danes to its most appealing advantage. The building in which it is housed is relatively new, and the labyrinth you'll find inside can be fun and very adult. The music that plays here is recorded, not live, but in view of the fact that it's the most popular adult disco in town, no one seems to mind. Barring that, consider a drink or two in the historic, 200-year-old premises of **Club 42,** Skomagergade 42 (☎ **46-35-17-64**). Open nightly, it's vaguely patterned on an English pub where beer and aquavit (Danish schnapps) seem to be the drinks of choice. It's open nightly, and also contains a restaurant (see recommendation above).

South Zealand & Møn

The largest of the Danish islands—about the size of the state of Delaware—Zealand was said to have been carved from Sweden by the goddess Gefion. From Copenhagen, almost any point of Zealand can be reached in an hour and a half. For convenience of touring, we have divided the island into North Zealand (see chapter 6) and South Zealand.

The north of the island, admittedly, has more drama, including sites like Hamlet's Castle and the cathedral at Roskilde. But the less-developed south offers more tranquillity, with its rural towns and small farms that edge up to communities with white sandy beaches. And when you're this far south, you can also visit an extension of Zealand, the offshore islands of Falster and Lolland.

One of the most history-rich parts of Denmark, South Zealand was especially important in the Viking age. It was also vital in the Middle Ages, especially as a center for the Valdemar dynasty. In the 1600s some of the most epic battles between Sweden and Denmark took place here, especially in the seas off Køge. One of Denmark's greatest moments of shame—other than an attack by Hitler's forces—came in 1658 when King Gustave of Sweden marched across the fields of South Zealand heading for Copenhagen. Once there, he forced a treaty that nearly cost Denmark its sovereignty.

If your time is limited you may want to confine your visit to the highlights, which would include the former witch-burning town of Køge, but also the sleepy town of Søro, one of the area's most charming. South Zealand is also filled with medieval churches (we've previewed the best of them) and has a 1,000-year-old ring fortress at Trelleborg.

Motorists from Køge in the east heading to Korsør in the west (perhaps to cross the bridge over the Great Belt into Funen) would be wise to steer clear of the dull E20 motorway and follow the scenic and greener Route 150 which will take you through South Zealand's best kept villages and farmlands.

There is much to see and do here, and much that awaits discovery, as the area is almost ignored by the rushed North American visitor. But for those with the time to seek them, there are rewards, ranging from climbing the "Goose Tower" in the old town of Vordingborg to exploring Præstø with its charming harbor and extremely well-preserved market town atmosphere. There are often festivals of fine food and music throughout the summer, plus seemingly endless sailing clubs, which give the ports a real maritime atmosphere, filled with the heady scents of seaweed and tar.

For Zealand rail information, you can call the main station in Copenhagen (see chapter 4). For bus information in Zealand, call ☎ **36-45-45-45.**

1 Køge

40km (25 miles) S of Copenhagen; 24km (15 miles) SE of Roskilde

This old port city, now peppered with many industries, is south of Copenhagen on Køge Bay on the east coast of Zealand.

Better known in the Middle Ages than it is today, Køge was granted a charter by King Erik VI in 1288. The area grew up around a bustling natural harbor, a hub of trade with Germany to the south and a thriving fishing center. In the Middle Ages it was known as a witch-burning town, similar to Salem in Massachusetts.

The Battle of Køge Bay was fought here in 1677, one of the major conflicts in the eternal wars with Sweden. The Danish admiral, Niels Juel, defeated the attacking Swedish navy, thwarting their attempt to conquer Denmark. He subsequently became a national hero, like Admiral Nelson to the British.

Køge, still a bustling city today with a modern commercial harbor and home to 40,000, is visited mainly because it has preserved the narrow, historic streets of its inner core. A fire in 1633 leveled many of the buildings, but others were spared to greet visitors today, and still others were restored to their original appearance. The heart of the city is its Torvet, or town square. The streets worth exploring, such as Kirkestræde, radiate from this main square.

ESSENTIALS

GETTING THERE   Take the S-railway extension from Copenhagen. Service is every 20 minutes throughout the day. The trip takes 35 minutes. You can also reach Køge by train from Roskilde. From Roskilde the trip is only 25 minutes. There are also rail links with Næstved (trip time: 35 minutes). Bus no. 21 departs for Køge frequently from Copenhagen's Central Railroad Station.

By Car   From Copenhagen, head south along the express highway E47/E55. Motorists from Roskilde can take Route 6, connecting with Route 151 south into the heart of Køge. Parking is available at Torvet (but it's only for an hour at a time). You'll find less restrictive parking at Havnen, north of the yacht harbor.

VISITOR INFORMATION   Guided tours of Køge are arranged through the **Tourist Office,** Vestergade 1 (☎ **56-65-58-00**), open Monday to Friday year-round 9am to 5pm. From June to August Saturday hours are 9am to 5pm; off-season, Saturday hours are 10am to 1pm. English is spoken.

GETTING AROUND

While at the tourist bureau you can ask for a free brochure published by the Dansk Cyklist Forbund (Danish Cyclists' Union). It's in English and outlines five biking tours of the nearby area, ranging from a 25-mile tour that features Vallø Slot, or Castle, (see below) to a 3 ¾-mile route that visits the grave of Danish philosopher, Nikolai Frederik Grundtvig.

Renting a bicycle in Køge might remind you of renting a car somewhere else: You make a phone call to an out-of-town group dedicated to counseling and guiding teenagers (**De Unges Hus,** ☎ **46-15-12-76**), and a member of their team will deliver the bicycle within a few hours to your hotel, the tourist office, or wherever you specify.

Bikes rent for 50 DKK ($7.25) a day. They do not want drop-in visitors. That's why there's no address.

EXPLORING THE TOWN

Køge Bay is no longer the perfect place to watch naval battles between the Danish and the Swedish fleets. Today it's mainly a recreational area with a pleasure boat harbor and miles of lovely but chilly beaches.

The harbor lies only a short walk from the medieval center and it has the same significance for the people of Køge as Nyhavn does for Copenhageners. We enjoy the atmosphere here and like watching the action in the busy harbor, which is filled with Baltic freighters, fishing boats, and pleasure craft. If you walk to the North Pier, you'll find a number of eating places and cafés in old-fashioned houses. Here you can relax over a meal or order a cold Danish beer—and the day is yours.

Opening onto the bay is a monument, commemorating the battle in Køge Bay. You'll see it standing some 30 feet high near the harbor. This granite obelisk bears the name of the maritime hero, the already-mentioned Niels Juel, and another naval hero, Ivar Huitfeldt. Huitfeldt commanded the vessel *Danebrog*, which burst into flames when bombarded by Swedish forces in 1710. This brave naval hero continued to fight on until his ship finally exploded.

Before taking a look at the bay, set out to explore the historic medieval core of the old town. You'll pass fish markets selling freshly caught flatfish, herring, and eel, as you experience the bustling atmosphere of this busy yacht harbor. Stroll through the city parks and surrounding woodland, and peek into the courtyards of the old buildings left from the Middle Ages. In summer, live street entertainment will amuse you, and giving a few kroner to the young musicians is always appreciated.

The best street for wandering is **Kirkestræde,** lined with graceful old houses. A small building on the street, No. 20, is reputed to be the oldest half-timbered house in Denmark, dating back to 1527. A couple of porch stones from the Middle Ages, said to be the only pair in Denmark in their original position, are in front of a house at Smedegarden 13, near an ancient tree.

Of the town's churches, **Sankt Nicolai Church,** Kirkestæde 29 (☎ 56-65-13-59), 2 blocks north of Torvet, is of the most interest. This Gothic structure dates from 1450 to the beginning of the 16th century and was named after St. Nicholas, patron saint of mariners. History records that King Christian IV watched the Battle of Køge, in which Niels Juel sank many Swedish vessels, from the church tower. The church has a number of art treasures, including an altarpiece by Lorents Jørgensen and 100 tombs of Køge merchants. Note the carved angels on the pews. They are without noses, thanks to drunken Swedish troops who in the 1600s came this way, cutting off the noses with their swords. Look for a little brick projection at the east end of the church tower. Called Lygten, it was for centuries a place where a burning lantern was hung to guide sailors safely back into the harbor. Hours from mid-June to late-August are daily from 10am to 4pm; off-season, daily 10am to noon. Admission is free.

All streets invariably lead to the **Torvet** or town square. This is the marketplace where stocks once stood. Trials of witches—they were almost always found guilty—were conducted here, followed by their executions. Those dank memories are all but forgotten today, especially on Wednesday and Saturday morning when a lively market takes place here. The Saturday market is the far livelier of the two.

On the north side of the market square (Torvet) is the **Køge Rådhus,** believed to be the oldest town hall in Denmark that's still in business. The building in the rear was erected very early in the 17th century to serve as accommodations for King Christian IV on his trips between the royal palaces in Copenhagen and Nykøbing F (the "F" refers to the island of Falster). You can wander into the courtyard at the town hall to see a modern sculpture created by Jens Flemming Sørensen.

A path for walkers and cyclists leads along the Køge River with access from the center in several places. Go here to enjoy some peace and quiet—and take along a picnic lunch if the weather's fair. There are several little delis in town where you can pick up some open-faced sandwiches and drinks to take along. The park, Lovparken, is only a 5-minute walk from the Torvet. A wooden bridge takes you across the river, where you have a charming view of the riverside and its gardens.

The coastline near Køge offers several spots for fine bathing. For example, directly north of Køge you'll come upon a land of dunes and lymegrass with an excellent sandy beach on Ølsemagle Revle. Near the city center, Køge Sydstrand, or south beach, offers camping sites. A bit further south the beach at Strøby Ladeplads is ideal for windsurfers.

Among specific attractions, consider a visit to the following:

Køge Museum. Nørregade 4. ☎ **56-63-42-42**. Admission 11 DKK ($1.60). Children 9 and under free. June–Aug daily 11am–5pm, Sept–May Mon–Fri and Sun 1–5pm, Sat 11am–3pm.

This fine museum in an old merchant's home from 1610 and surrounded by a beautiful garden near the town square is devoted to the history of culture in South Zealand. It consists of six well-furnished rooms and a kitchen with implements used between 1640 and 1899. Displays of costumes, textiles, carriages, farm equipment, crafts from artisan's guilds, and other historical artifacts of the area are featured. Curiously, there is a windowpane where H. C. Andersen scratched the words (translated, of course): "Oh, God, oh, God in Køge." The museum also has a desk once owned by Nikolai Frederik Grundtvig, the Danish philosopher and theologian who used to live on the outskirts of Køge. Also on display are hundreds of recently discovered silver coins, forming a treasure trove that may have been hidden for safekeeping during the wars with Sweden in the 1600s. There's also a collection of 322 coins from all over Scandinavia and Europe—the oldest coin is a Palatinate *taler* from 1548. Your museum ticket, incidentally, is valid—if you use it on the same day—for admission to Vallø Slot, a charming castle that's recommended separately at the end of this section in "Easy Excursions from Køge."

Kunstmuseet Køge Skitsesambling. Nørregade 29. ☎ **56-63-34-14**. Admission 20 DKK ($2.90) adults, free for children under 10. Tues–Sun 11am–5pm.

This is a major modern art museum on the island of Zealand, exhibiting drawings, sculptures, and models by important Danish artists of the 20th century. A changing roster of special exhibitions is also presented. In English the museum's name translates as "art and sketch" collection. What makes this museum unique is that it traces the artist's creative process from conception to execution, from the advent of the idea to the unfolding of the "vision." Original drawings, clay models, and even mock-ups of a particular work are included so that the public can see how a piece of art looks while it is still in the conceptual stage. Sometimes a particular piece of art will undergo a tremendous change in concept along the way.

SHOPPING

The best time to go shopping here, even if you don't buy anything, is on Saturday morning. The town is crowded with people, many from the surrounding area. It's market day, a tradition going back to the Middle Ages. Most activity is found at Torvet, the main market square, but it spills over into neighboring streets as well. Fruits and vegetables, cheese, and smoked fish are sold side by side with Danish crafts and secondhand goods. You can wander from stall to stall as street musicians—most often jazz artists—entertain you from several courtyards nearby.

The best and largest selection of Danish gifts is found at **Jørgen Müller's eft.,** Torvet 3–5 (☎ **56-65-25-80**),on the market square. Here you can pick up Georg Jensen silver, Royal Copenhagen porcelain, Holmegaard glass—you name it. The best selection for women's fashion is **Rokkjoer,** Torvet 2 (☎ **56-65-02-58**), which has an impressive array of continental coats, blouses, and dresses—many in what they call "oversize."

If you'd like to survey some South Zealand antiques, the best outlet is **ANTIK-stuen,** Nyportstræde 2C (☎ **56-63-69-70**), with a good collection of clocks, furnishings, paintings, lamps, and mirrors, including some exceptional glassware from old estates. Less interesting but worth a trip is **Antik Bahuset,** Brogade 16E (☎ **56-66-17-19**), which sells old furnishings, pewter, brass, and a lot of pre-1900 items. It is only open Saturday from 10am to 1pm unless you call for an appointment at other times.

Another antique store worth a visit is **Tamalat Antik,** Brogade 16 (☎ **56-65-63-10**), with a wide selection of antiques, and good buys in paintings, jewelry, glass, and porcelain. Finally, **Krybben,** Torvet 19 (☎ **56-63-02-01**), offers a wide selection of clothing, crafts, shoes, and antiques, an odd mixture but intriguing nonetheless. A special feature of Krybben is an upstairs gallery exhibiting the works of a talented local painter, Anne Kureer.

For the novelty alone, you might want to visit **Købmandshandel,** Vestergade 6 (☎ **56-66-30-67**), a grocer's shop of yesterday. You can see how groceries were sold in the good old days. Two hundred different sorts of tea, and spices from around the world, as well as everything from olive oils to licorice root to rock candy, are on sale. You'll even find shoes, syrups, jams, and handmade candles.

Køge used to be known for its goldsmiths. Still thriving after all these years is **Guldsmedien Ejvind Sørensen,** Nørregade 31 (☎ **56-66-19-91**), in a charming old building from 1612. A large selection of gold and silver jewelry is sold here.

For the very best of Scandinavian design, not only furnishings but home accessories, head for **Hjelm's Bolighus,** Nørregade 32 (☎ **56-65-06-30**). This has been the leading Scandinavian design outlet in Køge for 40 years.

WHERE TO STAY

Best Western Hotel Niels Juel. Toldbodvej 20, DK-4600 Køge. ☎ **800/528-1234** in the U.S. or 56-63-18-00. Fax 56-63-04-92. 51 units. MINIBAR TV TEL. Sun–Thurs 1,015 DKK ($147.15) double. July and Aug and Fri–Sat year-round 695 DKK ($100.75) double. Rates include breakfast. AE, DC, MC, V.

Built in 1989, in a harbor-front location that shows off the white walls of its traditional gabled form, this is an attractive, stylish, and modern hotel that was named after a 17th-century naval hero. Catering to a clientele of business travelers and, to a lesser degree, vacationers, it contains a bar and a cozy restaurant, the Quintus, specializing in Danish and French food, including fresh salmon, oysters, and mussels. On the hotel's ground floor is an extremely well-stocked wine cellar that is often the setting for wine tastings for hotel guests. Bedrooms are furnished in a sleek Danish modern style, and though not overly large, are very clean and well-maintained, with good beds. Convention facilities that attract local entrepreneurs and corporations are on the premises. Guests relax over newspapers in the library or amuse themselves in the billiard and dart room. In addition, there is both a sauna and a solarium. The staff can also make arrangements for guests to play at a golf course less than a mile from the hotel.

Centralhotellet Køge. Vestergade 3, DK-4600 Køge. ☎ **56-65-06-96.** Fax 56-65-59-84. 12 units, 3 with bath. 450 DKK ($65.25) double without bath, 550 DKK ($79.75) double with bath. Rates include breakfast. No credit cards.

Set behind a pale blue façade in the heart of town, only a few feet from the tarmac of the street, this hotel was only converted into a hotel relatively recently and still has the feel of a cozy 19th-century house. Its main allure involves its low rates, which are ample justification for ultra-simple, stripped-down but clean bedrooms. None has any real electronic amenities, neither phone nor TV, but each is reasonably comfortable, if a bit small. Things are managed by a lackluster staff who may or may not speak English, depending on their mood. There's a small bar on the premises.

Hotel Hvide Hus. Strandvejen 111, DK-4600 Køge. ☎ **800/528-1234** in the U.S., or 56-65-36-90. Fax 56-66-33-14. www.hotelinfoplus.com/køge/hvidehus/htm. 127 units. Summer 695–1,015 DKK ($100.75–$147.15) double, off-season, 875–1,115 DKK ($126.85–$161.65) double. Year-round, 1,600 DKK ($232). Rates include breakfast. AE, DC, MC, V.

Built in 1963, about a mile east of Køge's center, this is a two-story, white-brick hotel constructed in an angular, glass and chrome style that evokes a tasteful version of the kind of architecture dating from the peak of the Cold War. Set about 200 yards from the beach, the hotel has blandly furnished but comfortable bedrooms that are outfitted in a Nordic modern style, with excellent mattresses. Many clients are business travelers from other parts of Scandinavia on overnight sales trips away from home. Views from the bedrooms encompass either the forest and a garden, or the sea as seen through clusters of trees.

Dining/Diversions: A comfortable, softly lit restaurant outfitted in pale earth tones offers well-prepared food, and there's an adjacent bar. Try such specialties as poached salmon with a white wine sauce served with new potatoes or roasted ox in an onion sauce. The chocolate and raisin ice cream for dessert is the unbeatable choice.

Amenities: Hotel concierge; a reception desk that can arrange car rentals; a sauna, solarium, and pleasant garden; and easy access to a beach less than 200 yards from the door. There's also a convention center that's popular with corporations in the surrounding region.

Thor's Hall Guest House. Vallørækken 1, Valløby, DK-4600 Køge. ☎ 56-26-72-10. Fax 56-26-63-11. E-mail: cirepost@12.tele.dk. 10 units (2 with bath). 480 DKK ($69.60) double without bath; 580 DKK ($84.10) double with bath. Rates include breakfast. No credit cards.

Pleasant, relaxing, and unpretentious, this hotel is the result of the recent transformation of a pair of century-old buildings into a streamlined new entity that the kindly owners refer to as a guesthouse instead of a hotel. It sits across the road from the village church, 3 miles south of Køge, beneath a terra-cotta roof, and behind white walls that are meticulously maintained by Erik and Aase Vedsegaard. Shortly after their arrival, hotel guests receive a key to the front door and are shown the location of an honor bar. Inside, great efforts were expended to have a clean and uncluttered interior, with windows opening on to views. Beds have good mattresses, are homey and comfortable, and hallway baths are adequate. No meals are served other than breakfast.

WHERE TO DINE

Kipperkroen. Havnen 25. ☎ **56-65-02-64.** Main courses 85–185 DKK ($12.35–$26.85). AE, DC, MC, V. Daily 11:30am–9:30pm. DANISH/INTERNATIONAL.

Set across the road from the edge of Køge's harbor, within a much-renovated 17th-century building, this is a well-maintained, well-managed testimonial to the pleasures of Danish wine, beer, and cuisine. There's a garden for dining and drinking outdoors, weather permitting, although throughout most of the year, clients dine in one of two areas inside. One of them contains two prominently displayed paintings by Denmark's Queen Margrethe II, which a staff member will point out if you ask. Menu items depend on the availability of local ingredients. One of the most appealing is plaice stuffed with shrimp, asparagus, and lobster meat; and the chef elevates the Danish staple of *bixemad* (beef hash with potatoes and onions, traditionally made with whatever happened to be lurking in a family's larder) to a high art form. Here, a platter of *bixemad,* with the promise of as many refills as you want, plus access to a salad bar, costs 85 DKK ($12.35), one of the best dining values in town.

Restaurant Arken. Køge Lystbådehavn 21. ☎ **56-66-05-05.** Reservations recommended. Main courses 118–155 DKK ($17.10–$22.45); set-price menu 148 DKK ($21.45). AE, DC, MC, V. Daily 11:30am–9:30pm. DANISH/FRENCH.

Set at the edge of the smaller of Køge's two harbors, this is a modern, big-windowed restaurant built in 1979, whose name, "The Ark," derives from its likeness to a large wooden boat that might have been envied by Noah. Within an interior that's flooded with sunlight, surrounded by lots of varnished wood that's reminiscent of what you might find aboard a yacht, you can order dishes that are tried-and-true to local Danish traditions. Menu items include *frikadeller* (Danish meatballs), grilled salmon with butter sauce, sautéed beefsteak with mashed potatoes and golden-fried onions, and English-style roast beef with horseradish sauce. During warm-weather months, a local version of fried eel with stewed potatoes is available as well, and a terrace that overlooks the harbor is available for additional seating.

✪ Richter's Gaard. Vestergade 16. ☎ **56-66-29-49.** Main courses 145–188 DKK ($21.05–$27.25). Set menus 198–238 DKK ($28.70–$34.50). AE, DC, MC, V. Daily 11:30am–10pm (last order). DANISH.

The setting for this restaurant is one of the most charming and evocative, and the third-oldest, in town. It was originally built in 1644 as a general store. Today, the brown brick, half-timbered façade adds spice and a sense of robust antiquity to the town center. You can opt for a table amid the heavy timbers of the interior, or if the weather permits, you can move toward the garden in back, sitting in the congenial Danish interpretation of a German beer hall. Menu items, served with panache, include *frikadeller* (Danish meatballs), trout stuffed with lobster and shrimp and served with a fish sauce and white potatoes, tournedos of veal with morel mushrooms, and a dessert treat of Danish seasonal berries served with ice cake. Although not experimental, the food has flair and flavor, and is prepared with market-fresh ingredients. If you only want a bottle of Carlsberg in the garden, it will cost you 22 DKK ($3.20). Every Saturday morning, between 11am and 2pm, some kind of live music is presented.

KØGE AFTER DARK

You can begin your nightly pub crawl, as the locals do, at **Toldboden,** Havnen 27 (☎ 56-65-50-75), a pub and bar built between 1833 and 1847. Carlsberg is served here on draft, and you can also order Guinness. In summer you can use the courtyard. Live music is presented every Friday evening and on Saturday afternoons, but mostly it's a place to gather and meet the locals, most of whom speak English.

Our favorite spot to meet friends for a friendly chat at night is **La Fontaine,** Torvet 28 (☎ 56-65-51-00), which somehow manages to have the coldest beer in town. It's right on the market square by the old fountain and stays open Sunday to Thursday from 10am to midnight, and on Friday and Saturday from 10am to 2am, late hours for sleepy Køge.

For young people the hottest place to be at night is the **Ritz Rock Café,** Torvet 22 (☎ 56-65-33-77). It is Køge's local version of the fabled chain of Hard Rock Cafés. People come here for the disco music and to eat and drink, partaking of the American and Tex-Mex cuisine. On a very busy night, it can hold up to 1,000 patrons. On the ground floor you'll find the most impressive sound and light equipment. But the second floor is smaller and more elegant, attracting a more mature clientele.

One of the most charming places for a quiet drink at night is **Hugos Vinkaelder,** Brogade 19 (☎ **56-65-58-50**), which spills over into the courtyard in fair weather. This cozy little wine bar retreat is found in the cellar of an antique building dating from 1392. Filled with atmosphere, it always has an interesting selection of wine, which it will sell by the half bottle if desired. Many locals come here to drink beer, however. The place is open Monday to Saturday 10am to 1am, Sunday 10am to 11pm.

Ask at the tourist office if there are any presentations of interest going on at **Køge Bugt Kulturhus,** Portalen 1 (☎ **43-97-83-00**). This is the Køge Bay Cultural Center and the venue for a wide range of concerts and theatrical performances. An exhibit of Danish and international art is displayed in its exhibition hall. Tickets for cultural events—whatever they may be—are sold at the tourist office. Of course, you might want to skip the theatrical performances if you don't speak Danish, but concerts and other entertainment would interest an English-speaking visitor.

EASY EXCURSIONS FROM KØGE

On the periphery of Køge lie some of Zealand's most interesting sights, all of which can be visited in just one day.

VALLØ AND ITS CASTLE

Lying just 4½ miles south of Køge, Vallø is the most charming hamlet in this entire part of Denmark, a little village of mustard-yellow houses and cobblestone streets from the Middle Ages. By car head south on Route 209, turning right onto Billesborgvej and left onto Valløvej. Bicycling is the ideal way to reach Valløvej, as there's a cycle route sign-posted from Køge. It's also possible to go by train; Vallø station is only two train stops from Køge.

Many visitors come here to see **Vallø Slot,** a castle that dominates the town. This castle with its French-style gardens was built between the 16th and 18th centuries, with sweeping gardens containing lakes, moats, rare trees, and rose and dahlia flowerbeds. Following a disastrous fire in 1893, the castle had to be completely rebuilt. Its towers—one square, another round—are a Vallø landmark. Once a royal palace, the castle was converted in 1738 into housing for "spinsters of noble birth." These days it houses old-age pensioners. You can't go inside since Vallø is now a private residence, but you can enjoy the elegant gardens, which are free and open April to October 10am to dusk.

On the grounds at the stables, **Hestestalden** (☎ **56-26-74-62**), there is an exhibition of the history of the castle dating from the days when it was the property of Queen Sophie Magdalene in 1737. It's open from April to October from 11am to 4pm. The cost of admission is 10 DKK ($1.45) for adults and 5 DKK (75¢) for children. The ticket, incidentally, is valid—but only if you use it on the same day—for a visit to the Køge Museum as well.

THE CHALK CLIFFS OF STEVNS KLINT

Only 15 miles south of Køge, near Rødvig, lie the chalk cliffs of Stevns Klint. These are not as impressive as the ones farther south on the island of Møn but are a worthy substitute if you can't visit the latter. This chalk escarpment extends along the coastline, opening onto a panoramic vista of the sea.

A white chalk crag, rising nearly 140 feet in the vicinity of Højerup, is the most stunning. A little church, Højerup Kirke, was built here in 1357. Legend claims this

Zealand's Link to the Continent

On June 14, 1998, one of the world's largest bridge links opened on the west coast of Zealand near the town of Korsør. Queen Margrethe II of Denmark was here to cut the ribbon shortly before driving across the 11-mile-long Great Belt Bridge. After 10 years of construction work, Zealand is now linked to the mainland of Europe via Funen, which already has a bridge link to Jutland on the European mainland. From Jutland, one can drive south into North Germany.

The bridge has cut traveling time across the Belt by more than 1 hour as compared to the ferries, which ceased operations with the opening of the bridge. At a speed of 65 miles per hour, crossing the Great Belt into Funen now takes only 10 minutes. By contrast, crossing by ferry took 1 hour, not including the waiting time at the port and embarkation and disembarkation from the ferries.

Fares are also cheaper crossing the bridge—a one-way fare for a private car, for instance, costs 210 DKK ($30.45). About 10,000 cars now cross the bridge each day; ferries transported about 8,000 cars daily.

The rail link across the Great Belt was opened in 1997. Since then, Danish State railways has seen a 60% rise in passenger volume on trains across the Great Belt. An average of 20,000 rail passengers cross the Great Belt each day.

Besides joining East and West Denmark, the bridge link across the Great Belt represents the first stage of an improved infrastructure between Scandinavia and the rest of Europe. Sometime around the millennium the Øresund Fixed Link between Denmark and Sweden will open. This will create a coherent traffic network and establish even more vital links between Copenhagen on the island of Zealand and Malmø, southern Sweden's largest city. With three million people living within a 31-mile radius of the link, the region has the largest population concentration in the Nordic area.

For more information about the bridge, call ☎ **33-93-52-00.**

church was erected by fishermen in gratitude for having been rescued at sea. There's another legend about this church as well. The sea continues to erode the chalk cliffs, and locals claim that each New Year's Eve the church moves a fraction inland to keep from falling into the sea. In 1928 it didn't move far enough and the choir collapsed, but the church has since been reinforced and made relatively safe. To visit the church costs 5 DKK (75¢) for adults, free for children. Hours are daily 11am to 5pm, but only April to September.

2 Ringsted

69km (43 miles) SW of Copenhagen; 24km (15 miles)W of Køge; 16km (10 miles) E of Sorø; 28km (17½ miles) N of Næstved

An important settlement in Viking times and a medieval ecclesiastical center, today Ringsted is a sleepy provincial town. But it has its aristocratic memories. This modern town of 30,000 people makes an ideal center for touring the heart of Zealand, offering excellent rail and road conditions. Route 14 from Næstved (see below) to Roskilde intersects the east-west highway (E20) from Køge to Korsør, where you can take the bridge over the Great Belt into Funen.

As late as the 4th century, Ringsted was the site of "the thing," or Landsting, as the regional governing body was called. Justice was dispensed on this site. In Torvet, the market square, you can still see a trio of three stones, the Tingstener, or "thing stones," recalling the early days when Ringsted was a power broker in Denmark. Also on the square is a 1930s statue of Valdemar I sculpted by Johannes Bjerg.

In times gone by, Ringsted was where Valdemar kings and many of their successors were laid to rest, in Skt. Bendts Kirke (St. Benedict's Church). The church dates from the 12th century and is one of the oldest brick churches in Denmark.

After a long period of slumber following the loss of its royal patronage, Ringsted revived again in the 19th century with the coming of the railway.

ESSENTIALS
GETTING THERE   Trains run frequently from Roskilde, taking only 18 minutes to reach Ringsted. Dozens of daily trains from Copenhagen pass through to Roskilde (see chapter 6 on North Zealand). There are also rail connections from Næstved (see below), taking just 20 minutes. The center of Ringsted can be reached in just a 10-minute walk north from the train depot.

By Car   At a crossroads, Ringsted is an easy target for motorists. It lies on Route 150 just off of the E20 motorway coming in from Copenhagen in the east or Funen in the west. From Roskilde follow Route 14 to Ringsted.

VISITOR INFORMATION   The **Ringsted Turistbureau,** Sankt Bendtsgade 10 (☎ **57-61-34-00**), stands opposite Sankt Bendts Kirke. From May to August its hours are Monday to Friday 9am to 5pm, and Saturday 9am to 2pm. Off-season hours are Monday to Friday 9am to 2pm. The tourist office will advise you of the best cycling routes in the Ringsted area.

GETTING AROUND
In Ringsted, mountain bikes can be rented from **Cykelsporten,** Sankt Hansgade 22 (☎ **57-61-82-82**). Rentals go for 100 DKK ($14.50) per day.

EXPLORING THE TOWN
Ringsted grew up around **Sankt Bendts Kirke,** Sankt Bendtsgade (☎ **57-61-40-19**), which was constructed by King Valdemar I (1157–82), on the site of a previous abbey church. His original intent was that the church serve as a burial site for his father, Duke Knud Lavard, who was slain by Magnus the Strong, son of King Niels (1104–34). The beloved Knud Lavard was entombed here, beginning a tradition of using the church as a burial site for the Valdemar dynasty. In 1169 Knud Lavard was canonized by the pope. The tradition of burying kings and queens of Denmark here continued until 1341. Valdemar I's larger motive in building the church was to use it to bring together the influences of the Catholic hierarchy and the Valdemar dynasty.

In the early 20th century, ill-advised restorers altered the style of the original church, but much remains from the Middle Ages, even the 11th-century travertine blocks from the older abbey church built on this site.

In 1885 King Frederik VII ordered that the royal tombs be opened. In a church chapel you can see the treasures found in these tombs, including a lead tablet from the tomb of Valdemar the Great, plus silks from the grave of Valdemar the Victorious.

The tombs themselves—marked by a series of flat stones—are beneath the nave on the aisle floor. Such notables as Valdemar III and his queen, Eleonora; the twice-married Valdemar II with his queens Dagmar and Benegærd; Knud VI; Valdemar I and his queen, Sofia; and the already mentioned Duke Knud Lavard, are all entombed here. Many long-forgotten royals suffered the indignity of having their tombs removed to make way for later royal personages. Chief among these was the beloved Queen Dagmar, born a princess in Bohemia and still revered in Danish folk ballads.

Much-loved by the people of Denmark, she died prematurely in 1212. When her gravesite was removed to make way for the tomb of Erik VI (Menved) and his Queen Ingeborg, a small gold cross with detailed enamel work was found. Called the Dagmar Cross, it is believed to date from 1000 A.D. Today, brides marrying in Sankt Bendts often wear replicas of this Dagmar Cross.

In the choir and on the cross vaulting you can see some notable chalk paintings. Some of Zealand's most interesting church frescoes are in the nave, especially a series depicting events in the life of King Erik IV. He was called "King Ploughpenny," because of a dreaded tax he imposed on ploughs throughout his kingdom. These frescoes were painted at the beginning of the 14th century in a failed attempt to have the king canonized (the Pope said no). One fresco shows Queen Agnes, wife of Erik IV, seated on a throne; another immediately to her left depicts the murder of Erik IV, his attackers stabbing him with a spear. In another fresco the king's corpse is being rescued at sea by fishermen.

Other notable features in the church include pews from 1591 with dragon motifs. The richly adorned altarpiece is from 1699, and the even older pulpit dates from 1609. The baptismal font is the oldest relic of all, believed to date from some time in the 1100s. From May to mid-September the admission-free church is open daily from 10am to noon and 1 to 5pm. Off-season hours are daily 1 to 3pm.

The other major attraction in town is the **Ringsted Museum,** Køgevej 37 (☎ 57-61-94-04), within walking distance of both the train station and the central market square. A modern museum of local culture and history, it presents artifacts gathered throughout the area, displaying the workaday life of locals long since departed. Beside the museum is a restored 1814 Dutch windmill, still in working order and still grinding flour which is sold at a kiosk on site. There's also a cafe. Hours are Tuesday to Sunday 11am to 4pm; admission is 14 DKK ($2.05) (closed in January).

The town hall, of only minor interest, was built in 1937 on land that had once belonged to a Benedictine Monastery whose origins were some time in the early Middle Ages. Designed by Steen Eiler Rasmussen, the famous Danish architect, the two-story brick building with a copper roof stands near a statue of Valdemar the Great.

A most unusual mechanized displays lies a mile northwest of Ringsted, the **Eventyrlandet Fantasy World,** Eventyrvej (☎ 53-61-19-30). It's especially appealing to families, who appreciate its mixture of fantasy and fairytales. Within a very large and echoing room, you'll walk along simulations of paths through a magic forest. In the forest's clearings, mechanical dolls, each about 18 feet high, simulate characters from the stories of Hans Christian Andersen as they dance, pirouette, and generally interact in their stiff but charming way. The assumption is that onlookers will have memorized the tales behind each tableau, but if you've forgotten one of them, virtually any Dane in the crowd will be able to encapsulate it for you. There are also tableaux depicting folkloric dances in Mexico and China, plus hunting scenes in Greenland. It's open year-round, every day from 10am to 5pm, with the exception of slow periods when very few tourists are in town. Opening dates are as follows: February 7 to 22, April 4 to 13, May 8 to August 30, and October 3 to December 30. Admission costs 60 DKK ($8.70) for adults, 40 DKK ($5.80) for children ages 2 to 11; and 20 DKK ($2.90) for children under 2. There's also an outdoor playground, a cafe, and a gift shop. Take bus no. 14, 15, or 401.

SHOPPING

Ringsted is right in the middle of the island and has a number of specialty shops. A covered shopping center, **Ringsted Centret,** Nørregade 13, stands right in the middle of town, enabling you to shop and browse without having to worry about the weather.

This is where you'll find the widest array of Danish products in various stores. The best place to go for copies of the Dagmar Cross (see Sankt Bendts Kirke above) is **Klints Guld & Sølv,** Torvet 2 (☎ **57-61-01-83**). The cross comes in gold, silver, and gold with enamel. In 1683 the cross—believed to date from 1000 A.D.—was discovered when Queen Dagmar's tomb site was moved. Today nearly all brides married in Ringsted wear a reproduction of this cross, which makes an intriguing piece of jewelry even if you aren't a bride.

WHERE TO STAY

Best Western Sørup Herregård. Sørupvej, DK-4100 Ringsted. ☎ **800/528-1234** in the U.S., or 57-64-30-03. Fax 57-64-31-73. 100 units. MINIBAR TV TEL. June–Sept 695 DKK ($100.75) double; Oct–May 995 DKK ($144.25) double. Suite 1,800 DKK ($261) year-round. AE, DC, MC, V.

The most atmospheric hotel in the area lies 4 miles east of town, in a redbrick building that was originally a manor house. Surrounded by 950 acres of rolling fields and forests, it was enlarged in the 1980s with lots of glassed-in additions that send light streaming into the interior. Bedrooms are conservatively decorated with comfortable beds, filled with the kind of furniture you might have found in an upscale private home and accessorized with engravings of bucolic landscapes. Frankly, the staff isn't too well trained here, many of them being very young, although we suspect that this will improve as they gain more experience.

Scandic Hotel Ringsted. Nørretorv 57, DK-4100 Ringsted. ☎ **57-61-93-00.** Fax 57-61-02-07. 75 units. MINIBAR TV TEL. Sun–Thurs 1,025 DKK ($148.65) double. Fri–Sat and June–Aug 650 DKK ($94.25) double. Rates include breakfast. AE, DC, MC, V.

This four-story redbrick hotel, a 5-minute walk south of the town center, opened in 1986, and has been the preferred choice in central Ringsted ever since. Despite the fact that it's newer and a lot less historic than the also-recommended **Sørup Herregård** hotel, we actually prefer it for its convenient location near the town center, and because the staff is a lot better organized. Its public areas host many of the region's conventions and business meetings, and bedrooms are uncluttered and streamlined, with writing tables and efficient modern furniture, including comfortable beds.

Dining/Diversions: There's a bar and a restaurant, Klosterhavn, on the premises, that's open for lunch and dinner daily.

Amenities: Exercise room with sauna, steam room, and solarium.

WHERE TO DINE

Italy & Italy. Torvet 1C. ☎ **57-61-53-53.** Reservations recommended. Main courses 99–169 DKK ($14.35–$24.50). AE, DC, MC, V. Mon–Thurs 11am–10pm; Fri–Sat 11am–11pm; Sun 5–11pm. ITALIAN.

Thanks to good food and an emphasis on the olive oil–based cuisine of Italy, this is the most consistently popular restaurant in Ringsted. It sits very close to Ringsted's most famous church, in a dining room that's flooded with sunlight from big windows and lined with paintings that commemorate the architectural grandeur of Italy. Menu items cover all aspects of a well-orchestrated Italian meal, and include marinated seafood and vegetarian *antipasti,* and such pastas as lasagna and fettuccine with bolognese sauce. Medallions of veal "Sct. Elisabeth" are flambéed in cognac, and veal with gorgonzola sauce is a perennial favorite.

Rådhus Kro. Sct. Bendtsgade 8. ☎ **57-61-68-97.** Reservations recommended. Main courses 65–150 DKK ($9.40–$21.75). AE, DC, MC, V. Mon–Sat 11am–9:45pm. DANISH.

Set across the street from the Rådhus (City Hall), after which it's named, this restaurant occupies one large room of a modern-looking building erected within the last

15 years. The dining room décor consists of a muted color scheme of soft oranges and greens. The menu is very, very Danish, and very traditional, and the restaurant is the haunt of a cross-sampling of virtually everyone who's active in Ringsted's business and government community. Menu items include mushroom bouillon with garlic croutons, Norwegian haddock with red wine sauce, veal steak with mushroom sauce, and filets of pork with white sauce and boiled potatoes.

RINGSTED AFTER DARK

You'll find pubs in virtually every neighborhood of town, but two of our favorites include the **Kong Valdemar Pub,** Nørregade 5 (☎ **57-61-81-32**), an antique-looking watering hole that has welcomed many generations of beer drinkers to its paneled interior. More modern, and an occasional venue for live music, is the **Apotekergarden,** Nørregade 12B (☎ **57-61-66-63**). Here you'll find an attractive crowd of Danish men and women, at least some of whom seem single, unattached, and available.

Another cozy gathering place at night is **Mettes Baghus,** Sct. Hansgade 31 (☎ **57-61-25-47**), a cozy little pub with a lovely garden. It's a nice place with a congenial crowd and a relaxed atmosphere. Kilkenny Irish beer is on tap, and you can also play pool or a game of darts.

3 Slagelse

99km (62 miles) SW of Copenhagen; 37km (23 miles) SE of Kalundborg; 19km (12 miles) NE of Korsør

In the Middle Ages this was a major trading center, with trade routes to Næstved in the south, Copenhagen in the east, and Kalundborg in the north. In the 11th century the town had its own mint, and its municipal charters were granted in 1288. Slagelse lies in the heart of Viking country and is the best center for visiting the nearby fortress at Trelleborg (see below).

Today the town of some 36,000 people is prospering, thanks largely to a lively economy. The area around here might be called Hans Christian Andersen Country, like Odense in Funen: The writer attended the local grammar school here for several years but found the town a "nuisance." Founded after the Reformation, it was an important school until it closed in 1852.

After its heyday in the Middle Ages, Slagelse declined considerably, the victim of various wars and some raging fires that burned its major buildings. But with the coming of the rail lines, the economy recovered. Canning factories, distilleries, and breweries beefed up its economy.

Today it is a major city of West Zealand, a route along the important traffic artery, the E20, linking Copenhagen with the bridge across the Great Belt into Funen and subsequently the continent. Though often bypassed by the rushed motorist, Slagelse has a number of treasures for those interested in the Viking period.

ESSENTIALS

GETTING THERE   Since Slagelse lies on the main east–west rail line between Copenhagen and the neighboring island of Funen (its subsequent link to the continent), trains run here frequently. The trip takes an hour. There are also easy connections from Roskilde, taking 35 minutes, and from Korsør (near the bridge over the Great Belt), taking only 12 minutes.

VISITOR INFORMATION   Lying a 10-minute walk south of the train depot, the **Slagelse Turistbureau,** Løvegade 7 (☎ **58-52-22-06**), provides information about its own attractions and Trelleborg (see below) to the west. Hours are Monday to Saturday 9am to 5pm, mid-June to August. Off-season, it is open Monday to Friday 10am to 5pm and on Saturday 10am to 1pm. The tourist office can arrange rooms in private homes with prices beginning at around 125 DKK ($18.15) per person for B&B, plus a 10 DKK ($1.45) booking charge. You can rent bikes here or at **HJ Cykler,** Løvegade 46 (☎ **58-52-28-57**).

EXPLORING THE TOWN

The town is dominated by its **Sct. Mikkels Kirke** (St. Michael's Church), Rosengade 4 (☎ **58-52-05-11**). Admission is free, and you can visit every day between 8:30am and 5pm. The church was constructed in 1333 in the redbrick Gothic style on the tallest hill in Slagelse. By the 1870s it had fallen into serious disrepair, however, and was restored. Although hardly the most interesting church in Zealand, it makes a worthy stop. A memorial here honors the Danish Resistance Movement in World War II. The sculptor, Gunnar Slot, designed it in 1959. Next to it is another sculpture entitled "Woman," the work of Keld Moseholm Jørgensen.

Slagelse has an even older church, **Sct. Peders Kirke** (St. Peter's Church), Brede- gade 7A (☎ **58-52-08-81**), which is open daily from 8:30am to 5pm. Admission is free. It was originally built in the Romanesque style around 1150, and later given a Gothic overlay. The vestry and porch date from around 1500. After its collapse, the church's original tower was reconstructed in 1664. The building contains many medieval graves, some of which can be viewed within an area used during the Middle Ages for storage of armaments that could be employed in the event of an attack upon the town or church. The most important tomb is that of St. Anders, who died in 1205, the first in a long line of vicars, and a major figure in the development of Slagelse. His tomb can be found in the northern part of the church.

Another attraction, lying south of Nytorv, the main commercial square of town, is the **Slagelse Museum,** Bredegade 11 (☎ **58-52-83-37**), inaugurated in 1984. It's an intriguing museum of local history with exhibitions devoted to arts and crafts, trade, and industry. Everything is here from a grocer's shop to a carpenter's and joiner's work- shop. The butcher, the barber, and even the blacksmith also get in on the act. Note the exquisitely set dining room. In all, there are 22 stands with exhibits. The museum has recently opened a new exhibition hall. From May to September it is open daily noon to 4pm; Saturday 3 to 5pm. In the off-season it is open only on Saturday 3 to 5pm. Admission is 10 DKK ($1.45).

If you follow the street, Fisketorv, it will lead to Gammel Torv, which for many decades was the thriving main part of town and a meeting place of locals. It is said that Queen Margrethe I crowned her 6-year-old son, Oluf, on this spot.

SHOPPING   Slagelse is home of the **Vestsjællands Center,** Jernbanegade 10 (☎ **58-50-63-90**), a shopping mall with about 40 stores that occupies a prominent position in the town center, and whose only real competitor is an equivalent shopping center 25 miles away.

If you're in the market for gold and silver jewelry, as well as the elegant products of Georg Jensen and Royal Copenhagen, the preferred outlet is **Guildsmed Carl Jensens,** Rosengade 17 (☎ **58-52-02-97**).

An intriguing collection of modern Danish paintings, along with gifts and sou- venirs, is found at **Gylling's Galleri & Værksted,** Skolegade 17 (☎ **58-86-00-85**). Finally, **Bahne,** City Arkaden (☎ **58-52-00-75**), is located in the shopping complex in the heart of Slagelse. It houses the largest collection of applied art in Slagelse, along with a wide range of pieces from Holmegård glass works and the Royal Danish Porce- lain Factory.

OUTDOOR ACTIVITIES

In summer there are many possibilities in the vicinity of the town to experience the great outdoors. The tourist office (see above) is helpful in hooking you up with any activities you might want to pursue and in providing detailed directions for hiking and walking.

The forest, **Bildsø Skov,** has the largest variety of trees in West Zealand. You can take a walk in its splendid surroundings, enjoying the natural environment. To reach Bildsø Skov from Slagelse, drive 6-miles east of town along Vej 277 (Route 277), following the signs pointing to Korsør.

The lagoon area in the northern part of the town is a series of lakes set up by city officials for the purification of waste water from the town. It is home to a wide variety of birds and attracts "birders" from all over Zealand. It is also the site of what is called the "people's woods," with many good possibilities for hiking. There are also panoramic views of Slagelse from here.

Finally, the city maintains clean and family-friendly beaches. The water and facilities at Bildsø and Stillinge Beach live up to Blue Flag conditions, the European designation for beaches with unpolluted waters. At Køngsmark Beach, you can go windsurfing.

WHERE TO STAY

Best Western Hotel Frederik den II. Idagårdsvej 3, DK-4200 Slagelse. ☎ **800/528-1234** in the U.S., or 58-53-03-22. Fax 58-53-46-22. 74 units. TV TEL. Mon–Fri 1,040 DKK ($150.80) double. Sat–Sun 825 DKK ($119.60) double. Suite for two, 1,350 DKK ($195.75) throughout the week. AE, DC, MC, V.

Set a 10-minute drive south of the center of town, at the junction of Route 22 and the E20 highway leading to Korsør, this is a sprawling, brick-built, motel-style establishment that's clean, convenient, well managed, and utterly without historic charm. Bedrooms are exactly what you'd expect from such a blandly international-looking building—comfortable, clean, respectable, and relentlessly standardized, but with excellent beds. Units lie on one of two floors—those on the ground floor have private patios; those upstairs contain balconies. There's a sauna, a bar, and a decent restaurant on the premises.

WHERE TO DINE

Nytorv 2. Nytorvet 2. ☎ **58-52-04-45.** Main courses 100–190 DKK ($14.50–$27.55). DC, MC, V. Mon–Sat 11am–10pm. DANISH.

Set in the heart of town, within the all-pedestrian shopping district, this is the only full-fledged restaurant in town that specializes exclusively in Danish food. You can dine on a brick-floored patio in back, surrounded by verdant potted plants, or in a conservatively decorated but comfortable dining room with a high ceiling and a polite, attentive staff. The house specialty is a "planck steak" that's prepared with ratatouille and a combination of béarnaise and pepper sauce and served on an oaken board. Several different preparations of plaice, as well as grilled salmon with spinach and rice, are also appealing, as are such desserts as fresh pastries with ice cream.

Pulcinilla. Rosengade 7C. ☎ **58-53-08-07.** Reservations recommended. Main courses 50–155 DKK ($7.25–$22.45). AE, DC, MC, V. Daily 5–11pm. ITALIAN.

This is a simple and likable dinner-only trattoria in the heart of Slagelse, with a white-walled interior whose roster of Italian art includes a blown-up version of the Mona Lisa. Menu items are flavorful and fun, and include a number of pizzas and pastas such as lasagna and fettuccine bolognese, soups and salads, and such main courses as veal parmigiana and entrecôte with pepper sauce. We won't pretend that this will be the finest Italian meal you've ever been served, but the food is well prepared with fresh ingredients, and it's good as a change of pace if you've tired of too much Danish fare.

SLAGELSE AFTER DARK

The municipality of Slagelse has converted an old power station into a splendid concert center, which is the venue for frequent musical events and also a center for changing art exhibitions. The old turbine hall can seat more than 400 patrons, and a cafe on site serves refreshments. The address is **Slagelse Musikhus,** Træskogården, Sdr. Stationsvej 1–3 (☎ **58-50-10-70**). Ask at the tourist bureau (see above) if any events are being staged at the time of your visit.

SIDE TRIPS: MEDIEVAL RUINS & VIKING RECONSTRUCTION

Slagelse makes a good base for exploring one of Scandinavia's major Viking reconstructions, Trelleborg, as well as a center for exploring Antvorskov, the ruins of a former royal palace and monastery. While still based at Slagelse, you can view both of these attractions in one very busy day.

★ **TRELLEBORG**   Although it's merely a mock representation, you can experience Viking life as lived 1,000 years ago at the reconstructed fortress of Trelleborg, Trelleborg Allé (☎ **58-54-95-06**), 4 miles west of Slagelse (for directions on how to get there, see below).

Trelleborg is the best preserved of the quartet of Viking ring fortresses in Denmark. Expect an agenda-loaded schedule once you arrive at Trelleborg: You can feel replicas of Viking tools, see household items used by Mrs. Viking plus the inevitable weapons of the day, soak up the atmosphere in a recreated Viking house, and, best of all, enjoy the beautiful Danish countryside surrounding Trelleborg. You can also take part in various events staged throughout the summer, including longbow archery, Viking cooking, sailing, martial arts, games, a Viking pageant, and a Viking market.

A reconstructed Viking house stands at the entrance to Trelleborg. It was built in the Viking stave style, with rough oak timbers rising above mud floors. The earthen benches inside were used by warriors and their families for both sitting and sleeping. The central hearth, as in this house, usually had an opening in the roof for venting smoke. This house and other reconstructions were based on finds excavated from an actual settlement on this site, which dated from 1000 to 1050.

The ring fortress consisted of a circular rampart with wooden stakes inserted in the earth. It could be entered through four different gates. From these entrances four lanes lead to the heart of the fortress. This divided the ring into four quadrants, with about 16 houses laid out in each quadrant. A moat protected the east side of the fortress, whereas the other three sides were secured by two small rivers and a marshland.

The relatively new Trelleborg Museum contains a fascinating shop selling Viking jewelry, books on the era, a film room, Viking exhibitions, ship models, ancient artifacts, and a cafe. The 20-minute video shown here will help you understand Trelleborg better before you actually explore it.

Visits are possible daily from 10am to 5pm. Allow at least an hour for a visit here, maybe a lot more if you find it intriguing. Admission is 35 DKK ($5.05) for adults, 20 DKK ($2.90) for children. A family ticket costs 100 DKK ($14.50).

If you're driving from Slagelse, follow Strandvejen until its termination at the village of Hejininge, where you'll see signs for Trelleborg, which is less than a mile away. You can also take bus no. 312 from Slagelse right to the gate. There are four buses Monday to Friday, but only one on Saturday (none on Sunday). We prefer to cycle our way here on a rented bike from Slagelse. The tourist office will give you a brochure outlining points of interest along the cycle trail.

ANTVORSKOV Today only the ruins of this former monastery and royal palace can be viewed, but much of Danish history happened on this spot, lying 1¼ miles south of the center of Slagelse near the road to Næstved. In 1164 King Valdemar I founded a monastery here, dedicated to the Order of St. John of Jerusalem. In time it became the major seat of the Order of St. John throughout the Nordic countries.

The monastery's chief legend centers around Hans Tausen (1494–1561), who preached a sermon in Antvorskov that paved the way for the Reformation in Denmark. This renegade monk, who trained at Antvorskov, then one of the richest monasteries in the country, became a disciple of Martin Luther, whom he had heard preach in Wittenburg. He became so inflamed at the abuses of the Catholic church that he delivered a fiery speech upon his return to Antvorskov. A museum dedicated to the reformer can be seen in Ribe (see chapter 10 on Southern Jutland).

When the Reformation did come, Antvorskov was confiscated by the king. It eventually was turned into a hunting manor. King Frederik II died here in 1588. In time it fell into disrepair and its buildings were sold and carted off. When it was deemed unsafe, the monastery church was torn down. The E20 motorway from Copenhagen has buried about half of the former grounds of the monastery. However, you can still see some of the brick foundations. To reach the site from Slagelse, follow Slotsalleén from the heart of town, turning right when you reach the end of this road, and then follow the signposts into Antvorskov.

Don't expect a formalized museum if you opt to visit this site, as it's little more than a ruin, with no guardian, no fence or barricades, no telephone contact point, no formal hours, and no admission fee.

BIRKEGÅRDENS HAVER This is a large, privately owned park set in one of the most beautiful parts of West Zealand. The fascinating grounds contain a stunning Japanese garden designed by the Danish landscape architect, H. C. Skovgård. The grounds also include a young oak forest with a little woodland lake. There are plenty of benches throughout the park, and packed lunches may be eaten in the courtyard garden. Here you can also see cows being milked, horses grazing, and goats, rabbits, and calves that come right up close to you. There's also a playground for children, a cafe offering refreshments, plus a kiosk selling ceramics, porcelain, and jewelry. Birkegårdens Haver lies at Tågerupvej 4 at Tågerup, near Kongsted (☎ **58-26-00-44**). It is open Wednesday to Sunday 10am to 6pm, Tuesday 10am to 9pm. Admission is 30 DKK ($4.35) for adults, 10 DKK ($1.45) for children. The gardens are only open annually from May 1 to October 19.

To reach the gardens from Slagelse, drive north for 17 miles from the town center, following the signs that point to Kalundborg.

4 Næstved

80km (50 miles) SW of Copenhagen; 25km (15½ miles) S of Ringsdted; 27km (17 miles) N of Vordingborg

The largest town in South Zealand, Næstved lies in an unspoiled countryside setting. With a population of some 45,000 and a historic core worth exploring, this port and industrial town stands on the southwest coast of Zealand at a point where the River Suså flows into the Karrebaek Fjord. This waterway forms a link between Næstved and Karrebæksminde Bay.

Næstved sprouted up around a Benedictine monastery, whose buildings today house Herlufen, Denmark's most famous boarding school, similar in prestige to Eton in Britain. In time, it became a major Hanseatic trading port. After a decline of fortunes, it came back with the coming of the rail lines in the 19th century.

Today it's a garrison town and home to the prestigious Gardehussar Regiment or Hussars of the Household Calvary. The best time to catch these guards is on Wednesday morning when they ride through the center of town amid much fanfare.

Today much of the outlying area of the town is industrial, devoted to such business as wood, paper, engineering, and even ceramics. But in the immediate surroundings, beyond the fringe of town, lie a number of charming places to visit, ranging from manors to mansions, and from abbeys to beautiful parks (see "Easy Excursions," below).

ESSENTIALS

GETTING THERE   Næstved lies on two major train routes, one going via Ringsted and taking 20 minutes, the other going via Køge and taking 38 minutes. Of course, Køge (see above), as well as Ringsted (see above), enjoy frequent rail connections from Copenhagen.

By Car   From Copenhagen, head south along E55 (also known as E47), cutting west along Route 54 into Næstved.

VISITOR INFORMATION   South of Axeltorv, **Næstved Turistbureau,** Havnen 1 (☎ **55-72-11-22**), is open from mid-June to August 9am to 5pm Monday to Friday, 9am to 2pm on Saturday. From September to mid-June, it is open Monday to Friday 9am to 4pm, Saturday 9am to noon.

GETTING AROUND

Bicycle riding is especially popular in Næstved, thanks to a relatively flat landscape and the fact that everyone in town seems to view it as a part of everyday life. You can rent a bike from **Rolsted,** Østergade 23–25 (☎ **55-72-07-52**). Bikes rent for around 50 DKK ($7.25) a day.

EXPLORING THE TOWN

Our favorite pastime here is a canoe ride on the River Suså, with its calm waters. The river runs through the west side of Næstved. It doesn't have rapids and its current is negligible, so maneuvering by canoe is fairly easy. On summer weekends, the river is crowded with others who like to go canoeing too. Canoes can be rented at **Suså Kanoudlejning,** Næsbyholm Allé 6, near Glumsø (☎ **57-64-61-44**). Charges are 70 DKK ($10.15) per hour or 290 DKK ($42.05) per day. The outlet for rentals lies at Slusehuset, at the southern end of Rådmanshavn.

As you stroll through the town, you'll come upon some interesting old structures, the most notable of which is **Apostelhuset,** a half-timbered house on Riddergade (just south of Sankt Morens Kirke) that dates from the Middle Ages. "Apostle House" has carved figures of the apostles on the beams of its 16th-century façade; each apostle carries an object that symbolizes his martyrdom. These are some of the oldest, certainly the best preserved, timber-frame carvings in the country. Nearby you'll see **Løveapoteket,** an old pharmacy in a restored half-timbered structure from 1853. The building is in the Dutch Renaissance style, and medicinal herbs and spices are still grown in a garden out back.

The central square of town is Axeltorv. All of the major sights of town are within a short walk of this historic area. The town center is graced with two Gothic churches, notably **Sct. Peders Kirke,** Sct. Peders Kirkeplads (☎ **55-72-31-90**), lying just to the south of Axeltorv. This is the largest Gothic church in Denmark, dating from the 1200s. When it was restored in the 1880s, wall paintings from 1375 were uncovered in the choir area. One of these paintings depicted Valdemar IV and his consort,

Hedwig, kneeling at a penitent's stool. A Latin inscription reads, "In 1375, the day before the feast of St. Crispin, King Valdemar died—do not forget that!" You can also see a choir screen by Abel Schrøder the Older (circa 1600), plus a crucifix by an unknown artisan dating from the 1200s, and a pulpit dated 1671. The church is open year-round, Tuesday to Friday 10am to noon. From May to August, it is also open Tuesday to Friday in the afternoon from 2 to 4pm. Entrance is free.

The other church worth a visit is **Sct. Mortens Kirke,** Kattibjerg 2 (☎ 55-73-57-39), lying halfway between the train depot and the landmark Axeltorv. Its façade is similar to that of Sankt Peders Kirke (see above). The artistic highlight inside is a tall altar carved in 1667 by Abel Schrøder the Younger; the pulpit, even older, was the work of his father, Abel Schrøder the Older. Admission is free, and the church is open year-round Monday to Friday 9 to 11am. From mid-June to mid-September it is also open Monday to Friday 2 to 5pm.

The town museum, **Næstved Museum,** Ringstedgade 4 (☎ 55-77-08-11), is also worth a visit. North of Axeltov, it is divided into two sections. One of these, in the 14th-century Helligåndshuset or "House of the Holy Ghost," the town's oldest building, is devoted to the cultural history of the area. Once this building was the town hospital. Its collection is known mainly for its medieval wood carvings, although some contemporary works are also featured. Other artifacts illustrate the agricultural history of the region and the tools the peasants used in their daily lives. The second section, Boderne, at Sct. Peders Kirkplads, displays local silver and crafts. The Holmegaard glass on display was made locally. The buildings housing this section of the museum are period pieces, made of medieval brick with arched windows imbedded in mortar. Called Stenboderne, these 15th-century "stone booths" are the only remaining medieval terrace houses in Denmark. Craftspeople used to occupy them before they were turned into a museum. Charging 20 DKK ($2.90) entrance for both sections of the museum (free for children under age 12), the museum is open Tuesday to Sunday 10am to 4pm.

SHOPPING   The thing to purchase here are products made by Holmegaards Glas-vaerker (see "Easy Excursions," below).

Of course, there's plenty of shopping in Næstved itself, with no fewer than three major shopping centers. Every day in summer the streets in the heart of town echo with the sounds of a jazz band, and there is a market at Axeltorv every Wednesday and Saturday morning. All the shopping malls in Næstved stage free exhibitions and shows.

The most important mall is the **Næstved Stor-Center,** Holsted Allée (☎ 55-77-15-00), which is widely recognized as the major shopping center for all of South Zealand, attracting shoppers from Møn, Falster, and hamlets for many miles around. Located about a mile north of the center, and accessible from the center of Næstved via bus no. 2, it's dominated by the giant Bilka supermarket (it's so large that they refer to it as a "hypermarket"). The mall's more than 50 specialist shops sell handcrafts, glass, jewelry, clothing, gifts, and dozens of other items.

WHERE TO STAY

✪ **Hotel Kirstine.** Købmagergade 20, DK-470 Næstved. ☎ **55-77-47-00.** Fax 55-72-11-53. 31 units. MINIBAR TV TEL. 765 DKK ($110.95) double; 875 DKK ($126.90) suite. Rates include breakfast. AE, MC, V.

The most appealing hotel in Næstved originated in 1745, when a local alderman created it as a venue for town meetings in a carpenter-derived design that's part neoclassical, part country baroque. Throughout most of the 1800s, it functioned as the home of the town's mayors, until around 1909, when it was transformed into a hotel that strictly prohibited any kind of alcohol on its premises. Today, the site is a half-timbered and romantic-looking monument to the elegant country life, thanks to millions of kroner spent on thoughtful accessories, a scattering of Danish antiques, and a meticulous allegiance in all the public areas to a kind of well-scrubbed, prosperous-looking integrity that many visitors associate with rural Denmark. Graceful touches abound, including a long, sun-flooded arcade where breakfast is served, and deep armchairs set in formal drawing rooms. Bedrooms are conservatively and comfortably furnished, with good, firm mattresses, but without the richly accessorized glamour of some of the public areas.

Dining/Diversions: A formal restaurant and a bar offer good food and an appealing 19th-century aura. There's also a nightclub and bar with granite walls, heavily timbered ceilings, and a dance floor that rocks to the sort of recorded pop music you might find at a Copenhagen disco.

Amenities: Conference center, and a golf course nearby.

Hotel Vinhuset. Sct. Peders Kirkeplads 4, DK-4700 Næstved. ☎ **55-72-08-07.** Fax 55-72-03-35. 57 units. MINIBAR TV TEL. 740–1,200 DKK ($107.30–$174) double. Rates include breakfast. AE, MC, V.

One of the most distinctive hotels in the region was built in 1768 atop vaulted cellars that local monks used to store wine as long ago as the 1400s. And although the site has always had a tradition of housing both overnight guests and the worldly goods of an order of monks, it entered the world of modern tourism in earnest sometime after World War II, when it was transformed into a working hotel. You'll find it across the square from Sankt Peders Kirke, behind a venerable brick façade whose large gables were inspired by country baroque designs. Inside, Persian carpets, antique furniture, and a romantic atmosphere add to the allure. Bedrooms are comfortable, high-ceilinged, and outfitted with a combination of modern furniture—especially good beds—and reproductions of antiques.

Dining/Diversions: The hotel has two comfortable restaurants, Bytinget and Les Baraques (see "Where to Dine," below). The hotel also has a cozy bar with beer on draught and a little nightclub, Copper Dance Floor.

Amenities: Conference facilities, patio garden, and concierge.

Mogenstrup Kro. Præstø Landevej 25, DK-4700 Næstved. ☎ **55-76-11-30.** Fax 55-76-11-29. www.firsthotels.com. E-mail: info@firsthotels.se. 99 units. MINIBAR TV TEL. Aug–June 995–1,095 DKK ($144.30–$158.80) double. July 595 DKK ($86.30) double. AE, DC, MC, V.

With origins that go back to its role as an old-time inn more than 200 years ago, this is a solid, well-respected resort that does a decent trade with weekenders escaping the urban congestion of Copenhagen. Quietly prosperous, and decorated in a pastel-colored tribute to the comfortable pleasures of the country life, it contains a cozy, highly reputable restaurant, and soft-toned bedrooms with big windows and accessories such as etchings of bucolic landscapes that evoke the interior of a Danish manor. Rooms are medium in size with good beds and fine plumbing and adequate towels in the baths.

Dining/Diversions: The hotel's formal restaurant features a top-rate Danish and international cuisine. On Saturday there is live music in the restaurant, but every evening guests gather in the cozy Jukebox Bar where you can choose your own music.

Amenities: Guests spend at least part of their time trekking through the rolling countryside nearby, or playing golf at an 18-hole course within a short drive of the hotel. Room service, laundry/dry cleaning, and concierge.

WHERE TO DINE

✪ **Restaurant Bytinget/Restaurant Les Baraques.** In the Hotel Vinhuset, Sct. Peders Kirkeplads 4. ☎ **55-72-08-07.** Main courses in Bytinget 99–198 DKK ($14.35–$28.70). Main courses in Les Baraques 198–278 DKK ($28.70–$40.30). AE, DC, MC, V. Mon–Sat noon–3pm and 6–9:30pm. DANISH (Bytinget) FRENCH/CONTINENTAL (Les Baraques).

In this small provincial town, it's unusual to have one organization (the previously recommended Hotel Vinhuset) making two separate restaurants available to diners. Both lie within the venerable 18th-century precincts of a country-baroque building that originally functioned as a warehouse for the wine and worldly goods of an order of Danish monks. The more Danish, and folkloric, of the two venues is Bytinget, where Danish staples such as *frikadeller,* Danish hash, browned steak with onions, and fillet of plaice with parsley-butter sauce, are among the culinary choices. The more formal and prestigious of the lot is Les Baraques, where the fare is upscale Danish and French. On the frequently changed menu you get morel cream sauce and *foie gras* accompanying many dishes, and such delights as tender veal filets and lobster. Both the roast lamb and duckling are superb here. The chefs are known for selecting only the finest ingredients on the market that day, but you'll pay for such culinary luxuries.

NÆSTVED AFTER DARK

Each of the hotels recommended within the "Where to Stay" section maintains a bar, but in addition to those, you'll find easy access to at least three pubs, any of which might act as a backdrop for some drinks, dialogue, and people-watching. Each of them follows an unpredictable, oft-changing schedule that incorporates an hour or two of live music, usually on Friday and/or Saturday nights beginning around 9pm. Everything in town, however, is very spontaneous, so be alert to whatever musical venue your hotel staff says is happening during the time of your arrival. A worthwhile bet for nautical atmosphere and camaraderie is **Rådhus Kroenm,** Skomagerrækken 8 (☎ **55-72-01-56**), rivaled only by **Underhuset Bar,** Axeltorv 9 (☎ **55-72-79-19**). Equally appealing is the **Step Inn,** Ramsherred (no phone).

EASY EXCURSIONS

Eight-miles northeast of Næstved, **Holmegaards Glasvaerker** (Holmegaard Glass-works) lies in the hamlet of Fensmark (☎ **55-54-62-00**). Founded in 1825, this is a genuine glass factory, inviting you to take a peek into a world where you can watch specialists performing a 2,000-year-old craft. You can watch the entire process, from the melting of the glass to the mouth-blowing and final forming. This company is the major producer of quality glass in Denmark. On site is a shop where you can purchase the company's products, plus a little museum. Admission is free, and it is open Monday to Thursday from 9:30am to noon and 12:45 to 1:30pm, and on Friday from 9:30am to noon only.

Another excursion can take you to **Herlufsholm,** known to educators throughout Europe as the site of a famous prep school that has been co-educational since the 1980s. Set about a mile northwest of the center of Næstved, it was founded at the dawn of the 13th century as a Benedictine monastery known as Skovkloster. The monastery, which was abandoned at the time of the Reformation, was eventually transformed into the **Herufsholm Academy,** Herlufsholm Allée (☎ **55-72-60-97**). To reach it from Næstved, take bus no. 6A or follow the Slagelsevej from the town center. You can always wander around the grounds of this place, assuming you don't interrupt the flow of the academics, but if your time is limited, the crown jewel of the academy grounds is the monastery church, **Stiftskirke Herufsholm.** Constructed in the late Middle Ages, it stands today as one of the oldest brick-built churches in all of

Denmark. It's especially noteworthy for its tombs, especially those of Admiral Herluf Trolle, who left an endowment to the monastery, and his wife, Birgitte Goye. The Gothic crucifix inside, made of ivory (artisan unknown), dates from around 1230; the baroque pulpit was the creation of Ejler Abelsen in 1620. The church, which has an unusually wide nave, can be visited every day of the year—except during religious services—during daylight hours. Entrance is free.

Of the many stately homes surrounding Næstved, none is more interesting than ✪ **Gavnø Slot & Park,** Gavnørej (☎ **53-80-02-00**). Located 2 ½ miles south of town, and accessible via bus no. 1A from the town center, it lies on a peninsula, on the opposite bank of the Karrebæk fjord from the rest of Næstved. The old rococo castle is surrounded by a delightful botanical garden, and is also the site of Butterfly World, where exotic tropical butterflies are allowed to fly free. A former nunnery, Gavnø reverted to private ownership in 1584. When Otto Thott (1703–85) took over the property, he had it converted into the rococo-style mansion you'll see today. Thott also accumulated one of the largest picture collections and private libraries (about 140,000 volumes) in Denmark. The premises also contain a valuable altar and pulpit carved by Abel Schroder the Elder. Although part of the interior remains a private residence, much of the castle can be visited, and much of the old collection is on display. The best time to visit is when the tulips bloom in spring. Later, these flowers give way to ornamental shrubs and roses. A ticket that combines admission to the castle, the castle gardens with its butterfly collection, and a nearby church (Gavnø Kirke) that has been associated with the castle for many generations, costs 60 DKK ($8.70) for adults, 30 DKK ($4.35) for children ages 5 to 11 (free age 4 and under). All three places are open between May and August, daily from 10am to 4pm.

The manor house we'd like to own in the area is ✪ **Gisselfeld Slot, Gisselfeldvej 3, 4690 Haslev** (☎ **56-32-60-32**). It's a beautiful, step-gabled, brick-built Renaissance home dating from 1557. Although it has been much altered and changed over the centuries, it forms an impressive sight today, set in a well laid-out park that evokes the countryside of England. The park contains a fountain, a small lake, a grotto, and even a waterfall. You will have to be content to view the house from the outside, but you can wander through one of Denmark's finest private gardens, with some 400 different species of trees and bushes, including a rose island and a bamboo grove. The gardens are at their best in the late spring. It is said that it was here that Hans Christian Andersen himself found inspiration for his fairytale, *The Ugly Duckling*. The gardens can be visited every day of the year from 10am to 5pm (from mid-June to mid-August, until 6pm), without charge. The only time the interior can be visited is during July, when guided tours can be pre-arranged, on a rotating and oft-changing schedule that must be reconfirmed prior to your arrival. For reservations, contact either the phone number listed above, or the **tourist office** in the hamlet of Haslev (☎ **53-31-52-00**).

5 Vordingborg

104km (65 miles) S of Copenhagen; 27km (17 miles) S of Næstved; 13km (8 miles)W of Møn

The little town of Vordingborg was much more important in the Middle Ages than it is today. It was from Vordingborg that the Danish kingdom was reunited in 1157—after several years of division—when Valdemar I (the Great) ascended the throne. Denmark's first constitution was written here in 1282. Before that, in 1241, the Jutland Code was first proclaimed here. This was one of the most significant doctrines of medieval times, codifying traditional law. The code's preamble— *"Mæth logh skal land byggiæs,*" or "with law shall a land be built"—is as familiar to Danish schoolchildren as the opening line of the Pledge of Allegiance is to American youth.

Because of its natural harbor, Vordingborg was an important launching point for the military campaigns of Bishop Absalon in the late 1100s against the warring Wends of eastern Germany. During the reign of the Valdemar kings, Vordingborg continued to remain in favor as a royal residence. The royal castle here was part of the system of Danish fortifications constructed along the Baltic as a protection against the Wends.

Valdemar IV (Valdemar Atterdag) was the king who in the 1360s extended the ring fortifications of the castle to their present-day dimensions. But in the 1400s the town lost its strategic importance when the Kalmar Union came into being. From that point on, Danish kings had such an expanded territory to be concerned about that they seemed to forget little Vordingborg, which declined in fortune.

The railroad came to the town in 1870, and by 1937 the Storstrøm Bridge replaced the ancient ferry link to the island of Falster. Today about 20,000 people live in and around Vordingborg. Although no longer the capital of Denmark, Vordingborg is thriving and is the site of many well-known local companies. Since it's only an hour's ride by rail from Copenhagen, many locals commute to the capital for work using Vordingborg as a virtual suburban community.

ESSENTIALS

GETTING THERE   Frequent trains throughout the day serve Vordingborg, arriving in just 80 minutes from the Danish capital. If you're already in Næstved (see above), the rail link is only 20 minutes. If you're planning to go on to Møn, you'll need to switch here from the train to the bus.

By Car   From Copenhagen take E55 south cutting west when you reach the junction of Route 22.

VISITOR INFORMATION   Just east of the Gåsetårnet or Goose Tower, **Vordingborg Turistbureau,** Algade 96 (☎ 55-34-11-11), is open Monday to Friday from 9am to 4pm and Saturday 9am to noon. From June to August it is also open until 5pm Monday to Friday and until 2pm on Saturday.

SPECIAL EVENTS   A good time to be in Vordingborg is the last week of July (dates vary) when a 4-day music festival is staged with some of the best known performers in Scandinavia. The Nordic Festival of Folk Song and Ballads is always a fascinating program reviving Scandinavia's great heritage dating from the Vikings. For tickets, programs, or information, call ☎ 55-36-08-00.

EXPLORING THE TOWN

Most of the town has been rebuilt in recent years in a modern but not unappealing style. The town's **Nordhavnen** or yacht harbor is the southernmost harbor of Zealand. Founded during the Valdemar kingdom, it still retains some of its old character, in spite of the many new facilities added.

Most tourists visit Vordingborg with one reason in mind, and that is to see the fabled "Goose Tower" (see below), but there are other attractions as well.

Once part of the sprawling royal castle and fortress that stood here during the Middle Ages, the 14th-century ✪ **Gåsetårnet (Goose Tower),** Slotsruinen 1 (☎ 53-77-25-54), is the best-preserved medieval tower in Scandinavia. It is the only structure that remains intact from the Valdemar era. The tower gets its name from 1368 when the king, Valdemar IV, ordered that a golden goose be placed on top of the tower to show his disdain for a declaration of war against Denmark by the Hanseatic League of Germany. He was hoping to suggest that the threats coming from the Hanseatic

League were no more ominous to him than a flock of cackling geese. The pointed copper roof of the 120-foot tower is still crowned by a golden goose, and the tower, of course, remains the town's landmark and source of historic pride.

From the top of the tower a panoramic view of the countryside unfolds. In its heyday the fortress had seven more towers but they were demolished over the centuries. In recent years excavations have been going on here to uncover the ruins of the castle. Queen Margrethe visited in 1997 to view the excavation of a Viking quay.

Visiting hours are June to August daily from 10am to 5pm; off-season, Tuesday to Sunday 10am to 4pm. If you arrive by train, stroll north from the station to the post office and then turn southeast onto Algade leading to Slotstorvet, in front of the fortress. An admission of 20 DKK ($2.90) for adults and 8 DKK ($1.15) for children covers entrance to the tower and the museum described below.

Opposite the Goose Tower and standing on the fortress grounds, the **Sydsjællands Museum** (South Zealand Museum) displays regional artifacts gathered from South Zealand since the Stone Age. It is a history not only of Vordingborg but also of nearby Langebæk and Præstø. Local antique tools are displayed in a number of rooms. The trade and craft exhibits from medieval times to the Renaissance are particularly interesting, including ecclesiastical decorations and also textiles. Look for a showcase exhibiting an *aquamanile,* a vessel from medieval times used to pour water over a priest's hands at mass.

When the castle fell into disrepair after the war with Sweden in 1660, a new fort and cavalry barracks were constructed. One of these buildings contains the museum. The museum keeps the same hours as the tower (see above).

After a visit you can stroll through the adjoining Botanical Garden, the first in Denmark, laid out in 1921. Plants grown here were originally used for medicinal reasons.

The town's most important church is **Vor Frue Kirke** (Church of Our Lady), standing on the Kirketorvet 14A (☎ **57-77-13-34**), on ground that was formerly the town moat. Its exact date of construction isn't known but was probably at the dawn of the 15th century. This brick-built church was financed by letters of indulgence that the Pope allowed parishioners; financial contributions were essentially rewarded with forgiveness for sins. Apparently, there were enough sinners in Vordingborg to finance the construction of the church. The nave and the aisle date from 1432–60, whereas the church tower was added around 1600, and the sacristy around 1700. In the choir, note the frescoes from the mid–15th century, depicting the *Adoration of the Magi* and the *Nativity* among other events. The altarpiece depicting the *Crucifixion* was the creation of Abel Schrøder the Younger and dates from 1642. The choir lattice gate was also created by Schrøder to isolate the clergymen from the laymen. Visiting hours are daily from 10am to noon.

The town is also noted for its **Prince Jørgen's Guard,** which comprises 50 boys from 8 to 23 years of age. In 1676 the chief of the regiment was Prince Jørgen, the youngest son of Frederik III and Queen Sophie Amalie. At his father's death in 1670 he inherited Vordingborg Castle. In recent times the guard has been revived, winning some 70 trophies for its marching, drumming, and prancing. Several experts now regard its marching as the best of any troop of guards in Denmark. Normally your chance of seeing the guard is best on Saturday mornings when they often parade down the main pedestrian street of the town, Algade.

Many interesting old sites await those who explore the environs of Vordingborg. **Knudshoved Odde** (Knudshoved Point), a 9-mile-long peninsula west of Vordingborg, is owned by the Rosenfeldt Estate and has been protected to preserve its unique Bronze Age landscape. Almost any type of Danish tree grows here—brackens as tall as people; thickets of brambles, honeysuckle, and ivy; and a wealth of wild flowers. The curiously named "zo tree frog" also survives here. A small herd of American buffalo was also imported to live here. You can park your car for 10 DKK ($1.45) and explore the park. The car park is halfway down the peninsula where the trail begins.

SHOPPING

Shopping here is limited but worthwhile. **Sandbirk,** Algade 48 (☎ **53-77-02-62**), is the exclusive outlet for the best porcelain, silver, and gold items in town, with all the big names represented: Jacob Jensen, Georg Jensen, and Flora Danica. If you don't find what you like here, a leading competitor is **Boe Andersen,** Algade 72 (☎ **53-77-05-73**). This is also the town's Seiko specialist. **Elmegårds Børnebutik,** Algade 38 (☎ **55-34-50-08**), carries a selection of gifts and crafts. If you're an inveterate antique collector, check out the selection at **Lulus Antik,** Algade 7 (☎ **55-34-14-18**). Finally, the best place for glass and porcelain is **IMERCO** (☎ **53-77-01-14**), which is particularly strong in Royal Copenhagen products and Holmegård Glas (glassware).

WHERE TO STAY

Hotel Kong Valdemar. Slotstorvet, DK-4760 Vordingborg. ☎ **55-34-30-95.** Fax 55-34-04-95. 60 units. MINIBAR TV TEL. 750 DKK ($108.75) double. Rate includes breakfast. DC, MC, V.

From the front, this hotel—the only one in town—looks like a modestly sized row house nestled comfortably among its neighbors. It's much bigger, however, than you might have thought, thanks to an enlargement in the 1980s, and thanks to the fact that its rooms sprawl out across a garden in back. Bedrooms are streamlined and efficiently decorated, not plush in any way, and vaguely reminiscent of a modern, no-frills college dormitory. Mattresses are a bit thin. On the premises are a bar and a restaurant which is separately recommended under "Where to Dine" (see below).

WHERE TO DINE

Den Gylden Gås (The Golden Goose). In the Hotel Kong Valdemar, Slotstorvet. ☎ **53-77-00-95.** Main courses 100–189 DKK ($14.50–$27.40). DC, MC, V. Daily noon–10pm. DANISH.

This competent, if not exactly exciting, dining room is associated with the previously recommended Hotel Kong Valdemar. Comfortably decorated, with window views that sweep out over some of the medieval buildings nearby, it offers such tried-and-true Danish specialties as shellfish and lobster soup with Noilly Prat; seafood salad (with salmon, sole, shellfish, herbs, and vinaigrette); Greenland halibut with white wine, chives, and new potatoes; pork cutlets with curry sauce and rice; and cognac-flamed pepper steak. Guests, many of whom are locals, enjoy the food here. It's a good place to take your Danish mother if you have one; the chefs probably cook like she does.

✪ **Restaurant Babette.** Kildemarksvej 5. ☎ **55-34-30-30.** Reservations recommended. Set menus 315–345 DKK ($45.70–$50.05). DC, MC, V. Tues–Sat noon–3:30pm and 6pm–2am. DANISH/INTERNATIONAL.

It was inevitable that at least one restaurant within this guide bears a name inspired by the brilliant European film "Babette's Feast," in which Danish and French characters interact with one another's appetites. And in Vordingborg, the most appealing and most interesting restaurant pays homage to the Babette of that film. It lies a half-mile north of the town center, near the headquarters of a local TV station (Channel 2), and within sight of Vordingborg's famous "Goose Tower." The menus at this place change every 14 days, based on the availability of fresh ingredients and the inspiration of co-chefs Henrik Pedersen and Vivi Schou. Cuisine is noteworthy for its zeal and intelligence and its sheer sense of style. Our most recent meal consisted of lobster cocktail with herbed Nantua sauce; fillets of halibut in a mousseline sauce; free-range chicken from a nearby organic farm, served with white truffles, spicy spinach, and new Danish potatoes; a selection of French and Danish cheeses; and a finale of fresh summer berries from nearby bogs, served with homemade ice cream.

Restaurant Påfuglen. Algade 88. ☎ **53-77-01-90.** Reservations recommended. Main courses 65–178 DKK ($9.40–$25.80). AE, DC, MC, V. Daily 11am–9pm (last order). INTERNATIONAL/DANISH.

This restaurant occupies a long, low, modern-looking veranda that's attached to a striking redbrick building that was originally conceived as a movie theater in the 1890s. Within a room that might remind you of a greenhouse because of its many windows along one side, you can enjoy a menu based mostly on seafood, but with lots of emphasis on steaks as well. Examples include grilled shrimp on a stick with sage sauce, fried Norwegian salmon with lobster sauce, and garlic steak with spicy butter and fried entrecôte with grilled tomatoes and béarnaise sauce. The place lives up to its moderate price tag and adheres to a fundamentally classical style of cookery. The dishes may be typical but they show a care and finesse when prepared by the kitchen staff.

VORDINGBORG AFTER DARK

A good place to begin your evening is **Amigo Bar,** Algade 35 (☎ **53-77-60-65**), right in the center of town. It seems to attract the most simpatico crowd. The best Bierstube is nearby: **Slots Kroen,** Algade 119 (☎ **53-77-02-61**). A lot of the locals will also direct you to **Willy Nilly,** Algade 1 (☎ **55-34-20-40**), a friendly English pub which seems to have the coldest beer in town. It is also the site of **Prinsen Diskotek,** Algade 1 (☎ **55-32-20-40**), which opens at 10 or 11pm, often staying open until 3 or 4 in the morning. It rarely charges a cover.

7 Møn

128km (80 miles) S of Copenhagen

The island of **Møn** lies just off of Zealand, in the southeast corner of Denmark. Its big attraction is 400-foot-high **Møns Klint,** 4 miles of white chalky cliffs that rise dramatically from the Baltic Sea. Møns Klint was cut by the Baltic Sea in a large pile of ice-transported chalk masses and glacial deposits. The chalk was formed from calcareous ooze 75 million years ago. The ooze enclosed shells of marine animals that are now fossils. The glacial deposits date from a million years ago. They originated partly as boulder clay deposited by inland ice and partly as bedded clay and sand containing marine mussels. The boulders on the beach have dropped from the cliff and have been rounded by wave erosion.

Although Møn's white chalk cliffs seem to be its main appeal, once you get here you'll find an island of rustic charm and grace well worth exploring. Less than 12,000 people live here, and the best way to get around is by car—or else by bike. There is no train system, and the bus service leaves much to be desired and takes an endless amount of time to get around.

The residents of Møn zealously guard their natural environment, and the beauty of their landscapes remain largely intact and unspoiled. Sheltered by dunes, the white sandy beaches are a summer attraction, so it's not just the wild cliffs that draw visitors here. The island also boasts beautiful forests with a wide variety of wildlife and a trio

Pottery Sales

As you drive about Møn, note the many signs advertising "keramik." On this slow-paced island people everywhere seem to have taken up ceramics and pottery and are only too willing to sell their products to you. This interest in ceramics originated because of the rich clay deposits found here.

of churches with the best frescoes in the country (more about that later), plus a lively market town in Stege.

Møn is also known for the prehistoric remains that are scattered about the island. For detailed information, the Stege tourist office (see below) publishes a booklet called "Prehistoric Monuments of Møn." Several Neolithic chambered tombs known as "giants' graves" were discovered. As the legend goes, the western part of the island was ruled by a "jolly green giant" called Green Huntsman, and the eastern part of the island was the domain of another giant, Upsal.

Møn lies at the eastern edge of the Størstrommen, a channel dividing the island of Zealand and the island of Falster (see below).

ESSENTIALS

GETTING THERE   From Copenhagen's Central Rail Station, take a train departing once an hour for Vordingborg in South Zealand. From Vordingborg take bus no. 62 or 64 to Stege, the capital of Møn. Once on the island, bus service is meager; you'll need a car to explore.

By Car   Cross over from the island of Zealand on the Dronning Alexandrines Bridge, then proceed through the old country town of Stege.

VISITOR INFORMATION The local tourist office, **Møns Turistbureau,** Storegade (☎ **55-81-44-11**), is open Monday to Friday 10am to 5pm, and Saturday 9am to noon.

GETTING AROUND   The major bus station is located at Stege. This is the departure point for all the island's bus routes. Fares are based on the number of zones traveled. Bus service is unreliable and varies according to weather conditions and the time of the year. The most popular route is traversed by bus no. 52, going from Stege to Klintholm Havn via Elmelunde and Magleby. From Monday to Friday service on this route is hourly, dropping to about every other hour on weekends. Magleby is the most easterly town on Møn. Bus no. 54 operates only in the peak of summer, usually late June to mid-August, taking passengers from Stege to the island's major attraction, Møns Klint. Service is about six times daily Monday to Friday, or four times daily on weekends. Finally, bus no. 53 goes from Stege to Ulvshale, with bus no. 64 serving the route from Stege to Bogø.

Many Danes prefer to explore Møn by bike. The best trail to follow is the signposted bike route going from the capital, Stege, to Møns Klint. Ask at the tourist office in Stege (see below) for a pamphlet outlining the best cycling tours of the island, which take in all of Møn's principal attractions.

In Stege, bikes can be rented at **Dækaingen Cykler,** Storegade 91 (☎ **55-81-42-49**). Rates average 35 DKK ($5.05) a day.

STEGE: THE ISLAND'S CAPITAL

After crossing the bridge from "mainland" Zealand on Route 59, take an immediate left and follow the road to the ancient market town of Stege, which is the ideal gateway to the island and the source of the best information about Møn (see "Visitor Information," above).

Time seems to have forgotten this sleepy little capital, and that is part of its charm. To the surprise of first-time visitors, Stege has preserved its moat and ramparts from the Middle Ages, whereas other Danish towns have torn them down. One of its original trio of town gates, Mølleporten, is still here to greet guests as in olden days. Mølleporten, which once allowed (or didn't allow) entry to the town, stands on Storegate. Meaning "mill gate" in English, the gate bears a resemblance to the Stege church tower. It's made of redbrick and lined with horizontal strips of white chalk from (where else?) Møns Klint.

EXPLORING THE TOWN

Known for its primitive frescoes, ✪ **Stege Kirke, Kirkepladsen** (☎ 55-81-40-65), is one of the largest churches in the country, with a massive tower striped in brick and chalk. Its oldest section, built in the Romanesque style, dates from the early 1200s. It was constructed by the ruler of the island, Jakob Sunesen, a member of the powerful Hvide family, which also claimed Bishop Absalon. In the latter 1400s the church was massively expanded to its present size.

The principal nave is flanked by two smaller naves on each side, filled with pointed arched windows and high vaulted ceilings. Rich fresco decorations are found in the choir and main nave. Long covered with whitewash, the frescoes were discovered and restored in 1892. Many are quite whimsical in nature. The aim of the fresco was to relate events in the Bible to illiterate peasants. Fresco artists were always at their best in depicting the horrible demons that stoked the fires of hell. Frescoes in the Stege church were painted only in black and ocher-red. In the post-Reformation era, Lutheran ministers found the frescoes "too evocative of Catholic themes," and ordered that they be whitewashed. Although this sounds bad, it was the whitewashing that actually preserved the frescoes so that they can still be enjoyed today. The frescoes were restored under the supervision of Denmark's national museum. The painter of the frescoes isn't known. He's a mystery to the centuries although popularly called Elmelundemesteren or Elmelunde master. Charging no admission, the church is open Tuesday to Sunday 8am to 4pm.

Next to the old Mølleporten or town gate stands **Empiregården,** Storegade 75 (☎ 55-81-40-67), housing the rather elegant **Møn Museum,** a repository of local cultural history. The collection is rich in artifacts from the Middle Ages, including coins and old pottery, but it also goes back to the Stone Age, displaying items like ancient fossilized sea urchins. The museum also displays Møn house interiors from the 1800s. It's open Tuesday to Sunday 10am to 4pm, charging 20 DKK ($2.90) for adults (free for children).

SHOPPING   The island is known for its ceramics and pottery, whose production keeps dozens of artisans working long hard hours. Two of the best places to see, and buy, some of the goods produced here include a warehouse-sized emporium 2 ½ miles east of Stege on the road leading to Møns Klint. **Ympelese,** Klintevej 110 (☎ 55-81-30-05), stocks some of the most appealing handmade candles in Zealand, as well as a roster of ceramic pots, plates, and vessels. There's even men's, women's, and children's clothing for sale, some of it fabricated by local seamstresses, and some of it designed to protect its wearer from the midwinter gales that sweep in from the Baltic and North Seas. A somewhat smaller competitor, with a worthy selection of island crafts, is **Imarco,** Storegade 43 (☎ 44-81-44-40), which has the added convenience of operating from a base in the commercial heart of Stege.

OUTDOOR ACTIVITIES

Many visitors come to Møn just to play golf at the **Møns Golf Course,** Klintevej
(☎ **55-81-32-60**), near the Præstekilde Kro & Hotel (see below). It remains open all
year, but you'd have to be a hearty golfer to play here in winter. However, die-hard
golfers have been seen batting a ball around patches of snow, weather permitting.
Conditions in the spring through autumn, and especially in midsummer, are often
ideal. Greens fees are 200 DKK ($29) Monday to Friday, rising to 250 DKK ($36.25)
on weekends. Anyone can play—not just members.

WHERE TO STAY

Hotel Stege Bugt. Langelinie 48 DK-4780 Stege. ☎ **55-81-54-54.** Fax 55-81-58-90.
27 units. MINIBAR TV TEL. June–Aug 400 DKK ($58) double, Sept–May 775 DKK ($112.35)
double. AE, DC, MC, V. Rates include breakfast.

An inviting town inn, long accustomed to putting up wayfarers, this is the leading
choice in the capital. A three-story motel-style building, it stands at the edge of town
near the sea. The English-speaking staff is helpful and welcoming. Bedrooms are fairly
streamlined with modern pieces and all the comfort you'll need. The most desirable
rooms have large windows with balconies. The hotel restaurant is also the finest in
Stege (see below). There's also a bar with a large TV screen and a clientele of local
sports fans and traveling salespeople.

Præstekilde Kro & Hotel. Klintevej 116, DK-4780 Stege. ☎ **55-86-87-88.** Fax 55-81-36-34.
www.sima.dk/praestekilde. 46 units. MINIBAR TV TEL. 715–815 DKK ($103.70–$118.20)
double, 925–1,025 DKK ($134.15–$148.65) jr. suite. Rates include breakfast. AE, DC, MC, V.

Its fans define this as the most opulent and glamorous hotel on Møns, partly because
of its upscale comforts, and partly because of its association with the island's nearby
golf course. Built in the early 1970s in a rambling compound of big-windowed, low-
slung buildings, it lies 3 miles east of Stege, about 1 ½ miles from the nearest beach,
Strand Wengensgaardsvej. Many, but by no means all, of the clients spend their day
on the golf links; others decompress on respites from urban life in Copenhagen,
walking through nearby fields and forests or relaxing beside the seacoast. Bedrooms are
more plush than those within most of the island's hotels, with thick upholstery and
color coordination of fabrics and accessories.

Dining/Diversions: There's a bar on the premises, and a well-regarded restaurant
with panoramic views over the surrounding fields and a nearby estuary. Full meals,
often presented as part of set-price menus, cost 200 DKK ($29) each.

Amenities: Indoor swimming pool lined with unusual contemporary murals,
immediate access to an 18-hole golf course, sauna, solarium, and billiard and table
tennis facilities.

WHERE TO DINE

Hotel Stege Bugt Restaurant. Langelinie 48. ☎ **55-81-54-54.** Reservations recommended. Main courses 78–168 DKK ($11.30–$24.35). AE, DC, MC, V. Daily noon–10pm.
DANISH.

Although Stege makes no pretense at being a gastronomic center, the food here is reliable and good, dished up by a friendly staff. Ingredients are fresh and deftly handled
by well-trained chefs. Offerings include grilled salmon made zesty with Danish yogurt
and fresh herbs, and sometimes accompanied by potatoes grown in the hotel's garden.
The grilled lamb with garlic potatoes and a crisp green salad is always a delight, as are
most other dishes on the menu. Desserts tend to be simple, like ice cream or fresh
fruit, but if you'd like a special dessert, call in advance and the kitchen will gladly
prepare it for you if they have the ingredients.

STEGE AFTER DARK

Persons under age 25 on the island are quick to point out that there are absolutely no full-time discos on Møn, unless a local church or civic group opts to hold a youth-group gathering in a communal basement somewhere. In lieu of that, you'll probably find that the most convivial gathering place is the bar at the previously recommended **Præstekilde Kro & Hotel,** Klintevej (☎ **55-86-87-88**). Here you'll find an inkling of big-city style a la Copenhagen, but not so much that you won't realize that you're very, very far from urban life. Still, the drinks taste good, and you're likely to meet a handful of other urbanites to swap stories with.

After leaving Stege you can follow a minor little road directly north with signposts that will lead you to:

ULVSHALE AND NYORD

Ulvshale, or Wolf's Trail in English, is a peninsula jutting west toward Zealand, a 4 mile trek north of Stege. It's one of the most beautiful spots on Møn, now preserved as a nature reserve, with gnarled old trees and rare birds such as snipe, razorbills, water-rails, and others, which prefer to live on the mud-flats. Ulvshale boasts one of the best beaches on the island and it also is home to one of the few virgin forests left in the country. The beach is Ulvshale Strand, and the main road, Ulvshalevej, runs right along it. The forest is crisscrossed with a network of hiking routes.

Once at Ulvshale you'll see a bridge connecting Møn with the little offshore island of **Nyord.** You can walk across the bridge to get to this tiny speck of an island, which means "New Word" in English. It's been set aside as a bird sanctuary for rare birds, including rough-legged buzzards, snow buntings, hen harriers, and others.

The birds are seen mainly in the east marshes. On the north side of the road, about half a mile after crossing the bridge, you'll come to a tower that is the best vantage point for watching the birds. The bridge itself is also a good bird-watching site.

The little village on the island is called Nyord too, and it's a time capsule from the 1800s, with old thatched houses. Other than a tiny yacht harbor and a little church from 1846, there aren't a lot of attractions, but it's such an idyllic place it's worth the effort to get here.

After a look at the birds, head back in the direction of Stege, but when you see a turnoff to Keldby, follow the signs into this hamlet, 3 miles east of Stege.

KELDBY

This agrarian community is mainly visited by those who want a look at ✪ **Keldby Kirke, Præstegårdstræde 1,** Keldby (☎ **55-81-33-05**). Built of brick between 1200 and 1250, this is one of the island's special churches, celebrated for its fresco paintings that span 200 years, the oldest dating from 1275. The frescoes, of course, are taken from biblical scenes such as stories from the book of Genesis. Both Old and New Testament scenes are included. No church in Denmark quite challenges Keldby in medieval frescoes—note especially the dramatic representation of Cain and Abel and the horror show depicting Doomsday. Shepherds pictured with their flocks create a more bucolic scene. In addition to the frescoes, the church also contains a number of other treasures, notably a carved pulpit dated 1586, and, in the vaulting, paintings by the Master of Elemunde, including a tender depiction of Joseph preparing gruel for his newly born infant son. A tombstone at the north side of the church dates from the mid–14th century. The church can be visited from April to September daily from 7am to 5pm; off-season daily 8am to 4pm. Admission is free.

If you have time after viewing the church, consider a visit to the manor **Hans Hansens Gård,** Skullebjergvej 15 (☎ **55-81-40-67**), which lies about a mile south of

Keldby Church. (Follow the signs to Keldbylille to reach it.) Dating from 1800, this is a thatch-covered building whose wings enclose an inner courtyard. Originally conceived as a farmhouse, it's the home of Møns Museumsgården, a monument that depicts what family life was like for homesteaders during the 1800s. The farm was kept in the same family for generations. When its last owner, a bachelor, Hans Hansens (for whom the property is named), died, he willed it to the people of Møns, who converted it into a museum. Furniture and utensils used by the Hansens family are on display. It's open from April to September, Tuesday to Sunday from 10am to 4pm. Admission is 15 DKK ($2.15).

The highway (Route 287) continues directly east to:

ELMELUNDE

This tiny rural hamlet, roughly equivalent to Keldby in size and layout, is about 4 ½ miles from Stege and is the site of the island's second-most-visited church, ✪ **Elmelunde Kirke, Klintevej, Elmelunde** (☎ **55-81-23-90**). Dating from around 1080, it's one of the oldest stone churches in Denmark. During the Romanesque era, the nave was expanded. Later, in the early 1300s, the distinctive tower was added, transforming it into a prominent landmark for sailors coming in from the sea. The interior of the church is known for its frescoes painted by the Master of Elmelunde. Here this rather mysterious artist left some of his masterpieces, including *Last Judgment, St. Peter with the Key to Heaven, Christ in Majesty, St. Paul with a Sword,* and his charming *Entry into Jerusalem,* along with the more sobering *Flagellation of Christ.*

He also painted lighter subjects, including autumn harvest and some plowing-the-fields scenes. Other frescoes depict Adam and Eve being thrown out of the Garden of Eden. The altar and pulpit were donated by the feudal lord, Corfitz Ulfeldt, and his consort, Queen Leonora Christina. The intricately carved and painted altar dates from 1646, the pulpit created about 3 years later. The carved pulpit is supported entirely on a figure of St. Peter. In 1460 the three-pointed vaults (seen over the altar) were added, and the Master of Elmelunde painted them as well. Year-round, the church is open daily from 8am to 5pm. Admission is free.

WHERE TO STAY

Hotel Elmehøj. Kirkebakken 39, Elmelunde, DK-4780 Stege, Møn. ☎ **55-81-35-35.** Fax 55-81-32-67. 23 units (none with bath). 370 DKK ($53.65) double. Rate includes breakfast. Half-board 660 DKK ($95.70), double occupancy. No credit cards. Closed Dec–Jan.

Set about 2½ miles inland from the sea, midway between Stege and Møns Klint, adjacent to the stop for buses that interconnect the two, this is one of the most stately looking guest houses in Møn. It occupies what was originally built between 1928 and 1930 as a retirement home, and sports a sheathing of ivy over what might remind you of an 18th-century manor house in England. In 1991, it was acquired by Brit Olifent, a woman born and reared on Møn, who runs it today with her Perth (Australia)-born husband Jonathan. Bedrooms are very simple and very clean, with few frills and a sense of regimented orderliness. There's little to do on the property, other than taking promenades in the well-tended garden, exploring the nearby beach and forest (each of which lie 2½ miles away), and visiting the 12th-century interior of the Elmelunde church, which lies within a 2-minute walk. A communal TV room and a public kitchen that some guests use to prepare light lunches and snacks are on the premises.

WHERE TO DINE

Kaj Kok. Klintevej 15, Elmelunde. ☎ **55-81-35-85.** Reservations recommended. Main courses 90–139 DKK ($13.05–$20.15). AE, DC, MC, V. Daily noon–9pm. Closed Mon–Tues Oct–Apr. DANISH.

Set within a big-windowed building from the 1970s, about a half-mile from the hamlet of Elmelunde, this is a well-recommended restaurant that has earned a reputation for serving well-prepared versions of time-honored Danish specialties. You'll recognize it by its red façade and a large garden in which tame goats munch on vegetables fed by well-wishers, where children play on mechanized toys. Within an interior whose modernity is disguised by a roster of old-fashioned decorative accessories, you can order crab and garlic bisque, marinated and/or smoked salmon, fillets of halibut in white wine parsley sauce, and a flavorful version of peppersteak. Lighter appetites appreciate the *smørrebrød,* which usually sell for 20 DKK ($2.90), except for a deluxe version, with lobster, that costs 40 DKK ($5.80). The restaurant's name, incidentally, translates as "Chef Kaj" in honor of its owner, Kaj Hansen.

After a meal at Kaj Kok, continue east along Route 287 through the hamlet of Borre where you'll pass a brick church built in the early 1200s. Continue through the village but turn left at the signpost to Sømarke. The next road to the right leads to Sømarkedyssen. At this point you'll come upon a round dolmen crowned by a huge capstone over an open chamber. From here there is a panoramic view over the entire island. After a look at the dolmen continue on the same road, going left up a very narrow lane. At the peak, turn right along the road for about 900 yards, which will lead to the entrance of:

LISELUND

This thatched palatial summer home from 1795 is surrounded by lovely park grounds with artificial lakes and canals in the northeastern part of the island. H. C. Andersen wrote The Tinder Box while staying at Swiss Cottage here. The park is called a "folly" of the 18th century, when it was constructed by Bosc de la Calmette, a royal chamberlain who was inspired by Marie Antoinette's La Hameau at Versailles. You can buy refreshments at a small chalet filled with antlers and antiques. The admission-free park is open daily until sunset year-round.

Other structures in the park were destroyed by a rockfall in 1905, but guided tours of the Old Castle are available. Call ☎ 55-81-21-78 for more details. Inside you'll find an architectural *mélange* of styles, with tiny canopied beds, a trompe l'oeil painting, and a Monkey Room painted with a jungle scene. Visits are possible May to October at 10:30am, 11am, 1:30pm, and 2pm. On Sunday there are two extra visits at 4 and again at 4:30pm. No visits are possible on Monday or Saturday. Admission is 20 DKK ($2.90) for adults or 10 DKK ($1.45) for children.

WHERE TO STAY & DINE

Liselund Ny Slot. Langebjergvej 6, DK-4791 Borre. ☎ **55-81-20-81.** Fax 55-81-21-91. 15 units. MINIBAR TEL. 735 DKK ($106.55) double, 1,300 DKK ($188.50) suite. MC, V.

Set amid the trees and rolling hills of a national park, this manor house was originally built in 1887 by a baron and his wife as an annex to a much older castle. Since the transformation of the original castle into a museum, most of the region's overnight guests seek accommodations in the yellow-colored stucco walls and soaring tower of the Ny Slot (New Castle). In 1994 new owners, the Matheisen family, acquired the hotel. The bedrooms are very simple, outfitted with minimalist furniture, and affording views over fields, forests, a pond with swans, and the sea. Many of the public rooms have frescoed ceilings and a high-ceilinged sense of their original grandeur.

Many nonresidents of the hotel opt for a lunch in the establishment's basement-level cafe (served from noon to 6pm), or for dinner in the more formal dining room (from 6:30 to 8pm). Menu items include preparations of Danish lamb in rosemary sauce, Baltic or North Sea fish, and steaks. There's also an occasional Chinese or Asian dish.

The restaurant is open daily in summer, with an occasional (unscheduled) closing 1 or 2 days a week in winter. Fixed-price three-course meals cost 300 DKK ($43.50).

MØNS KLINT

After a visit or even an overnight stay at Ny Slot, drive back to Route 287 and follow the road east to the highlight of the tour, ✪ **Møns Klint.** These impressive white chalk cliffs (see the introduction to Møn) stretch for several miles, with a sheer drop of 400 feet at their highest point. Formed by glacial deposits combined with the action of a turbulent sea, they are one of the most dramatic natural sights in Denmark. Møns Klint was pocked throughout with nearly 100 Neolithic burial mounds. Paths lead through woodland to the towering edge of the cliffs where one of the most spectacular views in all of Denmark awaits you. For decades photographers have delighted in capturing the image of these brilliantly white cliffs against the azure blue of the sea. When the sun is out, the scene is especially breathtaking.

Footpaths are cut into the cliffs, and visitors are fond of hiking these towering trails. It takes about an hour's walk to appreciate the magnificence of the site. There's a wide expanse of beech trees along the top of the cliffs, providing shelter for rare plants, including 20 species of orchids hidden in the undergrowth. For the best view, follow the signs to the peak called Sommerspiret and hope that the sky is clear at the time of your visit. Fossils of marine animals—some long extinct—have also been discovered on the beach below these cliffs. Two steep flights of steps lead from both Storeklint and Jydeleje down to the sea, but be prepared for an exhausting climb back to the top. Once you're at the bottom, you can join Danish families who hunt for blanched fossils on the beach, usually sea urchins. Captains at sea use the cliffs as a navigational point since they stand out from Zealand's relatively flat topography.

The most dramatic hike, of course, is along the towering cliffs. But if time remains, you can also hike through Klinteskoven (Klinte Forest), a woodland area that grows right up to the edge of the cliffs. Horse trails and a network of foot and hiking paths have been cut through this forest. Trails start from the edge of the cliffs, and the most interesting track to follow is a half a mile west of Storeklint, which will take you to Timmesø Bjerg. Here you'll see the meager ruins of a castle built circa 1100 A.D.

If you visit, facilities for tourists are found at Storeklint, including a cafeteria and a parking lot, along with some souvenir kiosks.

At **Rent-A-Horse,** Langebjergvej 1 (☎ **55-81-22-26**), an outfitter near a local youth hostel at Møns Klint, you can book 2-hour guided horseback tours of Møns Klint or the bay at its base, the Klinteskoven. Equestrian treks are priced at 125 DKK ($18.15) per person per hour.

WHERE TO STAY & DINE

Hotel Store Klint. Stengårdsvej 6, Store Klint, DK-4791 Borre. ☎ and fax **55-81-90-08.** 18 units (none with bath). 500–550 DKK ($72.50–$79.75) double. Rates include breakfast. No credit cards. Closed Mid-Oct to mid-Apr. Bus: "Store Klint" bus from Stege.

Built in 1910 on the pinnacle of the cliffs that soar above the extreme eastern seacoast of Møn, 9½ miles east of Stege, this is a white-walled three-story hotel that prides itself on the simplicity of its format and the ease with which guests re-familiarize themselves with the beauties of nature. Don't expect a large roster of amenities and activities, because other than a well-informed and polite staff, and cliff-top walks that stress the wonders of sunset-watching, the hotel offers very little in the way of amusement or diversions. Most visitors migrate to the fishing port of Klintholmhavn, 4 ½ miles to the southwest, for swimming and a choice of restaurants, although the hotel maintains a bare-boned "cafeteria," where drinks, salads, sandwiches, and simple platters of food are offered whenever there's enough business to warrant it. It's usually open from 10:30am to 8pm daily in summer, with reduced hours in spring and autumn, depending on the mood of the staff and how many visitors are expected. It's closed altogether between mid-October and mid-April. On very clear, calm days, you might be able to spot the coastlines of both Sweden and eastern Germany; otherwise, expect long vistas over blue-green Baltic water.

KLINTHOLM HAVN

Returning to the parking lot at Møns Klint, you can continue south along a minor little road to the hamlet of Sandvej. Once here, turn right at the T-junction in the direction of Mandemarke. Before reaching this village, take a left turn down a lane marked: KLINTHOLM HAVN. This will take you to an old village on the coast with a bustling fishing harbor and a modern marina. The seaside village, a bit of a holiday center, opens onto Hjelm Bay. It's best to visit here on a sunny day, as Klintholm Havn is mainly known for its beach.

Many wealthy Germans use the marina here to station their seagoing yachts. One harbor is filled with fishing boats, the other with these yachts, and the beach runs in both directions from these two harbors. We prefer the beach extending to the east. It's well maintained and set against a backdrop of low-lying dunes; the sands aren't pure white, however, but more of an oyster gray. But if you want to venture into these usually cold waters, the safest swimming is on the beach extending to the west of the harbors. There are public toilets and showers at the marina.

WHERE TO DINE

Chances are you'll be in the area for lunch. There are a few slightly formal places to eat, but our suggestion for a meal is to walk east along the coastal road from the fishing harbor until you come to a little outlet called **Klintholm Røgeri**. Here you can purchase fried or smoked fish and wash it down with a cold Carlsberg. This is an ideal place to enjoy a picnic, and there are picnic tables on site.

If you prefer, however, you can return to the village and have more formal service in a regular dining room.

Klintholm Søbad. Thyravej 19, Klintholm Havn, DK-4791 Borre. ☎ **55-81-91-23.** Reservations recommended. Main courses 99–110 DKK ($14.35–$15.95). Buffet meals 129 DKK ($18.70). No credit cards. Daily 12:30–3pm and 6–9:30pm. Closed Oct–Apr. Free parking.

Set in the center of Klintholm Havn, about 2 miles southeast of the hamlet of Borre, this yellow-walled *kro* is one of the most appealing and charming restaurants on Møn. Built a few steps from the sea, with views that extend southward as far as the coast of eastern Germany, it dates from 1927 and has been feeding visitors with traditional Danish-style food ever since. If you opt for the buffet, you won't be disappointed: it's laid out *smörgåsbord*-style and includes many of the traditional culinary specialties of Denmark. But if you opt for a la carte, the inn's signature dish is fried flatfish (a form of plaice) that's served with parsley-enriched butter sauce and new potatoes. Even more appealing, if it's to your taste, is the "herring buffet." Priced at 29 DKK ($4.20) per person, it includes four different preparations of herring (fried, marinated, in cream sauce, and in curry sauce), and satisfying chunks of fresh whole-wheat bread and butter. It's the kind of culinary experience that can be delectable, if you love this most Scandinavian fish.

On the premises are two simple, not very frequently occupied bedrooms, priced at 450 DKK ($65.25) for a double, and six cottages, each built in the 1980s, costing 550 DKK ($79.75) for between one and four occupants. Each comes with very few amenities (no TV, telephone, or kitchenette), but might be appropriate if you're looking for old-fashioned, bare-boned accommodations by the sea.

SIGHTS IN WEST MØN

After a visit to Møns Klint, you'll have to take the same route back into Stege. But there are other attractions in Møn if time remains. From Stege, head south along Route 287 to Grønjægers Høj, an impressive long barrow surrounded by a stone circle, 4 miles south of Stege near the hamlet of Æbelnæs. It's sign-posted. Called "The Hill of the Green Huntsman," it is a Stone Age "passage grave." The megolithic tomb of three chambers is surrounded by nearly 150 large stones, one of the largest such grave sites in all of Scandinavia.

The third church of Møn to have been decorated by the Master of Elmelunde lies in the area. To reach it, continue on Route 287 to the village of Damsholte, then go left on a minor road following the sign to ✪ **Fanefjord Kirke,** Fanefjordkirkevej, Fanefjord (☎ **55-81-70-05**). The frescoes in the chancel date from the mid–14th century, but the rest are by the master himself. The cycle of paintings were called "Biblia Pauperum" or "bible of the poor," since many of the peasants who formed the congregation did not read. Most of the themes of the frescoes were taken from the Old and New Testaments, but not all. Some are loosely based on Christian legends handed down through the centuries.

Depicted are such subjects as *Adoration of the Magi,* the *Baptism of Jesus,* the *Birth of Jesus,* and *The Annunciation,* among other subjects. *The Slaughter of the Innocents* is particularly moving. The most fun and amusing fresco is *St. George and the Fierce Dragon.* In the choir arch are some frescoes from the High Gothic period, around the mid-14th century, depicting St. Martin and St. Christopher, among other subjects. St. Christopher is seen carrying Christ across a fjord. The imagination that went into this cycle of frescoes shows amazing creativity and massive talent, and the refinement of color is also an outstanding achievement. They are well worth the detour here to reach them. The church itself overlooks Fanefjord and was constructed in the mid–13th century in the Gothic style. The church can be visited daily from 8am to 5pm Monday to Saturday, and on Sunday from 9:30am to 5pm. Admission is free.

After viewing the church, head 5 miles north of Fanefjord in the direction of Tostenæs, where you'll see a sign directing you to **Kong Asgers Høj,** a large passage grave, with a passageway leading to a vast burial chamber. The site lies in a farmer's field on Kong Asgers Vej. The burial chamber is 32½ feet long and some 6½ feet wide. Duck as you go in or you'll crown yourself.

One final attraction remains for Møn, and it's actually an island unto itself. The island of **Bogø** at the southwestern edge of Møn is reached by continuing along Route 287. A causeway leads to the island, which is called "The Island of Mills." Once many mills peppered the little island, but now there is only one remaining, Bogø Molle, which was constructed in 1852 and looks like a windmill from Holland.

Other than its bucolic charm, there isn't a lot to see and do on Bogø, but it has some of the most unspoiled rural scenery around and makes for a brief but satisfying drive.

In the little hamlet of Bogø you can pass by a medieval village church with some late-15th-century murals, but you will have seen better and more intriguing churches if you've already toured Møn. Once the hamlet was known for a famous navigation school, but it is long gone.

It isn't necessary to return to Møn to get back to Zealand. You can drive straight through Bogø until you come to the Farø bridges, which will connect you with Copenhagen in the north if you'd like to return to the capital, or to Falster in the south.

As you approach the ramp to the bridges, you'll see the **Farobroen Welcome Center,** with a cafeteria, money exchange office, and toilets. At the tourist kiosk here you can pick up brochures about Denmark.

8 Bornholm

Surrounded by the Baltic Sea, astride the important shipping lanes that connect St. Petersburg with Copenhagen and the Atlantic, Bornholm sits only 23 miles off the coast of Sweden, but about 95-miles east of Copenhagen and the rest of Denmark. Prized as a strategic Baltic military and trading outpost since the early Middle Ages, and the site of bloody territorial disputes among the Danes, Germans, and Swedes, it's home to 45,000 year-round residents. An additional 450,000 visitors arrive during the balmy months of summer. Besides tourism, which is growing rapidly, the economy relies on trade, fishing, herring processing, agriculture, and the manufacture of ceramics. Thanks to the island's deep veins of clay, ceramics has been an important industry since the 1700s.

Covering a terrain of granite and sandstone is a thin but rich layer of topsoil; the island's rock-studded surface is made up of forests and moors. The unusual topography and surprisingly temperate autumn climate—a function of the waters of the Baltic—promotes the verdant growth of plants: figs, mulberries, and enough lavish conifers to create the third-largest forest in Denmark (right in the center of the island). This forest, Almindingen, has the only rocking stone which still rocks. Rocking stones are giant erratic boulders weighing up to 40 tons that were brought to Bornholm by the advancing glaciers during the last Ice Age. In addition, one of Denmark's largest waterfalls, Døndalen, lies in the north of Bornholm in a rift valley. It can best be viewed from spring through fall.

The island covers 365 square miles and most of the inhabitants live along 87 miles of coastline. Not only do the flora and fauna of the island differ in many respects from the rest of Denmark, its geology is unique. The island is divided into two geologic zones: 1,500-million-year-old bedrock to the north and a 550-million-year-old layer of sandstone to the south.

Bornholmers traditionally have been fishers and farmers. Today their villages are still idyllic, evocative of the old way of life in their well-kept homesteads, as are fishing hamlets with their characteristic smokehouse chimneys, often used for smoking herring.

And the island is still sparsely populated. Gran Canaria (governed by Spain), an island off the coast of Africa, for example, is the same size as Bornholm, but while Gran Canaria has some two million residents in high season, the greatest number of people ever seen on Bornholm at one time is 100,000.

Hassle on Bornholm

Don't expect to enjoy a holiday on Bornholm without some inconvenience: Boats from Copenhagen take either 5 ½ or 7 hours each way. And if you plan to visit in midsummer, firm reservations are essential because of the large numbers of Danes who come for the sandy beaches and the Baltic sunshine.

The best beaches of Bornholm lie in the southwestern section of the island, between the towns of Balka and the main beach town of Dueodde.

Because of its location at the crossroads of warring nations, Bornholm has had a turbulent history even as late as 1945. Strongholds and fortified churches were necessary for the protection of local inhabitants when the island was a virtual plaything in the power struggle between royal and religious forces. It was plundered by pirate fleets, noblemen, and the Hanseatic towns of Pomerania. It didn't experience peace until it revolted against Swedish conquerors at the end of Denmark's war with Sweden in 1658. A group of liberators shot the island's Swedish Lord, and the Bornholmers handed their land over to the king of Denmark.

On a more modern and rather fanatical note, the liberation of Bornholm—unlike the rest of Denmark—was slow to come in 1945. Even when the Nazis had surrendered, the local German commandant on Bornholm refused to give up the island to the Allies. In response, the Soviets rained bombs down on Rønne and Nexø (the two main towns) and then invaded the island and occupied it for several months before returning it to the crown of Denmark. During the long Cold War, the Danes indulged in a little payback time with the Russians. Bornholm became one of NATO's key surveillance bases, spying on what Ronald Reagan called "The Evil Empire."

The island's cuisine is obviously influenced by the surrounding sea. Baltic herring, cod, and salmon are the traditional dishes. One of the most popular local dishes is called "Sun over Gudhjem," a specialty of smoked herring topped with a raw egg yolk in an onion ring. It's served with coarse salt and chives, or, most often, radishes. In autumn, the small Bornholm herring are caught and used for a variety of spiced and pickled herring dishes. Another local dish is salt-fried herring served on dark rye bread with beetroot and hot mustard.

ESSENTIALS

GETTING THERE   The most popular means of reaching the island from Copenhagen is the 7-hour ferryboat ride. Maintained by the **Bornholmstraffiken** (☎ **33-13-18-66**), these ferries depart from the pier at Kvæsthusbroen 1 every evening year-round at 11:30pm, with scheduled arrival the following morning at 6:30am. Between late-June and mid-August there's an additional departure at 8:30am every day except Wednesday. Passage costs 189 DKK ($27.40) per person each way, plus an optional supplement of 148 to 184 DKK ($21.45 to $26.70) to rent a private cabin. These ferries are most often used to transport a car from Copenhagen, which costs 451 DKK ($65.40) each way.

Bornholm Ferries, Havnen, at Rønne (☎ **56-95-18-66**), operates 2 ½-hour ferries from Ystad on the southern coast of Sweden, with up to four departures daily. These ferries have tax-free shops on board. A car with a maximum of five passengers costs 430 DKK ($62.35). You can also travel from Sassnitz-Mukran (Rügen) in North Germany for a 3 ½-hour crossing to Bornholm, arriving at Rønne. Tax-free shopping is also found on board on this crossing. From Germany, one-way passage for a car with a maximum of five passengers is 435 DKK ($63.05). Each of these ferries has a restaurant or bistro featuring a buffet with Danish and Bornholm specialties.

Mærsk Airlines (☎ **32-31-45-45** in Copenhagen, or ☎ 56-95-11-11 in Bornholm for reservations and information) has about eight flights a day from Copenhagen to Bornholm's airport (3 ½-miles south of Rønne). Depending on restrictions, round-trip fares range from 699 to 1,000 DKK ($101.35 to $145).

VISITOR INFORMATION   The tourist office, known as **The Bornholm Welcome Center,** Kystvej 3, Rønne (☎ **56-95-95-00**), is open June 1 through August 31 daily from 7am to 8pm; September 1 through May 31, Monday through Friday from 8am to 4pm, Saturday from 11:30am to 2:30pm, closed on Sunday.

GETTING AROUND   **Hertz,** Snellamark 19, in Rønne, adjacent to the ferryboat piers (☎ **800/654-3001** in the U.S., or ☎ 56-91-00-12), is the leading car-rental agency on the island. The cheapest cars rent for 1,550 DKK ($224.75) a day, but the price includes unlimited mileage, all insurance coverage, and the whopping government tax. **Avis** is located at Snellamark 19, in Rønne (☎ **800/331-2112** in the U.S., or ☎ 56-95-22-08).

During nice weather, biking around the island is almost as popular as driving. If you want to do as the Danes do, rent a pedal bike; the prices are pretty much the same throughout the island—about 55 DKK ($8) a day. Two suggested bike-rental companies in Rønne are **Bornholms Cykleudleijning,** Nordre Kystveg 5 (☎ **56-95-13-59**), and **Cykel-Centret,** Søndergade 7 (☎ **56-95-06-04**).

EXPLORING THE ISLAND

Even if you have a car available, you might want to bike the tour we've outlined below. Ask at any tourist office for a map of the island's more than 120 miles of bicycle trails, and divide this tour into several days, hitting the highlights mentioned below at your own speed.

The tour begins at Rønne, but you could join in at almost any point; basically, the route goes counterclockwise around the island's periphery. Be aware that Bornholm's highways do not have route numbers; even though some maps show the main east-west artery as Route 38, local residents call it "the road to Nexø." Consistent with local custom, this tour suggests that you follow the directional signs pointing to towns you'll eventually reach en route.

1 Rønne

The capital and administrative city of Bornholm, Rønne lies on the western coast facing the island of Zealand. The island's major harbor and airfield are found here.

Rønne is an elongated town with many single family dwellings, both large and small. If you arrive by boat, you'll notice St. Nicolai Church, dedicated to the patron saint of seafarers, on Harbour Hill, towering over the small South Boat Harbor just below.

It wasn't until the 18th century that locals moved ahead with plans for a large trading harbor here. Even today the harbor is still expanding to service ferries and the many cruise ships that call at Rønne in increasing numbers.

Soviet aerial attacks in 1945, mentioned previously, left most of Rønne in shambles. So what you see today is essentially a modern town with a population of 15,000. Many of the houses look older than they are, because the town was carefully rebuilt in the post-war years in the old style. That means the town is full of narrow streets with cross-timbered houses. Many are painted in bright colors such as yellow and orange.

On the vast stretches of sand both south and north of Rønne are popular bathing beaches.

Bornholm

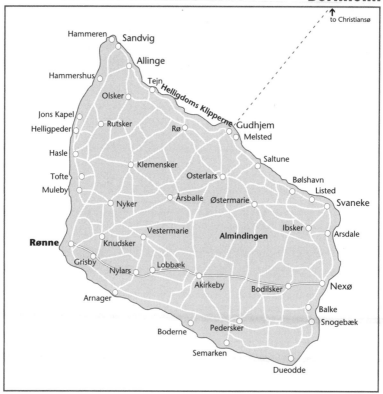

to Christiansø

Hammeren Sandvig
Allinge
Hammershus Tejn Helligdoms Klipperne
Olsker
Jons Kapel
Helligpeder Rutsker Rø Gudhjem
Melsted
Hasle Saltune
Tofte Klemensker Osterlars Bølshavn
Muleby Årsballe Østermarie Listed
Nyker Svaneke
Vestermarie Almindingen Ibsker Arsdale
Rønne Knudsker
Grisby Nylars Lobbæk
Akirkeby Bodilsker Nexø
Arnager Balke
Snogebæk
Boderne Pedersker
Semarken
Dueodde

SEEING THE SIGHTS

Hjorth's Fabrik (Bornholm Ceramic Museum). Krystalgade 5 (☎ **56-95-01-60**). Admission mid-Apr to mid-Oct, 25 DKK ($3.60) adults, 5 DKK (75¢) children; mid-Oct to mid-Apr, 10 DKK ($1.45) adults, free for children. May–Sept, Tues–Sat 10am–5pm; Oct–May, Tues–Fri 1–5pm, Sat 10am–1pm.

The unusual geology of Bornholm includes deep veins of a kind of clay that potters have appreciated for many generations. Since the 1700s hundreds of island residents have produced large numbers of unusual pots, plates, and cups, many of which are whimsical and highly idiosyncratic reminders of another way of life. In 1858 a small-scale factory, Hjorth's Ceramics, was established to make pottery from the island's rich deposits of clay, and it survived until 1993. In 1995 the island's newest museum was established in the company's original factory, a simple but solid building dating back to 1860. Inside, you'll find an intriguing hybrid between an art gallery and an industrial museum. You'll see the island's best examples of the dark-brown, yellow, and gray pottery that was produced in abundance beginning in the 1700s, samples of the dishes and bowls made by the Hjorth company over the years, and some of the work of Bornholm's modern-day potters. Throughout the year several ceramic artists maintain studios inside, casting, spinning, or glazing pots in full view of visitors. Small-scale and charming, the museum is run by two women descendants of the Hjorth family. The museum shop sells modern-day replicas of Hjorth ceramics, and many exhibits trace the production process from start to finish.

Museum of Bornholm (Bornholms Museum). Skt. Mortensgade 29. ☎ **56-95-07-35.** Admission 25 DKK ($3.60) adults, 5 DKK (75¢) children. Mid-Apr to mid-Oct, Mon–Sat 10am–5pm; mid-Oct to mid-Apr, Tues, Thurs, and Sat 1–4pm.

This is the largest and most distinguished museum on Bornholm. It focuses on the island's unique position in the Baltic. Set in what was formerly the island's hospital—a bland, stucco-covered brick building dating back a century—it has displays on archaeology, local traditions and costumes, ethnology, and the seafaring and agrarian traditions that made the island what it is today. Several rooms are outfitted with 19th-century antique furniture, toys, island-made silverware, and accessories. Of special interest is the collection of Bornholm-made clocks, copied from a shipment of English clocks that was salvaged from a Dutch shipwreck in the late 1700s.

Ericksson's Gård (Farm). Laksegade 7. ☎ **56-95-97-35.** Admission 25 DKK ($3.60) adults, free for children. June to mid-Oct, Tues–Sat 10am–5pm. Closed mid-Oct to May.

Set on the outskirts of Rønne, just a short walk from the town center, this is the island's best-preserved example of an old-fashioned farm—the kind that once flourished on Bornholm. Originally constructed in 1806, it's a half-timbered, tile-covered building filled with antique furniture and oil paintings, and flanked with a garden that horticulturists admire for its 160 species of old-fashioned (that is, non-hybrid) roses and flowers. Some of the objects inside commemorate the marriage of a descendent of the farm's original owners—the Ericksson family. An Ericksson daughter married the Danish poet Holger Drachmann (1846–1908), whose works are studied by virtually every schoolchild in Denmark.

Forsvarsmuseet. Kastellet Galløkken. ☎ **56-95-65-83.** Admission 15 DKK ($2.15) adults, 10 DKK ($1.45) children ages 4–10 (free age 3 and under). May–Sept Tues–Sat 10am–4pm.

Housed within a citadel built around 1650 by the Danish king, this Defense Museum is in the southern part of town. With its massive round tower, this old castle is filled with weapons, maps, and models of fortifications. There is also a collection of antique armaments and military uniforms. In our view, the most interesting displays depict the Soviet aerial bombardment of Bornholm in 1945 and the subsequent Russian occupation of the island.

If you have a car or are a great biker you can also view some attractions in the environs. **Brogårdsten** lies 5 ½ miles along the road to the hamlet of Hasle to the north of Rønne. This is the most significant runic stone on the island. First found in 1868, it dates from the beginning of the 12th century. Some long-ago Viking wrote this inscription: "Svenger had this stone placed here for his father Toste and for his brother Alvlak and for his mother and sisters." Obviously women weren't considered important enough to list their actual names.

If you visit Borgårdsten you might as well go another 1 ½ miles up the coast to the little port of **Hasle,** with its stone church from the 1300s and a half-timber tower. Inside the church is an intricately carved and painted altar, the work of an unknown artisan from Lübeck, dating from the mid–15th century. Although it sounds like something from a bad TV sitcom, in July a "herring festival" is celebrated here.

If you'd like to check out a west coast Bornholm beach, you'll find one south of Hasle. It's quite sandy and set against a backdrop of pine trees.

While at Hasle you can see five smokehouses in a row, lying on the coastline. One of the smokehouses (which can be visited for free) is preserved as it was originally built in 1897. It is Silderøgerierne I Hasle, Sdr. Bæk 16-20 (☎ **56-96-44-11**). In one of the other smokehouses, you can watch herring and other kinds of fish being smoked, the traditional way in open chimneys. In the morning you can see how the fish are prepared. Later on you can purchase smoked fish, pick up a beer, and find a nearby spot for an idyllic and very Bornholmer experience.

SHOPPING

Despite its isolation in the middle of the Baltic, Bornholm offers many options for the acquisition of some serious merchandise. Most of the island's shops line either side of streets funneling into the Lille Torv and the Store Torv. Part of the fun involves wandering aimlessly from shop to shop, but if you want specific addresses and ideas, consider any of the following.

For antiques, many of which carry a Baltic/mariners' theme, opt for a visit to **Anne-Lotte Antikviteter,** Lille Torv 14 (☎ **56-95-33-95**). If you're interested in buying more luggage as a means of hauling your loot off of Bornholm, head for **Bagere,** Rothes Konditori, Snellmark 41 (☎ **56-95-02-42**). An outlet for Danish-language books, with a small selection of English titles as well, is **Rønne Bio,** Heindalsvej 19 (☎ **56-95-81-25**). Want to offer some flowers to the object of your most recent affections? Head for **Lilliendal Plantecenter,** Sagavej 1 (☎ **56-95-47-24**).

And if you're looking for a garment of any degree of formality for the child or children you left behind, the best children's clothing store on the island is **Kids' Shop,** Sct. Mortensgade 4 (☎ **56-91-00-17**). Is your camera running out of film? Whatever you need in terms of film supply or film development is available at **Ilsted Bech,** Snellmark 25 (☎ **56-95-00-23**).

Two well-respected art galleries include **Gallerie Jessen,** Lille Torv 12 (☎ **56-49-81-82**), where the oils and watercolors of some of the island's many artists are displayed on an oft-changing basis, and to a lesser extent, **Hakon Holm ApS.,** Borgmester Nielsens Vej 24 (☎ **56-95-24-44**).

A major outlet for some of the art glass produced in abundance on Bornholm is **Pernille Bülow Glas,** Lille Torv (☎ **56-95-43-05**). A purveyor of some of the most unusual wrought iron in the Baltic is the **Dansk-Svensk Stål,** St. Torvegade 7 (☎ **56-95-14-42**). For a catch-all emporium selling everything from cheap souvenirs of your time on Bornholm to rather exotic handmade goods that you're not likely to find on the Danish "mainland," head for **Joker,** Torvegade 4 (☎ **56-95-09-13**).

The island is known for its unique Bornholmer grandfather clocks. The tradition began in 1744 when a Dutch ship was stranded on the way from Helsingør in Denmark to Talinn in Estonia. In its hold were five clocks and a cask with weights for them. Dexterous young men made models of the clocks and, in so doing, founded a Bornholm clock-making tradition, a craft that virtually disappeared at the end of World War II. The craft has now been revived, and the island's largest clockmaker workshop is located in Rønne. **Nye Bornholmerure,** Torneværksvej 26 (☎ **56-89-31-08**), sells the finest handmade grandfather clocks in Denmark, although, depending on the model, they can be very expensive. These clocks sound the hour with music—everything from Mozart to Andrew Lloyd Weber.

Many Swedes come over to Bornholm just to shop for the island's famous ceramics. Excavations in the old part of Rønne have revealed the kinds of ceramic kitchen utensils used by former inhabitants (some of these specimens are on view at the Museum of Bornholm). **Michael Andersen,** Lille Torv 7 (☎ **56-95-00-01**), still preserves the old ceramics-making traditions, but also manufactures many modern products as well.

The island's best goldsmith—and he's a stunning talent—is Jørn-Ole Thomsen, who works at **Guldhuset,** Bornholmercentret (☎ **56-95-02-70**), on Store Torv. Thomsen makes fine jewelry, not only for the local shop, but also for Georg Jensen, the world famous silver and goldsmith company.

WHERE TO STAY

Best Western Hotel Fredensborg. Strandvejen 116, DK-3700 Rønne. ☎ **800/528-1234** in the U.S., or ☎ 56-95-44-44. Fax 56-95-03-14. www.hotelfredensborg.dk. E-mail: www. info@hotelfredensborg.dk. 73 units. TV TEL 895–995 DKK ($129.75–$144.25) double; 900–1,100 DKK ($130.50–$159.50) suite. Rates include breakfast buffet. AE, DC, MC, V.

This is one of the few hotels on the island that remains open year-round. Situated in a quiet forest, adjacent to a beach about a mile south of Rønne's harbor-front, it was built during the 1960s in a comfortable, not particularly ornate style that includes Danish modern furniture and comfortable bedrooms; prices vary according to season and views of the water.

Dining: On the premises are two restaurants serving well-prepared food. The less formal of the two, Fisken, is open only from April to late-October, daily for lunch and dinner. The more formal restaurant, De 5 Stâuerna, remains open for lunch and dinner year-round. On warm summer evenings when the weather's clear, the hotel staff offers a barbecue on the terrace, with a view of the garden and the Baltic Sea. Every Thursday during summer, a large fish buffet is featured.

Amenities: Sauna, tennis court, billiards, and bike rentals.

Hotel Griffen. Kredsen 1, DK-3700 Rønne. ☎ **56-95-51-11.** Fax 56-95-52-97. 140 units. TV TEL. 745–945 DKK ($108–$137) double, 1,050 DKK ($152.25) suite. AE, DC, MC, V.

Set near the heart of Rønne, a 5-minute walk from the beach, the town center, and an upscale marina, this circa-1976 hotel is the largest on Bornholm. It's divided into four impressively large buildings, each with terra-cotta roofs and proportions that were vaguely influenced by 18th-century hip-roofed manor houses. Two of the buildings have multiple balconies and are reserved for lodgings; because of their isolation from bars, dining rooms, and convention facilities, they tend to be quiet and very peaceful. Furnishings in bedrooms are contemporary and minimalist, but with occasional touches of elegance and glamour that are enhanced by floor-to-ceiling windows and glass doors affording views of the sea. Expect lots of corporate conventions here, and a sometimes anonymous staff that might be a bit jaded from too constant exposure to large groups checking in simultaneously. Despite that, the hotel is comfortable and up-to-date, even though you won't necessarily feel a sense of country-rustic coziness.

Dining/Diversions: Restaurant Viktoria is a well-maintained, rather formal venue with a contemporary decor, an emphasis on Danish cuisine, and meals that average from 125 to 250 DKK ($18.15 to $36.25), depending on what you order. There's also a cocktail lounge.

Amenities: 24-hour room service, sauna, solarium, ping-pong tables, an indoor swimming pool, and a staff that can guide you toward most of the other outdoor diversions on Bornholm.

Hotel Hoffman. Ndr. Hystvej 32, DK-3700 Rønne. ☎ **56-95-03-86.** Fax 56-95-25-15. 69 units, 16 apts. with kitchen but without maid service. TV TEL. 745–875 DKK ($108–$126.85) double with breakfast. 335–585 DKK ($48.55–$84.80) apt. with kitchen, double occupancy. In apts., breakfast 65 DKK ($9.40) extra per person. One-time expense of 300 DKK ($43.50) for end-of-rental cleaning costs. AE, DC, MC, V.

This hotel is mainly appealing for its monochromatic and well-designed bedrooms, each of which contains the kind of big-city contemporary furnishings you might have expected from a stylish business-oriented hotel in Copenhagen. Built in the 1970s, it rises three brick-sheathed stories from a position about a block from the city's inner harbor. It's a member of the nationwide Dansk Kroferie chain, and as such, appeals to a broad audience based on the widely publicized similarities between it and many equivalent chain members across the country. The apartments here have kitchenettes and are more bare-boned than the conventional accommodations, requiring the payment of a one-time cleaning fee that's imposed at the end of every rental even if it's only 1 day.

Dining: There's a restaurant on the premises, open daily for lunch and dinner, whose tables spill out into the hotel's sheltered courtyard.

Amenities: Table tennis, billiards, sauna, and a solarium.

Hotel Ryttergaarden. Strandvejen 79, DK-3700 Rønne. ☎ **56-95-19-13.** Fax 56-95-19-22. 102 units, 28 apts. with kitchenette. MINIBAR TV TEL. 720–860 DKK ($104.40–$124.70) double. Rates include breakfast. Apts. for up to six occupants 1,795–5,000 DKK ($260.25–$725) per week, without breakfast, plus an obligatory one-time fee per apt. of 275 DKK ($39.90) for cleaning, plus 145–260 DKK ($21.05–$37.70) per unit per week for electricity. AE, DC, MC, V. Closed Oct–Apr. Bus from Rønne: 23 or 24.

Set about 1 ¼-miles south of Rønne, less than 200 yards from a sandy beach, this hotel was built between 1986 and 1998 as a compound of at least seven angular, big-windowed modern structures. Parts of its architecture might remind you of the buildings surrounding an international airport, because of their boxy, hyper-modern shapes and their ample use of glass. Overall, it's a good, albeit somewhat anonymous, choice for a holiday beside the sea. Bedrooms are cozy and modern, with varnished blond wood and sliding glass doors that open onto balconies facing the sea. On the premises are an indoor swimming pool, a sauna, a solarium, a restaurant, and a bar.

Svere's Small Hotel. Snellmark 2, DK-3700 Rønne. ☎ **56-95-03-03.** Fax 56-95-03-92. 33 units (17 with bath and TV). 360–460 DKK ($52.20–$66.70) double without bath, 480–530 DKK ($69.60–$76.85) double with bath. MC, V. Rate includes breakfast.

Set about a block from Rønne's harbor front, this ocher-colored antique building was originally established as a coaching inn around 1850. This is a clean, well-maintained, and completely unpretentious hotel that's an extremely good choice if you don't mind a half-mile trek to a worthwhile beach. Bedrooms are simple but cozy, with wall-to-wall carpeting, touches of wood trim, and in most cases, at least one chair for reading or talking with a roommate. Breakfast is the only meal served, although the neighborhood around the hotel offers many different dining choices.

WHERE TO DINE

✪ **De 5 Stâuerna.** In the Hotel Fredensborg, Strandvejen 116. ☎ **56-95-44-44.** Reservations recommended. Main courses 78–228 DKK ($11.30–$33.05). Fish platter of the day 68 DKK ($9.85); Set-price "menu dégustation" 265 DKK ($38.40). AE, DC, MC, V. DANISH/INTERNATIONAL.

This is the best and most upscale restaurant in Rønne, with a clientele that tends to select it for celebratory meals of any ilk, including family gatherings during important rites of passage. Its name translates as "the five rooms," each of which is outfitted in a rustic country-Danish style, with white walls and light that's filtered through yellow-tinted windows. There's always a platter of the proposed fish of the day, which is invariably prepared in a simple, Danish-derived style, usually fried in butter and served with new potatoes in a way that Bornholmers have witnessed since their childhood. Other, more elaborate, options include Hereford beefsteak prepared Cordon Bleu style, with salted cured ham and Emmenthaler cheese; tournedos of beef flambéed in Calvados and served with apples and onions; an exotic sautéed fillet of ostrich with Mexican pimentos and peppers; marinated and minced beefsteak with chili; and a dish that we personally prefer more than almost anything else on the menu, Bornholm lamb served with a sauce concocted from rosemary, olive oil, and tarragon.

Rådhuskroen. Nørregade 2. ☎ **56-95-00-69.** Reservations recommended on weekends. Main courses 75–145 DKK ($10.90–$21.05). AE, DC, MC, V. Daily noon–9pm. DANISH.

This is the most visible and, in its own way, most charming restaurant in Rønne. It's situated in the darkened and intimately illuminated cellar of the Town Hall, a 140-year-old building with a long history of feeding island residents in a cozy setting protected from blustering midwinter winds. Wall sconces cast romantic shadows over a collection of antique furniture and accessories, as a well-trained service staff serves such dishes as super fillet of salmon in a "summer sauce" of fresh tomatoes, chives, and herbs, and two different sizes of tender and well-prepared beefsteak ("Mr. Beef" and "Mrs. Beef"). This restaurant is open year-round.

RØNNE AFTER DARK

Its role as Bornholm's largest settlement forces Rønne into the sometimes unwanted role as nightlife capital of the island. Don't expect too much glitter. Things on Bornholm tend to stay quiet.

The most visible and popular disco on the island for high-energy members of the under-30 generation is **Sputnik,** Sct. Mortensgade 48, in Rønne (☎ **56-95-48-01**). Victim to oft-changing ownership within the past decade, it offers high-volume mania that's associated with nightlife in bigger cities. The venue is a dark-painted much-used environment with prominent bars, battered sofas and chairs, and a dance floor lit by colored lights whose rhythms might tempt you to dance, dance, dance. A 30 DKK ($4.35) cover charge is imposed on Friday and Saturday; otherwise, entrance is free. If you're less interested in hanging out with the Lolita/Lolito crowd, consider a pint of Guinness at **O'Malley's Irish Pub,** Store Torvegade, in Rønne (no phone), where clients older than 30 appreciate the Celtic conviviality and the recorded music.

FROM RØNNE TO NEXØ

From Rønne, drive east along the island's modern highway, A38, following the signs toward Nexø. About 3-miles later, stop in **Nylars,** a town that's known as the site of the best-preserved of Bornholm's four round churches. The **Nylarskirke,** (☎ **56-97-20-13**), built around 1250, and rising prominently from the center of a community with no more than about 50 buildings, contains frescoes that depict the Creation and the ejection of Adam and Eve from the Garden of Eden. The cylindrical nave has three floors, the uppermost of which was a watchman's tower in the Middle Ages. You can also view two fragments of a runic stone. From Rønne, bus no. 6 runs here if you don't have a car, and the bike path from Rønne to Åkirkeby also passes by the church. It's open between May 12 and October 20, daily from 9am to 5pm. Admission is free.

Continue driving another 3-miles east until you reach **Åkirkeby,** the only inland settlement of any size. Its economy is based on farming and on a factory (the Boværk Company) that produces vegetable fodder for farm animals. Small-scale and sleepy, this is Bornholm's oldest settlement (its town charter dates from 1346).

The little town was important in medieval times when islanders had to move inland to avoid attacks from enemies at sea. The island's regional council met here until 1776, and Åkirkeby was also the ecclesiastical center of Bornholm.

It's also home to the island's oldest and largest church, **Åkirke,** Torvet (☎ **56-97-41-03**), originally built around 1250. Although this church isn't as eccentric as some of the others, it's a sandstone-fronted monument built with defense in mind, as you'll note from the small windows. Notice the Romanesque baptismal font incised with runic inscriptions; it's believed that they were carved by the master craftsman Sigraf on the island of Gotland. Other runic inscriptions appear on the cloverleaf-shaped arches. The church is open daily from 10am to 4pm; there is a charge of 6 DKK (85¢) for visitors.

Åkirkeby is a good point to cut inland if you wish to see some of Bornholm's woodlands, among the densest in Denmark. Forests are filled with oak, hemlock, fir, spruce, and beech trees. The tourist office in Rønne (see above) will give you a map outlining the best of the trails that cut through Bornholm's largest forest, **Almindingen,** in the center of the island. It can be reached by following a sign-posted road north from Åkirkeby. The forest is also the location of the island's highest point, **Rytterknægten,** a 526-foot-high hill with a lookout tower, Kongemindet, which you can scale for a panoramic view of the dense woodlands.

You can also pick up information at a minor, rarely used tourist office that's much less visible than the island's main office in Rønne. It's the **Sydbornholms Turistbureau,** Torvet 2 (☎ 56-97-45-20) at Åkirkeby. From mid-May to mid-September, it's open Monday to Friday from 9am to 5pm, and Saturday from 8am to 1pm. The rest of the year, it's open Monday to Friday from 9am to 4:30pm, and closed on Saturday and Sunday.

A minor museum that's interesting to specialists and devoted automobile fans is the **Bornholms Automobilmuseum,** Grammegardsvej 1 (☎ 56-97-45-95). Its displays include vintage cars and motorcycles, plus some farm equipment and tractors that highlight the 20th century's advances in agrarian science. Antique cars and tractors derive from such manufacturers as Delahaye, Opel, Ford, Adler, Singer, Jaguar, and Fiat. It's open from May to October every Monday to Saturday, from 10am to 5pm. The rest of the year it's closed. Admission costs 25 DKK ($3.60) per person.

From Åkirkeby, cut southeast for 2 ¾ miles, following the signs to **Pedersker,** a hamlet with only three shops (which close down during the cold-weather months). Four miles later you'll reach **Dueodde,** the name of both a raffish beachfront community and the entire region around the southernmost tip of the island. The village of Dueodde marks the southern edge of a stretch of coastline that some people believe is the finest beach on the island. (The oceanfront bounty—and the best beaches on the island—stretch northward and eastward to the town of **Balka,** 3-miles beyond, encompassing stretches of white sand whose grains are so fine that they were used for generations to fill hourglasses.) The towns themselves are little more than backdrops for seasonal kiosks and a scattering of holiday homes for mainland Danes and Swedes. Most of the landscape, however, is a virtual wilderness of pine and spruce trees, salt-tolerant shrubs, and sand dunes, some of which rise more than 40 feet above the nearby sea.

The focal point of this southeastern coastline is the **Dueodde Fyr** (Dueodde Lighthouse), the tallest on the island, built in 1962 to warn ships away from the extreme southern tip of the island. Weather permitting, you can climb to its top during daylight hours between May and October for a fee of 5 DKK (75¢), which you pay directly to the lighthouse keeper. For information, call ☎ **56-48-80-42.**

From Dueodde, continue along the coast in a northeasterly direction, passing through the unpretentious fishing hamlets of **Snogebæk** and **Balka,** a sleepy midsummer resort that's even sleepier in winter.

Immediately north of Balka the road will deliver you north to Nexø, the second major town of the island after Rønne, opening onto the eastern coast facing Sweden.

2 Nexø

Nexø, 16-miles east of Rønne, has a year-round population of 3,900, which makes it the largest fishing port on the island. Part of the charm of this community can be found in the excellent replicas of the privately owned 17th- and 18th- century buildings that were architectural highlights of the island before World War II.

In May 1945 Nexø was heavily bombed by the Russians during 2 days of horror; this happened several days after the rest of Denmark had been liberated from the Nazis. Nexø was a final holdout of Nazi soldiers during the closing days of the war. Ironically, Bornholm was the last area of Denmark to get rid of its Soviet "liberators," although they didn't completely evacuate the island until 1946.

The destruction of most of the town's 900 buildings and their subsequent restoration along original lines is the stuff of which legends are made. Since the region around Nexø is composed mostly of sandstone, much of the town's masonry is tawny colored, rather than the granite gray found elsewhere on the island.

Before exploring the area, you can pick up good information at the **Nexø-Dueodde Turistbureau,** Aasen 4 (☎ **56-49-32-00**). From mid-May to mid-September, it's open Monday to Friday from 9am to 5pm, and Saturday from 8am to 1pm. The rest of the year, it's open Monday to Friday from 9am to 4:30pm, and closed on Saturday and Sunday.

One of the town's more eccentric and idiosyncratic monuments is the **Nexø Museum,** Havnen (☎ **56-49-25-56**), which is open only from May to September, daily from 10am to 4pm. For an entrance fee of 15 DKK ($2.15), you'll see displays of fishing-related equipment that has sustained the local economy, and memorabilia of the Danish author Martin Andersen (1869–1954)—better known as Martin Andersen Nexø, a pen name he adopted in honor of his native village. His novel, *Pelle the Conqueror,* which was set in Bornholm and later made into an acclaimed film, revealed how Danish landowners in the early 20th century exploited Swedish newcomers to the island.

WHERE TO STAY

In this southeastern corridor of Bornholm you aren't limited just to Nexø for accommodations. In summer you can also stay at the seaside hamlets of Dueodde or Snogebæk immediately south of the town of Nexø. These are more scenic places to stay and they also open onto the island's best beaches.

Since Nexø was heavily bombed during the war and isn't of much scenic interest, either Snogebæk or Dueodde might make a better alternative choice for lodgings. Dueodde is Bornholm's number one beach area, and the entire stretch of coast is filled with rolling dunes and endless strips of white sand. Snogebæk is a little seaside settlement with holiday homes, but there is no village attached to Dueodde; it's just a scattering of buildings along the coast. For the most part, residents who live in Dueodde or Snogebæk use Nexø for their services and supplies.

AT NEXØ

Hotel Balka Søbad. Vestre Strandvej 25, DK-3730 Nexø. ☎ **56-49-49-49.** Fax 56-49-22-33. 106 units. TV TEL. 710–1,040 DKK ($102.95–$150.80) double. Rates include breakfast. Supplement for half-board 50 DKK ($7.25) per person per day. MC, V. Closed Nov–Apr. From Nexø, drive 2-miles south, following the signs to Sogebæk.

Set in an isolated position on a flat and sandy sea-fronting plain 2-miles south of Nexø, this hotel consists of five white-walled modern buildings, each constructed between 1972 and 1976, encircling a common area with an outdoor swimming pool. Each of the bedrooms has wall-to-wall carpet, a kitchenette, a balcony or terrace, and simple, durable furniture that's consistent with the hotel's role as a beach resort catering to families with children. On the premises are a sauna and two tennis courts, but most of the guests spend the bulk of their time on the sands of the beach, the waters of which lie no more than 100 yards from the hotel.

Hotel Balka Strand. Boulevarden 9, DK-3730 Nexø. ☎ **56-49-49-49.** Fax 56-49-49-48. 96 units, half with kitchenettes. TV TEL. 870–1,090 DKK ($126.15–$158.05) double without kitchenette; 955–1,175 DKK ($138.50–$170.40) double with kitchenette. Rates include break-fast and dinner. AE, DC, MC, V. From Nexø, drive 1 ½-miles south along the coastal road, fol-lowing the signs to Balka and Dueodde.

This is the only hotel along Bornholm's beach-fringed eastern coast that remains open throughout the year, so as such, it's busier than you might have thought, even in mid-winter. Originally built in the 1970s, and doubled in size in 1992 (all the rooms with kitchenettes were added in this later stage), it has a design whereby accommodations encircle a heated outdoor swimming pool (open May to September only), within a short walk of the hotel's outdoor tennis court. Meals are served, with an emphasis on Danish recipes, in a big-windowed, modern dining room that concludes most of its evenings with live music, dancing, or some kind of entertainment.

AT SNOGBÆK

Pension Blomstergården. Dueoddevej 2–4, D-3730 Snogebæk. ☎ **56-48-88-06.** Fax 56-48-92-18. http://home3.inet.tele.dk/blomst/. E-mail: bloomst@post3.tele.dk. 23 units (4 with bath). 395 DKK ($57.30) double without bath; 475 DKK ($68.90) double with bath. No credit cards.

Set 3 ½-miles south of Nexø, on the outskirts of the hamlet of Snogbæk, this pension evolved from what was originally conceived as a village schoolhouse in the 1930s, and later transformed into a youth hostel. Today, thanks to the hard work and attention to detail of owner Stig Thomsen, it caters to beach and nature lovers and, in many cases, persons involved in bike rides around Bornholm. Bedrooms are comfortable and idio-syncratic, and might remind you of stripped-down versions of what you might have found in a private home. If advance notice is given, the owners will prepare a Danish-style light evening meal, for residents only, for 50 DKK ($7.25) per person.

Snogebæk Hotelpension. Ellegade 10, DK-3730 Snogbæk. ☎ **56-48-80-80.** Fax 56-48-81-31. E-mail: henrikch@post8.tele.dk. 25 units. TV TEL. 540–680 DKK ($78.30–$98.60) double. Rates include breakfast. MC, V. Closed Oct–Apr.

Set about a half-mile west from the center of Snogbæk, in an inland position a half-mile walk, drive, or bike ride from the beach, this hotel originated around the turn of the century as a rustic-looking farmhouse. After a massive renovation in the late 1980s, the farmhouse's beamed interior was converted into the establishment's restau-rant and social center, and newer, motel-style wings were added, extending into the garden. Bedrooms are small, not at all plush, and would be more claustrophobic if they didn't open directly into the well-maintained greenery that surrounds the hotel. On the premises is a swimming pool set within a greenhouse-style outbuilding, but despite its appeal, most clients spend most of their days at the nearby beach.

AT DUEODDE

Dueodde Badehotel. Poulsker, DK-3730 Nexø. ☎ **56-48-86-49.** Fax 56-48-89-59. http://home9.inet.tele.dk/due_odde. E-mail: Dueodde_Badehotel@bornnet.dk. 48 apts., each with kitchenette. TV TEL. 300–700 DKK ($43.50–$101.50) double. Closed Nov–Apr. AE, DC, MC, V. From Nexø, drive 5 ½-miles south along the coastal road, following the signs for Dueodde.

Well-designed and tasteful, this two-story motel-like structure was built in 1978, and remains the most southerly hotel in Bornholm. It is surrounded by scrub-covered sand dunes and is a short walk from the beach, which seems to be at the forefront of most of the thoughts and activities of a clientele that in some cases returns year after year. Each accommodation is laid out something like an efficiently designed suite aboard a cruise ship, with compact dimensions, a color scheme of blue and white, modern furniture, and in every case, a separate seating area and a balcony or terrace. Each has a radio and a safe for valuables. There's a tennis court on the premises, and a comfortable restaurant that charges 80 to 110 DKK ($11.60 to $15.95) for well-prepared Danish meals.

Hotel Bornholm. Pilegårdsvej 1, Dueodde, DK-Nexø. ☎ **56-48-83-83.** Fax 56-48-85-37. 44 apts., 7 cottages. 540–690 DKK ($78.30–$100.05) double per night, 2,525–5,800 DKK ($366.15–$841) cottage for four per night. Rates include breakfast. Half-board 159 DKK ($23.05) extra per person per day. MC, V. Closed Oct–Apr. From Nexø, drive 3 ½-miles south along the coastal road, following the signs to Dueodde.

Set beside the white sands of the island's most popular beach (Dueodde), this hotel was built between 1972 and 1982, in a design that evokes a stateside motel surrounded by a verdant garden. Each unit opens directly into a garden replete with roses, flowering shrubs, and small patches of lawn, an effect that gives the impression of camping out directly in a natural setting. Furnishings in each are durable, efficient, and practical—designed for hard use by couples and families on holiday at the beach. The resort contains both indoor and outdoor swimming pools, a tennis court, and an exercise room.

WHERE TO DINE
AT NEXØ
Hotel Balka Strand. Boulevarden 9. ☎ **56-49-49-49.** Reservations required for non-hotel guests. Main courses 80–135 DKK ($11.60–$19.60). AE, DC, MC, V. Daily noon–3 and 6:30–9:30pm. DANISH.

Although much of its dining room is occupied by residents of the (previously recommended) hotel that contains it, this restaurant opens its doors to well-meaning outsiders who phone ahead for reservations. Within an airy, sparsely decorated dining room whose angularity goes well with the stark seaside landscapes around it, you can enjoy such traditional menu items as marinated or fried herring, various kinds of omelets, soups such as a creamy version of borscht, fried steak with onions, and a roster of fresh fish that includes halibut with herbed wine sauce. Dessert might be a slice of chocolate layer cake, or perhaps a *flan* inspired by the chef's most recent visit to Spain. The cuisine, although not richly varied, is always reliable and dependable, and fresh ingredients are carefully prepared and briskly served. Portions tend to be quite large and filling. If you're lucky enough to arrive when there's live music, you might enjoy dancing at least part of the night away.

AT SNOGEBÆK
Den Lille Havefrue. Hovedgaden 5, Snogebæk. ☎ **56-48-80-55.** Reservations recommended. Main courses 100–170 DKK ($14.50–$24.65). AE, DC, MC, V. Daily 11:30am–10pm. Closed Oct–Apr. DANISH.

Housed in a cozy modern building erected in the 1950s, this is one of the least pretentious but best-recommended restaurants on the island. Its woodsy setting is accented with dozens of pottery pieces crafted by the local artist Kirsten Kleman. The hardworking staff will suggest any of various fish and meat dishes prepared according to long-established, traditional methods, including salmon with lobster sauce (a perennial favorite), codfish with potatoes and onions, beefsteak and calf's liver, and broiled plaice with lemon and parsley-butter sauce. The menu includes an ample selection of soups, salads, and simple desserts. The cookery is always reliable here, and never makes any pretense of being anything but that.

3 Svaneke

After Nexø, the topography of the island will gradually change from tawny sandstone to a more heavily forested area with thin topsoil, deep veins of clay, and outcroppings of gray granite.

Continue driving 3 ½-miles north along the coastal road, following the signs to **Svaneke,** Denmark's easternmost settlement, with fewer than 1,200 year-round residents. It lies 12 ½-miles east of Rønne. It bears some resemblance to certain eastern regions of the Baltic with which it has traded, and it still has many 17th- and 18th-century cottages along cobblestone streets leading to the harbor where fishing boats bob idyllically at anchor.

Many writers, sculptors, and painters are acquiring homes in Svaneke, an idyllic retreat from the urban life of Copenhagen. Svaneke is the most photogenic town on Bornholm; in 1975 it won the European Gold Medal for town preservation. Its most famous citizen was J. N. Madvig, Denmark's influential philologist, who was born here in 1804.

For information about the area, contact **Svaneke Turistbureau,** Storegade 24 (☎ 56-49-32-00). From June to August, it's open Monday to Friday from 9:30am to 4:30pm, Saturday from 9am to noon. The rest of the year, from September to May, it's open Monday to Wednesday from 10am to 4pm, and Thursday to Friday from 11am to 5pm.

Sights are few here and easily covered on foot. It is the appealing town itself that is the attraction, filled with red-tile buildings.

The town's main square is the Torv. Directly south of here is Svaneke Kirke, which has a runic stone dating from the mid–14th century. The church itself was largely reconstructed in the 1800s and is only of minor interest.

In and around the area are a number of windmills, including an old post mill on the north side of town. At a point 2-miles south of Svaneke, in the hamlet of Årsdale, there is an old working windmill where corn is still ground and sold to locals.

SHOPPING   Bornholm's east coast, particularly around Svaneke, contains the highest percentage of artists, many of whom display their creations within such art galleries as **Gallerie Hvide Hus,** Rand Kløvej 15, in the hamlet of Saltuna (☎ 56-47-03-33). Set midway between Svaneke and Gudhjem, it specializes in crafts, ceramics, and paintings, usually by Danish or Swedish artists, many of whom reside on the island.

WHERE TO STAY

Hotel Østersøen. Havnebryggen 5, DK-3740 Svaneke. ☎ **56-49-60-20.** Fax 56-49-72-79. 21 apts., all with kitchenettes. TV TEL. Sept–June 350–825 DKK ($50.75–$119.60) double. 700–1,000 DKK ($101.50–$145) quad. July–Aug (weekly rentals required) 4,350–5,450 DKK ($630.75–$790.25) per week double, 6,650 DKK ($964.25) quad. Obligatory end-of-rental cleaning fee of 250 DKK ($36.25) for two persons, 350 DKK ($50.75) for four. AE, DC, MC, V.

Rich with many of the architectural quirks of its original construction 300 years ago, this complex of apartments with kitchenettes is more charming and more authentically old-fashioned than its nearby competitors. It sprawls along a goodly portion of Svaneke's harbor-front, wrapping itself around three sides of an open-air courtyard, in the center of which is an outdoor swimming pool. Within the courtyard are well-maintained flowerbeds and a graceful art nouveau water nymph crafted from bronze. Apartments themselves are an appealing blend of old-fashioned buttresses (the original antique beams, now painted white, are visible within many of them), modern kitchenettes, and summery, airy furnishings. Overall, the venue is comfortable, cozy, and attractively positioned.

Pension Solgården. Skolebakken 5, Aarsdale, DK-3740 Svaneke. ☎ **56-49-64-37.** Fax 56-49-65-37. 18 units (9 with bath). 430 DKK ($62.35) double without bath; 540 DKK ($78.30) double with bath. Rates include breakfast. No credit cards. Closed Sept–May.

The only problem with this solidly built guesthouse involves the fact that it's open only 3 months a year during the peak of midsummer. It was originally conceived in the 1930s as the quintessential redbrick schoolhouse, with a panoramic position adjacent to the sea, 2-miles south of Svaneke, beside the road leading south to Nexø. The interior contains lots of exposed brick and big windows overlooking the sea. The simple but cozy bedrooms are outfitted with the kind of furnishings you might have seen within your college dormitory of long ago. There's a dining room on the premises, but it's open only to residents of the hotel. Outside you'll find lawns strewn with tables for sea-gazing and sun-worshipping.

Siemmsens Gaard. Havnebryggen 9, DK-3740 Svaneke. ☎ **56-49-61-49.** Fax 56-49-61-03. 50 units. 750 DKK ($108.75) double. Rates includes breakfast. AE, DC, MC, V.

Until about 5 years ago, this hotel sported one of the oldest physical structures on Bornholm. In the early 1990s, however, a bolt of lightning struck one of the establishment's two buildings, burning it to the ground, and necessitating a rebuilding of about half of the hotel rooms. Today, you'll face a hotel with old and new rooms, both types of which are cozy and rustically appealing as weather-tight getaways. Its location a few steps from the Svaneke harbor front adds a lot of charm to this property, as does the pub-like cocktail lounge and restaurant, which is separately recommended below. There's also a sauna and solarium on the premises.

WHERE TO DINE

Siemmsens Gaard. Havnebryggen 9. ☎ **56-49-61-49.** Reservations recommended. Lunch main courses 85–105 DKK ($12.35–$15.25); lunch *smørrebrød* 40 DKK ($5.80). 130–170 DKK ($18.85–$24.65). AE, DC, MC, V. Daily 7am–10:30pm. DANISH.

Set directly on the Svaneke harbor-front, the building that contains this restaurant is one of the oldest in town. Half-timbered, and with a pale yellow façade that evokes a historic *kro,* it was constructed 400 years ago as the home of a wealthy merchant. About half of its interior is devoted to bedrooms associated with the hotel that's separately recommended in "Where to Stay," above. The other half contains an artfully rustic and simple series of dining rooms whose thick walls and harbor views evoke the Denmark of the early 20th century. If you're not sure about what to order at lunch, consider a medley of *smørrebrød* (open-faced sandwiches) that some culinary experts think are almost too attractive to eat. An average lunch might consist of two or three of these. More substantial fare might include a selection of several kinds of herring arranged onto the same platter, steaming bowls of cream of shellfish soup, smoked and marinated salmon with *crème fraîche,* grilled monkfish or haddock with herbs and red wine sauce, grilled sirloin with herbs and mustard sauce, and a dessert specialty of *crêpes* with almond cream and fresh berries.

FROM SVANEKE TO GUDHJEM

From Svaneke, you can leave the Baltic coastline and head inland through the northern outskirts of the third largest forest in Denmark, **Almindingen.** (The western part of this forest is best explored by heading north from Åkirkeby—see above.) Dotted with creeks and ponds, and covered mostly with hardy conifers, it's known for the profusion of its wildflowers—especially lily-of-the-valley—and well-designated hiking trails. Head first for **Østerlars,** home to the largest of the island's distinctive round churches, the **Østerlarskirke,** at Gudhjemsveg 28 (☎ **56-49-82-64**). It's open between early-April and mid-October, Monday to Saturday from 9am to 5pm. The entrance fee is 5 DKK (75¢) for adults, free for children. It was originally built around 1150 by the Vikings, with rocks, boulders, and stone slabs. The church was dedicated to St. Laurence and later enlarged with chunky-looking buttresses; it was intended to serve in part as a fortress against raids by Baltic pirates. Inside are several wall paintings that date from around 1350, depicting scenes from the life of Jesus. Bus no. 9 from Gudhjem makes the run here.

After exploring the area and dipping south along forest roads you can follow the signposts to Østerlars, southwest of Gudhjem, or else drive back along the coast to Svaneke and take the coastal road northwest into Gudhjem.

4 Gudhjem

From Østerlars, drive 2-miles north, following the signs to **Gudhjem** ("God's Home"), a steeply inclined town that traded with the Hanseatic League during the Middle Ages. Most of its population died as a result of plagues in 1653–54, but the town was repopulated some years later by Danish guerrilla fighters and sympathizers following its territorial wars with Sweden. You'll find a town that—because of its many fig and mulberry trees, plus steep slopes—has a vaguely Mediterranean flavor.

Before setting out to explore actual sights in the town, you might want to call first at the **Gudhjem Turistbureau,** Åbogade 9 (☎ **56-48-52-10**), a block inland from the harbor. It's open only in summertime, between May and September. From May 1 to mid-June, and from mid-August to the end of September, hours are Monday to Saturday from 1 to 4pm. During the peak of midsummer, from mid-June to mid-August, hours are Friday to Wednesday from 10am to 4pm. It's closed the rest of the year.

Especially charming are Gudhjem's 18th-century half-timbered houses and the 19th-century smokehouses, known for their distinctive techniques of preserving herring with alderwood smoke. Its harbor, blasted out of the rocky shoreline in the 1850s, is the focal point for the town's 1,200 permanent residents.

Landsbrugs Museum (Bornholm Agricultural Museum). Melstedvej 25 (half a mile south of Gudhjem). ☎ **56-48-55-98.** Admission 25 DKK ($3.60) adults, 5 DKK (75¢) children. Mid-May to mid-Oct, Tues–Sun 10am–5pm. Closed mid-Oct to mid-May.

This museum is located inside a half-timbered, thatched-roof farmhouse originally built in 1796. It displays the kind of farm implements that were commonplace as recently as 1920; also on view are a group of pigs, goats, cows, and barnyard fowl that are genetically similar to those that were bred on Bornholm a century ago.

Gudhjem Museum. Stationsvej 1. ☎ **56-48-54-62.** Admission 15 DKK ($2.15), free for children ages 15 and under. Mid-May to mid-Sept, daily 10am–5pm. Closed mid-Sept to mid-May.

This museum is housed in Gudhjem's old railway station (an early 20th-century building that closed in 1952 with the demise of the island's railways). Its exhibits honor the now-defunct railways that once crisscrossed the island. There are locomotives and other train-related memorabilia.

SHOPPING For some of the best glass objects in the area, head for **Gallerie Baltic See Glass,** Melstedvej 47 (☎ **56-48-56-41**), lying 2-miles south of Gudhjem along the coastal road. Although much of this glass has a practical value, some works are so stunningly beautiful they should be treated like objects of art.

One of the best art galleries in the area is **Gallerie Kaffslottet,** Duebakken 2 (☎ **56-48-56-18**).

WHERE TO STAY

Casa Blanca. Kirchevej 10, DK-3760 Gudhjem. ☎ **56-48-50-20.** Fax 56-48-50-81. 33 units. 285–350 DKK ($41.30–$50.75) double. Rates include breakfast. Supplement for half-board 95 DKK ($13.75) per person. AE, DC, MC, V. Closed Oct–Apr.

Efficient, matter-of-fact, and carefully scrutinized throughout its summer-only rental season by owners Elly and Preben Mortensen, this is a three-story, red-roofed structure that rises, motel-style, from the center of Gudhjem. Three sides of it encircle a freshwater swimming pool, a site that—along with the separately recommended restaurant, the Flagermusen—functions as a social center for residents. Bedrooms are white-walled, somewhat cramped, and outfitted with simple furniture that, in some instances, is covered with leather upholstery. Glass doors open in every instance onto private balconies or terraces.

Gudhjem Hotel & Feriepark. Jernkåsvej 1. DK-3760 Gudhjem. ☎ **56-48-54-44.** Fax 56-48-54-55. 102 apts. with kitchen and TV. 360–835 DKK ($52.20–$121.05) double, per day. Supplemental charges include 45 DKK ($6.50) for electricity, a nominal fee for the rental of linens and towels, and a one-time cleaning charge of 275 DKK ($39.90). Discounts available for stays of three days or more. AE, DC, MC, V. Closed Nov–Apr.

This holiday complex consists of a tastefully designed compound of masonry-sided cottages, each with a steep, often sky-lit, terra-cotta roof, and a cement patio that extends the living area inside out onto the carefully clipped lawns. It sits a short walk south of Gudhjem, about midway between it and the satellite hamlet of Melsted, a 5-minute walk from the center of either. Many of the cottages surround an outdoor swimming pool, which guests seem to use less frequently than the wide, sandy expanse of beachfront that lies just a few steps from the hotel. Inside, accommodations are cozy, simple, and just a bit anonymous, although because of the wide expanses of beachfront a short walk from the hotel, most clients tend to live outdoors most of the time anyway.

Melsted Badehotel. Melstedvej 27, DK-3760 Gudhjem. ☎ **56-48-51-00.** Fax 56-48-55-84. 24 units (16 with bath). 400–500 DKK ($58–$72.50) double without bath; 540–720 DKK ($78.30–$104.40) double with bath. Rates include breakfast. AE, DC, MC, V. Closed mid-Oct to Apr. Bus: 7.

Originally built in 1942, during the darkest days of World War II, in a boxy, modern format with white-painted bricks and soft blue trim, this is the most prominent and visible building in the seaside hamlet of Melsted, a half-mile south of Gudhjem. Part of its allure derives from its location just 40 feet from the edge of the sea—occupants of its well-maintained and cozy bedrooms can hear the sounds of the surf throughout the night. Most rooms have private terraces or balconies; and on the premises is a coffee shop/bistro that serves simple lunches every day when the hotel is open, but never dinner. Much of this establishment's conviviality is exhibited on the wooden terrace that extends out over the sands, where outdoor tables, sun parasols, and chairs provide a space for sunbathing, people-watching, and the consumption of the meals that are available in the hotel's above-mentioned bistro.

Pension Koch. Melstedvej 15, DK-3760 Gudhjem. ☎ **56-48-50-72.** Fax 56-48-51-72. www.Sima.dk/pension-koch. 18 units. MINIBAR TV TEL. 460–560 DKK ($66.70–$81.20) double. AE, DC, MC, V. Closed Oct 25–early Apr.

Sheltered from the weather with pale yellow stucco and terra-cotta roof tiles, this small-scale hotel, originally built in 1938, has some of the most charming architecture in Gudhjem. Set within a 10-minute walk east of the town center, it offers a pleasant garden, an interior with big windows and lots of varnished paneling, and simple bedrooms with modern, unfussy furniture, a coffeemaker, and an empty refrigerator. Today, your hosts, members of the Koch family, are third-generation descendants of the original founders.

WHERE TO DINE

Bokulhus. Bokulvej 4. ☎ **56-48-52-97.** Reservations recommended. *Smørrebrød* and *smørrebrød* platters 45–110 DKK ($6.50–$15.95). Main courses 75–175 DKK ($10.90–$25.40).

AE, DC, MC, V. Daily 11:30am–10pm. Closed Tues mid-Apr to May and Sept to mid-Oct. Closed mid-Oct to mid-Apr. DANISH.

Its name derives from the Bokul, which in Gudhjem refers to the highest elevation in town—an undulating, gentle knoll that's within a 5-minute walk of the harbor-front. It was built in 1932 as a private home that retains its original yellow-brown façade and some of its original accessories. Menu items are authentically Danish, and in many cases, designed so that a platter of food is all most warm-weather diners really want. Examples include a "Dansk-platte," at 110 DKK ($15.95), that's loaded with herring, salmon, an assortment of cheeses, chickpeas, and hand-peeled shrimp. Other well-prepared choices include beef tournedos with baked sweet peppers, yellow-fin tuna with saffron sauce, and veal cutlets with potatoes and a shallot and parsley sauce. Overall, this is our favorite restaurant in Gudhjem.

Restaurant Flagermusen. In the Casa Blanca, Kirchevej 10. ☎ **56-48-50-20.** Main courses 60–120 DKK ($8.70–$17.40). Set-price menu 55 DKK ($8). AE, DC, MC, V. DANISH.

Some locals consider this wood-paneled restaurant as the highlight of the simple (and also-recommended) hotel that contains it. Some aspects might remind you of a brasserie with a Danish accent and frequent references to Carlsberg, a beer most of the clients seem to prefer. Meals might begin with mushroom or cream of clam soup, followed by smoked salmon, grilled Norwegian haddock with béarnaise sauce, turkey croquettes, fried herring or steak, or fillets of plaice with butter and parsley sauce. Service is personalized and polite, albeit a bit slow.

GUDHJEM AFTER DARK
Consider a drink at the **Café Klint,** Egn Mikkelsensvej (☎ **56-48-56-26**), where a cozy ambience that might remind you of a Danish version of an English pub welcomes you with pints of ale in an old-fashioned setting. And for something a bit more electronic, with more emphasis on rock-and-roll music, have a drink or two at the **Café Gustav,** St. Torv 8 (☎ **56-91-00-47**), where at least one or two of the many artists living on the island's east coast are likely to congregate.

FROM GUDHJEM TO ALLINGE
Continue driving west along the coastal road. Between Gudhjem and Allinge (a distance of 9 miles), you'll enjoy dramatic vistas over granite cliffs and sometimes savage seascapes. The entire coastline here is known as **Helligdoms Klipperne** ("Cliffs of Sanctuary"), for the survivors of the many ships that floundered along this granite coastline over the centuries.

Midway along the route you'll see the island's newest museum, the **Bornholms Kunstmuseet** (Art Museum of Bornholm), Helligdommen (☎ **56-48-43-86**). Opened in 1993, it contains the largest collection of works by Bornholm artists, including Olaf Rude and Oluf Høst. It's open from May to September, Tuesday to Sunday, from 10am to 5pm. Admission is 30 DKK ($4.35), free for children ages 15 and under. From the rocky bluff where the museum sits, you can see the isolated and rocky island of **Christiansø** (see below), about 7-miles offshore, the wind-tossed home to about 120 year-round residents, most of whom make their living from the sea.

At the base of the museum is a pier that serves as the summer home (June 25 to August 15) of the motor launch *Thor Båd* (☎ **56-48-54-01**); for 55 DKK ($8) per person each way, it will take you from the museum back to the port of Gudhjem, a ride of about 40 minutes. This ride enables visitors to appreciate the northern coast's dramatic cliffs as viewed from the sea. The boat makes five trips a day. *Note:* If you park your car at the museum, you'll probably want to come back from Gudhyjem on the *Thor*'s return trip. In all, allow about 2 hours for the round-trip.

5 Christiansø

Tiny Christiansø lies in the open sea east of Bornholm and is part of the archipelago known as Ertholmene. One of the most remote sites in Denmark, Christiansø is one of only two inhabited islands within the Ertholmene chain, the others being set aside as bird sanctuaries.

Ferryboats depart between 1 and 7 times a day, depending on the season. For ferryboats from Allinge and Gudhjem, call ☎ **56-48-51-76.** For ferryboats from Svaneke, call ☎ **56-49-64-32.** Round-trip transit of between 60 and 90 minutes costs 135 DKK ($19.60). There are no cars allowed on any of the Ertholmene islands. Christiansø, the largest, can be circumnavigated by a pedestrian in about half an hour. Once you're here, the most charming accommodation is recommended below.

WHERE TO STAY & DINE

✪ **Christiansø Gæstgiveriet.** DK-3740 Christiansø. ☎ **56-46-20-15.** Fax 56-46-20-86. 7 units (none with bath). 420 DKK ($60.90) double. Rate includes breakfast. AE, DC, MC, V. Closed: Mid-Oct to mid-Apr.

The most desirable place to stay in the archipelago is this solidly built, antique-looking inn, which was originally constructed in the 1700s as the home of the local naval commander. Bedrooms are cozy, outfitted in a style that is reminiscent of a room within a 1910 private home, and oddly nostalgic for a seafaring life of long ago. There's a nautically decorated bar on the premises, and a restaurant that serves lunch platters for 35 to 70 DKK ($5.05–$10.15); dinner platters for 65 to 120 DKK ($9.40–$17.40). Basically, the only entertainment you'll find here is what you'll create for yourself, talking with fellow guests, or exploring the local bird and wildlife habitats. Don't even consider, especially during July and August, heading out here from Bornholm without an advance reservation, as it's very popular in midsummer.

6 Allinge/Sandvig

Continue driving northwest until you reach the twin communities of **Allinge** and **Sandvig.** Allinge, whose architecture is noticeably older than that of Sandvig, contains 200- and 300-year-old half-timbered houses built for the purveyors of the long-ago herring trade, and antique smokehouses for preserving herring for later consumption or for export abroad.

The newer town of Sandvig, a short drive to the northwest, flourished around the turn of the century when many ferryboats arrived from Sweden. Sandvig became a stylish beach resort, accommodating guests at the Strandhotellet.

The forest that surrounds these twin communities is known as the **Trolleskoe** (Forest of Trolls), home to wart-covered and phenomenally ugly magical creatures that delight in brewing trouble, mischief, and the endless fog that sweeps over this end of the island.

From Allinge, detour inland (southward) for about 2 ½ miles to reach **Olsker,** site of the **Olskirke** (Round Church of Ols), Lindesgordsvej (☎ **56-48-05-29**). Built in the 1100s—the smallest of the island's round churches—it was painstakingly restored in the early 1950s with its conical roof and thick walls. Dedicated to St. Olav (Olav the Holy, the king of Norway who died in 1031), it looks something like a fortress, an image that the original architects wanted very much to convey. From June to September, and from October 12 to 16, it's open Monday to Saturday from 9am to noon and from 2 to 5pm. During April and May, and from October 1 to 11, it's open Tuesday to Thursday from 9am to noon. It's closed the rest of the year. Entrance costs 5 DKK (75¢).

Now retrace your route back to Allinge and head northward toward Sandvig, a distance of less than a mile. You'll soon see **Madsebakke,** a well sign-posted open-air site containing the largest collection of Bronze Age rock carvings in Denmark. Don't expect a building, any type of enclosed area, or even a curator. Simply follow the signs posted beside the main highway. The carvings include 11 depictions of high-prowed sailing ships of unknown origin. The carvings were made in a smooth, glacier-scoured piece of bedrock close to the side of the road.

From here, proceed just over a mile to the island's northernmost tip, **Hammeren,** for views that—depending on the weather—could extend all the way to Sweden. Here you'll see the island's oldest lighthouse, **Hammerfyr** (built in 1871).

FROM ALLINGE & SANDVIG BACK TO RØNNE

Now turn south, following the signs pointing to Rønne. After about a mile you'll see the rocky crags of a semi-ruined fortress that Bornholmers believe is the most historically significant building on the island—the ✪ **Hammershus Fortress,** begun in 1255 by the archbishop of Lund (Sweden). He planned for this massive fortress to reinforce his control of the island. Since then, however, the island has passed from Swedish to German to Danish hands several times; it was a strategic powerhouse controlling what was then a vitally important sea lane. The decisive moment came in 1658, when the Danish national hero Jens Kofoed murdered the Swedish governor and sailed to Denmark to present the castle (and the rest of the island) to the Danish king.

Regrettably, the fortress's dilapidated condition was caused by later architects, who used it as a rock quarry to supply the stone used to construct some of the buildings and streets (including Hovedvagten) of Rønne, as well as several of the structures on Christiansø, the tiny island 7-miles northeast of Bornholm. The systematic destruction of the fortress ended in 1822, when it was "redefined" as a Danish national treasure. Much of the work that restored the fortress to the eerily jagged condition you'll see today was completed in 1967. Interestingly, Hammershus escaped the fate of the second-most-powerful fortress on the island, Lilleborg. Set deep in Bornholm's forests, Lilleborg was gradually stripped of its stones for other buildings after its medieval defenses became obsolete.

Some 2 ½-miles south of Hammershus—still on the coastal road heading back to Rønne—is a geological oddity called **Jons Kapel** (Jon's Chapel); it can be seen by anyone who'd like to take a short hike (about a mile) from the highway. Basically it's a rocky bluff with a panoramic view over the island's western coast where, according to ancient legend, an agile but reclusive hermit, Brother Jon, preached to the seagulls and crashing surf below. For those who would like to enjoy a marvelous view, signs point the way from the highway.

From here, continue driving southward another 8 miles to Rønne, passing through the hamlet of **Hasle** en route.

9

Funen

Funen, the second-largest Danish island, separates Zealand from the mainland peninsula, Jutland. Known as "Fyn" in Danish, it offers unique attractions, from a Viking ship to runic stones.

Hans Christian Andersen was born in Funen in the town of Odense. A visit to the storyteller's native island is a journey into a land of roadside hop gardens and orchards, busy harbors, market towns, castles, and stately manor houses.

Funen has some 700 miles of coastline, with wide sandy beaches in some parts, whereas woods and grass grow all the way to the water's edge in others. Steep cliffs provide sweeping views of the Baltic or the Kattegat.

Although ferryboats have plied the waters between the islands and peninsulas of Denmark since ancient times, the government's leaders have always regretted the lack of a network of bridges. In 1934 the first plans were developed for a bridge over the 8-mile span of water known as the **Storebaelt** (Great Belt), the 12-mile silt-bottomed channel that separates Zealand (and Copenhagen) from Funen and the rest of continental Europe. After many delays caused by war, technical embarrassment, and lack of funding, and after the submission of 144 different designs by engineers from around the world, construction began in 1988 on an intricately calibrated network of bridges and tunnels.

On June 14, 1998, her majesty, Queen Margrethe II, cut the ribbon shortly before driving across the Great Belt Bridge. Today the islands of Zealand and Funen are now linked by bridge. (The rail link across the Great Belt has operated since June of 1997.)

The western terminus of this massive bridge is at Nyborg, on Funen; the eastern terminus is an isolated headland on the island of Zealand. The project's eastern and western segments connect with one another midway across the Great Belt, on the windblown island of Sprogø, 25% of which is devoted to interchanges, merging lanes, and service facilities for the bridge. The staggering scale of this project is surpassed only by some aspects of the Chunnel, which goes under the English Channel.

The Danish project incorporates both railway and road traffic divided between a very long underwater tunnel and both low and high bridges. The sea lane (and the routes of all but the smallest of ocean-going vessels) are on the eastern side of Sprogø, passing above a deeply buried tunnel (for trains) and below one of the highest and longest suspension bridges in the world.

Visitors can view exhibitions about the bridge at the **Great Belt Exhibition Center** (located at the entrance to the bridge and hard to

Funen

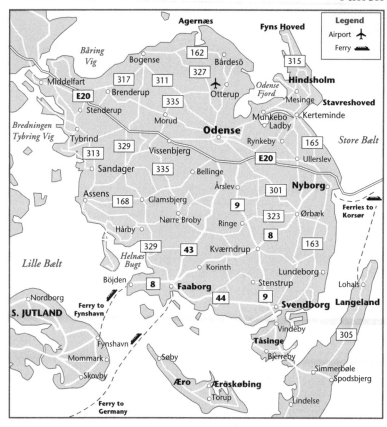

miss), open May to September, Tuesday through Sunday from 10am to 8pm; and October to April, Tuesday through Sunday from 10am to 5pm. The cost of admission is 30 DKK ($4.35) for adults, 15 DKK ($2.15) for children. For more information, call ☎ 58-35-01-00.

1 Nyborg: Gateway to Funen

129¹/₂ km (81 miles) W of Copenhagen; 33 ¹/₂ km (21 miles) E of Odense

After crossing the bridge from Zealand to Funen, you'll arrive at this old seaport and market town, a perfect place to explore before you head to Odense. Founded some 700 years ago, Nyborg is one of the oldest towns in Denmark. Its location in the middle of the trade route between Zealand in the east and Jutland in the west has helped boost its importance. In medieval times, from about 1200 to 1413, Nyborg was the capital of Denmark. Medieval buildings and well-preserved ramparts are testaments to that era. Nyborg's town square, the **Torvet,** was created in 1540, when a block of houses was demolished to make room for the royal tournaments of Christian III.

In summer, Denmark's oldest open-air theater, **Nyborg Voldspil,** is the setting for an annual musical or operetta under the leafy beeches on the old castle ramparts. Throughout the summer, classical music concerts (featuring international soloists) are performed in the castle's Great Hall. Inquire at the tourist office (see "Essentials," below) for further details; for tickets call ☎ 65-31-64-44.

For any rail information or rail schedules throughout Funen, call ☎ **70-13-14-15.** For bus routes on the island, dial ☎ **66-11-71-71.**

Dating from the mid-1600s, the "Tattoo" is an ancient military ceremony with musical accompaniment. This old custom has been revived to honor the corps who played an important role in the Schleswig wars in 1848 and again in 1864. In tribute to the old corps, the present-day Tattoo participants wear a green uniform with its characteristic cap, or *chakot*. The corps march through the center of town at 9pm for the first time each year on June 30, thereafter every Tuesday in July and August.

ESSENTIALS

GETTING THERE   You can reach Nyborg by train or bus (via ferry). Trains leave Copenhagen every hour, and there's frequent bus service from Copenhagen as well. Trains arrive twice an hour from Odense.

VISITOR INFORMATION   Go to **Nyborg Turistbureau,** located at Torvet 9 (☎ **65-31-02-80**), open June 15 to August, Monday to Friday from 9am to 5pm and Saturday from 9am to 2pm; September to June 14, Monday to Friday from 9am to 4pm and Saturday from 9am to noon.

SEEING THE SIGHTS

Mads Lerches Gård (Nyborg Og Omegns Museet). Slotsgade 11. ☎ **65-31-02-07.** Admission 10 DKK ($1.45) adults, 5 DKK (75¢) children. June–Aug daily 10am–4pm; Mar–May and Sept–Oct, Tues–Sun 10am–3pm. Closed Nov–Feb. Bus: 1, 3, or 4.

The finest and best-preserved half-timbered house in Nyborg, this building rises two floors and was built in 1601 by Mads Lerche, the town mayor. The 30 rooms of the house, painted a reddish pink, contain exhibitions of local history.

Nyborg Slot. Slotspladen. ☎ **65-31-02-07.** Admission 20 DKK ($2.90) adults, 10 DKK ($1.45) children. June–Aug, daily 10am–4pm; Mar–May and Sept–Oct, Tues–Sun 10am–3pm. Closed Nov–Feb. Bus: 1,2, or 3.

Founded in 1170, Nyborg Castle, with its rampart still intact, is the oldest royal seat in Scandinavia. Denmark's first constitution was signed in this moated castle by King Erik Glipping in 1282, and Nyborg Castle was the seat of the Danish parliament, the Danehof, until 1413. The present furnishings date primarily from the 17th century, when Nyborg was a resplendent Renaissance palace. It's located directly north of Torvet in the town center.

Vor Frue Kirke. Adelgade. ☎ **65-31-16-08.** Free admission. June–Aug, daily 9am–6pm; Sept–May, daily 9am–4pm.

Dating from the late 14th and early 15th century, the church of Our Lady has a fine Gothic spire, three aisles, wood carvings, old epitaphs, candelabra, and model ships. Nightly at 9:45, the Watchman's Bell from 1523 is rung—a tradition that dates far back in the town's history. Opposite the church is the 12th century **chapter house** of the Order of St. John (Korsbrødregård), with a fine vaulted cellar now converted into a gift shop. The church, located at the end of Kongegade in the town center, can be entered through the south door.

M/S Kong Frederik IX. Nyborg Havn. ☎ **65-30-28-09.** Admission 35 DKK ($5.05) adults, 20 DKK ($2.90) children. May–Aug daily 10am–5pm, Sept daily noon–4pm. Closed off-season.

At Nyborg harbor you can visit this living museum devoted to the flourishing ferry era in Denmark. You'll have almost unlimited access to the whole ship, including the bridge with its advanced equipment, the royal salon, or the engine room's machinery. The train deck presents a wealth of railway equipment, and alternating exhibitions illustrate the story of the ferries.

SHOPPING   A wide range of antiques and gift items are found at **Nyborg Antik,** Nørregade 11 (☎ **65-30-31-40**). Look especially for the Royal Copenhagen figurines, china, and old Funen furniture. A candle factory, **Danehof Lysstoberi,** operates at Bøjdenvej 71A (☎ **65-30-38-38**). Candles come in beautiful shapes and colors. One of the town's leading art galleries is **Tegneriet,** Mellemgade 15 (☎ **65-30-20-06**). The open workshop of a talented potter and "keramiker" can be visited at **Ida Rostgård,** Fiskerivej 5 (☎ **65-30-23-02**).

For a unique shopping adventure, head for **Purrekrogen,** Kokhaen 2 (☎ **65-36-15-10**), which exhibits the work of 15 East Funen exponents of various types of arts and crafts. The site, standing in a scenic landscape near Nordenenhuse on the coastal road between Nyborg and Kerteminde, has been tastefully restored in a rustic style. When not shopping you can enjoy a picnic lunch on Purrekrogen's terraces in parklike surroundings. The site is open daily from 10am to 5pm.

WHERE TO STAY

✪ Hotel Hesselet. Christianslundsvej 119, DK-5800 Nyborg. ☎ **65-31-30-29.** Fax 65-31-29-58. 46 units. MINIBAR TV TEL. 1,290–1,490 DKK ($187.05–$216.05) double Mon–Thurs, 1,290 DKK ($187.05) double Fri–Sun; 1,800–2,500 DKK ($261–$362.50) suite. Rates include breakfast. AE, DC, MC, V.

In a woodland setting of beech trees, with a view across the Great Belt with its bridge, this redbrick building with a pagoda roof is one of the most stylish hotels in Denmark. Completely refurbished in 1996, it offers spacious bedrooms, good-size baths, Oriental carpets, leather couches, a fireplace, a tasteful library, and sunken living rooms, which create a glamorous aura.

Dining: The hotel's gourmet restaurant, with a view of the Great Belt, is one of the finest on Funen. Main dishes are likely to include pink-fried breast of duck with fennel or poached tenderloin of veal. The hotel's Tranque Bar is a chic rendezvous.

Amenities: These include an indoor swimming pool, sauna, solarium, and two tennis courts. Nearby is an 18-hole golf course.

Hotel Nyborg Strand. Østersvej 2, DK-5800 Nyborg. ☎ **800/528-1234** in the U.S., or ☎ 65-31-31-31. Fax 65-31-37-01. E-mail:nyborgstrand@nyborgstrand.dk. 248 units. TV TEL. 815–1,015 DKK ($118.20–$147.15) double Mon–Thurs, 600–695 DKK ($87–$100.75) double Fri–Sun. Rates include breakfast. AE, DC, MC, V. Closed Dec 9–Jan 3.

Dating from 1899, the Nyborg Strand is one of the largest and most popular conference hotels in Funen, but it provides a suitable overnight stopover for casual visitors as well. Lying a mile east of the rail station, near the beach, it is a solid and reliable choice. Surrounded by forests, it offers modern comforts in its medium-sized bedrooms, which have standard furnishings and good-size baths. Bedrooms are furnished with sleek Nordic styling in light Scandinavian hues such as pale blue.

Dining: The hotel's dining facilities, often featuring a view of the water, serve both Danish and international dishes in its Bistro, and its more formal restaurant. Cookery is of a very high standard, especially the roast meats.

Amenities: A pair of saunas, a private sand-and-pebble beach, and an indoor swimming pool.

WHERE TO DINE

Danehofkroen. Slotsplads. ☎ **65-31-02-02.** Reservations recommended. Main courses 130–188 DKK ($18.85–$27.25); fixed-priced menu 189–325 DKK ($27.40–$47.15). MC, V. Tues–Sun 12:30–9pm (last order). DANISH/FRENCH.

A well-managed dining choice since the Jensen family took over in 1993, this restaurant was originally built as a barracks in 1815 for the soldiers who guarded the nearby castle. Painted a vivid yellow, with a red-tile roof, it's a low-slung building with two dining rooms outfitted like an elegantly old-fashioned country tavern. The tasty menu items include fish soup with saffron, fried duck liver flavored with bacon and leeks, turbot with mushroom sauce, a delectable veal fried with chanterelle mushrooms, and a dessert specialty of raspberry parfait with fresh melon.

Restaurant Østervemb. Mellengade. ☎ **65-30-10-70.** Reservations recommended. Lunch platters 60–110 DKK ($8.70–$15.95); dinner main courses 170–200 DKK ($24.65–$29). DC, MC, V. Mon–Sat noon–3pm and 5–9pm. DANISH/FRENCH.

Set behind a distinctive bright-red-with-green trim façade, this restaurant in the heart of town has flourished since it was established in 1924. Inside, on two floors devoted to dining and drinking facilities, you can order platters piled high with three different preparations of herring, cold potato soup with bacon and chives, breast of Danish hen served with spinach and mushrooms, curried chicken salad with bacon, and slices of grilled beef tenderloin with a fricassée of oyster mushrooms and tarragon-flavored glaze. The cookery is heart-warming, like that provided to a hungry crew by a nourishing Danish aunt.

NYBORG AFTER DARK

The region's most comprehensive nightspot is **Sophie's Kælder,** Nybrogade 2 (☎ 65-31-05-00), which occupies a building in the heart of town that was originally constructed in 1875. Named after a young niece of the owner, it includes a restaurant that's open from 11am till at least midnight, a very active series of bars where it's relatively easy to strike up a dialogue with locals, and where live music is presented on Fridays and Saturdays. Supplementing all this, in the cellar, clients can dance at **Discothek Blue,** which everyone agrees is the busiest and most appealing disco in town. It's open only Fridays and Saturdays from 10:30pm till around 5am. Charges include a cover of 20 DKK ($2.90). The entire complex is closed down on Sunday and Monday nights.

2 Odense: Birthplace of Hans Christian Andersen

96km (60 miles) W of Copenhagen; 33 ¹/₂ km (21 miles) W of Nyborg; 43km (27 miles) NW of Svendborg.

Leaving Nyborg, our next stop is Odense. This ancient town, the third largest in Denmark, has changed greatly since its famous son, H. C. Andersen, walked its streets. However, it's still possible to discover a few unspoiled spots.

In the heart of Funen and home to more than 185,000 inhabitants, Odense is one of the oldest cities in the country, with a history stretching back some 1,000 years. The Danish king Canute, or Knud, was murdered in St. Alban's Church here in 1086, and some 15 years later he was canonized by the pope. Long before Odense became a pilgrimage center for fans of Hans Christian Andersen, it was an ecclesiastical center and site of religious pilgrimage in the Middle Ages.

Although touristically, Odense virtually lives off of the memory of the fairytale writer, Andersen never felt appreciated in his native town, a resentment which some have read "between the lines" in his story *The Ugly Ducking.*

Odense

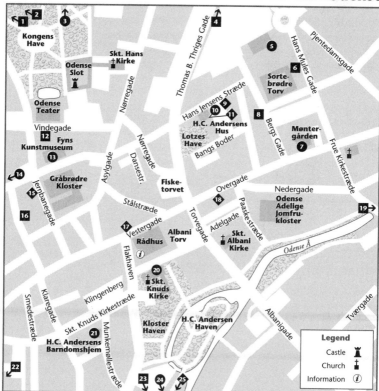

Attractions:

Bymuseet Møntergården
(Odense City Museum) **7**

Carl Nielsen Museet **5**

Danmarks Jernbanemuseum
(Railway Museum) **3**

Den Fynske Landsby
(The Fyn Village) **24**

Fyns Kunstmuseum **13**

H.C. Andersens
Barndomshjem
(Andersen's childhood home) **21**

H.C. Andersens Hus **10**

St. Canute's Cathedral **20**

Superbowl **14**

Accommodations:

City Hotel Odense **6**

Hotel Ansgar **2**

Hotel Domir/Hotel Ydes **16**

Hotel Knudens Gaard **23**

Næsbylund Kro **4**

Odense Congress Hotel **19**

Odense Plaza Hotel **1**

Radisson SAS H.C. Andersen Hotel **8**

Scandic Hotel Odense **22**

Windsor Hotel **12**

Dining:

Den Gamle Kro **18**

Den Grimme Æling **9**

Målet **15**

Marie Louise **17**

Sortebro Kro **25**

Under Lindetaeet **11**

Odense today is no fairytale town but an industrial might in Denmark, its harbor linked by a canal to the Odense Fjord and thus the Great Belt. It is a center of electro-technical, textile, and steel, iron, and timber production.

In summer Odense takes on a festive air, with lots of outdoor activities, including all types of music, drama, and street theater taking place on its squares and in its piazzas. Cafes and pubs are lively day and night.

The city's name stems from two words—Odins Vi (Odin's shrine), suggesting that the god Odin must have been worshipped here in pre-Christian times.

ESSENTIALS
GETTING THERE
BY PLANE   The only airline servicing Odense is **Muk Air** (☎ 75-33-22-44), a small-scale operator that maintains several domestic flights into Odense from Copen-hagen, and to a lesser degree, a daily flight into Odense from Århus, Esbjerg, Aalborg, and Billund. Because of the completion of the bridges connecting Funen to Zealand, and the new-found convenience of driving into Odense from other parts of Denmark, the future of some of these flights is in doubt.

BY TRAIN OR BUS   You can easily reach Odense by train or bus from Copen-hagen. About 12 trains or buses a day leave Copenhagen's Central Railroad Station for Odense (travel time: 3 hours).

BY CAR   From Nyborg, head west on E20 to Allerup and then follow Route 9 north to Odense.

VISITORS INFORMATION   Check with the **Odense Tourist Bureau,** Rådhuset, Vestergade 2A (☎ 66-12-75-20), open mid-June to August, Monday to Saturday from 9am to 7pm and Sunday from 11am to 7pm; September to mid-June, Monday to Friday from 9:30am to 4:30pm and Saturday from 10am to 1pm.

Besides helping you arrange excursions, the tourist bureau sells the **Odense Adven-ture Pass,** giving you access to 13 of the city's museums, 6 indoor swimming pools, and unlimited free travel on the city buses and DSB trains within the municipality. It also entitles you to reductions on river cruises, entrance to the Odense Zoo, and admission to the summer-only presentation of the city's H. C. Andersen plays (see below). The pass is valid for either 1 or 2 days: a 2-day pass costs 90 DKK ($13.05) for adults, 45 DKK ($6.50) for children age 13 and under; a 1-day pass goes for 50 DKK ($7.25) for adults, 25 DKK ($3.60) for children.

GETTING AROUND
You can rent a bicycle from **City Cykler,** Vesterbro 27 (☎ 66-13-97-83), for prices that range from 50 to 150 DKK ($7.25–$21.75) per day, depending on the type of bicycle.

SEEING THE SIGHTS
The Odense Tourist Bureau (see above) offers a 2-hour walking tour that's conducted between mid-June and the end of August, every Tuesday, Wednesday, and Thursday, at 11am from a meeting place behind the tourist office. Advance reservations are rec-ommended. Covering the town's major sites, it costs 30 DKK ($4.35) per adult and 10 DKK ($1.45) per child.

Also at the tourist office, you can get information about the **Hans Christian Andersen plays,** which are presented every year from mid-July to mid-August. The plays are given on an outdoor stage in the Funen Village, where members of the audience stand (if it's raining or if the ground is wet) or sit on the grass (often on blankets, if it's dry).

Even if you don't understand Danish, there's lots of entertainment value in the visuals. Plays begin every day at 4pm, last around 90 minutes, cost 60 DKK ($8.70) for adults and 35 DKK ($5.05) for children, and are usually mobbed with H. C. Andersen fans and their children.

About a mile west of the city center, accessible via bus nos. 91 or 92, is **Superbowl,** Grøneløkkenvej (☎ **66-19-16-40**), a complex of amusements and diversions that are entirely devoted to popular American culture. It incorporates facilities for indoor go-cart racing, an indoor version of American-style miniature golf, several bowling alleys, and a small-scale collection of rides and games inspired by the theme parks of Florida. Each individual element within the park maintains its own hours and entrance policies, but the best way to appreciate this site's diversity is to head here daily anytime between 10am and 6pm, when for an all-encompassing fee of 60 DKK ($8.70), you'll have unlimited access to all of them. Our favorite subdivision of this complex is the **Elvis Presley Museum.** Chock-full of more than 1,000 pieces of memorabilia that cover every major phase of Elvis's life, it's the compound's most appealing exhibit, celebrating the era of fast American cars, big-haired blondes, and easy conquests. The museum is open daily from 10am to 7pm. Admission cost 30 DKK ($4.35) for adults and 15 DKK ($2.15) for children.

Other more formal attractions include the following.

Bymuseet Møntegården (Odense City Museum). Overgade 48–50. ☎ **66-13-13-72.** Admission: 15 DKK ($2.15) per adult, and 5 DKK (75¢) per child ages 5–11 (free age 4 and under). Tues–Sun 10am–6pm.

Not the typical dull city museum of dusty artifacts, this museum traces Odense history back to the Viking era and also has a number of half-timbered houses from the 1500s and 1600s that you can actually walk through. It is particularly rich in artifacts from the Middle Ages, and there are not only interiors from the 17th and 18th centuries, but exhibits that go right up to the 1950s. In the Nyborgladen—the open storehouse of the museum—there are thousands of items exemplifying everyday life from the Middle Ages to the present day. The coin collection virtually spans a millennium.

Carl Nielsen Museet. Claus Bergsgade 11. ☎ **66-13-13-72.** Admission 15 DKK ($2.15) adults, 5 DKK (75¢) children ages 5–14, free for children age 4 and under. Tues–Sun 10am–4pm. Bus: 2.

Adjoining the Odense Concert Hall, this museum documents the life and work of composer Carl Nielsen, and his wife, the sculptor Ann Marie Nielsen. Visitors hear excerpts of Nielsen's music while they look at the exhibits and a biographical slide show. Parking is available outside the concert hall.

Denmarks Jernbanemuseum (Railway Museum). Dannebrogsgade 24. ☎ **66-13-66-30.** Admission 30 DKK ($4.35) adults, 10 DKK ($1.45) children. Year-round daily 10am–4pm. Bus: 2.

Original locomotives and carriages from the past century depicting Denmark's railway history are displayed, including the first railroad from 1847. One of the oldest locomotives in the collection, a "B-Machine," dates from 1869. Also on display are three royal coaches, a double-decker carriage, and a model railway. The museum is adjacent to the train station.

Den Fynske Landsby/Funen Village. Sejerskovvej 20. ☎ **66-13-13-72.** Admission 30 DKK ($4.35) adults, 10 DKK ($1.45) children. June–Aug daily 9:30am–7pm; Apr–May and Sept–Oct Tues–Sun 10am–5pm. Nov–Mar Sun only 11am–3pm. Bus: 21 or 22 from Flakhaven to the museum, 1 ½-miles south of the town center.

A big open-air regional culture museum, this is an archive of 18th century and 19th century Funen life. Located in the Hunderup Woods, old buildings—a toll house, weaver's shop, windmill, farming homestead, jail, vicarage, village school, and even a brickworks—were reassembled and authentically furnished. Plays and folk dances are staged at the Greek theater. In addition, you can visit workshops and see a basket maker, spoon cutter, blacksmith, weaver, and others at work.

Fyns Kunstmuseum. Jernbanegade 13. ☎ **66-13-13-72.** Admission 25 DKK ($3.60) adults, 15 DKK ($2.15) for children. Tues–Sun 10am–4pm.

Showcased within a dignified Greco-Roman style building, this museum displays Danish art from 1750 up to the present. Everything is here from paintings by old masters to the most abstract modern works of today. An array of artists whose names are widely familiar in Denmark but only in art circles elsewhere include Jens Juel, C. W. Eckersberg, Dankvart Dreyer, Franciska Clausen, and Henrik B. Andersen. A collection of works by young Danish sculptors has been set up, and there are also special exhibits devoted to Danish and international art.

H. C. Andersens Barndomshjem (H. C. Andersen's Childhood Home). Munkemøllestraede 3. ☎ **66-13-13-72.** Admission 5 DKK (75¢) adults, 2 DKK (30¢) children. June–Aug daily 10am–4pm; Sept–May daily 11am–3pm. Bus: 2.

Visit Andersen's humble childhood home, where the fairytale writer lived from age 2 to 14. From what is known of Andersen's childhood, his mother was a drunken, superstitious washerwoman, and Andersen was a gawky boy, lumbering and graceless, the victim of his fellow urchins' cruel jabs. However, all is serene at the cottage today; in fact, the little house has a certain unpretentious charm, and the "garden still blooms," as in *The Snow Queen.*

✪ H. C. Andersens Hus. Hans Jensensstraede 37–45. ☎ **66-13-13-72.** Admission 25 DKK ($3.60) adults, 10 DKK ($1.45) children ages 5–14, free for children age 4 and under. June–Aug daily 10:30am–7pm; Sept–May daily 10am–4pm. Bus: 2.

The object of most Funen pilgrimages is the *hus* and museum of H. C. Andersen, popular with both adults and children. A lot of Hans Christian Andersen memorabilia is here: his famous walking stick, top hat, and battered portmanteau, plus letters to his dear friend Jenny Lind and fellow writer Charles Dickens. In addition, hundreds of documents, manuscripts, and reprints of his books in dozens of languages are displayed.

St. Canute's Cathedral. Klosterbakken 2. ☎ **66-12-61-23.** Free admission. June–Aug Mon–Sat 10am–5pm, Sun and holidays noon–3pm; May 15–30 and Sept 1–14 Mon–Sat 10am–4pm; Apr–May 14 and Sept 15–30 Mon–Sat 10am–4pm; Oct–Mar Mon–Fri 10am–4pm, Sat 10am–2pm. Bus: 21 or 22.

Despite its unimpressive façade, this is the most important Gothic-style building in Denmark. A popular feature of this 13th-century brick building is the elegant triptych gold altar screen, carved by Calus Berg in 1526 at the request of Queen Christina. King Canute, the patron of the church, was killed by angry Jutland taxpayers in 1086 and then canonized 15 years later. The church stands opposite the Town Hall.

NEARBY ATTRACTIONS

Carl Nielsen's Barndomshjem. Odensevej 2A, near Lyndelse. No phone (contact the tourist office; see above). Admission 5 DKK (75¢) adults, 2 DKK (30¢) children. Tues–Sun 11am–3pm. Closed Sept–Apr. Bus: 960 or 962.

Eight miles from Odense, the childhood house of the famous composer is now a museum and archive of his life. Nielsen lived here during the last 5 years of his childhood until his confirmation in 1879. Two studies have been made into commemorative rooms, where the collections illustrate the composer's life.

☉ Egeskov Castle. Egeskovgade 18, Kvaerndrup. ☎ **62-27-10-16.** Castle, park, maze, playground, and museum, 105 DKK ($15.25) adults, 55 DKK ($8) children age 4–12, free for children age 3 and under; park, maze, playground, and museum only, 55 DKK ($8) adults, 27.50 DKK ($4) children age 4–12, free for children age 3 and under. July, park (including maze, playground, and museum), daily 9am–8pm; castle, daily, 10am–8pm. June and Aug, park, daily 9am–7pm; castle, daily 10am–5pm. May and Sept, park and castle, daily 10am–5pm. Closed Oct–May. Train: from Odense and also from Svendborg every hour. Bus: 920 from Nyborg.

This 1554 Renaissance water castle with magnificent gardens, northeast of Faaborg at Kvaerndrup, is the most romantic and splendid of Denmark's fortified manors. The castle was built on oak pillars in the middle of a moat or small lake. International experts consider it the best-preserved Renaissance castle of its type in Europe.

Every year some 200,000 visitors roam the 30-acre park and castle located on the main road between Svendborg and Odense. There's a vintage automobile, horse carriage, and airplane museum on the grounds as well. Chamber-music concerts are held in the Great Hall of the castle on 10 summer Sundays beginning in late June, starting at 5pm.

The most dramatic story in the castle's history is about an unfortunate maiden, Rigborg, who was seduced by a young nobleman and bore him a child out of wedlock. Banished to the castle, she was imprisoned by her father in a tower from 1599–1604.

Frydenlund. Skovvej 50, Naarup, near Tommerup. ☎ **64-76-13-22.** Admission 40 DKK ($5.80) adults, 20 DKK ($2.90) children. Easter–May and Sept daily 10am–4pm; June–Aug daily 10am–6pm. Closed Oct–Easter.

This bird sanctuary and park is 12¼ miles southwest of Odense near the village of Tommerup. Some 200 different species of pheasants, ducks, geese, storks, ostriches, parrots, and owls, among other, from all parts of the world, live here. There are more that 120 aviaries and some 20 parkland areas in an old farm setting, with many flowers, bushes, and trees. You can enjoy coffee and homemade pastries in the cafe or bring your own lunch.

Funen Aquarium Rold (Aquatic World). Roldvej 53, Rold, Vissenbjerg. ☎ **64-83-14-12.** Admission 40 DKK ($5.80) adults, 20 DKK ($2.90) children. Apr–Oct daily 10am–7pm, Nov–Mar daily 10am–6pm. Take the E20 expressway 10-miles west from Odense until the turnoff to Vissenbjerg (the aquarium is sign-posted from here). Bus: 831 from Odense.

Although no longer the largest aquarium in Europe, this attraction still merits a visit, as it contains 30 aquariums under 1 roof. Enter an undersea world of some 3,000 specimens, including sharks, electric eels, piranhas, and dragon fish—seemingly everything swimming in the North Sea and more.

Ladbyskibet. Vikingevej 123, Ladby. ☎ **65-32-16-67.** Admission 20 DKK ($2.90), free for children age 14 and under. May 15–Sept 14 daily 10am–6pm; Mar–May 14 and Sept 15–Oct daily 10am–4pm; Nov–Feb Wed–Sun 11am–3pm. Bus: 482 from Kerteminde, reached by bus from Odense.

Ladby, 12-miles northeast of Odense, is the site of a 72-foot-long 10th-century Viking ship, discovered in 1935. Remains of the ship are displayed in a burial mound along with replicas from the excavation (the originals are in the National Museum in Copenhagen). A skeleton of the pagan chieftain buried in this looted ship was never found, just the bones of his nearly dozen horses and dogs.

SHOPPING

Inspiration Zinch, Vestergade 82–84 (☎ **66-12-96-93**), offers the widest selection of Danish design and handcrafts on the island of Funen. All the big names are here, everything from Royal Copenhagen to Georg Jensen, but you will also come across younger and more modern designers, with whose names you might be unfamiliar. In the heart of the old town, opposite Hans Christian Andersen's house, you'll find a display of Danish crafts and Christmas decorations in a typical atmosphere of Old Funen at **Klods Hans,** Hans Jensens Staede 34 (☎ **66-11-09-40**). Merchandise might be anything. Another interesting outlet is **Smykker,** 3 Klaregade (☎ **66-12-06-96**), which offers museum jewelry copies from the Bronze Age, the Iron Age, and the Viking Age—all made in gold, sterling silver, and bronze in the outlet's own workshop. **College Art,** Grandts Passage 38 (☎ **66-11-35-45**), has assembled a unique collection of posters, lithographs, silk screens, original art, and cards. The best gallery for contemporary art is **Galleri Torso,** Vintappperstraede 57 (☎ **66-13-44-66**). Finally, if none of the above shops has what you want, head for **Rosengårdcentret** at Munkerisvej and Ørbaekvej. It's Denmark's biggest shopping center, with nearly 110 stores all under one roof.

WHERE TO STAY

Parking is free at all the hotels below.

EXPENSIVE

Odense Plaza Hotel. Østre Stationsvej 24, DK-5000 Odense. ☎ **800/233-1234** in the U.S., or ☎ 66-11-77-45. Fax 66-14-41-45. www.bestwestern.com. 68 units. MINIBAR TV TEL. July–Aug, 695 DKK ($100.75) double; 995 DKK ($144.25) suite. Sept–June, 1,095 DKK ($158.75) double; 1,195 DKK ($173.25) suite. Rates include breakfast. AE, DC, MC, V. Bus: 31, 33, 35, or 36.

Lying a quarter mile from the town center, this is one of the most alluring hostelries in town. It is also the classic hotel of Odense. It was built in 1915 and has been welcoming visitors ever since, its rooms opening onto scenic views. Bedrooms evoke an English country home, and many were renovated in 1997, making them better than ever. Muted colors and chintz add to the glow. Some are spacious; others medium-sized. Non-smoking units can be requested.

Dining/Diversions: You can relax and order a drink before dinner on the terrace overlooking a park and garden. The dining room has large picture windows opening onto the park and serves a refined Danish and international cuisine.

Amenities: Room service, concierge.

Radisson SAS H. C. Andersen Hotel. Claus Bergs Gade 7, DK-5000 Odense. ☎ **800/ 333-3333** in the U.S., or ☎ 66-14-78-00. Fax 66-14-78-90. 145 units. MINIBAR TV TEL. 675–1,135 DKK ($97.90–$164.60) double. Rates include breakfast. AE, DC, MC, V. Bus: 4 or 5.

With a 1960s Nordic modern design throughout, this brick-built structure in the heart of the old city lies next to a former residence once inhabited by Hans Christian Andersen. It is one of the premier hotels of Funen. The reception, with its glass-roofed section and southern exposure, is inviting and welcoming. Guests—usually business clients—are shown to accommodations often decorated in bold colors of burgundy and forest green. The quietest accommodations open onto the interior. Rooms come in a variety of sizes, some large, others a bit cramped. Baths tend to be small but have thoughtful extras such as makeup mirrors and hair dryers. Non-smoking accommodations can be requested, and some units are suitable for those with disabilities.

Dining/Diversions: Overlooking the market square, the hotel's formal restaurant is known for catering to special requests, such as vegetarians or diets. It serves a refined international and Danish cuisine and does so exceedingly well, using market-fresh ingredients. Two bars provide cozy settings for drinks. On site is one of only six casinos in Denmark, where you can play blackjack, roulette, and baccarat.

Amenities: Sauna, solarium, room service, concierge.

Scandic Hotel Odense. Hvidkærvej 25, DK-5250 Odense SV. ☎ **66-17-66-66.** Fax 66-17-25-53. E-mail: Odense@scandic-hotels.se. 100 units. MINIBAR TV TEL. June–Aug 650 DKK ($94.25) double, Sept–May 1,075–1,125 DKK ($155.90–$163.15) double. Rates include breakfast. AE, DC, MC, V. Bus: 11, 12, 31.

Comfortable and international in both its mentality and its sales promotions, and designed in a low-slung, three-story format that dates from 1986, this hotel lies 3 miles southwest of the center, in a drab industrial neighborhood that's conveniently close to the E20 highway. Inside, you'll find a polite and accommodating staff, a comfortable and uncontroversial contemporary décor, and tasteful bedrooms that each have hardwood floors, good-size baths, a seating area, and a writing table that's much appreciated by anyone who has to do paperwork during the course of an overnight stay.

Dining/Diversions: On-site restaurant serving Danish and international food, and a bar.

Amenities: Fitness room, sauna, solarium, billiard and pool tables; children's playroom, room service, and a concierge.

MODERATE

City Hotel Odense. Hans Mules Gade 5, DK-5000 Odense. ☎ **66-12-12-58.** Fax 66-12-93-64. 43 units. TV TEL. Mon–Fri 795 DKK ($115.30) double. Sat–Sun 695 DKK ($100.80) double. Rates include breakfast. AE, DC, MC, V. Bus: 41.

Set in the heart of the city, less than 2 blocks from the railway station, this hotel, a postmodern cluster of old-fashioned Danish cottages set at 90-degree angles to each other, was built in the late-1980s in an ocher-colored format. Favored by many of Odense's corporations as an appropriate and comfortable site for lodging participants in conventions, it offers a sundeck above its uppermost floor, and a bland, culturally neutral décor within each of its not particularly large but comfortably modern bedrooms. Other than breakfast, no meals are offered in this hotel, although a 300-year-old Danish inn, Den Gamle Kro, run by the same owner, serves flavorful meals a 5-minute walk away.

Hotel Ansgar. Østre, Stationsvej 32, DK-5000 Odense. ☎ **66-11-96-93.** Fax 66-11-96-75. 44 units. TV TEL. June–Aug 550 DKK ($79.75) double; Sept–May 595–695 DKK ($86.25–$100.75) double. Additional bed in double room 150 DKK ($21.75) extra. AE, DC, MC, V.

Originally built a century ago as an affiliate of a local church, this hotel dropped its religious connections many years ago. Set in the heart of town, behind a brick-and-stone façade, it boasts a very modern interior. Double-glazing on the bedroom windows cuts down the noise from traffic considerably. All the rooms are well furnished but come in a variety of sizes, ranging from spacious to small. Likewise, bathrooms may be medium-sized or cramped. All rooms come with a shower and toilet as well as a trouser press; in most units you'll also find a mini-bar. The hotel also has a reasonably priced restaurant on site, serving Danish food. Of particularly good value is the fixed price two-course dinner at 89 DKK ($12.90). The location is a 5-minute walk from the train depot.

Hotel Knudens Gaard. Hunderupgade 2, DK-5230 Odense. ☎ **800/528-1234** in the U.S., or ☎ 63-11-43-11. Fax 63-11-43-01. www.bestwestern.com. 62 units. TV TEL. June–Aug and Sat–Sun year-round, 650–750 DKK ($94.25–$108.75) double. Sept–May 735–850 DKK ($106.55–$123.25). Rates include breakfast. AE, DC, MC, V.

This motel, built in 1955 and renovated in the early 1990s, lies on Route 1A at the A9 junction, a mile south of the town center. The motel grew out of a half-timbered farmhouse. It offers compact and well-furnished bedrooms, and is a family favorite. Seventeen of the accommodations contain a mini-bar. A well-appointed first-class restaurant is on the premises, serving French and Danish cuisine.

Odense Congress Hotel. Ørbækvej 350, DK-5220 Odense. ☎ 66-15-55-35. Fax 66-15-50-70. E-mail: hotel@occ.dk. 109 units. MINIBAR TV TEL. Mon–Fri 950 DKK ($137.75) ($137.75) double, Sat–Sun 750 DKK ($108.75) double. Rate includes breakfast. Bus: 61.

This hotel is directly connected to the largest convention and conference facility in Funen, which was built with a combination of public and private money in 1986. Set 3 miles east of Odense's center, it has an angular redbrick façade, bland-looking but well-designed public areas that might remind you of an airport, and comfortably contemporary bedrooms filled with enough electronic amenities to keep you entertained and diverted during your stay here. There's a restaurant and bar on the premises, a small-scale exercise room, a sauna, a pool table, and a collection of dart boards.

INEXPENSIVE
Hotel Domir/Hotel Ydes. Hans Tausensgade 11 and 19, DK-5000 Odense C. ☎ 66-12-14-27. 63 units. TV TEL. 430–448 DKK ($62.35–$64.95) double. Rates include breakfast. AE, DC, MC, V.

There are so many similarities between these nearly adjacent hotels, that many travel journalists simply describe them as different manifestations of the same organization. Each was built a century ago, more or less, and each shares the same owner. Each has cozy, comfortable bedrooms, with the Ydes (with a total of 28 rooms) focusing a bit more on wooden paneling and old-fashioned décor, and the Domir (with 35 rooms) going for brighter colors and a more indulgent approach to pop culture and recently defined decorative accessories. Frankly, you'll have a greater sense of camaraderie at the Domir, where a live receptionist will check you in; at the Ydes, a TV monitor will beam you the instructions from the manager (who works out of an office in the Domir). Both lie less that 30 yards from one another.

Næsbylund Kro. Bogensevej 105–117, DK-5270 Odense. ☎ 66-18-00-39. Fax 66-18-29-29. 45 units. MINIBAR TV TEL. 650 DKK ($94.25) double. Rate includes breakfast. AE, DC, MC, V. Bus: 91.

Despite its self-image as a *kro* (a usually antique Danish inn), this roadside hotel 2½ miles north of Odense was built in 1983 in a style that's unabashedly modern. It's composed of two separate buildings, each of which is sheltered by a terra-cotta roof. One of the buildings contains balconies;, conservatively modern bedrooms, which, although comfortable, are relatively impersonal-looking; the other is devoted to a restaurant, the Carolinenkilde. There, only dinner is served, nightly from 5 to 9:30pm, with set-price menus going for 105 to 185 DKK ($15.25–$26.85).

Windsor Hotel. Vindegade 45, DK-5000 Odense. ☎ 66-12-06-52. Fax 65-91-00-23. 550–645 DKK ($79.75–$93.55). Rates include breakfast. AE, DC, MC, V.

Built in 1898, this cozy, well-furnished redbrick hotel occupies a street corner close to the center of town near the rail station. It is not a plush hotel in any sense, but is cozily comfortable. The high-ceilinged bedrooms are well maintained and inviting, although small for many tastes, with equally small baths. Furnishings are in sleek Nordic style. Double glazing on the bedroom windows cuts down the noise level. There's a good restaurant on site, serving dinner only from Monday to Thursday from 6 to 9:30pm; a two-course Danish menu costs only 89 DKK ($12.90). The food is simple but prepared with fresh ingredients.

WHERE TO DINE
EXPENSIVE
Den Gamle Kro. Overgade 23. ☎ 66-12-14-33. Reservations recommended. Main courses 135–230 DKK ($19.60–$33.35). Set-price meals 230–290 DKK ($33.35–$42.05). AE, DC, MC, V. DANISH/FRENCH.

With a history of serving food and drink that goes back to 1683, this historic Danish inn has very little in common with the postmodern, 10-year-old hotel with which it shares its management. Set within the city limits, a 5-minute walk from the center, it offers separate drinking and dining facilities, and a complex that includes a cellar-level bar that's lined with antique masonry, and a street-level restaurant with a beamed ceiling and references to old-fashioned Danish values. Two of the best menu items here are trout fried in butter and herbs, served with creamed potatoes, asparagus, and parsley; and beef tenderloin with herbs and green vegetables.

✪ **Marie Louise.** Lottrups Gaard, Vestergade 70–72. ☎ **66-17-92-95.** Reservations recommended. Main courses 95–210 DKK ($13.75–$30.45); fixed-price menu 160 DKK ($23.20). AE, DC, MC, V. Mon–Sat noon–2pm and 6–9:30pm. Closed July. Bus: 2. FRENCH.

A centrally located antique house painted yellow is the home of Odense's smallest and most exclusive restaurant. Its dining room is a white-walled re-creation of an old-fashioned country tavern, although closer inspection reveals a decidedly upscale slant to the furnishings, accessories, silver, and crystal. Well-planned dishes based on French recipes are served by a polished staff. Delectable specialties include a salmon-and-dill mousse with shrimp sauce, platters of fresh fish, turbot in riesling or champagne sauce, lobster in butter or provençal sauce, and an array of delectable desserts, many laid out like temporary (and well-flavored) works of art.

Under Lindetraeet. Ramsherred 2. ☎ **66-12-92-86.** Reservations required. 3-course fixed-price lunch 195 DKK ($28.30), 3-course fixed-priced dinner 325 DKK ($47.15), 4-course fixed-price dinner 395 DKK ($57.30). Main courses 164–220 DKK ($23.80–$31.90). DC, MC, V. Mon–Sat 11am–11pm closed July 4–24. Bus: 2. DANISH/INTERNATIONAL.

This inn, 2½ centuries old, is located across the street from Hans Christian Andersen's house. For more than a quarter of a century this has been a landmark restaurant, whose menu is based on fresh and high-quality ingredients. Skillfully prepared dishes include tender Danish lamb, fillet of plaice with butter sauce, shrimp, escalope of veal in sherry sauce, fried herring with new potatoes, and an upscale version of *laubscaus,* the famed sailors' hash. The atmosphere is Old World, and in summer, meals and light refreshments are served outside under linden trees. Artists often sit here to sketch Andersen's house.

MODERATE

Sortebro Kro. Sejerskovvej 20. ☎ **66-13-28-26.** Reservations are required. Cold buffet 135 DKK ($19.60), main courses 65–150 DKK ($9.40–$21.75). AE, DC, MC, V. Apr–Dec Mon–Sat noon–8:30pm, Sun noon–4pm. Jan–Mar daily noon–4pm. Closed Dec 23–Jan 12. Bus: 21 or 22 from Flakhaven. DANISH.

Outside the entrance to Funen Village, the open-air culture museum, about 1½ miles south of the center, Sortebro Kro is a coaching inn that dates from 1807. The interior is an attraction in its own right: long refectory tables, sagging ceilings with overhead beams, three-legged chairs, florid handmade chests, and crockery cupboards. Country meals are served featuring a popular all-you-can-eat Danish cold board.

INEXPENSIVE

Den Grimme Æling. Hans Jensens Stræde 1. ☎ **65-91-70-30.** Access to buffets 69.50 DKK ($10.10) Mon–Fri, 79.50 DKK ($11.55) Sat–Sun. AE, DC, MC, V. Daily noon–3pm and 5:30–10:30pm. DANISH.

Part of its charm derives from its name (which translates as "The Ugly Duckling") and its location very close to the former home of Hans Christian Andersen. It is set on a cobble-covered street in Odense's historic core, within an ocher-colored building from around 1850 that emulates an old-fashioned Danish *kro.* It specializes in well-stocked buffets manned by uniformed staff members who will cook your steak, fish, omelet, or whatever into virtually any Danish-inspired configuration you want. There are no *smørrebrod*, but because the lunch buffet contains a roster of sliced cheeses, breads, meats, and condiments, you can always manufacture your own. The staff speaks English perfectly, and if buffet dining appeals to you, you might have a perfectly wonderful time here.

Målet. Jernbanegade 17. ☎ **66-17-82-41.** Reservations recommended. Main courses 45–125 DKK ($6.55–$18.15). No credit cards. Sun–Mon 3–9pm; Tues–Sat 11am–9pm. Daily until midnight. DANISH.

One of the most vivid theme restaurants in Odense is guaranteed to please sports aficionados because of its tongue-in-cheek admiration for the nuances of soccer in general and Odense municipal soccer teams in particular. Don't expect the hi-tech, big-screen prowess of sports bars you might have visited in Miami or Chicago. Instead, you'll see only a cramped bar for around 15 drinkers in 1 corner, 2 small-screen TVs projecting sports events from anywhere, and years of collected memorabilia pertaining to soccer. No one will mind if you simply drink your way through the evening with the locals. Beer costs from 18 to 30 DKK ($2.60–$4.35). But if you want a meal, try the house specialty, a very large portion of pork schnitzel, priced at 79 DKK ($11.45), served with potatoes, and prepared in any of 10 different ways. Otherwise, you can order fish or beefsteaks, and even an occasional vegetarian dish, but know in advance that at this place, the schnitzels are simply the most appealing dish in the house. *Målet,* incidentally, translate as "soccer goalpost," and for your amusement, management has erected one as an admittedly ugly decorative centerpiece in a prominent position against one wall.

ODENSE AFTER DARK

There are lots of cultural events in Odense, foremost among which are performances by the Odense Symphony Orchestra. Throughout much of the year, concerts are presented within the Carl Nielsen Hall, Claus Bergs Gade 9 (☎ **66-12-00-57** for ticket information). Tickets cost 190 to 800 DKK ($27.55–$116), depending on the event. During the warm-weather months, the orchestra's role is less formal. In August, for example, the group is more likely to play outdoors, at the main marketplace, in front of the vegetable stands. Because of their location, these performances have been referred to as "the Vegetable Concerts." Likewise, every Thursday at 7pm between mid-June and August, the orchestra presents live (free) music at the edge of the Kongshavn.

Odense offers several places for dancing as well. By far the most popular and entertaining is **Congress Disco,** Asylgade 9 (☎ **66-11-63-02**), which opens at 10pm every Wednesday to Saturday, and which offers a sometimes crowded dance floor in its cellar, and upstairs, very high ceilings which help reduce the noise a bit. Only a bit less visible is **Boogies,** Nørregade 21 (☎ **66-14-00-39**), which attracts the most mixed crowd in town, including in most cases members of Odense's gay and lesbian population, who blend in with an otherwise straight clientele. Another choice that focuses on pop and disco hits from the '70s, '80s, and '90s, is **Crazy Daisy Disco,** Klingenberg 14 (☎ **66-14-67-88**). More rowdy, sometimes so much so that you might want to avoid it altogether, is the **James Dean Dansebar,** Mageløs 12 (☎ **66-11-90-54**), which features punk-rock, and high-volume, electronic rock music inspired by the clubs of London. Other than hanging out at Boogies (see above), gay people either drive to nearby Copenhagen for evening events, or stay alert to the special activities sponsored by **Lambda** (☎ **66-17-76-92**), which offers a Friday and/or Saturday (depending on the schedule) disco in the cellar of Vindegade 100.

Located at Odense's railway station, **Frank A.'s Café,** Jernbanegade 4 (☎ **66-12-27-57**), operates as a cafe throughout the day, and as such, draws a respectable crowd of drinkers and diners who appreciate the simple Danish platters which cost from 39 to 180 DKK ($5.65–$26.10). But the real heart and soul of the place doesn't become visible until after 10pm, when all pretenses of culinary skill is abandoned, and the place is transformed into one of the loudest, wildest, and most raucous nightlife venues in town. Then, live music—either Brazilian, Mexican, or simple rock-and-roll—transforms the place into everybody's favorite rendezvous. Come here to be convivial, amid a setting that's loaded with kitschy bric-a-brac and dozens of single or wannabe-single local residents. Food service is daily from 10am to 10pm; nightlife action runs from 10pm to at least 2am, and sometimes later.

3 Svendborg

43km (27 miles) S of Odense; 145¹/₂ km (91 miles) W of Copenhagen

This old port on Svendborg Sound has long been a popular boating center where you can see yachts, ketches, and kayaks in the harbor. The town still retains some of its medieval heritage, but much of it has been torn down in the name of progress. Visitors find that Svendborg makes a good base for touring the Danish châteaux country and the South Funen archipelago as well.

With 42,000 inhabitants, Svendborg is the second biggest town of Funen and the major commercial hub for South Funen. Until 1915 Svendborg was the home port for a big fleet of sailing ships because of its position on the lovely Svendborg Sound, which provides convenient access to Baltic ports.

Today Svendborg is a lively modern town, with much of interest, including museums, constantly changing art exhibitions, and sports. It has swimming baths, a brand new lido (or beach), and a yachting school. Its beach, Christiansminde, is one of several beaches in Funen flying the Blue Flag, indicating its waters are not polluted.

Svendborg is a market town. On Sunday morning, visit the cobblestoned central plaza where flowers and fish are sold. Wander through the many winding streets where brick and half-timbered buildings still stand. On **Ragergade** you'll see the old homes of early seafarers. **Møllergade,** a pedestrian street, is one of the oldest streets in town, with about 100 different shops.

Literary buffs will be interested to know that the German writer Bertolt Brecht lived at Skovsbo Strand west of Svendborg from 1933 to 1939, but he left at the outbreak of World War II. During this period he wrote *Mother Courage and Her Children.*

ESSENTIALS

GETTING THERE   You can take a train from Copenhagen to Odense, where you can get a connecting train on to Svendborg, with frequent service throughout the day.

By Car   From our last stopover in Odense, head south on Route 9, following the signs into Svendborg.

VISITOR INFORMATION   Contact the **Svendborg Tourist Office,** located at Centrumpladsen (☎ **62-21-09-80**), open June 14 to August, Monday to Friday from 9am to 7pm and Saturday from 9am to 3pm; and January 2 to June 13 and September to December 22, Monday to Friday from 9am to 5pm and Saturday from 9:30am to 12:30pm (closed December 23 to January 1).

SEEING THE SIGHTS

Viebaeltegård. Grubbemøllevej 13 (near Dronningemaen). ☎ **62-21-02-61.** Admission 20 DKK ($2.90) adults, free for children when accompanied by an adult. May 1–Oct 24 Mon–Fri 10am–5pm; Off-season Mon–Fri 10am–4pm.

The headquarters for the Svendborg County Museum's four branches, Viebaeltegård is in the town center housed in a former poorhouse/workhouse constructed in 1872, the only one of its kind still existing in a Danish town. These social-welfare buildings, including the garden, are now a historical monument. Inside, see displays from ancient times and the Middle Ages, including excavation finds from old Svendborg and South Funen. You can also visit crafts workshops, and watch goldsmiths, potters, and printers at work. There's a big museum shop, and you can picnic in the garden.

Anne Hvides Gård. Fruestraede 3. ☎ **62-21-76-15.** Admission 15 DKK ($2.15) adults, free for children when accompanied by an adult. June–Oct 20 daily 10am–5pm; off-season by arrangement with the main office.

The oldest secular house in Svendborg, a branch of the County Museum, it was built around 1558. It's a beautiful half-timbered structure with 18th- and 19th-century interiors and collections of Svendborg silver, glass, copper, brass, and faïence. It's located in the direct center of Torvet, the old market square.

St. Nicolaj Church. Skt. Nicolajgade 2B. ☎ **62-21-12-96.** Free admission. May–Aug daily 10am–4pm; Sept–Apr daily 10am–noon.

Svendborg's oldest church is situated among a cluster of antique houses off of Kyseborgstraede, in the vicinity of Gerrits Plads. Built before 1200 in the Romanesque style and last restored in 1892, its redbrick walls and white vaulting complement the fine altarpiece and stained-glass windows. Enter through the main door.

St. Jørgen's Church. Strandvej 97. ☎ **62-21-14-73.** Free admission. Daily 8am–4pm.

The beauty of St. George's church is exceeded only by the Church of St. Nicolaj (see above). The core of the church is a Gothic longhouse with a three-sided chancel from the late 13th century. During restoration of the church in 1961, an archaeological dig of the floor disclosed traces of a wooden building believed to be a predecessor of the present house of worship. Note the glass mosaics in the interior.

Svendborg Zoologiske Museum. Dronningemaen 30. ☎ **62-21-06-50.** Admission 15 DKK ($2.15) adults, 10 DKK ($1.45) children. Apr–Sept daily 9am–5pm; Oct–Mar Mon–Fri 9am–4pm, Sat–Sun 10am–4pm. Bus: 205, 206, or 208.

Danish zoological specimens and large dioramas showing animal immigration and habitats are displayed. Many exhibits have sound effects. Make sure to stop in at the whale house where you can view the skeleton of a 56-foot-long whale that beached itself on Tåsinge island in 1955.

Vor Frue Sogn. Frue Kirkestraede 4. ☎ **62-22-31-17.** Free admission. Daily 10am–noon.

On the hill where the old Castle Swineburg stood, this Romanesque-Gothic church, dating from 1253, has a carillon of 27 bells, which ring 4 times a day. Since 1660 the bells have rung at noon. From the tourist office at Torvet, walk up the steps leading to the rise on which the church stands, overlooking the Old Town and the harbor.

SHOPPING

The widest selection of Danish design, from household utensils to prestigious china from Royal Copenhagen, and even silver from Georg Jensen, is found at **Inspiration Zinck,** in the Svendborg Bycenter, Tinghusgade (☎ **62-22-35-93**). The best source of glass is **Glasblaeseriet,** Brogade 37 (☎ **62-22-83-73**), where glass can be blown to your own design specifications. Of course, regular glass products, created by others, are also for sale. At **Apollolys,** Smørmosevej 3 (☎ **62-20-53-30**), on Thurø, you can come in and color dip your own candles.

CYCLING IN SOUTH FUNEN

Little narrow roads along the coast, through the woods and past charming little villages, manor houses, and orchards, make South Funen an ideal destination for bikers. Biking routes and maps are available at the tourist office (see above). Rentals, ranging from 35 to 50 DKK ($5.05–$7.25) per day, can be obtained at the Hotel Svendborg, Centrumpladen 1 (☎ **62-21-17-00**).

WHERE TO STAY

Hotel Christiansminde. Christiansmindvej 16, DK-5700 Svendborg. ☎ **62-21-90-00.** Fax 62-21-60-82. 87 units. TV TEL. 675 DKK ($97.90) double. Rate includes breakfast. AE, MC, V. Bus: 201 from Svendborg.

Clean-cut, modern, accommodating, and comfortable, this hotel was built in the 1970s about 2 miles east of Svendborg's center, on a verdant and grassy slope that's close to the edge of the sea. It's divided into four separate buildings, each of which uses the color red in either its walls or its roof. Many visitors come here for a summer holiday beside the beach; others arrive as part of corporate conventions whose sponsors rent virtually every room inside for inspiration-building discussions over long weekends. Each of the bedrooms has a balcony or private terrace, and simple, functional, unpretentious furniture with clean lines. Some of them contain small kitchens, although there's no additional cost for such added facilities within any of the rooms. On the premises is a restaurant, plus a series of convention rooms, each with up-to-date electronic and broadcast amenities. There's a solarium and a small, indoor swimming pool on site, which visitors tend to avoid except during the coldest weather in favor of dips in the nearby sea. Walks into Svendborg are made easier thanks to a network of hiking trails, most of which avoid active roadways. Other than that, there aren't a lot of sport facilities and diversions at this property—only easy access to the great Danish outdoors and the nearby sea.

Hotel Royal. Toldbodvej 5, DK-5700 Svendborg. ☎ and fax **62-21-21-13.** 24 units (4 with bath). 400 DKK ($58) double without bath, 650 DKK ($94.25) double with bath. MC, V. Bus: 200, 208, or 980.

A 1930s hotel of modest comforts, this is for those who prefer a central location opposite the bus and rail stations. Rooms are simply furnished, each equipped with hot and cold running water. Two of the rooms with baths have a view of the harbor. Adequate bathrooms are on each floor. Only breakfast is served, although a bar and cafe are on the premises.

Hotel Svendborg. Centrumpladsen 1, DK-5700 Svendborg. ☎ **62-21-17-00.** Fax 62-21-90-12. www.hotel-svendborg.dk. E-mail: booking@hotel-svendborg.dk. 87 units. 785–825 DKK ($113.80–$119.60) double. June to mid-Aug 725 DKK ($105.10) double. Rates include breakfast. AE, DC, MC, V. Bus: 200 or 204.

This clean and stylish hotel offers the best accommodations in Svendborg. Built in the 1950s, with 90% of the rooms undergoing a radical overhaul in 1994, it rises four floors above the commercial core of town. Except for five or six of the rooms (which are a bit more outmoded), bedrooms are outfitted in Scandinavian modern furniture and pale colors, and are very comfortable, with good, clean bathrooms. On the premises is a restaurant with high ceilings and international food, and a cafe-bar with its own glassed-in front terrace overlooking the pedestrian traffic outside. There's also a facility on-site for suntanning.

Hotel Tre Roser. Fåborgvej 90, DK-5700 Svendborg. ☎ **62-21-64-26.** Fax 62-21-15-26. 70 units. TV TEL. 510 DKK ($73.95) double. AE, DC, MC, V.

This hotel, built in 1975, offers attractively furnished units—58 with kitchenette—that all cost the same with or without such facilities. The units are short on frills, but clean and comfortable. About a mile's drive south of Svendborg, the hotel contains a bistro-style restaurant, sauna, billiard room, and facilities for table tennis. Although it's situated about 3 miles from the nearest bathing beach, there's a big swimming pool and children's playground on the premises, and a golf course within a 5-minute drive.

Missionshotellet Stella Maris. Kogtvedvaenget 3, DK-5700 Svendborg. ☎ **62-21-38-91.** Fax 62-22-41-74. 25 units (15 with bath). 410–450 DKK ($59.45–$65.25) double without bath, 480–600 DKK ($69.60–$87) double with bath. Rates include breakfast. DC, MC, V. Bus: 202. From Svendborg head west along Kogtvedvej.

Missionshotellet Stella Maris is an old-fashioned place, the former dormer house of a large estate, built in 1904. The bedroom furniture may be dated, but all is comfortable and the patina of time has given the hotel a certain dignity. Sea-view units opening onto Svendborg Sound are more expensive. A private park leads directly to the sound. The restaurant serves meals daily from noon to 2pm and 6 to 7pm. It is one of the most reasonable places to eat in town if you demand no more than typical Danish regional fare, with main courses costing 110 to 140 DKK ($15.95–$20.30).

NEARBY ACCOMMODATIONS AT OURE

Majorgården. Landevejen 155, DK-5883 Oure. ☎ **62-28-18-19.** 4 units (none with bath). 400 DKK ($58) double. Rates include breakfast. AE, DC, MC, V. Bus: 901 running between Svendborg and Nyborg.

On the coast road, 7 miles from Svendborg and 20 miles from Nyborg, this 1761 white-brick inn has been cherished by such illustrious Danes as tenor Lauritz Melchior. Outside, a bower of roses grows against the walls, low white tables sit on the lawn for coffee, and a little pond at the rear is filled with ducks. An old horse stable has been turned into a bar. The rooms sit cozily above the restaurant under the roofline. Two have old-fashioned fixtures and furnishings, and the others are much more modern. If you're just driving by, stop in for a "plate of the inn"—two kinds of herring, plaice, meatballs, meat sausages, liver paste, and cheese. A large selection of fish and meat dishes is also available. Fixed-price menus cost 96 to 140 DKK ($13.90–$20.30) and meals are served every day from noon to 9:30pm.

WHERE TO DINE
AT SVENDBORG

✪ **Restaurant Gaasen.** Kullinggade 1B. ☎ **62-22-92-11.** Reservations recommended. Main courses 150–230 DKK ($21.75–$33.35). Set menus 205–355 DKK ($29.75–$51.50). MC, V. Mon–Sat noon–2pm and 5:30–10pm. DANISH/SEAFOOD.

Set at the edge of Svendborg's harbor-front, and housed within the solid masonry walls of what was originally an ironmonger's smithy, this is one of the most appealing and congenial restaurants in town. Its creative force derives from chef and owner Claus Holm, who invents many of the dishes that attract a steady stream of local business. There is an obvious willingness to invest in every aspect of what's needed to serve a fine cuisine, not only in the skill of the chef but in the devotion to quality ingredients. For the owner, it is clearly a labor of love. Three specialties of which he is the most proud include grilled freshwater crabs with a saffron-flavored bouillon and homemade lobster-stuffed ravioli; veal stuffed with black truffles and sweetbreads, and served with madeira sauce; and gray mullet with herbs, *beurre blanc* (white butter), and sautéed spinach. The establishment's name (which means "goose") derives from its location a few steps from the site where live poultry was bought and sold throughout the Middle Ages.

Svendborgsund. Havnpladsen 5A. ☎ **62-21-07-19.** Reservations recommended. Main courses 80–150 DKK ($11.60–$21.75); lunch *smørrebrød* 40–60 DKK ($5.80–$8.70) each. No credit cards. Daily 11am–midnight. DANISH/FRENCH.

A 5-minute walk south of the commercial center, this waterfront restaurant is the oldest in town, built in the 1830s in a stone house painted white. From its windows or summer terrace you can see the harbor with its ferryboats, trawlers, and pleasure yachts. The chef specializes in fresh fish and meat, and does so exceedingly well, especially with the very filling *biksemad* (meat, potatoes, and onions). The separate bar is popular with the locals.

AT VESTER SKERNINGE

Vester Skerninge Kro. Kravej 9, Vester Skerninge. ☎ **62-24-10-04.** Main courses 75–165 DKK ($10.90–$23.90). No credit cards. Wed–Mon 11am–9pm.

In the hamlet of Vester Skerninge, 7 miles west of Svendborg along Route 44, this *kro* (inn) was established in 1772, and has been dispensing generous portions of simple Danish food ever since. Behind a half-timbered façade, guests can order such dishes as clear or cream-based soups, English or French beefsteak, and Wiener schnitzel. Other specialties include *mediste pølse,* a mild grilled sausage, and *aeggkage,* a fluffy omelet concocted from smoked bacon, chives, and fresh tomatoes.

SVENDBORG AFTER DARK

The most popular disco in town, with the most appealing clients, is **Crazy Daisy,** Frederiksgade 6 (☎ **62-21-67-60**). Outfitted with bright lights and loud music deriving from Los Angeles, New York, and London, it spreads its clients over two floors that have easy access to three separate bars. Upstairs is disco music from the 1980s; downstairs, the dance music is newer, more cutting-edge, and more experimental. It's open only on Wednesdays, Fridays, and Saturdays from 10pm till dawn. The entrance charge is 40 DKK ($5.80). Also popular, but never as much as Crazy Daisy, is **Chess,** Vestergade 7 (☎ **62-22-17-16**), which offers music that alternates between disco from the '70s and '80s and more cutting-edge fare. People in their 40s and 50s appreciate the oldies fare generated at **Bortløbne Banje,** Klosterpladsen 7 (☎ **62-22-31-21**), whose opening is irregular, and based mostly on their ability to procure live musicians. And during the warm-weather months, the outdoor decks of the ship **Orangi,** Jessens Mole (☎ **62-22-82-92**), is a late-night venue for drinks and live jazz, but only between May and September from 9pm till around 1am.

NEARBY ATTRACTIONS ON THURØ

This horseshoe-shaped island, connected to Funen by a causeway, is filled with orchards and well-cared-for gardens, giving it the title "The Garden of Denmark." The island was once the property of the manor house, Bjornemose, but the Thurineans wanted liberty, so they joined together to buy back Thurø in 1810, an event commemorated by a stone proclaiming freedom from manorial domination.

It is the island itself that is the attraction, because of its scenic beauty. However, if you want a specific target to visit, make it **Thurø Kirke** (☎ **62-20-50-92**), which is open daily 8am to 6pm, charging no admission.

The best beaches on Thurø can be found at Smørmosen, Thurø Rev, and Grasten.

ON TÅSINGE

The largest island in the South Funen archipelago, Tåsinge has been connected to Funen by the Svendborg Sound Bridge since 1966. **Troense,** the "skipper town" of Tåsinge, is one of the best-preserved villages in Denmark, where many half-timbered houses still stand on Badstuen and Grønnegade, the latter declared Denmark's prettiest street.

The island was the setting for a famous tragic love story depicted in the film *Elvira Madigan*. After checking out of a hotel in Svendborg, Danish artist Elvira Madigan and her lover, Sixten Sparre, a Swedish lieutenant, crossed by ferry to Tåsinge, where together they committed suicide. The "Romeo and Juliet" of Denmark were buried in the Landet Kirkegård, Elvira Madigansvej, at Landet, in the middle of Tåsinge, where many brides, even today, throw their wedding bouquets on their graves. The 100th anniversary of the death of these two lovers was widely observed in 1989 throughout Scandinavia; many ballads were written to commemorate the date.

The island is best explored by car—drive over the causeway bridge (follow Route 9), or you could take local bus no. 200. However, the most important attraction, Valdemar's Slot, can be seen by taking the vintage steamer, *MS Helge* (☎ **62-50-25-00** for information), which departs several times daily from the harbor at Svendborg. The steamer operates May 11 to September 8. A one-way ticket costs 30 DKK ($4.35); a round-trip, 50 DKK ($7.25). Tickets are sold on board or at the Svendborg Tourist Office (see above).

SEEING THE SIGHTS

Bregninge Kirkebakke. Kirkebakken 1, Bregninge. Admission to tower 5 DKK (75¢) adults, 2 DKK (30¢) children. Church admission free. Tower daily 6am–10pm. Church Apr–Sept daily Mon–Sat 8am–6pm; Sun 8am–noon. Oct–Mar Mon–Sat 8am–4pm; Sun 8am–noon. Bus: 980 from Svendborg.

If the weather is clear, be sure to climb the **Bregninge church tower** for panoramic views of the island and the Funen archipelago. To the south are the Bregninge Hills, whose wooded slopes are popular for outings. Originally Romanseque, the church's porch dates from the 16th-century and its north wing from the 18th-century. Inside you'll see a Romanesque granite font, a head of Christ on the north wall dating from about 1250, and a 1621 pulpit with rich ornamentation. In the porch is a tombstone with arcade decoration, the image of a vicar, and runic letters.

Sofartssamlingerne I Troense. Strandgade 1, Troense. ☎ **62-22-52-32.** Admission 20 DKK ($2.90) adults, 10 DKK ($1.45) children and seniors. May–Sept daily 10am–5pm; Oct–Apr Mon–Fri 10am–5pm, Sat 9am–noon. Cross the causeway to Tåsinge, turn left and then left again, heading down Bregingevej toward the water; turn right at Troensevej and follow the signs to the old port of Troense and to the village school (now the museum) on Strandgade.

The Maritime Museum (a branch of the County Museum), housed in a 1790s school, traces maritime history from the early 19th-century to the present. Pictures of ships, panoramas, yachting models, and memorabilia of the trade routes to China and East India—including Staffordshire figures, Liverpool ware, Sunderland china, ropework art, and ships in a bottle—are displayed.

Tåsinge Skipperhjem og Folkemindesamling. Kirkebakken 1, Bregninge. ☎ **62-22-71-44.** Admission 10 DKK ($1.45) adults, 4 DKK (60¢) children. May 5–June 20 Mon–Fri 10am–5:30pm, Sat–Sun 10am–5pm. June 21–Aug 15 daily 10am–5pm. Closed Aug 6–May 4. Bus: 980 from Svendborg. From Valdemars Slot (see below), turn right by two thatched cottages and left again at the next junction; follow the signs to Bregninge.

Set in an 1826 school building, this private historical collection contains model and bottled ships, a coin collection, and revealing archives of Tåsinge history. A small collection of memorabilia is associated with the tragic love drama of Elvira and Sixten. In another building you can see what a typical sea captain's house looked like some 100 years ago.

Valdemars Slot. Slosalléen 100, Troense. ☎ **62-22-61-06.** Admission 50 DKK ($7.25) adults, 35 DKK ($5.05) children. May–Sept daily 10am–5pm; Apr–May and Oct 1–18 Sat–Sun 10am–5pm. Closed Oct 19–Mar. Take the *MS Helge* from Svendborg Harbor. By car, from Troense, follow Slotsalléen to the castle.

Valdemars Slot was built between 1639 and 1644 by order of Christian IV for his son, Valdemar Christian. In 1678 it was given to the naval hero Niels Juel for his third victory over the Swedes in a Køge Bay battle. The Juel family still owns the slot, which is in considerably better condition than when the admiral arrived. He found that the enemy Swedes had occupied the estate, sending the copper roof home to make bullets and stabling horses in the church. The castle is now a museum.

Valdemars Castle Church, in the south wing, was cleaned up by Admiral Juel, consecrated in 1687, and has been used for worship ever since. Two stories high, it's overarched by three star vaults and illuminated by Gothic windows.

WHERE TO STAY

Det Lille Hotel. Badstuen 15, Troense, Tåsinge, DK-5700 Svendborg. ☎ **62-22-53-41.** 8 units (none with bath). 450 DKK ($65.25) double. Rate includes breakfast. AE, DC, MC, V.

Set directly beside the harbor, in the center of Troense, this is one of the most appealing small hotels in the district. It was built 150 years ago as housing for a family that worked at a nearby castle (Valdemar Slot). It's a half-timbered building with a straw roof, cozy dimensions, and exterior walls that are painted a deep shade of red. None of the bedrooms has private baths (all facilities are shared, and accessible via the central hallway), but the hotel's quirky old age, and the kindness of its owner, Birgit Erikssen, more than compensate. Bedrooms are cozy, cramped, but comfortable, and very likable. Other than breakfast, the only meals served are those prepared by Ms. Erikssen herself, which are priced at 75 DKK ($10.90) each, but only if you pre-announce your intention of dining in-house several hours in advance.

Hotel Troense. Strandgade 5–7, Troense, DK-5700 Svendborg. ☎ **62-22-54-12.** Fax 62-22-78-12. 31 units (28 with bath). TV. 665 DKK ($96.45) double. Rates include breakfast. AE, DC, MC. V. Bus: 200.

Since 1905 this establishment has been both a hotel and a restaurant. It was last renovated in 1993. Most pleasingly furnished rooms are in the main white-walled building, but several are in comfortable but lackluster annexes nearby. Accommodations cost the same whether with or without bath. In the nautically decorated restaurant, which is also open to the general public, specialties include: fillet of lemon sole; plaice stuffed with shrimp, asparagus, and mushrooms; and medallions of pork with cream-and-curry sauce. The restaurant is open for lunch and dinner every day.

WHERE TO DINE

Restaurant Lodskroen. Strandvej 80, Troense. ☎ **62-22-50-44.** Reservations recommended. Main courses 155–200 DKK ($22.50–$29.00). Fixed-price menus 218–300 DKK ($31.60–$43.50). No credit cards. May–Aug Sat–Sun noon–4pm; daily 6–10pm. Sept–Apr only Sat–Sun noon–4pm and 6–10pm. DANISH.

This restaurant is positioned 4 miles south of Svendborg, on the island of Troense, which is accessible from Svendborg by means of a toll-free bridge. The building that contains it was constructed 200 years ago as an inn, and still retains its thick, white-painted exterior walls and thatch roof. Inside, you'll find two cozy dining rooms, plus two outdoor terraces, one of which faces the sea. Menu items are well-flavored, and served by an overworked staff to the accompaniment of a demanding management. The best dishes are beefsteak marinated in rum and herbs, then grilled; John Dory with buttered parsley, or perhaps wine sauce; and a simple but highly flavorful version of salmon that's grilled and served with fresh vegetables and butter.

✪ **Restaurant Slotskaelderen.** In Valdemars Slot, Slotsalléen 100, Troense. DK-5700 Svendborg. ☎ **62-22-59.00.** Fax 62-22-72-67. www.valdemarsslot.dk. E-mail: slot@valdemarsslot.dk. French restaurant, three-course fixed-price menu 365 DKK ($52.95). Danish bistro, main courses 38–98 DKK ($5.50–$14.20). AE, MC, V. June to mid-Sept daily 11am–9pm; Apr–May and mid-Sept to Oct daily 11am–5pm. Closed Nov–Mar. DANISH/FRENCH.

Set inside the thick stone walls of one of the region's most foreboding castles, the restaurant is divided into an unpretentious Danish bistro, where such dishes as schnitzels, *laubskaus* (hash), and rouladens of beef are served with Danish beer and *aquavit*, and a more upscale and somewhat more elegant French restaurant.

If you'd like to stay overnight, there are five luxurious bedrooms (four with private bath) and one suite located in a modern outbuilding of the historic castle. Expect luxury, charm, and grace if you decide on an overnight stay here. Doubles without bath cost 840 DKK ($121.80), doubles with bath are 940 DKK ($136.30), and the suite goes for 1,450 DKK ($210.25).

4 Faaborg

27km (17 miles) W of Svendborg; 179km (112 miles) W of Copenhagen; 37km (23 miles) S of Odense

Like Svendborg, Faaborg (also written Fåborg), a small seaside town of red-roofed buildings, is a good base for exploring southwestern Funen. Crowned by an old belfry, Faaborg has a number of well-preserved buildings, among them the medieval **Vesterport,** all that's left of Faaborg's walled fortifications.

You'll find one of the best collections of Funen paintings and sculpture, particularly the work of Kai Nielsen, an important modern Danish sculptor. One controversial sculpture by Nielsen that has been denounced as obscene by some and praised by others is *Ymerbrond* (Ymer Wall), displayed in the market square (a copy is displayed in the Museum of Faaborg). The sculpture depicts a man drinking from the udder of a bony cow while the cow licks a baby.

ESSENTIALS
GETTING THERE
BY BUS   From Odense, bus nos. 960, 961, or 962 run hourly from sunrise to about 11pm, taking 1¼ hours. Bus no. 930 from Svendborg also arrives frequently throughout the day, taking 40 minutes. The bus station lies on Banegårdspladsen, site of the old rail train depot at the southern rim of town. (There is no longer a train service for Faaborg.)

BY CAR   From Svendborg, head west on Route 44; from Odense, go south on Route 43.

VISITOR INFORMATION   The **Faaborg and District Tourist Association,** Banegårdspladsen 2A (☎ **62-61-07-07**), is open May to mid-September Monday to Friday 9am to 6pm and Saturday 9am to 6pm and Saturday 10am to 6pm.

For bike rentals, try **Bjarnes Cykler,** Svendborgvej 69 (☎ **62-61-24-61**), at the Faaborg Vandrerhjem. The cost is 55 DKK ($8) per day.

SEEING THE SIGHTS
Den Gamle Gaard (The Old Merchant's House). Holkegade 1. ☎ **62-61-33-38.** Admission 25 DKK ($3.60) adults, free for children. May 15–Sept 15 daily 10:30am–4:30pm. Closed Sept 16–May 14.

This 1725 house was established as a municipal museum in 1932 and displays Faaborg life in the 18th and 19th centuries. Various furnishings (some of which were the property of Riborg Voight, an early love of H. C. Andersen's), glass, china, and faïence indicating Faaborg's past importance as a trade and shipping center, are also on view. Exhibits from Lyk, including beautiful textiles and embroidery, are in the back. The museum lies in the town center near the marketplace and harbor.

Faaborg Museum. Grønnegade 75. ☎ **62-61-06-45.** Admission 30 DKK ($4.35) adults, free for children. Apr–May and Sept–Oct daily 10am–4pm, June–Aug daily 10am–5pm, Nov–Mar daily 11am–3pm.

Located near the bus station, the museum has a rich collection of work by Kai Nielsen. Aside from his works, the museum displays paintings by such outstanding local artists as Peter Hansen, Johannes Larsen, and Fritz Syberg. In the octagonal rotunda of the museum is a huge statue commissioned by Mads Rasmussen, a wealthy art patron who bore the nickname "Mads Tomato." The museum has a cafe, open daily, serving lunch and coffee.

Klokketårnet. Tarnstraede. ☎ **62-61-04-78.** Admission 10 DKK ($1.45) adults, 2 DKK (30¢) children. Mon–Fri 11am–4pm; Sat 10am–1pm. Closed mid-Sept to mid-June.

This old belfry is the Faaborg's main landmark—it's all that's left of the 13th-century Church of Sct. Nicolai, the first church in town, which was demolished around 1600. The town's old fire sledge is also here. The carillon bells play hymns four times a day. The belfry is directly in the town center near the marketplace.

SHOPPING   Svendborg offers appealing shops that include outlets for all the luxury goods produced in Denmark. Many line both sides of a shopping thoroughfare—Østergade—that's reserved, except for deliveries, for pedestrians. The best outlet for acquiring upscale porcelain, crystal, and china is **Imerco,** Østergade 6 (☎ **62-61-00-17**). Two highly appealing outlets for antiques include **Antik Faaborg,** Holkegade 6 (☎ **62-61-13-61**), which specializes in old-fashioned porcelain from Denmark, Germany, and France; and **Henstra Antiks,** Bøjestræde 14 (☎ **62-61-42-64**), which features upscale antiques from around 1900, in many cases crafted from mahogany. And if you're looking for an inexpensive keepsake of your time in Svendborg, a commemorative ashtray, dinner bell, or key chain, you'll find lots of them at the town's biggest news kiosk, **Waters Kiosk,** Mellengade 6 (☎ **62-61-00-87**).

WHERE TO STAY

Hotel-Pension Mosegård. Nabgyden 31, DK-5600 Faaborg. ☎ **62-61-56-91.** Fax 62-61-56-96. 20 units (10 with bath). 430–490 DKK ($62.35–$71.05) double without bath, 560–620 DKK ($81.20–$89.90) double with bath. Rates include breakfast. DC, MC, V.

Originally built in the 1960s, this hotel is in an isolated spot surrounded by fields and forests, beside the sea, about 3 miles east of Faaborg. Most clients are Danish vacationers on holiday, and many opt for stays of at least a week or more. Rooms are clean, conservative, comfortable, and snug. Those with private bathrooms also contain TVs. Most of the accommodations on the top floor have a view of the sea, and some of the accommodations contain their own private balconies. Fixed-price meals in the hotel's dining room cost 118 DKK ($17.10) for two courses or 138 DKK ($20) for three courses. The cuisine is typically Danish regional fare, including roast veal in a brown sauce with mixed vegetables and boiled potatoes or breaded plaice *meunière* with lime and boiled potatoes.

Interscan Hotel Faaborg Fjord. Svendborgvej 175, DK-5600 Faaborg. ☎ **62-61-10-10.** Fax 62-61-10-17. www.nordiskhotelgruppe.dk/faaborg. E-mail: ihf@nordiskhotelgruppe.dk. 131 units. TV TEL. 695–995 DKK ($100.75–$144.25) double. Rates include breakfast. AE, DC, MC. V.

Built in 1975 and enlarged about a decade later, this hotel lies across the road from a sweeping view over one of Denmark's most famous fjords. Set in its own park at the eastern edge of town, this modern year-round hotel has comfortable rooms, each with a balcony/terrace. An indoor swimming pool and sauna are among the amenities. The restaurant offers a panoramic sea view, good food, and an excellent wine cellar. A two-course fixed-price menu goes for 130 DKK ($18.85), with a three-course fixed-price meal costing 190 DKK ($27.55). Main courses range from 115 to 145 DKK ($16.65–$21.05). Dishes are typically Danish but often with a French influence, including poached trout in a *beurre blanc* (white butter) sauce or poached fish delicately flavored with lemon.

Korinth Kro. Reventlowsvej 10, DK-5600 Faaborg. ☎ **62-65-10-23.** 32 units (10 with bath). 430 DKK ($62.35) double without bath, 525 DKK ($76.15) double with bath. Rates include breakfast. AE, DC, MC, V.

Five miles northeast of Faaborg along Route 8, this hotel features comfortably old-fashioned bedrooms (a few with TV), a children's playground, and a rear garden. The 1758 building was originally intended as a school where local farm girls could learn weaving, but it became an inn in 1801. Today it's shielded from the main road by a screen of architectural gingerbread, a red-tile roof, and scores of climbing vines. If you wish, you can just drop in for lunch or dinner. A fixed-price five-course menu costs 215 to 235 DKK ($31.15–$34.05).

NEARBY ATTRACTIONS
AT MILLINGE
✪ **Falsled Kro.** Assensvej 513, Falsled, DK-5642 Millinge. ☎ **62-68-11-11.** Fax 62-68-11-62. www.falsledkro.dk. E-mail: Falsledkro@vip.cybercity.dk. 19 units. TEL. 1,690–1,850 DKK ($245.05–$268.25) double; 2,150–2,650 DKK ($311.75–$384.25) suite. AE, DC, MC, V. Bus: 930.

The epitome of a Danish roadside inn, this former 15th-century smuggler's inn has been converted into a premier hotel, the finest in Funen. A Relais & Châteaux property, it offers tradition and quality in its colony of thatched buildings clustered around a cobblestone courtyard with a fountain. Each accommodation is elegantly furnished and comfortable—some in converted outbuildings, others in cottages across the road. Eleven rooms have a TV and seven are fitted with mini-bars. A garden leads to the water and a yacht harbor. It's located west of Faaborg on Route 329.

Dining: Many critics rate the hotel restaurant the best in Denmark (see "Where to Dine," below).

Amenities: Room service, laundry, baby-sitting, luggage service, translation and guide service. Fishing and bathing areas, helipad, parking area; tennis courts 500 yards away; horseback riding 3 miles away.

AT BØJDEN
Hvedholm Slot. Hvedholm Slot 1, DK-5600 Faaborg. ☎ **62-60-22-57.** Fax 62-60-17-44. E-mail: Royal-Classic@Internet.dk. www.royal-classic.dk/Hvedholm. 34 units at press time, with 9 more envisioned during the lifetime of this edition. 895 DKK ($129.75) double. Rate includes breakfast. AE, DC, MC, V. Drive 4½ miles west of Faaborg, following Route 8 and the signs pointing to Bøjden. Bus no. 920, which originates in Faaborg's center, will drop you off a quarter-mile from the hotel.

One of the region's most evocative castles enjoys a recorded history going back to 1231, and a sweeping view over the fjord and the Faaborg harbor-front, 4½ miles away. The grand and ornate brick-and-sandstone façade you'll see today was rebuilt during the late 19th-century, when it gained the soaring tower and elaborate gables and ornamentation that make it so charming. When its owners ran out of money after World

War I, the contents were sold at auction by the Danish government, and the site functioned as a mental hospital beginning in 1928.

In 1996, it was bought by a team of bold and imaginative entrepreneurs (Gorm Lokdam and Ann Vibeke) who added it to their already-functioning chain of three other stately hotels in Denmark. Regrettably, none of the original art or antiques remain from this historic home's heyday: Instead, you'll find a tasteful medley of conservative reproductions vaguely inspired by what you might have expected within the stately homes of England. Decor of each of the bedrooms is different from its neighbors, each employing a color scheme, furniture, and fabrics of its own.

Although someone on the staff might prepare you a platter of food by special request around noontime, breakfast and dinner are the only scheduled meals ever served. Dinner is daily from 6 to 10pm, and priced as part of table d'hôtel meals at 188 DKK ($27.25), plus drinks. Non-residents who phone in advance are welcome. During our visit, the dinner consisted of a platter of smoked fish with an avocado cream sauce, followed by breast of duck with a spinach soufflé, mushrooms, and fried potatoes, followed by a medley of Danish cheeses and pastries. There's a great deal of charm about this place, and a vivid history, despite a certain spartan look and a format that, at this writing, still carries a vague sense of a glamorous-hotel-in-the-making.

✪ **Steensgaard Herregårdspension.** Steensgaard, DK-5642 Millinge. ☎ **62-61-94-90.** Fax 62-61-78-61. 18 units (17 with bath). MINIBAR TEL. 780 DKK ($113.10) double without bath, 830–1,090 DKK ($120.35–$158.05) double with bath. Rates include breakfast. AE, DC, MC, V. Bus: 920 or 930.

Few places in Denmark are evocative of a bygone manorial life as much as this brick-and-timber house, one of the most ideal places in Funen for a relaxing weekend. It is set in an area of scenic beauty within a very large park with a private lake. About 4 miles northwest of Faaborg, the oldest section dates from 1310, possibly earlier. Bedrooms are comfortably and tastefully furnished, often with antiques.

You can drive here even if you don't have the opportunity of staying overnight, but if you aren't a guest you should reserve a table. Dinner is served nightly from 6:30 to 9:30pm with a three-course menu costing 325 DKK ($47.15). You can also visit for lunch daily from 12:30 to 2pm, a three-course fixed price menu going for 200 DKK ($29). There is only one price for main courses: 195 DKK ($28.30). Typical dishes include champagne soup, roe deer with juniper berries, or salmon *en papillote* with local herbs. Fresh from the sea, Danish lobster or baby shrimp are also featured.

WHERE TO DINE

Restaurant Klinten. Klintallée 1. ☎ **62-61-32-00.** Reservations recommended. Main courses 95–138 DKK ($13.75–$20). Fixed-price lunch 110 DKK ($15.95), fixed-price dinner 148 DKK ($21.45). MC, V. Daily 11am–4pm and 6–8:30pm. DANISH.

This attractive restaurant, overlooking the water a quarter-mile east of the commercial center, enjoys a forest setting near the sea. The building was erected in 1977, and the restaurant is known for its big windows and panoramic view of a verdant offshore island. The cookery has a lot of flavor and shows a respect for fresh ingredients. Try the fresh salmon in puff pastry with spinach and lobster as a starter, following with such main courses as spicy steak in a tomato sauce, served with a medley of fresh vegetables, or else the salmon cutlet in a white wine sauce. In summer the terrace is popular when the weather's right. On the terrace is a barbecue grill with a salad bar. Occasionally they have all-you-can-eat barbecues here for 100 DKK ($14.50).

Tre Kroner. Strandgade 1. ☎ **62-61-01-50.** Reservations recommended. Lunch main courses 50–70 DKK ($7.25–$10.15); dinner main courses 130–150 DKK ($18.85–$21.75). No

23

‑ignoreread

credit cards. Daily 11am–3pm and 6–9pm. Bar daily 10am–11pm or midnight, depending on business. DANISH.

This is the oldest pub and restaurant in Faaborg, with a pedigree going back to 1821, when it was established as an inn, and a stone-sided architectural layout that dates back to sometime in the 1600s. The place is the first to be cited by townsfolk as a cozy site for drinks in a venerable, informal, and somewhat cramped setting. Meals focus on traditional Danish recipes, and include a lunchtime roster of *smørrebrød*, platters of herring, soups, and salads. Dinners are more elaborate, featuring chicken breasts in mushrooms and brandy sauce, grilled steaks, calf's liver with onions, and roasted pork with braised red cabbage.

NEARBY DINING AT MILLINGE

✪ **Falsled Kro.** Assensvej 513, Falsled, Millinge. ☎ **62-68-11-11.** Reservations essential. Main courses 265–370 DKK ($38.40–$53.65). Fixed-price menus 410–610 DKK ($59.45–$88.45) three-courses, 730 DKK ($105.85) five-courses. AE, DC, MC, V. Mon noon–2:30pm; Tues–Sun noon–2:30pm and 6–9:30pm. Closed Mon Oct–Mar. DANISH/FRENCH.

Hailed as Denmark's finest dining choice, this *kro* (inn) may just well be the culinary highlight of your stay. Growing many of its own vegetables, the *kro* uses only fresh, seasonal produce. Food preparation has been inspired by French cuisine. Some of this restaurant's most noted dishes are among the simplest; for example, a succulent version of salmon, which is smoked on the premises in one of the outbuildings. Other choices include a warm salad of smoked haddock with roast eggplant, scallop salad with basil sauce, a fish-and-shellfish soup with sorrel, fiery lobster in the style of "Tiger Lee," French duck liver with wild rice and sweet corn relish, and a saddle of rabbit or braised beef in red-wine sauce. The owners breed quail locally and cook and serve them with a port-wine sauce. The chef's seafood platter is a gift to put before Neptune. Try salmon grilled or flamed over fennel. Game dishes predominate in autumn. The kitchen also bakes its own bread and cakes, and the wine list is well chosen.

FAABORG AFTER DARK

Our leading choice for a drink in cozy and historic surroundings is a site previously recommended as a restaurant, **Tre Kroner.** Even at the peak dinner hours, someone is likely to be here just for drinks, and after the rush of the evening meal service ends (around 9:15pm), the entire place is re-invented as a pub until closing at around midnight.

A viable competitor for the after-dark favors of Faaborgians is **Kinografen,** Banegårdspladsen 21 (☎ **62-61-33-55**), which occupies the premises of what was originally built as a movie theater. Its pub section opens daily at noon, and continues until at least midnight. Live music is heard on Friday and Saturday nights from 9pm till closing. A weekend disco transforms the place into a rock-and-roll emporium every Friday and Saturday night from 10pm until around 6am. Entrance to the disco costs 25 DKK ($3.60).

5 Ærø

29km (18 miles) across the water S of Svendborg; 176km (110 miles) W of Copenhagen; 73 1/2 km (46 miles) S of Odense

An interesting Denmark excursion is to the Baltic Sea island of Ærø, 22 miles long and 6 miles wide. The island has little seaside and country hamlets linked by winding, sometimes single-lane roads, with thatch-roofed farmhouses in pastures and cultivated fields. Ærø possesses both sand and pebble beaches. The best towns to make your center on the island are Søby, Ærøskøbing, or Marstal.

There are many good places on Ærø to eat and sleep—cozy inns in the country and comfortable little hotels in town. Try some of the local rye bread; it's said to be the best in Denmark. With your *aquavit* (schnapps), asks for a dash of Riga balsam bitters, a tradition that started when Ærø men sailed to Riga, found these bitters, and used them ever since in their *aquavit.*

As you drive across Ærø, you'll note the landscape dotted with a number of windmills evoking the fields of Holland. Some of the mills are new; others much older but well preserved. Regrettably, they are not open for interior visits but can be viewed from the outside. The mills are particularly visible at Risemark where you can see 11 of them. There are other mills outside the towns of Bregninge, Søby, Haven, and Marstal. All these mills still provide power for the people of Ærø, creating as little pollution as possible.

ESSENTIALS
GETTING THERE   The only way to reach Ærø is by ferry. Car-ferries depart from Svendborg six times daily. The trip takes about an hour. For a schedule, contact the tourist office or the ferry office at the harbor in Svendborg. Bookings are made through **Det Æroske Faergegraf-Ikselskab** in Ærøskøbing (☎ 62-52-40-00).

GETTING AROUND   It's best to take a car on the ferry since there's limited **bus service** on Ærø (call ☎ 62-53-10-10 in Ærøskøbing for bus information). Bus: 990 runs every hour on the hour in the afternoon between Ærøskøbing, Marstal, and Søby. There's only limited morning service. Tourist offices (see below) provide bus schedules, which change seasonally. Tickets costing 46 DKK ($6.65) for the day can be bought on the bus.

If you'd like to take a bus tour of the island, call **Jesper "Bus" Jensen** (☎ 62-58-13-13.)

EXPLORING THE ISLAND
Most visitors go to Ærøskøping, perhaps Marstal, then return to the pleasures of South Funen. But if you like to cycle or have rented a car in Funen you can explore the southern tier of the island, going from Marstal, the port in the east, all the way to Søby at the northern and far western tip of Ærø. There are several attractions along the way, although you can just enjoy the landscape for its own idyllic beauty.

Take the coastal road going west from Marstal (sign-posted Vejsnaes). From here continue west following the signs to Store Rise, where you can stop and visit **Rise Kirke,** originally a Romanesque church dating from the latter part of the 12th century. Later, vaults were added and the church was enlarged twice, the last time in 1697. The altarpiece inside dates from 1300 and depicts the suffering and resurrection of Christ. Its carved work is from the town of Schleswig in northwestern Germany. The tower is similar to that of the church at Bregninge. It was originally roofed in oak tiles but these were replaced in 1957. In the churchyard wall facing the vicarage garden an old porch known as "the Monks Door" can be seen, dating from circa 1450.

In a field in the rear of the church you can view **Tingstedet,** a 175½ foot-long Neolithic passage grave. It is believed that this site is 5,000 years old, maybe a lot older. Archaeologists have claimed that the cup-like markings in the biggest stone (close to the church) indicate the site may have been used by a "fertility cult." A footpath leading from the church to the Neolithic site is clearly marked, and it's only a short walk to get here.

If you'd like to break up the driving tour, you can drive a mile south of the village to **Risemark Strand,** one of the island's few sandy beaches. Many of the other beaches on Ærø consist of shingles.

Cycling Around the Island

Ærø is one of the best islands in Denmark for cycling because of its low-lying terrain and scenic paths. Local tourist offices provide maps outlining routes for 15 DKK ($2.15). You can use these maps for bike rides but also for walks. Cycle trails around the coast are marked by numbers 90, 91, and 92. Bike rentals cost 40 DKK ($5.80) a day, and rentals in Ærøskøbing are available at the **Ærøskøbing Vandrerhjem,** Smedevejen 15 (☎ **62-52-10-44**); at Marstal at **Nørremark Cykelforretning,** Møllevejen 77 (☎ **62-53-14-77**), and at **Søby Cykelforretning,** Langebro 4A (☎ **62-58-18-42**).

The road continues west to Tranderup where you can visit **Tranderup Kirke,** a Romanesque building with Gothic vaulting. Inside, the large carved figure depicting Mary and the infant Jesus dates from around the 14th century and is one of the oldest ecclesiastical pieces on the island. The triptych is from circa 1510, and the large mural over the chancel arch reveals the date of its execution in 1518. Originally the spire of Tranderup resembled those of Rise and Bregninge (see below). But they were rebuilt in a neoclassical style in 1832; the largest bell was cast in 1566 and is still in use.

After a visit follow the signs west to the village of **Vodrup,** which originally grew up in the 13th century and is mentioned for the first time in 1537 under the name of Wuderup. The village disappeared in the 17th century when the land became part of Vodrup Estate. When the estate was dissolved, the village came back.

The area is visited today for its stunning cliffs, ✪ **Vodrup Klint.** The geology is unusual: large blocks of land have slipped down and now resemble huge steps. The soil lies on top of a layer of gray clay, which can be seen at the base of the cliffs by the beach. The layer of clay is full of snail and cockle shells, left here by the sea. Water seeping down through the earth is stopped by a layer of clay. If enough water is absorbed by the clay, it becomes so "movable" that it acts as a sliding plane for the layers of earth above. The last great landslide here occurred in 1834.

Vodrup Klint is one of the most southerly points in Denmark, attracting creatures such as lizards and many species of plants that thrive here—for example, the carline thistle grows on these cliffs, blooming from July to September. An unusual characteristic of the cliffs is a proliferation of springs, where water bubbles out by the foot of the slopes. When the cattle need water, farmers need only push a pipe into the cliff face and let the water collect in a pool.

Fyn County has bought the cliffs, roughly 87 acres, and set them aside for the use of the public, which has access to the area. Animals are allowed to graze the fields in the summer months. You can walk on all areas of the land. Cycle trail 91 runs right past Vodrup Klint, so it is often a stopover for bikers.

The route continues west to Bregninge and **Bregninge Kirke,** originally a 13th-century building with grandiose vaults that were added during the latter 15th century. Its impressive spire shows the influence of East Schleswig (Germany) building traditions, and is roofed with oak tiles. The murals inside date from circa 1510—one, for example, depicts the Passion of Christ, another the life of John the Baptist. The magnificent triptych dates from shortly before the Reformation, and was made by Claus Berg. The crucifix in the nave is from the latter Middle Ages, and the 1612 pulpit was executed in the Renaissance style.

After your visit along the southern part of Ærø, you can continue northwest into Søby (see below).

ÆRØSKØBING

The neat little village of ❂ **Ærøskøbing** is a 13th-century market town, which came to be known as a skippers' town in the 17th century. Called "a Lilliputian souvenir of the past," with its small gingerbread houses, intricately carved wooden doors, and cast-iron lamps, few Scandinavian towns have retained their heritage as much as Ærøskøbing. In the heyday of the windjammer, nearly 100 commercial sailing ships made Ærøskøbing their home port.

Lying in the middle of the island, the town looks as if it were laid out by Walt Disney—in fact, it's often known as "the fairlytale town" because it looks more like a movie set than a real town. Filled with cobblestone streets, hollyhocks, and beautifully painted doors and windows, the town itself is far more interesting to wander and explore at random than are any of its minor attractions.

During the summer its shops, cafes, and restaurants are bustling with life. At the old market square you can still see the pumps that supplied the town with its water until 1952, and they are still in working order.

The marina and nearby beach are ideal spots for enjoying outdoors activities. At the end of a busy day, we suggest you stroll over to the Vesterstrand where the sunset (in our view) is the most romantic and evocative in all of Denmark.

The town of Ærøskøbing was founded in the 12th century, and it was granted town privileges in 1522 on orders of King Christian II. As visitors wander through the town, many wonder why the houses are still original and weren't torn down to make way for modern structures. The main reasons were the hard times and poverty that prevented many citizens from tearing down their old structures and rebuilding. However, when prosperity did come, the locals realized their old buildings were a treasure, so instead of tearing them down they restored them—and they're waiting for you to see them today. Preservation societies are particularly strong on the island.

ESSENTIALS

VISITORS INFORMATION   **Ærøskøbing Turistbureau,** Vestergade 1 (☎ **62-52-13-00**), is open from June 15 to August 31 Monday to Saturday from 9am to 5pm. Off-season hours are Monday to Friday from 9am to 4pm and Saturday 9am to noon.

SEEING THE SIGHTS

Ærøskøbling Kirke, Søndergade 43 (☎ **62-52-11-72**), was built between 1756 and 1758 to replace a rather dilapidated church from the Middle Ages. In the present reconstructed church, the 13th-century font and the pulpit stem from the original structure. They were donated by Duke Philip of Lyksborg in 1634, the year he bought Gråsten County on the island of Ærø. The year before he had inherited the market town of Ærøskøbing and an estate in Voderup. The altarpiece is a copy of Eckersberg's picture hanging in Vor Frue Kirke in Svendborg. The colors selected for the interior of the church, along with the floral motifs, were the creation of Elinar V. Jensen in connection with an extensive restoration project carried out in 1950. The church can be visited every day between 8:30am and 5pm; entrance is free.

Flaskeskibssamlingen, Smedegade 22 (☎ **62-52-29-51**), is a nautical museum. The seafaring life is documented in this museum of Peter Jacobsen's ships in bottles, which represents his life's work. Upon his death in 1960 at the age of 84, this former cook, nicknamed "Bottle Peter," had crafted more than 1,600 bottled ships and some 150 model sailing vessels built to scale, earning him the reputation in Ærøskøbing of "the ancient mariner." The museum also has Ærø clocks, furniture, china, and carved works by sculptor H. C. Petersen. Admission is 25 DKK ($3.60) for adults, 10 DKK ($1.45) for children; open daily 10am to 5pm.

Ærø Museum, Brogade 35 (☎ 62-52-29-50), is the best local museum, found at the corner of Nørregade and Brogade. In the old days it was inhabited by the bailiff, but today you'll find a rich collection of the island's past. The collection includes antiques and paintings from the mid-1800s. It is open Tuesday to Sunday from June 13 to August 23 from 10am to 4pm. Off-season hours are Tuesday to Sunday from 10am to 1pm. Admission is 10 DKK ($1.45).

Of minor interest, **Hammerichs Hus,** Gyden 22 (☎ 62-52-27-54), stands on the corner of Brogade and Gyden. It was the home of sculptor Genner Hammerich and is now a museum with a collection of his art and tiles. The half-timbered house also has a collection of period furnishings, antiques, and china, all gathered by the artist in the hamlets of Funen and Jutland. In one of the rooms you'll find a pair of porcelain dogs, which were brought home from England by sailors. Once, prostitutes placed these dogs on their window sills. If the dogs faced each other, callers were welcome as it signaled that the coast was clear, meaning a previous customer had cleared out. Since prostitutes were not allowed to charge for their favors, they sold the dogs to their customers as payment. It is said that the North Sea is paved with porcelain dogs that the sailors did not dare bring home. It is open Wednesday to Monday 11am to 3pm June through August. Admission is 10 DKK ($1.45).

SHOPPING

Shopping options in Ærøskøbing blossom like flowers in summer, but are greatly reduced after the crush of seasonal tourist retreats. Two particularly worthwhile options that remain open most of the year include **Ærøskøbing Antiks,** Vestergade 60 (☎ 62-52-10-32), which sells a remarkable collection of antiques, many of them nautical in their inspiration, and some of them imported during the great days of Ærø's maritime heyday from faraway St. Petersburg, Estonia, or northeastern Germany. Gift items, souvenirs of Ærø, newspapers, and books in Danish, German, and English are available from **Creutz Boghanel,** Vestergade 47 (☎ 62-52-10-22). And in addition to those year-round staples, some of the best shopping is available simply by wandering among the seasonal kiosks and boutiques that line either side of the Søndergade and the Vestergade, the town's main shopping emporiums.

WHERE TO STAY

Det Lille Hotel. Smedegate 33, DK-5970 Ærøskøbing. ☎ 62-52-23-00. 6 units, none with bath. 550 DKK ($79.75) double. Rates include breakfast. No credit cards.

Lying 100 yards from the ferry and harbor, Det Lille Hotel began its life in 1844 as a private home. Today you can rent simple but cozy bedrooms. Open year-round, the hotel is also a good dining choice, serving meals daily from 11:30am to 2pm and 6 to 9pm. You can sample such dishes as asparagus soup, pork chops with vegetables, ham cutlets with mushrooms, beef steaks, fried chicken, and hash.

Hotel Ærøhus. Vestergade 38, DK-5970 Ærøskøbing. ☎ 62-52-10-03. Fax 62-52-21-23. 70 units, 55 with bath. MINIBAR TV TEL. 460 DKK ($66.70) double without bath, 700 DKK ($101.50) double with bath. Rates include breakfast. AE, DC, MC, V. Closed Dec 24–Feb 1.

Painted in a salmon pink, this typical Danish inn has a tile roof and black half-timbers. Dormer windows peer like eyes from its steeply pitched roof. Inside it's charming, with many traditional features, such as copper kettles hanging from the ceiling and warm lamps glowing. The bedrooms are traditional—vaguely French boudoir–style—although they've been modernized. You can also enjoy good Danish meals here. In summer there's dining in the large garden. The hotel, a 3-minute walk from the harbor, offers live music on summer weekends.

NEARBY ACCOMMODATIONS

Vindeballe Kro. Vindeballe Vej 1. DK-5970 Ærøskøbing. ☎ **62-52-16-13.** Fax 62-52-23-49. 6 units (none with bath). 350 DKK ($50.75) double. Rate includes breakfast. MC, V.

This charming country inn, built in 1888, is located on the road between Søby and Marstal, 2½ miles south of the old town of Ærøskøbing and is close to the sea. Rooms are without frills, but comfortable, and guests share the lounge, which has a TV. The inn also has a simple restaurant (see "Where to Dine," below). Non-residents can drop in for a well-prepared meal daily from noon to 2pm and 6 to 9pm.

WHERE TO DINE

Ærøskøbing Røgeri. Havnen 15. ☎ **62-52-40-07.** Platters 16–52 DKK ($2.30–$7.55). No credit cards. Daily 10am–6pm (till 7pm from mid-June to mid-August). Closed Sept–Apr. SMOKED FISH.

The setting is anything but glamorous, and the food you order will be served on paper plates with plastic knives and forks. And if you're looking for wine to accompany your meal, forget it, as the beverage of choice is beer. But despite those drawbacks, this is one of the most popular places in town, a culinary landmark that nearly everyone describes with nostalgia and affection. Set within a raffish-looking house built in the old Ærø style beside the harbor, it serves only fresh fish that has been smoked (usually that morning) in electric and wood-fired ovens on the premises. You'll specify what kind of fish you want (salmon, herring, fillet or whole mackerel, trout, or shrimp) and which of a half-dozen seasonings you want (dill, parsley, pepper, paprika, garlic, or "provençal"), then you carry your plate to outdoor seating overlooking the harbor, or haul it back to wherever you're staying for consumption later. The most expensive thing on the menu is a slab of fresh-smoked salmon accompanied with bread, butter, and a portion of potato salad; the least expensive is a make-it-yourself *smørrebrød* that includes a smoked herring, a slice of rough-textured bread, and fresh Danish butter.

Restaurant Mumm. Søndergade 12. ☎ **62-52-12-12.** Main courses 115–170 DKK ($16.65–$24.65). AE, DC, MC, V. June–Aug 15 daily 11:30am–2:30pm and 6–9:30pm; May and Sept Tues–Sun 11:30am–2:30pm and 6–9:30pm. Closed Oct–Apr. AMERICAN/INTERNATIONAL.

In a simple house whose foundation dates from 1780, this restaurant enjoys a reputation for well-prepared dishes that sometimes carry a North American (or at least an international) flavor. Inside, you'll find a pair of dining rooms; the less formal one offers a view into a very busy kitchen. There's also a terrace set up in the garden in back, where parasols and candles usually adorn the outdoor tables. The restaurant offers an unusual combination of American-and-Danish-style dishes (a former owner had been a chef at a Florida resort). There's a copious salad buffet, well-flavored steaks, and an abundance of seafood (most of which comes directly from local waters), including fillet of plaice, grilled salmon with hollandaise sauce, sole in parley-butter sauce, mussels in wine sauce, and various preparations of shrimp and snails.

Restaurant Pilebækken. Vestergade 55. ☎ **62-52-19-91.** Reservations recommended. Main courses 74–148 DKK ($10.75–$21.45.) AE. Thurs–Mon 6–9pm. Closed Mid-Sept to Apr. DANISH.

Small, charming, and authentically Danish, this restaurant is set in a house that hasn't changed much since 1900, and whose infrastructure dates from around 1701. Inside, you'll find a menu with new, mostly Danish, items that are added and deleted every day, as well as an ongoing roster of dishes, such as herring platters and fried beef with onions and herbs, that remain constant throughout the summer. Especially worth-while are fillets of plaice stuffed with shrimp and asparagus, chicken breasts with mushrooms and cream sauce, and platters of smoked whitefish with horseradish.

NEARBY DINING

Vindeballe Kro. Vindeballe Vej 1, Vindegballe. ☎ **62-52-16-13.** Reservations recommended. Main courses 68–184 DKK ($9.85–$26.70). MC, V. Daily 11am–2:30pm and 6–9pm. From Ærøskøbing, drive 2 ½-miles south, following the road signs to Søby. DANISH.

This is the restaurant that's associated with the previously recommended guesthouse (see above), whose half-dozen simple bedrooms occupy a late 19th-century farmhouse and inn near the geographic center of the island. The restaurant is better-known, and better-recommended by local residents, than the hotel section of this place, especially since it's one of the few die-hard eateries that's open year-round, even after the hordes of tourists go home for the winter. There's room for only about 30 diners at a time, who occupy the violet-and-cream-colored dining room whose paneling evokes old-fashioned Ærø of long ago. Menu items include "flat fish" (a form of plaice) with parsley and butter sauce; Danish beef that's fried with onions; beef tenderloin with baked potatoes; veal Schnitzels fried in butter; pan-fried eel (a specialty of Ærø) served with potatoes; turkey steak with gorgonzola sauce; and grilled steaks with your choice of béarnaise, tomato, or Mexican-style sauce. Some of the tables are arranged around a bar that attracts a local clientele that's separate from that of the restaurant.

ÆRØSKØBING AFTER DARK

In summertime, you'll find sidewalk cafes and bars that come and go with the seasons (and which sometimes don't return the following year) along either side of the Vester-gade and the Søndergade. One of the most reliable and enduring of these seasonal joints is the **Café Andelen,** Søndergade 28A (☎ **62-52-17-11**), which presents live jazz that begins around 9pm most nights between June and August. Two year-round pubs that tend to be favored by local residents and fishers are **Aarebo Pub,** Vestergade 4 (☎ **62-52-28-50**), which offers some kind of live music every Friday and Saturday throughout the year, and its nearby competitor, **Landborgården Pub,** Vestergade 54 (☎ **62-52-10-41**), which is a site just for drinking and socializing.

MARSTAL

Marstal, a thriving little port on the east coast of Ærø, has had a reputation in sailor's circles since the days of the tall ships. The harbor, protected by a granite jetty, is still busy, with a shipyard producing steel and wooden vessels, an engine factory, a ferry terminal, and one of Denmark's biggest yacht basins. The street names of Marstal attest to its seafaring background: Skonnertvej, Barkvej, and Galeasevej (Schooner, Bark, and Ketch roads).

ESSENTIALS

VISITOR INFORMATION   The Marstal Turistbureau, Havengade 5 (☎ **62-53-19-60**), a 5-minute walk south of the harbor, is open from mid-June to August Monday to Friday from 10am to 5pm and on Saturday from 10am to 3pm. In July, the peak month to visit Ærø, it is also open Sunday 10am to noon. Off-season hours are Monday to Friday 9am to 4pm.

SEEING THE SIGHTS

Maren Minors Minde. Teglgade 9. ☎ **62-53-23-31.** Admission 5 DKK (75¢) adults, 2 DKK (30¢) children. Daily 11am–3pm. Closed Sept to mid-June.

This is the once-prosperous, once-private home of a successful sea captain, Rasmus Minor, whose other bequests to Ærø included an orphanage and a retirement home. In the 1950s his widow, Maren Minor, willed the house and its collection of nautical artifacts to the municipality as a museum.

Marstal Søfartsmuseum. Prinsensgade 1. ☎ **62-53-23-31.** Admission 20 DKK ($2.90) adults, 10 DKK ($1.45) children. Oct–Apr Tues–Fri 10am–4pm, May and Sept daily 10am–4pm; June and Aug daily 9am–5pm, July daily 9am–9pm.

This museum contains collections of ship models, old maritime equipment, objets d'art, and junk brought home by sailors from foreign shores. It's only of passing interest.

Marstal Kirke. Kirkestrade 14. ☎ **62-53-10-38.** Free admission. Daily 9am–5pm.

Built in 1738, the church was enlarged twice—once in 1772 by adding an extension and later in 1920 with a tower to commemorate the reunification of Southern Jutland with Denmark. Seven votive ships inside indicate the growth of shipping in the town from the 18th up to the 20th century, and the town's close links to the sea. The front dates from the Middle Ages. The blue color of the benches symbolizes the sea and eternity, whereas the red colors of the altar and pulpit are supposed to evoke the blood shed by Christ. Red is also the color of love. The altarpiece from 1881 was painted by Carl Rasmussen, a maritime artist who usually specialized in the motifs of Greenland. It depicts Christ stilling a storm. In the old churchyard are memorials and tombstones honoring the sailors of Marstal who died at sea during two world wars.

Finally, in summer, consider a side trip to **Birkholm Island** lying offshore. It is ideal for exploring, relaxing, and swimming. Twice a day a mail boat takes a limited number of passengers on this 45-minute trip from Marstal. Except for service and utility vehicles, there are no cars allowed on the island. For information and reservations, you can contact the captain of the mail boat, Gustav Gensen, at ☎ **62-54-17-77.** The price of round-trip passage from Marstal to Birkholm Island is 110 DKK ($15.95).

SHOPPING   Marstal's most densely inventoried shopping streets are the Kirkestræde (which is transformed into an all-pedestrian walkway during July and August) and Kongengade. Many of the boutiques and kiosks that flourish there during midsummer disappear altogether the rest of the year, so the best way to appreciate the shopping scene involves spontaneously dropping in and out of boutiques as they catch your fancy. The best, and more enduring, venue for souvenirs from Ærø and the rest of Denmark is Emerto, Kirkestræde 10 (% 62-53-13-91). Its owner, Bille Knusen, accumulates porcelain, crystal, woodcarvings, nautical memorabilia, and pots and pans into an all-inclusive emporium. Nearby is Fruhøst, Kongensgade 22 (☎ **62-53-24-09**), a store specializing in odd bits of handmade paraphernalia that for the most part are made on Ærø. Inside, owner Elizabeth Jørgensen sells weavings, homemade wine, homemade chocolates, candles, and bric-a-brac.

WHERE TO STAY

Ærø Kongreshotel. Egehovedvej 4, DK-5960 Marstal. ☎ **62-53-33-20.** Fax 62-53-31-50. 100 units. TV TEL. 650 DKK ($94.25) double; 870 DKK ($126.15) suite. Rates include breakfast. DC, MC, V. Closed Dec 18–Jan 2. Bus: 990 to Marstal.

A 5-minute walk south of the center of town and a quarter mile from the beach, this hotel, opened in 1989, is the largest and most up-to-date on the island. Set in a windswept landscape of seagrass and sweeping vistas, the rooms are first class, decorated in pastel colors, with all the amenities such as private baths. The suites are twice the size of regular rooms. There's an excellent restaurant, Østersøen, and one bar.

Hotel Marstal. Droningstraede 1A, DK-5960 Marstal. ☎ **62-53-13-52.** 7 units (none with bath). 375 DKK ($54.35) double. Rates include breakfast. MC, V.

This old-fashioned hotel offers clean but functionally furnished bedrooms in a very regional atmosphere. In the town center, 2 minutes from the harbor, it contains medium-sized bedrooms with large windows and dark paneling. Two rooms opening onto a view of the sea are the most frequently requested. Baths are a bit small, but mattresses are firm. Towels are a bit skimpy, but the price is so fair there are few complaints. The good news is that the hotel operates one of the most reliable restaurants in town. You may want to patronize it even if you aren't a guest. See "Where to Dine," below.

WHERE TO DINE

Den Gamle Vingård. Skolegade 15. ☎ **62-53-13-25.** Reservations recommended. Pizzas and pastas 50–63 DKK ($7.25–$9.15); main courses 80–135 DKK ($11.60–$19.60). No credit cards. May and Sept daily 5–10pm. June–Aug noon–10pm. Closed Oct–Apr. DANISH.

On the main square (Torvet) of Marstal, this restaurant is set within a relatively new building, despite the fact that its name translates as "the old vineyard." It is, nonetheless, one of the best restaurants in Marstal, with a décor that includes engravings and oil paintings of antique ships and lots of woodsy-looking memorabilia of old Ærø. Your meal might consist of something as simple as a pasta or pizza, or more substantial fare, which would include steaks, veal, chicken, fried fillets of pork, or any of a half-dozen kinds of fresh fish. Each of these is prepared with firm guidance from the kitchen as to the sauce or preparation best suited to their individual flavors: Salmon, for example, is grilled and accompanied with an herb and butter sauce; herring is best either marinated, or fried and served with a lime-vinegar sauce. Plaice, depending on the mood of the chef, might be stuffed with shrimp and asparagus.

The Restaurant in the Hotel Marstal. Dronningestræde 1A. ☎ **62-53-13-52.** Reservations recommended. Main courses 110–148 DKK ($15.95–$21.45). AE, MC, V. Daily noon–2pm and 5:45–11pm. STEAKS/SEAFOOD.

One of the best restaurants in town is this dark-toned replica of an English pub, where lots of varnished paneling, tones of brown and forest green, flickering candles, and nautical accessories contribute to a general coziness at all times of the year. There's lots of beer on tap, and a menu that focuses on grilled steaks, some of them with pepper sauce; veal Cordon Bleu; and fresh seafood that might have arrived that morning from local fishers. Especially flavorful are any of the beef dishes, or the grilled salmon steak with potatoes, asparagus, and either a lemon-butter or hollandaise sauce.

MARSTAL AFTER DARK

Two of our favorite pubs on Marstal include **Toldbohus,** Prinsensgade 7 (☎ **62-53-15-41**), which opens every day at 8am and which transforms itself from a cafe into a bar and pub as the day progresses; and **Lanternen,** Straandstræde 45 (☎ **62-53-19-20**), which opens around 2pm.

South Jutland 10

South Jutland (Jylland in Danish) is part of the larger landmass of Jutland, connected to the mainland of Europe, with Germany its immediate neighbor to the south. This landmass is part of the general Jutland peninsula that is dotted with heather-covered moors, fjords, farmlands, lakes, and sand dunes. The mainland of Jutland opens onto the North Sea, and it's 250 miles from the northern tip of Jutland to the German frontier. The North Sea washes up on miles of sandy beaches, making this a favorite holiday place.

The meadows of Jutland are filled with rich bird life and winding rivers. Nature walks are possible in almost all directions. Gabled houses in the marshlands of South Jutland add to the peninsula's charm. Two of the most popular vacation islands are Rømø and Fanø, off of the southwestern coast. Here many traditional homes of fishermen and sea captains have been preserved. Of all the towns of South Jutland, none has more particular appeal and charm for the tourist than Ribe, fabled for its storks' nests.

The Little Belt Bridge at Middlefart connects the island of Funen with the mainland of Jutland.

You can do as the Danes do and go cycling through the countryside of South Jutland, which is crisscrossed by a fine network of cycle paths. Stop in at one of the tourist offices and pick up a detailed map of the region, which often outlines the best paths for cycling.

A dike evocative of the Netherlands stretches along the coast of southwest Jutland. It was built to protect the land here from the tempestuous North Sea. Nature lovers flock here to enjoy walks along the Wadden Sea, and at low tide they can even explore the sea-bed itself. You can also cycle along the dike, but the westerly winds make this a difficult run.

Some of the finest beaches in Northern Europe are found in South Jutland, especially on the island of Rømø (see below). When the winds blow, these long beaches are ideal for kite-flying.

In the little villages and towns, the past meets the present, as you walk along narrow, cobbled streets, admiring the half-timbered houses that look as if they've stepped intact from a Hans Christian Andersen fairytale. To experience an authentically Danish meal, order the traditional lunch of pickled herring, rye bread, and schnapps.

There are many museums of local history, showing you how life was lived long before you arrived. Many of these museums include workshops where artisans still practice the old crafts—for example, the lace making that made Tønder famous in the 18th century.

Mainly, South Jutland is a place to go to recharge your batteries.

1 Kolding

208km (130 miles) SW of Copenhagen; 91km (57 miles) E of Esbjerg; 81$^1/_2$ km (51 miles) N of the German border; 69$^1/_2$ km (43$^1/_2$ miles) SW of Århus

The lively port of Kolding in the east is the gateway to South Jutland. Nestled on a fjord of the same name, Kolding dates from 1321. Several roads converged here in the Middle Ages, and in 1248 the crown ordered that Koldinghus Slot be erected here. It was torn down and rebuilt several times over the centuries. In wars against Schleswig-Holstein, Kolding was occupied by German troops, but the Treaty of Vienna in 1864 put the town clearly in Danish hands.

Today, Kolding, a city of some 60,000 people, is the fifth largest city of Jutland. The town continues its role as Denmark's largest cattle exporter, and has a number of prosperous industries, including engineering, iron, and textiles.

ESSENTIALS

GETTING THERE   Trains run frequently between Kolding and Padborg on the northern German border (trip time: 70 minutes). Frequent trains also arrive from Frederikshavn in the north of Jutland, taking 4 hours. Trains also cut across Jutland, reaching Esbjerg (see below) in the west in just under an hour.

By Car   After taking the bridge from Funen in the east, follow Route 161 into Kolding. If you're already in West Jutland, perhaps in Esbjerg, you can cut across Jutland along motorway E20 until you reach Kolding as you near the east coast.

VISITOR INFORMATION   Kolding Tourist Information, Akseltorv 8 (☎ **76-33-21-00**), is open Monday to Friday 9:30am to 5:30pm and Saturday 9:30am to 1pm. On the first Saturday of every month hours are extended to 9:30am to 3pm. From June 15 to August 31, Saturday hours are 9:30am to 4:30pm.

SEEING THE SIGHTS

Kolding Fjord attracts anglers, swimmers, and boaters, and **Kolding Marina** is one of the largest in Denmark. The fjord is also lined with beaches with plenty of recreational areas.

The town's major sight remains its castle, **Koldinghus Slot,** in the center of town (☎ **75-50-15-00**), lying immediately to the north of Akseltorv. King Erik V ordered that a fortress be built on this site in 1268 to protect Danish interests against the Duchy of Schleswig to the south. Christian IV spent much of his boyhood here, adding a landmark tower around 1600. Over the years the castle was attacked and destroyed many times. The oldest parts of the present building that still remain are from around the mid–15th century. In 1808, Denmark was allied with France under Napoléon Bonaparte. Napoléon commanded Spanish troops because his brother occupied the Spanish throne, and at the time Spanish soldiers were billeted in Koldinghus Slot. The Spanish soldiers, not used to Danish winters, built a roaring fire that not only kept them warm, but set the castle on fire.

Until 1890 the castle was left in ruins. A north wing was restored to house a museum. Reconstruction continued very slowly over much of the 20th century, with the Christian IV tower restored by 1935. Today the castle shelters a Historical and Cultural Museum, with exhibitions tracing the town's history. The exterior has a baroque façade evocative of the 18th century. The castle is rich in Romanesque and Gothic sculptures, plus such handcrafted articles as silver, stoneware, and porcelain. A special exhibit documents the wars against Prussia in 1848–50 and 1864. Special exhibitions, theatrical and operatic performances, along with classical concerts, are held in

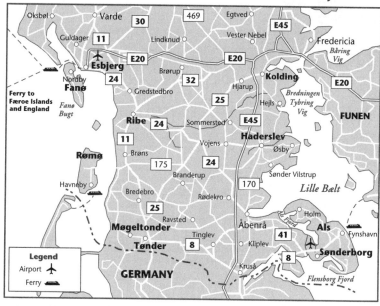

the great hall and courtyard. From the top of the tower there are panoramic views over the town and surrounding area. Hours are daily 10am to 5pm, adults paying 40 DKK ($5.80), although children under 16 are admitted free.

Equally intriguing as the castle is the ✪ **Kunstmuseet Trapholt,** Æblehaven 23 (☎ **75-54-24-22**), reached by bus no. 4 from the center of the city. On the eastern periphery of Kolding, it opens onto the north side of Kolding Fjord. In a park and launched in 1988, it is home to a vast collection of contemporary Danish paintings and applied art, such as textiles, design, and ceramics. Its angular glass walls and shrill white interiors flood the art with natural light. You'll see works by such artists as Egill Jacobsen, Anna Archer, and Richard Mortensen. Trapholt also houses a Museum of Furniture opened in 1996 and dedicated to modern Danish furniture design. Furniture from as far back as 1900 is exhibited, but the collection is centered mainly around some of the biggest names in Danish design, including Arne Jacobsen, Finn Juhl, Poul Kjærholm, Mogens Koch, Børge Morgensen, and Hans J. Wegner. From May to September the museum is open daily 10am to 5pm. During other months hours are Monday to Friday noon to 4pm and Saturday and Sunday 10am to 4pm. Admission is 30 DKK ($4.35); children under age 16 free.

Also worth a visit is ✪ **Geografsisk Have og Rosehave** (Geographical Garden), at Chr. d. 4 Vej (☎ **75-50-38-80**), reached by bus no. 2 from the town center. This garden on the southern periphery of town was laid out by Axel Olsen, the owner of a local tree nursery. Today it has some 2,000 species of trees and shrubs from all over the globe, including North and South America, and even Burma. It gets its name because it was designed on geographical lines. It is home to the longest bamboo grove in Northern Europe. You can also enjoy a picnic lunch outdoors or in one of the on-site garden pavilions. The gardens are open April to September daily from 10am to 6pm. During other months, hours are Monday to Friday 8am to 2:30pm, Saturday and Sunday 8am to 5pm. Admission is 30 DKK ($4.35) adults, 15 DKK ($2.15) children ages 12–16; free for children age 11 and under.

SHOPPING

There is a network of pedestrian streets flanked with shops in the town center. On Tuesday and Friday from 7am to 1pm there is an open-air market at Akseltorv where traders sell flowers, fruit, vegetables, cheese, fish, and much more.

One of the largest shopping malls in Denmark, **Kolding Storcenter,** Skovbrybnet (☎ **75-50-74-88**), lies 2 ½-miles north of Kolding's center. (To reach it, follow the signs to Vejle from the town center.) Home to some 60 shops, and entirely enclosed in one climate-controlled complex, it was built in 1993 and attracts an astonishing 80,000 visitors a week. In a style that might remind you of a mega-mall in California, it's especially crowded whenever it's raining, when hundreds of local residents seem to come here just to hang out.

Another intriguing shopping possibility is the **Kolding Antiques & Stall Market** held at Haderslevvej and Sdr. Ringvej on Saturday and Sunday from 10am to 5pm.

Visitors can make their own candles by dropping in at **Klintenborg Candlemaker,** Stubdrupvej 98, Harte (☎ **75-53-70-11**). As noted, Kolding is a center of textiles. You can visit the best textile shop—part of a mill—by going to **Damaskvæveriest,** Dieselvej 1 (☎ **75-52-27-00**). You must arrive Monday to Friday from 9am to 5pm. Since this is on the outskirts, you can take bus no. 3 to reach it.

The best art galleries in town are **Galleri Elise Toft,** Låsbygade 58 (☎ **75-50-78-55**), and **Galleri Pagter,** Adelgade 3 (☎ **75-54-09-30**).

WHERE TO STAY

✪ **Hotel Koldingfjord.** Fjordvej 154, Strandhuse, DK-6000 Kolding. ☎ **75-51-00-00.** Fax 75-51-00-51. 115 units. MINIBAR TV TEL. 675–1,265 DKK ($97.90–$183.40) double. AE, DC, MC, V. From Kolding, follow the signs to the E45 highway, then (before you reach it), detour northward along the Lushojalle and drive 2 miles.

Set on the opposite bank of the Kolding Fjord, a 3-mile drive from the center, this is one of the most ostentatiously grandiose buildings in the region. It originated in 1903, when the postmaster general of Denmark initiated a charity drive to raise money, through the sale of Christmas seals, for the construction of a sanatorium for tubercular children. In 1911, a neoclassical palace reminiscent of something occupied by a member of the royal family was erected on 50 acres of forested land adjacent to the Kolding Fjord in an area noted for its pure air. After a long stint as a hospital and a boarding school, the site was transformed in 1988 into a comfortable hotel that's today noted as one of the most appealing in the region. Bedrooms are more contemporary-looking than the building's stately façade would imply, each with streamlined and comfortably unfussy furnishings and a scattering of reproductions of modern paintings. They're scattered between the main building and three of its original outbuildings. Also on the premises are a brand new, very large, state-of-the-art convention center, an indoor pool, a sauna, solarium, pool room, and outdoor tennis court. The in-house restaurant is recommended separately in "Where to Dine."

Hotel Scanicon Comwell. Skovbrynet 1, DK-6000 Kolding. ☎ **75-50-15-55.** Fax 75-50-15-68. 160 units. TV TEL. 900–1,085 DKK ($130.50–$157.30) double. Rate includes breakfast. AE, DC, MC, V. Bus: 1, 5, or 6.

The newest hotel within the city limits opened in the late 1980s, about a mile northwest of the center, adjacent to a small lake. It was deliberately designed in a low-rise (three-story) format that doesn't protrude too obviously above the residential neighborhood around it. The place is saturated with contemporary Danish design, sophisticated (usually halogen) lighting, exposed and varnished pinewood trim with touches of brass, big windows, and, at least within the public rooms, a stylish kind of minimalism. Bedrooms aren't particularly spacious, but are comfortable, bright, cheerful, and well-maintained, always with touches of laminated pine and usually primary colors of blue, soft reds, and yellows. Amenities include such features as a wood-burning fireplace within one of the public lounges, an indoor pool with its own sauna and fitness room, and a billiard table. The hotel's restaurant, La Cocotte, is separately recommended in "Where to Dine."

Hotel Tre Roser. Byparken, DK-6000 Kolding. ☎ **75-53-21-22.** Fax 75-50-40-64. 95 units. TV TEL. 725 DKK ($105.10) double. AE, DC, MC, V.

The one-story design of this early 1970s hotel might remind you of an American-style motel more than any other accommodation in town. Bordered by one of Kolding's public parks on one side and by a group of quiet private homes on the other, it affords a chance to relax within calm, quiet surroundings that seem very far from the urban world. Bedrooms are comfortable but anonymous-looking, outfitted with contemporary Danish furnishings and accessories. On the premises are an indoor swimming pool, health club, sauna, and solarium. There's also a steakhouse-style restaurant staffed by chefs in toque hats, plus a bar.

Kolding Byferie. Kedelsmedgangen 2, DK-6000 Kolding. ☎ **75-54-18-00.** Fax 75-54-18-02. 85 apts., each with kitchenette. TV TEL. Three nights stay, double occupancy 1,195–1,895 DKK ($173.25–$274.75); three nights stay for four occupants 1,395–2,495 DKK ($202.25–$361.80). Three night minimum stay is required in any season. AE, DC, MC, V.

One of the most unusual hotels in the district sits at the edge of the water, within a roughly defined "amphitheater" created by the other, older buildings of the town center surrounding it. The hotel consists of at least 15 very modern, cement-and-glass buildings, each erected in 1994, and each shaped into a different whimsical form. From the top, looking down, their shapes include squares, rectangles, octagons, circles, stars, and in some cases, free-form units with angular sides. The result is an award-winning compound that has excited great interest in architectural circles throughout Denmark, and which provides unusual floor plans for occupants who are required to pay for a minimum stay of at least three nights. This is not a particular hardship since you can be based here and explore nearly all of Jutland using Kolding as your center. None of the units has a private veranda, but since the oversized windows of each unit slide open, occupants get the idea that their entire unit can be transformed into an outdoor terrace at will. Furnishings inside are simple, angular, and virtually indestructible, and as such, are often occupied by families with children. There are very few amenities (i.e., no restaurant, bar, pool, or sauna) on the premises, but the dining, drinking, and public sports facilities of Kolding lie within a short walk, and the staff is well-versed in providing ideas on how and where clients might want to spend their free time.

Scandic Hotel. Kokholm, DK-6000 Kolding. ☎ **75-51-77-00.** Fax 75-51-77-01. 120 units. TV TEL. Mon–Thurs 1,125 DKK ($163.15) double; Fri–Sun 650 DKK ($94.25) double. Rate includes breakfast. AE, DC, MC, V. From the E45 highway, 4-miles north of Kolding, the hotel lies adjacent to Exit 63.

Its brochures refer to it as "the gem of the motorway," and while that might not exactly thrill your sense of adventure, it accurately reflects this hotel's role as a provider of clean, safe, predictable lodgings that are convenient for motorists. Built in the early 1980s, the hotel rises six floors in a design that's repeated by other members of its chain throughout Scandinavia. Bedrooms are clean, well-maintained, comfortable, and streamlined, with good beds and small but adequate baths. On the premises are a restaurant, bar, solarium, sauna, billiard room, and small health club.

WHERE TO DINE

La Cocotte. In the Hotel Scanicon Comwell, Skovbrynet 1. ☎ **75-50-15-55.** Reservations recommended. Lunch buffet 155 DKK ($22.45) per person. Set-price dinners 300–410 DKK ($43.50–$59.45). Main courses 160–210 DKK ($23.20–$30.45). AE, DC, MC, V. Daily noon–10pm. Buffet daily noon–2pm. Bus: 1, 5, or 6. DANISH/FRENCH.

The only drawback to this well-orchestrated restaurant is its lack of a view over the nearby lake. Other than that, the place is cozy, inviting, and warmly appealing thanks to well-prepared food, a copious lunchtime buffet (the best in town), and a medley of striking contemporary oil paintings that are dramatically lit from above. The buffet includes an all-Danish medley of hot and cold dishes that feature *frikadeller* (meatballs), many different preparations of herring, salads, casseroles, an impressive collection of fresh-baked breads, and an artful medley of Danish and European cheeses. A la carte dishes change with the seasons and the inspiration of the chef, but are likely to include such choices as Dover sole *meunière;* tournedos of beef with onions and a *confit* of sweet peppers; a *ragoût* of angler-fish with scallops and fresh vegetables; and North Sea turbot with white asparagus stalks, baby cabbage, and a reduction of fresh tomatoes.

Hotel Koldingfjord. Fjordvej 154, Strandhuse. ☎ **75-51-00-00.** Reservations recommended. Main courses 135–225 DKK ($19.60–$32.65). AE, DC, MC, V. Daily noon–2pm and 6–10:30pm. From Kolding, follow the signs to the E45 highway, then (before you reach it), detour northward along the Lushojalle and drive 2 miles. DANISH/CONTINENTAL.

Set within one of the high-ceilinged and formal reception rooms of the previously recommended hotel, this is one of the most appealing restaurants in Kolding. Food is well-prepared, but an experience here has the added benefit of a view over the fjord and an insight into the charitable origins of one of the grandest buildings in the region. Menu items change with the seasons, but might include a garden salad garnished with lobster and fresh asparagus, warm salmon pudding with spinach, crabmeat bouillon with fresh tomatoes, fillet of monkfish with either citrus sauce or *beurre blanc* (white butter), gratin of fresh tuna with a ragoût of fish roe and tomatoes, and a seasonal dessert specialty consisting of a medley of summer berries with freshly made vanilla cream.

KOLDING AFTER DARK

Three after-dark sites compete with one another for the title of most popular nightlife option in Kolding. They include the **English Pub,** A.L. Passagen (☎ 75-50-80-44), which opens at 10am and serves hundreds of pints of English and Danish beer every night until closing around midnight. Equally popular, but with shorter hours, is the **Crazy Daisy,** Jernbanegade (☎ 75-54-16-88), a pub and disco that's open for drinking every night from 9pm till midnight, and which functions as a disco every Tuesday, Friday, and Saturday night from 9pm till around 4am. A fashionable venue that combines hi-tech decor with food service and occasional bouts of live jazz is the **Blue Café,** Lilletorv (☎ 75-50-65-12). Light platters of simple food are served daily from 10am till around 9:30pm; cappuccino, wine, beer, and schnapps are available every day till at least midnight, and sometimes later, depending on the crowd.

EASY EXCURSIONS FROM KOLDING

Directly to the south of Kolding, a distance of 5 ½ miles (to reach it from Kolding, follow the signs pointing to Christiansfeldt), is one of the most powerful but understated monuments of Denmark, **Skamilingsbanken.** A rolling hill that rises to a height of 370 feet, it commemorates the survival of the Danish language and the Danish nation against German incursions throughout the centuries. Its location marks the frontier between Denmark and North Schleswig, a hotly contested territory that was bounced around between Germany and Denmark repeatedly throughout modern times. In 1920, as part of the settlement at the end of World War I, the Danish-German border was moved to a point 51 miles to the south, where it has remained ever since. Today, very few Danes will articulate the reason for the emotionalism associated with this site. (In the words of one tourist official, "Today, we're all part of the European Community and we really don't like to talk about that.") For reasons of tact, since the 1960s, the site has been downplayed within the Danish national psyche, although beginning in 1998, it has been the site of a one-day-a-year concert presented the first Sunday in August, where the Royal Danish Opera travels down from Copenhagen to present operatic works by archetypal German and Danish composers Richard Wagner and Karl Nielsen. The event is free, with further details provided by the tourist office in Kolding (see above).

2 Haderslev

248km (155 miles) SW of Copenhagen; 30^1/$_2$ km (19 miles) S of Kolding; 51km (32 miles) E of Ribe

At the head of the Haderslev Fjord, this appealing town of 32,000 inhabitants is known for having one of the oldest and best preserved historic cores in Denmark. In 1995 it was awarded the Europa Nostra Prize for its old, beautifully restored buildings. In spite of some minor attractions, there is nothing more interesting here than walking through its narrow, cobbled streets with buildings dating back all the way to 1570. As a result of a massive preservation effort launched in 1971 the town of Haderslev looks better than ever.

Although built on the banks of a fjord, Haderslev actually lies 9 ½ miles inland. It has always depended on trade for its livelihood, and by 1292 it already had a city charter. Christian I came here in 1448, signing a charter allowing him to become king of Denmark. Another Christian (this time King Christian IV) came here in 1597 to celebrate his wedding to Anne-Catherine of Brandenburg. From 1864 to as late as 1920 Haderslev was part of the duchy of Schleswig-Holstein and controlled by Prussia. When the Duchy of Schleswig was divided in 1920, Haderslev became part of Denmark.

VISITOR INFORMATION   The **Haderslev Turistbureau,** Honnørkajen (☎ 74-52-55-50), is open from mid-June to August, Monday to Friday 9am to 5pm and on Saturday and Sunday 9:30am to 2:30pm. In the off-season it is open Monday to Friday 9am to 4pm and on Saturday from 9:30am to 12:30pm.

EXPLORING THE AREA

Haderslev is situated in a ✪ **subglacial stream trench** which is 15-miles long and which stretches from the Little Belt to the neighboring town of Vojens. A beautiful landscape has been created by nature. In 1994 Denmark's second largest nature reservation opened south of Haderslev Dam, stocked with fallow deer. Near the reservation, the large marsh area of Hindemade was flooded. Today, the whole area has a rich bird and animal life, and Hindemade has been designated a bird sanctuary by the European Union. You can walk about in the area along the Tunneldal paths, which run through most of the subglacial trench between Haderslev and Vojens.

Back in the center of Haderslev, you can, as mentioned, wander through the town's historic core, an area so well preserved it was voted European town of the year in 1984. The old town grew up around its Domkirke (see below), which stands on high ground. One of the oldest and most interesting houses is at Slotsgade 20, dating from the 16th century. It now houses the **Ehlers-samlingen** (Ehlers Collections), and has been turned into a museum of Danish pottery dating from the medieval era until the beginning of the 20th century. At this point, regional distinctions in Danish pottery began to erode. This is an attractive timber-framed building from 1577 that has preserved many of its original decorative wall panels. You can also see many antique domestic items and some 16th-century wall paintings. The collection can be viewed Tuesday to Sunday from 10am to 5pm and Saturday and Sunday from 2 to 5pm. It is closed on Wednesday and Friday in winter. Admission costs 10 DKK ($1.45) for adults and children. For more information, call ☎ **74-53-08-58.**

✪ **Haderslev Domkirke,** Torvet (☎ **74-52-36-33**), is a redbrick cathedral that's one of the most interesting buildings of its kind in the country. The structure has been entirely whitewashed, enhancing the light coming through the tall windows in the 15th-century chancel. The transept and nave are the most ancient parts of the cathedral, dating from the mid-13th century. Many additions, however, were made over the years. The bronze font is from the late 1400s, and the baroque pulpit was added in 1636. A restored Sieseby organ has a beautifully clear sound, and is played regularly. At the altar you'll see a Romanesque crucifix, probably from the beginning of the 14th century, and statues of Mary and John along with alabaster figures of the Apostles. The church played an important part in the Reformation, becoming the first Lutheran church in the country. A disastrous fire swept over the Domkirke in 1627, destroying much of the building, but the restoration had been completed by 1650. When Haderslev reunited with Denmark in 1920, a new diocese was established, making the Domkirke a true cathedral. Admission is free, and the cathedral is open 10am to 5pm Monday to Saturday (from 11:30am to 5pm on Sunday) from May to September. It is open daily off-season from 10am to 3pm. In August concerts are given on the previously mentioned church organ at 8pm on Tuesday and again at 4:30pm Friday. Know in advance that these days might vary, depending on the availability of performers, so a call in advance to the tourist office might clear up any confusion. The Friday concert is usually free, while admission to the Tuesday concert costs 75 DKK ($10.90) per person.

Half a mile northeast of the Torvet stands the **Haderslev Museum,** Dalgade 7 (☎ **74-52-75-66**). This has one of the peninsula's best collections of archaeological artifacts gathered in the region. There are also local historical exhibitions and reconstructed street scenes, with entire rooms decorated as they would have been in the 19th century. In addition, there is an open-air museum with an old farm, and even a windmill, among other period structures. From June to August hours are Monday to Friday 10am to 5pm and Saturday and Sunday noon to 5pm. Off-season the museum is open Tuesday to Sunday 1 to 4pm. Admission is 15 DKK ($2.15) for adults, free for children age 12 and under.

SHOPPING   Two of the most appealing shops in Haderslev include **Stentebjerg,** Storegade 8 (☎ **74-52-02-09**), which specializes in pottery from the region and from throughout Denmark. For lots of options on how to make your home or apartment look a little more Danish, head for **Stolen,** Møllepladsen 2 (☎ **74-53-33-87**).

WHERE TO STAY

Hotel Harmonien. Gåskærgade 19, DK-6100 Haderslev. ☎ **74-52-37-20.** Fax 74-52-44-51. 28 units. TV TEL. 820 DKK ($118.90). AE, DC, MC, V.

Haderslev's most antique-looking, and most authentically charming hotel lies in the town center, behind a façade that has been painted a soft red for as long as anyone can remember. Originally established in 1844, it was the site of a visit from King Christian VII in the late 19th century, and a full-blown artist's dinner attended by Queen Margrethe II and her family in May of 1998. Although much of the allure of this place derives from the cozy restaurant, which is recommended separately in "Where to Dine" below, its bedrooms are attractively decorated, thanks to an intelligent renovation during a radical overhaul of the historic inn back in the 1970s. Each has uncomplicated but comfortable furnishings, and a sense of the old-time, off-the-beaten-track Europe of long ago. There are virtually no additional facilities or amenities associated with this hotel, but in view of the hotel's sense of history, none of the clients really seem to mind.

Hotel Norden. Storegade 55, DK-6100 Haderslev. ☎ **74-52-40-30.** Fax 74-52-40-25. 67 units. MINIBAR TV TEL. Sept–June 950 DKK ($137.75) double; July–Aug 700 DKK ($101.50) double. Rate includes breakfast. AE, DC, MC, V.

This is the biggest, best-accessorized, and newest hotel in Haderslev, large enough to accommodate many corporate conventions, and even the occasional tour bus making stops at historic sites throughout Jutland. Within a three-story, white-fronted building a 5-minute walk north of the town center, you'll find a well-trained staff, and clean, comfortable accommodations that are outfitted with touches of varnished pine and a neutral, Danish modern style that's equivalent to what you might have expected in Copenhagen. On the premises is a swimming pool, sauna, exercise room, cafe and bar, and a restaurant that's recommended separately in "Where to Dine."

WHERE TO DINE

Restaurant Harmonien. In the Hotel Harmonien, Gåskærgade 19. ☎ **75-52-37-20.** Reservations recommended. Main courses 109–239 DKK ($15.80–$34.65). Daily 6–9:30pm. AE, DC, MC, V. Closed Dec 20–Jan 2. DANISH.

The most historically charming restaurant in Haderslev occupies a circa 1844 *kro* (inn) whose soft red façade complements a terra-cotta roofline. Set in the town center, it's the restaurant most often cited as a place for a cozy, country-style Danish meal without too much emphasis on big-city glamour. Within a long and narrow dining room that contains only about 10 tables and an oversized fireplace that's usually blazing on cold evenings, you can order such Danish specialties as venison with red wine sauce, tournedos of beef with several kinds of peppercorns, fillet of Dover sole prepared *meunière*-style, and roasted breast of duck with a piquant sauce. These dishes are expertly prepared and exquisitely seasoned. There isn't culinary greatness here, but you get the sense that the kitchen staff really cares about what it serves its guests.

The Restaurant of the Hotel Norden. Storegade 55. ☎ **74-52-40-30.** Reservations recommended. Main courses 78–210 DKK ($11.30–$30.45). AE, DC, MC, V. Daily noon–5pm and 5–10pm. DANISH/FRENCH.

Modern, airy, high-ceilinged, and spacious, this restaurant's setting is radically different from that of its leading competitor, the antique dining room of the Hotel Harmonien, which is also recommended. Surrounded with unusual art and a welcome sense of space, you'll be offered a roster of well-prepared menu items that might include North Sea turbot roasted with lemon juice and wine, served with white asparagus and braised cabbage; beef tournedos with baked sweet peppers; Danish veal cutlet with a panade of ham, shallots, parsley, and morel sauce; and *noisettes* of lamb sautéed in virgin olive oil, served with Dijon mustard and Swiss-style spätzle. On our last visit, everything was flawlessly prepared and beautifully presented by a helpful staff, who are both unobtrusive and prompt.

HADERSLEV AFTER DARK

Most of the after-dark activities in town take place at one of only two hangouts. One of them, **Buch's Vinstue,** Nørregade 9 (☎ **74-53-09-53**), is an old-fashioned Danish beer and wine house that gets very crowded with friends and acquaintances from throughout the district. They select it as a rendezvous point for ongoing dialogues about politics, art, business, or just idle gossip. It opens daily at 2pm. A competitor that's a bit more modern in its approach to entertainment is **Huset,** Nørregade 10 (☎ **74-53-43-73**). Opening at around 6pm, it functions as a well-used bar most nights, except on Thursdays and Fridays, when live music is presented beginning around 10pm. There's never any cover charge, and the under 40 residents of Haderslev tend to be very alert to the changing musical fare at this local legend.

3 Tønder

277 km (173 miles) SW of Copenhagen; 77 km (48 miles) S of Esbjerg; 85 km (53 miles) SW of Kolding

Tønder, on the banks of the River Vidå, is called the capital of the marshland, the oldest town in Denmark holding official town rights, with a municipal charter granted in 1243. In medieval times, it was an important port and a place of disembarkation for horses and cattle. Its surrounding marshland, even Tønder itself, was often flooded by the North Sea. By the middle of the 15th century, townspeople started to erect dikes. But the end result was that Tønder lost its position as a port. The sea eventually receded, leaving Tønder landlocked.

In the 17th century the townfolk turned to lace-making, and eventually 12,000 lace-makers were employed in the town and its surrounding area. The many rich lace dealers built the beautiful patrician houses adorning the streets today.

From 1864 Tønder and the region of North Slesvig were part of Germany. But a plebiscite in 1920 lead to the reunion of North Slesvig with Denmark. Even so, Tønder is still heavily influenced by Germany and its traditions, as it lies only 2½-miles north of the German frontier. The town still holds a German school, kindergarten, and library, and a German vicar is attached to Tønder Christ Church.

ESSENTIALS

GETTING THERE   The train depot lies on the west side of Tønder, half a mile from Torvet (the market square) and reached by going along Vestergade. From Monday to Friday, trains arrive every hour during the day from Ribe (trip time: 50 minutes) and from Esbjerg (trip time: 1 ½ hours). There is less frequent service on Saturday and Sunday.

By Car   From Kolding (see above) take Route 25 southwest to the junction with Route 11 which will carry you for the final lap to the turn-off for Tønder, reached along Route 419 heading west.

VISITOR INFORMATION   The **Tønder Turistbureau,** Torvet 1 (☎ 74-72-12-20), is open June 15 to August Monday to Friday 9:30am to 5:30pm and Saturday 9:30am to 3pm. Otherwise, hours are Monday to Friday 9am to 4pm and Saturday 9am to noon.

SPECIAL EVENTS   Beginning rather modestly in 1975, the **Tønder Festival** every year from August 27–30 has turned into an international musical event. The Tønder Festival covers a wide range of folk music. Musicians from all over the world present blues, bluegrass, cajun, zydeco, jazz, gospel, and traditional Irish, Scottish, English, and American folk music. Known as well as unknown musicians play their instruments in the streets, squares, pubs, and on seven official stages. More than 25,000 visitors flock to Tønder annually for this event. For information, contact Tønder Festivalen, Vestergade 80 (☎ **74-72-46-10**).

GETTING AROUND

Bikes costing from 40 DKK ($5.80) a day are for rent at **Tønder Campingplads,** Holmevej 2A (☎ **74-72-18-49**). Bicycling maps are available at the tourist office. From mid-May until mid-August, water bikes can also be hired here daily, costing 40 DKK ($5.80) per day.

SEEING THE SIGHTS

To see the now antique homes built by the lace-makers during the heyday of Tønder's prosperity, wander up and down the main street which changes its name several times: Østergade, becoming Storegade, and finally Vestergade. Most of the stately mansions along this street (or streets) were built in the 17th and 18th centuries. They are characterized by richly carved portals. The actual lace-makers lived on the smaller side streets, Uldgade and Spikergade, and their houses were more modest, but still interesting to explore. Most of these houses on the latter two streets were built in the 1600s with bay windows. Actually, in our view, Uldgade is the most colorful lane in Tønder. A cobblestone narrow street, it is in many ways the most characteristic street in Tønder that evokes old Denmark.

The best collection of regional artifacts are showcased at the **Tønder Museum,** Kongevej 55 (☎ **74-72-26-57**), which is established in the gatehouse of the old Tønder Castle, all that remains of the former schloss. Exhibitions reflect the local history of the area, and naturally there is an emphasis on the city's lace-making heyday. You can also view regional costumes, wall tiles, antiques, and even elegant table silver once owned by prosperous merchants in the area. The wooden figure with the cane, Kagmand, once stood at Torvet, the market place. At one time any citizen who had committed a crime was tied to this figure and publicly whipped.

In the same building as the Tønder Museum is the **Sønderjyllands Kunstmuseum,** Kongevej 55 (☎ **74-72-26-57**), which holds a fine collection of Danish surrealistic art, and a still-growing collection of contemporary works. Besides the permanent exhibitions, special and always changing art shows are staged here as well.

A short walk away is the **Museumstårnet & H. J. Wedgner udstilling,** Kongevej 55 (☎ **74-72-26-57**). In 1995, the town's antique water tower was converted into an exhibition center for the works of the celebrated furniture designer, native son H. J. Wedgner, whose designs during the 1950s and 1960s were later defined as seminal in the creation of the style that later became known as Danish modern. The uppermost floor of the tower has been converted into a room offering panoramic views over the surrounding marshlands.

The price of an all-inclusive admission to all three of Tønder's above-mentioned museums—the Tønder Museum, the Sønderjyllands Kunstmuseum, and the Museumstårnet—is 15 DKK ($2.15) for adults, free for children. Opening hours for all three museums are the same: From May to October, they're open Tuesday to Sunday from 10am to 5pm; the rest of the year Tuesday to Sunday 1 to 5pm.

Dröhse's Hus, Storgade 14 (☎ **74-72-49-90**), is a small museum set within Tønder's pedestrian zone. The exhibitions inside focus on artifacts relating to lace-making, antiques, and a collection of old glass. The painstaking art of old-fashioned lace-making that once made the town famous is still demonstrated here by women in period costumes. From May to October, it's open Tuesday to Sunday from 10am to 5pm. The rest of the year, it's open Tuesday to Sunday 1 to 5pm. Admission costs 10 DKK ($1.45) for adults and children.

Kristkirken, Kirkepladsen (☎ 74-72-20-80), is located on the northeast side of Torvet. This church from the 1500s is one of the richest in Denmark in terms of furnishings from the Renaissance and baroque era. The 50-meter tower here is actually from an earlier church that stood on this site. In the old days, when Tønder was a port (before the North sea receded), the tower served as a navigational marker for mariners. The font inside is from the mid–14th century; the pulpit created in 1586. A series of memorial tablets or epitaphs were hung by wealthy cattle and lace dealers in the 15th and 16th centuries. The church is open daily from 9am to 4pm; admission is free.

SHOPPING According to long tradition, the shopkeepers of Tønder—dressed in old-fashioned costumes—arrange a pedestrian zone market in the center of town from July 17–18. On Saturday, the final market day, there are live music and drinks in the main square, Torvet. Another shopping adventure occurs on August 1 of every year when there is a "feast" in the pedestrian zone in the historic core of the city. Shops remain open until 10pm, offering amusements to visitors. There is plenty of food and drink, climaxed by a concert in the main square (Torvet).

On Tuesday and Friday local vendors sell fish, fruit, cheese, and fresh vegetables in the main square. We always like to gather the makings for a picnic here, to be enjoyed later in the marshland surrounding Tønder.

For such a small town, Tønder has a large number of specialty shops. Many Germans drive across the border to shop here. Various gifts and souvenirs can be purchased at **Andersen & Nissen,** Storegade 26 (☎ 74-72-13-42).

For the best of Danish design, head for **Dan Designs,** Østergade 5 (☎ 74-72-19-65), where a collection of artfully produced textiles, some of them from the mills, are sold either by the meter or as part of table settings, bath towels, napkins, and bedcovers. They're also crafted into fashionable garments (especially winter coats) for men and women. Look for colors that reflect either the monochromes of a Danish winter, or the brighter forest and earth tones of a Scandinavian summer. They also sell playful paintings (animal prints are a specialty), or accessories for the table or desktop. The venue is fun and whimsical, rather than formal, and very Danish in its inspiration.

Din Grønne Skobutik, Østergade 3 (☎ 74-72-48-93), features one of the best collections of women's shoes in town, everything from high heels to the kinds of boots a woman might want for treks through the marshes and forests of Denmark.

Gaveboden, Østergade 10–12 (☎ 74-72-58-29), sells sweaters—the kind of garment that wards off the fog and damp of a Danish winter yet still manages to make its wearer look appealing. Specialties of the store include alpaca, angora, and woolen tops with unusual patterns, including plaids. There's even a scattering of garments by Finnish designer Marimekko.

At the sprawling **Blue Willi's Sweater House,** Vestergade 1 (☎ 74-72-58-81), the most prevalent color is indigo blue—indigo blue jeans, denim jackets, indigo-colored leggings that look fetching on ski slopes or volleyball courts, or denim backpacks and shoulder bags. There's also enough knitwear for both men and women, in a variety of colors that manage to bring out either the motorcycle enthusiast or the Hollywood star or starlet, depending on the image you're trying to cultivate. Don't come here looking for formal wear: Instead, augment your wardrobe for your next semester at university, or gather together a rough-and-tumble wardrobe for your next weekend fling.

W. Ø. Larsen, Vestergade 66 (☎ 74-72-48-44), is everybody's favorite stopover for the kind of luxury goods that are usually imported from far away, and which tend to add grace notes and frills to the good life. Inside a shop whose décor might remind you of an upscale apothecary from the 19th century, look for specialty tobaccos, coffee, teas, wines, and cigars. There's also a collection of pipes and cigar humidors.

OUTDOOR ACTIVITIES

In the region around Tønder is a stream system stretching for 56 miles, the various tributaries of which offer variable fishing possibilities. The tourist bureau sells a 1-day fishing license for 70 DKK ($10.15). If you want to rent a canoe, a local firm, **Tønders Kano,** Grænsevej 16 (☎ 74-72-42-50), will charge you 125 DKK ($18.15) a day, or 150 DKK ($21.75) if you opt to keep the vessel throughout the course (Saturday and Sunday) of a weekend.

WHERE TO STAY

Bowler Inn. Ribe Landevej 56, DK-6270 Tønder. ☎ **74-72-00-11.** Fax 74-72-65-11. E-mail: mail@hotelbowlerinn.dk. 10 units. TV TEL. 595 DKK ($86.25) double. AE, MC, V.

Few other hotels in the region pursue as aggressive a devotion to one particular sport. In this case, the passion is bowling, and to make it possible, this hotel's designers and investors added 10 state-of-the-art bowling alleys in a long, low, interconnected building when they constructed this place in 1993. Don't fret that you won't fit in if you opt not to go bowling, as rooms are more modern, more comfortable, and better-accessorized than many competitors in the same price range nearby. The complex, set within the city's outskirts, about a half-mile north of the center, contains an English-inspired pub of the type you might have expected in London, a restaurant serving mostly Danish food, and the above-mentioned bowling alleys, which are the site of many local competitions. Rental of a bowling alley for up to six players costs 90 to 125 DKK ($13.05 to $18.15), depending on the time of day.

Hostrups Hotel. Søndergade 30, DK-6270 Tønder. ☎ **74-72-21-29.** 23 units. 590–700 DKK ($85.55–$101.50). Rates includes breakfast. AE, MC, V.

Set on the southern perimeter of town, adjacent to a spot where the river widens to one of its broadest points, this hotel was built around the turn of the century, and today projects an aura of calm, well-manicured charm. The interior, including the bedrooms, has been much modernized into a streamlined venue of high ceilings, monochromatic color schemes, and patterned upholstery that, combined, contribute to a restful sense of calm. Most contain both TV and phone, and all of them have good beds. There's a restaurant, and also a bar, on the premises, and a staff that speaks virtually no English.

Hotel Tønderhus. Jomfrustien 1, DK-6270 Tønder. ☎ **74-72-22-22.** Fax 74-72-05-92. 42 units. TV TEL. 575–1,000 DKK ($83.40–$145). AE, DC, MC, V.

One of the most oft-rebuilt structures in the town center, with numerous reconstructions due to various fires and catastrophes, this is the best hotel within the Tønder city limits. Constructed from redbrick in two distinctly different structures (one antique-looking, the other much more modern), it's a U-shaped monument that encircles three sides of a formal courtyard. Originally built in 1818, and respected as the first hotel in town that everyone automatically thinks of, it has well-maintained and unpretentious bedrooms. There's also a basement-level party room with a glass ceiling that was originally conceived as a cistern. A glass-sided cafe serves simple snacks and coffee, and a cozy restaurant is recommended separately in "Where to Dine."

WHERE TO DINE

Hotel Tønderhus. Jomfrustien 1. ☎ **74-72-22-22.** Main courses 105–250 DKK ($15.25–$36.25). Set-price menu 115 DKK ($16.65). AE, DC, MC, V. Daily noon–2pm and 6–9pm. DANISH.

One of Tønder's many appealing restaurants lies on the street level of this previously recommended hotel. Within an artfully old-fashioned setting accessorized with rustic implements from the agrarian Denmark of long ago, you can order copious portions of such tried-and-true Danish specialties as cold potato soup with bacon and chives, fresh-fried fish cakes of the house, a platter of assorted marinades of herring, brisket of beef with horseradish, and a savory afterthought that might include fried camembert with black currant jam. Between the lunch and dinner hour, the place remains open for coffee, tea, drinks, and a limited selection of such cold platters as marinated herring with various types of Danish cheeses.

Torvets Restaurant. Storegade 1. ☎ **74-72-43-73.** Reservations recommended in restaurant, not necessary in bistro. In restaurant, main courses 79–200 DKK ($11.45–$29); in bistro, platters 35–120 DKK ($5.05–$17.40). AE, DC, MC, V. Daily noon–11pm. DANISH.

Set beside the main shopping street of Tønder, these twin-tiered restaurants occupy what was originally built during the 1930s as a bank. Today, the building's stately looking main floor is divided equally into a formal, antique-laden restaurant, and a less elegant, less prestigious bistro where food is cheaper and culinary pretensions a lot lower. Within the bistro, you can order platters of *smørrebrød*, pastas, pizzas, and cold assortments of Danish cheese, herring, and fresh vegetables. Within the restaurant, expect more elaborate concoctions that change with the season and are likely to include lobster bisque; slices of air-cured beef with arugula, parmesan cheese, and truffle oil; fillets of lemon sole *meunière* with roasted mushrooms and spinach, served with butter sauce and new potatoes; oven-baked salmon with hollandaise sauce; and such two-fisted beef dishes as filet steak béarnaise and chateaubriand with wine sauce.

Victoria Restaurant. Storegade 9. ☎ **74-72-00-89.** Reservations recommended. Main courses 130–160 DKK ($18.85–$23.20). AE, DC, MC, V. Mon–Fri 9am–11pm; Sat 9am–1am; Sun 2–10pm. DANISH.

Set within a century-old building in the heart of town, this restaurant serves well-prepared, completely unpretentious platters of Danish food that usually arrive cheerfully and in generous portions. In summer, tables and chairs that match the green and white façade of this place are set out on the cobblestones in front, creating an aura much like that of a Tivoli-inspired bistro-cafe in faraway Copenhagen. Menu items reflect time-tested Danish traditions, and usually include such dishes as smoked salmon with a morel-flavored dill sauce, platters heaped with three different kinds of herring, egg salad with shrimp imported form the waters off of Greenland, breast of Danish hen with spinach and mushrooms, and a dessert specialty that might include a citrus-flavored *bavarois* with wild berry sauce.

TØNDER AFTER DARK

There isn't much activity. Your best bet is **Hagge's Musik Pub,** Vestergade 80 (☎ 74-72-44-49), which lies opposite the post office. Here you can order pub grub and both Irish and Danish beer on draft. Although it's not an every night event, it is a frequent venue for live music including blues, jazz, and Danish or Scottish folk.

A VISIT TO OLD WORLD MØGELTØNDER

Even if you have to skip Tønder itself, head for the little village of ✪ **Møgeltønder,** lying only 2½ miles west of Tønder and reached via Route 419. Bus no. 66 from Tønder also runs here about every hour during the day; the trip taking only 10 minutes.

Once at Møgeltønder, you'll find a charming old-world village. Filmmakers have even suggested it is a "fairytale setting," with its long and narrow street, called Slotsgade. This street is lined with low gabled houses, most of them dating from the 1700s and some of them with thatched roofs. The street is also planted with a double row of lime trees, making it even more colorful and photogenic.

At the end of the street stands a small castle, **Schackenborg Slot,** which can only be viewed from the outside, as it's owned by the Queen of Denmark and currently functions as the principal residence of her younger son, Prince Joachim, and his wife, Alexandra. The king presented Field Marshall Hans Schack with the castle in 1661, in the wake of his victory over the Swedes during the battle of Nyborg. His descendants occupied the castle for centuries. Although security is tight and you can't visit the interior of the castle, you can tour through the moat-enclosed grounds that begin on the opposite side of the street, but only under very carefully monitored circumstances. During June, July, and August, two 30-minute tours are conducted every day, beginning at 1pm and 1:30pm. The price is 15 DKK ($2.15) for a supervised trek through the gardens. The rest of the year, visits to the gardens are not possible.

At the other end of the Slotsgade stands the 12th-century **Møgeltønder Kirke,** Slotsgade (☎ 74-73-85-96), which contains some interesting frescoes, the oldest of which dates from 1275, and which are found under the chancel's arch. In the chancel itself are some frescoes from the mid-16th century. The altarpiece probably dates from the beginning of the 16th century, and you can also see such treasures as a Romanesque font and a baroque pulpit from the end of the 1600s. The church organ was made in Hamburg in 1679. The church is open daily from 8am to 5pm, closing at 4pm October to March. Admission is free.

WHERE TO STAY

✪ **Schackenborg Slotskro.** Slotsgaden 42, Møgeltønder, DK-6270 Tønder. ☎ **74-73-83-83.** Fax 74-73-83-11. www.slotskro.com. E-mail: schackenborg@slotskro.dk. 12 units. TV TEL. 900–1,200 DKK ($130.50–$174) double. Rate includes breakfast. AE, DC, MC, V.

One of the most unusual hotels in southern Jutland lies a very short walk from the 17th-century foundations of a royal palace still occupied by the Danish queen and her French-born husband. The hotel is a venerable, thick-walled 17th-century structure set on the historic, picture-perfect main street of the hamlet Møgeltønder. Owned but not operated by the queen's son, Prince Joachim, and his Hong Kong–born wife, Alexandra, the inn takes great pains to project an aura of aristocratic well-being and glamour, despite occasional touches of streamlined modern intrusions in an otherwise Old World setting. Each of the bedrooms is named after one of the palaces or fortresses of Denmark, and contains an encapsulated history of its namesake as part of the reading material within each room. Expect jewel-toned colors, rich upholstery, and a not overly large but relatively luxurious Danish manor house at its most intimate. Even if you opt not to spend the night, consider a meal within the formal dining room, which frankly, is a lot more appealing than the hotel that contains it.

WHERE TO DINE

Schackenborg Slotskro. Slotsgaden 42, Møgeltørder. ☎ **74-73-83-83.** Reservations recommended. Main courses 165–245 DKK ($23.90–$35.55). Set menus 325–465 DKK ($47.15–$67.45). AE, DC, MC, V. Daily noon–2pm and 6–8:30pm. Closed occasional Mondays because of private parties. DANISH/INTERNATIONAL.

The most stylish and prestigious restaurant in the neighborhood lies on the street level of a previously recommended, very upscale inn that's owned by Prince Joachim, one of the sons of Queen Margrethe and her husband Prince Henrik. Within an ocher-colored dining room that reeks of 18th century respectability, you'll be seated at formally accessorized tables. The dish for which the restaurant is famous is a distinctive specialty—salmon soufflé encased in a fish mousse. Your version will come with a number indicating where it falls on the historical tally (at this writing, the restaurant had served more than 70,000 of them). Other items include quail cooked in Madeira sauce, and various versions of seafood. Expect a leisurely, rather elegant reflection of the image that's preferred by Denmark's royal family, and a bit of social posturing on the part of the other guests.

A TRIP TO LØGUM KLOSTER AND MEMORIES OF A MONASTERY

A final and worthwhile excursion is to the hamlet of Løgum, 11-miles north of Tønder. (To get here from Tønder, follow the road signs to Ribe, then the signs to Kolding and, a bit later, the signs to Løgum Kloster.) **Løgum Kloster** (Løgum Abbey), Klostervej (☎ **74-74-52-40**), once competed with Tønder as a lace-making center. Built in what was then an uninhabited and marshy plain, the abbey—today an ecclesiastical administrative center—was founded in 1173. Once impressive in size, the abbey today has been reduced to its east wing, with the sacristy, library, chapter house, and church remaining. Constructed from redbrick, the abbey church grew and changed over a period of years from 1230 to 1330. It was built when Europe was changing from the Romanesque to the Gothic style, so the abbey reflects both periods of architecture. In the nave are traces of frescoes, and other treasures include a winged altar and elegantly carved choir stalls from the early 16th century, and a reliquary with wings and a Gothic triumphal cross (circa 1300). Opposite the main building stands an 80-foot tower with a carillon named in honor of King Frederik IX. It strikes a concert daily at 8am, 11am, 3pm, 5pm, 6:30pm, and 9pm.

Between May and October, the abbey church can be visited Monday to Saturday from 10am to 6:30pm; Sunday from noon to 5pm. The rest of the year, it can be visited Monday to Saturday from 10am to 4pm; and Sunday from noon to 4pm. Admission is free.

4 Rømø

288km (180 miles) SW of Copenhagen; 14 ½ km (9 miles) W of Skærbæk; 5km (3 miles) N of Sylt

Off of the west coast of Jutland, **Rømø**, a North Frisian island, is the largest Danish island in the North Sea. It is about 5 ½-miles long and 4-miles wide. The western shore opens onto the North Sea, whereas the east coast facing the mainland is bounded by tidal shallows. The northwest corner of the island is a restricted military zone.

The island, which is separated from the German island of Sylt by the **Lister Dyb** (Lister Deep), has a wild, windswept appearance and is particularly known for its nude sunbathing, as is the German island of Sylt. In summer, Rømø is filled with tourists, especially Germans, but off-season it's one of the sleepiest places in Europe.

Midway between Ribe and Tønder, Rømø is connected to the mainland by a 6-mile causeway that passes over a panoramic marshland filled with wading sea birds and grazing sheep in summer. Exposed to the North Sea, the western edge of the island is the site of the best sandy beaches and is a magnet for windsurfers. The most popular beach area is at Lakolk on the central western coastal strip. Here the beach is about half a mile wide. The main hamlets are on the eastern coast along a 4-mile stretch from the causeway south to the little port of Havneby.

ESSENTIALS

GETTING THERE   To reach Rømø, take the 6-mile stone causeway from mainland Jutland, a half-hour's drive on Route 175 from either Tønder or Ribe (there are no tolls en route). You can take a bus south from Ribe to Skærbæk and then bus

Wildlife on Rømø

Many visitors come to Rømø to seek out its plentiful bird life on the west coast, which is also home to some 1,500 seals. You can see them sunbathing during the day.

no. 29 across the tidal flats to Rømø. Skærbæk is linked by rail to the towns of Tønder, Ribe, and Esbjerg.

If you'd like to continue your trip to Sylt from Rømø, take a car-ferry from the Danish fishing village of Havneby to the far northern German town of List. Trips take 1 hour and depart six times a day. For schedules and more information, call **Rømø/Sylt Linie** (☎ 74-75-53-03).

VISITOR INFORMATION   **Rømø Turistbureau,** Havnebyvej 30 (☎ 74-75-51-30), is open 9am to 5pm Monday to Friday and 10am to 4pm on Saturday and Sunday. It's closed every Sunday off-season from November to April.

GETTING AROUND

The best way to get around Rømø is by bike. Rentals, costing from 30 DKK ($4.35) a day, are available at **Garni,** Nørre Frankel at Havneby (☎ 74-75-54-80).

EXPLORING THE ISLAND

The island of Rømø has one of the widest beaches in Denmark, flying the Blue Flag, a European designation for clean bathing water. The nude beach, often frequented by Germans, is at Sønderstrand on the southwesterly extremity of the island. Windsurfing is popular on the island, mainly focused on the west coast. The best area for windsurfing is at the southern side of Lakolf. However, windsurfers bring their own equipment to Rømø, so there is no outlet locally to rent equipment.

At the rear of the tourist office (see above) you'll find the **Naturcentret Tønnisgård,** Havnebyvej 30 (☎ 74-75-52-57), in an old thatched farmhouse from the island of Rømø. It contains modest displays of the island flora and fauna, and there is also a cafeteria serving drinks and Danish pastries. Tønnisgård is open daily from 10am to 4pm except from November through January. Admission is 20 DKK ($2.90) for adults and 10 DKK ($1.45) for children. The center also conducts 90-minute nature tours of the local wetlands between June and September. Between four and five of these depart every day during that period, depending on demand, each of them priced at 30 DKK ($4.35) per participant. Phone ahead for schedules and departure times.

Other attractions include **Kommandørgården** (The National Museum's Commander House), Guvrevej 60, in the hamlet of Toftum (☎ 74-75-52-76). The house dates from 1748 and is evocative of the great prosperity enjoyed by ship's commanders in the sailing heyday of Rømø in the 18th century. The house is fully restored, including its panels, ceilings, and doors. The walls are covered with Dutch tiles and the furnishings are lavish. About 50 sailors from Rømø served simultaneously as captains on Dutch and German ships which sailed on whaling expeditions to Greenland. From May to September the house is open Tuesday to Sunday from 10am to 6pm. In October it is open Tuesday to Sunday from 10am to 3pm. Closed off-season. Admission costs 15 DKK ($2.15) for adults, 10 DKK ($1.45) for children under 12.

In the little village of **Jurve,** there is a fence made of whale jawbone in 1772. It has been preserved and is now under the protection of the National Museum in Copenhagen. As no wood or stone was available on the island at the time, the locals made use of this unusual building material, a remnant of the whaling ships' catches in Greenland.

Rømø Kirke at Kirkeby also merits a visit. The church was originally built in the late Gothic style, but was greatly extended in the 17th and 18th centuries. It is consecrated to St. Clemens, the patron saint of seafarers, and contains a number of ship models, as well as three large chandeliers, all donated by sailors. Admission is free, and it is open year-round from 8am to 4pm Tuesday through Friday only.

OUTDOOR ACTIVITIES

Other than the beaches and windsurfing (see above), the most popular outdoor pursuit is horseback riding, available at **Rømø Ranch,** Lakolk Strand (☎ 74-75-54-11), a stable right on Lakolk Beach. It offers rides to experienced as well as novice riders, and most rides take place right on the beach, costing 45 to 75 DKK ($6.50–$10.90) per hour.

SHOPPING

The best selection of chic-looking sporting clothes—ideal for wearing on your jaunts around Rømø—are found at **Skandia,** Havnebyvej 71, Kongsmark (☎ 74-75-55-74). It specializes in Blue Willi's pure indigo cotton.

At the center of the island in Kongsmark, you'll find Rømø's major gallery, known by the English name **Art House,** Gamle Skolevej #8A (☎ 74-75-61-36). Here you can experience and purchase Danish and European handcraft products. From April to October, a new exhibition of glass and pottery by leading Danish and international artisans is presented every month. If weather allows, you can enjoy freshly brewed coffee and other refreshments in a beautiful garden surrounding the Art House. In July and August hours are Monday to Friday 11am to 6pm, Saturday 10am to 1pm. During other months, hours are Wednesday to Friday from 11am to 4pm and on Saturday from 10am to 1pm.

WHERE TO STAY

In addition to the recommendations below, Havneby Kro (see "Where to Dine," below), also rents some simple and basic rooms.

✪ **Hotel Færgegaarden.** Vestergade, DK-6792 Havneby. ☎ **74-75-54-32.** Fax 74-75-58-59. 35 units. MINIBAR TV TEL. 780 DKK ($113.10) double. Rate includes breakfast. AE, DC, MC, V.

Set on the southern stretches of the island, a short drive from the island's best beaches, one of the most charming hotels on Rømø is an authentic, thatch-roofed inn that has welcomed overnight guests since it was originally built in 1813. Set behind its deep-red façade are cozy, much-restored bedrooms, each with a scattering of old-time accessories and traditional copies of Danish furnishings. Although they're comfortable and solid, the real appeal of the place derives from its high-ceilinged restaurant, where beamed ceilings and many reminders of the Denmark of long ago contribute to a feeling of well-being. Meals are served daily from noon to 10pm, with set dinners at 115 DKK ($16.65), and main courses priced from 168 to 238 DKK ($24.35 to $34.50). On the premises is a separate building, erected in 1987, that contains an indoor swimming pool, sauna, and solarium. There's also a tennis court within the garden, and a clientele that's more cosmopolitan than you might have expected with visitors from as far away as Florida, Washington, and California.

Hotel/Motel Rømø. Kongsmark. DK-6792 Rømø. ☎ **74-75-51-14.** 35 units. TV. 395 DKK ($57.30) double. No credit cards. Closed Nov–Apr.

This is one of the least expensive and simplest hotels on Rømø. Built in the early 1970s in two cost-effective buildings on the island's eastern shore, it has virtually no architectural fantasy, no sense of old-time Denmark, and no decorative frills or graceful notes. Despite that, the place is usually booked solid, thanks to low prices, clean rooms that have big windows and a sense of retro-kitsch in the angular furniture, and a feeling of isolation from the cares and concerns of mainland Europe. On the premises is a simple restaurant that serves generous portions of traditional Danish food every day from noon to 9:30pm. A set-price menu is a relative bargain at 90 DKK ($13.05). Although the sea is only a few steps from the hotel, the nearest beach lies 2 ½-miles to the south, on Rømø's southern tip.

Hotel RIM & Feriecenter. Vestergade 159, DK-6792 Rømø. ☎ **74-75-57-75.** Fax 74-75-57-36. 207 units, each with kitchenette and TV. 597–900 DKK ($86.55–$130.50) apts. for 1–4 occupants; 690–995 DKK ($100.05–$144.25) apts. for 1–6 occupants. AE, DC, MC, V.

This is the largest and most visible hotel on Rømø, with a North European clientele (Danish, Dutch, and German) that tends to stay for several days or more. The setting is a compound of gabled brown-brick houses, each of which contains between two and four apartments, and each of which was built between 1979 and 1986. Inside, you'll find simple, angular furnishings, lots of exposed wood, and an unfrilly, anonymous setting that's in keeping with the resort's high turnover. Don't expect verdant gardens or forests, as the venue is based on the fragile ecology of tenacious sea grasses that grow under streaming sunlight and almost constant ocean winds. On the premises are a restaurant, cafe, bar, two indoor pools, two outdoor pools, sauna, solarium, and health club. There's also easy access to the largest beach in northern Europe, a windswept stretch of sand almost 2-miles wide by 4 ½-miles long. Unlike many other apartment-style beachfront hotels in Denmark, this one remains open throughout the year.

WHERE TO DINE

✪ **Havneby Kro.** Skansen 3, Havneby, DK-6792 Rømø. ☎ **74-75-66-44.** Reservations necessary in midsummer. Main courses 70–140 DKK ($10.15–$20.30). MC, V. Daily 6–10pm. Closed Dec 26–Jan 6. CONTINENTAL.

This is the best restaurant in Rømø, with a turn-of-the-century setting overlooking the harborfront, and with service rituals that are more elaborate than those at any other establishment on the island. Despite that, the prices are less expensive that you might have supposed, especially considering the roster of antique tables and chairs within the cozy dining room, and the care that the chef takes with the food. Menu items are inspired by international cuisine, especially that of Germany, Italy, and Denmark, and might include such dishes as steak with gorgonzola sauce, chicken with curry sauce and bananas, fried herring with beans and potatoes, and fillets of plaice with crabmeat and fresh tomatoes. Don't overlook the possibility of a drink or two at the elaborately carved bar before or after a meal here: It was crafted in the *art nouveau (Jugendstil)* style in 1905, and hauled in by barge after it was acquired in Belgium by the owner several years ago. It's open every night from 6pm to 1am. Incidentally, management maintains three rooms, none with private bath, on the upper floors of this place, marketing them almost as an afterthought to its primary business of managing the restaurant. No breakfast is served, and although they're clean and cozy, none of the rooms have any particularly graceful notes. The price for a double room is 250 DKK ($36.25) per night.

Otto & Ani's Fisk. Havnepladsen, Havneby. ☎ **74-75-53-06.** Main courses 30–115 DKK ($4.35–$16.65). No credit cards. June–Sept daily 10am–8pm. Oct–May daily 10am–6:30pm. SEAFOOD.

You'll either find this place authentic and appealingly raffish, or hopelessly informal, depending on your temperament. Except for the fact that it avoids frying all of its fish in deep fat, it might remind you of a seafront fish-and-chips stand in England. Expect a self-service format within a brown brick building that's among the least stately-looking in Rømø. English-speaking proprietor Susan Jensen will help you select from a Danish-language menu that lists various platters of fish, most of which comprise a filling meal in its own right. Examples include everything from a simple portion of fillet of cod served, sandwich-style, with fresh bread, butter, and a handful of freshly peeled shrimp; or a more substantial platter that contains a dinner-sized portion of fillet of sole with baked potato, mixed salad, and—again—a handful of shrimp. Beer or wine might accompany your meal, which you'll consume either at picnic tables set up outside, or within a severe-looking all-white room with absolutely no sense of architectural fantasy. Despite its shortcomings, the place has thrived because of its low prices and flavorful fish for more than a dozen years.

RØMØ AFTER DARK

There are very few options for nightlife on an island that is notoriously sleepy, even by the standards of Danish islands. Our best suggestion is to have a drink at the **Havneby Kro** (see above), where the staff defines at least part of their function as the administration of a busy pub and bar.

If you'd like to follow drinks in a tavern with a dance club, the island's best is **Make Up Diskotek,** Lakolk Butikstorv (☎ 74-75-59-23), open Thursday to Saturday 10pm to 4am. From Sunday to Wednesday, hours are 10:30pm to 2am. Admission is 45 DKK ($6.50). Of course, this is a summer-only disco.

5 Ribe

32km (20 miles) S of Esbjerg; 297^1/$_2$ km (186 miles)W of Copenhagen; 46^1/$_2$ km (29 miles) N of Tønder

Ribe, a town of narrow cobblestone lanes and half-timbered and crooked houses, became legendary because of the graceful (and, sadly, endangered) storks that build their nests on top of its red-roofed medieval houses. Every year the residents of Denmark's oldest town ponder the question: Will the storks return in April?

This port was an important trading center during the Viking era (9th century) and became an Episcopal seat in 948, when one of the first Christian churches in Denmark was established here. It was also the royal residence of the ruling Valdemars around 1200.

In medieval days Ribe was linked by sea-trade routes to England, Germany, Friesland, the Mediterranean, and other ports, but then its waters receded. Today it's surrounded by marshes, much like a landlocked Moby Dick. The town watchman still makes his rounds—armed with his lantern and trusty staff—since the ancient custom was revived in 1936.

ESSENTIALS

GETTING THERE   You can easily reach Ribe by train; there is hourly service from Copenhagen (via Bramming). The schedules of both trains and buses are available at the tourist office.

By Car   From Kolding (see above) head west across Jutland on the motorway (E20), but cut southwest when you reach Route 32, which will carry you into Ribe.

VISITOR INFORMATION   The **Ribe Turistbureau,** at Torvet 3 (☎ 75-42-15-00), is open June 15 to August, Monday to Saturday from 9:30am to 5:30pm, and Sunday from 10am to 2pm; April to June 14 and September to October, Monday to Friday from 9am to 5pm and Saturday from 10am to 1pm; and November to March, Monday to Friday from 9:30am to 4:30pm and Saturday from 10am to 1pm.

Ribe

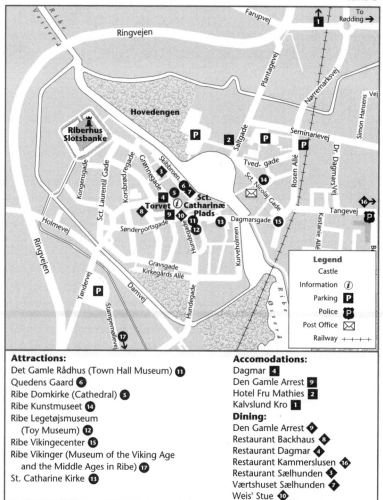

Attractions:
Det Gamle Rådhus (Town Hall Museum) **11**
Quedens Gaard **6**
Ribe Domkirke (Cathedral) **5**
Ribe Kunstmuseet **14**
Ribe Legetøjsmuseum
(Toy Museum) **12**
Ribe Vikingecenter **15**
Ribe Vikinger (Museum of the Viking Age
and the Middle Ages in Ribe) **17**
St. Catharine Kirke **13**

Accomodations:
Dagmar **4**
Den Gamle Arrest **9**
Hotel Fru Mathies **2**
Kalvslund Kro **1**
Dining:
Den Gamle Arrest ◆ **9**
Restaurant Backhaus ◆ **8**
Restaurant Dagmar ◆ **4**
Restaurant Kammerslusen ◆ **16**
Restaurant Sælhunden ◆ **3**
Værtshuset Sælhunden ◆ **7**
Weis' Stue ◆ **10**

GETTING AROUND

If you'd like to bike your way around the area, you can rent bikes for 55 DKK ($8) at **Ribe Vandrerhjem (Youth Hostel),** Sct. Pedersgade 16 (☎ **75-84-19-26**).

SEEING THE SIGHTS

Det Gamle Rådhus (Town Hall Museum). Von Støckends Plads. ☎ **79-89-89-55.** Admission 20 DKK ($2.90) adults. 10 DKK ($1.45) children ages 7–14, free for children age 6 and under, June–Aug, daily 1–3pm; May and Sept. Mon–Fri 1–3pm. Closed Oct–Apr.

In the oldest existing town hall in Denmark, originally built in 1496, the medieval Town Hall Museum houses Ribe's artifacts and archives. Included are a 16th-century executioner's sword, ceremonial swords, the town's money chest, antique tradesmen's signs, and a depiction of the "iron hand," still a symbol of police authority.

✪ **Ribe Domkirke.** Torvet (in the town center off of Sønderportsgade). ☎ **75-42-06-19.** Admission 10 DKK ($1.45) adults, 3 DKK (45¢) children. June–Aug, daily 10am to 6pm; May and Sept, daily 10am–5pm; Oct–Apr, Mon–Sat 11am–3pm, Sun 1–3pm.

This stone-and-brick cathedral, this little town's crowning achievement, was under construction from 1150 to 1175. Inspired by Rhineland architecture, it's a good example of the Romanesque influence on Danish architecture, despite its Gothic arches. A century later a tower was added; climb it if you want to see how the storks view Ribe—and if you have the stamina. Try to see the legendary "Cat's Head Door," once the principal entranceway to the church, and the granite tympanum—*Removal from the Cross*—the most significant piece of medieval sculpture left in Denmark. The mosaics, stained glass, and frescoes in the eastern apse are by the artist Carl-Henning Pedersen.

Ribe Vikinger (Museum of the Viking Age and the Middle Ages in Ribe). Odins Plads. ☎ **75-42-22-22.** Admission 40 DKK ($5.80) adults, 15 DKK ($2.15) children. June 15–Sept 14, daily 10am–5pm; Apr–June 14 and Sept 15–Oct, daily 10am–4pm; Nov–Mar, Tues–Sun 10am–4pm.

Opened in 1995, this museum traces the story of Ribe through exhibitions. Beginning in A.D. 700, it depicts the Viking age and the medieval period. Actual archaeological finds of that era are displayed, along with such reconstructed scenes as a Viking age marketplace, dating from around 800, and a church building site from around 1500.

Ribe Vikingecenter. Lustrupvej 4. ☎ **75-42-22-22.** Admission 30 DKK ($4.35) adults, 15 DKK ($2.15) children ages 3–14 (age 2 and under free). May 12–Sept 25 Tues–Sun 11am–4pm.

Lying a mile south of the town's historic core, this Viking center, affiliated with Ribe Vikinger (see above), is still under construction. Here life as lived in the Viking era comes alive again. Based on excavations made in the surrounding area, the Viking marketplace here is a reconstruction of what a marketplace from Viking times looked like in 720. Whenever possible materials discovered in excavations were used. At the market place you can see craftspeople at work, practicing blacksmithing, wood turning, bow making, and archery. Potters work side by side with amber cutters, basket makers, and textile workers. A great house from the year 980 is being constructed (it's the equivalent of a manor house). The structure is scheduled to be completed in 1999. In 1998 the center launched the "building of a town milieu from the year 1050." Town houses from the late Viking period will form a background for the urban life of the period.

Quedens Gaard. Overdammen 12. ☎ **75-42-00-55.** Admission 40 DKK ($5.80) adults, 15 DKK ($2.15) children. June–Aug, daily 10am–5pm; Mar–Apr and Sept–Oct, Tues–Sun 11am–3pm; Nov–Feb, Tues–Sun 11am–1pm.

In the rooms of an old merchant house, you can see how life was lived in Ribe "upstairs and downstairs," covering the period from 1600 to 1900. Different interiors from those centuries are shown, along with an old kitchen. A collection of silver made by Ribe craftsmen is displayed, along with artifacts illustrating the industrial development of Ribe.

Ribe Kunstmuseet. Skt. Nicolai Gade 10. ☎ **75-42-03-62.** Admission 30 DKK ($4.35) adults, free for children age 15 and under. June 15–Aug, daily 11am–5pm; Feb–June 14 and Sept–Dec, Tues–Sat 1–4pm, Sun 11am–4pm. Closed Jan.

An extensive collection of Danish art is displayed at the Ribe Kunstmuseet, including works by acclaimed Danish artists like Eckersberg, Kobke, C. A. Jensen, Hammershøj, and Juel. Housed in a stately mid–19thcentury villa in a garden on the Ribe River, many paintings are from the golden age of Danish art. Occasionally the museum changes exhibitions.

⭐ **St. Catharine Kirke.** Skt. Catharine's Plads. ☎ **75-42-05-34.** Church, free; cloisters, 3 DKK (45¢) adults, 1 DKK (15¢) children age 13 and under. May–Sept, daily 10am–noon and 2–5pm; Oct–Apr, daily 10am–noon and 2–4pm. Closed during church services.

The Black Friars (Dominicans) came to Ribe in 1228 and began constructing a church and chapter house (the east wing of a monastery), and parts of the original edifice can still be seen, especially the southern wall. The present church, near Dagmarsgade, with nave and aisles, dates from the first half of the 15th century, and the tower dates from 1617. Extensive restorations have made this one of the best-preserved abbeys in Scandinavia. Only the monks' stalls and the Romanesque font remain from the Middle Ages. The handsome pulpit dates from 1591 and the altarpiece from 1650.

You can walk through the cloisters and see ship models and religious paintings hanging in the southern aisle. Tombstones of Ribe citizens from the Reformation and later can be seen along the outer walls of the church.

Ribe Legetøjsmuseum (Toy Museum). Von Støckens Plads 2. ☎ **75-41-14-40.** Admission 30 DKK ($4.35) adults, 15 DKK ($2.15) children ages 3–12 (age 2 and under free). Family ticket 90 DKK ($13.05). Jan–Mar and Nov–Dec, Mon–Sat 1–4pm; Apr–May and Sept–Oct, daily 1–5pm; June–Aug, daily 10am–noon and 1–5pm.

This exhibition on two floors contains a unique collection of several thousand toys, covering a period from 1850 to 1980. There are more than 500 dolls alone, along with toy cars ranging from the first horseless carriages to today's model cars. Motorcycles are also represented. There are also wooden toys, old games, robots, antique teddy bears, and much more.

SHOPPING

Ribe has some of the best shopping in Jutland. The best antiques stores are **Antik Ripen,** Grydergade 5 (☎ 75-41-18-08), and **Ribe Antik,** Nygade 4 (☎ 75-41-18-00). The best clothing store is **Mr. Lundgaard,** Saltgade 3 (☎ 75-42-02-91), which has the town's largest selection, everything from high quality clothes to Marlboro classics. The shop caters to both women and men. A wide range of footwear for adults and children is available at **City Sko,** Skoringen Ribe, Tømmergangen 3 (☎ 75-42-02-46). At **Ribe's Broderi & Garn,** Dagmarsgade 4 (☎75-42-16-75), you'll find the finest selection of needlework (some exquisite pieces) and woolen items. **Bentzons Boghandel,** Mellemdammen 16 (☎ 75-42-00-41), is the best bookstore, with many English language titles. **Alisson-Dansk Naturkosmetik,** Nederdammen 32 (☎ 75-41-09-01), is an intriguing store with a varied selection of products from a well-known Danish company, Alisson of Denmark. They are makers of skin care and cosmetic products.

If your tastes run to handcrafts, gifts, and souvenirs, you'll find that Ribe is loaded with boutiques. The most amusing outlet is **Ryk Ind,** Sønderportsgade 7 (☎ 75-42-29-69), which is stuffed with gifts—everything from classic model cars to china dolls. A large assortment of artwork, porcelain, glass, paper collages, and mobiles, plus other decorative items for the home, is sold at **Overdammens Idebutik,** Overdammen 5 (☎ 75-42-14-14). For generations, Ribe citizens have patronized **Børge Bottelet Guldsmedie,** Mellemdammen 14 (☎ 75-42-02-26), for jewelry.

OUTDOOR ACTIVITIES

You can evoke yesteryear by riding a horse-drawn carriage through the cobble-covered streets of Ribe. In summer, you can hire a carriage in Torvet, the central market square. The cost is 40 DKK ($5.80) per person for a ride of about 15 minutes. Carriages hold up to 5 passengers each. For more information, call ☎ **75-42-19-94.**

Anglers and fishers head for **Storkesøen,** an interconnected trio of artificial lakes that government employees keep well stocked with fish, especially trout. Known for their appeal to escapists and for their verdant beauty, they lie less than a mile south of Ribe. A permit allowing 4 consecutive hours of fishing costs 90 DKK ($13.05); 7 hours costs 125 DKK ($18.15); 9 hours costs 150 DKK ($21.75); and a permit good for 24 hours of fishing costs 225 DKK ($32.65). For more information, contact Storkesøen, Haulundvej 164 (☎ 75-41-04-11).

Horseback riding in the area can be arranged through **Gelsådalens Ridelejr,** Ribelandevej 17 at Gram (☎ 74-82-21-22). The cost is 60 DKK ($8.70) per hour.

WHERE TO STAY

Weis' Stue and Restaurant Backhaus (see "Where to Dine," below) also rent rooms. Parking at the following hotels is available on the street.

✪ **Den Gamle Arrest.** Torvet 11, DK-6760 Ribe. ☎ **75-42-37-00.** 12 units (3 with bath). 490–640 DKK ($71.05–$92.80) double without bath; 640–940 DKK ($92.80–$136.30) double with bath. Rates include breakfast. No credit cards.

One of the town's most evocative and charming hotels occupies what was originally built in 1546 as the town jail. Set on the main square of Ribe and constructed of the same russet-colored bricks that formed most of the important buildings of the town, it was a jail until as late as 1989, when it was sold to the present entrepreneurs for transformation into the cozy hotel you'll find today. Bedrooms are snug, often with exposed brick, and enough old-fashioned amenities to remind you of a gentrified version of the building's original function. On the premises is a well-recommended restaurant, described separately below.

Hotel Fru Mathies. Saltgade 15, DK-6760 Ribe. ☎ **75-42-34-20.** 6 units (4 with bath). MINIBAR TV. 550–640 DKK ($79.75–$92.80) double with or without bath. AE, DC, MC, V.

Set behind a bright yellow stucco façade, a very short walk from the city's pedestrian zone, this hotel was named after its present guardian and supervisor, Fru (Mrs.) Inga Mathies. There's a shared TV/living room on the premises, and bedrooms are simple but cozy affairs, each with a radio and modest numbers of old-fashioned accessories. Breakfast is the only meal served.

✪ **Dagmar.** Torvet 1, DK-6760 Ribe. ☎ **800/528-1234** in the U.S., or ☎ 75-42-00-33. Fax 75-42-36-52. 50 units. MINIBAR TV TEL. 925–1,275 DKK ($134.15–$184.90) double. Rates include breakfast. AE, DC, MC, V.

A Denmark legend, this historic 1581 hotel claims the most glamorous address in the region. Converted from a private home in 1850, it's named after a medieval Danish queen. The bedrooms are well furnished and comfortable, roomy, and with lovely traditional pieces, plus state-of-the-art baths. On Friday and Saturday nights (except in summer) there's music and dancing. The hotel's restaurant is recommended in "Where to Dine," below.

Kalvslund Kro. Koldingvej 105 (at Kalvslund), DK-6760 Ribe. ☎ **75-43-70-12.** 5 units, none with bath. 300 DKK ($43.50) double. Rate includes breakfast. No credit cards. Bus: 57 or 921 from Ribe. Closed Oct–Apr.

An 1865 Danish inn 5 ½-miles north of Ribe via Route 52, the Kalvslund Kro offers comfortable rooms but few frills. The furniture, according to the management, "is old but not antique." The restaurant serves home-style cooking. The food we've sampled was well prepared and well presented. Full meals include such dishes as asparagus soup, Danish beef with sautéed onions, and pork cutlets. From May to September, the restaurant is open daily from 11am to 10pm; the rest of the year it opens only with advance reservations and agreed-upon times.

WHERE TO DINE

Den Gamle Arrest. Torvet 11. ☎ **75-42-37-00.** Reservations recommended. Main courses 120–160 DKK ($17.40–$23.20). AE, DC, MC, V. June–Sept only, daily noon–3pm and 6–9pm. DANISH.

One of the newest restaurants in Ribe, and housed in one of the most unusual buildings, this redbrick monument was originally built in the 1500s as the town's debtor's prison and jail. You'll be able to stroll within the courtyard that functioned for centuries as an area where prisoners could exercise, although your experience will be much, much more pleasant than the ones they undoubtedly endured. Menu items include such Danish staples as grilled fillets of salmon with spicy herb sauce, filet of ox meat with fresh vegetables and red wine sauce, and roasted turkey served with a mango-flavored chutney sauce. There is nothing served here that overtaxes the imagination of the chef, but the cookery is good and tasty, the portions filling, and the ingredients fresh.

Restaurant Backhaus. Grydergade 12, DK-6760 Ribe. ☎ **75-42-11-01.** Reservations recommended. Main courses 60–120 DKK ($8.70–$17.40). DC, MC, V. Daily 11am–9:30pm. DANISH.

The brick-fronted, antique building that contains this place has served as some kind of restaurant or inn for as long as anyone in Ribe can remember. Today, under the hardworking sponsorship of one of Ribe's most prominent matrons, it continues the tradition with steaming platters of all-Danish food that arrive in generous portions at reasonable prices. Menu specialties include a Danish platter containing artfully arranged presentations of herring, cheeses, and vegetables that taste wonderful with the establishment's earthy, rough-textured bread; tomato soup with sour cream and a surprising but refreshing dab of horseradish; tender pork schnitzels served with potatoes and braised red cabbage; and sautéed strips of beef tenderloin with fried onions that hits the spot on a cold, windy day. Dessert might be a hazelnut pie with vanilla ice cream.

On the premises are seven simple bedrooms, each of which is a stripped-down but comfortable hideaway that's very clean and completely without artifice or pretension. With breakfast included, doubles cost 500 DKK ($72.50). With the exception of about a week every year at Christmas, the hotel is open year-round.

Restaurant Dagmar. In the Hotel Dagmar, Torvet 1. ☎ **75-42-00-33.** Reservations required. Main courses 139–255 DKK ($20.15–$36.95); fixed-price menu 175 DKK ($25.40) at lunch, 265–395 DKK ($38.40–$57.30) at dinner. AE, DC, MC, V. Daily noon–10pm. DANISH/INTERNATIONAL.

Opposite the cathedral (near the train station), the Hotel Dagmar's four dining rooms are a 19th-century dream of ornate furnishings and accessories. The international cuisine is the best in town, and it's impeccably served and complemented by a good wine list. Generally two different fresh North Sea fish dishes of the day are offered. Among meat and poultry selections, try the fried quail stuffed with mushrooms on *beurre blanc* (white butter), or veal tenderloin with shallot mousse in port sauce. There's also a cozy cellar dining room.

Restaurant Kammerslusen. Bjerrumvej 30, DK-6760 Ribe. ☎ **75-42-07-96.** Fax 75-42-29-32. Reservations recommended. Main courses 85–165 DKK ($12.35–$23.90). Set-price menu 155 DKK ($22.45). DC, MC, V. Daily 11am–9pm. DANISH.

Built in 1997 in a position abutting both the seacoast and the canal that connects Ribe to the sea, this is one of the newest restaurants in Jutland. To reach it, drive 9 ½-miles east of Ribe, across flat and sandy terrain, until you eventually reach a redbrick, old-fashioned-looking hideaway that's permeated with Danish hospitality and respectability. There is no public transport to this hotel. Menu items derive from long-standing regional traditions, and include fried fillets of eel with white sauce and new potatoes, poached red salmon with au gratin potatoes, and a particularly popular house specialty of grilled steak with barbecue sauce and fried onions. The cookery is always reliable and tasty, and it's easy to understand why this has suddenly blossomed into a local favorite.

✪ **Restaurant Sælhunden.** Skibbroen 13, DK-6760 Ribe. ☎ **75-42-09-46.** Reservations recommended. Main courses 80–126 DKK ($11.60–$18.25). DC, MC, V. Apr–Oct, 11am–9:45pm (last food order); Nov–Mar, 11am–8:45pm (last food order). Beer served till midnight. DANISH/INTERNATIONAL.

One of the most evocative and cheerful restaurants in Ribe occupies a venerable but cozy brick building whose history goes back to 1634. Set beside the river that flows through Ribe, within full view of the craft that kept its commerce alive during its mercantile heyday, it has flourished as a restaurant since 1969. Today, you're likely to find an engaging staff deriving from every corner of Europe, and an antique format whose size is doubled during mild weather thanks to an outdoor terrace. Menu items include at least three kinds of steaks that include T-bone, French-style entrecôte, and something known as "English steak," that presumably gives British visitors access to the kinds of meat that is no longer legal in England. There's also fried fillets of plaice cooked in white wine with leeks; platters of meatballs or smoked salmon; and a local delicacy, smoked and fried dab, a flat fish not unlike flounder that flourishes in the local estuaries. The cuisine appeals to discerning tastes. Products are well chosen for quality and are fresh. Sauces are light but dishes are well seasoned. The cookery is imaginative and versatile, catering to a wide assortment of tastes. No one will mind if you come here just for a beer or a simple snack. In summertime, it's one of the closest approximations in town to the kind of beer garden you might have expected in Hamburg, with Carlsberg priced at 20 to 29 DKK ($2.90–$4.20), depending on its size.

Værtshuset Sælhunden. Skibbroen 13. ☎ **75-42-09-46.** Main courses 50–100 DKK ($7.25–$14.50). DC, MC, V. Daily noon–9pm. DANISH.

This charming little restaurant stands amid stately trees near the edge of the town's narrow canal just north of the cathedral. The low-slung brick building dates from the 1600s, although in the 18th and 19th centuries it was the town's shoe factory. The dining room, the **Seals Room,** is decorated with many pictures and seal skins. Regional dishes include *skipperlavskovs* (beef, potatoes, and onions concocted into a hash) served with brown bread and a beetroot salad. Also featured are clear bouillon with meatballs, and fried fillet of plaice. The chef also specializes in ostrich, which is grown on a farm nearby. Here the bird is roasted and served with a tomato sauce, potatoes, and sweet peas. For dessert, there is a homemade strawberry jelly served with thick cream, or else you may opt for the homemade nougat and walnut ice cream. In summer you can sit in the cozy yard.

Weis'Stue. Torvet 2, DK-6760 Ribe. ☎ **75-42-07-00.** Reservations recommended. Main courses 85–175 DKK ($12.35–$25.40); two-course fixed-price menu 125 DKK ($18.15). MC, V. Daily 11am–10pm. DANISH.

Small and charming—and infused with a sense of history—this brick-and-timber inn is located on the market square adjacent to the cathedral. Originally built in the 1500s, and gradually enlarged over the centuries, it derives most of its income from the restaurant, although overnight guests can choose from one of four upstairs bedrooms. None of these has a private bathroom, but the accommodations are cozy, not overly large, and antique. With breakfast included, a double costs 450 DKK ($65.25).

Food in the ground-floor restaurant is plentiful and well prepared. Menu items might include shrimp with mayonnaise and marinated herring with raw onions, smoked Greenland halibut with scrambled eggs, liver paste with mushrooms, sliced ham and Italian salad, filet of beef with onions, and two sorts of cheese with bread and butter.

RIBE AFTER DARK

Your best bet is to head for the Hotel Dagmar (see previous recommendation). It is the most happening place in Ribe. If it's winter, visit **Vægterkælderen,** Torvet (☎ 75-42-36-52), the place to enjoy a good meal in informal and traditional surroundings, or else to stop in for a glass of frothy, newly drawn ale in the company of locals. The kitchen serves homemade pickled herring, fresh fish dishes, and juicy steaks, but many locals just come in for a drink. In the summer months you might want to sit outside in the Dagmar's courtyard, enjoying the **Pavillionen,** Torvet (☎ **75-42-00-33).** Hot drinks are served on cooler days, but if it's hot you can order draft beer or even lemonade. Light summer meals, including fresh fish, are served. You can listen to the bells in the cathedral tower, admire the storks in their nests, and if you're still around at 10 o'clock at night, see the night watchman as he prepares for his rounds.

The market square is also the home of the **Stenbohus Pub & Bar,** entered at Stenbogade 1 (☎ **75-42-01-22),** where live music can be heard at least once a week—folk, rock, soul, or blues. Otherwise, it's one of the most congenial taverns in town to meet locals over a glass of beer with a good head on it. **Vægterkælderen** (see above) is a classier joint for a drink; this one is more informal, attracting a more youthful crowd.

✪ A SIDE TRIP TO MANDØ

The island of Mandø, 6 miles off the coast of Jutland southwest of Ribe, is one of the most tranquil island hideaways in Denmark. Surrounded by the Wadden Sea, it has remained virtually untouched by tourism, partly because of the sheer awkwardness involved with getting here. Other than privately owned watercraft, the only way of reaching the island is via a bumpy stone-and-gravel drive (the Låningsvejen) that's completely submerged during high tide, usually twice a day.

Under normal conditions, and whenever seas aren't particularly rough, access is possible some 15 to 18 hours during every 24-hour period in summertime. The island itself is a low-lying marshland that's protected from erosion by a man-made dike that surrounds it, and by massive sandbanks and dunes that are infertile, uninhabited, completely surrounded by water during high tides, and which change their size and locations after storms.

To reach Mandø from Ribe, drive 6-miles southwest of town to the coastal hamlet of Vester Vedsted, which marks the debut of the above-mentioned Låningsvejen. The distance from Vester Vedsted to Mando is 7 miles, of which 3 ½ miles are, as mentioned above, submerged by the high tides of the Wadden Sea. If you respect the clearly posted safety notices and the schedule of tides, a conventional car can make the trip out to Mandø without incident. You can also enlist as a passenger in the **Mandø Bussen** (Mandø Bus), a heavy-duty tractor-bus that's equipped with large-tread tires. It departs from the car park just to the west of Vester Vedsted at least twice a day between May and September, charging 50 DKK ($7.25) per passenger. Except under optimum circumstances, it doesn't run at all between October and April. For information about departure times, call either the tourist office in Ribe or the Mandø Bussen at ☎ **75-44-51-57.**

The first recorded mention of Mandø appeared in 1231, when it was claimed in its entirety by the Danish monarchs. However, in 1741, the inhabitants purchased the island from the king at auction. Then, and throughout the rest of the 18th and 19th centuries, the island's men were involved with shipping while the women took care of the farms. In 1890, the island's population was 262; today, the island has a year-round population of only 70.

A few yards from where the bus stops in Mandø village stands **Mandøhuset** (☎ 75-44-60-52), an old skipper's home, now a museum of local artifacts. Entrance is 5 DKK (75¢) for adults and 3 DKK (45¢) for children. Visits are possible Monday to Friday from 10am to 4pm.

To the south stands **Mondø Kirke,** dating from 1639. The entrance costs 2 DKK (30¢) but you have to call for an appointment to have the church opened (☎ 75-44-51-80). An old mill, built in 1860, can be seen in the northern part of the village.

Bird life here is outstanding, with thousands of breeding pairs, including eider ducks, sandpipers, and oyster catchers.

The tidal flats on the island are neither land nor sea. One moment they are dry, but for 6 hours a day they are covered by vast quantities of water. These flats are spawning grounds for several species of edible fish including plaice and cod. It is estimated that every year 10 to 12 million birds fly over these tidal flats.

In all, these flats are Denmark's largest nature reserve. For those who like bird-watching, the spring and autumn migration periods are the best times to visit.

If you look anywhere to the southwest of Mandø, you'll get a view of what's some-times referred to as Denmark's largest desert, an uninhabited expanse of sand dunes surrounded like an island by tidal flats that are submerged during high tides and storms. With borders and channels (*prieler*) whose positions are constantly changing because of storm and wave actions, the dunes and sand deposits are known as **Kore-sand.** Although a visit in winter is not advisable, during calm seas in summer, the site attracts ecologists and bird-watchers as part of twice-per-week half-day tours that are arranged by the same entrepreneurs who manage the above-mentioned **Mandø Bussen** (☎ 75-44-51-57 for reservations and departure times).

Visitors depart from and return to Mandø within open trailers drawn by tractors that resemble the Mandø Bussen described earlier. En route, you'll pass some of the largest seal colonies in the Baltic. (These are most active and interesting during the month of August.) You'll also be able to see the island of Rømø to the south and the island of Fanø to the northwest. There's usually the chance to search for amber on the beaches of Koresand, depending on the waves and the weather. The whole experience covers about 15 ½ miles and takes about 2 hours. The cost of the excursion is 50 DKK ($7.25) for adults and 25 DKK ($3.60) for children under 12.

WHERE TO STAY AND DINE

Accommodations on Mandø are available at an establishment that's part private home, part B&B, at least whenever there are enough guests in residence to justify its trans-formation.

Solid, unsurprising, and reliable, **Mandø Kro,** Mandø Buvej, Mandø DK-6760 Ribe (☎ 75-44-60-83), rents five rooms, none with private bath, that are simple, function-ally decorated, and completely unpretentious. Set on the west side of the island, it's open only from April to October, charging 500 DKK ($72.50) for a double room, a rate that includes breakfast and dinner for two occupants. Credit cards are not accepted.

6 Esbjerg

93km (58 miles) W of Vejle; 168km (105 miles) SW of Århus; 277km (173 miles) W of Copen-hagen

Esbjerg's harbor, on the west coast of Denmark, with its easy accessibility to the North Sea, is a perfect shipping point for large agricultural exports to Great Britain, making it Denmark's largest fishing port. In recent years the oil and natural gas deposits in the North Sea have made Esbjerg the country's oil city. Many ships here are used as supply vessels for Danish oil rigs.

Esbjerg is laid out with straight, wide streets, square town sections, and a large town square. There's a long pedestrian street, plus many specialty shops and large shopping centers. Within the town are parks and lakes with wooded areas.

Denmark's youngest major city can also be used as a base for exploring one of the country's prime holiday areas, a landscape of beaches, nature experiences, medieval towns, and amusement parks.

After Denmark lost the Schleswig/Holstein region to Germany in 1864, it needed an export harbor for the shipping of grain to Britain. In what had previously been farmland, the town at Esbjerg was founded in 1868, with the port opening in 1874. It was granted its city charter in 1898. The population has steadily grown to 82,000, making Esbjerg the fifth largest city of Denmark. The down side here is that since the city is relatively new, it doesn't have the old-time historic core that attracts visitors to most cities, such as Ribe (see above). However, in spite of that, there is much here to amuse.

ESSENTIALS

GETTING THERE   By Plane   Esbjerg Airport (☎ 75-16-02-00), receives 5 or 6 flights a day from Copenhagen on **Mærsk Airlines** (☎ 75-16-07-77), and several flights a week from both Aberdeen and Dundee in Scotland on **Business Air,** whose bookings are made through the staff at Mærsk Airlines (see above). There are also daily flights into Esbjerg from Stavanger in southern Norway, and daily flights into Esbjerg from Newcastle upon Tyne in England, both via **Danish Air Transport** (☎ 75-18-14-22).

By Train   About three buses depart every day for Esbjerg from Frederikshaven, Ålborg, Viborg, and Herning.

By Car   From all corners of Denmark, highways lead to Esbjerg. From the German border in the south, take Route 11 north, heading left at the junction with Route 24. From Funen in the east, take the E20 express highway west across Jutland.

By Ferry   Esbjerg has three weekly ferryboat departures heading for Harwich in England throughout the year. Travel time, each way, is around 19 hours. For information and reservations, contact **Scandinavian Seaways** at ☎ 79-17-97-17. You can also connect by ferry with Fanø (see below). Ferries to Fanø take only 10 minutes from Esbjerg and service in summer is every 20 minutes during the day or every 40 minutes off-season. Information is available by calling **Fanø-overfarten** (☎ 75-13-45-00).

VISITOR INFORMATION   The **Esbjerg Tourist Office,** Skolegade 33 (☎ 75-12-55-99), is open Monday through Friday from 9am to 5pm and on Saturday from 9am to 1pm (until 5pm in summer).

SEEING THE SIGHTS

The town landmark is the **Esbjerg Vandtårn,** or Esbjerg Watertower, lying 2 blocks south of Torvet (market square) at Havnegade 22 (☎ 75-12-78-11). It was erected in 1897 by C. H. Clausen, the town architect at the time, so don't be taken in by its look, evocative of the Middle Ages. Since Esbjerg was so new, town fathers at the time wanted the tower to give the town a more medieval look, even if it were merely the mock. You can climb the tower from June 1 to September 15 from 10am to 4pm. Off-season hours are only on Saturday and Sunday from 10am to 4pm. Admission is 10 DKK ($1.45) adults, 5 DKK (75¢) children.

Esbjerg Havn (Esbjerg Harbor), is one of the most important in Denmark—Christian IX in 1868 called it "Denmark's gateway to the west." The oldest section is

Den gamle Dokhavn and England Quay, the latter being the terminal that sees the arrival of some 200,000 ferry passengers between Denmark and England annually.

Just west of the Den gamle Dokhavn lie the ferry terminals taking passengers to the holiday island of Fanø (see below).

Close to the ferryboat terminal for boats headed to Fanø, at Esbjerg Havn, the museum lightship, *Horns Rev* (☎ **75-45-91-88**), lies permanently anchored. The vessel offers visitors an excellent impression of what life was like on board the ship, which helped to protect shipping off of the dangerous west coast of Jutland until 1984. It can be visited between May and September every Monday, Tuesday, and Thursday from 9:30am to 2pm. Entrance costs 10 DKK ($1.45) per person.

If you have a passion for things maritime, and if the idea of a waterside view of the port of Esbjerg appeals to you, consider a round-trip passage aboard *M/S Sønderho,* which leaves from the docks at Færgehavnen. Tours of the harbor last 75 minutes each, are conducted from late June to early September, and depart as follows: Monday to Thursday at 11am, 1pm, and 3pm; Friday at 11am and 1pm. Adults pay 35 DKK ($5.05); children under age 12, 17 DKK ($2.45).

At the southern end of the harbor lies Vestkraft power plant, which boasts Denmark's highest chimney stack—812 ½-feet tall. Vestkraft supplies the entire south and west Jutland area with electricity as well as providing inexpensive heat for some 80,000 of the region's inhabitants. At the far end of the harbor lies Østerhavn, which is used as a base for shipping supplies and equipment to the many offshore oil and gas production facilities in the North Sea.

Although the fish auctions aren't what they used to be when the industry was more important for Esbjerg, they are still held at 9:30am on Wednesday in July and August in a large auction hall (clearly visible) at the harbor. Fishing for edible fish has declined, although Esbjerg is still a leading producer of fish meal and fish oil—some 600 tons of fish are processed here annually for that purpose.

The newest landmark in Esbjerg—also at the harbor—has attracted a lot of attention, both from visitors and locals. Called "Esbjerg's new giants," they are four chalky white figures, the late Svend Wiig Hansen's giant sculpture, "Man Meets the Sea," located at Sædding Strand, on a 180-square-yard area of the shore opposite the fishing museum (see below). These concrete figures, gazing out across the mysterious sea, are 259-feet high. They sit upright like Greek columns. The four figures are completely alike, radiating a kind of classical beauty. The images evoke the massive monuments of ancient Egypt, perhaps something found in the Valley of the Kings.

Bogtrykmuseet. Borgergade 6. ☎ **75-12-78-11.** Admission 15 DKK ($2.15) adults, 10 DKK ($1.45) children. Tues–Fri 1–4pm, Sat–Mon noon–4pm. Bus: 1, 5, 6, 8, or 9.

The largest working presswork museum in Denmark, it's built and furnished like a medium-size Danish printing office. Exhibits of printed work and presses trace the craft of printing through 500 years. You can see the process as it developed from handset type and printing on cumbersome man-powered presses to today's fast, accurate production with modern state-of-the-art equipment.

Esbjerg Kunstmuseum (Esbjerg Art Museum). Havnegade 20. ☎ **75-13-02-11.** Admission 30 DKK ($4.35) adults, 15 DKK ($2.15) children. Daily 10am–4pm.

The city's museum of art focuses both on its permanent collection and constantly changing exhibitions of contemporary art, mainly from Europe. The museum is one of the finest in Denmark for displaying the works of the country's artists. Outstanding artists on exhibit include Richard Mortensen, Robert Jacobsen, and Per Kirkeby. The museum lies in the central park area of the city.

Esbjerg Museum. Nørregade 25. ☎ **75-12-78-11.** Admission 20 DKK ($2.90) adults, 10 DKK ($1.45) children. Tues–Sun 10am–4pm. Closed Jan 1, June 5, and Dec 24–25. Bus: 1, 5, 6, 8, or 9.

From the train and bus station, follow the signs for a quarter of a mile to this museum, off of Torvetgade. It tells the story of amber, called "the Danish gold." The museum exhibits hundreds of amber objects, some nearly 10,000 years old. The west coast of Jutland is famed for its amber, and the museum tells how amber was gathered over the centuries, and how people have used it from the Mesolithic Age until today. A Viking Age exhibition is also presented.

Fiskeri-og-Søfartsmuseet, Salt-Vandsakvariet & Sælarium (Museum of Fishing & Shopping). Tarphagvej 2. ☎ **75-15-06-66.** Admission 55 DKK ($8) adults, 30 DKK ($4.35) children. June–Aug daily 10am–6pm, Sept–May daily 10am–5pm. Bus: 22, 23, or 30.

Lying 2 ½-miles northwest of the city center, this unusual attraction is an aquarium containing some 50 species of fish. There is an outdoor sea pool where you can attend seal feedings at 11am and 2:30pm daily. Down below you can watch the antics of the seals underwater and through glass.

SHOPPING   Esbjerg is the major city for shopping in South Jutland. Everything from fresh food and delicacies to fashion and decorative art is found along **Torvet-gade,** a main shopping thoroughfare. If you don't find it here, chances are Esbjerg doesn't sell it. The other major shopping venue is **Kongensgade,** one of the biggest centers for shopping in West Jutland, with some 156 specialty shops. One of the widest assortments of interesting gifts and Danish crafts, such as glassware, is found at **Chess,** Torvetgade 7 (☎ 75-12-33-05). There's a stunning collection of Georg Jensen pipes for the smoker in the family at **Vinstokken,** Kongensgade 102 (☎ **75-12-06-19**). If you're planning to do a lot of picture taking in South Jutland, replenish your camera supplies at **PhotoCare,** Kongensgade 21 (☎ **75-13-50-44**). **Christine Jør-gensen** became world famous in the 1950s as a man called George who journeyed to Copenhagen for a sex change operation, and became a legend, although operations such as that are relatively commonplace today. Christine Jørgensen—not the person, but a shop of the same name—is found at Kirkevej 85 (☎ **75-12-63-77**), selling the most delectable chocolates in South Jutland.

WHERE TO STAY
EXPENSIVE

✪ **Hotel Hjerting.** Strandpromenaden 1, DK-6710 Esbjerg V. ☎ **75-11-76-77.** Fax 75-11-76-77. www.sima.dk/hotel hjerting. 45 units. MINIBAR TV TEL. 750–850 DKK ($108.75–$123.25) double. Rate includes breakfast. AE, DC, MC, V. Bus: 3 from Esbjerg.

One of the most appealing hotels in Esbjerg lies 4-miles northwest of the center, a very short walk from the beach, at the top of a rocky seawall that breaks up the power of destructive waves during storms. Capped with a red roof and painted the traditional yellow of a Danish *kro,* it was originally built a century ago, and was expanded in 1987 and again in 1992 with two additional extensions and wings containing traditionally furnished, spacious, and comfortable bedrooms with medium-size tiled baths with generous towels. Today, most of the clients come here to unwind from urban stress and experience the sea in some direct way, either through swimming during mild weather or merely by gazing over its surface from its terraces or from either of its well-recommended restaurants.

    Dining/Diversions: The more formal of the hotel's restaurants is the Strand-pavilion, where set menus priced at 169 DKK ($24.50) focus on fresh ingredients, seasonal variety, and Danish and French traditions. Less formal, and cheaper, is the cozy, brick-and-wood-sheathed Ship Inn, an English-style pub serving set menus for 69 DKK ($10) each. Both sites are open daily, year-round, for both lunch and dinner.

Amenities: Virtually every activity on the premises centers around the nearby beach. The reception staff can arrange golf games at nearby golf courses, or give directions to the attractions that are available within the surrounding region, such as Legoland.

Scandic Hotel Esbjerg. Strandbygade 3, DK-6700 Esbjerg. ☎ or fax **75-18-11-08.** www.scandic-hotels.com. 86 units. MINIBAR TV TEL. Sun–Thurs 1,095 DKK ($158.75) double; Fri–Sat year-round 750 DKK ($108.75) double. Mid-June to mid-Aug, 650 DKK ($94.25) double. Rate includes breakfast. AE, DC, MC, V.

Built in a bulky, boxy-looking, four-story format in the 1970s, this member of a national hotel chain is the largest hotel in Esbjerg's center. Drawing on the experience of other Scandic hotels in other parts of Scandinavia, it's the best bet within the town center for clean, well-maintained accommodations with a blandly standardized, uncontroversial international flavor. Bedrooms are color-coordinated, conservatively modern, very comfortable, and often occupied by business travelers from other parts of Scandinavia.

Dining/Diversions: Both Danish and international food is served in the dining room, Restaurant Scandic Olympic, which offers a fixed-price two-course menu for 195 DKK ($28.30) and a fixed-price three-course menu for 225 DKK ($32.65). The restaurant is spacious, stylish, and formal, relying on good well-trained chefs and market-fresh ingredients. There's also a cozy bar for relaxation.

Amenities: Room service, concierge, sauna, and a solarium.

MODERATE

Hotel Ansgar. Skolegade 36, DK-6700 Esbjerg. ☎ **75-12-82-44.** Fax 75-13-95-40. 55 units. TV TEL. Fri–Sat and June 20–Aug 7, 590 DKK ($85.55) double. Sun–Thurs 725 DKK ($105.10) double. Rate includes breakfast. AE, DC, MC, V.

Set behind an elaborate and dignified white-painted façade near the town's most centrally located square, this is Esbjerg's grande dame hotel, with a pedigree that goes back to the 1920s and an architecture that evokes the building styles of the early 20th century. In 1997, it was radically renovated, and in some cases, walls were knocked out as a means of making some units bigger than they had been originally. Bedrooms are impeccably maintained, clean, cozy, and modern, usually with pale colors and tones of blue-gray and white. Most contain a mini-bar. One of the most appealing sites within this hotel is its restaurant, which is recommended separately in "Where to Dine" (see below). The hotel lies a 5-minute walk from the sea.

Hotel Britannia. Torvet, DK-6701 Esbjerg. ☎ **75-13-01-11.** Fax 75-45-20-85. 79 units. MINIBAR TV TEL. June–Aug 695 DKK ($100.75) double, Sept–May 880 DKK ($127.60) double. Rates include breakfast. AE, DC, MC, V.

One of the best hostelries in town for those seeking middle-bracket lodgings, this four-story hotel was constructed in a rather bland format typical of the 1960s, but was enlarged, upgraded, and improved in 1985. The medium-size bedrooms with small tile baths are comfortable and outfitted in a traditional international modern style, convenient and accommodating, if short on character. On the premises is a moderate restaurant serving a standard international fare, with some Danish regional specialties. A two-course menu costs 245 DKK ($35.55), with three courses going for 265 DKK ($38.40).

INEXPENSIVE

Palads Hotel Cab Inn. Skolegade 14, DK-6700 Esbjerg. ☎ **75-18-16-00.** Fax 75-18-16-24. 94 units. TV TEL. 510–595 DKK ($73.95–$86.25). Rates include breakfast. AE, DC, MC, V. Bus: 2.

Although its accommodations are far from being the most plush or luxurious in town, the exterior of this hotel retains all the dignity and quirky stateliness of its construction in 1912, when it functioned as the most upscale and glamorous hotel in town. Today, the detailed red brickwork and the conical twin towers of its façade remain intact, despite numerous renovations and many, many stripping-downs of its original opulence into efficient, cost-effective lodgings. The larger and more gracious of the bedrooms here are identified by the staff as "Palace Rooms" and lie near the front of the hotel. The smaller, more bare-boned of the rooms lie in the back, and are known as Cab Inn rooms after the nationwide chain (the Cab Inns) that the hotel belongs to. Regardless of which category of rooms you select, there's something akin to the feel of a college dormitory about both categories, partly because of the formica-sheathed amenities that are durable but not at all glamorous, and a sense of budget-conscious living that pervades the place. Breakfast is the only meal served.

WHERE TO DINE

Munkestuen. Smedegade 21. ☎ **75-18-17-44.** Reservations recommended. Main courses 138–198 DKK ($20–$28.70). AE, DC, MC, V. Mon–Sat 11:30am–3pm and 6:30–9:45pm. DANISH/FRENCH.

In light of the fact that Esbjerg is a relatively new city, its owners cite the 1890s house that contains this restaurant as one of the oldest in town. Until 1985, it functioned as a private home, but at that time, the present owners radically upgraded its interior, added a lot of gaslight-era kitsch, and opened for business as one of the most consistently popular restaurants in town. You'll see chandeliers and candelabrum that might have appealed to Liberace, big portraits of big women enjoying their gin, and references to the railways that helped propel Esbjerg into the mercantile city you'll see today. Menu items include an oversized platter containing three or four kinds of fried fresh fish; medallions of veal served with oysters, rosemary, thyme, and brandy sauce; and one of the best versions of pepper steak (a house specialty) in town. The cookery at times has a certain flair and remains consistently good. This is among the more dependable choices in town.

Papa's Cantina. Torvet. ☎ **75-13-08-00.** Main courses 95–120 DKK ($13.75–$17.40). All-you-can-eat Mexican buffet (available Mon–Thurs only) 99 DKK ($14.35). MEXICAN.

You'll get the feeling here that the local Jutlanders appreciate the Mexican theme that dominates this place, using it as an excuse to really let down their hair and play at being "faux-Latinos." Outfitted with Mexican weavings and rustic Mexican artifacts, it's one of the most consistently popular restaurants in town, thanks to a well-prepared roster of nachos, empanadas, tostitas, chimichangas, and tortillas. Recorded salsa and merengue music plays as you enjoy any of four kinds of margaritas (including banana, lime, strawberry, and a mélange of fruits that the local Danes refer to as a "tutti-frutti") at a large bar that's positioned in the center of the dining room. Many clients head for the all-you-can-eat Mexican buffet, which includes both a salad bar and an ice cream bar, the best value in town. On Friday and Saturday nights, from midnight to 6am, the site is transformed into a disco. Entrance is free on Friday night, and priced at 25 DKK ($3.60) on Saturday night.

Restaurant Ansgar. In the Hotel Ansgar, Skolegade 36. ☎ **75-12-82-44.** Reservations recommended. Main courses. 125–135 DKK ($18.15–$19.60). AE, DC, MC, V. Daily 11:30am–2pm and 5:30–9:30pm. DANISH/INTERNATIONAL.

Set within the street level of the previously recommended hotel, this is a solidly reliable, eminently respectable restaurant that has at one time or another received visits from virtually every politician or businessperson within the region. High-ceilinged and formal-looking, it offers dishes that include clear soup with meatballs; shrimp cocktail with home-baked bread; French-style steaks sizzled in butter sauce; Indian-style curried chicken; chateaubriand with morels; and for dessert, a medley of ice creams and pastries made on the premises. The cooking is dependable, the ingredients are fresh, but the kitchen rarely creates any culinary excitement here.

Restaurant Pakhuset. Dokvej 3. ☎ **75-12-74-55.** Reservations required. Main courses 140–210 DKK ($20.30–$30.45). Five-course fixed-price menu 375 DKK ($54.35). AE, DC, MC, V. Tues–Sat noon–3pm, and 6–10pm. DANISH.

The redbrick building was constructed in 1902 as an auction hall for the tons of fish hauled from nearby waterways. Set a few paces from the ferryboats that depart for Fanø, the building (whose name translates as "warehouse") now functions as a restaurant and art gallery. In a heavily trussed and beamed interior similar to that of a high-ceilinged chapel, oil paintings by Danish artists are displayed and often purchased by diners. Launch yourself with a summer salad with a *confit* of baby onions, going on to a perfectly prepared Danish filet of veal with an essence of basil, or perhaps steamed fillets of fjord salmon with red bib lettuce. Many Danes prefer to end their repast with a selection of cheeses from both Denmark and Eastern France; others request something from the dessert trolley, perhaps an assortment of chocolates perfumed with essence of orange and orange zest, often garnished with the sorbets of the day.

ESBJERG AFTER DARK

If there's a major cultural event being presented in Esbjerg—ballet, opera, or whatever—its venue will be the stunningly designed **Musikhuset Esbjerg,** Havnegade 18 (☎ 76-10-90-00). The tourist office (see above) will have complete details of what might be presented (if anything) at the time of your visit. The chalk-white tiled building—the work of Jørn and Jan Utzon—rises up like some huge, tempting lump of sugar in the old city park area between the main square and the waterfront. Jørn was the world-famous architect of the Sydney Opera House. Jan is his son, also an architect.

The city boasts several symphony orchestras, and the Esbjerg Ensemble presents numerous concerts throughout the year. On a number of Wednesdays in summer, city officials offer free summer entertainment under an open sky (the tourist office will have details).

Rock and jazz concerts, along with theatrical performances, are also presented at **Multihus Tobaksfabrikken,** Gasværksgade 2 (☎ 75-18-02-22), a spectacular "mecca" seating an audience of 750. Here musical events are presented year-round, ticket prices again depending on the different shows booked here.

A pub that can provide conversation and diversion for a while is **You'll Never Walk Alone,** Kongensgade 10 (☎ 75-45-40-60), which celebrates Esbjerg's close ties with Britain and Ireland, thanks to English and Celtic folk musicians who sometimes appear here. Also, don't overlook the possibility of disco fever, beginning at midnight on Fridays and Saturdays, within the premises of what was previously recommended as a restaurant, **Papa's Cantina,** Torvet (☎ 75-13-08-00), where cover charges rarely exceed 25 DKK ($3.60), and which attracts as hard-core a crowd of nightlife addicts as Esbjerg can provide.

Walking Tours in Marbæk

Seven-miles north of Esbjerg between Ho Bay and the Varde River lies the scenic Marbæk area, spread over 3,250 acres. This area has now been designated a nature reserve. The name first appears in the 17th century, but it wasn't until the beginning of the 20th century that interest was shown in this wide, desolate stretch of heath where all traces of the original forests have long disappeared. In 1904, a local barrister, E. M. Hansen, began to plant trees, and today these woodlands cover 1,125 acres of the total. Trees range from sitka spruce to different types of pine.

During the last Ice Age the area was largely leveled by waters of the melting snows of the Arctic spring. Up until around the time of Christ, the North Sea came right into the mainland. But gradually the sea deposited new sandflats along the coast. In time Ho Bay was formed, and the cliffs of Marbæk became relatively sheltered.

In a relatively small space one can view many different species of plants, such as lyme grass, sea purslane, sea milkwort, and the stalkless obione. The heathland ranges from dry crowberry heath to swampy heath. Gorse is also found. Wildlife abounds here too, notably foxes, deer, hares, kestrels, and the common buzzard, along with pheasants, snipe, and sparrow hawks. In the spring by the lakes and ponds you can see web-footed birds such as the pochard, tufted duck, mute swan, coot, and moorhen.

The best trails to follow are named after colors. The red trail, called the Strandtur or beach trail, is 3-miles long and takes about 90 minutes to walk. The trail starts on the beachfront at Hjerting. The green trail, called the Nordturen or north trail, is 3-miles long and also takes about 90 minutes to walk. It starts at the parking area, called Pax. The blue trail or Søtur (sea trail) is 2 ½-miles long and takes about 70 minutes to walk. This trail runs from the parking area near Marbækgård. The yellow trail, called Skovtur or woodland trail, is also 2 ½-miles long and also takes about 70 minutes to walk. This trail starts at the parking lot in the middle of Marbæk plantation.

From Esbjerg you can drive in the direction of Oksbol along a road called Vestkystvejen as far as the Varde River, or along the coast road through Hjerting and Sjelborg, then take minor roads (sign-posted) into the area itself. Bus no. 8 also runs here from Esbjerg.

7 Fanø

46¹/₂ km (29 miles) NW of Ribe; 281¹/₂ km (176 miles) W of Copenhagen

Off the coast of South Jutland, this is one of the most beautiful of North Sea islands. Consisting of a landmass of some 21 square miles, with a population of some 3,500, it is known for its white sandy beaches, which have made it a popular holiday resort in summer. In addition to its beaches, heathland and dunes also dominate the landscape. The best beaches are in the northwest, mostly in and around the hamlets of Rindby Strand and Fanø Bad.

Nordby, where the ferry arrives, is a logical starting point for exploring the island of Fanø. Here you'll find heather-covered moors, windswept sand dunes, fir trees, wild deer, and bird sanctuaries. From Ribe, Fanø makes for a great day's excursion (or longer if there's time).

Fanø is a popular summer resort among the Danes, Germans, and English. **Sønderho,** on the southern tip, and only 8 ½ miles from Nordby, with its memorial to sailors drowned at sea, is our favorite spot—somewhat desolate, but that's its charm.

A summer highlight on Fanø is the **Fannikerdagene festival,** the second weekend in July, which offers traditional dancing, costumes, and events connected with the days when sailing ships played a major part in community life.

If you miss the festival, try to be on Fanø the third Sunday in July for **Sønderho Day.** The high point of the festival day is a wedding procession that passes through the town to the square by the old mill. Traditional costumes and bridal dances are some of the attractions.

It was a Dutchman who launched Denmark's first bathing resort at Nordby in 1851. It consisted of a raft on which some bathing huts had been set up. The bathers entered the huts, undressed, put on different clothes, pulled down an awning to the water's surface, and bathed under the awning.

Until 1741 Fanø belonged to the king, who, when he ran short of money, sold the island at auction. The islanders themselves purchased it, and the king then granted permission for residents to build ships, which led to its prosperity.

From 1741 to 1900 some 1,000 sailing vessels were constructed here, the islanders often manning them as well. Inhabitants built many beautiful houses on Fanø with monies earned. Some of these charming, thatched Fanø homes stand today to greet visitors. There are some in the northern settlement of Nordby, but more in the south at Sønderho.

Although Nordby and Sønderho are the principal settlements, beach lovers head for the seaside resort of Fanø Bad. This is also a popular camping area. From Fanø Bad the beach stretches almost 2 ½ miles to the north. Bathing here is absolutely safe as a sandy bottom slopes gently into the North Sea. There are no ocean holes and no dangerous currents.

Fanø adheres to old island traditions almost more than any other island in Denmark. As late as the 1960s some of the elderly women on Fanø still wore the "Fanø costume," the traditional dress, although today you'll see it only at special events and festivals. This dress originally consisted of five skirts, but today's costumes are likely to have only three. When the skirt was to be pleated, it was wetted, laced up, and sent to the baker who steamed it in a warm oven.

ESSENTIALS

GETTING THERE   From Ribe, head north on Route 11 to Route 24. Follow Route 24 northwest to the city of Esbjerg where you can board a ferry operated by **Scandlines** (☎ **75-13-45-00** for information and schedules). From May to October, ferries depart Esbjerg every 20 minutes during the day for the 12-minute crossing. In winter, service is curtailed, with departures during the day every 45 minutes. A round-trip ticket costs 25 DKK ($3.60) for adults or 12 DKK ($1.75) for children. One average-size car, along with five passengers, is carried for 280 DKK ($40.60) round trip.

VISITOR INFORMATION   The **Fanø Turistbureau,** Færgevej 1, Nordby (☎ **75-16-26-00**), is open Monday to Friday from 8:30am to 5:30pm, Saturday from 9am to 1pm, and Sunday 11am to 1pm. From June 6 to August 23, hours are Monday to Friday 8:30am to 6pm, Saturday 9am to 7pm, and Sunday 9am to 5pm.

GETTING AROUND

Local buses meet passengers at the ferry dock. They crisscross the island about every 40 minutes, with vastly curtailed service in winter. The bus will take you to the communities of Nordby in the north to Sonderhø in the south, with stops at Rindby Strand and Fanø Bad. For information, call **Fanø Rutebiler** at Sonderhø (☎ **75-16-40-10**). The tourist office also keeps a bus timetable.

Many visitors like to explore Fanø by bike. Bikes, costing from 40 DKK ($5.80) per day, can be rented at **Fanø Cykler,** Hovegaden 96 (☎ **75-16-25-13**), at Nordby, and at **Fanø Cykler,** Fanø Bad (☎ **75-16-25-13**).

SEEING THE SIGHTS

Most explorations of the island begin where the ferry docks at the settlement of Nordby. While here, and before setting out to explore the rest of Fanø, you can stop in at the **Fanø Skibsfarts-og Dragtsamling** (Fanø Shipping & Costume Collection), Hovedgaden 28 (☎ **75-16-22-72**). The museum traces the maritime heyday of the island in the 19th century, known as its "boom period." You learn that Fanø at the time had the largest fleet outside of Copenhagen. Exhibits reveal that husbands often left their families for years at a time for a life at sea. The maritime collection incorporates many ship models, details of Fanø's fleet, and displays depicting a sailor's life aboard ship and in port. The costume collection shows both the working dress of the island women and those special costumes they wore for festivals. In May and June and in August and September, the museum is open Monday to Saturday, 10am to noon and 2 to 5pm; on Sunday from 2 to 5pm. In July it is open Monday to Saturday, 10am to 5pm, and on Sunday from 2 to 5pm. Off-season, it is open Monday to Saturday from 10am to noon. Admission costs 15 DKK ($2.15) for adults, and 7.50 DKK ($1.10) for children under age 12.

Housed in a 300-year-old building, another interesting museum at Nordby is the **Fanø Museum,** Skolevej 2 (no phone). This museum houses a comprehensive collection of period furniture, utensils, tools, and other island artifacts. There's also an exotic collection of mementos sailors have gathered on their voyages. The museum is open in June Monday to Saturday from 10am to 1pm, and in July and August Monday to Friday 11am to 4pm and Saturday 10am to 1pm. In September it is open Monday to Friday 10am to 1pm. Admission is 15 DKK ($2.15) for adults, 7.50 DKK ($1.10) for children under age 12.

Near the most southerly tip of the island, in the settlement of Sonderhø, you can visit what's acknowledged as the island's most beautiful building, **Sonderhø Kirke,** Strandvejen (☎ **75-16-40-32**), which is open daily, year-round, during daylight hours. The church has a strong maritime influence—in fact, it displays 14 votive ships, more than any other church in Denmark. The baroque altarpiece dates from 1717, the pulpit from 1661, and the organ loft with an original painting from 1782. This is an assembly hall church, seating some 800 members of a congregation. There's no charge for admission.

While at Sonderhø you can also visit **Fanø Kunstmuseum,** Norland 5 (☎ **75-16-40-44**). In 1992 this museum opened in Kromanns Hus, a former store and factory. The old shop dating from 1868 has been restored and now serves as the entrance to the museum. Throughout the past century Fanø has attracted a number of artists who moved here, and this museum showcases the most outstanding of their works. The collection is based on pictures first assembled by Ruth Heinemann who founded an art association on Fanø. The aim of the museum is to show art inspired by the Frisian coast, past and present, with both permanent and temporary exhibitions. From April 5 to June 14, the museum is open daily Tuesday to Sunday 2 to 5pm; June 15 to August 31, daily 1 to 5pm; and September 1 to October 18, Tuesday to Saturday 2 to 5pm. Admission is 15 DKK ($2.15) for adults, 7.50 DKK ($1.10) for children under age 12.

A quarter of a mile north of Sonderhø, on the road to Nordby, stands the **Sonderhø Mølle,** Vester Land 44 (no phone), a restored windmill. Once islanders were obliged to use the crown mill at Ribe, but in 1701 they received permission to construct one here. Several mills since that time have stood on this site. One burned down in 1894 but was replaced by another the following year, and this one was in use until 1923. A preservation-minded group purchased the mill in 1928 and restored it. It is now open to the public from June to September daily from 3 to 5pm. Admission is 15 DKK ($2.15) for adults, 7.50 DKK ($1.10) for children under age 12.

Hannes Hus, Øster Land 7 (☎ 75-16-40-02), is one of the most typical and characteristic of old Fanø structures, and it's appropriately set in Sonderhø, which contains Denmark's highest proportion of protected buildings. Hannes Hus faithfully maintains the atmosphere of a 17th-century captain's home. Hanne, a captain's widow, and her daughter, Karen, lived in this house until 1965, when it was acquired by the Village Trust. Inside are original furnishings, a stove, pictures, a sheep stable, and souvenirs from the captain's travels. Here's your chance to see what a Fanø sailor's private home looked like. It is open June to August daily from 3 to 5pm and in September on Saturday and Sunday 3 to 5pm. Admission is 15 DKK ($2.15) for adults, 7.50 DKK ($1.10) for children under age 12.

SHOPPING

In Nordby there's an interesting collection of crafts and gift items at **Tove's Gavebod,** Hovedgaden 41 (☎ 75-16-24-62). Look for Danish crafts, ceramics, and even bone carvings. For an antique store, combined with a flea market, head for **Vestergårdens Antik,** Vestervejen 47 (☎ 75-16-68-00), also at Nordby. A competitor also merits a visit. Try **Fanø Antik,** Strandvejen 10A (☎ 75-16-29-20), where you'll find well-crafted porcelain, furnishings, and glass, among other items.

For the best collection of the tiles for which the island is known, head for **Den lille butik,** Landevejen 3 (☎ 75-16-43-58), at Sønderho. You'll also find an array of exquisite silk items, much of it handmade, at **Jane Heinemann,** Landevejen 15 (☎ 75-16-42-90), also at Sønderho. An art gallery at Sønderho, **Galleri Anne,** Østerland 15 (☎ 75-16-43-05), is open in July and August daily from noon to 3pm.

WHERE TO STAY

Fanø Krogaard. Langelinie 11, Nordby, DK-6720 Fanø. ☎ **75-16-20-52.** Fax 75-16-23-00. 9 units, 7 with bath. TV. 340 DKK ($49.30) double without bath, 590 DKK ($85.55) double with bath. Rate includes breakfast. AE, DC, MC, V.

This old-fashioned inn, originally constructed in 1624, has been welcoming wayfarers ever since. Located 100 yards from the ferry dock, its rooms are simple but cozy, comfortable, and nautical. The rooms without bath are in the less preferred century-old annex a short walk from the main building. The inn has some of the best food on the island. Even if you don't stay here, consider the inn for its dining possibilities (see below). There's also a popular bar, open daily from 8am to midnight, and an outdoor terrace used in summer for Saturday jazz sessions.

Hotel Fanø Badeland. Strandvejen 52–56, DK-6720 Fanø. ☎ **75-16-60-00.** Fax 75-16-60-11. 126 units, each with kitchenette. TV TEL. 645–795 DKK ($93.50–$115.25) one-bedroom unit for up to four occupants; 845–995 DKK ($122.50–$144.25) two-bedroom unit for up to six occupants. Discounts offered for stays of 5 nights or more. AE, DC, MC, V. Bus: 631.

This hotel takes no chances with the frequent possibility that fog or rain might spoil the ability of its clients to go swimming. Although it sits on Fanø's western edge, a few hundred yards from one of the best beaches on the island, it has the added benefit of a glass-enclosed complex of indoor pools whose waterslides and Jacuzzis create an impressive complex of year-round swimming options. Built between 1984 and 1992, and located 2-miles south of the hamlet of Nordby, it's composed of a sprawling complex of modern-looking buildings whose low lines and modern angularity fit gracefully into the windswept scrubland that surround it on all sides. Bedrooms are urban-looking, minimalist, and angular, with small kitchenettes nestled into one corner of a living room. Each has either one or two bedrooms outfitted with simple, durable furniture and no-nonsense accessories. You'll pay an additional 50 DKK ($7.25) per person for a package containing sheets and towels, unless you opt to bring your own. On the premises is a restaurant and a bar, as well as an indoor tennis court, squash court, and the above-mentioned indoor complex of swimming pools.

○ **Sønderho Kro.** Kropladsen 11, Sønderho, DK-6720 Fanø. ☎ **75-16-40-09.** Fax 75-16-43-85. E-mail: sdrhokro@post6.tele.dk. 12 units. TEL. 780–1,190 DKK ($113.10–$172.55) double. Half-board 325 DKK ($47.15) per person extra. AE, DC, MC, V.

A 1722 thatched-roof, ivy-covered inn, this National Trust House nestled behind the sand dunes is an unbeatable choice. Each room has a distinctive character, yet all fit into the traditional atmosphere of the inn. Antiques add a nice touch. The first-floor lounge offers views of the tidal flats, and the dining room is atmospheric as well. The cuisine is superb and plentiful, with meals beginning at 305 DKK ($44.20) for three courses. The Sønderho Kro is 8-miles south of the Nordby ferry dock; a bus connects with ferry arrivals.

WHERE TO DINE

Fanø Krogaard. Langelinie 11, Nordby. ☎ **75-16-20-52.** Reservations recommended. Main courses 49–160 DKK ($7.10–$23.20). MC, V. Daily noon–2pm and 5:30–9pm. Mid-May to Sept daily 11:30am–10pm. DANISH.

Set within 100 yards of the point where ferryboats arrive from the Danish "mainland," this is one of the most historic inns on the island. Originally built of russet-colored bricks in 1624, with a well-deserved patina that has accumulated thanks to many generations of diners and drinkers, it offers three cramped but cozy dining rooms that specialize exclusively in Danish food. You'll find the usual array of herring, fried beef with onions, and roasted chicken you'd expect in such a conservative setting, as well as a house specialty consisting of roasted rack of veal with a cream sauce, fresh green beans, two kinds of potatoes, and a garnish that consists of a hollowed-out apple filled with red currant jelly. The food is good, filling, reasonable in price, well-prepared, and nutritious.

Kromann's Fisherestaurant. Kropladsen, Sønderho. ☎ **75-16-44-45.** Reservations recommended. Main courses 100–150 DKK ($14.50–$21.75). No credit cards. Easter–Oct, daily noon–4pm and 6–10pm. Closed Nov–Easter. DANISH/GERMAN.

Set in the heart of the village, near its famous church, this restaurant occupies the premises of a redbrick building that was originally constructed as a private house during the early years of World War I. Menu items include a wide roster of meats and fish, especially plaice and salmon, which the chef prepares in any of at least three different ways. There's also shrimp, crayfish, and fried eel served in the traditional way—with potatoes and parsley. The cookery is solid and reliable—nothing more, nothing less.

○ **Sønderho Kro.** Kropladsen 11, Sønderho. ☎ **75-16-40-09.** Reservations necessary. Main courses 186–225 DKK ($26.95–$32.65). Set menus 255–395 DKK ($36.95–$57.30). AE, DC, MC, V. Daily noon–2:30pm and 6–9pm. Closed Wed from Sept–Apr. INTERNATIONAL.

Designated as a Relais & Châteaux, this is the most prestigious and elegant restaurant on the island, and one of the very best restaurants in central Jutland. The setting is adjacent to the harborfront within what was established as an inn in 1722, and which has gained steadily in influence and glamour ever since. Your meal is likely to include some form of smoked fish, prepared in-house with smoke from juniper wood, within a custom-built oven whose construction was inspired by designs perfected by the Inuit of Greenland.

Only the very best local produce is used by the hotel chefs who even make their own jams and preserves (using only the classiest fruits, of course). You can purchase some of the hotel's products to take home—for example, strawberry jam with almonds and French black currant liqueur. Any of their dishes are good, especially some of the best beef sausage you are likely to ever taste—it's smoked with juniper wood. A juniper snaps sausage and a superb smoked leg of lamb are also likely to be offered. These meats are without artificial coloring and have a low fat content. Move on to an array of perfectly prepared dishes, a splendid gourmet feast that comes as a surprise in a country inn. Save room also for one of the harmoniously composed desserts. The international wine list is no less delightful than the friendly, efficient service.

FANØ AFTER DARK

Your best bet is any event sponsored by the **Fanø Jazzklub,** Strien, Lindevej 5 (☎ 75-16-23-98), at Nordby. The club sponsors various events in summer. The tourist office will have a schedule. Tickets cost 75 DKK ($10.90) and can be purchased at the door.

Don't expect glitter or glamour on Fanø, as virtually everyone who lives here seems to believe in honest industry and an early-to-bed kind of entertainment agenda. But in Nørdby, two possible contenders for your nightlife include the previously recommended **Fanø Krogaard,** Langelinie 11 (☎ 75-16-20-52), where a cozy bar with a cold-weather fireplace keeps you warm. Newer, with a greater influence on staying abreast of trends in places like faraway Copenhagen, is **Bar Titanic,** Hovedgade 57 (☎ 75-16-22-29). Here, the legend associated with history's most notorious shipwreck is perpetuated within a nautically inspired interior, among a clientele that has included at one time or another virtually everyone under age 35 on Fanø. In Sønderho, a worthwhile bar is **Nanas Stue** (☎ 75-16-40-25), a cozy and old-fashioned environment where the winds blowing in from the North Sea seem a lot less blustery, thanks to stiff drinks and companionable dialogue.

The central part of Jutland, connected to the mainland of Europe, cuts across a broad swath of the country, extending from the gateway city of Fredericia in the south to Viborg and Limfjord (a large inland fjord) in the north. The east side of Central Jutland contains more desirable land than the west, which is a wide plain of windswept moors bordered by a rugged coastline of beach flats and sand dunes.

Small farms and rich fertile land characterize the rolling hills of the central belt's eastern shores. But since the 19th century much of the land in the west has also been reclaimed; great parts of it have been turned into pastureland and cultivated fields for growing sugar beets against the competition of North Sea winds.

The landmass of Central Jutland takes in some of the most sparsely populated regions of Denmark, although it has cities too—notably Århus (the largest city), as well as Silkeborg, Viborg, Randers, and others.

Central Jutland, either east or west, is one of the most hospitable regions of Denmark. Locals are proud of a landscape that ranges from wide expanses of heathland to lovely fields of heather to charming, clean, town environments. Central Jutland also has some of the best beaches in Denmark, with miles and miles of white sand. Art museums, galleries, concerts, and beautiful old churches add to the allure.

The best and most interesting towns in East Central Jutland are Jelling, Vejle, and Århus. If you'd like to center your travels from the Lake District, favorite spots include Ebeltoft, Silkeborg, and Ry. In the interior, Randers and Viborg make the best stopovers, and if you want an anchor on the central west coast, make it Ringkøbing.

Jelling is one of the most historic spots in Denmark, and **Legoland** is Jutland's most visited attraction; anyone who grew up playing with Lego blocks will tell you why. The liveliest and most diverse cultural venue is found at Århus, Denmark's second largest city with some quarter of a million residents.

For rail information to any town, call ☎ **70-13-14-15;** for bus connections and schedules, call ☎ **98-90-09-00.**

1 Vejle

198$^{1}/_{2}$ km (124 miles) W of Copenhagen; 72km (45 miles) SW of Århus; 29$^{1}/_{2}$ km (18$^{1}/_{2}$ miles) N of Kolding; 25km (15$^{1}/_{2}$ miles) NW of Fredericia

The thriving town of Vejle lies near the top of the blue waters of Vejle Fjord, and stands in an area of scenic beauty, with tall wooded slopes, dales, and deep gorges. Since ancient times, it's been something of a holiday resort.

Lying in a sheltered hollow, the city has a thriving economy based on exports of bacon, textiles, and chewing gum, among other products, as well as an ever-increasing tourist industry. Highway 3 goes through the town, and the railway also brings passengers and goods here.

Vejle opens onto the coast of East Jutland, and lies north of Kolding and northwest of Fredericia. The entire Vejle region stretches from the Vejle Fjord through Grejsdalen to Jelling, going through the river valley of Vejle Adal to Egtved. This area in Denmark is known for its beautiful, hilly countryside.

The town was granted its charter in 1327. But wars with Prussia did not help its economy, and Vejle suffered great hardship in the 1600s. In the 1820s the construction of a new harbor brought it increased prosperity. By that time, the making of akvavit, or schnapps, played an important role in its economy. In the wars of the 19th century with Schleswig-Holstein in the south, Vejle was occupied several times by German troops. Until 1956, it was a garrison town.

ESSENTIALS

GETTING THERE   Trains arrive frequently throughout the day from Copenhagen, as Vejle lies on the main Jutland line. The town also has good rail links to the other main towns of Jutland—for example, it's only 45 minutes by rail to Århus or 35 minutes to Kolding.

By Car   If you've used Fredericia as your gateway to Central Jutland, follow Route 28 northwest into Vejle.

VISITOR INFORMATION   The **Velje-engens Turistbureau,** Søndergade 14 (☎ 75-82-19-55), is open June to August from 9:30am to 5:30pm Monday to Saturday (closing at 3pm off-season).

SEEING THE SIGHTS

Charming small squares, old houses, courtyards, and one of the most attractive pedestrian streets in the country provide the town center with a distinctive atmosphere. Even from the center of town, there are views of the blue waters of Vejle Fjord and its forest-clad hills.

Vejle Kuntsmuseum, Flegborg 16 (☎ 75-72-31-00), founded in 1899, is a museum of art housing some 12,000 prints and drawings, including foreign prints from 1450 to 1800. In addition, there are collections of Danish paintings, sculpture, prints, and drawings—mostly from the 20th century. A variety of special exhibitions are also mounted every year. Hours are Tuesday to Sunday 11am to 4pm, costing 20 DKK ($2.90) for adults, free for children.

Another notable attraction, **Vejle Museum,** Flegborg 18 (☎ 75-82-43-22), also founded in 1899, presents an exhibition entitled "Man and Nature—archaeology in the Vejle area." A series of other special exhibitions are also held here. The rest of its attractions lie at Søndergade 14, a museum tracing the history of the town over the past 8 centuries. Among the subjects covered are medieval life, Vejle as a theater of war in the 17th century, and Vejle as an industrial town in the 19th century. The museum at Flegborg is open Tuesday to Sunday from 11am to 4pm. The Søndergade 14 address is open April to October, Tuesday to Sunday 11am to 4pm; November to March, Tuesday to Saturday 1 to 4pm. Admission is free at both addresses.

Another intriguing attraction is **Sankt Nicolai Kirke,** Kirketorvet (☎ 75-82-41-39), a 10-minute walk from the tourist office. The Gothic church is one of the town's oldest buildings, its north wall dating back to the mid–13th century. The church contains one of Denmark's finest bog findings, an Iron Age woman from the year 450 B.C.,

Central Jutland

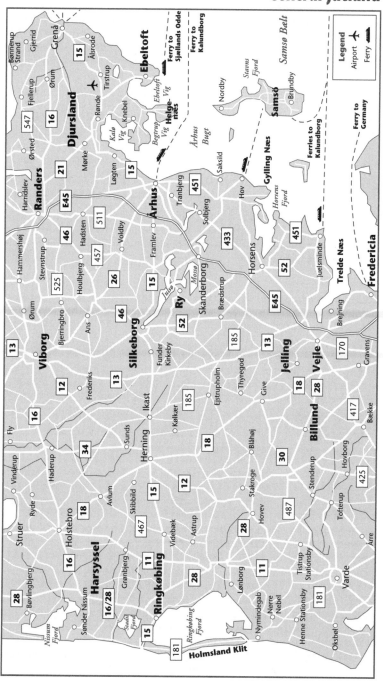

discovered in the Haraldskaier bog in 1835. She can be seen through a glass-topped case. Many guidebooks report that this is the preserved body of the Viking queen, Gunhilde. However, recent scientific studies have shown that the corpse is much older, dating in fact from the early Iron Age. The skulls of 23 beheaded robbers caught in the Nørreskoven woods some 3 centuries ago have been bricked into the outer north wall of the church. Special features of the church include a classical reredos (the screen behind the altar), the work of sculptor Jens Hiernoe in 1791, plus a 16th-century Renaissance pulpit and a processional crucifix. It's open Monday to Friday from 9am to 5pm, Saturday and Sunday from 9am to noon. Entrance is free.

For your farewell to Vejle, you can take a moving stairway in town up to **Munkebjerg** to the southeast of Vejle. At an elevation of 300 feet, you'll enjoy a panoramic view of Vejle and the fjord. The yew, that old Scandinavian forest tree, and other rare trees and plants can be seen here.

If you have a car, you can arm yourself with a good map (available at the tourist office) and explore **Grejsdalen,** lying 4½ miles from Vejle. This valley is one of Denmark's most beautiful areas, with densely wooded hillsides and many lookout points. The preserved part of the valley is also the home of a richly varied birdlife. Near Grejs itself are some limestone deposits resembling cliff caverns.

SHOPPING

The main pedestrian street alone features more than 220 specialty shops, restaurants, and department stores, so there's a wealth of shopping opportunities here, more so than nearly any other place in Jutland.

The best and most sophisticated ceramics are sold at **Ulla Møller,** Havnegade 21 (☎ 75-83-71-21). For a gift shop featuring local crafts, head for **Allehånde,** Søndergade 14 (☎ 75-83-83-66). An intriguing collection of antiques is always on display at **Borring Antiques,** Grejsdalsvej 326A (☎ 75-85-34-00). The town's most stylish leather goods are sold at **Neye,** Torvegade 36 (☎ 75-82-01-65), a tradition since 1881.

WHERE TO STAY

Andersen's Hotel. In the Torvehallerne, Kirketorvet 12, DK-7100 Vejle. ☎ **79-42-79-10.** Fax 79-42-79-01. 31 units. MINIBAR TV TEL. 895 DKK ($129.75) double. Rate includes breakfast. AE, MC, V.

Its construction in 1993 was viewed as a vital part of the success of the Torvehallerne—Vejle's largest conglomeration of cultural, dining, drinking, and nightlife facilities. Consequently, you'll be able, in any season or weather, to migrate from your room at this three-story hotel through the big-windowed, greenhouse-inspired spaces of the market hall for drinking, dining, diversions, and mall-gazing of the kind you might have expected in California. Other than breakfast, no meals are served within the hotel itself, but considering the many nearby options—including a French and an Italian restaurant in Torvehallerne, both within a few steps of the reception area—no one really cares. Bedrooms are well-maintained, comfortable, and contain simple and angular furnishings, yet despite their efficiency, rooms look a bit more plush than the usual. Much of this stems from reproductions of unusual paintings by Danish artists that range from the mannered and the baroque to the contemporary, each selected for its drama and theatricality. Color schemes within each room, which run the spectrum from the dark and dramatic to all-white, were chosen as a means of presenting each painting in its most flattering light.

Hotel Australia. Dæmningen 6, DK-7100 Vejle. ☎ **76-40-60-00.** Fax 76-40-60-01. www.Nordishhotelgruppe.dk/australia. 102 units. MINIBAR TV TEL. Mon–Fri 1,095 DKK ($158.75) double; Sat–Sun 795 DKK ($115.25) double. Extra bed 200 DKK ($29) all week long. Rate includes breakfast. AE, DC, MC, V.

One of the most modern and state-of-the-art hotels in Central Jutland, and the only four-star hotel within the nationwide Interscan chain, rises 11 stories from a central location in the heart of town. Originally built in 1958, and radically upgraded in 1996, the hotel has a name that derives from its creator's fascination for Australia, thanks to the many trips he took there. As such, the hotel has been one of the most visible advertisements for tourism to Australia in Jutland, and has (unofficially) spurred a flood of Danish visitors to Australia since it was inaugurated. Inside, you'll find all the amenities that several corporations would need to host simultaneous conventions. Public rooms are spacious, modern, and pleasantly decorated, usually with wood-veneer paneling, contemporary but conservative furnishings, and potted plants. Bedrooms are larger-than-usual and clean, well-maintained, and outfitted in a culturally neutral kind of modernism of the kind you might expect at many upscale chain hotels throughout Europe. Each offers free video movies, trouser presses, and a hair dryer in the small baths. The hotel includes a bar, restaurant, and sauna, but surprisingly for a hotel of this size and stature, it doesn't have a swimming pool or health club.

✪ **Munkebjerg Hotel.** Munkebjergvej 125, DK-7100 Vejle. ☎ **76-42-85-00.** Fax 75-72-08-86. E-mail: info@munkebjerg.dk. 148 units. TV TEL. Mon–Thurs 1,125–1,795 DKK ($163.15–$260.25) double; Fri–Sun 685–960 DKK ($99.30–$139.20) double. 2,250–2,750 DKK ($326.25–$398.75) suite all week long. AE, DC, MC, V. From Vejle's center, drive 4 ½-miles south, following the signs to "Vejle Sid."

This is the most stylish and prestigious hotel in the region, with the most panoramic setting and a staff that's more accustomed to dealing with delicate temperaments than any other hotel in or around Vejle. South of the center, it sits in isolated and contemporary grandeur on a panoramic hilltop within the Munkebjerg Forest. Originally built in 1967, and renovated and enlarged many times since, it's the preferred stopover for clients as diverse as Little Richard and Chuck Berry, as well as the prime minister of Denmark. Expect dramatic, impeccably maintained public areas in a big-windowed and angular modern style, and very comfortable, soothing accommodations. Bedrooms are flooded with sunlight thanks to sliding glass windows overlooking a private balcony and forest, and contain furniture with soft, well-upholstered angles, deep cushions, comfortable mattresses, and pale, easy-to-live-with colors.

Dining/Diversions: The hotel contains the only casino within 65 miles. (Its nearest competitor is in Århus.) Open daily from 7pm to 4am, it contains blackjack, poker, roulette, and about 50 slot machines, and charges an admission fee of 50 DKK ($7.25). On the premises is an artfully illuminated cocktail lounge, and a middle-bracket restaurant, the Panorama, featuring lunch and dinner daily and sweeping views over forests and lakes. There's also one of the most glamorous, *haute-cuisine* restaurants in Central Jutland, Treetops, which is separately recommended in "Where to Dine."

Amenities: The Vejle Golf Club lies within a short drive from the hotel, and offers tee-off times to residents of the hotel. There's also an outdoor tennis court, an indoor swimming pool, a sunbed, and an exercise room. There are also several state-of-the-art conference rooms within the hotel's convention center.

WHERE TO DINE

Restaurant Baghuset. Dæmningen 42. ☎ **75-72-41-41.** Reservations recommended. Main courses 94–184 DKK ($13.65–$26.70). Fri and Sat night carvery (dinner only), 135 DKK ($19.60) per person. DC, MC, V. Mon–Sat 11:30am–10:30pm (last order); Sun 5:30–10:30pm (last order). DANISH/INTERNATIONAL.

Before it was transformed into this well-managed steakhouse, this address functioned as Velje's community center, providing a grange-like meeting space whose walls and ceilings were massively trussed with heavy beams. In its present role as a restaurant, the old-time décor works as an appropriate backdrop for the generous portions of time-tested favorites that emerge from the kitchens. Food items include several kinds of steak, each seasoned with your choice of sauces; roasted turkey and lamb; and such seafood as steamed or fried salmon, lobster, and trout. Every Friday and Saturday, from 5:30pm till closing, the establishment's (otherwise unused) second floor is opened as a carvery-style buffet. Priced at 135 DKK ($19.60) per person, it's one of the best weekend food values in town.

✪ **Treetops Restaurant.** In the Munkebjerg Hotel, Munkebjergvej 125. ☎ **76-42-85-00.** Reservations necessary. Main courses 255 DKK ($36.95) each. Set menus 315–495 DKK ($45.70–$71.75). Daily 6:30–9:30pm. AE, DC, MC, V. From Vejle's center, drive 4½ miles south, following the signs to "Vejle Sid" and the Munkebjerg Hotel. DANISH/ INTERNATIONAL.

This restaurant in the previously recommended hotel is celebrated throughout the region for its contemporary glamour and its devotion to fine cuisine. A meal is always prefaced with a guided tour of the establishment's wine cellar, where a glass of something bubbly is preferred as part of the experience. After that, a table is prepared within a high-ceilinged room that's spanned with artfully arranged tree limbs that provide a cozy, forest-like tone. Menu items change frequently, according to the seasons and the creative ideas of the chefs. Examples include lime-marinated salmon with sundried tomatoes and olives; crisp red snapper on summer lettuce, served with a frothy and whipped version of crayfish bouillon; poached fillets of sole, with lobster and a tomato-flavored *beurre blanc* (white butter) sauce; or parmesan-glazed monkfish with a thyme and chili-flavored cream sauce. More substantial fare includes a succulent version of filet of lamb roasted with garlic and served with a lemon-grass gravy, and tournedos of veal with ratatouille and balsamic vinegar. Dessert might be ice cream flavored with fresh raspberries and served with a white chocolate mousse and mint sauce. Finely balanced sauces are highlights. The chefs are expert cooks, carefully tuned to what the best produce is in any given season.

VEJLE AFTER DARK

At the **Casino Munkebjerg Vejle,** Munkebjergvej 125 (☎ **75-42-40-00**), you can play roulette, blackjack, the machines, and—only if you're willing to learn—"Viking poker." A photo ID is required to gain entrance. The major cultural venue for the city is the **Musik Theatret Vejle,** Vedelsgade 25–31 (☎ **75-83-66-00**), the setting for operas, musicals, shows, and theater. You can check with the tourist office (see "Visitor Information," above) if any events at the time of your visit would appeal to you.

Also consider a visit to the complex **Torvehallerne,** Kirketorvet 12 (☎ **79-42-79-00**). Here, a large, spacious palm garden, Væksthuset, forms the center of a complex that includes restaurants, a hotel, a cafe, a stage, and a pub. There is always something going on here—jazz, dancing under the palm trees, concerts, or theatrical performances. We can't predict what will be going on at the time of your visit, but it's always a lively place to drop in on at night.

Vejle is also a town rich in pub life, our favorites being **The Irish Cat Pub,** Norregade 61 (☎ **75-72-38-00**), and **Seven Oaks,** an old English-style pub at Dæmningen 42G (☎ **75-72-07-77**).

2 Jelling

11km (7 miles) NW of Vejle; 144km (90 miles) W of Copenhagen

This sleepy little village is historically important as the 10th-century seat of Danish kings Gorm the Old and Harald Bluetooth, Gorm's son. These two kings left behind two large burial mounds and two runic stones, known as the Jelling stones. They have provided crucial information about early Danish history. Although the village of Jelling enjoys idyllic surroundings, set against a backdrop of forest and lakes, it is visited mainly for its runic stones and not because it's a lovely place.

In 1994 Jelling had its Viking monuments listed with those most worthy of preservation in the world, which includes the Egyptian pyramids and the Acropolis, among others. The decision was made at a UNESCO convention.

At the peak of the Viking era, a thousand years ago, Jelling was the Danish Royal Seat. Gorm is important in Danish history because the royal line began with him and proceeds unbroken to the present Danish monarch, Queen Margrethe. The line, though tortuous, is still intact.

ESSENTIALS

GETTING THERE   Jelling is a 20-minute train ride from Vejle on the run to Struer and Herning. Trains depart about once an hour Monday through Friday, less frequently on weekends. Connections are possible from Vejle's bus station; take bus no. 211.

By Car   From Vejle, take Route A18 north. If you're using Fredericia as your gateway to Central Jutland, go first to Vejle, then continue the final lap into Jelling.

VISITOR INFORMATION   The **Jelling Turistbureau,** Gormsgade 4 (☎ 75-87-13-01), is open daily from June to September, 10am to 6pm. At other times of the year, contact the tourist office at Vejle (see above).

DISCOVERING A VIKING PAST

In the center of town, **Jelling Kirke** (☎ 75-87-13-20), was erected at the beginning of the 12th century, and is one of the oldest churches in Denmark. The church would be of interest in itself, but it's visited mainly because of its two well-preserved runic stones, which sit just outside the door. Nevertheless, you should look inside the church as well to see its restored 12th-century frescoes. Admission is free, and the church is open Monday to Friday 10am to 5pm, and on Saturday from 10am to 2pm. It's closed for visits on Sunday because of mass. You can attend mass then, but casual sightseeing in the church is discouraged at times that it's being used as a place of worship.

Both ✪ **Gorm the Old (883–940),** and his son, **Harald Bluetooth** (940–85), lived in Jelling and left behind monuments to prove it. They left two large burial mounds and two runic stones—one small, one large. The small runic stone bears the inscription: "King Gorm made these sepulchral monuments to Thyra, his wife, the grace of Denmark." The large runic stone is inscribed: "King Harald had these sepulchral monuments made to Gorm, his father, and Thyra, his mother, the Harald who conquered all Denmark and Norway and made the Danes Christians."

The latter part of the inscription has often been called Denmark's baptismal certificate, though this is something of an exaggeration. But King Harald and his people were undoubtedly converted to Christianity, even if it was a century before the country as a whole can be said to have become Christian.

The north's oldest depiction of Christ appears over this part of Harald's runic lettering. The Christlike figure appears with his arms spread out but without a cross. This may have been because the artist at the time wanted to depict Christ as a victorious Viking king—hence no cross. The significance of the other depiction on the stone isn't known. It depicts a snake locked into a deadly combat with a mythical animal. The stones, decorated in the typical Viking style, with interlacing leaf and creeper-work, were originally painted in bright colors.

Excavations of the two barrows began in 1820 when the north barrow was dug up. It revealed a burial chamber but no human remains, only a few objects and fragments, including a little silver goblet, later dubbed the Jelling goblet. Graverobbers may have plundered the site over the years. In 1861 the south barrow was excavated by King Frederik VII, who had a keen interest in archaeology, but it didn't even have a burial chamber. In general it is believe that both Gorm and Thyra had been buried in the north mound and that the empty south barrow was but a memorial mound.

In modern times the area beneath the church was excavated, and archaeologists discovered the remains of three wooden churches which had replaced each other. The oldest church was King Harald's and was even bigger than the present Jelling Kirke, earning the nickname the "Cathedral of the Viking Age."

The discovery of a burial chamber beneath the choral arch revealed human bones, but they were in complete disorder, indicating that they had been moved. The skeletal remains discovered are believed to be those of Gorm, which were probably moved over from the north mound when his son Harald became Christian. It has never been determined where Queen Thyra was buried.

SHOPPING   If you'd like a souvenir of your trip to Jelling, your best bet is to go to **Impuls,** Gormsgade 17 (☎ **75-87-12-98**), which sells gifts and souvenirs along with arts and crafts.

WHERE TO STAY

✪ **Jelling Kro.** Gormsgade 16, DK-7300 Jelling. ☎ **75-87-10-06.** Fax 75-87-10-08. 6 units (1 with bath). 495 DKK ($71.75) double with or without bath. Rate includes breakfast. AE, MC, V. Bus: 214.

The most evocative and appealing hotel in town occupies the severely dignified, yellow-fronted premises of what has functioned since 1780 as a *kro* (old-fashioned inn). Capped with a terra-cotta roof and positioned in the center of town, across from the country's most famous burial site, the hotel offers a well-recommended restaurant (which is described separately in "Where to Dine"), and simple but clean bedrooms that were revamped in the mid-1980s into a modern, contemporary style. Each has slight decorative differences from its neighbor, and most have a shared bath positioned within each of the hallways. Another repainting of each of the rooms occurred around 1993. If you opt to stay in this hotel, know in advance that you'll share it with good company. In 1842, just before an overnight visit from the Danish king, it was reclassified as one of only about 30 hotels in Denmark suitable then and thereafter for overnight visits from a Danish monarch. Although that classification is no longer an iron-bound rule, it nonetheless adds a *cachet* to the allure of this historic hotel.

Tøsby Kro. Bredsten Landevej 12, DK-7300 Jelling. ☎ **75-88-11-30.** Fax 75-88-14-03. 6 units (none with bath). 300 DKK ($43.50) double. MC, V. Lies 4½ miles west of Jelling.

Isolated amid many acres of undulating fields, this is a century-old *kro* (inn) that gives the curious impression of belonging in a time warp from another era. The side that's presented to the road evokes a late-19th-century inn, with a steep roof and white-painted façade. In back, forming an open courtyard, are additional buildings that are used for housing a team of Icelandic ponies. Don't expect to go riding, because in the words of the owners, Else and Søren Jensen, "you can talk to them, but you can't ride them." Four of the six bedrooms are upstairs from the establishment's restaurant. Very simple, but clean, they include virtually no amenities of any kind, yet are worthy for short-term, uncluttered stays with virtually no grace notes. On location is a TV lounge that's used for socializing. Two additional rooms are in the Jensen family's private home, a modern farmhouse located about a mile away. There's a busy pub on the premises, the social high point for the region around it, and a wood-paneled, old-time restaurant that serves lunch and dinner every day from noon to 3pm and 5 to 9pm. Menu items are old-fashioned and Danish, and served in generous farmer's-style portions. A house specialty is a Danish omelet, made with three eggs whipped with cream for added fluffiness, and garnished with bacon, tomatoes, onions, and herbs.

WHERE TO DINE

Jelling Kro. Gormsgade 16. ☎ **75-87-10-06.** Reservations recommended. Main courses 98–169 DKK ($14.20–$24.50). Set-menus 130–150 DKK ($18.85–$21.75). AE, MC, V. Sept–May, Wed–Sun 5–9pm. June–Aug daily 5–9pm. DANISH.

The most appealing restaurant in Jelling lies within the previously recommended hotel, behind an ocher-colored façade that evokes 19th-century Denmark in all its rustic charm. The dining room is much more modern than the historic setting would imply, although some of the angularity of the modern décor is softened with a worthy collection of paintings by a local artist, Albert Bertelsen, a resident of nearby Vejle. Menu items change according to the availability of the ingredients, but usually stress fish that's parceled out into several kinds of fish platter, served either as a starter or in a more elaborate form as a main course configured into a "symphony of fish." Although the composition of each platter changes daily, according to availability, you can almost always expect an emphasis on marinated salmon and fresh shrimp. Other excellent dishes include cream of leek soup with bacon, tournedos of beef garnished with mushroom stew and "today's potato," or breast of chicken with white wine sauce.

3 Billund/Legoland

228km (142¹/₂ miles) W of Copenhagen; 58¹/₂ km (36¹/₂ miles) NE of Esbjerg; 27km (17 miles) W of Vejle

The "Disneyland of Denmark," Legoland, an amusement park lying less than half a mile north of the small Central Jutland town of Billund, is the second most visited tourist attraction in the country, after Tivoli in Copenhagen. Since 1968 when it opened, some 27 million visitors from around the world have shown up here. It can be fun if you're traveling as a family. Adults exploring Denmark without children in tow might want to seek other diversions.

ESSENTIALS

GETTING THERE Billund Airport is just across the road from Legoland—it's only a 5-minute walk from the arrival lounge of the airport to the park. Air Mærsk (☎ **75-33-22-44**) has frequent flights daily from Copenhagen, and also provides service from such international cities as London, Stockholm, Frankfurt, Brussels, and Amsterdam. There is no train service. Rail passengers get off at Vejle (see above), then take a bus marked Legoland for the final lap of the journey. In summer, seasonal buses run from Vejle (☎ **75-12-16-00**). There is also bus service from Esbjerg (☎ **75-16-26-00**).

By Car After crossing the bridge linking Funen and Jutland, continue northwest toward Vejle on the E20, linking up with Route 18, which connects with Route 28 going west into Billund.

VISITOR INFORMATION The **Legoland/Billund Turistbureau** (☎ **76-50-00-55**) lies on the grounds of Legoland itself. From mid-June to the end of August, it's open daily from 10am to 9pm. From May to mid-June, and during September and October, it's open daily from 10am to 8pm. From February to April, it's open Monday to Friday from 9am to 4pm. It's completely closed during November, December, and January.

AMUSEMENT PARK FUN

This is a theme park constructed from plastic Lego blocks. The greatest attraction at Legoland is Castleland, which opened in 1997. Home to the King's Castle, a faux-medieval fairytale castle, it offers an action adventure ride on one of two 212-seat "dragons," waiting to show you this re-created world. On the upper floor the Knight's Barbecue, a restaurant decorated with suits of armor and shields.

Miniland is the second major attraction, with miniature models of famous buildings or monuments from around the world, all made of Lego bricks. The entire medieval town of Ribe is re-created, for example, as is Amalienborg Castle in Copenhagen. Other thematic attractions in the park include Logoredo Town, a re-creation of a western town with an Indian camp and a sheriff's office, plus Pirateland, where you can take a boat trip through caves. There's even a Lego Safari, where children steer small zebra-striped jeeps on a ride through a faux savannah. There are dozens of amusement rides galore, mostly for children, including merry-go-rounds and Ferris wheels. All the rides, including the miniature train and boat trips, are included in one admission price.

From April 1 to June 19, hours are daily 10am to 8pm; June 20 to August 30, daily 10am to 9pm, August 31 to October 25 daily 10am to 8pm. Admission is 115 DKK ($16.65) for those over the age of 14, or 105 DKK ($15.25) for ages 3–13 (free for children age 2 and under). For more information, call ☎ **76-50-00-55.**

WHERE TO STAY

Hotel Legoland. Aastvej 10, DK-7190 Billund. ☎ **76-50-00-55.** Fax 75-35-31-79. 126 units. TV TEL. 1,150 DKK ($166.75) double; 1,800 DKK ($261) junior suite. AE, DC, MC, V. Free shuttle bus to the hotel from the airport at Billund.

This is the only hotel associated with Jutland's most famous theme park, and as such, it does a thriving business selling overnight accommodations to families with children in summer. During the winter, the clientele shifts to more of a business-oriented crowd, many of whom check in as part of an ongoing schedule of corporate conventions. It was originally built in 1968, and despite frequent upgrades and renovations, some of which were completed between 1995 and 1997, still carries a pervasive sense of the slightly dated aesthetics of the 1970s. Built for the most part in a low-rise format of between one and three stories, with most of it devoted to a big-windowed one-story design, it's permeated with a Legoland theme. There are lots of Disney-style Legoland sculptures in the lobby, and a chipper and perky multilingual staff that's often preoccupied with the care, feeding, and amusement of children. Like everything else in Legoland, a bit of this goes a long way, especially if you happen to be traveling without children in tow. Bedrooms are outfitted with neutral colors, non-committal contemporary furniture, and less of an emphasis on the Legoland theme than you'll find in the public areas. Suites are larger, but outfitted in an equivalent style, and contain minibars.

Dining/Diversions: Residents of the hotel receive a discount on the price of entrance to the theme park, paying 75 DKK ($10.90) per person (both adult and child) as opposed to the regular fee of 130 DKK ($18.85) for adults and 120 DKK ($17.40) for children aged 3 to 13. They can enter through a separate entrance that funnels directly into the hotel. Room service is available 24 hours a day. There's a cocktail lounge (the Concorde Bar) on the premises, a hotel dining room open daily for lunch (noon to 3pm) and dinner (6 to 10pm). It specializes mostly in all-you-can-eat buffets priced at 154 DKK ($22.35) at lunchtime and 184 DKK ($26.70) at dinner. The hotel's more glamorous restaurant, Le Petit, is described separately in "Where to Dine."

Amenities: Concierge and reception staff well-versed in catering to the needs of children; and all the amenities of Legoland, which lies a few steps from the hotel.

WHERE TO DINE

Le Petit. In the Hotel Legoland, Aastvej 10. ☎ **76-50-00-55.** Reservations recommended. Main courses 170–190 DKK ($24.65–$27.55). AE, DC, MC, V. Daily 6–10pm. DANISH/INTERNATIONAL.

The creation of this restaurant in 1998 was part of Legoland's (accurate) perception that its pervasive kiddie theme might have grown a bit tired among the corporate convention crowd that dominates its client roster throughout the winter. Consequently, you might be relieved to discover a mostly adult, and attractively formal, venue within the resort's only hotel. The décor is urban, urbane, and postmodern, and cuisine draws its inspiration from big-city venues in places that, depending on the inspiration of the chef, might include Munich, Milan, and Paris. Don't expect a wide variety of menu items, as there might be only three or at most four starters, main courses, and desserts listed as part of an oft-changing cuisine based on market availability of ingredients and the inspiration of the staff. Examples include roe of salmon garnished with red onions and sour cream, air-dried beef (*Bündnerfleisch*) with Parma ham served with exotic lettuces and marinated artichokes, a savory *ragoût* of halibut and shellfish in a saffron sauce with wild rice, tuna steak with fresh spinach in a pasta basket on a bed of tomato sauce, and a succulent version of tenderloin of lamb with *Rösti* potatoes with rosemary-flavored gravy and glazed onions. One particularly delicious dessert is a chocolate basket filled with berries of the season and served with a Grand Marnier–flavored parfait. A drink within the Concorde Bar is a welcome preface to a meal here.

4 Ringkøbing

320km (200 miles) W of Copenhagen; 9km (5¹/₂ miles) E of the North Sea; 85km (53 miles) W of Silkeborg

This old market town, lying on the north side of the lagoon-like Ringkøping Fjord, is the capital of a regional government, albeit a tiny one, with only 9,000 inhabitants. Its oldest known municipal charter dates from 1443, but the earliest archaeological finds establish its origins some time around the mid–13th century. At that time there was no outlet from the western end of Liim Fjord to the North Sea, so Ringkøping Fjord was the only natural harbor in the area. It became one of the most important harbor cities on the west coast of Denmark with trading links extending to Norway, Germany, and Holland.

In time, though, especially during the 17th century, the approach at Nymindegab began to sand up and move south. With the opening of the West Jutland trunk line in 1875, shipping for Ringkøping stopped almost immediately, leaving the town to reinvent itself. It wasn't until a lock at Hvide Sande was constructed in 1931 that Ringkøping was once again assured of a passage to the North Sea. However, its role as a port for ships was never to return to its former glory. It did, however, become the first small town in Denmark to provide free universal education.

That fall-off in commerce is what has probably kept Ringkøping looking as old fashioned and splendid as it does today. The townspeople also have a lively spirit. For example, the town's 7 miles of coastline is cleaned by local residents at a beach-combing event to ensure that the blue flags (symbol of unpolluted waters) fly over their beaches in summer.

ESSENTIALS

GETTING THERE Ringkøping lies on the main DSB rail lines between Esbjerg (trip time: 1 ¼ hours) and Struer (trip time: 1 hour). In summer, a little ferry, *MF Sorte Louis,* sails across Ringkøping Fjord between Ringkøping and Hvide Sande. For tickets, information, or schedules call ☎ **97-32-42-88.**

By Car From Silkeborg (see below) continue west along Route 15 into Ringkøping.

VISITOR INFORMATION **Ringkøping Turistbureau,** Torvet (☎ **97-32-00-31**), is open between mid-June and September every Monday to Friday from 9am to 5pm; every Saturday 10am to 2pm. The rest of the year (from October to mid-June), it's open from 9:30am to 5pm Monday to Friday and from 10am to 1pm on Saturday.

GETTING AROUND

The surrounding scenic flatlands are ideal for cyclists. Bikes can be rented at **Børgensen Cykler,** Nørredige (☎ **97-32-36-01**). Bicycles rent for 50–60 DKK ($7.25–$8.70) per day.

SEEING THE SIGHTS

Ringkøping's townscape takes its general outline from houses built from 1700 to 1800 in the main. The dominant building style—dark red houses with white cornices and semi-hipped rooftops—developed in the late 18th century. Ringkøping's leading citizens were its merchants, whose large houses lined the narrow streets, particularly Algade and Østergade. Some have remained in a well-preserved condition, notably the addresses of Nørregade 2 and Algade 4–6. Much effort still goes into preserving Ringkøping's pleasant old-town atmosphere, and a walk through the town's narrow cobbled streets brings its own reward.

If you're standing at the marketplace (Torvet) seeking a way to the harbor, the obvious choice is **Vester Strandgade.** This is an old street whose earliest homes date from the early 1800s. The street was always known for its merchants, including a plumber, butcher, bakery, grocer, bike shop, shoemaker, and inn. You can still smell fresh bread from the local bakery, and can stop for a delicious Danish pastry at a coffee shop.

Once you arrive at the harbor, you'll see a facility dating from 1904. Once this was a bustling fishing harbor until Ringkøping lost out to Hvide Sande to the south. Today the harbor is used mainly by pleasure craft and fjord fishing boats. Fishers from the fjords land their fish here at the harbor and every day at 9:30am hold an auction in a red wooden building at the harbor's edge. Everything from salmon, trout, flounder, perch, and eel to sea trout is sold here to the highest bidder.

At the edge of the town center, **Alkjær Lukke** is a lovely park, idyllic for a picnic lunch. Ducks quacking in the pond tell you they want to be fed. In the airy beech wood the forest floor is covered with wood anemones, buttercups, and lily of the valley. It's a nice place to stop and listen to the flowers grow.

The town's main attraction—other than the town itself—is **Ringkøping Museum Østerport** (☎ **97-32-16-15**). Lying a few blocks east of the market square (Torvet), this museum is a virtual attic of local history, including coins and ecclesiastical artifacts, ships' figureheads, and even pictures of stranded ships in the North Sea. Someone at the museum is likely to show you what a chastity belt from 1600 looked like. We find the most intriguing exhibits to be those devoted to Ludwig Mylius-Erichsen (1872–1907), who led an expedition to Greenland in 1906. Regrettably, he died on the return journey. From mid-June to August the museum is open daily from 11am to 5pm; the rest of the year (September to mid-June) it's open Monday to Thursday from 11am to 4pm, and Sunday from 1 to 4pm. It's closed every Friday and

Saturday during off-season. Entrance costs 20 DKK ($2.90) for adults, 10 DKK ($1.45) for children under 12.

SHOPPING

The best and biggest gift shop is **Imerco,** Nygade 2 (☎ **97-32-01-06**), featuring many well-known Danish brands. If you're seeking Scandinavian woolen items, head for **Tvistholm,** Vesterhede 11 (☎ **97-32-12-91**), a mile-and-a-half north of town. It has the widest selection. Some of the town's most sophisticated ceramics are sold at **Keramikkens Hus,** Ndr. Ringvej 14 (☎ **97-33-14-01**).

Actually, one of the most intriguing shopping prospects is not in Ringkøping itself, but directly south of the town at the hamlet of Stauning. Follow the secondary road along the east side of Ringkøping Fjord until you come to the village where you'll see a sign indicating **Bousøgaard,** Bousøvej 6, at Stauning (☎ **97-36-91-72**). This is an old thatched West Jutland farm with four wings. The attractive barn is an art gallery, the biggest in West Jutland, with oils, graphics, and sculptures by well-known Danish artists. There is also an on-site potter's workshop, where the old potter's craft is still practiced. Next to the workshop is a museum of Danish decorated pottery from the 1800s until circa 1950. Hours are Monday to Saturday 11am to 5pm.

WHERE TO STAY

Hotel Fjordgården. Vesterkær 28, DK-6950 Ringkøping. ☎ **800/528-1234** in the U.S., or ☎ 97-32-14-00. Fax 97-32-47-60. 98 units. MINIBAR TV TEL. Sun–Thurs 1,015 DKK ($147.15) double. Fri–Sat and June 1 to Aug 15, 695 DKK ($100.75) double. AE, DC, MC, V.

The best hotel in Ringkøping lies a quarter-mile north of the town center, on sandy flatlands near the coast. Built in 1967 in a sprawling, generously proportioned format with between one and two stories, white walls, and a prominent brown roof, it has the most comfortable accommodations, and better dining, than any other hotel in town. The rooms are good-sized with firm beds and small but spanking-clean baths. The beneficiary of many upgrades and renovations since its construction, it contains rooms filled with vibrant but tasteful colors, big-windowed views over the surrounding land and seascapes, and in many cases, exposed brick walls.

Dining/Diversions: One of Ringkøping's two best restaurants is the Helten, a cozy and eminently tasteful enclave of good service and stylish cuisine with views over the dunes. See "Where to Dine," below. There's also a bar, a concierge who can arrange for the rental of cars and bicycles, and 24-hour-a-day room service.

Amenities: The hotel's indoor pool duplicates the aesthetics and the temperature of the subtropics. Flanked with big windows and shaped like a kidney, it contains a water chute, a children's pool, a separate whirlpool, a fitness center, and a solarium.

Hotel Ringkøping. Torvet 18, DK-6950 Ringkøping. ☎ **97-32-00-11.** Fax 97-32-18-72. 16 units. TEL. 550 DKK ($79.75) double. Rate includes breakfast. MC, V.

Set on a cobble-covered square in the heart of town, near a quartet of linden trees that were each planted in the late 1700s, this is the second-oldest hotel in Jutland, surpassed in age only by one in Ribe. Established in its present format in 1833, within a much-enlarged, frequently renovated building from the 1600s, it has a terra-cotta roof that's attached to a richly half-timbered façade. The hotel is cozy and somewhat kitschy. Don't expect the same antique charm within the bedrooms that you'll see on the building exterior, as accommodations are somewhat banal, even a bit dowdy, thanks to overly frilly bedcovers and somewhat clumsy attempts at gussying up some relatively plain spaces with gewgaws that include ersatz canopies above the beds. Two of the accommodations lie within a nearby annex. On the premises are an English-style pub serving lots of suds and occasional live rock-and-roll sessions, and a restaurant that looks like it hasn't been redecorated since someone added a lot of accessories in the 1960s.

WHERE TO DINE

Restaurant Den gamle Toldbod. På havnen (at the harbor). ☎ **97-32-66-66.** Reservations recommended. Lunch main courses 68–188 DKK ($9.85–$27.25); fixed-price lunch 118 DKK ($17.10). Dinner main courses 128–188 DKK ($18.55–$27.25). DC, MC, V. Mon–Sat 11:30am–2pm; daily 5:30–10pm. DANISH/INTERNATIONAL.

This, rivaled only by the also-recommended Helten restaurant, is the best dining room in town. It's set within what was originally built in 1843 as a customs house, where taxes were assessed on the contents of every ship that pulled into Ringkøping's harbor. Today, you'll find three separate dining rooms (two upstairs, one on street level) accented with exposed stone walls and the vibrantly colorful paintings of the establishment's owner, Bente Merrild. Although furnishings date in many cases from around 1910, the food items are considerably more modern. Lunches tend to focus on very fresh versions of traditional Danish recipes, combining smoked fish, cheese, and meats into savory salads, pastas, sandwiches, and platters. Dinners are more elaborate, focusing on unusual versions of fresh fish and seasonal vegetables. Examples might include roasted monkfish served with a vinegar-enhanced *beurre blanc* (white butter) sauce; filet of veal baked with sun-dried tomatoes, fresh morels, and feta cheese; and breast of young chicken stuffed with a soufflé of mushrooms and covered with a light mushroom and herb sauce. The cookery is extremely competent and well flavored here, and locals often attend for family celebrations.

Restaurant Helten. In the Hotel Fjordgården, Vesterkær 28. ☎ **97-32-14-00.** Reservations recommended. Lunch buffet 160 DKK ($23.20). Dinner main courses 138–198 DKK ($20–$28.70); fixed-price dinners 195–225 DKK ($28.30–$32.65). AE, DC, MC, V. Daily noon–2pm and 6–10pm. DANISH/INTERNATIONAL.

This is the showplace dining room of the only four-star hotel in Ringkøping, and as such, you're likely to receive more internationally conscious culinary finesse, and more diligent service, than in less well-funded competitors. Within a very modern dining room with a view of the dunes and the sea and a plum-colored decor, you'll find a lunch venue centered around one of the most appealing buffets in town. Look for a savory collection of soups, salads, open-faced sandwiches, Danish cheeses, smoked meats and fish, seasonal berries, and pastries. Dinners are more elaborate. We highly recommend, when it's available, a platter of smoked *helten* (a small, herring-shaped fish that's the restaurant's namesake). Found only in the nearby fjord, and traditionally served salted or smoked, it's prized as one of the unusual delicacies of Denmark. This might be followed with curried crab, *carpaccio* of beef filet with onions, pepper steak, lamb cutlets with onion and rosemary sauce, or monkfish braised in a lemon-butter sauce. Dessert might be a traditional Jutlander version of apple pie with ice cream.

RINGKØPING AFTER DARK

The most fun place in town, attracting not only young people but many middle-aged patrons, too, is **Watchman's Pub,** Hotel Ringkøping, Torvet 18 (☎ **97-32-00-11**). Live music is often presented, and the suds flow freely. It has an English pub ambience.

EXPLORING RINGKØBING FJORD

Long straight sandy beaches, nature reserves, drifting North Sea sands, and heath-covered dunes create a dramatic West Jutland landscape on the narrow isthmus running south from Ringkøbing along Route 181. To reach the road that takes you along the western side of the fjord, head directly east of Ringkøbing along Route 15, turning south when you see the junction with Route 181, going to the small town of Hvide Sande.

Your first major stopover will be:

HVIDE SANDE   Midway along the isthmus, this is a typical West Jutland fishing town, founded in 1931 when it grew up around the large lock and sluice between the North Sea and Ringkøbing Fjord. Today, with its splendid beach on the seaside, it is the fifth largest fishing port in Denmark. A path follows along the windswept dunes between the sea and Ringkøbing Fjord, with panoramic views in all directions.

The most intriguing attraction here is, naturally, the fishing harbor, the heartbeat of the town. You can walk around and hopefully photograph the harbor. Catches of edible fish are unloaded at the auction building here. The auction is held every Monday to Friday at 7am and again at 10am if the catch has been heavy. A small nod or a lifted eyebrow is caught immediately by the auctioneer, and the purchase is registered. When the fish is sold, the catch is taken by truck for processing at local plants or exported directly in large refrigerated vans to such cities as Copenhagen.

While in the area, you can visit the **Vestkyst Aquarium** (also known as Fiskeriets Hus), Nørregade 2B (☎ 97-31-26-10), a museum devoted to anything and everything to do with fishing. The museum has a saltwater aquarium with fish from both the North Sea and Ringkøbing Fjord. The museum also includes tanks for large fish such as piked dogfish, rays, and big gadoids. From April to October 31, the fish are fed every Tuesday and Friday at 3:30pm. Displays also include fishing tackle, and children can go on a voyage in the wheelhouse of a real cutter. While below deck, visitors experience the cramped conditions under which fishermen live at sea. From April to October, it's open daily from 10am to 6pm; from November to March, it's open Tuesday to Sunday from 10am to 4pm. Admission costs 40 DKK ($5.80) for adults, 20 DKK ($2.90) for children under age 12.

At Hvide Sande (whose name translates as "white sands") you'll find information available at **Holmsland Klit Turistforening,** at offices they maintain on the premises of the **Vestkyst Aquarium,** Nørregade 2B (☎ 97-31-18-66). The office is open year-round, Monday to Friday from 10am to 5pm. It's also open during midsummer (June to August) every Saturday from 9am to 5pm and on Sunday from 11am to 4pm.

WHERE TO DINE IN HVIDE SANDE

Restaurant Slusen. Bredgade 3. ☎ **97-31-27-27.** Reservations recommended. Main courses 118–248 DKK ($17.10–$35.95); fixed-price menu 248 DKK ($35.95). AE, DC, MC, V. Daily 11:30am to 2:30pm and 6–9pm. Closed Sunday night and all day Monday during Jan–Feb. SEAFOOD/DANISH.

Set within a building from the 1940s, in a location that's directly astride the harbor front, this is the most appealing restaurant in Hvide Sande, thanks to well-conceived cuisine and a tactful staff. Outfitted with bright colors and a collection of landscape paintings that depict the local seacoast, it contains only 40 seats and a menu that changes with the availability of ingredients. Menu items include fried fillets of plaice or turbot, different preparations of herring and salmon, a succulent seafood platter, and fillets of catfish with mustard sauce. Lobster is available, kept fresh in an on-site aquarium. The dessert specialty is a Grand Marnier soufflé served on a purée of fresh peaches. The helpings are generous, the food flavorful, the fish fresh and well prepared, and the price right. Not only that, but the staff assured us readers will have "great fun" here. What more could be asked?

THE ROUTE SOUTH

You can continue south to Nymindegab, the gateway to the isthmus, if you're coming from Esbjerg. In times gone by, Nymindegab was the home of a small fishing harbor. From here you can explore:

Windsurfing on Ringkøbing Fjord

Ringkøbing Fjord is one of the most popular places for windsurfing in the north of Europe. The area has Denmark's best wind statistics, and friendly shallow fjord waters are ideal for beginners. When the wind blows from the west, it comes in directly from the North Sea. Having passed the dunes, it accelerates across the fjord, creating a strong and constant wind. A wind from the east brings heat and sun, which in turn ensures increasing winds in the afternoon, so that surfing is generally possible every day. The wind is strongest in March and April and again in autumn during September and October.

The best conditions are found at Hvide Sande, the venue for international and national speed weeks. This is the largest center around the fjord with Denmark's best shallow water area for speed and slalom surfing. The center has a well-stocked shop with a school providing windsurfing instruction, equipment for hire, and a cafeteria with wind gauge. You'll be kept up-to-date on weather forecasts. You can stop in at **Westwind Nord** (☎ **97-31-25-99**), where you can get an introductory 3-hour course for 350 DKK ($50.75). They also rent gear.

✪ **TIPPERNE NATURE RESERVE**   A small road, sign-posted from Nymindegab, leads into this tiny peninsula jutting into Ringkøbing Fjord. The flats and water areas surrounding the peninsula are one of the most important bird sanctuaries in West Jutland. The area's bird life was protected some years ago to establish undisturbed breeding. Today it is a favorite stopover for migratory birds. During both spring and autumn, thousands of ducks, geese, and waders stop here to rest. In July and August, when migration is at its peak, the sandpiper, curlew, snipe, and golden plover are some of the many species to be seen here. In the winter season, the swan, Denmark's national bird, is one of the species finding shelter at Tipperne. From April to August, the bird reserve is open to visitors Sunday from 5 to 10am only. From September to March, the reserve can be visited every Sunday only from 10am to noon. You should continue by car until you reach a building marked Tipperhuset. You're not allowed to stop until you reach the parking lot, but once there you can climb a viewing tower to observe the birds. A 1-mile nature path departs from the bird tower. All walking in the area is restricted to this one path.

5 Ry

256km (160 miles) W of Copenhagen; 24km (15 miles) SE of Silkeborg; 35km (22 miles) SW of Århus

In the very heart of Jutland, the little old town of Ry makes a less commercialized center than Silkeborg (see below) for visiting the mid–Jutland Lake District, which is one of the most beautiful areas of Denmark. Ry lies in a countryside of extensive forests and rolling hills, valleys, gorges, and lakes, all linked by the Gudenå (also spelled Gudenåen), the longest river in Denmark. The region is filled with numerous sites of historical interest, including old churches, abbey ruins, villages with thatched roofs, and a number of small museums. Other than a walk through the town of Ry itself, there aren't many notable sights in the historic center. Most visitors use Ry as a base, branching out to see attractions in its environs.

ESSENTIALS

GETTING THERE   Ry lies on the main rail route linking Silkeborg (trip time: 20 minutes) and Århus (trip time: 30 minutes). There's also a bus from Århus, but it takes twice as long.

By Car   From Silkeborg (see below) take Route 15, heading east, and following the signs to Århus. Veer right (south) when you reach the town of Låsby, following the signs to Ry.

VISITOR INFORMATION   The **Ry Turistbureau,** Klostervej 3 (☎ **86-89-34-22**), is open June 15 to August 31 Monday to Saturday from 9am to 4:30pm. Off-season hours are Monday to Friday 9am to 4pm and Saturday 9am to noon.

GETTING AROUND

For many Danes, the only way to see the lake district and its little hamlets is by bike. **Ry Cykel,** Skanderborgvej 19 (☎ **86-89-14-91**), will rent you a bike for the day for 50 DKK ($7.25).

Instead of a bike, you might prefer to explore the river and the beautiful lakes in the area by canoe. Brochures about canoeing are available from the Ry Turistbureau (see above) or from **Ry Kanofart,** Kyhnsvej 20 (☎ **86-89-11-67**), which will rent you a canoe for 250 DKK ($36.25) per day.

EXPLORING THE AREA

Lying only a 10-minute ride west of Ry via Route 445, ✪ **Himmelbjerget,** or sky mountain, is the most visited spot in the Lake District. You can also get here by taking bus no. 104 from the train depot at Ry. Himmelbjerget rises 482 feet above sea level, the highest point in Denmark. In 1871 the Danish crown obtained the property and turned it over to the people of Denmark as a sightseeing attraction.

Himmelbjerget towers majestically over the surrounding countryside, not only when viewed from the lake, but from the many footpaths in the woods. Two modern tourist boats, the *Viking* and the *Turisten,* run summer cruises between Ry and Himmelbjerget. For information and schedules, call ☎ **86-82-88-21** in Ry. The cost is 35 DKK ($5.05) one way for adults and 20 DKK ($2.90) one way for children.

The **Himmelbjerget Tower,** rising 82 feet, was erected in commemoration of King Frederik VII who, on June 5, 1849, gave the Danish people a free constitution. The tower was designed by the architect L. P. Fenger. From the tower you'll have the most panoramic view of the area. It is open daily in May and June from 10am to 5pm; in July, daily 10am to 9pm; from August to September 15, daily 10am to 6pm; and from September 16 through October, only on Saturday and Sunday from 10am to 5pm. Admission is 5 DKK (75¢).

Even more interesting than Ry itself is the old hamlet of **Gamle Ry,** lying directly west of Ry and reached along Route 461. This is called the "village of kings and springs." Its original name was "Rye," but this was changed to Gamle Ry. The name "Rye" comes from rydning, Danish for clearing. In the Middle Ages this was a spiritual center of Denmark because of its "holy springs." The village gets its royal associations through Frederik II, who built a hunting mansion here in 1582.

From the center you can follow a sign directing you to Sct. Sørens spring in Rye Sønderskov (Rye Southwood). This is a wonderful walk through a subglacial stream trench, called Jammerdalen or "The Vale of Tears." The curative water of this spring attracted many pilgrims, launching Gamle Ry on its heyday of medieval glory. In gratitude, pilgrims contributed to the funding of a granite church on the nearby hill where the present Sct. Sørens Kirke is situated. After the Reformation, when the pilgrimages stopped, the church fell into disrepair. It was far too big for local parishioners to maintain. However, in 1912, a rich farmer had the old tower reconstructed. The original church here was the scene of the election of Christian III as king of Denmark on July 4, 1534. The election led to the collapse of the Catholic church in Denmark.

From the church you go east past a mill to Galgebakken (The Gallow Hill), a protected nature reserve set in lovely heather-clad hills.

East of Gamle Ry, if you cross the Gudenå at Emborg bridge, you will come to the ruins of the largest Cistercian abbey in Denmark, the **Øm Kloster** (Monastery). In the 12th century a group of Cistercian monks left the Vitskøl Kloster monastery in Himmerland and, after considerable roaming, arrived at Øm, where they founded the Øm Kloster monastery in 1175. The Cistercians were skilled farmers and preferred sites in forests and remote areas, where their hard work turned barren land into exemplary farms. During the Reformation, the monastery ceased to exist and the lands were taken over by the king. The monastery itself was pulled down. However, excavations in modern times have revealed one of the best preserved ground plans of a medieval monastery to date. For information, call ☎ **86-89-81-94.** There is a little museum here open daily in April, 10am to 4pm; in May, 10am to 5pm; from June to August, 10am to 6pm; in September, 10am to 5pm; and from October 1 to 20, 10am to 4pm. The cloister is always closed on Monday. Admission is 30 DKK ($4.35) adults, 12 DKK ($1.75) children. This minor museum has a historical medical exhibition, an herb garden, and a collection of skeletons discovered in the area. The plants in the herb garden date back to the days when the monastery flourished here.

You can take Route 461 south from Gamle Ry until you see the turnoff east to the hamlet of Emborg. This takes you to **Mossø,** the largest lake in Jutland. To the west of the lake are the Højlund Forest and the Sukkertoppen Hill, rising 354 feet.

The longest watercourse in Denmark, the Gudenå, also passes through Mossø en route from Tinnet Krat to Randers Fjord. Closer to the river are valley terraces created by water melting from the Ice Age. The sandy surfaces are covered with heather and coniferous plantations, but make for poor farmland.

Mossø is the habitat of many types of birds. The sanctuary at Emborg Odde is a breeding site for a colony of black-headed gulls, which are extremely aggressive, thus providing protection from predators. The black-necked grebe takes advantage of this and breeds among the gulls. In the late summer, grebes can be seen along the edges of the reed banks, feeding on small animals.

Because of its size and varying depths, Mossø has always housed a wide variety of fish—some 20 species—the most numerous being perch, roach, and ruffe, along with pike-perch, eel, and lake trout.

SHOPPING   The hamlet of Gamle Ry has a number of specialty stores. The best collection of ceramics and stoneware is found at **Gamle Rye Pottemageri,** Nyvej 9 (☎ **86-89-86-30**). You can also visit an antique mart here: **Gamle Rye Antik,** Emborgvej 4 (☎ **86-89-80-70**).

FISHING THE LAKES

The lakes in the Ry area offer excellent possibilities for catching perk, pike, trout, and zander. Fishing passes, costing 30 DKK ($4.35) daily, and fishing licenses, going for 25 DKK ($3.60) daily, are available from the Ry Turistbureau (see above).

WHERE TO STAY

Gamle Rye Kro. Ryesgade 8, DK-8680 Ry. ☎ **86-89-80-42.** 30 units (25 with bath). 420 DKK ($60.90) double without bath; 540 DKK ($78.30) double with bath. AE, DC, MC, V. From Ry, drive 3-miles southwest, following the signs to Gamle Ry.

The most historic (but not the most luxurious) hotel in Ry lies 3 miles to the southwest, in the center of a satellite town known as Gamle (Old) Ry. The place looks like a large white farmhouse, set 200-yards north of the village church and the town market square. It has a history stretching back 400 years, to the time when pilgrims heading for the nearby (now ruined) monastery extolled the healing powers of local springs. What you'll see today is a well-maintained, white-walled inn with a red tile roof, lots of modernizations, and a new wing that contains many of the simple, efficiently decorated bedrooms. Some (but not all) have TV and telephone. Don't expect accommodations, or even public rooms, dripping with a sense of antique nostalgia, as part of the inn's antique charm has been washed out during the renovations of the early 1990s. Overall, however, there's a sense of hospitality from the youthful and entrepreneurial staff, and a restaurant, separately recommended in "Where to Dine", with worthwhile, albeit conservative, Danish cooking. On the premises are a heated indoor swimming pool, and a solarium.

Hotel Himmelbjerget. Ny Himmelbjergvej 20, DK-8680 Ry. ☎ **86-89-80-45.** Fax 86-89-87-93. 19 units (none with bath). TEL. 450 DKK ($65.25) double. Rate includes breakfast. Bus: 411.

Set at a higher altitude than any other hotel in Denmark, this hotel was built in 1922 in a charming, rustic, old-fashioned venue that has changed very little, despite subtle modernizations, ever since. It lies 4½ miles northwest of the center of Ry, on a rocky plateau of its own, within a 10-minute walk of the soaring monument built around the turn of the century by a Danish king to celebrate his nation's highest peak. Bedrooms still retain some of their old-time paneling and accessories, and in many cases have either terraces or balconies. Accommodations overlook the nearby tower, or the fields, lakes, and forests of this loftiest district in Denmark. Each has a writing table, chairs, and twin beds that can be separated or moved together, according to the wishes of the room's occupants. On the premises are a bar and an appealing old-fashioned (separately recommended) restaurant that serves generous portions of conservative, time-tested Danish recipes that taste especially flavorful because of the illusion that you're actually at a high altitude. The hotel's name, incidentally, translates from the Danish as "Heaven Mountain."

Ry Park Hotel. Kyhnsvej 2, DK-8680 Ry. ☎ **86-89-19-11.** Fax 86-89-12-57. E-mail: ry_hotel@post5.tele.dk. 76 units. TV TEL. 645–895 DKK ($93.50–$129.75) double. AE, DC, MC, V.

Set in the center of Ry, this is at the same time one of the oldest and newest hotels in town. Originally built in 1888, it was radically reconfigured into a more streamlined and comfortable venue exactly a century later. Parts of the interior are outfitted in a woodsy, pine-sheathed motif that evokes the northern forests; others are filled with furniture inspired by old-fashioned English models. About 20 of the bedrooms lie within a comfortable annex across the road, and throughout the hotel, bathrooms are sheathed in layers of polished white marble. The hotel is frequently reserved almost exclusively for participants in corporate conventions, who ask the hotel's staff to arrange fishing, canoeing, kayaking, bicycling, and yachting excursions whenever possible. On the premises are an indoor swimming pool, sauna, solarium, billiards room, restaurant, and cocktail bar.

NEARBY ACCOMMODATIONS

Nørre Vissing Kro. Låsbyvej 122, Nørre Vissing, DK-8660 Skanderborg. ☎ **86-94-37-16.** Fax 86-94-37-57. 14 units. TV TEL. 650 DKK ($94.25) double. Rate includes breakfast. AE, DC, MC, V. Drive north from Ry, following the signs from Låsby. At Låsby, turn southwest, following the signs to Nørre Vissing.

Set 7 miles northwest of Ry, amid rolling farmlands dotted with stately trees, this century-old inn has received many awards during the late 1990s for the excellence of its cuisine. (As such, its restaurant is recommended separately, below.) But in addition to the well-deserved accolades it receives for its food, it also maintains artfully decorated and stylish bedrooms, that are a lot more interesting than those within some of the region's more modern hotels. Each is outfitted in varying shades of blue, the owner's favorite color, and each has a scattering of rustic antiques that were in most cases acquired within Jutland. There are very few amenities per se, other than a grouping of comfortable chairs near the buttery-yellow reception area where guests congregate for a drink, in some cases interacting with the very hip staff and very charming owners.

WHERE TO DINE

Gamle Rye Kro. Ryesgade 8. ☎ **86-89-80-42.** Reservations recommended. Main courses 55–200 DKK ($8–$29). AE, DC, MC, V. Daily noon–10pm. From Ry, drive 3 miles southwest, following the signs to Gamle Ry. DANISH.

This is the most appealing component of one of the oldest inns in the region, thanks to generous portions of traditional Danish food, and a cozy, albeit much-renovated, overly-modernized interior design. Menu items include all the traditional Danish staples, such as *frikadeller* (meat balls), platters with several different preparations of herring, cream of mushroom soup, smoked salmon with chive-flavored cream sauce, roasted pork with red cabbage and onions, Dover sole *meunière*, and fillet of plaice stuffed with asparagus and baby shrimp. Fried eel is even available on occasion. The cookery is always reliable in the best grandmotherly tradition.

Restaurant Himmelbjerget. Ny Himmelbjergvej 20. ☎ **86-89-80-45.** Reservations recommended. Main courses 140–180 DKK ($20.30–$26.10). AE, DC, MC, V. Daily 10am–10pm. Bus: 411 from Ry. DANISH.

Set at a higher altitude than any other restaurant in Denmark, in a location 4½ miles northwest of Ry, this is an appealingly old-fashioned restaurant where white napery, high ceilings, and old-world service are still enforced. You might preface or follow your meal with a 10-minute uphill hike to the highest point in Denmark, where a medieval-looking stone tower was built as a landmark around the turn of the century. Menu items include most of the traditional specialties of Denmark, including marinated salmon with mustard and dill sauce and fresh-baked bread, fillet of beef with onions and red wine sauce, fillet of veal with fresh vegetables and mushroom sauce, cold potato soup with bacon and chives, brisket of beef with horseradish sauce, or tenderloin of beef with fried onions. Any of these might be followed with selections from a carefully arranged platter of Danish cheeses. The recipes seemingly haven't changed in a century—and that's exactly what the locals like to depend on when they come here.

NEARBY DINING

✪ **Nørre Vissing Kro.** Låsbyvej 122, Nørre Vissing, DK-8660 Skanderborg. ☎ **86-94-37-16.** Reservations recommended. Lunch main courses 95–140 DKK ($13.75–$20.30); dinner main courses 160–210 DKK ($23.20–$30.45). Fixed-price dinner menus 195–405 DKK ($28.30–$58.70). AE, DC, MC, V. Daily noon–3pm and 6–9:30pm. Drive north from Ry, following the signs from Låsby. At Låsby, turn southwest, following the signs to Nørre Vissing. FRENCH/ITALIAN/DANISH.

This is one of the most sophisticated and urbane restaurants in Jutland, with a string of recent awards based on culinary excellence and flair. Most of the dinner guests here combine their meal with an overnight stay in any of the inn's 14 bedrooms (see above), an arrangement that's encouraged by the establishment's copious wine list and the strict rules of Denmark against driving and drinking. Luncheons, however, tend to include greater numbers of guests en route to somewhere else, and tend to be lighter and less elaborate. The dining room is a spacious, all-blue affair dotted with country antiques and artfully chosen accessories. Menu items change with the seasons, and depend on the inspiration of the chef on the day of your arrival. A well-conceived meal, however, might include *foie gras* with cherry sauce served on a bed of sautéed summer cabbage; poached lobster with a spinach flan and orange sauce; a medley of European cheeses from France and Italy; and a layer cake stuffed with summer berries marinated in rum, served with strawberry sorbet. There is a robust quality to the cuisine, yet each dish is imbued with a subtle texture that only a master chef can achieve, one who knows how to turn simple, natural produce into a gastronomic experience of unmistakable quality.

6 Silkeborg

43km (27 miles) W of Århus; 278 1/2 km (174 miles) W of Copenhagen; 37km (23 miles) S of Viborg

In the heart of the Danish lake district, the small city of Silkeborg is surrounded by large forests, beautiful lakes, and the Gudenå River, the longest in Denmark. This provincial town lies on the shores of Lake Longsø, its two major sights being the Kunstmuseum and the Silkeborg Museum. In 1845, Michael Drewsen, whose statue is seen in the town square, built a paper mill here on the east side of the river. He, in so doing, founded the town, and the mill and other industries grew until, today, Silkeborg has a population of some 35,000 citizens.

ESSENTIALS

GETTING THERE   From Århus, follow Route 15 west to Silkeborg. If you aren't driving, there's frequent train service from Copenhagen to Silkeborg via Fredericia. Trains also run frequently between Silkeborg and Århus, going via Ry. An express bus (no. 913E) makes a 50-minute run between Århus and Silkeborg twice daily.

By Car   From Århus (see below) follow Route 15 west.

VISITOR INFORMATION   Contact the **Silkeborg Turistbureau,** Godthåbsvej (☎ **86-82-19-11**), open June 15 to August Monday to Friday 9am to 5pm, Saturday 9am to 3pm, and Sunday 9:30am to 12:30pm. Off-season hours are Monday to Friday 9am to 4pm, Saturday 9am to noon.

GETTING AROUND BY BIKE

One of the best ways to visit the lake district is by renting a bike, available at **Silkeborg Cykeludlejning,** Århusvej 51 (☎ **86-82-28-24**). Rental fees start at 50 DKK ($7.25) a day. Bicycle route maps are available from the Silkeborg Turistbureau (see above).

EXPLORING THE AREA

The most intriguing way to see Sky Mountain and the surrounding countryside is aboard the paddle steamer *Hjejlen,* which has operated since 1861 and sails frequently in summer. For schedules and information, call **Hjejlen Co. Ltd.,** Havnen (☎ **86-82-07-66**). A round-trip ticket costs 79 DKK ($11.45) for adults, half price for children. Departures from Silkeborg Harbor are daily at 10am and 1:45pm from mid-June until mid-August.

✪ **Silkeborg Museum.** Hovedgaardsvej 7. ☎ **86-82-14-99.** Admission 20 DKK ($2.90) adults, 5 DKK (75¢) children. May to mid-Oct, daily 10am–5pm; mid-Oct to Apr, Wed and Sat–Sun noon–4pm. Bus: 10.

This 18th-century manor by the Gudenå River, directly east of Torvet, houses the 2,200-year-old **Tullund Man,** discovered in a peat bog in 1950. His face is the most unspoiled of all early people found to date. His body was so well preserved, in fact, that scientists were able to determine the contents of his last supper: flax, barley, and oats. His head capped by fur, the Tollund Man was strangled by a plaited leather string—probably the victim of a ritual sacrifice. Equally well-preserved is the Elling Woman, who was found near the same spot. Scientists estimate that she was about 25 years old when she died in 210 B.C.

The museum also has a special exhibition of old Danish glass, a clogmaker's workshop, a collection of stone implements, antique jewelry, and artifacts from the ruins of Silkeborg Castle. In the handcraft and Iron Age markets, artisans utilize ancient techniques to create iron, jewelry, and various crafts.

Silkeborg Kunstmuseum. Gudenåvej 9. ☎ **86-82-53-88.** Admission 20 DKK ($2.90) adults, free for children under age 16. Apr–Oct Tues–Sun 10am–5pm, Nov–Mar Tues–Fri noon–4pm, Sat–Sun 10am–4pm. Bus: 10.

This museum offers unique exhibitions, including Asger Jorn's paintings and ceramics. The museum also displays paintings by members of the COBRA School (**Co**penhagen, **Br**ussels, and **A**msterdam, where the artists originated). Much of their work was produced between 1948 and 1951. Special exhibitions are also staged. The façade of the building features a large ceramic relief by Jean Dubuffet.

AQUA Ferskvands Akvarium og Museum. Vejsøvej 55. ☎ **89-21-21-89.** Admission 55 DKK ($8) adults, 30 DKK ($4.35) children. June–Aug daily 10am–6pm; off-season Mon–Fri 10am–4pm, Sat–Sun 10am–5pm.

This freshwater aquarium and museum on the south side of town offers visitors an intriguing journey underwater. AQUA is a "converse aquarium," designed so that visitors feel as though they're underwater. Come and see rare otters hunting and at play, or watch the diving ducks, lurking pikes, and many other fish and plants in their natural surroundings. You can also have lunch in the park or pay a visit to the AQUA Café.

NEARBY ATTRACTIONS
Jysk Automobilmuseum (Jutland Car Museum). Skovvejen, Gjern. ☎ **86-87-50-50.** Admission 45 DKK ($6.50) adults, 20 DKK ($2.90) children. Apr 1–May 15 and Sept 16–Oct 31 Sat–Sun and holidays 10am–5pm; May 16–Sept 15 daily 10am–5pm. Closed Nov 1–Mar. Located 10 miles northeast of Silkeborg, it's accessible from Silkeborg by following the road signs to the town of Hammil, then turning off when you see the signs for Gjern and the Jysk Automobilmuseum. There's also a bus that departs once an hour from Silkeborg that's marked "Randers" as its final destination.

Near Silkeborg at Gjern, this is the only automobile museum in Jutland, featuring 140 vintage automobiles dating from 1900 to 1948. Sixty-eight different makes are represented, among them the V12 cylinder Auburn, V12-cylinder Cadillac, 1947 Crosley, the famous Renault Taxis de la Marne, Kissel, Hotchkiss, Jordan, Vivinus, Rolls-Royce, and Maserati. The museum was established in 1967 by a local mechanic, Mr. Aagi Louring, who collected and restored only Danish cars, motorcycles, trucks, and fire engines. Today, although the collection is still privately owned, it has expanded its collections into the international cornucopia of antique cars you'll see today. Mr. Louring, who is something of a local celebrity, still makes it a point to drop in on the collection at regular intervals.

SHOPPING
The main market is held at Torvet (the town's central square) on Saturday mornings, getting started around 7am. It's always best to go before noon. A smaller market begins about the same time every Wednesday at Nørretorv. Among specialty stores, **Bon Sac,** Søndergade 2C (☎ **86-82-60-55**), has an intriguing collection of fashionable leather goods. **Inspiration,** Østergade 5 (☎ **86-82-50-11**), offers a large collection of gift items for the home.

WHERE TO STAY

The Silkeborg Turistbureau (see above) can book you into nearby **private homes.**

⭐ **Best Western Hotel Louisiana.** Chr. 8 Vej 7, DK-8600 Silkeborg. ☎ **800/528-1234** in the U.S., or ☎ 86-82-18-99. Fax 86-80-32-69. www.louisiana.dk. E-mail: info@louisiana.dk. 43 units. MINIBAR TV TEL. 913.50–1,015 DKK ($132.45–$147.15) double; 1,250 DKK ($181.25) suite. Rate includes breakfast. AE, DC, MC, V.

One of Silkeborg's most deeply entrenched hotels was built in 1940, in a position a few blocks south of the center of town, behind a pinkish-gray, three-story façade. In 1998, a massive renovation was completed, an act that brought its interior up to the standards of the most modern hotels in town. Part of the charm of this place derives from a particularly attentive staff, an unusual collection of modern art, and a deep concern with protecting and preserving the natural environment. (A percentage of every kroner taken in by the hotel is donated to environmental causes.) Bedrooms are a bit larger than you might have expected, and conservatively decorated with unassuming furniture, including good beds and ample baths. On the premises is a worthy steakhouse, The Angus. Open only for dinner, nightly from 5 to 10pm, it charges 130 to 180 DKK ($18.85–$26.10) for main courses.

Gammel Skovridergaard. Marienlundsvej 36, DK-8600 Silkeborg. ☎ **86-82-11-55.** Fax 86-80-19-30. 69 units. TV TEL. 885 DKK ($128.30) double, 950 DKK ($137.75) suite. Rates include breakfast. AE, DC, MC, V. From Silkeborg, drive a half-mile south of town, following the signs to Horsens.

This historic and luxurious property is devoted to conventions and conferences more than virtually any other hotel in the region, and as such, rooms (especially during the peak of convention season in winter) might not be available. But during those periods when rooms are available (usually during midsummer) a stay here can be extremely pleasant and comfortable. Set within a well-maintained park, the hotel originated in the 1700s, when the manager of the surrounding game reserve and forest built a well-appointed home for himself. In the mid-1980s, under the ownership of Silkeborg's largest bank (which books at least 30% of all convention space for its own managers and staff members) it was expanded into the convention center and hotel you'll see today.

Bedrooms are larger than you might have expected, and filled with comfortably upholstered, even plush furnishings that any business executive might have selected for his or her private home. Cafe tables are set up on the hotel's verdant lawns during mild weather, and the hotel's restaurant offers well-prepared, carefully choreographed meals. The in-house restaurant merits special mention because of its ability to cater to large groups or individuals with aplomb. Only set menus are offered, each priced at 190 DKK ($27.55). Lunches are almost always configured as a buffet; dinners are sit-down, internationally-inspired meals served by a staff at artfully decorated tables. Other than that, this site doesn't really indulge its visitors with a lot of sports and recreation facilities on-site.

Hotel Dania. Torvet 5, DK-8600 Silkeborg. ☎ **86-80-20-04.** 47 units. TV TEL. Mon–Thurs 1,080 DKK ($156.60) double. Fri–Sun and during July–Aug 880 DKK ($127.60) double. Rate includes breakfast. AE, DC, MC, V. Free parking. Bus: 3.

Set directly on Silkeborg's main square, within a 5-minute walk of the railway station, this is the oldest and most venerable hotel in town. Behind a yellow-with-white-trim façade, it was established in 1848, and had a radical upgrade and renovation performed on each of its bedrooms in 1997. While antiques fill the corridors and reception lounge, the rooms have been completely renovated in a functional, modern style. Outdoor dining on the square is popular in summer, and the hotel restaurant

(The Underhuset) serves typical Danish food along with Scandinavian and French dishes. The hotel's dining room, incidentally, is the longest restaurant in Denmark: a corridor-like room with windows along one side, it stretches more than 150 feet, encompassing one end of the ground floor of two different buildings.

Hotel Impala. Vestre Ringvej 53, DK-8600 Silkeborg. ☎ **86-82-03-00.** Fax 86-81-40-66. E-mail: impala@vbip.cibercity.dk. 60 units. MINIBAR TV TEL. 840 DKK ($121.80) double. Rates include breakfast. AE, DC, MC, V.

One of the best hotels in the area, the Impala has streamlined rooms with angular Danish-modern furniture and private balconies. Outside, gardens slope past an artificial pond to the highway. Its rustic core was built as a farmhouse in 1890, and several modern chalet extensions were added in 1975 when it became a hotel. It's located west of Langsø Lake. Lunch and dinner are served daily in the upstairs dining room to hotel guests and the general public. A full list of European wines is available.

Scandic Hotel Silkeborg. Udgårdsvej 2, DK-8600 Silkeborg. ☎ **86-80-35-33.** Fax 86-80-35-06. 117 units. MINIBAR TV TEL. June–Aug 650 DKK ($94.25) double, Sept–May 1,095 DKK ($158.75) double (Sun–Thurs), 750 DKK ($108.75) double (Fri–Sat). Suite 1,400 DKK ($203) year round. AE, DC, MC, V. Bus: 3 from rail station.

Launched in 1990, the largest hotel in Silkeborg lies 1½ miles west of the town center in a residential neighborhood surrounded by fields and forests. Each room is well furnished and decorated in strong violets, greens, and blues. The bedrooms and tile baths are a bit cramped, but generally comfortable. The hotel dining room, Guldanden (Golden Duck), is a glamorous setting for a Danish and international cuisine, with meals beginning at 200 DKK ($29). Facilities include an indoor pool, sauna, health club, and solarium.

NEARBY ACCOMMODATIONS
In Laven

Hotel Silkeborgsøerne. Himmelbjergvej 106, Laven DK-8600 Silkeborg. ☎ **86-84-12-01.** Fax 86-84-17-40. 43 units. MINIBAR TV TEL. 1,015 DKK ($147.15) double; 1,250 DKK ($181.25) suite. AE, DC, MC, V. From Silkeborg, follow Route 15 and the signs to Århus, then veer south, following the signs to Laven.

Set on a panoramic hillside 8½ miles west of Silkeborg, on the north shore of the region's largest lake (Lake Julsø), this is a low-rise, angular, and modern hotel whose design you might have imagined on a hilltop in New Mexico. Designed and built in 1971, and radically upgraded and renovated in 1996, it's the holiday home of North European urbanites who value the many points of natural beauty that stretch out among the many nearby lakes and forests. Overall, the venue is extremely simple, with staff and owners that live close to nature and the changing seasons. Meals in the dining room are served a la carte to whomever happens to show up, including non-residents of the hotel who might be camping in tents in the surrounding region. Main courses in the modern, big-windowed dining room, cost from 95 to 170 DKK ($13.75–$24.65), and usually follow the tenets of traditional Danish cuisine. Bedrooms are small but sunny, illuminated with sliding glass doors that lead onto private verandas, and outfitted with furnishings designed in the modern Scandinavian style.

In Ans

✪ **Kongensbro Kro.** Gamle Kongevej 70, DK-8643 Ans. ☎ **86-87-01-77.** Fax 86-87-92-17. 15 units. TEL. 650–800 DKK ($94.25–$116) double. Rate includes breakfast. AE, DC, MC, V. Closed Dec 23–24 and Dec 31–Jan 5.

Although a tavern stood on this site from 1663, it was little more than a ruin when members of the Andersen family bought and rebuilt it in 1949. The family's matriarch, Else, authored five Danish-language cookbooks during her active years here, and became something of a legend throughout Denmark. Today the charming and well-kept inn is directed by her son, Øle, and his hardworking staff. Accommodations are pleasant and cozy, and some contain TVs.

Meals are served daily from noon to 3pm and 6 to 9pm. A two-course fixed-price menu is available at lunch and dinner for 105 DKK ($15.25), although most serious gastronomes opt for a la carte meals with main courses ranging from 80 to 180 DKK ($11.60 to $26.10). Delectable menu items include the best *frikadeller* (Danish meatballs) in Jutland, served with red cabbage, or else you might opt for the alluring quail, which is quite delectable in its port-wine sauce. The finest thing on the menu is likely to be Danish trout, often served in puff pastry with a creamy dill sauce. The inn lies between Ans and Århus, about a 10-minute drive north of Silkeborg.

✪ **Svostrup Kro.** Svostrupvej 58, Svostrup, DK-8600 Silkeborg. ☎ **86-87-70-04.** 15 units (10 with bath). 520 DKK ($75.40) double without bath; 680 DKK ($98.60) double with bath. Rate includes breakfast. AE, DC, MC, V. From Silkeborg, drive 6 miles north, following the signs to Randers, and then the signs to Svostrup. Bus: 313 from Silkeborg.

This is one of the least-modernized inns around Silkeborg, with more of its original architectural features than many of its equivalently historic competitors. On farmland between the Gudenå River and the Gjern hills, it was built in the 1600s as a bargeman's inn, and designated by the Danish monarchy in 1834 as one of the inns that would be suitable for a visit from the Danish king. Because of its aesthetic authenticity and its hardworking, tactful staff, it's sought out by aficionados of old Danish inns, who appreciate its antique paneling and an interior that evokes the Denmark of long ago. Bedrooms are an appealing mixture of antique, or at least old, furnishings, with enough touches of dowdiness to keep them interesting. On the premises is a restaurant that's open from 7am to 11pm every day. Main courses at lunch range from 38 to 228 DKK ($5.50–$33.05); main courses at dinner cost from 148 to 288 DKK ($21.45–$41.75). Many of the food items include old-fashioned Danish cuisine such as herring platters with new potatoes, or fried steak with onions. Others are more modern, such as venison steak braised with red wine, and served with caramelized apples, nuts, celery, mushrooms, and a *confit* of baby onions.

WHERE TO DINE

Piaf. Nygade 31. ☎ **86-81-12-55.** Reservations recommended. Lunch platters 48–67 DKK ($6.95–$9.70). Dinner main courses 95–178 DKK ($13.75–$25.80). DC, MC, V. Mon–Sat noon–3pm and 5:30–10:30pm. MEDITERRANEAN.

The most exotic and deliberately counter-culture restaurant in town occupies the solid brick premises of an 80-year-old building in the historic core. It was named after the uncanny resemblance of its owner, Anni Danielsen (who's known for her fondness of black dresses), to the late French *chanteuse*, Edith Piaf. Artwork within the restaurant is offset with brick walls, potted plants, poster-image testimonials to the late Gallic sparrow, and deliberately mismatched tables, plates, ashtrays, and accessories. Lunch platters tend to be light, airy, and flavorful; dinners more substantial with excellently chosen ingredients—always fresh and flavorful—deftly handled by a skilled kitchen staff. Both are inspired by the tenets of southern European (i.e., Spanish, Greek, Provençal, and Italian) cuisine. Look for heaping platters of paella, bouillabaisse, roasted lamb with rosemary, carpaccio, and sliced veal. What's the only item you're likely not to find on the menu? Pork, since it reminds most of the clients of the cuisine served in Denmark during their childhoods, and which is consequently something avoided within this consciously exotic setting.

Spiesehuset Christian VIII. Christian VIII Vej 54. ☎ **86-82-25-62.** Reservations required. Main courses 165–190 DKK ($23.90–$27.55); four-course fixed-price menu 325 DKK ($47.15); 3-course fish menu 255 DKK ($36.95). AE, DC, MC, V. Mon–Sat noon–3pm and 5:30–9:30pm. DANISH/FRENCH.

One of the best restaurants in Silkeborg, this establishment was founded about a decade ago in what was originally a late-1700s private house. It seats only 30 people in a dining room painted in what the owners describe as the color of heaven (cerulean blue) accented with crystal, fine silverware, and dramatic modern paintings. Delectable food items include lobster ravioli, carpaccio of marinated sole and salmon served with a saffron sauce, fillet of beef with truffle sauce, medallions of veal stuffed with a purée of wild duck and herbs, and a tender rack of Danish lamb with garlic sauce. Service is attentive and professional.

SILKEBORG AFTER DARK

One site that draws a high percentage of after-dark revelers is the **Jortin Pub,** Tværgade 6 (☎ **86-82-93-20**), where food, beer, schnapps, and dialogue seem to flow within a not particularly historic but very charming environment in the heart of town. Older and more historic is the **Underhuset Pub,** part of the dining and drinking facilities within the also-recommended Hotel Dania, Torvet 5 (☎ **86-82-01-11**). And for a bout of dancing with the Danes of Silkeborg, check out the laser lights and electronic pulsations at the **Chaplin Disco,** Nygade 18B (☎ **86-82-12-73**). Here, beginning around 10:30pm every Wednesday to Saturday, a cover charge of 35 DKK ($5.05) will get you entrance to a site where locals dance till they drop amid peers who rarely seem to be older than around 45.

7 Århus

158¹/₂ km (99 miles) NE of Fanø; 174¹/₂ km (109 miles) W of Copenhagen

Jutland's capital, the second-largest city in Denmark, Århus is a cultural center—a university town combined with a lovely port. Aside from enjoying the city's many restaurants, hotels, and nighttime amusements, you can use Århus as a good base for excursions to Silkeborg, Ebeltoft, and the moated manors and castles to the north.

To some, Århus is the "alternative capital of the west," since Copenhagen is so far to the east and the country as a whole lacks geographical unity. On the east coast of Central Jutland, it lies on a wide bay whose waters are sheltered by the Helgenæs peninsula. Its economic growth today is based on communications, the food industry, electronics, textiles, iron and steel, and Danish design, as well as the harbor which is now the second most important in Denmark, rivaled only by Copenhagen.

Originally Århus was a Viking settlement, probably founded as early as the 10th century; its name, Aros, meaning estuary, comes from its position at the mouth of a river, Århus Å. The town experienced rapid growth and by 948 it had its own bishop. An Episcopal church was built here in 1060, and a cathedral was launched at the dawn of the 13th century. This prosperity came to a temporary end in the late Middle Ages when the town was devastated by the bubonic plague. The Reformation of 1536 also slowed the growth of Århus. But the coming of the railway in the 19th century renewed prosperity, which continues to this day.

GETTING THERE   By Plane   Århus Airport is in Tirstrup, which lies 27 miles northeast of the city. **SAS** (☎ **800/221-2350** toll free within North America, or ☎ 70-10-20-00 in Århus) operates some 12 flights a day, Monday to Friday from Copenhagen, and about 6 on Saturday and Sunday. SAS also operates an afternoon

Århus

Attractions:

Århus Domkirke
  (Cathedral of St. Clemens) ⑮
Århus Kunstmuseum ④
Bæsættelsesmuseet ⑰
Den Gamle By ⑦
Det Danske
  Brandværnsmuseum ⑥
Forhistorisk
  Museum-Moesgård ㉗
Kvindemuseet ⑯
Marselisborg Slot ㉙
Naturhistorisk Museum ②
Rådhuset (Town Hall) ㉑
Steno Museet ①
Vikingemuseet ⑬
Vor Frue Kirke ⑩

Accommodations:

Atlantic Hotel ㉛
Eriksen's Hotel ㉓
Hotel Kong Christian den X ㉕
Hotel La Tour ③
Hotel Marselis ㉖
Hotel Mercur ㉚
Hotel Royal ⑫
Plaza Hotel Århus ㉔
Radisson SAS Scandinavia
  Hotel Århus ㉒

Dining:

Den Gremme Ælleng
  (The Ugly Duckling) ⑲
Kellers Gaard ⑱
Kroen I Krogen ㉘
Le Canard ⑳
Munkestruen ⑪
Prins Ferdinand ⑤
Restaurant de 4 Arstider
  (Four Seasons) ⑧
Rio Grande ⑨
Teater Bodega ⑭

Legend

Church	†
Information	ⓘ
Parking	🅿
Police	🄿
Railway	┼┼┼┼

flight most days between Århus and London. An airport bus runs between the train depot at Århus and the airport, meeting all major flights. The cost of a one-way ticket is 50 DKK ($7.25).

By Train About five or six trains a day make the 4½ hour trip from Århus to Copenhagen. Some 20 trains a day connect Aalborg with Århus, taking an hour and 40 minutes. From Frederikshavn, the North Jutland port and ferry-arrival point from Norway, some 20 trains a day run to Århus, taking 3 hours.

By Bus Two buses daily make the 4-hour run to Århus from Copenhagen.

By Car From the east, cross Funen on the E20 express highway, heading north at the junction with the E45. From the north German border, drive all the way along the E45. From Frederikshavn and Aalborg in the north, head south along the E45.

VISITOR INFORMATION   The tourist office, **Tourist Århus,** is located in the Rådhuset, Park Allé (☎ **89-40-67-00**). It is open mid-June to mid-September, Monday to Friday 9:30am to 6pm, Saturday 9:30am to 5pm, and Sunday 9:30am to 1pm. Off-season times are Monday to Friday 10am to 5pm and Saturday 10am to 1pm.

Århus offers a **tourist ticket** costing 45 DKK ($6.50) which can be purchased at the tourist office or at newsstands (kiosks) throughout the city center. This ticket is valid for 24 hours and for an unlimited number of rides within the central city. It's also valid for a 2½-hour guided tour of Århus. You can purchase a regular bus ticket, valid for one ride, on the rear platform of all city buses for 13 DKK ($1.90). Finally, there's the **Århus Pass,** allowing unlimited travel by public transportation and free admission to many museums and attractions in town. The pass also includes a free 2½-hour guided tour. A 2-day pass costs 110 DKK ($15.95) for adults and 55 DKK ($8) for children; a pass that's valid for a week goes for 155 DKK ($22.45) for adults and 75 DKK ($10.90) for children. The Århus Pass is sold at the tourist office, as well as at many hotels, camping grounds, and various kiosks throughout the city.

SEEING THE SIGHTS

For the best introduction to Århus, head for the town hall's tourist office, where a 2½-hour **sightseeing tour** leaves daily at 10am from June 24 to August 31, costing 45 DKK ($6.50) per person (free with the Århus Pass; see above).

In addition to the more major museums listed below, you can also visit two museums on the grounds of Århus University, Nordre Ringgade. They include **Steno Museet,** C. F. Møllers Allé (☎ **89-42-39-75**), which displays exhibits documenting natural science and medicine. You'll see beautiful 19th-century astronomical telescopes, a 1920s doctor's surgery, and some of the first computers made in Denmark in the 1950s. Posters, models, and do-it-yourself experiments, including tests of Galileo's demonstrations of gravity and of electromagnetism, are also on display. In addition, you can walk through an herbal garden with some 250 historical medicinal herbs. There is also a planetarium with shows daily at 11am, 1pm, and 2pm, as well as 8pm on Wednesday. Hours are Tuesday to Sunday 10am to 4pm. From October to March it is also open from 7 to 10pm. Admission is 30 DKK ($4.35) for adults and 10 DKK ($1.45) for children. To see a planetarium show costs another 30 DKK ($4.35) for adults, 20 DKK ($2.90) for children.

Also on site at the university is a **Naturhistorisk Museum,** Block 210, Universitetsparken (☎ **86-12-97-77**), filled with stuffed animals from all over the world. Some of them are displayed in attractive dioramas. The collection of Danish animals, especially birds, is unique within Denmark. Skeletons, minerals, and a display devoted to the evolution of life are some of the other exhibits. It is open daily 10am to 4pm (until 5pm in July and August). It is closed on Mondays from November to March. Admission is 30 DKK ($4.35) for adults, free for children.

Århus Kunstmuseum. Vennelystparken. ☎ **86-13-52-55.** Admission 30 DKK ($4.35) adults, free for children. Tues–Sun 10am–5pm. Bus: 1, 2, 3, 6, or 9.

One of the oldest and best collections of Danish paintings is assembled here, as well as sculptures and drawings dating from 1750 to the present day. The romantics, the realists, the impressionists—they are all here, featuring modern works from Denmark and abroad, including Germany and the United States. Special exhibitions are often staged here, at which time adults pay 40 DKK ($5.80) (children free). The museum is south of the university. On Sunday there are free guided tours at 3pm.

Bæsættelsesmuseet. Mathilde Fibigers Have 2. ☎ **86-18-42-77.** Admission 15 DKK ($2.15) adults, 5 DKK ($0.75) children. June–Aug Tues–Sun 10am–4pm; off-season Sat–Sun 10am–4pm.

This museum illustrates dramatic events as well as everyday life in Århus during the Nazi takeover of the city, from 1940 until liberation in 1945. The museum is housed in the old city hall, which lies off Domkirkepladsen. This was the Gestapo headquarters during the war. In the basement of the building, this Occupation Museum details a most troubled time, depicting Allied air raids on Århus, weapons, documents, World War II photo displays, guns, and even instruments of torture. The museum also describes sabotage carried out by the local resistance movement. An interesting display documents Allied, Nazi, and Danish propaganda.

Århus Domkirke (Cathedral of St. Clemens). Bispetorvet. ☎ **86-12-38-45.** Free admission. May–Sept, Mon–Sat 9:30am–4pm; Oct–Apr, Mon–Sat 10am–3pm. Bus: 3, 11, 54, or 56.

This late-Gothic redbrick, copper-roofed cathedral, crowned by a 315-foot spire, begun in the early 13th century and completed in the 15th, is the longest cathedral in Denmark, practically as deep as its spire is tall. Of chief interest here are the Renaissance pulpit, 15th-century triptych, and 18th-century pipe organ. (After the cathedral, we suggest a visit to the nearby medievalesque **arcade** at Vestergade 3, with half-timbered buildings, a rock garden, aviary, and antique interiors.)

✪ **Den Gamle By.** Viborgvej 2. ☎ **86-12-31-88.** Admission 55 DKK ($8) adults, 15 DKK ($2.15) children. June–Aug, daily 9am–6pm; May and Sept, daily 9am–5pm; Apr, Oct, and Dec, daily 10am–4pm; Jan–Mar and Nov, daily 11am–3pm. Bus: 3, 14, or 25.

The top sight in Århus, Den Gamle By displays more than 75 buildings representing Danish urban life from the 16th to the 19th century, re-created in a botanical garden. This open-air museum differs from similar museums near Copenhagen and Odense, where the emphasis is on rural life. Here visitors walk through the authentic-looking workshops of bookbinders, carpenters, hatters, and more. There's also a pharmacy, a school, and even an old-fashioned post office. A popular attraction is the Burgomaster's House, a wealthy merchant's antique-stuffed, half-timbered home, built at the end of the 16th century. Make sure to see the Textile Collection and the Old Elsinore Theater, erected in the early 19th century. The museum also houses a collection of china, clocks, delftware, and silverware; inquire at the ticket office. Summer music programs are staged, and there's a restaurant, tea garden, bakery, and beer cellar.

Det Danske Brandværnsmuseum. Tomasgervej 25. ☎ **86-25-41-44.** Admission 40 DKK ($5.80) adults, 15 DKK ($2.15) children. Apr–Oct daily 10am–5pm; Nov–Mar Tues–Sun 10am–5pm. Bus: 12 or 18.

This is the largest firefighting museum in Europe, with some 100 fire engines from the 19th century up to the present day. These vehicles are both horse-drawn and engine driven. Children delight in the playroom where they can have a hands-on experience with real firefighting equipment. The location is 3 miles west of the historic core of Århus and just off of Viby Ringvej.

Forhistorisk Museum-Moesgård. Moesgård Manor. Moesgård Alle 20, Højbjerg. ☎ **89-42-11-00.** Admission 45 DKK ($6.50) adults; free for children under 15. Apr–Sept daily 10am–5pm; Oct–Mar Tues–Sun 10am–4pm. Bus: 6 from railway station. Positioned 5½ miles south of Århus' center.

The former Århus Museum is now an archeological and ethnographic museum in a country setting about 5 miles from town, at Moesgård Manor. It owns the incredibly well-preserved 2,000-year-old Grauballe man, who had lain since the Iron Age in a bog in central Jutland. Outside in the park and woods is an open-air museum that displays prehistoric reconstructions and a prehistoric "trackway." If you're driving from the center, follow the signs to Odder and the Moesgård Manor.

Kvindemuseet. Domkirkepalds 5. ☎ **86-13-61-44.** Admission 20 DKK ($2.90) adults, free for children. June 1–Sept 15 daily 10am–5pm; off-season Tues–Sun 10am–4pm.

This museum is devoted to the history of women, their history and culture, their everyday life, their art, and even work done by women's hands. The museum has collected objects and documents, photos, slides, and biographies to document the lives and heritage of women and to record their changing roles over the centuries. The museum documents the legacy of both famous and forgotten women. Three or four special exhibitions devoted to women are staged here annually.

Rådhuset (Town Hall). Rådhuspladsen. ☎ **89-40-20-00.** Admission: Guided tour, 10 DKK ($1.45); tower only, 5 DKK (75¢). Guided tours, Mon–Fri at 11am; tower, at noon and 4pm (closed Sept–June 23). Bus: 3, 4, 5, or 14.

A crowning architectural achievement in the center of Århus, the Rådhuset was built between 1936 and 1941 to commemorate the 500th anniversary of the Århus charter. Arne Jacobsen was one of the designers—and it's been the subject of controversy ever since. The modern marble-platted structure with lots of airy space and plenty of glass can be seen only on a guided tour. There's an elevator (or 346 steps) to the top of the 197-foot tower, where a carillon occasionally rings.

Vikingemuseet. St. Clemens Torv 6. ☎ **89-42-11-00.** Free admission. Mon–Wed and Fri 9:30am–4pm, Thurs 9:30am–6pm. Bus: 3, 11, 54, or 56.

In the basement of the Unibank, close to the cathedral of Århus, original and reproductions of Viking objects can be seen. These objects are unearthed in an excavation on this very site in 1963 and 1964. Remains of the town's old Viking walls can be seen. Behind the museum, you'll find reconstructions of Viking houses—that is, a stave church and one of the small pit houses found during the excavation at the site. Objects illustrate how life went on in this bustling merchant city from its foundation in about 900 A.D. until around 1400.

✪ Von Frue Kirke. Frue Kirkeplads. ☎ **86-12-12-43.** Free admission. Sept–Apr Mon–Fri 10am–2pm, Sat 10am–noon; May–Aug Mon–Fri 10am–4pm, Sat 10am–noon. Bus: 7, 10, or 17.

"The Church of Our Lady" lies to the northwest of Århus Domkirke. It was built between the 13th and 15th centuries but was originally part of a Dominican priory. The original Århus Cathedral was erected on this site in 1060. Today's church, built of redbrick, has a largely whitewashed interior. It is mainly a Gothic building with frescoes and a significant altarpiece from the workshop of Claus Berg, painted in 1520. The altarpiece depicts a scene from the Passion, in a stunningly expressive style that is often compared to the work of Pieter Bruegel the Elder. Restoration work was begun here in the 1950s, and the crypt of the original Romanesque church from 1060 was uncovered under the chancel. Its early date makes it the oldest vaulted building in all of Scandinavia. This vaulted krypta is now virtually "a church within a church." In addition, a chapter house, which once was a hospital for the elderly in the Reformation era, has been dedicated as a church and incorporated into the general structure. So "Our Lady" is actually three churches in one. Wall paintings from the Middle Ages adorn the walls of the chapter house. Because of all these multiple layers beneath the surface, Vor Frue Kirke is often likened to a Russian matryoshka doll.

NEARBY ATTRACTIONS

The summer residence of Denmark's royal family, **Marselisborg Slot,** at Kongevejen 100, less than 1½ miles south of Århus' center, is one of the most famous and symbolic buildings in Denmark. If you visit, you can see the changing of the guard at noon every day Her Majesty and family are in residence. It's announced on the local news and in the newspapers when Her Majesty is here. This white manor house has been used by the royal family since 1902.

It is not possible to visit the interior of the palace, but the castle grounds, even the Queen's rose garden, are open to the public when the castle is not occupied. Admission-free visits are possible from 9am to 5pm. The hamlet of Marselisborg itself lies less than a mile from the center of Århus and can be reached by bus nos. 1, 18, and 19.

The setting is in a large forest belt stretching for some 6 miles along the coast. The entire area is ideal for hikes, as nature trails have been cut through the forests. Bikers also like the terrain. Less than a mile from the royal palace on the main road south lies **Dyrehaven** (deer park), a protected forest area where you can see fallow deer, and even sika deer. The more elusive wild roe deer also live here, even wild pigs, although you're unlikely to spot the latter.

THE MANOR HOUSES OF EAST JUTLAND

Clausholm. Voldum, Hadsten. ☎ **86-49-16-55.** Admission (including guided tour) 45 DKK ($6.50) adults, 15 DKK ($2.15) children. June and Aug Sat–Sun 11am–4pm, July daily 11am–4pm. Closed Sept–May. Bus: 221 from Randers.

Some 8 miles southeast of Randers and 19 miles north of Århus, 17th-century Clausholm is a splendid baroque palace—one of the earliest in Denmark. It was commissioned by Frederik IV's chancellor, whose adolescent daughter, Anna Sophie, eloped with the king. When Frederik died, his son by his first marriage banished the queen to Clausholm, where she lived with her own court until her death in 1743.

The rooms of the castle have been basically unaltered since Anna Sophie's day, but few of the original furnishings remain. The salons and ballroom feature elaborate stucco ceilings and decorated panels, and an excellent collection of Danish rococo and Empire furnishings have replaced the original pieces. The Queen's Chapel, where Anna Sophie and her court worshipped, is unchanged, and contains the oldest organ in Denmark. In 1976 the Italian baroque gardens were reopened, complete with a symmetrically designed fountain system.

Gammel Estrup. Jyllands Herregårdsmuseum, Randersvej 2–4, Auning. Manor house, 50 DKK ($7.25) adults, 35 DKK ($5.05) senior citizens and children; agricultural museum, 50 DKK ($7.25) adults, 35 DKK ($5.05) senior citizens, free for children. Manor house, Apr–Sept, daily 9am–5pm; Oct–Mar, Tues–Sun 11am–3pm. Agricultural museum, daily 9am–5pm. From Randers, take Route 16 east to Auning. Bus: 214.

This Renaissance manor was owned by two families for 6 centuries, but today it houses the **Jutland Manor House Museum** (☎ **86-48-30-01**) in the main building and the **Danish Agricultural Museum** (☎ 86-48-30-01) in the outbuildings. Built on medieval fortified grounds, Gammel Estrup dates back to the 14th century, with major rebuilding of the present structure in the early 1600s. The Manor House Museum, with the Great Hall, chapel, and many other rooms, is richly decorated with stucco ceilings, tapestries, and paintings from the 17th and 18th centuries. The Agricultural Museum has tools and machines used over several centuries and a special exhibit highlighting "the year of the farmer."

✪ **Rosenholm Slot.** Hornslet. ☎ **86-99-40-10.** Admission 45 DKK ($6.50) adults, 20 DKK ($2.90) children ages 6–12 (free age 5 and under). June 20–Aug, daily 10am–5pm, May–June 19 and Sept Sat–Sun 10am–5pm. Closed Oct–Apr. Bus: 119 or 121 from Århus's Central Bus Station.

On an islet 13 miles north of Århus and half a mile north of Hornslet, this moated Renaissance manor has been the home of the Rosenkrantzes for 4 centuries. The four-winged castle, encircled by about 35 acres of parkland, houses a Great Hall (its most important room), as well as a large collection of Flemish woven and gilded leather tapestries, old paintings, Spanish furniture, a vaulted gallery walk, and pigskin-bound folios.

SHOPPING

Århus is the biggest shopping venue in Jutland, with some 400 specialty stores, each of them tightly clustered within an area of more than a half-mile square. The centerpiece of this district is the Strøget, whose terminus is the Store Torv, dominated by the Århus Domkirke. You might try a large scale department store first. One of the best is **Salling,** Søndergade 27 (☎ 86-12-18-00), with some 30 specialty boutiques, all under one roof. A wide range of articles is sold here for the whole family, including body care items, clothing, gifts, toys, music, and sports equipment. **Magasin du Nord,** Immervad 2–8 (☎ 86-12-33-00), is the largest department store in Scandinavia, in business for more than 125 years. The staff will assist foreign visitors with tax-free purchases.

"The greatest silversmith the world has ever seen," is the name often used to describe **Georg Jensen,** Søndergade 1 (☎ 86-12-01-00). A tradition since 1866, George Jensen is known for style and quality, producing unique silver and gold jewelry, elegant clocks and watches, and stainless steel cutlery, among other items. The biggest goldsmith outside Copenhagen, **Boye,** Søndergade 36 (☎ 86-19-21-22), has been in business in Århus for more than 50 years. It offers an impressive selection of jewelry, much of it made in the company's own workshops. Another leading goldsmith, **Hingelberg,** Store Torv 3 (☎ 86-13-13-00), is the licensed Cartier outlet, and offers a wide selection of top quality designer jewelry.

Galleri Bo Bendixen, Store Torv 14 (☎ 86-12-67-50), offers the brilliant, colored, top quality designs of Bo Bendixen, the famous Danish graphic artist. The shop also sells a wide range of gifts and garments for both children and adults. **Volden 4 Kunsthåndværk,** Volden 4 (☎ 86-13-21-76), specializes in top quality applied art, including silk garments hand-painted in elegant designs, and even glass made by some of the leading artisans of the country. Silver, copper, and brass ornaments are for sale, as are exclusive bronze candlesticks. **Ordning 7 Reda,** Volden 23 (☎ 86-19-03-41), sells an attractive range of Scandinavian and paper design products for the home and office. The range includes photograph albums, notebooks, calendars, and writing papers, as well as bags by Marimekko. For the best in Danish knitwear design, head for **Marianne Isager Yarn,** Volden 19 (☎ 86-19-40-44).

Bülow Duus Glassblowers, Studsgade 14 (☎ 86-12-72-86), is a working glassblowers open to the public. At an attractive old house in the heart of the city, you can watch the fascinating work of glassblowing. Drinking glasses, candlesticks, bowls, and other items are for sale. Another good glass outlet is **Glasmenageriet,** Møllestien 50 (☎ **86-13-81-81**), which displays the work of 25 of the country's leading glassblowers. For traditional Danish pottery, head for **Favlhuset,** Møllestien 53 (☎ **86-13-06-32**).

If you haven't found what you're looking for yet, head for **Inspiration Buus,** Ryesgade 2 (☎ **86-12-67-00**), which sells top quality gifts, kitchenware, tableware, and toiletry articles, much of it of Danish design.

WHERE TO STAY

Low-cost accommodations in this lively university city are limited. Those on a modest budget should check with the tourist office in the Rådhuset (☎ **86-12-16-00**) for bookings in **private homes.**

Depending on the time of the week or the time of the year you check in, rooms in many of the hotels labeled inexpensive aren't inexpensive at all, but more moderate in price.

EXPENSIVE

Atlantic Hotel. Europlads 12–14, DK-8000 Århus. ☎ **86-13-11-11.** Fax 86-13-23-43. E-mail: ATL@nordiskhotelgruppe.dk. 102 units. MINIBAR TV TEL. June–Aug 695 DKK ($100.75) double; Sept–May 1,189 DKK ($172.40) double. Rate includes breakfast. AE, DC, MC, V.

A favorite of commercial travelers, the Atlantic was built in 1964 and fully renovated again in 1994. One of the city's tallest buildings, it rises 11 floors. Bedrooms are comfortably streamlined in a Nordic modern style, each with a balcony. Bathrooms are newly tiled and well maintained, a bit small, but with decent towels and plenty of hot water. Ask for a room with a sea view if it's available.

Dining/Diversions: Breakfast is the only meal served, but many eateries are close at hand. The hotel does have a cozy bar, however.

Amenities: Access to nearby health club and tennis courts, and dry-cleaning/laundry.

Hotel Kong Christian den X. Christian X's Vej 70, Postbox 2262. DK-8100 Århus (Viby J). ☎ **86-11-61-11.** Fax 86-11-74-00. www.christiandx.dk. E-mail: hotel@christiandx.dk. 80 units. MINIBAR TV TEL. Mon–Thurs 925–1,095 DKK ($134.15–$158.75). Fri–Sun 595–705 DKK ($86.25–$102.25). AE, DC, MC, V. Bus: 11.

This hotel caters mostly to business travelers from a location in the suburbs, 2 miles south of the commercial center. Upscale and respectable, with an angular, big-windowed design that its detractors have compared to the departure terminal of an airport, it opened in 1987. Once you get used to the glistening modernity of the place, however, you'll discover a well-organized hotel with a polite, hardworking staff and bedrooms that are comfortable, well furnished, and quiet, despite a bland modern décor that's somewhat noncommittal. Baths are tiled and well maintained though a bit small.

Dining/Diversions: There's a big-windowed modern-looking restaurant that's often the venue for mealtime gatherings of participants in corporate conventions, and artfully laid-out breakfast buffets. There's also a cocktail lounge and a bar.

Amenities: A health club with exercise equipment and a sauna, and a wading pool for children. Room service is available daily from 7am to 11pm.

Hotel Marselis. Strandvejen 25, DK-8000 Århus C. ☎ **86-14-44-11.** Fax 86-11-70-46. 101 units. MINIBAR TV TEL. Mon–Thurs 1,240 DKK ($179.80) double, Fri–Sun 1,720 DKK ($249.40) suite. Discounts of 30% are offered Fri–Sun. Rate includes breakfast. AE, DC, MC, V. Bus: 6.

This is the most isolated and nature-conscious of the grand modern hotels of Århus, thanks to a long, narrow format that rambles along a grass-covered bluff, a few steps from the sea, in a location about 3 miles south of the city center. Built of earth-colored bricks in 1967, it plays up its views over the water and an interior décor that's more nautical and seafaring than that of any other hotel with which it competes. Bedrooms are smaller than those in, for example, the SAS Radisson, and less imaginatively decorated, but overall, the setting is soothing and well-maintained. Corporate conventions sometimes come here, but less often than the hotel would really like.

Dining/Diversions: The Restaurant Marselis, and its bar, the Café Nautilus, provide food, piano music, drink, and a log-burning fireplace, always within a dark environment with colors that match the nearby seascape. A less formal dining and drinking venue, open only during mild weather, is the Beach Café, whose tables are arranged on a sunny terrace.

Amenities: This is one of the few modern hotels in Århus with its own swimming pool, an indoor affair with big windows overlooking the sea. There's also a sauna, room service (daily from 6:30am to 10:30pm) and a reception/concierge staff that provides information and ideas about diversions in the nearby region.

✪ **Hotel Royal.** Stove Torv 4, DK-8000 Århus. ☎ **86-12-00-11.** Fax 86-76-04-04. 102 units. MINIBAR TV TEL. 1,345–1,695 DKK ($195–$245.75) double, 2,900 DKK ($420.50) suite. Rate includes breakfast. AE, DC, MC, V. Parking 150 DKK ($21.75). Bus: 56 or 58.

This is the most glamorous accommodation in town. The date in gilt letters on its neo-baroque façade commemorates the hotel's establishment in 1838. There have been numerous additions and upgrades since. The Royal stands close to the city's symbol, its cathedral. After you've checked-in, a vintage elevator will take you to one of the bedrooms, many of which are quite spacious. Bedrooms are modernized, with good-size bathrooms and plenty of towels. Beds are newly refurbished with strong, durable mattresses, and accommodations are fitted with high quality commercial furniture, carpeting, and fabrics.

Dining/Diversions: The mezzanine greenhouse restaurant, the Queen's Garden, has an excellent chef who always experiments (happily so) and turns out a succulent cuisine that might begin with salmon ravioli and "honey gravy" or a halibut carpaccio. Follow with such delights as a grilled Norway lobster salad or truffle-flavored turbot on apple chutney with a spinach sauce. His desserts are worth saving some room for, especially the strawberry gazpacho with an anise parfait. The hotel also has the only casino in Århus, but it's definitely not Las Vegas.

Amenities: Sauna, car-rental desk, room service, dry cleaning/laundry, and a solarium.

Plaza Hotel Århus. Banegårdsplads 14, DK-8100 Århus C. ☎ **87-32-01-00.** Fax 87-32-01-99. 168 units. TEL. 820–895 DKK ($118.90–$129.75) double, 1,295 DKK ($187.75) suite. Rate includes breakfast. DC, MC, V. Bus: 3, 17, 56, or 58.

A quiet, dignified, and traditional hotel that until recently was known as the Ansgar, the Plaza is close to the Town Hall and all city center attractions. Completely renovated and vastly improved in 1997, it is part of an original hotel that opened back in 1930. Greatly redecorated, the hotel is now first class, with tastefully done bedrooms—most of which are medium size—and modern, completely refitted tile baths. Bedrooms have modern furnishings and good beds (with new mattresses).

Dining: Café Brasserie Agnete & Havmanden offers lunch specialties with meats that are prepared by the hotel's own butcher. The more formal Restaurant Brazil features a Latin American barbecue with a main course consisting of 5 to 7 different kinds of meat, according to the season. The meats are prepared on a special barbecue and served at table on large skewers. Vegetables are stir fried in a deep wok, and spicy relishes and sauces accompany the feast.

Amenities: Room service, concierge, Jacuzzi, sauna.

Radisson SAS Scandinavia Hotel Århus. Margrethepladsen 1, DK-8000 Århus C. ☎ **800/ 333-3333,** or ☎ 86-12-86-65. Fax 86-12-86-75. 233 units. MINIBAR TV TEL. June to mid-Aug and Fri–Sun year-round, 775–975 DKK ($112.35–$141.40) double. Mon–Thurs Mid-Aug to May, 850–1,860 DKK ($123.25–$269.70) double. Suites 1,900–3,000 DKK ($275.50–$435) year-round. Rate includes breakfast. AE, DC, MC, V. Bus: 1, 2, 6, or 16.

This is one of the most modern and dynamic modern hotels in Denmark, and a city showplace that municipal authorities proudly show off to dignitaries visiting on trade missions from abroad. It was built in 1995 directly above the largest convention facilities in Jutland, and as such, maintains a closer contact with the dynamics of huge conventions and their planners than any other hotel in the region. Bedrooms occupy floors 4 to 11 of a glass- and stone-sheathed tower that's visible from throughout the city. Lower floors contain check-in, dining, drinking, and convention facilities. Bedrooms are outfitted in plush upholsteries with bright colors. Each has a décor that's different from its immediate neighbor, incorporating Scandinavian, English, Japanese, or Chinese themes. Most of them are more tasteful and upbeat than the bland and relatively noncommittal décors that are the norm in many of this hotel's competitors. Each has a trouser press, hair dryer, and large-windowed views over the city.

Dining/Diversions: There's a well-managed restaurant, Scenario, on the premises, and a very stylish modern bar whose décor is based on a series of sinuous curves, soft lighting, verdant plants, and carefully varnished paneling. Room service is offered daily from 7am to 11pm.

Amenities: There's a health club and a sauna, and a staff that's well-versed in providing information and advice on local attractions in a wide medley of languages.

MODERATE

Hotel La Tour. Randersvej 139, DK-8200 Århus. ☎ **86-16-78-88.** Fax 86-16-79-95. 101 units. TV TEL. 845 DKK ($122.50) double. Rate includes breakfast. AE, DC, MC, V. Bus: 2, 3, or 11.

Since its construction in 1956, and its rebuilding in 1986, this hotel has followed a conscious policy of downgrading its accommodations and facilities from a once-lofty status to a decidedly middle-brow formula that has attracted hundreds of foreign visitors. The result is a hotel that's far from being the best in town, but which seems secure in its middle-bracket niche that it has worked hard to create. Set 2¼ miles north of Århus' center, and built in a not particularly imaginative two-story format, it offers clean but unpretentious bedrooms with small baths, but fewer of the facilities (including sauna and exercise room) that used to be part of its premises. There's a patio-style restaurant serving competently prepared Danish and international food, a bar, and a children's playroom which closes down completely between October and April. The staff is hardworking and articulate, and deeply committed to the hotel's middle-brow marketing vision.

Hotel Mercur. Viby Torv, DK-8260 Århus, Viby J. ☎ **86-14-14-11.** Fax 86-14-46-41. 90 units. TV TEL. Mon–Thurs 650–800 DKK ($94.25–$116) double; 850 DKK ($123.25) suite. Fri–Sun 450–600 DKK ($65.25–$87) double; 650 DKK ($94.25) suite. Rate includes breakfast. AE, DC, MC, V. Bus: 5, 15, and 25.

This is one of the most appealing ultra-modern hotels in town. Set 2½ miles south of town, about a half-mile from the park that surrounds Queen Margrethe's summer house (Marselisborg Slot), it was designed in a six-story concrete-and-glass format in the 1970s. Overall, it's warmer and cozier than some of its most visible competitors, such as the Kong Christian den X. Its stone-floored lobby is rendered less angular and modern thanks to lots of exposed wood and a scattering of Oriental carpets. Today, views from its masculine-looking and conservatively contemporary bedrooms encompass panoramas over the town and the seacoast. Some of these have narrow, rarely-used balconies of their own, and a monochromatic color scheme of earth tones and grays. The hotel, incidentally, is not associated with the low-budget France-based hotel chain, Mercure, with which it's often confused, and whose accommodations are much less plush.

There's a restaurant, the Mercur, and a bar, on the premises, both of which are appealing and warmly decorated.

There are also two bowling alleys in the hotel's cellar, and a much larger bowling alley complex lies within a few blocks of the hotel. There's also a shopping mall, Viby Centret, with about 50 shops, on Skanderborgvej, a short walk from the hotel.

INEXPENSIVE

Eriksen's Hotel. Banegardsgade 608. DK-8000 Århus. ☎ **86-13-62-96.** Fax 86-13-76-76. 18 units (none with bath). 420 DKK ($60.90) double. Rate includes breakfast. DC, MC, V. Bus: 16 or 17.

This hotel is the best bargain in the vicinity of the train depot. More rooming house than hotel, Eriksen's is utilitarian, clean, and recently modernized. Decent showers are just outside the rooms, but plumbing is not a major reason to stay here (towels are a bit skimpy). The mattresses have been used by many, many clients before you checked in. Windows are double-glazed so sleeping is usually tranquil here, especially if you get a room in the rear. In addition to breakfast, the hotel also serves an inexpensive lunch of soup and sandwiches and it's also licensed for beer.

WHERE TO DINE
EXPENSIVE

✪ **Le Canard.** Kannikegade 10–12. ☎ **86-13-80-00.** Reservations recommended. Set menus 295–530 DKK ($42.80–$76.85). AE, DC, MC, V. Mon–Sat 5–9pm. FRENCH.

One of Århus' most appealing French bistros is set in what used to be a shop in the pedestrian-only zone of the downtown shopping district. Behind lace curtains, and within a room decorated with paintings of flowers and artfully arranged vegetables, you can order any of several fixed-price menus that the staff has composed in ways that are as sophisticated as at any other restaurant in town. An expensive but very worthy meal might begin with a creamy, saffron-flavored soup studded with chunks of lemon sole, lobster, and leeks. Or else you may prefer a platter of succulent grilled scallops with mushrooms. *Foie gras* appears in a classic Normandy style, garnished with apples and a dash of Calvados. The tenderloin of veal is perfectly tender, its flavor enhanced by a basil sauce with fresh tomatoes. For your grand finale, you can select a dessert platter piled high with a medley of the pastry chef's grandest creations, or opt instead for a plate of Danish, French, and Italian cheese. The service is just as first-rate as the cookery.

✪ **Prins Ferdinand.** Viborgvej 2. ☎ **86-12-52-05.** Reservations recommended. Main courses 95–175 DKK ($13.75–$25.40) at lunch, 150–235 DKK ($21.75–$34.05) at dinner; fixed–price menu 195–225 DKK ($28.30–$32.65) at lunch, 375–450 DKK ($54.35–$65.25) at dinner. AE, DC, MC, V. Tues–Sat 11am–3pm and 6–9pm (last orders). Bus: 3. DANISH/INTERNATIONAL.

Set on the edge of Århus' historic center in a yellow-fronted structure originally built in 1933 as a tea salon, this is one of the city's finest restaurants. It was established in 1988 by Per Brun and his wife, Lotte Norrig, who create a version of modern Danish cuisine that has won favor with the region's business community. In a pair of pink-toned dining rooms laden with flickering candles and flowers, you can order a platter of fresh smoked salmon served with a tartare of salmon and a pepper-cream sauce, turbot with Russian caviar and a drizzling of olive oil, sea devil with lobster prepared in the Thai style with lemon grass, boneless pigeon stuffed with fresh goose liver served with a raspberry sauce, and a dessert specialty of pears cooked with elderberries and served with vanilla ice cream, nougat, and almonds. The restaurant's array of dessert cheeses, the most unusual in Jutland, are produced by small farmers whose highly esoteric products are not otherwise very widely distributed.

○ **Restaurant de 4 Arstider (Four Season).** Aboulevarden 47. ☎ **86-19-96-96.** Reservations required. Main courses 200–220 DKK ($29–$31.90); fixed-price menu 290–430 DKK ($42.05–$62.35). AE, DC, MC, V. Mon–Sat 6–10pm. Closed July. Bus: 1, 2, 3, 6, 9, or 16. FRENCH.

This restaurant presents a carefully crafted cuisine based on the specialties of the season. In spring that means fresh asparagus (sometimes with *foie gras*), along with the catch of the day, perhaps red snapper in a zesty sauce. Of course, succulent preparations of veal and lamb are always featured, and in the autumn you can enjoy game dishes. Since the menu is always changing, we can't recommend specific specialties, but over the years it's always been a heart-warming experience to arrive on the doorstep to discover the chef's surprises for the evening. You can order an apéritif in the lounge with its antiques and comfortable settees.

MODERATE

Kellers Gaard. Frederiksgade 84–86. ☎ **86-12-35-66.** Reservations recommended. Lunch main courses 68–148 DKK ($9.85–$21.45); lunch set menus 118–168 DKK ($17.10–$24.35); dinner main courses 168–218 DKK ($24.35–$31.60); dinner set menus 298–389 DKK ($43.20–$56.40). AE, DC, MC, V. Mon–Fri noon–4pm; Mon–Sat 5–10pm. Bus: 52 or 55. DANISH/FRENCH.

One of the best-recommended upscale restaurants in Århus occupies an antique blue-sided house that's set a few paces from the city's most visible concert hall, the Musikhuset. Inside, there's an all-white dining room whose only color derives from rack after rack of wine bottles artfully arranged against the walls. Food is as cultivated as anywhere else in Århus. Based on French models, with lots of fresh shellfish and fish, the menu might include a heaping platter of lobster and mussels dressed with a saffron-flavored *fumet,* cream of mussel soup, codfish with a *fumet* of lobster, roasted pigeon with balsamic vinegar and roasted nuts, or fillet of veal with rosemary sauce and Swiss-style *Rösti* potatoes. And for the culinary finale, hazelnuts, solidified chocolate, and homemade ice cream that's fashioned into a tower that juts upward from a dessert platter. The place provides dependable quality, and we're somewhat impressed with it, mainly because of the helpful staff and the fresh ingredients used.

Kroen I Krogen. Banegårdspladsen 4. ☎ **86-19-24-39.** Lunch platters 26–128 DKK ($3.75–$18.55); dinner main courses 98–158 DKK ($14.20–$22.90). Set menus 108–128 DKK ($15.65–$18.55). AE, DC, MC, V. Daily noon–10pm. DANISH.

This restaurant has established a loyal clientele since it was established as "the inn in the corner" (a translation of its name) across from the railway station in 1934. Inside, you'll find one of the most unusual décors in town, thanks to walls that are richly adorned with mahogany and decorated with about two dozen panels depicting local artist Michale Fisher's interpretation of the history of Århus from the 14th to the mid–20th centuries. They were painted shortly after World War II on the back of canvas sacks holding coffee beans, since more conventional art supplies simply weren't available.

Menu items focus on tried-and-true interpretations of conventional Danish cuisine. You can order something as straightforward and simple as grilled sausage with black bread—a worthy foil for a glass of beer—or a house specialty known as *kroens Anretning,* a platter with two kinds of herring, a fish fillet, a handful of shrimp, and a small steak with fried onions. Other items include a savory orange-marinated salmon, perfectly grilled ribeye steaks, and hazelnut cake with sorbet. Between April and September, at least 50 additional seats are made available on an outdoor terrace. Recent visits from the glitterati? Most recently, Maria Montell, well-known Danish pop star and girlfriend-of-the-minute of Prince Frederik, younger son of Queen Margrethe, was spotted sipping cappuccino here with a group of friends.

INEXPENSIVE

Den Gremme Ælleng (The Ugly Duckling). Østergade 12. ☎ **86-13-99-63.** Reservations recommended. All-you-can-eat buffet lunch 99.50 DKK ($14.45), buffet dinner 225 DKK ($32.65). AE, DC, MC, V. Daily noon–2:30pm and 5:30–10:30pm. Bus: 2, 6, or 17. DANISH BUFFET.

This cost-conscious member of a chain whose restaurants are scattered throughout Denmark offers a self-service Danish buffet. At lunchtime, dishes include at least 10 different preparations of herring, Nordic meatballs, and an amply varied salad bar. In the late afternoon a different array is laid out. These usually include such hot dishes as casseroles, meats, and vegetables, plus Danish cheeses and a salad bar.

Munkestruen. Klostertorvet 5. ☎ **86-12-95-67.** Reservations required. Main courses 80–120 DKK ($11.60–$17.40). No credit cards. Daily 11am–midnight. Closed July 1–7. Bus: 1, 2, 6, or 9. DANISH/INTERNATIONAL.

Almost invariably you stumble upon this charming old place if you're out sightseeing. This small and cozy inn with a courtyard is in the old Klostertorv across from Frue Kloster Abbey. Menu choices depend on seasonal fresh produce. The owner, Lise Poulsen, says that she's inspired by the culinary traditions of the world, but still cooks everything "the Danish way." Her produce is market fresh, and her meals are tasty and filling.

Rio Grande. Vestergade 39. ☎ **86-19-06-96.** Reservations not required. Main courses 85–119 DKK ($12.35–$17.25), two-course fixed-price menu 89 DKK ($12.90). AE, DC, MC, V. Daily 5–11pm. Bus: 7, 10, or 17. MEXICAN.

This was the first Mexican restaurant to open in Jutland, providing what is for many a much-appreciated contrast to a too-constant diet of Danish food. In the one large dining room outfitted in desert colors with Mexican artifacts, you can order tacos, chimichangas, burritos, tostadas, enchiladas, and such tequila-rich drinks as margaritas, which are priced at 29 DKK ($4.20). We won't pretend it's as good as the fare you can find in America's Southwest, much less in Mexico, but coming upon this place in the heart of Denmark is a bit of a culinary adventure.

Teater Bodega. Skolegade 7. ☎ **86-12-19-17.** Reservations recommended. Main courses 79–165 DKK ($11.45–$23.90), lunch *smørrebrød* 30–79 DKK ($4.35–$11.45). Three-course fixed-price lunch or dinner 198 DKK ($28.70). DC, MC, V. Mon–Sat 11am–11:30pm. Bus: 6. DANISH.

Originally established at a different address in 1907, Teater Bodega in 1951 moved across the street from both the Århus Dramatic Theater and the Århus Cathedral. It tries to provide an amusing dining ambience for theater and art lovers. The walls are covered with illustrations of theatrical costumes along with other thespian memorabilia. The food is solid and flavorful in the Danish country style. Various kinds of Danish hash, including *biksemad,* are served along with regular or large portions of Danish roast beef. There's also English and French beef, fried plaice, and flounder.

NEARBY DINING

Restaurant Skovmøllen. Skovmøllenvej 51. ☎ **86-27-12-14.** Reservations recommended. Lunch main courses 35–150 DKK ($5.05–$21.75); dinner main courses 95–150 DKK ($13.75–$21.75). Set menus 168–198 DKK ($24.35–$28.70). AE, DC, MC, V. From downtown Århus, take bus no. 6. DANISH/INTERNATIONAL.

Since it was constructed of straw, wood, and stone more than 300 years ago, this building has functioned as a farmhouse, a gristmill, and a simple cafe. It's set beside the Giber River, 6 miles south of Århus, close to the Moesgaard Museum of Danish prehistory. Beneath a beamed ceiling and frequent reminders of old-time Denmark, you can order platters that are all-Danish at lunchtime, and straightforward, not particularly esoteric dishes that are just a bit more cosmopolitan at night. Lunches might include meatballs, *smørrebrød,* herring platters, or roasted pork with onions and braised cabbage. Dinners are more elaborate, featuring shrimp cocktails, steak with French fries, stuffed fillets of plaice with new potatoes, and salmon chops with garlic-flavored butter sauce. The place is always dependable, the cookery always reliable, but its main allure is that it's a charming getaway visit from the city center to absorb a country flavor.

ÅRHUS AFTER DARK

There's more happening here after dark than anywhere else on Jutland. The Århus Symphony Orchestra and the Danish National Opera perform frequently, among other attractions.

CULTURAL ÅRHUS

The city of Århus has the richest and most varied cultural life in Jutland. Its chief attraction, and a major venue for cultural events, is the Musikhuset Århus (see below). However, for a look at what's happening in many other venues, pick up a copy of the monthly booklet, *What's On in Århus,* at the tourist office (see above).

You'll have to speak Danish to enjoy most productions at the **Århus Theater,** Bispetorv (☎ **89-33-26-22**), which has five stages with a total of 1,200 seats. It was designed by Hack Kampmann and opened in 1900. Local actors and visiting stars entertain in a wide repertoire from early September to mid-June.

Svalegangen, Rosenkrantzgade 21 (☎ **86-13-88-66**), presents an up-to-date repertoire, the latest in Danish drama, music, cabaret, modern dance, and guest artists. On the other hand, **MBT Danseteater,** Frederiks Allé 20 (☎ **86-13-70-67**), is the only provincial modern dance theater in Denmark. The company stages about 40 productions annually. **Entré Scenen,** Grønnegade 93B (☎ **86-20-15-36**), is an experimental feature of Århus's dramatic life. A varied range of performances, often by foreign artists, appeal to a wide spectrum of ages here. Guest opera and dance theater productions are also staged at **Gellerupscenen,** Gudrunsvej 78 (☎ **86-25-03-66**).

Opened in 1982, ✪ **Musikhuset Århus,** Thomas Jensens Allé (☎ **89-31-82-00**), is the concert hall and home of the Århus Symphony Orchestra and the Danish National Opera. Tickets for most events range from 50 to 1,000 DKK ($7.25–$145). Programs are presented on the great stage, the small stage, and the cabaret stage, as well as in the amphitheater and on the foyer stages where free performances are presented year-round. The foyer, open daily from 11am to 9pm, is the site of the booking office, information desk, a cafe/restaurant, and souvenir shops.

The concert hall adjoins a good restaurant catering primarily to cultural devotees: **Le Premier** (☎ **89-31-82-90**), which is open from 5:30pm to midnight on performance nights. A superb Danish/international cuisine is served, with main courses costing 95 to 165 DKK ($13.75–$23.90) (AE, DC, MC, V). There is also an on-site cafe open daily from 11am to 8pm.

Dance Clubs

The following clubs usually—but not always—impose a cover charge that can range from 30 to 50 DKK ($4.35 to $7.25), depending on what entertainment is offered.

The most popular, charming, and fun disco in town is **Train,** Toldbodgade (☎ **86-13-47-22**), where a crowd that's under 35 or 40-ish tends to dance on any of three floors of what used to be a warehouse down beside the waterfront. The top floors feature older disco music from the '70s and '80s; while the middle and lower levels are devoted to an English-style pub and louder, more jarring technomusic. The site is also a venue, at irregular intervals, for live concerts.

Its leading competitor is **Blitz,** Klostergade 34 (☎ **86-12-94-11**), which is very large and (if you happen to drink too much) very confusing because of the way it's arranged into a labyrinth of corridors and side rooms. Set within the city center, it's the disco that's recommended, along with Train (see above), as the most appealing and animated in town. Both of them don't start to get busy until around 10pm. The valentine-colored hideaway of **La Belle,** Mindegade 6 (☎ **86-12-52-55**), on the ground floor of an apartment building in the center of town, has provided a venue for midnight dancing and romantic trysts since it was established in the 1970s. Inside, you'll find a changing roster of live dance bands who provide everything from your favorite 1960s-era rock-and-roll songs to the kind of music where you'd feel comfortable dancing arm-in-arm, or cheek-to-cheek, with someone attractive. Many of the clients come back again and again, in some cases tripping the light fantastic multiple times with various partners through multiple marriages, hobnobbing with their cronies en route. This is not at all a place for teeny-boppers; clients tend to be in their mid-30s to late 50s. Whisky with soda, depending on the brand, sells from 55 DKK ($8); platters of food—including Danish meatballs, or roasted and shredded duck breast with homemade black bread and butter—cost 25 to 65 DKK ($3.60 to $9.40). There's live music every Monday through Friday. On Saturday, the place functions merely as a bar, and as such attracts its share of singles or single wannabes. It's open Monday to Saturday 10am to 5pm.

An Amusement Park

Tivoli-Friheden, Skobrynet (☎ **86-14-73-00**), is a pale imitation of the world famous Tivoli in Copenhagen, built on a smaller scale, but with some of the same sense of fantasy. Set in a forest about 2 miles south of Århus, it's bright and modern, appealing to families and couples from the city and the surrounding communities. Entertainment includes an open-air theater, art shows, concerts, clowns, rides, and a scattering of restaurants. The park is open only from late-April to mid-August. Although the park opens every day at noon, the rides and attractions don't open until 2pm. Everything closes down at 11pm. Admission is 35 DKK ($5.05) adults or 15 DKK ($2.15) for children. Bus no. 4.

The Town's Only Casino

Hotel Royal Casino. In the Hotel Royal, Stove Torv 4. ☎ **86-19-21-11.**

This casino in the town's most prestigious hotel (dating from 1838) was added in 1991, making it one of only four in Jutland and one of a handful in the entire country. Blackjack—also French roulette on weekends—plus other games of chance are offered daily from 3pm to 4am. Admission is 40 DKK ($5.80) until 7pm when entrance goes up to 50 DKK ($7.25). No jeans and no sports shoes are allowed, although a tie isn't necessary (a jacket is preferred).

Bar Hopping

Århus abounds in bars and taverns, most of which charge no cover unless there is live music of some sort on special nights. To get you going, drop in at **Paddy Go Easy,**

Åboulevarden 60 (☎ **86-13-83-33**), with its Irish musical fare. The premises are decorated with Celtic art painted on the walls. A lovely Irish brogue permeates the atmosphere on some nights. The oldest hostelry in town, **Thorups Kælder,** Store Torv 3 (☎ **86-12-04-14**), was founded by Cisterian monks in the 13th century. Here you can quench your thirst in historic surroundings. The only Aussie bar in Århus, **The Billabong Bar,** Skolegade 26 (☎ **86-13-27-15**), is a typical outback-style bar, its raw edge adding to its charm. There is live music every weekend, and sports fans gather here to watch major events on TV, all the time sipping Australian beverages such as beer. **Musikcaféen,** Mejlgade 53 (☎ **86-19-22-55**), is the venue for rock, techno, and the like. There's dancing and youth at **Valdemar Natterdag,** Store Torv 3 (☎ **86-19-21-22**), but the minimum age for entry is 23.

Bryggeriet Sct. Clemens, Kannikegade 10–12 (☎ **86-13-80-00**), is a combined brewery and public house which serves freshly tapped, frothy draft beer brewed in coppers in the cellar, matured and served in glasses. The bartender's special is a 1-liter "kwak glas." Regardless of which beer you select, this glass is designed for massive consumption. In addition to the pub, you can also order various Danish dishes here if you decide to stick around and dine. Gays and lesbians gather to dance and enjoy the cafe at **Pan Club,** Jægergårdsgade 62 (☎ **86-13-43-80**).

8 Ebeltoft

96km (60 miles) E of Silkeborg; 53km (33 miles) NE of Århus; 334$^1/_2$ km (209 miles) W of Copenhagen

A well-preserved town of half-timbered buildings, Ebeltoft ("apple orchard" in English) is the capital of the Mols hill country. This is a village of cobblestone streets, hidden-away lanes, old inns, and ruddy-faced fishermen who still carry on the profession of their ancestors.

Ebeltoft's Viking Age wooden boats have given way today to yachts and modern ferries. Life at Ebeltoft developed around its harbor and the beautiful bay of Ebeltoft Vig.

The thriving port was prosperous in the Middle Ages, enjoying trade with Germany and Sweden as well as Copenhagen. However, in 1659 the Swedish army invaded, sacking the port and setting fire to its merchant fleet. Ebeltoft never really recovered until tourists—ironically the Swedes—began to arrive in the 1960s. Because it slumbered for so long, Ebeltoft retained its old look of timber-framed brick buildings topped with red-tile roofs.

ESSENTIALS

GETTING THERE   There's no direct train service to Ebeltoft. From Copenhagen, take the train (via Fredericia) to Århus; at Århus Central Station, board bus no. 123 for Ebeltoft.

By Car   From Silkeborg head east on Route 15 through Århus and continue around the coast, then follow Route 21 south to Ebeltoft.

VISITOR INFORMATION   Contact the **Ebeltoft Turistbureau,** Strandvejen 2 (☎ **86-34-14-00**), open June 15 to August, Monday to Saturday from 10am to 6pm and Sunday from 11am to 4pm; and September to June 14, Monday to Friday from 9am to 4pm and Saturday from 10am to 1pm.

GETTING AROUND

Bikes can be rented at **L&P Cykler,** Nørre Allé 5 (☎ **86-34-47-77**), open Monday to Friday from 8am to 5:30pm, Saturday from 8am to noon. Rental fees cost around 50 DKK ($7.25) per day.

SEEING THE SIGHTS

Farvergårdeb. Adelgade 13–15. ☎ **86-34-13-82.** Admission 15 DKK ($2.15) adults, 5 DKK (75¢) children. June 1–Aug 31 daily 11am–5pm. Closed Sept–May.

Dating from 1772, the oldest part of this dyeworks goes back to 1683. Exhibits include the living quarters with original furniture, the dye facilities with a pressing room, a dye room with boilers, a printing room, and a stable wing with a coach house dating from the early 18th century. It's located directly west of Torvet in the town center.

✪ **Fregatten** *Jylland.* Strandvejen 4. ☎ **86-34-10-99.** Admission 50 DKK ($7.25) adults, 20 DKK ($2.90) children. Daily 10am–6pm.

The *Jylland,* dating from 1860, is the oldest man-of-war in Denmark and the world's longest wooden ship. The frigate is moored in the harbor. The restoration of the frigate to its original state was completed in 1994, and it now stands as a monument to Denmark's role as a seafaring nation. The frigate saw active duty until 1887, and was a veteran of the battle of Heligoland. You can wander through it to look at the galley, the captain's room, the bridge, and you can see a 10½ ton pure copper and pewter screw. The Pomperanian pine figurehead is quite voluptuous. The renovation of this three-masted tall ship was financed by Mærsk McKinney Møller, the Danish shipping tycoon. It is a frigate with rigging, wood carvings, and a cleft-end flag, serving as a reminder of a past when ships of similar character were a familiar sight in Ebeltoft.

Det Gamle Rådhus. Torvet. ☎ **86-34-13-82.** Admission 20 DKK ($2.90) adults, 5 DKK (75¢) children. June–Aug 10am–5pm. Closed off-season.

The Town Hall looks as if it had been erected just for kindergarten children to play in—don't miss this 1789 building, a museum housing an ethnographic collection from Thailand and artifacts from the town's history. It's located in the town center north of Strandvejen.

Glasmuseum. Strandvejen 8. ☎ **86-34-17-99.** Admission 40 DKK ($5.80). Mid-May to mid-Sept daily 10am–5pm; off-season daily 1–4pm.

At Ebeltoft harbor stands one of Denmark's most important glass museums, housed in a building that was once a customs and excise house. It displays both decorative and functional glass, ranging from the symbol-laden works of Swedish glass guru Bertil Vallien to the luminous gold pavilions of Japanese artist Kyohei Fujita. The artists being exhibited decide themselves which of their pieces they want to be represented by. This has resulted in a large permanent exhibition. From May until September young glass students work with blowing irons and modern "syrupy" blobs of glass in the museum garden.

Vindmølleparken. Færgehaven. ☎ **89-52-11-11.** Free admission. Mon–Fri 10am–4pm.

Set 3 miles south of Ebeltoft, adjacent to the ferryboat terminal, this is one of Denmark's largest windmill parks, wherein 16 windmills on a curved spit of land open to gusts of wind from the Baltic to generate electricity for some 600 families. To see it, drive south of town, following the signs toward the hamlet of Øer, or the signs pointing to the ferryboat to Zealand. If you phone in advance, in some rare instances, a 30-minute guided tour can be arranged by the city council, free anytime during opening hours.

SHOPPING

Since the mid-1980s, Ebeltoft has become "Denmark's glass kingdom." There are no fewer than six local glassworks producing and selling blown glass items. At several of the studios, it's possible to see the workshops where glass bowls, vases, wine glasses, and beautiful dishes are created in the glowing furnace. You can visit various workshops and purchase glass at such outlets as **Glasværkstedet,** Skindergade 5 (☎ **86-34-08-89**); **Glaspusteriet,** Adelgade 62F (☎ **86-34-49-58**); and **Ebeltoft Glas,** Nedergade 19 (☎ **86-34-35-66**).

WHERE TO STAY

Hotel Ebeltoft Strand. Nordre Strandvej 3, DK-8400 Ebeltoft. ☎ **86-34-33-00.** Fax 86-34-46-36. E-mail: ebelstra@pip.dknet.dk. 72 units. MINIBAR TV TEL. 775 DKK ($112.35) double for a few weeks in midsummer (dates vary), 1,085 DKK ($157.30) double the rest of the year. Rate includes breakfast. AE, DC, MC, V. Bus: 123 from Århus.

Centrally located, this comfortable two-story hotel was constructed in 1978 and most recently renovated in 1995. Its well-furnished bedrooms—each with a balcony or terrace—overlook Ebeltoft Bay. Facilities include tennis courts, horseback riding, an indoor swimming pool, and a sauna. The hotel also has a restaurant, bar, open fireplace, and playground. It's located about a 5-minute drive from the ferry and a 15-minute drive from Tirstrup Airport.

Hotel Hvide Hus. Strandgårdshøj 1, DK-8400 Ebeltoft. ☎ **86-34-14-66.** Fax 86-34-49-69. E-mail: hotelpost3.tele.dk. 104 units. MINIBAR TV TEL. 840–1,040 DKK ($121.80–$150.80) double, 1,330 DKK ($192.85) suite. Rate includes breakfast. AE, DC, MC, V. Closed Dec 18–Jan 4. Bus: 123 from Århus.

An elegant establishment built in 1963, Hvide Hus has kept abreast of the times and today provides well-furnished bedrooms with standard but comfortable pieces, including terraces, refrigerators, and medium-size baths with good towels. If you're a guest, its restaurant is worth a look, offering an array of Danish and international dishes nightly, with main courses going for 75 to 170 DKK ($10.90–$24.65), or a two-course menu a great value at 125 DKK ($18.15). The restaurant serves daily from 5 to 10pm. Recreational facilities on site include a sauna, solarium and swimming pool, along with a bar/night club.

Hotel Vigen. Adelgade 5, DK-8400 Ebeltoft. ☎ **86-34-48-00.** Fax 96-34-44-20. 11 apts., each with kitchenette. TV TEL. 500–600 DKK ($72.50–$87) per day for a unit suitable for up to four occupants, 700–800 DKK ($101.50–$116) per day for a unit suitable for up to six occupants. AE, DC, MC, V.

This is a comfortable, well-maintained apartment house that's set within a sprawling old-fashioned villa, surrounded by scrubland, in the center of Ebeltoft, very close to the Old Town Hall. The establishment combines elements of an apartment house (nine of the units are owned outright, in most cases by Copenhagen-based investors who use the place on weekends) with those of a laid-back hotel where you might see the staff rarely, if ever. No meals of any kind are served, since most guests opt to prepare meals within their individual kitchens. Sheets and towels can be rented for a one-time charge of 60 DKK ($8.70). Although there's no restaurant on the premises, at least one lies within a short walk. The hotel sits on scrub-covered sands that slope down to the sea, but if you want to go swimming, it's advisable to walk or drive to the town's beach, which lies about a half-mile away. On the premises is an indoor swimming pool.

✿ Mols Kroen. Hovegaden 16, Femmøller Strand, DK-8400 Ebeltoft. ☎ **86-36-22-00.** Fax 86-36-23-00. www.molskroen.dk. E-mail: molskroen@aclr.dk. 18 units. 1,280–1,680 DKK ($185.60–$243.60) double, 3,200 DKK ($464) suite. Rate includes breakfast. DC, MC, V. Closed Dec 24–Jan 8. Bus: 123 from Århus.

This hotel was vastly upgraded in 1998, and its prices rose dramatically too. Nevertheless, it's one of the better places to stay in the area, with its rooms—often with terraces—overlooking Mols Hills with a fine white sandy beach only 350 feet away. The *kro* (inn) is in the center of an area of summer houses built for the most part in the 1920s and 1930s. The premises still retain somewhat of the aura of an old seaside hotel and summer boarding house combined. Bedrooms have been vastly improved. Medium in size, they are sleek, functional, and most comfortable, with freshly tiled baths and generous towels. All the beds and mattresses have been renewed.

Dining: The sound of crackling logs on the fire often greet you in this restaurant, which has a cozy, friendly ambience. Opt for one of the fish dishes, especially the oyster soup flavored with fresh herbs, or the fried angler on spinach with baby vegetables. You can also order an all-vegetarian menu as well.

Amenities: Don't expect any, but this is a worthy choice nonetheless.

WHERE TO DINE

✪ Ane Kirstine. Adelgade 62. ☎ **86-34-44-66.** Reservations recommended. Lunch main courses 90–110 DKK ($13.05–$15.95); dinner main courses 150–200 DKK ($21.75–$29). Set lunch 168 DKK ($24.35); set dinners 298–418 DKK ($43.20–$60.60). AE, DC, MC, V. DANISH/FRENCH/ITALIAN.

Our favorite restaurant in Ebeltoft presents a sophisticated, carefully choreographed cuisine that's a step above the more nationalistic cuisine that's featured at many of its competitors. Named after the grandmother ("Anna Christine") of a former owner, it occupies what was originally built in the heart of town as a general store in 1775. Within a pair of dining rooms (one yellow, one white) that are accented with dramatic modern paintings by Jutland artists, you'll appreciate the delicate and urbane cuisine of one of the region's best chefs, Poul (Paul) Erik Jensen. Part of its allure derives from his training as a chef in the classical French tradition at grand restaurants in other parts of Denmark. Lunches tend to include stable and relatively conservative platters, the most popular of which include salmon fishcakes with salad and fresh bread, and plates piled high with an assortment of various preparations of herring. Dinners are more elaborate, with menus that change frequently, according to the season, but which might include veal roasted with a *ragoût* of locally picked forest mushrooms, turbot with a saffron sauce, or fillets of plaice served with a lemon-butter sauce. Any of these can be preceded with such exotica as Mediterranean-inspired *carpaccio Piemontese* with truffle oil, or hot pecorino cheese drizzled with hot maple syrup.

Restaurant "Mellem Jyder." Juulsbakke 3. ☎ **86-34-11-23.** Reservations recommended. Main courses 90–170 DKK ($13.05–$24.65). Set menus 100 DKK ($14.50) (available only from 11am to 6pm); and 170 DKK ($24.65) (available anytime). MC, V. Wed–Mon 11am–9pm. DANISH.

The oldest and most historically evocative restaurant in Ebeltoft occupies a circa-1610 half-timbered building a few steps from the old Town Hall. Inside, within four dining rooms whose paneling and accessories have been compared to those of a museum, you can order a roster of conservative and ultra-traditional Danish food whose authenticity seems to go well with the antique setting. Menu items include roasted or marinated salmon with dill sauce; fillet of sole *meunière,* or in some cases, fried and served with parsley and butter sauce; roasted pork with cabbage, fresh salad, French fries, and béarnaise sauce; and an old-fashioned hash dish known as *biksemal.* On afternoons, a beer garden in back, like you might have expected in neighboring Germany, is popular during mild weather.

EBELTOFT AFTER DARK

The best place to gather in the evening is **Den Skæve Bar,** Overgade 23 (☎ **86-34-37-97**), an English-style pub from 1683. Often this is the venue for live music, including folk, rock, blues, and jazz.

9   Viborg

297^1/$_2$ km (186 miles) W of Copenhagen; 57^1/$_2$ km (36 miles) W of Randers; 65^1/$_2$ km (41 miles) NW of Århus

"Viborg is like a mother to Jutland," wrote a historian some 4 centuries ago. That could still be true today. It's been called "Jutland in a nutshell," and a "cocktail of all good things from sea to sea on the Jutland peninsula." To the west of Viborg is rolling countryside, dominated by pine forests. The east side of town is blessed with hilly, fertile farmland, with the Nørreå River meandering through the valley between the hills.

South of town lies a deep lake, Hald Sø, at the foot of Dollerup Bakker, an area dominated by Denmark's largest oak forest and ancient beach woods. Viborg itself doesn't open onto the sea, however, even though Limfjord tries to reach Viborg with its salty tongue, Hjarbæk Fjord. The hamlet of Hjarbæk, to the north of town, is Viborg's link with the sea today, and Hjarbæk is also home to a unique fleet of skiffs— the brown-sailed fjord boats.

A stroll through the town will give you a sense of its history, which was launched in the Middle Ages, although settlements here may date from as far back as 700. Once the town was called Wibjerg; "wi" is the old Viking word for sacred, and it is believed that the site of present-day Viborg was once a pagan cult worship center. By 1065 Viborg was the see of a bishop. At that time it was also the capital of Jutland.

Danish kings were elected in Viborg, a tradition that continued until 1340. Even after it lost that role, Danish nobles continued to pay homage to the newly elected king of Denmark here, at least for another three centuries. It remained the largest town in Jutland until 1650. Even as late as 1850 it was the seat of the provincial governing assembly, or *Landsting,* as it's called in Danish.

In 1525 and again in 1529, Hans Tausen, a preacher, made Viborg a center of the Reformation, which led to the closing of the monasteries and abbeys. At its peak Viborg had 25 churches and abbeys. In 1567 and again in 1727, fires swept over Viborg, destroying much of the town.

Today it is a lively town of commerce and industry, no longer enjoying its illustrious royal and ecclesiastical associations, having long lost that role to Copenhagen in the east.

ESSENTIALS

GETTING THERE   Trains from Århus (see above) arrive during the day on the hour (less frequently on Saturday and Sunday). The trip takes just 70 minutes.

By Car   From Randers, our last stopover, follow Route 16 directly west into Viborg.

VISITOR INFORMATION   Viborg Turistbureau, Nytorv 9 (☎ **86-61-16-66**), is open in summer Monday to Saturday 9am to 5pm. Off-season hours are Monday to Friday 9am to 4pm and Saturday 9:30am to 12:30pm.

SEEING THE SIGHTS

The narrow, steep, and winding streets of the historic core reveal Viborg's medieval origins. Viborg is pedestrian friendly, and motorists had best park outside and cover the inner city on foot. The city's main attraction is **Viborg Domkirke,** Sct. Mogens Gade (☎ **87-25-52-50**). This is one of Denmark's largest granite churches. It is a round-arched Romanesque structure, constructed in 1876 in a style similar to the original great church that stood here in the 12th century. Even before that, a wooden structure was built on this site in the Viking era. Many churches, mostly constructed of stone, followed in the wake of the Viking church. The ravages of time and many fires left their mark on the church, although there are still traces of its first stone crypt from 1130.

The crypt is worth examining in detail. In the leather-clad coffin of one of the crypt chapels lies the embalmed body of the alchemist Valdemar Daa, described so movingly by Hans Christian Andersen in his story, *The Wind Tells of Valdemar Daa and His Daughters.*

The cathedral's most distinctive features are its twin towers with their pyramidal roofs. The interior is known for the Biblical wall paintings of Joakim Skovgaard, created between 1901 and 1906.

The black stone in the floor in front of the altar marks the grave of the murdered Danish king Erik Glipping, who received no less than 50 sword and dagger thrusts through his body when spending the night in Finderup, just southwest of Viborg, in 1286. Hours are Monday to Saturday 11am to 4pm and on Sunday from noon to 5pm; admission is free.

Skovgaard Museet, Domkirkestræde 2-4 (☎ **86-62-39-75**), fronts the cathedral. The museum is housed in the old town hall of Rådhus, a Baroque structure designed by Claus Stallknecht of Hamburg, Germany. He came to Viborg to help rebuild the city after the last major fire in 1726. The museum here today is devoted to the paintings, sketches, and sculptures of Joakim Skovgaard (1856–1933), known mainly for his work in Viborg Domkirke (see above). The museum owns his preliminary sketches for his frescoes for the cathedral. You can also see works by some of his fellow artists and friends, including Johan Thomas Lundbye, Niels Larsen Stevns, and Thorvald B. Bindesbøll. Works by 20th-century artists can also be viewed. The museum is open May to September daily from 10am to 12:30pm and 1:30 to 5pm. Off-season hours are daily 1:30 to 5pm. Admission is free.

A final museum, **Viborg Stiftsmuseum,** Hjultorvet 9 (☎ **87-25-26-10**), is housed in a building that was once the headquarters of the local health society, with statues of some of the society's pioneers. The museum relates the history of the city going back to the Ice Age, although exhibitions range up to modern times as well. There are also artifacts discovered in the area that date back to the Stone Age, the Iron Age, and, of course, the Viking era. An intriguing section of the museum displays commercial art as interpreted by the artists of the 1500s and 1600s. The museum is open May to August daily from 11am to 5pm. Off-season hours are Tuesday to Friday 2 to 5pm and Saturday and Sunday 11am to 5pm. Admission is 15 DKK ($2.15) adults; free for children under 15.

SHOPPING   Most of the shopping outlets in Viborg line either side of the all-pedestrian Sct. Mathiasgade. Two of the most appealing of them include **Inspiration,** Sct. Mathiasgade 54–56 (☎ **86-62-59-00**); and **Bahne,** Sct. Mathiasgade 14–18 (☎ **86-62-63-55**). Both sell the kinds of housewares, gift items, and kitchen equipment that make you want to ship a box or two loaded with gadgets and art objects back to wherever you live.

WHERE TO STAY

Restaurant Jagtstuen on the outskirts of town (see "Where to Dine," below) also rents rooms.

Golf Hotel Viborg. Randersvej, DK-8800 Viborg. ☎ **86-61-02-22.** Fax 86-61-31-71. E-mail: golfvib@pip.dknet.dk. 133 units. MINIBAR TV TEL. 950–1,250 DKK ($137.75–$181.25) double. Rate includes breakfast. AE, DC, MC, V.

Few other hotels in the region convey as much of a sense of spaciousness, thanks to a sprawling interior, a location on a peninsula jutting into a freshwater lake, and an architectural design that emphasizes strong horizontal lines, red roofs, verdant lawns, and pale, clear colors. Set less than a half-mile east of the town center, the hotel was built in the mid-1980s as a getaway site for overstressed urbanites, many of whom spend part of their day on the links at the nearby Viborg Golf Club. (Residents pay between 150 to 170 DKK [$21.75–$24.65] for greens fees—about 30% less than non-residents at the same course.) Much of the floor space here is devoted to a state-of-the-art series of conference rooms, which in winter are booked by corporations as far away as Copenhagen for the continuing education and R&R of their employees and management. Bedrooms are stylish and modern, with big windows, and such elegant touches as leather-upholstered armchairs, copies of Oriental carpets, and whimsical artworks.

Dining/Diversions: Restaurant Brænderigaarden and Restaurant Golf Salonen provide some of the most upmarket dining in the area. The cuisine at either is solidly reliable, giving an injection of cosmopolitan flair. The chefs display a fine native understanding of raw ingredients, which they shape into the most winning combinations. After dinner you can dance in the hotel nightclub.

Amenities: There's an indoor swimming pool sheathed with blue and white tiles in country-baroque, usually floral patterns; a sauna, a fitness center, and a golf course and convention facilities.

Kongenshus Hotel. Daugbjerg, DK-8800 Viborg. ☎ **97-54-81-25.** 9 units (3 with bath). 450 DKK ($65.25) double without bath; 550 DKK ($79.75) double with bath. No credit cards. From Viborg, drive 12 miles along the Viborgvej, heading southwest of town, following the signs to Holstebro and Daugbjerg.

This hotel enjoys a location in the rolling foothills and scenic backdrop of Mindepark, southwest of Viborg. It was built as an imitation of a Danish manor house in 1953, and paid for by a consortium of local farmers and ecologists who wanted to protect the grass and heather-covered heath to keep it the way most of Jutland looked in the 1700s. Fronted by a soaring flagpole from which flies the Danish flag, the venue contains sturdy modern furniture and a restaurant where main courses cost 150 to 180 DKK ($21.75–$26.10) at dinner, and 45 to 60 DKK ($6.50–$8.70) at lunchtime. Bedrooms contain the high ceilings and big casement windows of the building's original construction, pale colors, and cost-conscious and angular modern furniture, much of it made from laminated birch or plywood with birch veneers. If you opt for a stay here, expect a genteel setting where the natural beauty of the surrounding heath is the main allure, and a roster of fellow guests who might tend to devote many hours to hiking over its surfaces.

Palads Hotel. Sct. Mathias Gade 5, DK-8800 Viborg. ☎ **86-62-37-00.** Fax 86-62-40-46. 75 units. MINIBAR TV TEL. 840–995 DKK ($121.80–$144.25) double; 1,495 DKK ($216.75) suite. AE, DC, MC, V.

Its façade is grander than that of any other hotel in Viborg, and memorable because of its neoclassical detailing and touches of art nouveau. Inside, you'll find a gracefully modernized, high-ceilinged collection of public areas that convey a light and airy feeling thanks to modern Scandinavian design and pale Nordic colors. Bedrooms contain more hardwood veneers than you might have expected, and comfortable but simple furnishings. Although there's a restaurant on the premises, it was closed at the time of this writing, with an uncertain future. For an unusual way to spend 5 minutes or so, head to the pavement outside this hotel. Here, sunk into the masonry of the sidewalk, you'll find a Danish interpretation of the handprints in the concrete near Los Angeles' Grauman's Chinese Theater. Look for the handprints of actors and actresses you might never have heard of (Max Hansen, Paul Hagen, Ghita Nørby, and Fritz Helmuth), each of whom is a household name throughout Denmark.

WHERE TO DINE

Arthur's. Vestergade 4. ☎ **86-62-21-26.** Reservations recommended. Lunch platters 29–89 DKK ($4.20–$12.90); dinner main courses 155–175 DKK ($22.45–$25.40). Set menus 185–225 DKK ($26.85–$32.65). AE, DC, MC, V. Mon–Sat 11:30am–3pm and 6–10pm. DANISH/INTERNATIONAL.

The most charming small-scale restaurant in Viborg is set within the town's most central shopping district, adjacent to a thoroughfare that's usually reserved just for pedestrians. Originally conceived around 1900 as a hotel but no longer in the business of renting rooms, it contains a cafe within a front room, and a more substantial-looking restaurant in back.

Décors in both are based on antique-looking brick walls and lots of potted plants, and depending on where you want to sit, both can serve the following food items in either room. Lunches tend to be relatively light, and include salads, open-faced sandwiches, pastas, omelets, burgers, and marinated or smoked fish. Menu items at dinner are offbeat and idiosyncratic, often based on ideas gathered by the staff during their holidays abroad. Examples include a terrine of guinea fowl seasoned with cognac and port; fillet of veal with braised celery, new potatoes, and mushroom sauce; and French-style chocolate cake with orange sauce and a medley of fresh berries. The cookery is soundly based on classical principals, with a little imagination thrown in for good measure. Upmarket dishes show considerable technical skills.

Brugger Bauer. Sct. Mathiasgade 61. ☎ **86-61-44-88.** Reservations recommended. Lunch main courses 53–79 DKK ($7.70–$11.45). Dinner main courses 68–180 DKK ($9.85–$26.10). AE, DC, MC, V. Mon–Sat 11:30am–5pm and 5–9pm. DANISH.

A temperance brewery that specialized in non-alcoholic beer was established on the main street of Viborg as early as 1840. All of that changed in 1872, when it was bought by a Hungarian-born entrepreneur named Bauer—who was nicknamed Brugger Bauer, or "Bauer the Brewer." He immediately changed the establishment's reliance on alcohol-free beer and began brewing the real thing in custom-built underground cellars the same year he acquired it. Today, those cellars house one of Viborg's busiest and most atmospheric restaurants. Built of russet-colored bricks, and set 24-feet beneath Viborg's main shopping street, they're appealingly outfitted with tables, chairs, a tactful staff, and very good cuisine. A premier main course specialty is a "beerbones" platter, consisting of pork fillet boiled in beer, then fried with dill and served with sweetened and fried Danish potatoes. Also popular are salmon steak with lobster sauce and boiled white potatoes, and a traditional, all-Danish version of fried beefsteak with fried onions and potatoes.

Den Gyldne Okse. Store Sct. Peders Stræde. ☎ **86-62-27-44.** Reservations recommended. Lunch main courses 45–79 DKK ($6.50–$11.45). Dinner main courses 140–190 DKK ($20.30–$27.55). DC, MC, V. Mon–Sat 11am–3pm and 5–10pm (last order). DANISH.

Although its food is less imaginative than you might have hoped for, the setting of this 400-year-old Danish *kro* (inn), a few steps from Viborg's town hall, evokes the mercantile days of Denmark during the 1600s. Both the outside and inside feature rich half-timbering and the patina left by many generations of cigarette smoke, spilled beer, and the noise and animation of hundreds of diners and drinkers. Lunches are lighter, quicker, and less formal than dinners, and might include a selection of sandwiches, salads, and simple platters such as salmon cakes with herb sauce and fresh-baked rye bread. Dinners are a bit more elaborate, with a limited number of steaks, most of which are imported from the U.S. midwest, and are served with pepper sauce, béarnaise, or fresh mushrooms. Fish dishes include all the standard sea creatures swimming around Denmark, including various preparations of salmon, shrimp, and sole. No one will mind if you drop in just for a bottle of Carlsberg and a snack, but if you want a full-blown meal, the hardworking but bemused staff will think that's just fine too. The food is good and reliable, without being sensational in any way.

Restaurant Jagtstuen. In the Rindsholm Kro, Gammel Århusvej 323, DK-8800 Viborg. ☎ **86-63-90-44.** Fax 86-63-97-44. Reservations recommended. Main courses 86–186 DKK ($12.45–$26.95). AE, DC, MC, V. Daily 4–8:30pm (last order). From Viborg's center, drive 3½ miles southeast, following the A26 highway and the signs to Århus. DANISH/ INTERNATIONAL.

Located in contemplative rusticity in an isolated position, midway between the new and the old highways leading between Viborg and Århus, this two-story, yellow-fronted inn offers well-prepared food and a limited handful of simple bedrooms which are maintained almost as an afterthought to the dining and drinking facilities.

The solid and symmetrical building you'll see today dates from 1906. It was enlarged in the 1930s, and fully "winterized" for year-round use in the 1960s. It occupies the site of an inn that flourished during the 1600s, a fact whose historic implications are deeply important to the kind-hearted owners, Hanne and Frode Hansen. If you ask, they'll point out some of their prized historic mementos, including the body (but not the engine) of an American tank used during the invasion of Normandy (it occupies a prominent spot in their garden), and bullets, cannonballs, and diary entries that attest to the blood-soaked hand-to-hand combat that broke out in 1849 between Danish and Prussian soldiers in the woods a few steps from the site of their present home.

Menu items are artfully prepared, and include such delicious-tasting dishes as breast of wild duckling with port wine and game sauce, medallions of venison with black currant sauce, and fish hauled in directly from Denmark's western coast. These might include fillets of plaice with parsley and butter, or catfish with lime sauce.

Upstairs, the family maintains seven simple but cozy bedrooms, only one of which has a bathroom. With breakfast included, doubles without bath cost 490 DKK ($71.05); the lone double with bath rents for 575 DKK ($83.40).

VIBORG AFTER DARK

If there is a major cultural or musical event, it will no doubt take place at **Kongres-og Musikjhus,** Tingvej (☎ 86-62-62-65), the town's cultural center. The tourist office (see above) has complete details of any events staged here.

You can rock and roll in Viborg's shadows at the bar within the previously recommended **Brugger Bauer,** St. Mathiasgade 61 (☎ 86-61-44-88), or head to one of its most visible competitors, **Messing Jins,** Sct. Mathiasgade 48 (☎ 86-62-02-73). Old, historic, and loaded with the patina of many generations of clients, it's a good choice for some beers and maybe a dance or two to recorded music. More closely geared to dancing than either of the two sites mentioned above is the American-inspired **Doc Holliday Bar & Disco,** Grauene 20 (☎ 86-61-51-33). Although you can get a drink here virtually any day of the week after 2pm, it's most popular every Thursday, Friday, and Saturday, when it rocks and rolls as Viborg's premier disco.

12 Northern Jutland

Separated from the rest of Jutland (and also the mainland of Europe) by the Limfjord, Northern Jutland is a land unto itself. It is a landscape of North Sea beaches, coastal hamlets, fishing harbors, and wild heathlands. It has only one large city, Aalborg, which lies at the narrow point of Limfjord, plus a number of mid-sized towns, notably Frederikshavn and Hjørring. Any of these would be a suitable base, but for sheer scenic beauty we'd choose to stay in Skagen, which has long attracted some of Denmark's leading artists and artisans. Skagen stands at the northernmost boundary of Denmark.

Come to North Jutland for nature, its rugged people, and the unspoiled environment. Because of bridges linking Funen with Zealand and Jutland, you can drive to North Jutland from Copenhagen in just 4 ½ hours.

"Why do we live here in such a rugged environment?" asked a painter in Skagen, then answered his own question. "The real Denmark is a winter day at the North Sea with the wind blowing back your hair and making your skin salty, a trip in the autumn forest to gather mushrooms, or a romantic stroll in the newly leafed beech forest."

You will not be among the first to visit North Jutland. The first visitors arrived some 4,000 years ago in a land that was created by the Ice Age some 10,000 years earlier. Many places in Vendsyssel (the name of the province) still bear traces from the Stone Age, the Iron Age, and certainly from the Viking Age. You can see history at many ancient monuments and relics of antiquity on display in the area.

In 1859, Hans Christian Andersen, enraptured with North Jutland, said it best: "If you are a Painter then follow us here, here are Subjects for you to paint, here is Scenery for Writing." In the 19th century, the Skagen painters—the Danish equivalent of the French Impressionists—were attracted to North Jutland for its special, intense light, the region's rough natural surroundings, the sea, and the people. A large collection of their paintings can be viewed today at the Skagens Museum. Some of their homes have also been turned into museums.

After a long, long slumber, the towns of North Jutland are more alive than ever. Young people, who used to leave the folks at home and head for the bright lights of Copenhagen, are often remaining to live in the area of their birth, bringing new energy and excitement to its once dull towns and hamlets.

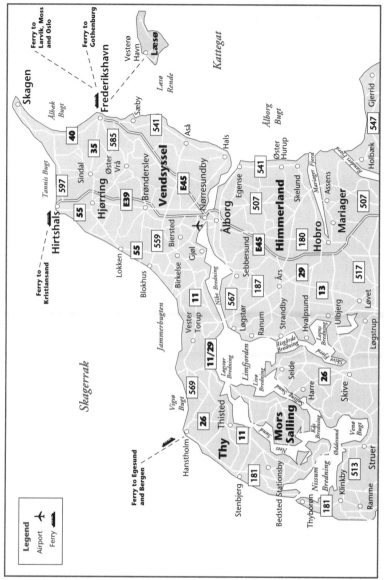

The new emphasis of town planners is on quality of life and aesthetics. In Hjørring the main street has been renovated and in some old back alleys, shops, cafes, and craft stores have opened. In Hirtshals both town and harbor have been spruced up and linked by a new external sculptural staircase. Frederikshavn has worked creatively with street spaces and has brought life and light to previously rundown, dull streets. A tour of North Jutland and a view of its natural environment will make you understand why the landscape inspired such writers as Henrik Ibsen and Herman Bang.

And then there are monuments, many of them erected in memory of the members of the Resistance who struggled against Nazi oppression during the German takeover of Denmark for most of World War II. Other monuments commemorate lifeboatmen

A Breath of Fresh Air

The air in Northern Jutland is among the purest in Europe. Locals are fond of pointing out that the nearest factory chimney is 500 miles to the west in Scotland.

who died while rescuing shipwrecked sailors. Almost everywhere there are reminders that the North Sea is something with which one must live daily. Many monuments note that the sea both gives life but can brutally claim it as well.

For rail information to any town, call ☎ **70-13-14-15;** for bus connections and schedules call ☎ 98-90-09-00.

1 Mariager

57¹/₂ km (36 miles) N of Århus; 341km (213 miles) NW of Copenhagen

Aalborg-bound motorists with time should stop over at Mariager. In a charming setting overlooking Mariager Fjord, the town has quaint cobblestone streets and half-timbered, red-roofed buildings.

Mariager was only a small fishing hamlet at the ferry crossing on the way between Randers and Aalborg before the foundation of Bridgettine Abbey in 1410. The abbey led to a flourishing trade and commerce in the area, and the town became a popular resort for the worshipping nobles. However, with the coming of the Reformation in 1536, the tide turned. When Mariager was granted its city charter in 1592, only 500 inhabitants remained. Many of the old buildings constructed in Mariager's heyday remain, however. Industrialization did not come until 1960, and by that time the town had become preservation-minded as a walk through its cobbled streets will reveal.

ESSENTIALS

GETTING THERE   There is no direct train to Mariager. Trains run from Aalborg to Hobro, east of Mariager, every 30 minutes, and trains from Århus to Hobro run hourly. Take the bus from Hobro. Buses to Mariager run hourly from Hadsun, Hobro, or Randers. The ride on all three takes about half an hour.

By Car   Take the E45 north from Randers and head east at the junction of Route 555.

VISITOR INFORMATION   The **Mariager Tourist Association,** Torvet 1B (☎ **98-54-13-77**), is open June 15 to August Monday to Friday 9am to 5pm, Saturday 9am to 2pm. Off-season hours are Monday to Friday 9am to 4pm, Saturday 9am to noon.

SEEING THE SIGHTS

Mariager is connected to the Baltic via the Mariager Fjord, a deep but narrow saltwater inlet favored by sailors and yacht enthusiasts because of its smooth surface. You can sail aboard a small-scale cruise ship, the *Svanen,* as it circumnavigates the western recesses of the fjord. About four times a day, the ship touches down at such fjord-side towns as Mariager, Hadsund, and Hobro, taking 2 ½ hours for a complete circuit that's priced at 70 DKK ($10.15) per person. You can get off at any of five villages en route, and wait for the next boat to pick you up and carry you on to the next town. There's a cafeteria on board, and a sun deck where guests can improve their suntans during the short Nordic summer. En route, between Mariager and Hadsund, you'll see one of the biggest areas in Denmark for the harvesting of mussels. The tourist office in Mariager (see above) is the best source of advice about schedules and itineraries.

Although it is the old town itself that is the most alluring attraction, you may want to call on the abbey church, **Mariager Kirke Klostervej** (☎ 98-54-15-95), which was constructed in the 15th century as part of a nunnery. It was given to the town as its parish church following the Reformation. Although it has been largely reconstructed over the years, it is still a fine and lofty building with a magnificent carved altarpiece depicting the Last Supper and the Crucifixion, surrounded by 11 of the apostles. A memorial tablet to the last abbess in the south transept can be seen. Hours are Monday to Saturday 8am to 3:30pm; admission is free.

One of the most beautiful buildings in Mariager is the old merchant's house, now the **Mariager Museum,** Kirkegard 4B (☎ 98-54-12-87). In the museum you can see an attractive collection of domestic utensils and tools. The museum also contains relics from the ancient history of both Mariager and the surrounding district. Of special interest is a reconstruction of the abbey and its church, an exhibit established in 1981 in connection with the 500th anniversary of the church. It is open May 15 to September 15 daily 3 to 5pm. Admission is 15 DKK ($2.15) for adults; free for children.

Danmarks Saltcenter, Haven (☎ 98-54-18-16), opened in 1998. It is the only science center devoted to salt in the country. Lying on the harbor at Mariager, close to the water, it traces the methods for extracting salt since the Middle Ages. Called white gold, salt was formed some 250 million years ago, or so you learn at the museum. You can go exploring in the tunnels of the salt mine and experience what it was like to work in a mountain salt mine a century ago. You can watch a foreman at the salt works boil the salt in a boiling hut as they did in the Middle Ages. The salt garden is planted with plants that obviously can tolerate salt, and this is the setting for the museum's Salt Café where, naturally, dishes connected with salt are served. There are also many activities for children, including, among others, shallow pools in the outdoor water playground. Tickets are 50 DKK ($7.25) for adults and 30 DKK ($4.35) for children ages 3–11 (free for age 2 and under). Hours are May 15 to August 31 daily 10am to 6pm. Off-season hours are Monday to Friday 10am to 4pm and Saturday and Sunday 10am to 5pm.

SHOPPING   As a shopping curiosity, **Second-Hand Geschäft** operates out of the old merchants house, now the Mariager Museum, Kirkegard 4B (☎ 98-54-12-87). Here you can purchase secondhand clothes of all sorts, shapes, and sizes. Prices, naturally, are very reasonable.

WHERE TO STAY

If you can't find a hotel room, the Mirager Tourist Association (see above) will help book you into a **private home** or boardinghouse.

Hotel Postgården. Tovert 6A, DK-9550 Mariager. ☎ **98-54-10-12.** Fax 98-54-24-64. 14 units. TV. 600 DKK ($87) double. Rate includes breakfast. AE, DC, MC, V.

The most authentically historic hotel in Mariager has extended hospitality to travelers since it was established in 1710 in the heart of town, near the main square and Town Hall. It was restored in 1982, and upgraded many times since, including once in 1992, just before it was selected by the courtiers of Queen Margrethe as a place for her to spend a few hours before an inspection she made of some Danish naval vessels floating offshore. The building's façade and public areas, especially its pub and restaurant, are authentically historic and old-time. But about two-thirds of the bedrooms have been stripped of their historic charm and upgraded to a modern international look that's comfortable and cozy, albeit culturally neutral. If you really insist on an antique decor, request room 305 (one that the hotel usually assigns to anyone claiming to be a honeymooner); or, to a lesser extent, rooms 201, 203, or 307.

Motel Landgangen. Oxendalen 1, DK-9550 Mariager. ☎ **98-54-11-22.** 6 units. TV. 450 DKK ($65.25) double. Rates include breakfast. AE, DC, MC, V.

Set beside the river, a 5-minute walk north of the abbey, this is not a dreary motel, even though its white exterior and simple architecture date from the late 1960s. Its small rooms are cozy and inviting, well kept and neat, including the baths. The place is even better known for its restaurant, which is open in summer daily from noon to 8pm and off-season only Friday through Wednesday from noon to 8pm. Its dining room features Danish specialties and cozy furniture with a view of the water. A platter of the day costs 58 DKK ($8.40) at lunch, and you can order a dinner beginning at 130 DKK ($18.85) for two courses. Otherwise, regular main courses range from 65 to 140 DKK ($9.40–$20.30).

WHERE TO DINE

Restaurant Postgården. In the Hotel Postgården, Torvet 6A. ☎ **98-54-10-12.** Reservations recommended. Lunch main courses 30–130 DKK ($4.35–$18.85). Dinner main courses 100–178 DKK ($14.50–$25.80). Set-price menus 98–228 DKK ($28.70–$33.05). AE, DC, MC, V. Daily 11am–11pm. DANISH/FRENCH.

Many diners appreciate this restaurant for its old-time décor and the sense of intimacy created by its trio of small-scale but bustling dining rooms. During mild weather, tables are set up outside, thereby expanding the restaurant's floor space and popularity. There's nothing particularly avant-garde about the food served here, although that's exactly the cuisine that many of the regular clients seem to crave. Luncheon favorites include such tried-and-true favorites as *smørrebrød* (open-faced sandwiches) piled high with baby shrimp or Danish ham, and platters of herring or roasted pork with red cabbage and new potatoes. Dinners are more elaborate, and usually include filets of veal with mushroom sauce, steaks with red wine sauce, a very tasty brisket of beef with horseradish sauce, and perfectly cooked chicken breasts with a gratin of potatoes. Any of these might be followed with selections from a platter of local cheeses, or a slice of hazelnut pie with vanilla ice cream.

AFTER DARK

One of the town's most consistently popular pubs lies within the previously recommended **Hotel Postgården,** Torvet 6A (☎ **98-54-10-12**). Within a room sheathed with old-fashioned paneling, near a bar with antique-looking beer pulls, you're likely to find an animated crowd of office workers and after-dinner refugees from the confines of their homes, with lots of options for meeting and making new friends. Open daily from 11am to 11pm, it serves platters of food, including herring, that taste good with the Carlsberg, and which cost from 30 to 55 DKK ($4.35–$8) each. Beer costs around 20 DKK ($2.90) a bottle.

2 Aalborg

131km (82 miles) NW of Ebeltoft; 381km (238 miles) W of Copenhagen

The largest city in northern Jutland, with a population of 160,000, Aalborg (Ålborg) is known worldwide for its *aquavit.* Although essentially a shipping town and commercial center, Aalborg makes a good base for sightseers, with its many hotels, attractions (a blend of old and new), more than 300 restaurants, and diverse nightlife. It is the natural center of North Jutland.

History is a living reality in Aalborg. The city was founded 1,000 years ago when the Viking fleets assembled in these parts before sailing on their predatory expeditions. The historic atmosphere of Aalborg has been preserved in its old streets and alleys.

Aalborg

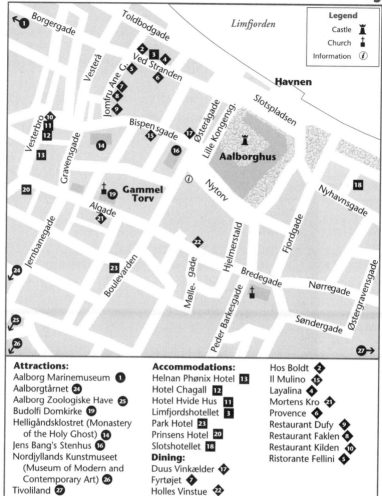

Attractions:
Aalborg Marinemuseum ❶
Aalborgtårnet ㉔
Aalborg Zoologiske Have ㉕
Budolfi Domkirke ⑲
Helligåndsklostret (Monastery
   of the Holy Ghost) ⑭
Jens Bang's Stenhus ⑯
Nordjyllands Kunstmuseet
   (Museum of Modern and
   Contemporary Art) ㉖
Tivoliland ㉗

Accommodations:
Helnan Phønix Hotel ⑬
Hotel Chagall ⑫
Hotel Hvide Hus ⑪
Limfjordshotellet ❸
Park Hotel ㉓
Prinsens Hotel ⑳
Slotshotellet ⑱
Dining:
Duus Vinkælder ⑰
Fyrtøjet ❼
Holles Vinstue ㉒

Hos Boldt ❷
Il Mulino ⑮
Layalina ❹
Mortens Kro ㉑
Provence ❻
Restaurant Dufy ❾
Restaurant Faklen ❽
Restaurant Kilden ❿
Ristorante Fellini ❺

Near the Church of Our Lady are many beautifully restored and reconstructed houses, some of which date from the 16th century.

Denmark's largest forest, **Rold,** where robber-bandits once roamed as they did in Sherwood, England, is just outside town. Also, **Rebild National Park** is the site of the annual American Fourth of July celebration.

Not far from Aalborg, on the west coast of northern Jutland, are some of the finest beaches in northern Europe, stretching from Slettestrand to Skagen. The beach-resort towns of **Blokhus** and **Løkken** are especially popular with Danes, Germans, and Swedes.

ESSENTIALS
GETTING THERE   If you aren't driving, you can fly from Copenhagen to Aalborg; the airport (☎ **98-17-11-44**) is 4 miles from the city center. **SAS** (☎ **98-17-33-11**) flies 10 times daily between Copenhagen and Aalborg. On most international flights, you'd fly first to Copenhagen, then to Aalborg. However, **MUK Air** (☎ **98-19-03-88**)

flies Monday to Friday to Oslo (only 1 flight per day). A bus costing 30 DKK ($4.35) each way is timed to coincide with flight arrivals. It takes air passengers into the center of Aalborg. The average taxi fare between the airport and the heart of town is about 100 DKK ($14.50) each way. There is frequent train service from Copenhagen (via Frederica) to Århus; here you can connect with a train to Aalborg, a 90-minute ride. Express buses run daily to Copenhagen in 6 hours, to Århus in 2 ¼ hours, and to Esbjerg in 3 ½ hours. For bus information and schedules, call any of three separate phone numbers: ☎ **70-10-00-30** for information about buses to and from Copenhagen; ☎ **86-78-48-88** for information about buses headed to Århus; and ☎ **98-90-09-00** for information about buses going to other parts of Jutland. Since Aalborg's bus station is the transportation center for northern Jutland, buses reach Aalborg from all directions. For all bus information in northern Jutland, call **Nordjyllands Trafikselskab** (☎ **98-11-11-11**).

By Car   From Ebeltoft (see chapter 11 on Central Jutland) follow Route 21 north until you reach the junction with Route 16; then drive west on Route 16 until you come to E45, the motorway which you take north into Aalborg.

VISITOR INFORMATION   Contact the **Aalborg Tourist Bureau,** Østerågade 8 (☎ **98-12-60-22**); it's open June to August, Monday to Friday 9am to 6pm, Saturday from 9am to 5pm; and September to May, Monday to Friday from 9am to 4:30pm and Saturday from 10am to 1pm.

Special Events   The **Aalborg Carnival** on May 21 is one of the major events of spring in Jutland. Streets are filled with festive figures in colorful costumes strutting in a major parade. Up to 100,000 people participate in this annual event, marking the victory of spring over winter's darkness. The whole city seems to explode in joy. There's also the **Aalborg Jazz and Blues Festival** from June 4–7. Jazz seemingly fills the whole city at dozens of clubs, although most activity centers around C. W. Obels Plads. Every year on the 4th of July, Danes and Danish-Americans meet to celebrate America's Independence Day in the lovely hills of Rebild.

GETTING AROUND

All city buses depart from the city center, usually from Østerågade and Nytorv. The bus fare is 11 DKK ($1.60) for adults or 5.50 DKK (80¢) for children ages 4–14 (free for age 3 and under). You can purchase a 24-hour tourist pass for 70 DKK ($10.15) for adults or 35 DKK ($5.05) for children.

SEEING THE SIGHTS

The easiest way to see the sights is to take an organized tour, available in English from late June to mid-August. A bus tour covers the highlights of Greater Aalborg in just 3 hours, costing 60 DKK ($8.70) for adults or 30 DKK ($4.35) for children. Information and tickets are available at the Aalborg Tourist Bureau (see above).

Another possibility is to hire an English-speaking taxi driver who will take you past the city's highlights. The maximum number of passengers allowed is four, and the average tour lasts a half hour, costing 450 DKK ($65.25) for a quartet. For more details, ask at the tourist bureau.

Aalborg Marinemuseum. Vester Fjordvej 81. ☎ **98-11-78-03.** Admission 40 DKK ($5.80) for adults 20 DKK ($2.90) for children ages 5–12 (free for age 4 and under) May–Aug daily 10am–6pm; off-season daily 10am–4pm.

This museum of marine exhibits is next to the harbor, Vestre Bådehavn. You can see the *Springeren,* a 75-foot-long submarine; *Søbjørnen,* the world's fastest torpedo boat; or the inspection ship *Ingolf,* which was on active duty in the waters around

Greenland until 1990. Various exhibits depict life at sea, the port of Aalborg, and activities at the Aalborg shipyard. At the Café Ubåden (submarine), you can order food and drink. There's also a playground on site.

Aalborgtårnet. Søndre Skovvej, at Skovbakken. ☎ **98-12-04-88.** Admission 20 DKK ($2.90) for adults, 10 DKK ($1.45) for children. June 17–Aug 11, daily 10am–7pm; May–June 16 and Aug 2–Sept 15, daily 10am–5pm. Closed Sept 16–Apr. Bus: 8 or 10.

From this tower rising 325 feet above sea level, there's a perfect view of the city and the fjord. You may enjoy a snack at the top of the tower or else a simple meal such as roast chicken and French fries. They also serve coffee, soda, and beer here.

Aalborg Zoologiske Have. Mølleparkvej 63. ☎ **98-13-07-33.** Admission 60 DKK ($8.70) for adults, 30 DKK ($4.35) for children ages 4–11, free for children age 3 and under. May–Aug, daily 9am–6pm; Apr and Sept–Oct, daily 10am–4pm; Nov–Mar, daily 10am–2pm. Bus: 1 or S3.

Mølleparken is a large park with a lookout where you can see most of Aalborg and the Isle of Egholm (look for Roda Reilinger's sculpture *Noah's Ark*). In the park is the second-largest zoo in Scandinavia, where some 800 animal specimens from all over the world wander freely in surroundings designed to duplicate an open African range. Often you can come face to face with endangered species. Aalborg Zoo helps to ensure these animals' survival by cooperating internationally with regard to their breeding; some are released back into their natural habitat. It's like a trip through Africa, seeing the suricats' rocky abode, the crocodiles on the river bank, the giraffe house, the bear forest, and even the Anteaters' pampas. Apes and beasts of prey are kept under minimal restrictions. There's a good bistro inside the zoo, and snack bars located here and there.

Budolfi Domkirke. Algade. ☎ **98-13-49-28.** Free admission. Mon–Fri 9am–2pm. Bus: 3,5 10, or 11.

This elaborately decorated and whitewashed cathedral is dedicated to St. Botolph, patron saint of sailors. The baroque spire of the church is Aalborg's major landmark. The church you see today is the result of 800 years of rebuilding and expansion. On the south wall is a fresco depicting St. Catherine of Alexandria and some grotesque small centaurs. In the body of the church, notice the altarpiece from 1689 and the pulpit from 1692—both carved by Lauridtz Jensen. The marble font from 1727 was a gift to the church. Note too the gallery in the north aisle with its illustrations of the ten commandments. A similar gallery in the south aisle illustrates the suffering of Christ and also bears the names of a number of prominent Aalborg citizens from around the mid-17th century. A carillon sounds daily every hour from 9am to 10pm.

Helligåndsklostret (Monastery of the Holy Ghost). C. W. Obels Plads (call the tourist office for information). Guided tour 25 DKK ($3.60) for adults, 10 DKK ($1.45) for children. Late June to mid-Aug guided tour Mon–Fri at 2pm. Bus: 1.

This vine-covered monastery is the oldest social-welfare institution in Denmark, as well as the oldest building in Aalborg. Built near the heart of town in 1431, and designed with step-shaped gables, it contains a well-preserved rectory, a series of vaulted storage cellars—some of which occasionally functioned as prisons—a whitewashed collection of cloisters, and a chapter house whose walls in some areas are decorated with 16th-century frescoes. The complex can only be visited as part of a guided tour.

۞ Jens Bang's Stenhus. Østerågade 9. Bus: 3, 5, 10, 11.

This six-floor mansion, built in 1624 in a glittering Renaissance style, once belonged to a wealthy merchant, Jens Bang. It is hailed as the finest example of Renaissance domestic architecture in the north of Europe. Bang was gifted but also argumentative and obstinate. He deliberately made his house rich with ornamentation and ostentation as a "challenge" to the other good citizens of the town. It was rumored that he revenged himself on his many enemies by caricaturing them in the many grotesque carvings on the façade of the house. In spite of his wealth, he was never made a member of the town council, and to this day his image is depicted on the south façade sticking his tongue out at the Town Hall. The historic wine cellar, Duus Vinkjaelder, is the meeting place of the Guild of Christian IV. On the ground floor is an old apothecary shop. The mansion itself is still privately owned and is not open to the public.

Nordjyllands Kunstmuseet (Museum of Modern and Contemporary Art). Kong Christians Allé 50. ☎ **98-13-80-88.** Admission 30 DKK ($4.35) for adults, free for children. July–Aug, daily 10am–5pm; Sept–June, Tues–Sun 10am–5pm. Bus: 1, 4, 8, 10, or 11.

This museum building is a prime example of modern Scandinavian architecture. Built from 1968 to 1972, it was designed by Elissa and Alvar Aalto and Jean-Jacques Baruël as a showplace for 20th-century Danish and international art, with changing exhibits. The museum was created from two private collections, the oldest being that of Anna and Kresten Krestensen, acquired in 1967. This collection shows the development from naturalism to abstract art. Works are displayed by such artists as Edvard Weie, Harald Giersing, and Vilhelm Lundstrøm, although the heart of the exhibition comprises works acquired in the 1940s and 1950s. The collection also contains many foreign works, as exemplified by artists such as Victor Vasarely and Serge Poliakoff. The second private collection donated was in 1986, a gift of Kirsten and Axel P. Nielsen. This collection places a strong emphasis on experimental art from the beginning of the 1960s until today. There are galleries, scepter gardens, two auditoriums, a children's museum, an outdoor amphitheater, and a restaurant, the Museumscafeen.

NEARBY ATTRACTIONS

Less than 2 ½-miles north of Aalborg, you'll find the remains of the Viking settlement of Nørresundby. It's the site of more than 700 cremation graves, and contains the charred remains of more than 150 Viking boats and ships that were ceremonially burned as part of the above-mentioned cremations. Set within a park, the excavations are open to the public 24-hours-a-day, year-round. Further details about the excavations, however, are on view within the **Lindholm Høje Museet,** Vendilavej 11 (☎ **98-17-55-22**). The museum is open from Easter to mid-October every day from 10am to 5pm. From mid-October to Easter, it's open Tuesday to Sunday from 10am to 4pm. Admission costs 25 DKK ($3.60) for adults, 14 DKK ($2.15) for children ages 5–11 (free for age 4 and under). From the center of Aalborg, you can reach this site on bus no. 6, which departs at intervals of between 15 and 25 minutes.

Most of the graves are marked with stones placed in the form of a triangle, an oval, or a ship. The deceased person was usually cremated. North of the burial ground lay the associated village where the finds include the remains of houses, fences, wells, and fire pits. The area was subject to drifting sand. About 1000 A.D., the whole burial ground became covered with sand, which meant that the stone markings and even a newly ploughed field were preserved until this day. A museum on site contains the archeological finds from the excavations and illustrates how the inhabitants of Lindholm Høje lived at home and when trading abroad.

Voergård Slot, Flauenskjold (☎ **98-46-90-72**), a Renaissance-era castle dating from 1588 positioned 22-miles north of Aalborg, is filled with sculpture, Louis XVI furniture, a banqueting hall, grand salon, and paintings by Goya and Rubens. Admission costs 35 DKK ($5.05) for adults; 20 DKK ($2.90) for children. Take the E45 from Aalborg, cutting east on Route 559 to Droningland, and then follow the signs to Voergård Slot from there. From mid-June to August, it's open daily from 10am to 5pm. From April to mid-June, and from mid-August to the end of September, it's open only on Saturday from 2 to 5pm, and on Sunday from 10am to 5pm. It's closed to the public between October and March.

Americans who are in Jutland for the Fourth of July should make a beeline to the **Rebild National Park,** 18-miles south of Aalborg. On these heather dunes, Danes, Danish-Americans, and Americans celebrate America's Independence Day. The program often features opera singers, folk dancers, choirs, and glee clubs, together with well-known speakers. In the park is the **Lincoln Memorial Log Cabin and Immigrant Museum** (☎ 98-39-14-40), which is devoted to mementos of Danish immigration to the United States, and the after-effects of the exodus both within Europe and the New World.

A 1-hour drive from Aalborg takes you to the resort town of **Blokhus** and the broad white beaches of the North Sea coast. Not far from here is a 124-acre amusement park, **Fårup Sommerland & Waterpark.** Admission costs 115 DKK ($16.65) for adults and children alike, although kids under age 4 enter for free. Expect lots of noise, lots of families, and lots of emphasis on good, clean fun in a style that might remind you of a small-scale version of Disneyland with water wings. It's open mid-May to August, daily from 10am to 7pm. Take bus no. 200 from Aalborg to reach it.

SHOPPING

If it's a Wednesday, head for **House of Crafts,** Kattesundet 20 (☎ 98-12-52-32), a typical half-timbered Aalborg building from about 1630. It was originally part of a trading house. Today it's a center for "endangered" handcrafts. Keeping alive the artisan traditions of yesterday, the center is filled with several workshops—a blacksmith, a coppersmith, a watchmaker, even painters. It is open every Wednesday 10am to 5pm.

Even if you're not in Aalborg on a Wednesday, you'll find that this North Jutland city abounds in specialty stores. For the best collection of gold and silver jewelry, patronize **Aalborg Guld- & Solvhus,** Gravensgade 8 (☎ 98-16-57-11). The best and most sophisticated handcrafts—many quite amusing—are sold at **Lange Handicrafts,** Hjelmerstald 15 (☎ 98-13-82-68). To watch a glassblower in action, and perhaps make some purchases, go to **Lene Højlund,** Norregad 6 (☎ 98-13-01-20).

The largest shopping center in North Jutland lies about 4-miles south of Aalborg's center. (Take bus no. 8 to reach it.) The **Aalborg Storcenter,** Hobrovej 452 (☎ 98-18-23-10) contains at least 50 specialty shops and kiosks, as well as the all-inclusive **Bilka Department Store** (☎ 98-18-24-00).

Aalborg also has some other department stores that bring a vast array of Danish merchandise together under one roof, including **Salling,** Algade (☎ 98-16-00-00), with 30 specialty shops. It has the city's largest selection of fashion, plus lots of other good stuff, including books and toys. A major competitor is **Magasin,** Nytorv 24 (☎ 98-13-30-00). If you're into Scandinavian design for your home, the most refined selection is found at **Trend House,** Østeraa 27 (☎ 98-10-22-47). **Gavlhuset** at Algade 9 (☎ 98-12-18-22), has a little bit of everything—Indian silver, "dancing beans," old Kelim carpets, masks from around the globe, knitted goods, "gods" in bronze, exotic spices, wooden toys in bright colors, and even African wood carvings.

The finest antique dealer is **Vejgaard Antik,** Hadsundvej 59 (☎ 98-11-90-99). To look at and perhaps purchase some of the city's best contemporary art, head for **Galerie Wolfsen,** Tiendeladen 6 (☎ 98-13-75-66).

WHERE TO STAY

The Aalborg Tourist Bureau (see above) can book a room for you in a private Danish home—double or single, with access to a shower. Bed linen is included in the price, and all rooms are situated within the city limits and reached by bus. In July and August, the peak tourist months for visiting Aalborg, Helnan Phønix slashes its rates and becomes a moderately priced choice. Although many rooms at the Limsford-hotellet are labeled expensive, the hotel throughout the year also rents dozens of more affordable accommodations as well.

EXPENSIVE

☯ **Helnan Phønix Hotel.** Vesterbro 77, DK-9000 Aalborg. ☎ **98-12-00-11.** Fax 98-10-10-20. E-mail: hotel@helnen_phonix.hotel.dk. 201 units. MINIBAR TV TEL. July–Aug 900 DKK ($130.50) double, 1,500 DKK ($217.50) suite. Sept–June 1,100 DKK ($159.50) double, 2,000 DKK ($290.00) suite. AE, DC, MC, V. Bus: 8, 10, or 11.

This is the oldest, largest, most historic, and most prestigious hotel in Aalborg, with an old-fashioned series of public rooms that disguise, at first glance, any indication of how modern it really is. It originated in 1783 on the main street of town as the brick-fronted private home of the Danish brigadier general assigned to protect it from assault by such foreign powers as England and Sweden. In 1853, it was converted into a hotel, and entered the modern age after it was massively enlarged three separate times, in the 1960s, '70s, and '80s. Today, it appears deceptively small if you view it from Aalborg's main street, and very imposing if you see its modern wings from the back. Bedrooms are painted in shades of cream, and outfitted with a combination of dark-grained furniture based on turn-of-the-century English models and light-grained pieces of Danish modern.

Dining/Diversions: The hotel's restaurant, Brigadieren, serves a sophisticated Danish and international cuisine. There's also a cocktail lounge.

Amenities: There's a reception/concierge staff dispensing information on what's interesting within the region, a health club that was renovated and upgraded in 1997, and a solarium.

Hotel Hvide Hus. Vesterbro 2, DK-9000 Aalborg. ☎ **98-13-84-00.** Fax 98-13-51-22. www.hhhaalb.dk. E-mail: hhhaalb@pip.dknet.dk. 200 units. TV TEL. 1,020–1,220 DKK ($147.90–$176.90) double. Rates include breakfast. AE, DC, MC, V. Free parking. Bus: 1, 4, 8, 10, or 11.

The 1970s "White House Hotel" is set in Kilden Park, about a 12-minute walk from the heart of Aalborg. This is a first-rate hotel that many international businesspeople are now using instead of the traditional Hotel Helnan Phønix. In cooperation with well-known Danish galleries, the hotel is decorated with works by some of Denmark's leading painters. The bedrooms are well furnished in a fresh Scandinavian-modern style; all have private balconies with a view of Aalborg.

Dining: On the 15th floor is the Restaurant Kilden, offering Danish and international specialties. See "Where to Dine," below.

Amenities: Room service and laundry are available, and the hotel also has a sauna and swimming pool.

Limsfordhotellet. Ved Stranden 14–16, Dk-9000 Aalborg. ☎ **98-16-43-33.** E-mail: limhotel@pip.dknet.dk. 188 units. MINIBAR TV TEL. 895–1,250 DKK ($129.75–$181.25) double; 2,050 DKK ($297.25) suite. Rates include breakfast. AE, DC, MC, V. Closed December 24–26. Parking 40 DKK ($5.80). Bus: 1, 4, 40, or 46.

With its daring design, this is the most avant-garde hotel in town. The hotel was constructed in stages—the first part in the late 1970s, the second half 8 years later. It's located near Jomfru Anegade, a street packed with bars and restaurants. In the center of town, within a 3-minute walk east of the cathedral, the hotel opens onto the famous Limsjorden Canal. The public rooms are sparsely furnished with modern, streamlined furniture. Many of the comfortable bedrooms overlook the harbor. Rooms are of medium size, with good-sized tile baths with towels thick enough to do their job. Mattresses are firm, and everything is maintained in state-of-the-art condition.

Dining/Diversions: The hotel has a good restaurant, serving both international and Danish regional dishes. We'd recommend it, however, only if you're a guest. Although the food is good and the staff courteous and efficient, it's not worth the effort to cross town to dine here. In the reception area is a piano bar, an autumnal fantasy of warm shades of brown, open Monday to Saturday from 5pm to 1 or 2am. There's also a casino, open daily from 8pm to 4am, charging an entrance fee of 40 DKK ($5.80) unless you're a guest of the hotel.

Amenities: Jacuzzi in suites, car-rental desk, room service, dry cleaning/laundry, solarium, and a fitness club.

Slotshotellet. Rendsburggade 5, DK-9100 Aalborg. ☎ **98-10-14-00.** Fax 98-11-65-70. E-mail: Slotsho@post5.tele.dk. 155 units. TV TEL. 1,115 DKK ($161.65) double, 1,405 DKK ($203.75) suite. Rates include breakfast. AE, DC, MC, V. Bus: 1, 3, 5, or 7.

Stylish and comfortable, this tasteful and well-designed hotel opened in 1986. Located a few blocks from the town center within view of the harbor, the hotel lies adjacent to the most important waterway in Aalborg, the Limsjorden Canal, and is about a 2-minute walk east of the cathedral. There's a cafe and a bar, and the bedrooms are comfortable, functionally furnished, and well maintained with good, firm mattresses on the beds. Baths, although a bit small and without enough storage space, are well maintained and tiled; adequate but hardly special.

Dining: The best hotel breakfast in town is served daily, but there are no other dining facilities.

Amenities: Room service, concierge, solarium, fitness center, and table tennis.

MODERATE

Check into the Chagall on any Friday, Saturday, and Sunday night, and you'll find you're staying at an inexpensive hotel instead of a moderate one. Prinsens also rents a number of inexpensive rooms, although most of its accommodations are moderate. Likewise, the Park also rents a number of inexpensive rooms in addition to some pricey selections.

Hotel Chagall. Vesterbro 36–38, Postboks 1856, DK-9000 Aalborg. ☎ **98-12-69-33.** Fax 98-13-13-34. E-mail: chagall@aixl.danadata.dk. 71 units. Mon–Thurs 970 DKK ($140.65) double. Fri–Sun 690 DKK ($100.05). Rates include breakfast. AE, DC, MC, V. Bus: 1, 8, or 10.

Originally built in the 1950s in a boxy, five-story format that rises from a prominent position in the heart of town, this hotel was radically upgraded and redesigned in 1988 into the simple but well-managed three-star hotel you'll see today. Other than a cafe-style area serving breakfast, there are no restaurants and bars within the hotel, and very few amenities other than the well-maintained contemporary-looking bedrooms. Each of them is outfitted in shades of yellow or blue, a style influenced by modern Scandinavia design. Many of them contain at least one reproduction of a painting by Marc Chagall, the hotel's namesake.

Park Hotel. Boulevarden 41, DK-9100 Aalborg. ☎ **98-12-31-33.** Fax 98-13-31-66. E-mail: ccc20331@vip.cybercity.dk. 81 units. TV TEL. 675–1,055 DKK ($97.90–$153) double. Rates include buffet breakfast. AE, DC, MC, V. Bus: 2, 10, 11, or 13.

The original 18th-century atmosphere has been preserved but the hotel has been carefully modernized throughout the years. Rooms are clean, comfortable, and modern, but a bit small, although with good beds. The hotel also has a restaurant serving both

Scandinavian and international food, but the major restaurant street of Aalborg is just a 5-minute walk from the Park. Room service is provided, as is baby-sitting. Facilities include a health club.

Prinsens Hotel. Prinsensgade 14–16. DK-9000 Aalborg. ☎ **98-13-37-33.** Fax 98-16-52-82. 37 units. MINIBAR TV TEL. 695–845 DKK ($100.75–$122.50) double. Rates include breakfast. AE, DC, MC, V. Closed December 23–January 1. Bus: 1, 3, or 5.

Opposite the railroad station, this 1906 landmark is constantly updated and renovated. In spite of its age, bedrooms are decorated in a light, modern, Nordic style. The hotel is very well maintained, and the staff is welcoming. There is also a garden patio, plus a sauna, solarium, Jacuzzi, and table tennis. Guests gather in an inviting bar before going into the main restaurant, Gallay, where both Danish specialties and international dishes are served.

NEARBY ACCOMMODATIONS

Hotel Scheelsminde. Scheelsmindevej 35, DK-9100 Aalborg. ☎ **800-780-7234** in the U.S., or ☎ 98-18-32-33. Fax 98-18-33-34. www.bestwestern.com. E-mail: scheelsminde@scheelsminde.dk. 75 units. 920–1,315 DKK ($133.40–$190.65) double. Rates include breakfast. AE, DC, MC, V. Bus: 4, 6, 41, or 42.

One of the most popular hotels in the area lies 2 ½-miles south of Aalborg's center, in what was originally a manor house constructed in 1808. Many of the accommodations are in a modern addition, although the restaurant is housed in the original core. In classic surroundings, you can escape the noise of Aalborg and wander at leisure through the hotel's large private grounds. Each room is decorated in pastel colors with a light modern decor. Reservations are strongly advised during peak season, because of the hotel's popularity.

Dining/Diversions: You might also like to dine here, since the hotel chef is equally at home with Danish and international specialties. The restaurant was designed with large windows overlooking the park. Its open daily from 11am to 10pm, offering fixed-price meals at 110 DKK ($15.95) for two courses and 140 DKK ($20.30) for three courses.

Amenities: Fitness center and spa, nearby golf, laundry and valet services, indoor and outdoor pools, tennis, 24-hour room service, jogging area, sauna, and Jacuzzi.

WHERE TO DINE

Jomfru Anegade is the most famous restaurant street in Jutland. If you can't find good food here, you didn't try. It's got something for most palates and most pocketbooks.

EXPENSIVE

Hos Boldt. Ved Stranden 7. ☎ **98-16-17-77.** Reservations recommended. Main courses 130–318 DKK ($18.85–$46.10); fixed-price menu 100–400 DKK ($14.50–$58). AE, DC, MC, V. Monday–Saturday 5pm–midnight. DANISH/FRENCH.

One of Aalborg's most likable restaurants was established in 1992 in a 19th-century building that had functioned for many years as a simple tavern. Owned and operated by Hans Boldt and members of his family and team, it consists of two deliberately old-fashioned dining rooms filled with antique furniture and flickering candles. Menu items change with the availability of the ingredients, but might include such perfectly prepared dishes as steamed turbot with a julienne of leeks, consommé of veal with herbs and quail eggs, lobster bisque, a platter with various preparations of salmon, snails in a herb-flavored cream sauce, rack of Danish lamb in a rosemary-flavored wine sauce, and sea bass cooked in a salt crust.

♦ **Mortens Kro.** Algade 37. ☎ **98-12-48-60.** Reservations recommended. Set-price menu 400 DKK ($58). AE, DC, MC, V. Monday–Saturday 6–10pm. FRENCH/DANISH.

Set within what functioned as a store 65 years ago, this is a small, cozy, and artful restaurant with only 30 seats and an association with Morten Nealsen, one of the most gifted chefs in Aalborg. The only culinary option here is a set-price, six-course menu *gastronomique*, which showcases the seasonally inspired cuisine of the chef to its best advantage. Within a yellow-and-gold dining room, your meal might include fillets of red snapper with an apricot-flavored curry sauce, chicken with truffles, fillet of turbot with a lime-flavored mousseline and fresh spinach, and breast of duckling with pepper sauce. Dessert might include a Napoléon layered with pulverized raspberries and blueberries. This is really a top-rate restaurant with a certain flair. The cooking is defined by well-rehearsed rules of technique, and the classic schooling of French cuisine has been beautifully blended with Danish flavors. There is a simple honesty in the cuisine and a commitment to first-rate raw materials.

MODERATE

Il Mulino. Bispensgade 31. ☎ **98-12-39-99.** Reservations recommended. Main courses 139–149 DKK ($20.15–$21.60). AE, DC, MC, V. Mon–Sat noon–3:30pm and 5:30–10pm. Closed Sun Sept–Mar. Bus: 1. ITALIAN.

Set on the second floor of an inner-city building that was originally erected as a warehouse in 1737, this is an authentic and completely engaging Italian restaurant with a cuisine that includes specialties from throughout the Italian peninsula. Its pastas, which are made and rolled out fresh every day, are among the best in town. Seasoned with flair, they're likely to include ravioli stuffed with spinach and pulverized veal and pork, served with a pink sauce. There's also spaghetti with scampi; crespelle (crêpes) stuffed with salmon and shrimp, or with cheese and herbs; lasagna with broccoli and bacon; fettuccine with rabbit meat; and filets of veal with gorgonzola and fresh tomato sauce. If you're in the mood for something fairly simple, consider a fresh salad and a grilled steak that's served with fresh tomatoes.

Provence. Ved Stranden 11. ☎ **98-13-51-33.** Reservations recommended. Main courses 99–159 DKK ($14.35–$23.05). Set-price lunch 50 DKK ($7.25); set-price dinner 99–169 DKK ($14.35–$24.50). AE, DC, MC, V. Monday–Saturday 12:30–10pm, Sunday 5:30–10pm. Bus: 1, 4, 40, or 46. DANISH/FRENCH.

This is Aalborg's foremost purveyor of Danish cuisine that's influenced in almost every case by the culinary traditions of France. Set across from the Limsfordhotellet—with which it's not associated—in the center of town, it offers a cozy, small-scale brown-and-white interior that's illuminated by a stained-glass skylight. The only complaint ever expressed about this place is the fact that its younger staff is not as well-trained as those at some of its competitors, although in some cases their charm may compensate for their lack of skill. Your meal might begin with fresh oysters, a lobster cocktail, fish, soup, or lobster soup. Main courses include a fillet of Dutch sole with a salmon soufflé and fresh spinach; fired sea bass with leek sauce; or tournedos served either in its own juices, or layered with *foie gras*. Anything might be followed with a selection of cheeses from a trolley, or perhaps a chocolate mousse. Even if the service isn't always faultless, the cuisine often is. The food remains classical and always reliable.

Restaurant Dufy. Jomfru Anegade 8. ☎ **98-16-34-44.** Reservations required. Fixed-price menu 59 DKK ($8.55) at lunch, 99–249 DKK ($14.35–$36.10) dinner. Main courses 39–155 DKK ($5.65–$22.45). AE, DC, MC, V. Daily 11:30am–11:30pm. Bus: 1, 3, or 5. DANISH.

The inviting décor, attentive service, and good cuisine make this pair of restaurants the very best on a street crammed with places to eat. The same kitchen prepares the tempting specialties served in the downstairs bistro and in the more formal upstairs restaurant. The menu and prices are the same in both restaurants. Choices might include the best chunky lobster soup in the region, served with sour cream; followed by sautéed Skagen shrimp; an absolutely delectable fish *pâté*, and a perfectly cooked roast breast of duck with Madeira sauce or Dijon-style beef. There's dining on the outdoor terrace in summer.

Restaurant Faklen. Jomfru Anegade. ☎ **98-13-70-30.** Reservations recommended. Main courses 109–189 DKK ($15.80–$27.40). Set-price menus 139–169 DKK ($20.15–$24.50). AE, DC, MC, V. Mon–Sat noon–4pm and 6–10pm. Bus: 1, 3, or 5. DANISH.

This restaurant occupies one of the newer (circa 1973) buildings along a main thoroughfare that's otherwise devoted to older architecture. Inside, you'll find two dining rooms, each outfitted with tartan-patterned carpeting and a thistle motif inspired by Scotland, and staff members, both male and female, sporting kilts. (The pattern, in case you wondered, is copied from the Gordon clan.) Despite the emphasis on the Celts of north Britain, the food is thoroughly Danish, and includes such specialties as lobster soup, every permutation of salmon and herring you can think of, pepper steak, roasted pork with onions and braised cabbage, and one of the most famous old-fashioned desserts, pear belle Hélène. No one is daringly experimental here but the flavors are honest and pure, the staff gracious in their help and attentive service. The real secret is in the skill of the chef and the pristine nature of the ingredients.

Restaurant Kilden. In the Hotel Hvide Hus, Vesterbro 2. ☎ **98-13-84-00.** Reservations recommended. Lunch buffet 150 DKK ($21.75); lunch main courses 28–50 DKK ($4.05–$7.25); dinner main courses 140–195 DKK ($20.30–$28.30). AE, DC, MC, V. Daily noon–3pm and 6–11pm. Bus: 1, 4, 8, 10, or 11. DANISH/INTERNATIONAL.

Set on the second-highest (15th) floor of the Hotel Hvide Hus, in the center of town, this is a contemporary, stylish, and well-recommended restaurant that attracts crowds of office workers to its attractively priced luncheon buffet, and both local residents and hotel guests to its smoothly choreographed evening meals. Some of its allure derives from the views that sweep out over the nearby municipal park (the Kilden Park, after which the restaurant is named) and the seacoast. There's also a coziness formed by a color scheme of pink and burgundy, and a piano in the nearby bar. Although there's no pianist on hand to play, guests are welcome to entertain themselves and other patrons with their own talents, and frequently do. Menu items change with the season, but are likely to include lobster soup, pepper steak, sliced tenderloin of pork with mustard sauce, medallions of veal with truffle sauce, venison with cognac sauce, and roasted rack of lamb with garlic sauce. These are all elegant dishes, beautifully prepared by a skilled chef, using the freshest ingredients possible.

Ristorante Fellini. Jomfru Anegade 20. ☎ **98-11-34-55.** Main courses 125–195 DKK ($18.15–$28.30). Set-price menus 59–210 DKK ($8.55–$30.45). AE, DC, MC, V. Daily 11am–midnight. Bus: 1, 3, or 5. SOUTHERN ITALIAN.

Your best opportunity for a change of pace from too constant a diet of Danish food will be within this hardworking restaurant in the center of Aalborg. Here, staff members from Campania (the region around Naples) will offer a succulent array of Mediterranean dishes wherein the heat and style of southern Italy will be presented at its very best. There's a cozy bar that gracefully mingles the Nordic and southern European attitudes about liquor, and dining areas are accessorized with wood paneling and mementos of the faraway Mediterranean, and racks of Italian wines that the kindly staff will help you choose. Menu items include choices from a display of fish and marinated-vegetable antipasti; spaghetti *con vongole* (with clams); risotto *alla pescatore* (with shellfish and fish), an array of fresh shellfish that mingles that day's catch from the North and Baltic seas with Italian verve. There's also a particularly succulent version of lamb roasted with herbs and potatoes in a style perfected over the centuries by cooks in the highlands of Italy's south-central regions.

INEXPENSIVE

Duss Vinkjaelder. Østerågade 9. ☎ **98-12-50-56.** Snacks 15–49 DKK ($2.15–$7.10) wine by the glass 24 DKK ($3.50). MC, V. Mon–Fri 11am–1am, Sat 10am–2am. Bus: 1, 3, or 5. DANISH.

This old-world 1624 cellar lies beneath one of the most famous private Renaissance mansions (Jens Bang's Stonehouse), a 2-minute walk east of the cathedral. It features a selection of beer and wine (ever had Rainwater Madeira?), but it's a bit skimpy on the food. It's more of a snack restaurant and a wine bar than a full-fledged restaurant. However, you can order a plate of Danish *biksemad* (hash), a burger, or perhaps some *pâté.*

Fyrtøjet. Jomfru Anegade 17. ☎ **98-13-73-77.** Reservations recommended. Main courses 60–120 DKK ($8.70–$17.40). AE, DC, MC, V. Mon–Sat 11:30am–midnight, Sun noon–11pm. Bus: 1, 3, or 5. DANISH/INTERNATIONAL.

A cozy, small restaurant in the center of town, Fyrtøjet serves at outdoor tables in the summer. We suggest a Danish specialty, the *almueplatte* (peasant's plate), with marinated herring, curry salad, two warm rissoles, cold potato salad and chives, and deep-fried Camembert cheese with black currant jam. Other main dishes include stuffed plaice with shrimp, pepper steak, and breast of duck. The cookery is competent, good, and filling, though not exciting.

Holles Vinstue. Algade 57. ☎ **98-13-84-88.** Main courses 45–75 DKK ($6.50–$10.90); smørrebrød from 22 DKK ($3.20). Mon–Fri 11am–8pm, Sat 11am–4pm. Bus: 1, 3, or 5. DANISH.

A 4-minute walk west of Nytorv, this is a popular wine bar and restaurant, with an inviting atmosphere. Owners sell wine by the glass or bottle. Until 3pm you can fill up on some of the best *smørrebrød* (open-faced sandwiches) in town. Or else you can ask for more substantial meals, with many dishes designed to stand off the cold winds from the north. Sample a Wiener schnitzel, various omelets, and fish fillets, or else some "granny" stews or hashes. Much of the cookery is designed to appeal to the old Norsemen of the North Sea instead of food trendies.

Layalina. Ved. Stranden 7–9. ☎ **98-11-60-56.** Main courses 79–169 DKK ($11.45–$24.50); fixed-price dinner 89 DKK ($12.90) Sun–Thurs, 98 DKK ($14.20) Fri–Sat. AE, DC, MC, V. Daily 5–10pm. Bus: 1, 4, 40 or 46. DANISH.

Layalina means "our pleasant nights" in Arabic. Its owners are Lebanese, and they have decorated the restaurant warmly with handmade Middle Eastern artifacts. Exotic dishes such as *shish kebab* and *hummus* are served in an atmosphere of genuine Middle Eastern hospitality. The house special is three brochettes with lamb, meatballs, and spicy sausage. Although a true Lebanese might find fault with the cookery here, it comes as a wonderful change of pace for most of us after too many nights of Danish cuisine without variation.

AALBORG AFTER DARK

Hot summer days and long, mild evenings are ideal for open-air concerts of various kinds. Each year Aalborg hosts several major rock concerts in Mølle Park, with up to 16,000 attending. There are also rock concerts in Skovdalen, behind Nordjyllands

Kunstmuseum, all through the summer. Kilden Park is also a setting for summer concerts. Information about these summer concerts becomes available at the tourist office (see above) beginning in April of every year.

The home of the Aalborg Symphony Orchestra is **Aalborg Kongres og Kultur Center,** Vesterbro (☎ 98-13-46-33), north of Kilden Park. Opera and ballet performances are also presented here. The tourist office (see above) keeps complete data on all cultural events staged here.

FOR FAMILY FUN

Tivoliland, Karolinelundsvej (☎ 98-12-33-15), is an amusement park for the entire family, with lots of snap and sparkle, although a pale imitation of the more famous one in Copenhagen. A tradition since 1946 in the center of Aalborg, it is one of the most attended attractions in the north of Jutland. In addition to rides, there are beautiful gardens with thousands of flowers and fantastic fountains. You've seen it all before, but it's still an amusing and delightful way to spend an evening, as you can take everything from a flying carpet ride to a spin on Scandinavia's only boomerang roller coaster (with screws and loops both forward and backward). China Town is one of the most visited attractions, containing such attractions as the China dragon, the fun house, and a cycle fun rail. An open-air stage, restaurants, a pizzeria, dancing areas, and sing-alongs—it all makes for one big evening. The attraction is open from May to September 6, daily from 10am to 10pm. Admission is 40 DKK ($5.80) for adults or 20 DKK ($2.90) for children. However, you'll pay separately for the various attractions, with tickets ranging from 10 to 20 DKK ($1.45 to $2.90). An unlimited ticket for all rides, good for one day only, costs 160 DKK ($23.20).

DANCE CLUBS

Mature audiences head for **Ambassadeur,** Vesterbro 76 (☎ 98-12-62-22), originally built in the 1950s as a private residence. It was later expanded into the largest and most popular nightlife complex in the region. Its street level contains the Dancing Palace, where traditional dance music is performed by live bands for crowds who enjoy dancing cheek to cheek. Conceived as a supper club, it serves typically Danish specialties. Upstairs, electronic music is broadcast to a hyperactive and much younger crowd in Annabell's Disco. The Bossan Bar in the cellar is sometimes transformed into a disco if business warrants it. The cost of admission allows anyone to wander at will between all three venues. Beer costs from 30 DKK ($4.35), and admission is 20 DKK ($2.90) on Tuesday to Thursday, rising to 40 DKK ($5.80) on Friday and Saturday. Admission is refunded to anyone who orders dinner, with a three-course fixed-price menu costing 169 DKK ($24.50). The club is open Tuesday to Thursday 9am to 5am and Friday and Saturday 7pm to 6am.

Young people often gravitate to **Musik Keller,** in the basement of the previously recommended Restaurant Provence, Ved Straden 11 (☎ 98-13-51-33). Neither the wildest nor the most conservative club in town, it's a bit staid by New York standards, although its DJ plays the most recent music arriving from London, Los Angeles, and elsewhere. There's never any live music, however. Admission is free, and the Keller is open Thursday to Saturday 10pm to 3am.

Gaslight, Jomfru Anegade 23 (☎ 98-10-17-50), is a specialist in rock-and-roll dance music for the under-30 set. **Rendez-Vous,** Jomfru Anegade 5 (☎ 98-16-88-80), offers drinking facilities on its street level, and a dance floor upstairs, simultaneously attracting university students and folks under 40. Or else head for **Over & Under Uret,** Jomfru Anegade 10 (☎ 98-10-30-10), a bar and disco that's open every Tuesday to Sunday from 8pm until the last client has wandered on to other venues.

A CASINO

On the site of the Hotel Limfjordshotellet, **Casino Aalborg,** Ved Stranden 14–16
(☎ **98-10-15-50**), offers such games of chance as American roulette, black jack, stud
poker, and the inevitable slot machines. It is open daily from 8pm to 4am, charging
50 DKK ($7.25) for entrance. No one under age 18 is allowed.

3 Frederikshavn

64km (40 miles) NE of Aalborg; 381km (238 miles) NW of Copenhagen; 40km (25 miles)
S of Skagen

For many, this coastal town in Eastern Jutland is their final stop in Denmark. From
here, ferry connections are possible to either Norway or Sweden (see below.) But the
town of some 26,000 people, the largest in Jutland north of Aalborg, is not just an
international ferry port.

Even though a relatively young town, it has a number of attractions but few historic
sites. At first glance, however, you'll think the whole town is one vast supermarket,
filled with Swedes or Norwegians on a shopping expedition. Danish food products are
cheaper here than they are back in Sweden or Norway.

A strong maritime aura permeates the town. There are seven municipal harbors
alone where the ferries leave or arrive from Norway and Sweden. Just north of Frederikshavn lies the fishing hamlet of Standby where most of the famous "Frederik-
shavner plaice" are landed.

In the Middle Ages the fishing settlement here was called Fladstrand. During the
Thirty Years War the site became a defense entrenchment. In time a powder tower surrounded by a wall was erected. But it wasn't until as late as 1818 that Fladstrand was
granted its municipal charter and the new name of Frederikshavn. In addition to
tourists, ferry passengers, and shoppers from other Scandinavian countries, Frederikshavn also depends on fishing to spark its economy, and is the site of such industries
as iron foundries, shipbuilding, and engineering.

ESSENTIALS

GETTING THERE   Trains leave from Aalborg hourly during the day. Frequent
buses run between Aalborg and Frederikshavn.

By Car   Head north from Aalborg along the E45 to Frederikshavn.

By Ferry   *Seacat* (☎ **96-20-32-00**), a catamaran, sails over the water between Frederikshavn and Gothenburg, on the west coast of Sweden, three times a day. The trip
between the cities takes 1 hour and 55 minutes. Passengers without cars pay from 70
to 150 DKK ($10.15–$21.75) each day, depending on the day of the week and the
season. Cars with a driver and up to four passengers are charged from 450 to 920
DKK ($65.25–$133.40) each.

Seacat's most viable competitor is **Stena Line** (☎ **96-20-02-00**), which operates
three catamaran crossings of its own every day, at fares that are equivalent to those on
the *Seacat* (see above). It also operates a conventional ferryboat service that's a lot
slower than the catamarans. Transit by ferryboat between Frederikshavn and Gothenburg takes 3 hours and 15 minutes. The cost of **Stena's** conventional ferryboat ranges
from 70 to 150 DKK ($10.15–$21.75) for a pedestrian, and from 400 to 1,200 DKK
($58–$174) for one-way transit of a car with a driver plus up to four passengers.

Stena also operates ferryboats between Frederikshavn and Oslo, an overnight trip
that takes 9 hours. Service is daily in summer, and continues in winter, weather permitting. Standard passenger fares range from 250 to 450 DKK ($36.25–$65.25) for

pedestrians without cars, and from 800 to 1,800 DKK ($116–$261) for a car with a driver plus up to four passengers. Rental of a cabin is required for passengers on this long transit, at fees that vary with the cabin category from 100 to 1,000 DKK ($14.50–$145) per person, double occupancy.

VISITOR INFORMATION   The **Frederikshavn Turistbureau,** Brotorvet 1 (☎ 98-42-32-66), near the ferry dock, is open during the summer season Monday through Saturday from 8:30am to 8:30pm and on Sunday from 8:30 to 11am and 4 to 8:30pm; the rest of the year, Monday through Friday from 9am to 4pm and on Saturday from 11am to 2pm.

SEEING THE SIGHTS

Although most of Frederishavn is modern, the oldest part of town, **Fiskerkylyngen,** lies to the north of the fishing harbor. Here you'll encounter a number of 17th-century houses, each well preserved. You can also see a former military fortification, Norde Skanse (North Entrenchments), which was constructed by the troops of Wallenstein during the Thirty Years' War.

Attractions are minor, but could easily occupy your time while you're waiting for a boat departure. If you're rushed for time, visit the only major attraction, the Bangsbro Museum (see below). Otherwise, some of the following sights are of minor interest.

Opposite the railway station rises Frederikshavn's most famous symbol, **Frederik-shavn Kirke,** Kirkepladsen (☎ 98-42-05-99). Most of it dates from 1690, although it was significantly rebuilt in 1892. Inside you can see its major attraction, an altarpiece painted by Michael Ancher, the Skagen artist. The cemetery at the church contains graves of both Allied and German soldiers killed in World War II. Admission is free, and the church is open Tuesday to Saturday 9am to noon.

You can climb the whitewashed gun tower, **Krudttårnet,** at Havnespladsen, a remnant of the famed citadel that stood here in the 1600s (call the tourist office for information). The tower actually stood at another place in Frederikshavn but when the shipyards had to be expanded it was moved here instead of being torn down. The former gun powder magazine, built of stone in 1688, has been turned into a Museum of Military History, displaying weapons from the 17th to the 19th centuries. Today the tower is the emblem of Frederikshavn. It is open daily from June 1 to September 15 from 10:30am to 5pm, charging 20 DKK ($2.90) for adults, 10 DKK ($1.45) for children ages 5 to 12 (free for children age 4 and under).

Another tower worth a visit is **Cloostårnet** (Cloos Tower) (☎ 98-48-60-69), lying 2 ½-miles to the southwest of town at an altitude of 540 feet above sea level. This observation tower rises 190 feet, offering panoramic views over the sea and the countryside of Vendsyssel. An elevator will take you to the top, and in fair weather you can see most of the surrounding district. Admission is 10 DKK ($1.45) for adults or 2 DKK (30¢) for children. Hours are May to mid-June Monday to Friday 1 to 5pm, Saturday and Sunday 10am to 5pm. From mid-June to mid-August it is open daily from 10am to 5pm. From mid-August until August 31, hours are daily 1 to 5pm. It is closed the rest of the year. It can be reached from the center of Frederikshavn by taking bus nos. 210 or 225.

Bangsbro Museum. Dronning Margrethsvej 6. ☎ **98-42-31-11.** Admission 25 DKK ($3.60) for adults, 5 DKK (75¢) for children. Apr–Oct, daily 10am–5pm; Nov–Mar, Tue–Sun 10am–5pm.

One of the premier open-air museums of the region, this place is located in a wooded area beside the Deer Park, 2-miles south of the town center, and contains a cluster of 18th-century buildings near the remnants of a 14th-century manor house. Of special interest is an old barn built in 1580, one of the oldest in Denmark, which houses antique farm equipment and implements. The main house has a collection of hand-crafts made from human hair, a large display of relics from World War II, and a nautical section including ship models, figureheads, and other mementos. An early ship, *Ellingå*, similar to the vessels used by the Vikings, is in one of the stable buildings. It is the reconstructed remains of a Viking-style merchant ship excavated 3-miles north of Frederikshavn.

SHOPPING

Frederikshavn is an active shopping town, with boutiques and emporiums that line both sides of the **Gågade,** one of the longest all-pedestrian thoroughfares in Denmark.

One of the most intriguing shopping possibilities, **Dot Keramik** is at Skagensvej 270, Nielstrup, Strandby (☎ **98-48-14-10**), 4 ½-miles north of Frederikshavn. Here you'll find a wide display of hand-thrown ceramics, plus an array of applied art, gift articles, and intriguing decorations. At **Birgitte Munch,** Daanmarksgade 42C (☎ **98-43-80-66**), you can see the town's most talented goldsmith producing jewelry according to the best traditions of workmanship. A wide range of jewelry, locally designed, is on sale, and quality is high.

WHERE TO SAY

In case you miss the boat and need a room, the Frederikshavn Turistbureau (see above) will book you into a **private home** if you'd prefer that to a hotel.

EXPENSIVE

Hotel Jutlandia. Postboks 89, Havnepladsen, DK-9900 Frederikshavn. ☎ **98-42-42-00.** Fax 98-42-38-72. 103 units. 910–1,070 DKK ($131.95–$155.15) double, 1,165–2,000 DKK ($168.95–$290.00) suite. Rate includes breakfast. AE, DC, MC, V.

This is the largest and the best-rated hotel in town, and as such, it's the site where members of the Danish royal family have stayed during several of their visits. It's also the closest hotel to the spot where the boats from Gothenburg stop, and it draws consistent business from travelers about to navigate their way through either Jutland or Sweden. Built in the 1960s, in a bulky, angular format, the hotel contains greater numbers of unusual art objects than you'd expect, and public areas that have felt the touch of some very skilled decorators. The lobby, a study in high-ceilinged, 1960s-style architecture, outfitted in cool grays and violets, is one of the best examples of Scandinavian design in town. Bedrooms are carpeted but in most cases, they're not excessively large. Except within some of the upper-tier categories, they might be more cramped than you'd really feel comfortable in. Luxury-category rooms, however, are very comfortable, outfitted with well-upholstered furniture and particularly plush mattresses. One truly exceptional accommodation is the Thai Suite, the largest in the building, outfitted in richly carved teakwood furniture that's as opulent and sinuous as anything you're likely to find in Frederikshavn. Don't expect the amenities of a resort if you opt for a stay here, as it caters to business travelers who aren't necessarily interested in swimming pools and sports facilities.

Dining/Diversions: One of the town's best restaurants, the Grå-Ander (Gray Duck), is recommended separately in "Where to Dine." There's also a durable, woodsy-looking English-style pub, and a library-style cocktail lounge on the premises.

Amenities: Limited room service (restricted to breakfast and dinner hours), and a concierge who can arrange business services and leisure activities, most of which will take place outside the hotel.

Stena Hotel Frederikshavn. Tordenskjoldsgade 14, DK-9900 Frederikshavn. ☎ **98-43-32-33.** Fax 98-43-33-11. 215 units. MINIBAR TV TEL. 950–1,200 DKK ($137.75–$174) double, 1,750 DKK ($253.75) suite. AE, DC, MC, V.

In the center of town, near the pedestrian shopping area and not far from the harbor, this 1987 hotel has long been one of the leading hotels in the area, although it's not as fancy or as highly rated as the Jutlandia. It's one of the largest hotels in Denmark outside of Copenhagen. All of its bedrooms are well furnished and well maintained, and 15 units are equipped for persons with disabilities. Some rooms can be converted into three- or four-bed units, so the Stena has long been a favorite with families.

Dining/Diversions: Good food is served in the hotel's premier dining room, Det Gulge Pakhus, or else you can dine more informally in the Brasserie Søhesten. There is also a coffee shop and a night club, Bonne Nuit.

Amenities: The hotel's primary attraction is its Aqualand, complete with water flume, foaming waterfalls, summery wavelets, and gentle whirls. Jacuzzi, room service, dry cleaning/laundry, solarium, fitness club, and heated indoor swimming pool.

MODERATE

Frederikshavn Sømandshjem & Hotel. Tordenskjoldsgade 15B, DK-9900 Frederikshavn. ☎ 98-42-09-88. Fax 98-43-18-99. 40 units (30 with bath). Aug–June, 530 DKK ($76.85) double without bath; 675 DKK ($97.90) double with bath. July, 600 DKK ($87) double without bath; 745 DKK ($108) double with bath. Rates include breakfast. AE, DC, MC, V.

In the center of town, near the shopping area and close to the harbor, this old-fashioned hotel was founded in 1880 as the Seamen's Mission. However, newly restored in 1998, it offers some of the best lodgings for your kroner in town. Many of its functionally furnished bedrooms can be converted into three- or four-bed units suitable for families. The restaurant at the hotel serves good Danish food of the meat-and-potatoes (with gravy) variety, with main courses costing from 50 to 100 DKK ($7.25–$14.50). Only dinner is served, daily from 5 to 7:30pm.

Hoffmann's Hotel. Tordenskjoldsgade 1, DK-9900 Frederikshavn. ☎ 98-42-21-07. Fax 98-42-21-07. 73 units (27 with bath). TEL. 500 DKK ($72.50) double without bath, 600 DKK ($87) double with bath. Rates include breakfast. AE, DC, MC, V.

This inn in the center of Frederikshavn provides a decent stopover at a reasonable price. It has long sheltered passengers staying overnight and waiting to catch ferries to either Sweden or Norway. Bedrooms are comfortable but functionally furnished and rather plain. Cleanliness is high, however. The free car park at the rear is convenient for ferry departures. Other than a breakfast room, facilities are at a minimum.

Hotel Lisboa. Søndergade 248, DK-9900 Frederikshavn. ☎ 98-42-21-33. Fax 98-43-80-11. E-mail: info@lisboa.dk. 32 units. TV TEL. 625–675 DKK ($90.65–$97.90). MC, V. From Frederikshavn, take bus nos. 1, 2, 3, or 4.

Outfitted in a blue-and-white color scheme, and with polished stone floors of the type you might have expected in a hotel in Portugal, this hotel was named in honor of a holiday that its founders had taken in Lisboa (Lisbon) just before its original construction in 1958. In 1978, it was enlarged with an annex, and the entire property has been upgraded and improved several times since. Designed in a two-story format that gives its simple bedrooms a good view of the sand dunes and the beach, it appeals to a nature-loving, escapist crowd year-round. Bedrooms are simple, spartan, and uncomplicated, with straightforward-looking furniture and few, if any, graceful notes. On the premises are a bar and a restaurant, where set menus cost 105 DKK ($15.25) and a la carte main courses cost from 95 to 140 DKK ($13.75–$20.30) each. Public areas and the restaurant are outfitted with the blue-and-white abstract paintings of Danish artist Peder Meinert.

Hotel 1987. Havnegade 8E, Damsgaards Plads, DK-9900 Frederikshavn. ☎ 98-43-18-87. Fax 98-43-19-42. 28 units. TV TEL. 560 DKK ($81.20) double. Rate includes breakfast. AE, DC, MC, V.

The name of this hotel derives from the fact that it was radically reconfigured in 1987 from what had originally been built 130 years before as a warehouse for the stockpiling of marine supplies and freight. Today, only the symmetrical yellow façade and an interior labyrinth of massive beams and trusses, artfully incorporated into the smooth white plaster and dark blue carpeting, remain from the original construction. Those beams and that color scheme extend throughout the public rooms and most of the bedrooms, which are comfortable, cozy, and snug. The staff is helpful, and although the hotel only serves breakfast, it's not far from the bars and restaurants of the rest of the town.

Park Hotel. Jernbanegade 7, DK-9900 Frederikshavn. ☎ **98-42-22-55.** Fax 98-42-20-36. 30 units (18 with bath). TEL. 550 DKK ($79.75) double without bath, 990 DKK ($143.55) double with bath. Rates include breakfast. AE, DC, MC, V.

An atmospheric choice with a certain charm, this hotel was built in 1880 in both an old French and an old English style. Many of the handsomely furnished traditional bedrooms have marble baths. All of the rooms have a phone, and some also contain a TV and mini-bar. The Park is known for its gourmet restaurant, Gastronomen, which serves an international cuisine (see separate recommendation under "Where to Dine," below). Room service is provided, and a swimming pool and health club are found next door.

INEXPENSIVE

Aktivitel. Knivholtvej 22, DK-9900 Frederikshavn. ☎ **98-43-23-77.** Fax 98-43-89-99. 94 units. 475 DKK ($68.90) double. Rate includes breakfast. MC, V. From Frederikshavn, take bus no. 14.

This is the most sports-oriented hotel in Denmark, with such a strong emphasis on tennis, soccer, handball, and hockey that school groups from throughout Europe sometimes book large blocks of its rooms as part of their pre-season workout strategies. Positioned 2-miles west of Frederikshavn, on sandy scrub-covered flatlands about a mile from the nearest beach, it was founded in 1989 by a championship ice hockey player, Søren Lauretsen. Since then, its durable, slightly battered premises have emerged as a household name throughout Denmark, known as a training ground for amateur, and in rare instances, professional sports teams.

Its accommodations are situated within a low-rise compound of interconnected cottages that might remind you of either an American-style motel or an army barracks, depending on your point of view. Bedrooms are small, spartan, and outfitted with durable furniture that has survived more or less intact under the punishment of clients who no doubt have a lot more energy than you. Each has twin beds, a chair, and two tables, one of which is formatted for writing. Frankly, this hotel might appeal to some readers, and absolutely horrify many others. Select it only if you have an abiding interest in sports (either performing them or teaching them), and only if you don't mind lots of youthful high-jinx pervading every aspect of your holiday retreat. Don't expect luxury, as it simply isn't a part of the experience here, but in its way, the place can be intriguing for a night or two.

A restaurant serves set-price menus priced from 98 to 175 DKK ($14.20–$25.40). Room service is not available. Amenities include at least four separate soccer fields, eight tennis courts, a handball court, and a basketball court. There's also space for "floor hockey" wherein participants on roller skates mimic the motions they would have performed on ice.

Hotel Mariehønon. Danmakrsgade 40, DK-9900 Frederikshavn. ☎ **98-42-01-22.** Fax 98-43-40-99. 32 units (18 with bath). 390–450 DKK ($56.55–$65.25) double without bath, 490–550 DKK ($71.05–$79.75) double with bath. AE, DC, MC, V.

Right in the heart of Frederikshavn, this hotel is among the most convenient in town, lying only 5 minutes from the ferry terminal and 3 minutes from the train depot.

Most of its guests are passengers waiting overnight to catch ferries to Oslo or Gothenburg. A family run hotel, Mariehønon offers rooms that are basic, functionally although comfortably furnished, and well maintained. Most of the bedrooms have TVs. A family-run place, it is known for providing a good night's sleep at a reasonable rate. The hotel's restaurant has long closed, but there are several places to eat nearby.

WHERE TO DINE
EXPENSIVE

Gastronomen. In the Park Hotel, Jernbanegade 7. ☎ **98-42-22-55.** Reservations required. Main courses 128–168 DKK ($18.55–$24.35). Reservations required. Two course fixed-price menu 238 DKK ($34.50), three-course fixed-price menu 298 DKK ($43.20). Mon–Sat 7am–10pm. FRENCH.

Long known for its cuisine, this gourmet restaurant in a previously recommended hotel has an engaging appeal and infectious charm. The food is several notches above a typical French bistro, relying heavily on quality ingredients, served in formal, traditional surroundings. The menu reads like an exciting assemblage of food, often served in perfect combinations, such as the Norwegian lobster with asparagus, or the grilled filet of beef in a velvety smooth tarragon sauce. As a nouvelle dish, the grilled tenderloin of veal appears with chanterelles and a raspberry sauce. Old Danish tradition is followed with the fried plaice with white potatoes and parsley, just like Ibsen liked it, but you can try more daring innovations as well, like the light and tasty watercress soup with champagne. Marinated salmon with freshly chopped herbs is always welcome, and the fish of the day is usually your safest bet. It depends on the catch of the day and can be grilled to your specifications. For your grand finale, opt for the walnut nougat cake served with rhubarb purée or some other concoction of the day, or else settle for a dish of sorbet or perhaps a selection of cheese.

✪ **Restaurant Grå-Ander (The Gray Duck).** In the Hotel Jutlandia, Havnepladsen. ☎ **98-42-42-00.** Reservations recommended. Lunch main courses 58–183 DKK ($8.40–$26.55); dinner main courses 140–200 DKK ($20.30–$29.00). Set-price menu 245 DKK ($35.55). AE, DC, MC, V. FRENCH.

This is one of the best-recommended dining rooms in Frederikshavn, with a reputation that the managers of the Hotel Jutlandia work hard to maintain. There's room inside for only 34 diners at a time, who enjoy their meal within a mostly blue (with touches of red) dining room, with windows that overlook the blue-gray expanse of the sea. Menu items are based on inspirations from France, and include classic dishes from the Gallic repertoire of fine food. Examples include duck liver pâté with apple salad; skewered and grilled scallops with fresh spinach and pepper sauce; monkfish grilled with fresh tomatoes and served with ratatouille; roasted codfish with white wine sauce, spinach, and parsley; and chicken breast layered with duck liver and served with sautéed mushrooms. Two dishes to rave about include lemon sole in a *ragoût* of mussels and curried cream, and quail with *foie gras* and a red-wine flambé.

Dessert might be a raspberry Napoléon with a honey parfait and chocolate sauce. The staff is justifiably proud of their food and the service, which is excellent. They also take pride in selecting the finest of ingredients and enhancing natural flavors once the produce arrives in the kitchen. There are many luxury ingredients on the menu but prices are not awe-inspiring.

MODERATE

Restaurant Bacchus. Lodsgade 8A. ☎ **98-43-29-00.** Reservations recommended. Main courses 152–199 DKK ($22.05–$27.25). Fixed-price lunches 168 DKK ($24.35); fixed-price dinners 198–238 DKK ($28.70–$34.50). AE, DC, MC, V. Mon–Sat 5–10pm. DANISH.

Set within a simple building dating from the 1850s near the harbor, this is an unassuming, unpretentious bistro with a hardworking team and a hard-nosed view of profits and every evening's bottom line. Although there's a well-chosen wine list, it's a lot less comprehensive than you might have assumed in view of the restaurant's name. Within an old-fashioned dining room with only 40 seats and lots of wood paneling, you can order one of the best versions of creamy fish soup in town (it's a house specialty), a "symphony" of fish (three or four kinds, arranged on a platter and served with a saffron and white-wine sauce), grilled turbot with *beurre blanc* (white butter) sauce, a perfectly cooked pepper steak, or veal steak whose flavor is perked up with Calvados. The restaurant was established on this site during the early 1990s.

INEXPENSIVE

Vinkaelderen. Havnegade 8. ☎ **98-42-02-70.** Main courses 69–165 DKK ($10–$23.90), fixed-price menu 123 DKK ($17.85). AE, DC, MC, V. Daily 11am–11pm. DANISH.

Lying midway between the harbor and the center of town, this restaurant is recognized by its redbrick façade, bull's-eye glass windows, and multiple carriage lamps. Originally established after World War II, it has a warmly rustic coziness enhanced by the racks of European wines on the walls. House wines cost 29 DKK ($4.20) per glass. Fresh fish and Danish beef dishes are specialties. The fixed-price menu is served day and night. This place is for those who want filling and flavorsome fare—all at a reasonable price—but don't expect "fireworks" for the palate.

FREDERIKSHAVN AFTER DARK

In Frederikshavn, nightlife simmers away in quiet, not particularly demonstrative ways, most visibly at the **John Bull Pub,** Havnepladsen (☎ **98-42-42-00),** an English pub clone adjacent to the Jutlandia Hotel. More Danish, and more accustomed to wine-drinkers, is the **Vinkaelderen,** Havnegade (☎ **98-42-02-70),** where a roster of wines from throughout the world are sold by the glass, within a setting whose décor was inspired by old-time Danish models of long ago.

4 Skagen

104km (65 miles) NE of Aalborg; 485km (303 miles) W of Copenhagen

Skagen is the "Land's End" of Denmark—the northernmost tip of Jutland on its eastern coast. It has been compared to a "bony finger" pointing into the North Sea. Pronounced *skane,* Skagen is the second-biggest fishing port in Denmark. A thriving artists' colony has done much to enliven the town.

This town of 13,000 people who live here year-round is set against a backdrop of dramatic scenery—moors covered with heather, undulating stretches of dunes, and some of the best—but not the warmest—sandy beaches in Europe.

This small, windswept town is known for its artists and craftspeople. For centuries it remained unspoiled and isolated. But in the 19th century, artists—attracted to the desolation of the place—began to arrive in increasing numbers. With the coming of the railway in 1890, with a link connecting Skagen with Frederikshavn, tourists began to discover the area as well.

ESSENTIALS

GETTING THERE   For those who aren't driving, there are several trains a day from Copenhagen to Århus, where you'll need to connect with another train to Frederikshavn; from Frederikshavn there are 12 daily trains to Skagen.

By Car   Continue on E45 northeast to Frederikshavn. From here, head north on Route 40 to Skagen.

VISITOR INFORMATION   Contact the **Skagen Turistbureau,** Skt. Laurentiivej 22 (☎ **98-44-13-77**); it's open June 22 to August 11, daily from 9am to 7pm; June 1–21 and August 12–31, Monday to Saturday from 9am to 5:30pm and Sunday from 10am to 2pm; in May and September, Monday to Friday from 9am to 5:30pm and Saturday and Sunday from 10am to 2pm; and October to April, Monday to Friday from 9am to 5:30pm and Saturday from 10am to 1pm.

SEEING THE SIGHTS

Since it opened in 1907 **Skagen Harbor** has been one of the major attractions of town. It's seen at its best when the boats come back to land their catches (times vary). For early risers, the fish auction "at the rack of the morning" is a popular attraction. From mid-May to mid-October the oldest part of the harbor is a haven for the boating crowds centered around a marina here. Many yachting people in Jutland use Skagen as their favorite harbor haven.

Old Town lies 1 ½ miles from the center of Skagen (signs point the way). The place was given its name of "Old Skagen" because it is thought that the original town of Skagen grew up here. Originally Gammel Skagen was the fishing hamlet—that is, until Skagen Havn (Skagen Harbor) opened in 1907. Today, Gammel Skagen is a little resort town with large beach hotels that are mainly timeshares.

The most important attraction in the town is the **Skagens Museum,** Brøndumsvej 4 (☎ **98-44-64-44**). It houses the works of many local artists who have painted in the area, and is especially rich in the works of artists from the 1930s. You'll see paintings by P. S. Krøyer (1851–1909), Michael Ancher (1849–1909), and Anna Ancher (1859–1935), among others. Admission is 40 DKK ($5.80); free for children age 14 and under. It's open May to September, daily from 10am to 6pm; in April and October, Tuesday to Sunday from 11am to 4pm; and November to March, Wednesday to Friday from 1 to 4pm, Saturday 11am to 4pm, and Sunday 11am to 3pm.

The homes of some former artists have been turned into museums. Now the **Michael & Ana Ancher Hus,** Markvej 2–4 (☎ **98-44-30-09**), is open to the public. If you visit the Skagens Museum (see above), you may have seen works displayed by these talented artists, who originally purchased this house back in 1884. After their daughter, Helga, died in the 1960s, it was converted into a museum of their works. It is preserved rather like it was in the lifetime of these artists. Admission is 30 DKK ($4.35) for adults, 10 DKK ($1.45) for children ages 6 to 16 (free for age 5 and under). In April and October hours are daily, 11am to 3pm; May to June 20 and August 16 to September, daily, 10am to 5pm; June 21 to August 15, daily, 10am to 6pm; November to March, Saturday, Sunday, and holidays, 11am to 3pm.

Drachmanns Hus, Han Baghsvej 21 (☎ **98-44-51-88**), is the home of the Danish poet and artist, Holger Drachmann. Built in 1828, the house was Drachmann's home until his death in 1908. Now a museum, it is filled with mementos of the artist. From June 1 to June 14, it is open Saturday and Sunday from 11am to 3pm; June 15 to August 15, daily, 10am to 5pm; August 16 to September 15, daily, 11am to 3pm; and September 16 to October 16, open only Saturday and Sunday, 11am to 3pm. Adults pay 20 DKK ($2.90) but children are admitted free.

An open-air museum worth a look, **Skagen By- & Egnsmuseum,** Fortidsminderne, P. K. Nielsensvej (☎ **98-44-47-60**), is in a compound where the homes of both rich and poor fishers were moved to create the aura of how people lived in this area a long time ago, mainly from 1830 to 1880. Today there's a maritime museum on-site devoted to shipwrecks, with photographs of vessels in distress. There is also a fisheries exhibition. You can also see a life-saving station, and there's even an original Dutch windmill here. The museum is a 15-minute stroll from the train depot. From March to April it is open Monday to Friday 10am to 4pm; May to September, daily, 10am to 5pm; and October and November, Monday to Friday 10am to 4pm. Adults pay 10 DKK ($1.45) to enter, children ages 7 to 14 pay 5 DKK (75¢), kids age 6 and under are free.

At the **Skagen Ravmuseum,** Bankvej 2 (☎ **98-44-47-33**), you'll find one of Denmark's greatest collections of amber. The museum displays, among other items, some 50,000 pieces of amber and amber-related exhibits: amber with insects trapped in it, old amber works, Stone Age amber, amber from all over the world, and even amber jewelry set in a riot of colors. The museum also displays a collection of *Jugenstil* (art nouveau) silver jewelry. Hours are as follows: March 1 to June 14, daily, 10am to 6pm; June 15 to August 14, daily, 10am to 10pm; and August 15 to February, daily, 10am to 5pm. Adults pay 15 DKK ($2.15) for admission, children 1-17, 10 DKK ($1.45).

An amusing curiosity is **Den Tilsandede Kirke** (☎ **98-44-43-71**), a church buried in sand dunes 1-mile south of town. The only part that's visible is the upper two-thirds of the tower. When Hans Christian Andersen visited in 1859, he called the church "The Pompeii of Skagen." The sand didn't exactly surprise a congregation at worship. The only things hidden under the dunes are the remnants of a wall and the old floor and perhaps the baptismal font. By 1775, the church had already fallen into disrepair and was used by fewer and fewer members. By 1795 it was completely closed down, and in 1810 it was partly demolished, the stones sold to people in the area as building materials for their private houses. Today red stakes in the ground indicate the placing and extent of the nave and vestry. The site is open June 1 to September 1 daily 11am to 5pm. Admission to the grounds is 8 DKK ($1.15) for adults, 4 DKK (60¢) for children.

A final attraction, and one well worth exploring, is **Rådjerg Mile,** a protected migrating dune moving at the rate of about 35 feet annually. Located 10-miles south of town, it can be reached via Kandestederne. This dune was formed on the west coast in the 16th century during the great sand drift which characterized the landscape until the 20th century. The dune continues to move yearly, eastward toward the forest.

SHOPPING

Since so many artists live in Skagen, many visitors purchase art here. The best gallery is **Galerie Skagen,** Trondsvej 16 (☎ **98-44-44-25**), which also has a tasteful collection of handcrafts. The most sophisticated collection of pottery is found at **Skagen Potteri,** Sct. Laurentivej 27 (☎ **98-44-69-29**). Stunningly designed modern jewelry is sold at **Smykkekunstner,** Niels Ottensvej 5 (☎ **98-44-33-60**), in Gammel Skagen. Some of Jutland's finest glass pieces—often works of art—are on display and for sale at **Skagen Glasvaerksted,** Sct. Laurentivej 95 (☎ **98-44-60-50**).

WHERE TO STAY

Finns Pension. Østre Strandvej 63, DK-9990 Skagen. ☎ **98-45-01-55.** 7 units (none with bath). 525–725 DKK ($76.15–$105.15) double. Rates include breakfast. No credit cards. Closed Nov–Mar.

This is the kind of old-fashioned Danish homestead that many residents of more modern hotels wished that they had had a more intimate view of. Originally built in 1909 in a style that the owner refers to as "a Norwegian wood house," it's sheathed mostly in age-darkened wood both inside and outside, and designed in a style that Scandinavian immigrants made popular during the 19th-century in American states such as Minnesota. Set within a residential neighborhood of Skagen, a 10- to 15-minute walk northeast of its commercial center, and a 3-minute walk from the beach, it's furnished with old furniture and antiques and with dark colors. Throughout, you'll find an old-fashioned aversion to computers and electronic devices (meaning no phones or TVs in the bedrooms). Many of the rooms have heavily beamed ceilings and a charming but vaguely claustrophobic allure that's consistent with the small-scale rooms and amenities of turn-of-the-century Denmark. Our only warning about this place involves a rigidity on the part of the hardworking managers and staff, who establish very clear-cut rules for new arrivals, aren't noted for their flexibility, and who maintain an aggressive "take it or leave it" approach to their unique hotel. If you give advance notification, they'll prepare a five-course evening meal, which is served only to residents, for an average price of around 160 DKK ($23.20) per person. If you agree to this, on pain of severe reproach, don't be late for dinner.

✪ **Strandhotellet/Strandhuset.** Jeckelsvej, Gammel Skagen, DK-9990 Skagen. ☎ **98-44-59-19.** Fax 98-44-59-19. 14 units, 6 suites with kitchenette. TV TEL. 785–950 DKK ($113.85–$137.75) double. 885–1,070 DKK ($128.35–$155.15) junior suite, 1,175–1,675 DKK ($170.40–$242.90) suite with kitchenette. Rates include breakfast. AE, DC, MC, V.

Our favorite hotel in Skagen lies 2 ½-miles south of the town's commercial center, close to Gammel Skagen, a sleepy hamlet with more historical interest and a more ancient pedigree. It consists of two well-crafted buildings, the older of which (Strandhotellet) was built in 1912 as a holiday home for a local matriarch whose fervor for solid construction has become something of a local legend, and the younger of which (Strandhuset) was constructed with a prominent hip roof in a symmetrical, historically appropriate style in the early 1990s. Both contain equivalent accommodations, except that the suites with kitchens tend to be focused within the Strandhuset. Throughout the establishment, furnishings are tasteful, and in many cases, artful; always accentuated with a collection of unusual modern paintings by a stable of talented artists living in or near Skagen. Bedrooms are evocative of the lodgings within an elegant and tasteful private home, where the owners just happen to have gobs of good taste and an appreciation for the serenity of the sand dunes nearby. Breakfast is the only meal served within the hotel. It's presented within a semi-circular greenhouse-style extension jutting out from one end of the house. A cozy turn-of-the-century restaurant, Sømærket, which is separately recommended, lies within a short walk.

WHERE TO DINE

✪ **Skagen Fiske Restaurant.** Fiskehuskai 13. ☎ **98-44-35-44.** Reservations recommended. Lunch platters 55–65 DKK ($8–$9.45). Dinner main courses 150–200 DKK ($21.75–$29). AE, DC, MC, V. May 29–Aug 29 daily noon–2:30pm and 6–10:30pm. FISH.

One of the best-known fish restaurants in Jutland occupies the red-sided premises of a gable-roofed building that was erected directly beside the harborfront in 1907. You'll enter a bar on the establishment's street level, where the floor is composed of the actual beachfront—nothing more than sand. Don't dismiss this place, however, as too rustic, as it's considered so charming that Denmark's Queen Margarethe schedules regular meetings here with the king of Norway, conducting the low-key equivalent of a Scandinavian summit meeting over platters of fish and *aquavit*. Other guests have included the king of Sweden and various dignitaries and ordinary folk looking for insights into the rustic seafaring Denmark of long ago. Climb to the nautically decorated dining room one floor above street level for meals. Lunches usually include flavorful platters that might contain fish cakes, Norwegian lobster, peel-your-own-shrimp, three different preparations of herring, or grilled fillets of sole with lemon sauce. Dinners are more elaborate, consisting of whatever fish has been hauled in that day by local fishers, prepared any way you specify, with virtually any sauce that's reasonably available. Frankly, the only drawback to this place involves its short, summer-only season.

Index

FROMMER'S® NATIONAL PARK GUIDES

Family Vacations in the
    National Parks
Grand Canyon

National Parks of the
    American West
Rocky Mountain

Yellowstone & Grand Teton
Yosemite & Sequoia/
    Kings Canyon
Zion & Bryce Canyon

FROMMER'S® GREAT OUTDOOR GUIDES

New England
Northern California

Southern California & Baja
Washington & Oregon

FROMMER'S® MEMORABLE WALKS

Chicago
London

New York
Paris

San Francisco
Washington D.C.

FROMMER'S® IRREVERENT GUIDES

Amsterdam
Boston
Chicago

London
Manhattan

New Orleans
Paris

San Francisco
Walt Disney World
Washington, D.C.

FROMMER'S® BEST-LOVED DRIVING TOURS

America
Britain
California

Florida
France
Germany

Ireland
Italy
New England

Scotland
Spain
Western Europe

THE COMPLETE IDIOT'S TRAVEL GUIDES

Boston
Cruise Vacations
Planning Your Trip to Europe
Hawaii

Las Vegas
London
Mexico's Beach Resorts
New Orleans

New York City
Paris
San Francisco
Walt Disney World
Washington, D.C.

THE UNOFFICIAL GUIDES®

Branson, Missouri
California with Kids
Chicago
Cruises
Disney Companion

Florida with Kids
The Great Smoky &
    Blue Ridge
    Mountains

Las Vegas
Miami & the Keys
Mini-Mickey
New Orleans

New York City
San Francisco
Skiing in the West
Walt Disney World
Washington, D.C.

SPECIAL-INTEREST TITLES

Born to Shop: Caribbean Ports of Call
Born to Shop: France
Born to Shop: Hong Kong
Born to Shop: Italy
Born to Shop: New York
Born to Shop: Paris
Frommer's Britain's Best Bike Rides
The Civil War Trust's Official Guide
    to the Civil War Discovery Trail
Frommer's Caribbean Hideaways
Frommer's Europe's Greatest Driving Tours
Frommer's Food Lover's Companion to France
Frommer's Food Lover's Companion to Italy
Frommer's Gay & Lesbian Europe
Israel Past & Present

Monks' Guide to California
Monks' Guide to New York City
The Moon
New York City with Kids
Unforgettable Weekends
Outside Magazine's Guide
    to Family Vacations
Places Rated Almanac
Retirement Places Rated
Road Atlas Europe
Washington, D.C., with Kids
Wonderful Weekends from Boston
Wonderful Weekends from New York City
Wonderful Weekends from San Francisco
Wonderful Weekends from Los Angeles